GW00705989

PHILIP'S

MOTORING ATLAS
Britain

Contents

First published in 2003 by
Philip's a division of
Octopus Publishing Group Ltd
2–4 Heron Quays, London E14 4JP
www.philips-maps.co.uk
Second edition 2004
First impression 2004

Cartography by Philip's
Copyright © 2004 Philip's

 Ordnance Survey®

This product includes mapping data licensed from Ordnance Survey®, with the permission of the Controller of Her Majesty's Stationery Office. © Crown copyright 2004. All rights reserved. Licence number 100011710

Information for Tourist Attractions in England supplied by the British Tourist Authority / English Tourist Board.

Information for National Parks, Areas of Outstanding Natural Beauty, National Trails and Country Parks in Wales supplied by the Countryside Council for Wales.

Information for National Parks, Areas of Outstanding Natural Beauty, National Trails and Country Parks in England supplied by the Countryside Agency.

Data for Regional Parks, Long Distance Footpaths and Country Parks in Scotland provided by Scottish Natural Heritage.

Gaelic name forms used in the Western Isles provided by Comhairle nan Eilean.

Data for the National Nature Reserves in England provided by English Nature.

Data for the National Nature Reserves in Wales provided by Countryside Council for Wales. Darparwyd data'n ymwneud â Gwarchodfeydd Natur Cenedlaethol Cymru gan Gyngor Cefn Gwlad Cymru.

Information on the location of National Nature Reserves in Scotland was provided by Scottish Natural Heritage.

Data for National Scenic Areas in Scotland provided by the Scottish Executive Office. Crown copyright material is reproduced with the permission of the Controller of HMSO and the Queen's Printer for Scotland. Licence number C02W0003960.

The town plans of Calais and Boulogne are based on data supplied by Hachette Livre. The road mapping of Northern France was supplied by Blay-Foldex SA Copyright © Blay-Foldex SA

Printed in Italy by Rotolito

Cover photograph: Grisedale, Cumbria
David Wrench, Leslie Garland Picture Library / Alamy

National Trust properties

Key to symbols

- 🏰 Castle
- 🏛 Historic house
- 🏠 Other buildings
- ✝ Church, chapel etc
- ✿ Garden
- 🌳 Park
- ⛰ Countryside
- 🌊 Coast
- 🗿 Prehistoric site
- ⚙ Industrial archaeology
- 🎭 Events
- 🐄 Farm / farm animals
- 🐦 Nature reserve
- ✖ Mill
- 🚶 Country walk
- 🗣 Guided tours

How to join the National Trust

For immediate membership you can join at almost all National Trust properties or shops. Alternatively contact National Trust Membership Department, PO Box 39, Warrington, WAS 7WD
☎0870 240 3207

Aberconwy House 🏛
Dating from the 14th-century, Aberconwy House is the last remaining medieval merchant's house in the old walled town of Conwy. Each room shows a different moment in time, reflecting the taste and character of some of the families who lived there.
Castle Street, Conwy LL32 8AY ☎(01492) 592246 83 D7

Aberdulais Falls ⛰ ⚙
For over 300 years this famous waterfall has provided the energy for industry from the first manufacture of copper in 1584 to present day remains of the Tinplate works. Today the Turbine House provides access to an interactive computer, fish pass and display panels.
Aberdulais, Neath SA10 8EU ☎(01639) 636674 34 D1

Acorn Bank Garden and Water-Mill ✿
Surrounded by ancient oaks and high sandstone walls, this is the largest culinary and medical herb collection in the north of England. **Temple Sowerby, nr Penrith, Cumbria CA10 1SP ☎(017683) 61467** 99 B8

A la Ronde 🏛
A unique 16-sided house built on the instructions of two spinster cousins, Jane and Mary Parminter, on their return from a grand tour of Europe. Completed c.1796, the house contains many 18th-century collections brought back by the Parminters.
Summer Lane, Exmouth, Devon EX8 5BD ☎(01395) 265514 10 F5

Alfriston Clergy House 🏛 ✿
Alfriston Clergy House was the first building to be acquired by the Trust in 1896. The building is half-timbered and thatched and contains a medieval hall, exhibition room and two other rooms open to the public, with a charming cottage garden.
The Tye, Alfriston, Polegate, East Sussex BN26 5TL ☎(01323) 870001 18 E2

Anglesey Abbey Gardens and Lode Mill 🏛 ✖ ✿ 🎭
The Abbey was founded in 1135 and for almost four centuries was a religious house. The gardens and Abbey as they stand today were created by Huttleston Broughton, the first Lord Fairhaven. His collections of sumptuous furnishings and rare works of art are displayed as he had laid them out. The gardens have all the grandeur of a mature 18th-century garden. **Lode, Cambridgeshire CB5 9EJ ☎(01223) 810080** 55 C6

Antony 🏛 🏠 ✿ 🌳 🌊 🗣
One of Cornwall's finest early 18th-century houses. The garden contains a national collection of day lilies, magnolias and summer borders. Also of note is an 18th-century dovecote and the 1789 Bath Pond House. **Torpoint, Plymouth PL11 2QA ☎(01752) 812191** 6 D2

Arlington Court 🏛 ✿ 🌳 ⛰ 🐄 🚶
A house full of collections, a stable block with horses and one of the finest carriage collections in the country. Walks through colourful gardens, grounds and woods, all set in miles of beautiful North Devon countryside.
Arlington, nr Barnstaple, Devon EX31 4LP ☎(01271) 850296 20 E5

Ascott 🏛 ✿
Ascott is the creation of Leopold de Rothschild. Anthony de Rothschild, Leopold's son, introduced the exceptional oriental porcelain collection that is so prominent a feature of this house. There are also collections of 18th-century English furniture and paintings. A giant sundial forms the highlight of the garden's topiary work. **Wing, nr Leighton Buzzard, Buckinghamshire LU7 0PS ☎(01296) 688242** 40 B1

Ashdown House 🏛 ✿ ⛰ 🗣
A 17th-century house built by 1st Lord Craven and dedicated to Elizabeth, sister of Charles I, who became Queen of Bohemia. The great staircase, rising from hall to attic, is impressive and the house contains important portraits of the Winter Queen's family. **Lambourn, Newbury, Berkshire RG16 7RE ☎(01793) 762209** 38 F2

Ashridge Estate 🏠 ⛰ 🚶 🎭
This magnificent estate runs along the main ridge of the Chiltern Hills. There are woodlands, commons and chalk downland, supporting a rich variety of wildlife and offering walks through outstanding scenery. The Visitor Centre comprises an exhibition room, shop, tea shop and facilities. **Ringshall, Berkhamsted, Hertfordshire HP4 1LT ☎(01442) 851227** 40 C2

Attingham Park 🏛 🌳 🚶
Designed in 1782 by the innovative Scottish architect George Steuart. The rich collections of furniture, paintings and silver together form one of the most complete representations of Regency taste. The top-lit picture gallery and circular painted boudoir are among the most important country house interiors to survive unaltered. **Shrewsbury, Shropshire SY4 4TP ☎(01743) 708162** 60 D5

Avebury ⛰ 🗿
One of the most important megalithic monuments in Europe. The great stone circle is approached by an avenue of stones. West of Avebury, the Iron Age earthwork of Oldbury Castle crowns Cherhill Down, along with the conspicuous Lansdowne Monument.
Nr Marlborough, Wiltshire SN8 1RF ☎Answerphone (01672) 539250 25 C6

Avebury Manor and Garden 🏛 ✿ 🏠
A much-altered house of monastic origin, the present buildings date from the early 16th century. The topiary and flower gardens contain medieval walls, ancient box and numerous 'rooms'. **Nr Marlborough, Wiltshire SN8 1RF ☎(01672) 539250** 25 B5

Baddesley Clinton 🏛 ✝ ✿ 🌳
A romantically-sited intimate medieval moated manor house dating from the 14th-century, and little changed since 1634. The contents owe much to Elizabethan antiquary Henry Ferrers. He introduced the rich oak panelling and highly decorated overmantels in many of the rooms. **Rising Lane, Baddesley Clinton Village, Knowle, Solihull, Warwickshire B93 0DQ ☎(01564) 783294** 51 B7

Barrington Court 🏛 🏠 ✿ 🎭
An enchanted formal garden influenced by Gertrude Jekyll and laid out in a series of 'rooms'. The Tudor manor house was restored in the 1920s by the Lyle family and is let to Stuart Interiors as showrooms with antique furniture for sale. **Nr Ilminster, Somerset TA19 0NQ ☎(01460) 241938** 11 C8

Basildon Park 🏛 ✿ 🌳
A classical 18th-century house by John Carr of York, in a beautiful setting overlooking the Thames Valley. Two octagonal rooms, important pictures and furniture. The early 19th-century pleasure grounds are currently being restored and there are waymarked trails through the 400 acre woodland.
Lower Basildon, Reading, Berkshire RG8 9NR ☎(0118) 9843040 26 B4

Bateman's 🏛 🏠 ✖ ✿ ⚙
Home to Rudyard Kipling from 1902 until his death in 1936, the rooms are still furnished as they were when he lived here. At the bottom of the tranquil garden with its yew hedges, pond and rose garden designed by Kipling and the wild/conservation area, you can find the 'little mill that clacks'.
Burwash, Etchingham, East Sussex TN19 7DS ☎(01435) 882302 18 C3

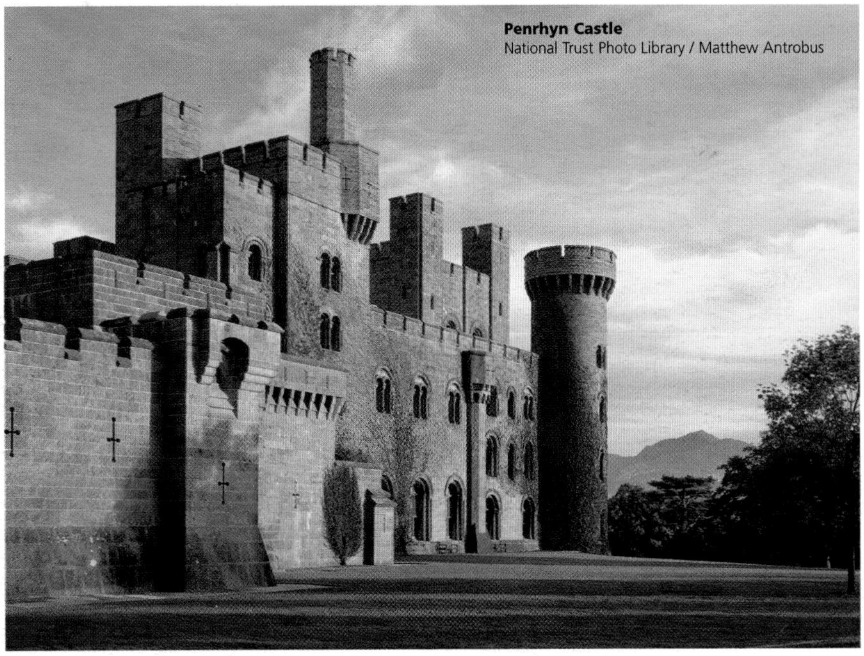

Penrhyn Castle
National Trust Photo Library / Matthew Antrobus

Beatrix Potter Gallery 🏠
Once the office of her husband and her solicitor, William Heelis, this largely unchanged interior now houses an annually changing exhibition of Beatrix Potter's original watercolour illustrations from her captivating children's story books. The gallery complements a visit to Hill Top, Beatrix Potter's house.
Main Street, Hawkshead, Cumbria LA22 ONS ☎(015394) 36355 99 E5

Belton House 🏛 🏠 ✝ ✿ 🌳 🚶 🗣
The serenity of Belton House has made it a favourite for royal visitors. Built late in Charles II's reign, the interiors are exuberantly baroque, with a stunning collection of Old Masters.There are formal gardens, orangery and magnificent landscaped park. **Grantham, Lincolnshire NG32 2LS ☎(01476) 566116** 78 F2

Bembridge Windmill ✖
Dating from around 1700, Bembridge is the only windmill to survive on the island. Much of the wooden machinery can still be seen.
Enquiries to: NT Office, Longstone Farmhouse, Strawberry Lane, Mottistone, Newport, Isle of Wight PO30 4EA ☎(01983) 873945 15 F7

Beningbrough Hall and Gardens 🏛 🏠 ✿ 🚶
Set on a slight rise above the water meadows of the River Ouse, this beautifully restored country house, has exquisite woodcarvings and an impressive cantilevered oak staircase, furniture and porcelain. The Great Hall, which is two storeys high, has one of the most impressive Baroque interiors in England.
Beningbrough, York, North Yorkshire YO30 1DD ☎(01904) 470666 95 D8

Benthall Hall (tenanted) 🏛 ✝ ✿
The exterior of Benthall Hall has changed little since it was built in the 16th century. The early 17th-century interior includes an intricately carved oak staircase, decorated plaster ceilings and oak panelling. The intimate garden is sheltered and enclosed by trees. **Broseley, Shropshire TF12 5RX ☎(01952) 882159** 61 D6

Berrington Hall 🏛 ✿
This elegant, compact house was designed by Henry Holland and built between 1778 and 1783. There is much fine furniture on show, including the Digby Collection of French Regency furniture. The gardens immediately surrounding the house contain many interesting and exotic plants. Lancelot 'Capability' Brown, Holland's father-in-law, laid out the extensive park in the 1780s.
Nr Leominster, Herefordshire HR6 0DW ☎(01568) 615721 49 C7

Biddulph Grange Garden ✿ 🎭
One of Britain's most exciting and unusual gardens. A series of connected 'compartments', designed in the mid-19th century by James Bateman to display specimens from his extensive and wide-ranging plant collection.
Biddulph Grange, Biddulph, Stoke-on-Trent, Staffordshire ST8 7SD ☎(01782) 517999 75 D5

Blewcoat School Gift Shop 🏠
The building was in use as a school until 1926, bought by the Trust in 1954 and restored in 1975. This is the NT London gift shop and information centre. **23 Caxton Street, Westminster, London SW1H 0PY ☎(020) 7222 2877** 28 B3

Blickling Hall, Garden and Park 🏛 🏠 ✿ 🌳 ⛰ 🚶 🎭
Blickling is a harmonious marriage of Jacobean and Georgian interior styles. A breathtaking garden and many miles of attractive lakeside and parkland walks with Temple, secret garden, orangery and plant centre. **Blickling, Norwich, Norfolk NR11 6NF ☎(01263) 738030** 81 E7

Bodiam Castle 🏰 ⛰ 🎭
One of the most famous and evocative castles in Britain, Bodiam was built in 1385, both as a defence and a comfortable home. The exterior is virtually complete and the ramparts rise dramatically above the moat below. Enough of the interior survives to give an impression of castle life, and there are spiral staircases and battlements to explore.
Bodiam, Robertsbridge, East Sussex TN32 5UA ☎(01580) 830436 18 C4

Bodnant Garden 🏠 ✿
Bodnant covers nearly 100 acres on a slope looking down to the River Conwy and across to Snowdonia. Above are a series of five Italianate-style terraces and formal lawns whilst below, in a wooded valley, a stream runs through the secluded wild garden. Magnificent 200-year-old native trees. Bodnant holds the National Collections of Rhododendrons, Magnolias and Eucryphias.
Tal-y-Cafn, Colwyn Bay LL28 5RE ☎(01492) 650460 83 D8

Bourne Mill ✖ ✿
This unusual little Tudor building is an exotic hotch-potch of stones, some from Roman remains. Built as a fishing lodge in Tudor times, the mill changed from cloth milling to corn in about the 1850s.
Bourne Road, Colchester, Essex CO2 8RT ☎(01206) 572422 43 B6

Bradley (tenanted) 🏛 ✝ ⛰
A small 15th-century medieval manor house with original decoration set in woodland and meadows. **Newton Abbot, Devon TQ12 6BN ☎(01626) 354513** 7 B6

Bredon Barn 🏠
A 14th-century barn, 132 ft (40 metres) long, with fine porches, one of which has unusual stone chimney cowling. The barn was restored with traditional materials after a fire in 1980.
Bredon, nr Tewkesbury, Worcestershire ☎Regional Office (01985) 843600 50 F4

Brownsea Island ⛰ 🌊 🐦 🚶 🎭
Brownsea Island is a beautiful wildlife haven in the middle of Poole Harbour, reached via a short crossing by boat. Lord Baden-Powell held his first scout camp on this island.
Poole Harbour, Dorset BH13 7EE ☎(01202) 707744 13 F8

Buckland Abbey 🏛 🏠 ✝ ✿ 🚶
Buckland Abbey holds the secret to over 700 years of history. Medieval monks established a Cistercian monastery. Sir Richard Grenville converted the Abbey into a dwelling place. Later, Sir Francis Drake lived at Buckland during the turbulent period of the Armada.
Yelverton, Devon PL20 6EY ☎(01822) 853607 6 C2

Buscot Park 🏛 ✿ 🌳
A late 18th-century house with pleasure grounds set within a park. **Faringdon, Oxfordshire SN7 8BU ☎(0845) 3453387 📠(01367) 241794** 38 E2

Calke Abbey 🏛 🏠 ✝ ✿ 🌳 🐄 🗣
Present house built in 1701-3 for Sir John Harpur, set in a park with ponds and oak woodland. Within the house is a magnificent 18th-century staircase and good examples of 18th- and 19th-century interiors, notably in the caricature and drawing rooms. Pleasure grounds and attractive walled gardens with an 18th-century orangery at their centre.
Ticknall, Derbyshire DE73 1LE ☎(01332) 863822 63 B7

Canons Ashby House 🏛 ✝ ✿ 🌳
Built in the 1550s by John Dryden and occupied by his descendants for over 400 years. The formal gardens, created by Edward Dryden, are now almost completely restored to reflect the taste of the early 18th-century, providing panoramic views of the surrounding parkland and the church.
Canons Ashby, Daventry, Northamptonshire NN11 3SD ☎(01327) 861900 52 D3

Carlyle's House 🏛
Thomas and Jane Carlyle moved from Scotland in 1834 to rent this Queen Anne home. They lived here until their deaths, hers in 1866 and his 15 years later. The house is still full of their furniture, books, personal relics and portraits. **24 Cheyne Row, Chelsea, London SW3 5HL ☎(020) 7352 7087** 28 B3

Castle Drogo 🏰 ✝ ✿ 🌳 ⛰ 🚶
The last castle to be built in Britain, this 20th-century home designed by Sir Edwin Lutyens incorporates modern conveniences with a medieval atmosphere. The garden is colourful from spring to autumn. A huge, circular croquet lawn is available for visitors.
Drewsteignton, nr Exeter, Devon EX6 6PB ☎(01647) 433306 10 E2

Charlecote Park 🏛 ✿ 🌳 🐄 🚶
Home of the Lucy family since 1247, the present house was built in the 1550s and was later visited by Queen Elizabeth I. Rich Victorian 'romantic' interiors were created from the 1820s onwards. The River Avon flows through the park, landscaped by 'Capability' Brown, which supports herds of red and fallow deer, reputedly poached by Shakespeare. **Warwick, Warwickshire CV35 9ER ☎(01789) 470277** 51 D7

Chartwell 🏛 ✿ 🚶
The home of Sir Winston Churchill from 1924 until the end of his life. The rooms have been left as they were in his lifetime. Two rooms are given over to a museum for his many gifts and uniforms. Terrace gardens descend towards the lake; the garden studio containing many of Sir Winston's paintings is also open.
Westerham, Kent TN16 1PS ☎(01732) 866368 29 D5

Chedworth Roman Villa 🗿
One of the best exposed Romano-British villas in Britain, the remains are those of the luxuri-

ous 4th-century house. The rooms are arranged in three wings around a large courtyard, and features include several 4th-century mosaics, two bath-houses and a water shrine with running spring. A small museum houses a fine selection of objects illustrating all aspects of life in Roman times. **Yanworth, nr Cheltenham, Gloucestershire GL54 3LJ ☎(01242) 890256 ✉(01242) 890544** 37 C7

Cherryburn
Visitors are welcomed with Northumbrian pipe music in the farmhouse which houses an exhibition on the wood engraver Thomas Bewick's life and works. You will find a roaring fire in the old kitchen range and there are demonstrations of wood engraving and printing in the press room. Across the cobbled farmyard is the cottage where Bewick was born in 1753. **Station Bank, Mickley, nr Stocksfield, Northumberland NE43 7DD ☎(01661) 843276** 110 C3

Chirk Castle
A magnificent, furnished marcher fortress now 700-years-old. A dramatic dungeon deep under the west range contrasts with the elegant state rooms which contain elaborate plasterwork, superb furniture, tapestries and portraits. A beautiful and fragrant garden. **Chirk, Wrexham LL14 5AF ☎(01691) 777701** 73 F6

Clandon Park
This is a remarkable combination: a Palladian (1730s) house with its cool 'Roman' style marble hall; the Gubbay collection of porcelain, furniture and needlework; Ivo Forde collection of Meissen Italian comedy figures; fine English 18th-century furniture; the Museum of Queen's Royal Surrey Regiment and to cap it all a Maori house in the garden! **West Clandon, Guildford, Surrey GU4 7RQ ☎(01483) 222482** 27 D8

Claremont Landscape Garden
One of the earliest surviving English landscape gardens. Lake, island with pavilion, grotto, turf amphitheatre, viewpoints and avenues. Splendid trees, including one of the finest cedars of Lebanon in England. **Portsmouth Road, Esher, Surrey KT10 9JG ☎(01372) 467806** 28 C2

Claydon House
This manor house remains the most perfect expression of rococo decoration in England, and has mementoes of Florence Nightingale, who often visited her sister Parthenope here. Within the grounds there is a peaceful little church, and a garden walk with views across the three lakes. **Middle Claydon, nr Buckingham, Buckinghamshire MK18 2EY ☎(01296) 730349** 39 B7

Clevedon Court
Clevedon Court was built about 1320 by Sir John de Clevedon and is one of the very few complete houses of its time that has survived. The house contains a number of collections plus Monuments of Engineering, part of a collection made by Sir Arthur Elton, 10th Baronet, which illustrates aspects of the Industrial Revolution. **Tickenham Road, Clevedon, Somerset BS21 6QU ☎(01275) 872257** 23 B6

Cliveden
Incomparably sited above a steep wooded escarpment plunging to the Thames. The mirror-and-panelling dining room was imported intact from Madame de Pompadour's hunting lodge in France and the portrait of Lady Nancy Astor, the first lady MP, watches over the hall. In the gardens are the sequestered Italian garden, formal lawns, miles of wooded walks and the water garden. **Taplow, nr Maidenhead, Berkshire SL6 0JA ☎(01628) 605069** 40 F2

Clouds Hill
A tiny isolated brick and tile cottage, bought in 1925 by T.E. Lawrence (Lawrence of Arabia) as a retreat. The austere rooms inside are much as he left them and reflect his complex personality and close links to the Middle East. **Wareham, Dorset BH20 7NQ ☎(01929) 405616** 13 E6

Clumber Park
Clumber Park is a unique mosaic of grassland, heath, woodland and lake. A memorable entrance of almost 3km (2 miles) can be made down the longest lime tree avenue in Europe, and although the mansion was demolished in 1938, many features of the estate survive, namely an outstanding Gothic revival chapel, the stableyard and garages, and ornate park entrance lodges. **Worksop, Nottinghamshire S80 3AZ ☎(01909) 476592** 77 B6

Coggeshall Grange Barn
Originally part of the Cistercian monastery of Coggeshall, this is one of the oldest timber-framed barns in Europe, dating from around 1140. **Grange Hill, Coggeshall, Colchester, Essex CO6 1RE ☎(01376) 562226** 42 B4

Colby Woodland Garden
Woodland garden set in a tranquil and secluded valley. Gentle strolls or extensive walks to explore the estate. A haven for bird watchers and gardeners alike. **Stepaside, Narberth, Pembrokeshire SA67 8PP ☎(01834) 811885** 32 D2

Coleridge Cottage
The home of Samuel Taylor Coleridge for three years from 1797, with mementoes of the poet on display. It was here that he wrote 'The Rime of the Ancient Mariner', part of 'Christabel' and 'Frost at Midnight'. **35 Lime Street, Nether Stowey, Bridgwater, Somerset TA5 1NQ ☎(01278) 732662** 22 F3

Coleton Fishacre House and Garden
This garden, developed by Rupert and Lady Dorothy D'Oyly Carte, lies in a stream fed valley amid the spectacular scenery of this National Trust coast. The subtropical climate and sheltered location provides a superb setting for the large collection of tender and exotic plants, started in the 1920s. The house reflects the Arts and Crafts tradition but has refreshingly modern interiors. **Coleton, Kingswear, Dartmouth, Devon TQ6 0EQ ☎(01803) 752466** 7 D7

Compton Castle
A fortified manor house with curtain wall, built at three periods: 1340, 1450, 1520, by the Gilbert family. It was the home of Sir Humphrey Gilbert (1539-83), coloniser of Newfoundland and half-brother of Sir Walter Raleigh: the family still lives here. **Marldon, Paignton, Devon TQ3 1TA ☎(01803) 875740** 7 C6

Conwy Suspension Bridge
Designed and built by Thomas Telford, the famous engineer, this elegant suspension bridge was completed in 1826, replacing the ferry. **Conwy LL32 8LD ☎(01492) 573282** 83 D7

Corfe Castle
The magnificent ruins of this 1000-year-old castle dominate the Isle of Purbeck. The castle ruins have many fine medieval defensive features and the 'Gloriette' features some of the most interesting Gothic architecture in England. **Wareham, Dorset BH20 5EZ ☎(01929) 481294** 13 F7

Cornish Mines and Engines
Following the expiry of the patent on the Boulton and Watt steam engine in 1800, Cornish engineers set about producing more efficient engines. The Trust owns several survivals from this great chapter in Cornish history. At the East Pool and Agar mine is the largest of the great beam engines left in Cornwall. **Pool, nr Redruth, Cornwall TR15 3NP ☎(01209) 315027** 3 B5

Cotehele
Built 1485-1627, and home of the Edgcumbe family for centuries, the house contains original furniture, armour and a remarkable set of tapestries and other textiles. There is a series of formal gardens near the house and a richly planted valley garden. Cotehele Mill has been restored to working condition, with adjoining workshops. **St Dominick, nr Saltash, Cornwall PL12 6TA ☎(01579) 351346** 6 C2

Coughton Court
An impressive central gatehouse dating from 1530 with Elizabethan half-timbered courtyard. It has important connections with the Gunpowder Plot and contains priests' hiding places. Some notable furniture, porcelain and portraits. There are two churches, a tranquil lake, riverside walk and newly created formal gardens. **Nr Alcester, Warwickshire B49 5JA ☎(01789) 400777** 51 C5

Cragside House, Gardens and Estate
Described by contemporaries as 'the palace of a modern magician', Cragside was the first house in the world to be lit by hydro-electric power, with state-of-the-art hydraulics powering both the revolutionary new lift systems and internal telephones which so mesmerised the guests of William Armstrong. The formal Victorian Garden is a short walk from the house. You can also explore the 1,000 acre estate. **Rothbury, Morpeth, Northumberland NE65 7PX ☎(01669) 620333** 117 D6

Croft Castle
Croft Castle, set in the beautiful countryside of north Herefordshire, with superb views southwards and westwards to the Brecon Beacons, has been the property of the Croft family since Domesday (with an intermission of 170 years). The house retains its ancient walls and corner towers although was modified over the centuries when the fine ceilings and Gothic staircase were installed. **Nr Leominster, Herefordshire HR6 9PW ☎(01568) 780246** 49 C6

Croome Park
Croome was 'Capability' Brown's first complete landscape, making his reputation and establishing a new parkland aesthetic which became universally adopted over the next fifty years. **NT Estate Office, The Builders' Yard, High Green, Severn Stoke, Worcestershire WR8 9JS ☎(01905) 371006** 50 E3

Dapdune Wharf
The old boat-building site for the Wey and Godalming Navigations, Dapdune Wharf has a collection of associated buildings that have been restored and refurbished to tell the fascinating story of this historic waterway. **Wey Navigations Office, Guildford, Surrey GU1 4RR ☎(01483) 561389** 27 D7

Dinefwr
A landscaped park attributed to 'Capability' Brown. The deer park has also been home to the ancient White Park Cattle since the 9th-century. The 12th-century Castle of Dinefwr, the home of the Princes of Deheubarth, and part of Newton House are also open. **Llandeilo, Carmarthenshire SA19 6RT ☎(01558) 823902** 33 B7

Dolaucothi Gold Mines
These unique Roman goldmines are set amid wooded hillsides overlooking the beautiful Cothi Valley on the Dolaucothi Estate. The Trust's Exhibition Centre and Miners' Way vividly illustrate the ancient and modern mine workings. **Pumsaint, Llanwrda, Carmarthenshire SA19 8RR ☎(01558) 650177** 47 E5

Dudmaston
This late 17th-century house of mellow red brick contains collections of modern art and sculpture. The house is surrounded by an extensive and impressive lakeside garden with a colourful rockery and woodland walks. **Quatt, nr Bridgnorth, Shropshire WV15 6QN ☎(01746) 780866** 61 F7

Dunham Massey
Georgian house with Edwardian additions set in a wooded deer park. Over 30 rooms are open, with fine furniture, paintings and outstanding Huguenot silver. The moat provides power for a working Jacobean mill. The large garden contains an 18th-century orangery, a Victorian bark house and well house. **Altrincham, Cheshire WA14 4SJ ☎(0161) 941 1025** 86 F5

Dunster Castle
The house and medieval ruins are magically framed with sub-tropical plants including the famous Dunster Lemon; the National Collection of Arbutus; palm trees and Kiwi fruit. Each winding path reveals a new secret, whether a rare shrub or a glimpse of the sea with the Welsh mountains beyond. **Dunster, nr Minehead, Somerset TA24 6SL ☎(01643) 821314** 21 E8

Dunster Working Water-Mill
Built on the site of a mill mentioned in the Domesday Survey of 1086, the present mill dates from the 18th century and was restored to working order in 1979. Note: the mill is a private business and all visitors, including NT members, are asked to pay the admission charge. **Mill Lane, Dunster, nr Minehead, Somerset TA24 6SW ☎(01643) 821759** 21 E8

Dyrham Park
The mansion at Dyrham Park lies at the foot of an ancient parkland situated at the end of the Cotswold Scarp. The deer park has been here since Saxon times. The present house dates from the time of William and Mary, much of the content of the house reflects that period. **Nr Chippenham, Wiltshire SN14 8ER ☎(01179) 372501** 24 B2

East Riddlesden Hall
A charming 17th-century West Yorkshire manor house with embroideries, pewter and a fine collection of Yorkshire oak furniture. The tranquil walled garden overlooking a grass maze has now been restored to its original design. **Bradford Road, Keighley, West Yorkshire BD20 5EL ☎(01535) 607075** 94 E3

Emmetts Garden
A hillside garden originally laid out around the turn of 19th century, with a fine collection of trees and shrubs, noted for its outlook with good views of the Weald of Kent. **Ide Hill, Sevenoaks, Kent TN14 6AY ☎(01732) 751509** 29 D5

Erddig
The most evocative 'upstairs-downstairs' house in Britain. The authentic kitchen, bakehouse, coach-house, smithy and joiners' shop show how 18th-and 19th-century servants lived and worked. Upstairs the state rooms display the exquisite furniture and textiles made for the house in the 1720s. Around the canal, the formal early 18th-century garden has been fully restored and also contains the National Ivy Collection. **Wrexham LL13 0YT ☎(01978) 355314** 73 E7

Farnborough Hall (tenanted)
A classical, mid 18th-century stone house. The entrance hall, staircase and two principal rooms are shown; the plasterwork is particularly notable. The grounds contain charming 18th-century temples, a terrace walk and obelisk. **Banbury OX17 1DU ☎(01295) 690002** 52 E2

Farne Islands
The islands provide a summer home for over 17 different species of seabirds including Puffin, Kittiwake, Eider duck, Guillemot, Fulmar, Tern. Large colony of grey seals. St Cuthbert died on Inner Farne in 687 and there is a chapel built to his memory in the 14th-century and restored in 1845. **Seahouses Information Centre, Northumberland ☎(01665) 721099** 125 F8

Felbrigg Hall Garden and Park
The 17th-century house owes much of its splendour to William Windham II who remodelled the interior to make it a suitable setting for his art treasures. The domestic wing has recently been restored offering a startling contrast between life above and below stairs. The walled garden is complete with greenhouses and is home to the National Collection of colchicums. **Felbrigg, Norwich, Norfolk NR11 8PR ☎(01263) 837444** 81 D7

Fell Foot Park
Fell Foot is a Victorian garden with space for children to play, and leisure facilities in season, and there are magnificent views of the Lakeland fells. The park has access to the lakeshore where there are boats for hire and fine picnic areas. **Newby Bridge, Ulverston, Cumbria LA12 8NN ☎(015395) 31273** 99 F5

Fenton House
Diarist Samuel Pepys may have watched with a mixture of dismay and relief as a small harpsichord dating from 1664 was hauled from the river by boat during the Great Fire on 2nd September 1666. It is now among the outstanding collection of instruments at this 17th-century house. **Windmill Hill, Hampstead, London NW3 6RT ☎(020) 7435 3471** 41 F5

Finch Foundry
Fascinating 19th-century forge, powered by three water wheels. The forge produced sickles, scythes and shovels for both agriculture and mining, and is in the centre of the picturesque village of Sticklepath with countryside and river walks adjoining. **Sticklepath, Okehampton, Devon EX20 2NW ☎(01837) 840046** 9 E8

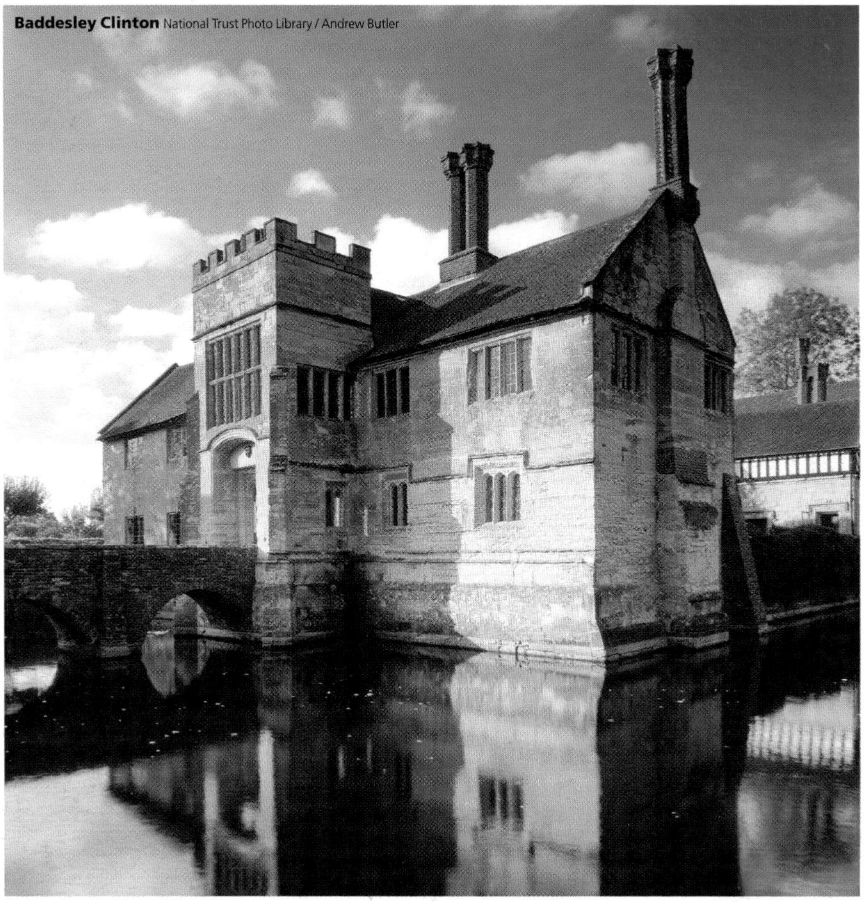
Baddesley Clinton National Trust Photo Library / Andrew Butler

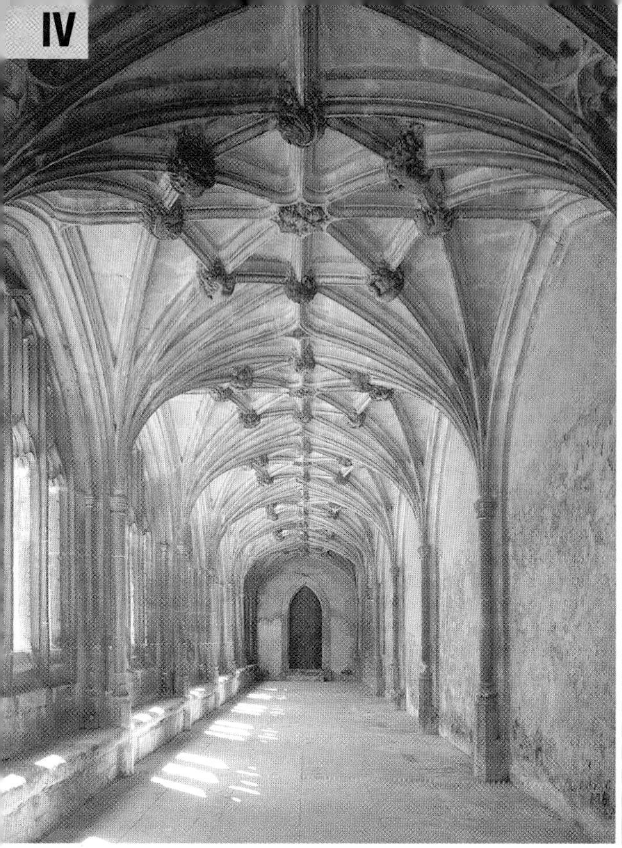

▲**Lacock Abbey** National Trust Photo Library / Andrew Butler

Flatford: Bridge Cottage
Flatford remains very much as John Constable saw and painted it 150 years ago. The thatched Bridge Cottage, upstream from Flatford Mill and right on the bank of the River Stour, is now restored and contains a display to help the visitor identify the actual spots from which the artist composed his famous paintings. **Flatford, East Bergholt, Colchester, Suffolk CO7 6UL** ☎ **(01206) 298260** 56 F4

Fountains Abbey and Studley Royal Water Garden
One of the most remarkable places in Europe and a World Heritage Site, comprising the spectacular ruin of a 12th-century Cistercian abbey, an Elizabethan mansion and one of the best surviving examples of a Georgian water garden. Elegant ornamental lakes, avenues, temples and cascades provide a succession of dramatic eye-catching vistas. St Mary's Church provides a majestic focus to the medieval deer park, home to over 600 deer.
Fountains, Ripon, North Yorkshire HG4 3DY ☎ **(01765) 608888** 95 C5

The White Cliffs of Dover
The gateway to Britain, the White Cliffs of Dover are internationally famous. A Gateway visitor centre has spectacular views and introduces the visitor to five miles of coast and countryside. Visitors can also tour South Foreland Lighthouse, a distinctive landmark used by Marconi for his first ship-to-shore radio experiments. **Langdon Cliffs, Dover, Kent CT16 1HJ** ☎ **(01304) 202756** 31 E7

Gawthorpe Hall
Built between 1600 and 1605, and restored by Sir Charles Barry in the 1850s; Barry's designs have been re-created in the principal rooms. Gawthorpe was the home of the Shuttleworth family, and the Rachel Kay-Shuttleworth textile collections are on display in the house. **Padiham, nr Burnley, Lancashire BB12 8UA** ☎ **(01282) 771004** 93 F8

George Inn
The only remaining galleried inn in London, famous as a coaching inn in the 18th and 19th centuries, and mentioned by Dickens in 'Little Dorrit'. The George Inn is leased and run as a public house. **The George Inn Yard, 77 Borough High Street, Southwark, London SE1 1NH** ☎ **(020) 7407 2056** 41 F6

George Stephenson's Birthplace
A small stone tenement built in 1760 to accommodate four pitmen's families. The furnishings are circa 1781, when George Stephenson was born. The room in which he was born is open to visitors.
Wylam, Northumberland NE41 8BP ☎ **(01661) 853457** 110 C4

Gibside
There is much to explore in this historic estate, along forest paths and above the river. The Palladian interior of the chapel is dominated by a rare triple-decker mahogany pulpit. The remains of the Orangery lie within the sight of a great avenue of ancient oaks: the remnants of one of the greatest 18th-century landscape designs. **Nr Rowlands Gill, Burnopfield, Newcastle-upon-Tyne NE16 6BG** ☎ **(01207) 541820** 110 D4

Glendurgan Garden
Set in a wooded valley rich in fine trees and rare and exotic plants, Glendurgan is one of the great sub-tropical gardens of the South West. The 1833 laurel maze, recently restored, and the 'Giant's Stride' (a pole with ropes to swing from) are unusual and popular features. **Mawnan Smith, nr Falmouth, Cornwall TR11 5JZ** ☎ **(01326) 250906** 3 D6

Gondola
The grand Victorian elegance of Steam Yacht Gondola and her plush interior evoke memories of a bygone age. Gondola provides a relaxing passenger service on Coniston Water in the heart of the Lake District.
NT Gondola Bookings Office, The Hollens, Grasmere LA22 9QZ ☎ **(015394) 41288** 99 E5

Great Chalfield Manor
Dating from 1480, the manor house is set across a moat between parish church and stables. No free-flow; guided tours only.
Nr Melksham, Wiltshire SN12 8NJ ☎ **(01225) 782239** 24 C3

Great Coxwell Barn
A 13th-century monastic barn, stone-built with stone-tiled roof, which has interesting timber construction. **Great Coxwell, Faringdon, Oxfordshire** ☎ **Coleshill Office (01793) 762209** 38 E2

Greys Court
16th-century house with later additions, set in the remains of a 14th-century fortified house. Beautiful grounds include walled gardens, early Tudor donkey wheel well-house and Archibishop's Maze. **Rotherfield Greys, Henley-on-Thames, Oxfordshire RG9 4PG** ☎ **(01491) 628529** 39 F7

Gunby Hall (tenanted)
A red-brick house with stone dressings, built in 1700 and extended in the 1870s. Inside, there is a good early 18th-century wainscoting and a fine oak staircase, also English furniture and portraits by Reynolds. Contemporary stable block, walled garden, lawns and borders. **Gunby, nr Spilsby, Lincolnshire PE23 5SS** ☎ **Regional Office (01909) 486411** 79 C7

Ham House
Outstanding Stuart house built on the banks of the River Thames in 1610 and enlarged in the 1670s. Ham House contains rare survivals of the 17th century including exquisite closets, furniture, textiles and paintings. **Ham, Richmond TW10 7RS** ☎ **(020) 8940 1950** 28 B2

Hanbury Hall
Hanbury Hall is every Englishman's idea of a substantial squire's house, tucked away in of parkland. Ten showrooms are open to the public with paintings by Sir James Thornhill, whose work can also be seen in St Paul's Cathedral, and the collection of fine porcelain and Dutch flower paintings given.
Droitwich, Worcestershire WR9 7EA ☎ **(01527) 821214** 50 C4

Hardwick Hall
A spectacular Elizabethan house built for the ambitious and formidable Bess of Hardwick – the richest woman in England after the queen. Elizabethan and later furniture, tapestries, needlework and a dramatic frieze in the High Great Chamber. Walled courtyards enclose fine gardens, orchards and a herb garden. Historic parkland with Longhorn cattle, and ponds. **Doe Lea, Chesterfield, Derbyshire S44 5QJ** ☎ **(01246) 850430** 76 C4

Hardy's Cottage
The small cob and thatch cottage where novelist and poet Thomas Hardy was born in 1840 and from where he would walk to school every day in Dorchester, six miles away. It was built by his great-grandfather and is little altered since. See also Max Gate. **Higher Bockhampton, nr Dorchester, Dorset DT2 8QJ** ☎ **(01305) 262366** 12 E5

Hatchlands Park
A handsome brick house built in 1758 for Admiral Boscawen, victor of the Battle of Louisburg; splendid interiors by Robert Adam. Since 1988 Hatchlands has been extensively redecorated and it now houses the Cobbe collection of keyboard instruments, paintings and furniture. **East Clandon, Guildford, Surrey GU4 7RT** ☎ **(01483) 222482** 27 D8

Hidcote Manor Garden
An Arts and Crafts garden on a hilltop. A series of small gardens within the whole, separated by walls and hedges of different species. Hidcote is famous for rare shrubs, trees, herbaceous borders, 'old' roses and interesting plant species. **Hidcote Bartrim, nr Chipping Campden, Gloucestershire GL55 6LR** ☎ **(01386) 438333** 51 E6

Hill Top
Beatrix Potter wrote her famous children's books in this little 17th-century farmhouse, which she bought in 1905. The original settings of several of the illustrations for her books can be found in the house.
Nr Sawrey, Ambleside, Cumbria LA22 0LF ☎ **(015394) 36269** 99 E5

Hinton Ampner Garden
Set in superb countryside, the garden combines formal design and informal planting, producing delightful walks with many unexpected vistas. The house was gutted by a fire in 1960, rebuilt and refurnished with fine Regency furniture, 17th-century Italian pictures and porcelain.
Bramdean, nr New Alresford, Hampshire SO24 0LA ☎ **(01962) 771305** 15 B6

Houghton Mill
The present, unusually large four-storey mill, with its gallery of local art (July and August), was raised in the 17th century on an artificial island on the River Ouse.
Houghton, Cambridgeshire PE28 2AZ ☎ **(01480) 301494** 54 B3

Hughenden Manor
Lovely grounds surround the home of the Prime Minister, Benjamin Disraeli. A feast for the addict of Victoriana, or the political browser, with papers and mementoes, and Dizzy's Gallery of Friendship, depicting distinguished contemporaries. **High Wycombe, Buckinghamshire HP14 4LA** ☎ **(01494) 755573** 40 E1

Ickworth House, Park and Garden
The eccentric Earl of Bristol, also Bishop of Derry, created this equally eccentric house, started in 1795 to display his European collection of art. A wonderful collection of paintings includes works by Titian, Gainsborough and Velasquez. The Georgian Silver Collection is considered the finest in private hands. There are many Mediterranean species in the unusual, Italianate garden. 'Capability' Brown parkland with many ancient oaks and beech trees. **Horringer, Bury St Edmunds, Suffolk IP29 5QE** ☎ **(01284) 735270** 60 B5

Ightham Mote
Ightham Mote is a beautiful moated manor house set in a wooded valley. Ranged around the cobbled centre courtyard are the old gatehouse, Great Hall, chapel and the Jacobean drawing-room. Lovely garden and woodland walks. **Ivy Hatch, Sevenoaks, Kent TN15 0NT** ☎ **(01732) 810378** 29 D6

Kedleston Hall
Built between 1759 and 1765 for the Curzon family and little altered since. Robert Adam designed the south front and the decoration of the magnificent state rooms. The rooms remain adorned with the important portrait, landscape and history painting which it was built to display. Includes an Indian Museum. The garden is restored in part to an 18th-century pleasure ground. **Derby, Derbyshire DE22 5JH** ☎ **(01332) 842191** 76 E3

Killerton
The house, built in 1778, is furnished as a comfortable family home. Upstairs, the Paulise de Bush collection of costumes from the 18th century to the present day is displayed in a series of period rooms. The spectacular hillside garden is beautiful throughout the year. **Broadclyst, Exeter, Devon EX5 3LE** ☎ **(01392) 881345** 10 D4

Kingston Lacy
The 17th-century house (later encased in stone by Sir Charles Barry) houses a magnificent collection of Old Masters; the celebrated 'Spanish Room', panelled in gilded leather-work and hung with Spanish paintings; and a ceiling shipped home from Venice.
Wimborne Minster, Dorset BH21 4EA ☎ **(01202) 883402** 13 D7

Knightshayes Court
Designed by William Burges and built in 1869, a rare example of the architect's High Victorian Gothic style. Of equal beauty is the garden. Originally designed by Edward Kemp, this glorious garden owes much to the late Sir John and Lady Joyce Amory, who devoted themselves to its development.
Bolham, Tiverton, Devon EX16 7RQ ☎ **(01884) 254665** 10 C4

Knole
Knole is the largest private house in England and sits within a magnificent deer park. The 13 state rooms open to the public contain a collection of historical portraits, including works by Van Dyck and Gainsborough and a room devoted to the works of Sir Joshua Reynolds. Silver, tapestries and a world-renowned collection of Stuart furniture and the prototype Knole Settee. **Sevenoaks, Kent TN15 0RP** ☎ **(01732) 450608/462100** 29 D6

Lacock Abbey
The abbey was founded in 1232, and was converted into a country house in the mid 16th century. The Museum of Photography commemorates the achievements of a former resident of the Abbey, William Fox Talbot, inventor of the modern photographic negative. The 13th-century village is also cared for by the National Trust. **Lacock, nr Chippenham, Wiltshire, SN15 2LG** ☎ **(01249) 730227** 24 C4

Lamb House (tenanted)
Home of the writer Henry James from 1898 to 1916 where he wrote the best novels of his later period. Also once home to the author E.F. Benson. **West Street, Rye, East Sussex TN31 7ES** ☎ **Regional Office (01892) 890651** 19 C6

Lanhydrock
One of the most beautiful houses in Cornwall, and the most complete house on show in the British Isles. A blend of High Victorian splendour and elements from the original house, almost destroyed by fire in 1881. Beautiful Victorian garden. **Bodmin, Cornwall PL30 5AD** ☎ **(01208) 265950** 5 C5

Lavenham: The Guildhall of Corpus Christi
Early 16th-century timber-framed Tudor building, originally the hall of the Guild of Corpus Christi, overlooks and dominates the market place. Displays of local history, farming, industry and the development of the railway, and a unique exhibition of 700 years of the medieval woollen cloth trade.
Market Place, Lavenham, Sudbury, Suffolk CO10 9QZ ☎ **(01787) 247646** 56 E3

Lindisfarne Castle
Built in the 1540s as a defence against border raids by the Scots, Lindisfarne lost its military importance after the unification of England and Scotland under James I. It was in ruins by 1901 when Edward Hudson, founder and proprietor of the magazine 'Country Life', bought it in 1902 and immediately commissioned Edwin Lutyens to restore it as a summer retreat. **Holy Island, Berwick-upon-Tweed Northumberland TD15 2SH** ☎ **(01289) 389244** 125 E7

Little Moreton Hall
Regarded as the most perfect example of a timber-framed manor house in the country, Little Moreton Hall remains exceptional among half-timbered houses of its time.
Congleton, Cheshire CW12 4SD ☎ **(01260) 272018** 74 D5

Llanerchaeron
A rare survivor of a Welsh gentry estate. The core area includes a principal house designed and built by John Nash in 1794-96, service wing and courtyard; model home farm, kennels and stables. The house opened to the public for the first time in June 2002.
Nr Aberaeron, Ceredigion SA48 8DG ☎ **(01545) 570200** 46 D3

Lodge Park
An exquisite 17th-century grandstand, built for the Dutton family. Recently restored, The Great Room features a stupendous fireplace.
Sherborne, Cheltenham, Gloucestershire GL54 3PP ☎ **(01451) 844130** 37 C8

Lower Brockhampton
A late 14th-century moated manor house, with an attractive detached half-timbered 15th-century gatehouse, a rare example of this type of structure. Also the ruins of a 12th-century chapel.
Bringsty, Worcestershire WR6 5UH ☎ **(01885) 488099** 49 D8

Lundy Island
An unspoilt island, with rocky headlands and fascinating animal and bird life, with no cars to disrupt the peace. The small island community includes a tavern, shop, castle and church. **Devon EX39 2LY** ☎ **(01237) 431831 www.lundyisland.co.uk** 20 C2

Lydford Gorge
The Gorge is perhaps best known for its spectacular White Lady Waterfall, a 90 ft (27.5 metre) cascade of water, and the Devil's Cauldron, a whirlpool of water where the River Lyd rushes through a series of potholes.
The Stables, Lydford Gorge, Lydford, nr Okehampton, Devon EX20 4BH ☎ **(01822) 820441/820320** 9 F7

Lyme Park
The exterior of Lyme Hall, one of the largest houses in Cheshire, is a splendid example of Palladian architecture containing Mortlake tapestries, Grinling Gibbons carvings and a unique collection of English clocks. The garden encompasses a sunken 'Dutch' garden, Victorian-style formal bedding, a lake, lawns, 'secret' paths, herbaceous border and rhododendron walk. **Disley, Stockport, Cheshire SK12 2NX** ☎ **(01663) 762023/766492** 87 F7

Lytes Cary Manor
A manor house with a 14th-century chapel, 15th-century hall and 16th-century great chamber. The home of Henry Lyte, translator of 'Niewe Herball' (1578).
Charlton Mackrell, Somerton, TA11 7HU ☎ **Regional Office (01458) 224471** 12 B3

Lyveden New Bield
The shell of an uncompleted 'lodge' or garden house, begun c.1595 by Sir Thomas Tresham, and designed in the shape of a cross. The exterior incorporates friezes inscribed with religious quotations and signs of the Passion.
Nr Oundle, Peterborough, Northamptonshire PE8 5AT ☎ **(01832) 205358** 65 F6

Max Gate (tenanted)
Designed by poet and novelist Thomas Hardy who lived here from 1885 until his death in 1928. The house is leased to tenants and only the garden, dining room and drawing room are open. **Alington Avenue, Dorchester, Dorset DT1 2AA** ☎ **(01305) 262538** 12 F5

Melford Hall
A turreted brick Tudor mansion, little changed since 1578 with the original panelled banqueting hall, an 18th-century drawing room, a Regency library and a Victorian bedroom, showing fine furniture and Chinese porcelain. There is also a special Beatrix Potter display and a garden. **Long Melford, Sudbury, Suffolk CO10 9AH** ☎ **(01787) 880286** 56 E2

Mendips
Home of John Lennon between the ages of five and 23, restored to how it would have been at the time. Access only by pre-booked guided minibus tour, which also visits Paul McCartney's childhood home. Donated to the National Trust by Yoko Ono. **251 Menlove Avenue, Woolton, Liverpool L25 7SA** ☎ **(0151) 708 8574 (a.m. tours) (0151) 427 7231 (p.m. tours)** 85 F8

Mompesson House

A perfect example of an 18th-century house, and one of the most distinguished in the Cathedral Close.A peaceful garden with traditional herbaceous borders, provides an oasis of peace in the city centre.
The Close, Salisbury, Wiltshire SP1 2EL
(01722) 335659 14 B2

Monk's House (tenanted)

A small village house and garden, and the home of Leonard and Virginia Woolf from 1919 until Leonard's death in 1969.
Rodmell, Lewes, East Sussex BN7 3HF
(01372) 453401 17 D8

Montacute House

Built between 1558 and 1601, this is a magnificent Elizabethan mansion in the tranquil setting of Montacute village. The garden includes colourful mixed borders and formal landscapes. **Montacute, Somerset TA15 6XP**
(01935) 823289 12 C2

Morden Hall Park

A green oasis in the heart of London suburbia, this former deer park has an extensive network of waterways, ancient hay meadows, an impressive avenue of trees and an interesting collection of old estate buildings.
Morden Hall Road, Morden, London SM4 5JD
(020) 8545 6850 28 C3

Moseley Old Hall

An Elizabethan house with later alterations. Charles II hid here after the Battle of Worcester and the bed in which he slept is on view, as well as the ingenious hiding place he used. The small garden has been reconstructed in 17th-century style with formal box parterre. **Moseley Old Hall Lane, Fordhouses, Wolverhampton, Staffordshire WV10 7HY**
(01902) 782808 62 D3

Mottisfont Abbey Garden, House and Estate

The setting of this 12th-century Augustinian Priory is one of great beauty and tranquillity. A tributary of the River Test flows close to the Abbey and the grounds contain a magnificent collection of huge trees. The Priory became a house after the Dissolution of the Monasteries in the 16th century. The National Collection of Old-Fashioned Roses is housed in the walled garden. **Mottisfont, nr Romsey, Hampshire SO51 0LP (01794) 340757** 14 B4

Mr Straw's House

A semi-detached house built at the turn of last century, belonging to William Straw and his brother, Walter. The interior has been preserved since the death of their parents in the 1930s with 1920s wallpaper, furnishings and local furniture.
7 Blyth Grove, Worksop, Nottinghamshire S81 0JG (01909) 482380 89 F6

Newhall Equestrian Centre (Killerton)

The finest range of vernacular farm-buildings on the Killerton Estate. They are now used as a livery yard and equestrian centre, with exhibitions of equestrian art, a small carriage museum and pets' corner.
Killerton, Broadclyst, Exeter, Devon EX5 3LW
(01392) 462453 10 D4

Nostell Priory

A fine Palladian house, built for the Winn family in the 18th century. An additional wing and many of the state rooms were designed by Adam. Fine collection of Chippendale furniture specially made for the house. There are also delightful lakeside walks through the grounds. **Doncaster Road, Nostell, nr Wakefield, West Yorkshire WF4 1QE**
(01924) 863892 88 C5

Nunnington Hall

A delightful, mainly 17th-century, manor house on the banks of the River Rye. A magnificent panelled hall with a fine carved chimneypiece; also, fine tapestries, china and the Carlisle Collection of Miniature Rooms. The delightful walled garden is a rare survival from the 17th-century which still bears traces of the original formal layout.
Nr Helmsley, North Yorkshire YO62 5UY
(01439) 748283 (01439) 748284 96 B2

Nymans Garden

One of the great gardens of the Sussex Weald comprising rare and beautiful trees, shrubs and plants collected from across the world. Walled garden with Italian fountain, hidden sunken garden, laurel walk and ancient bank of bird cherries. The picturesque ruins of the house overlook the lawns. Across the road is the wild flower garden, formerly known as the Tasmania Garden. The Messel family activity is much in evidence in Lady Rosse's library, drawing room and forecourt garden.
Handcross, nr Haywards Heath, West Sussex RH17 6EB (01444) 400321/400777 17 B6

Oakhurst Cottage

A very small 16th-century timber-framed cottage, restored and furnished as a simple cottager's dwelling. Delightful cottage garden with contemporary plant species.
Hambledon, nr Godalming, Surrey GU8 4HF
(01428) 684090 27 F7

Old Town Hall, Newtown

A delightful, small 18th-century brick and stone building that was once the focal point of the 'rotten borough' of Newtown. Copies of ancient documents of the borough are on display with a facsimile of the mace from the hall. An exhibition depicts the history of the famous 'Ferguson's Gang'. **Contact Custodian, Ken Cottage, Upper Lane, Brighstone, Isle of Wight PO30 4AT (01983) 531785** 14 E5

Ormesby Hall

Sir James Pennyman, 6th Baronet, ran through the fortune he inherited by enlarging Ormesby estate only to be forced to hand it over to the bailiffs on completion. A developing model railway exhibition is in the Old Wing. **Ormesby, Middlesbrough TS7 9AS**
(01642) 324188 102 C3

Osterley Park

Set in 375 acres of landscaped park and farmland with ornamental lakes and woodland walks, Osterley was transformed in the 18th century by Robert Adam from a crumbling Tudor mansion into an elegant neo-classical villa for the founders of Child's Bank. Its spectacular interiors contain one of the country's most complete examples of Adam's work.
Isleworth, Middlesex TW7 4RB Email: osterleypark@smtp.ntrust.org.uk (020)8232 5050 28 B2

Overbecks

A beautiful garden with many rare plants, shrubs and trees from around the world and with spectacular views over the Salcombe Estuary. The elegant Edwardian house contains collections of local photographs and inventions by its former owner, Otto Overbeck. **Sharpitor, Salcombe, Devon TQ8 8LW (01548) 842893** 6 F5

Oxburgh Hall, Garden and Estate

Built in 1482 the rooms and their contents range from Tudor to Georgian and Victorian. Mary Queen of Scots embroidery, and a wonderful tapestry map of Oxfordshire and Berkshire. Built on an island in the Fens, the land around is now drained and cultivated into a wonderful garden with delightful walks.
Oxborough, King's Lynn, Norfolk PE33 9PS
(01366) 328258 67 D7

Packwood House

Dating from the 16th-century, Packwood House has been extended and much changed over the years. This fascinating timber-framed house contains a wealth of fine tapestries and furniture. Cromwell's general, Henry Ireton, slept here the night before the Battle of Edgehill in 1642. The superb gardens are noted mainly for their yew topiary and Carolean Garden and the renowned herbaceous borders. **Lapworth, Solihull, Warwickshire B94 6AT (01564) 783294** 51 B6

Paycocke's House (tenanted)

Delightful cameos frolic along the intricately decorated wooden beam spanning the whole width of this fine half-timbered merchant's house dating from 1500. Inside there is a display of the lace for which Coggeshall was famous. **West Street, Coggeshall, Colchester, Essex CO6 1NS (01376) 561305** 42 B4

Peckover House and Garden

A lovely Georgian brick town house with a charming Victorian walled garden including summerhouses, Victorian fernery and an orangery.
North Brink, Wisbech, Cambridgeshire PE13 1JR (01945) 583463 66 D4

Penrhyn Castle

This dramatic neo-Norman castle was built by Thomas Hopper between 1820 and 1845. The extraordinarily grand staircase and extravagant stone carving of the interior create an almost cathedral-like atmosphere. The recently restored Victorian kitchens and servants' rooms complete the Penrhyn story.
Bangor LL57 4HN (01248) 353084 83 D6

Petworth House and Park

More of a palace than a conventional country house, Petworth is set in 'Capability' Brown's famous landscape park immortalised by Turner. Internationally known for its outstanding art collection, Petworth has over 300 paintings on display including works by Turner, Van Dyck, Titian, Gainsborough, Reynolds and Claude as well as fine collections of ancient and neo-classical sculpture, furniture and wood carvings by Grinling Gibbons. **Petworth, West Sussex GU28 0AE**
(01798) 342207 16 B3

Plas Newydd

Impressive 18th-century house by James Wyatt in unspoilt surroundings on the Menai Strait, with magnificent views of Snowdonia. The house contains Rex Whistler's largest wall painting and an exhibition devoted to his work. In the military museum are campaign relics of the Ist Marquess of Anglesey who commanded the Cavalry at Waterloo.
Llanfairpwll, Anglesey LL61 6DQ
(01248) 714795 83 D7

Plas Yn Rhiw

A small manor house with garden and woodlands, overlooking the west shore of Porth Neigwl (Hell's Mouth Bay) on the Llyn peninsula. The house is part medieval with Tudor and Georgian additions, with ornamental gardens. **Rhiw, Pwllheli LL53 8AB**
(01758) 780219 70 E3

Polesden Lacey

Polesden Lacey is still a peaceful country estate, surrounded by trees and green pasture. The house, an elegant Regency 'villa', was luxuriously furnished in Edwardian times by society hostess, The Hon. Mrs Greville. Her collection of furniture, paintings, porcelain and silver is remarkable. Lovely walled garden and stunning walks through the North Downs. **Nr Dorking, Surrey RH5 6BD**
(01372) 458203/452048 28 D2

Powis Castle

Perched dramatically above the late 17th-century garden terraces, Powis Castle is one of the finest country houses in Wales. Established in 1987, the Clive Museum, shows the treasures brought from India by Clive and his son. Built c.1200. The world-famous garden shelters rare and tender plants.
Welshpool SY21 8RF (01938) 551929 60 D2

Princes Risborough Manor House (tenanted)

A 17th-century red-brick house with Jacobean oak staircase. House and front garden by written arrangement only with tenant. **Princes Risborough, Buckinghamshire HP17 9AW Regional Office (01494) 528051** 39 D8

Prior Park Landscape Garden

A beautiful and intimate 18th-century landscape garden, created by local entrepreneur Ralph Allen with advice from the poet Alexander Pope and 'Capability' Brown, and set in a sweeping valley with magnificent views of the city of Bath. **Ralph Allen Drive, Bath BA2 5AH (01225) 833422** 24 C2

Quarry Bank Mill

Set in a country park with riverside and woodland walks, Quarry Bank Mill is a Georgian cotton mill, built in 1784 by Samuel Greg, and restored as Europe's largest working textile museum. The Apprentice House garden is a fascinating example of a Victorian utilitarian garden, growing fruits, vegetables and herbs using the same methods as 150 years ago.
Wilmslow, Cheshire SK9 4LA
(01625) 527468 87 F6

Quebec House

One of Britain's greatest military heroes, James Wolfe, spent the first eleven years of his life here. The 17th-century house is full of mementoes of his victory at Quebec when he defeated the French by scaling the Heights of Abraham above the town.
Westerham, Kent TN16 1TD
Chartwell Office (01732) 868381 29 D5

Rainham Hall (tenanted)

Conveniently close to the Thames, this elegant Georgian house was completed in 1729 for prosperous merchant, John Harle. Built in the domestic Dutch style, with dormers in the hipped roof, the interior has hardly changed. Bookings by written application to the tenant.
The Broadway, Rainham, Havering, London RM13 9YN London Office (020) 7447 6605 41 F8

Red House

Acquired by the National Trust in 2002, and designed in the late 1850s by Philip Webb for William Morris, one of his co-founders in the Arts and Crafts Movement, Red House is a landmark in the history of domestic architecture. The gardens inspired many of Morris's wallpaper patterns.
13 Red House Lane, Bexleyheath, Kent DA6 8JF (01494) 559799 29 B5

Rievaulx Terrace and Temples

Like Fountains Abbey the Cistercian abbey of Rievaulx was established in a secluded valley. Overlooking the ruins (owned by English Heritage), there is a fascinating 1 km long, grass-covered terrace and two mid-18th century temples. There is a permanent exhibition in the basement relating to English landscape design and natural history.
Nr Helmsley, North Yorkshire YO62 5LJ (01439) 798340 (01439) 748284 102 F3

Rufford Old Hall

There is a legend that William Shakespeare performed here for owner Sir Thomas Hesketh in the Great Hall of this, one of the finest 16th-century buildings in Lancashire. In the Carolean Wing, altered in 1821, there are fine collections of 16th- and 17th-century oak furniture, arms, armour and tapestries.
Rufford, nr Ormskirk, Lancashire L40 1SG
(01704) 821254 86 C2

Runnymede

Historic meadows where King John sealed Magna Carta in 1215; wooded slopes on Cooper's Hill overlook the meadows. Memorials dedicated to Magna Carta, John F. Kennedy and the Air Forces.
Egham, Surrey (01784) 432891 27 B8

St John's Jerusalem (tenanted)

A large garden, moated by the River Darent. The house is the former chapel of a Knight's Hospitallers' Commandery, since converted into a private residence. **Sutton-at-Hone, Dartford, Kent DA4 9HQ Regional Office (01372) 453401** 29 B6

St Michael's Mount

The spectacular castle on top of this famous rocky island dates from the 14th-century. Approached by a causeway at low tide, the castle has magnificent views towards Land's End. Fascinating early rooms, armoury, a rococo Gothic drawing room and, at the highest point, a 14th-century church.
Marazion, nr Penzance, Cornwall TR17 0EF
(01736) 710507 2 D4

Saltram

Stunning state rooms designed by Robert Adam, furniture by Chippendale and family portraits by Sir Joshua Reynolds. Superb Chinese wallpaper. The Great Kitchen is possibly England's most complete survival of a large country house kitchen. Set in romantic gardens and undulating parkland.
Plympton, Plymouth, Devon PL7 1UH
(01752) 333500 6 D3

Sandham Memorial Chapel

This red-brick chapel was built in the 1920s for the artist Stanley Spencer to fill with murals of his experiences in the First World War. Inspired by Giotto's Arena Chapel in Padua, this impressive project took five years to complete and is arguably Spencer's finest achievement. The chapel is set amidst lawns and orchards with views across Watership Down. **Burghclere, nr Newbury, Hampshire RG20 9JT (01635) 278394** 26 C2

Scotney Castle Garden

Often described as the most romantic garden in England, the ruins of the small 14th-century castle are reflected in its moat, forming the backdrop to a garden of breathtaking beauty and considerable importance to the garden-historian. **Lamberhurst, Tunbridge Wells, Kent TN3 8JN (01438) 820307** 18 B3

Shaw's Corner

An early 20th-century house, and the home of George Bernard Shaw from 1906 until his death in 1950. The rooms remain much as he left them with many literary and personal effects on show. Shaw's writing hut is hidden at the bottom of the garden, which has richly planted borders and views over the Hertfordshire countryside.
Ayot St Lawrence, nr Welwyn, Hertfordshire AL6 9BX (01438) 820307 40 C4

Sheffield Park Garden

A highly impressive garden, with four lakes, laid out in the 18th century by 'Capability' Brown. In early summer the 'Stream Garden' is particularly attractive and in the autumn hundreds of trees and shrubs, planted specially for their autumn colour, are a spectacular display. **Sheffield Park, East Sussex TN22 3QX (01825) 790231** 17 B8

Sheringham Park

One of Humphry Repton's most outstanding achievements, the landscape park contains fine mature woodlands, and the large woodland garden is particularly famous for its spectacular show of rhododendrons and azaleas (flowering at its best May to early June). There are stunning views of the coast and countryside from the viewing towers and many delightful waymarked walks. **Warden: Gardener's Cottage, Sheringham Park, Upper Sheringham, Norfolk NR26 8TB**
(01263) 823778 81 C7

Shugborough Estate

Shugborough is the magnificent estate of the Earls of Lichfield. Visit the servants' quarters and the restored working brew-house, the impressive collection of horse-drawn vehicles and the authentic Victorian schoolroom. The Park Farm houses a Rare Breeds Approved Centre and working corn mill; there is a Grade I historic garden and a unique collection of neo-classical monu-

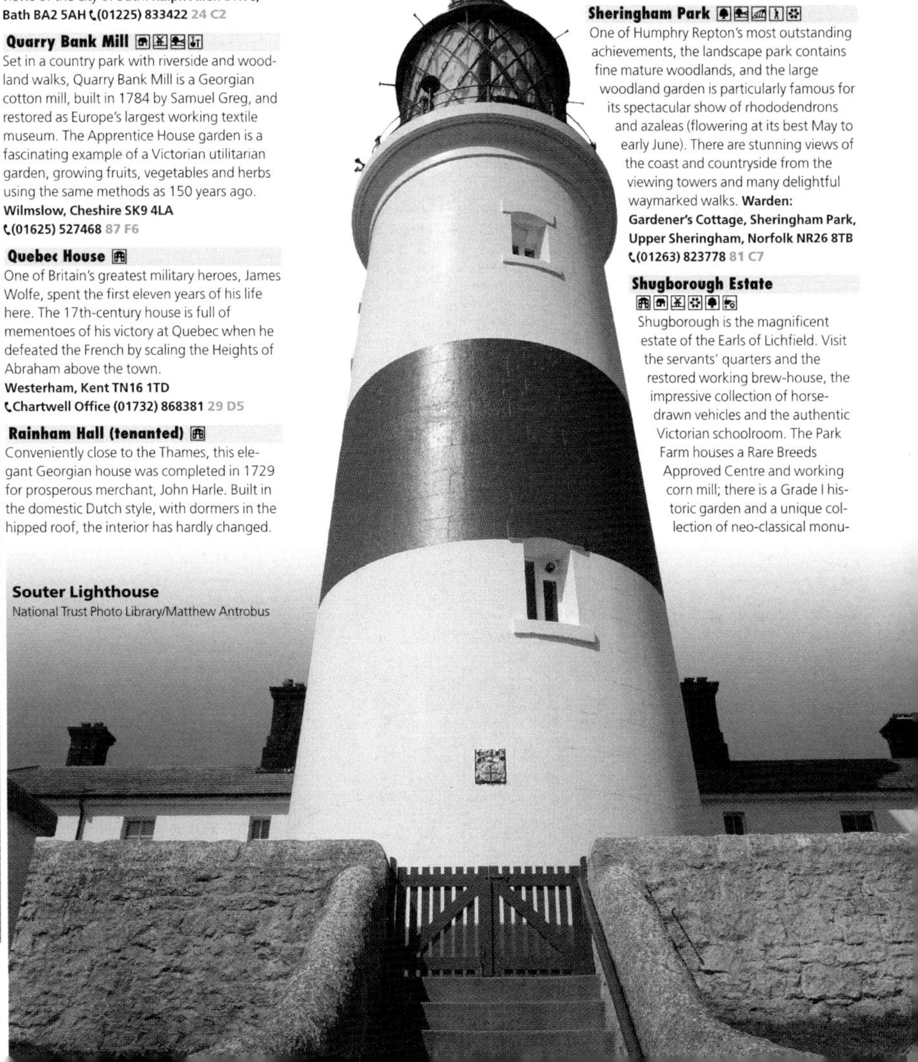

Souter Lighthouse
National Trust Photo Library/Matthew Antrobus

ments by James Stuart. **Milford, nr Stafford, Staffordshire ST17 0XB ☎(01889) 881388** 62 B3

Shute Barton (tenanted)
One of the most important surviving non-fortified manor houses of the Middle Ages. Begun in 1380 and completed in the late 16th century, then partly demolished in the late 18th century, the house has battlemented turrets, late Gothic windows and a Tudor gatehouse. Access to most parts of the interior for conducted tours only. **Shute, nr Axminster, Devon EX13 7PT ☎(01297) 34692** 11 E7

Sissinghurst Castle Garden
Of international acclaim, this connoisseur's garden was created by the late Vita Sackville-West and her husband, Sir Harold Nicolson, between the surviving parts of an Elizabethan mansion. A series of small enclosed romantic gardens or 'outdoor rooms' are the spring garden, orchard, white garden and herb garden. Also the study where Vita Sackville-West worked, and the Long Library. **Sissinghurst, nr Cranbrook, Kent TN17 2AB ☎(01580) 710701** 18 B5

Sizergh Castle
Sizergh was built over 760 years ago to withstand attack in the frequent border raids which troubled the region for centuries. The pele tower rises to almost 60ft and its Limestone walls are still formidable. Known for the decorative use of wood in its interior, Sizergh's unique feature is the Inlaid Chamber. **Nr Kendal, Cumbria LA8 8AE ☎(015395) 60070** 99 F6

Smallhythe Place
Legendary actress Dame Ellen Terry lived here for nearly 30 years, from 1899 until her death in July 1928. The house is a museum of the great actress's career and includes many personal and theatrical mementoes from the greats of Victorian drama. **Smallhythe, Tenterden, Kent TN30 7NG ☎(01580) 762334** 19 C5

Snowshill Manor
Snowshill Manor is no ordinary Cotswold manor house but the setting for Charles Paget Wade's 'Collection of Craftsmanship.' You will see English, European and Oriental furniture, musical instruments, clocks and model ships and other collections in nearly all the 21 rooms. The delightful garden is now organically managed. **Snowshill, nr Broadway, Worcestershire WR12 7JU ☎(01386) 852410** 51 F5

Souter Lighthouse
Souter was built after a disastrous year in 1869, when no fewer than 20 vessels came to grief between South Shields and Sunderland. Climb 76 steps up to the 76 foot (23 metre) high tower and see the automatic radio beacon and the light which shines out, 150 ft (46 m) above sea level – the original lighthouse was the first ever to be powered by a reliable electric current. **Coast Road, Whitburn, Sunderland SR6 7NN ☎(0191) 529 3161** 111 C7

Speke Hall
One of the most famous half-timbered houses in the country, its Elizabethan stone bridge still spans the now grassy moat. William Morris wallpapers, Jacobean plasterwork, as well as a fully-equipped Victorian kitchen and servants' hall. Also, newly restored Victorian farm building with new restaurant, shop and visitor reception. **The Walk, Liverpool, Merseyside L24 1XD ☎(0151) 427 7231 Infoline (local rate) 08457 585702** 86 F2

Standen
Built in the 1890s by the architect Philip Webb, whose friendship with William Morris led to the house being decorated with many of the famous designer's textiles and wallpapers. There is also a good collection of contemporary furniture, pottery and pictures. **East Grinstead,West Sussex RH19 4NE ☎(01342) 323029** 29 F4

Staunton Harold Church
Built by Sir Robert Shirley in an open act of defiance to Cromwell's Puritan regime, leading to death in the Tower of London, at the age of 27. The church survives, little changed. **Ashby-de-la-Zouch, Leicestershire LE65 1RW ☎(01332) 863822** 63 C7

Stembridge Tower Mill
The last thatched windmill in England, dating from 1822 and in use until 1910. **High Ham, Somerset TA10 9DJ ☎(01458) 250818** 23 F6

Stoneacre (tenanted)
A half-timbered mainly late 15th-century yeoman's house, with great hall and crownpost, and newly restored cottage-style garden. **Otham, Maidstone, Kent ME15 8RS ☎(01622) 862157 ⎙(01622) 862157** 30 D2

Stourhead
Stourhead garden is one of the most famous examples of the early 18th-century English landscape movement. Sheets of water reflect splendid mature trees, temples, a classical bridge, and a grotto in the best 18th-century tradition. The house contains a wealth of Grand Tour paintings and works of art, together with furniture designed by Chippendale the Younger. **The Estate Office, Stourton, Warminster, Wiltshire BA12 6QD ☎(01747) 841152** 24 F2

Stowe Gardens
One of the finest Georgian landscape gardens, made up of valleys and vistas, narrow lakes and rivers with more than 30 temples and monuments designed by many of the leading architects of the 18th century. **Buckingham, Buckinghamshire MK18 5EH ☎(01280) 822850** 52 F4

Sudbury Hall
A most individual Charles II house. The great staircase under the dome is the finest of its kind in an English house, and the long gallery is notable for the period. The National Trust Museum of Childhood in the old servants' wing houses the Betty Cadbury collection of playthings past. **Sudbury, Derbyshire DE6 5HT ☎(01283) 585305** 75 F8

Sutton Hoo
One of the most fascinating and important archaeological finds in this country's history. A fascinating story of Anglo-Saxon pagan kings, ship burials, treasure and warriors is revealed. **Sutton Hoo, Woodbridge, Suffolk IP12 3DJ ☎(01394) 389700** 57 E6

Sutton House
A rare example of a Tudor red-brick house in London's East End. Recent restoration revealed many 16th-century details which are now displayed when 'secret' panels are opened. **2 and 4 Homerton High Street, Hackney, London E9 6JQ ☎(020) 8986 2264** 32 D2

Tattershall Castle
A magnificent example of medieval brick architecture, with walls 14 ft (4.5 m) thick at the base, it rises through four floors to a rooftop courtyard and battlement walkway. Each floor contains a single enormous state room and many smaller rooms within the thickness of the walls. Surrounding the castle is a double moat. **Tattershall, Lincolnshire LN4 4LR ☎(01526) 342543** 78 D5

Tatton Park
One of the most complete historic estates open to visitors in England. The 19th-century Wyatt house, set in an extensive deer park, contains the Egerton family collections and specially commissioned Gillow furniture; servants' rooms and cellars. The gardens contain authentic Japanese and Italian gardens. Also, a medieval hall and 18th-century farm – working as in the 1930s – and many varieties of wildfowl. **Knutsford, Cheshire WA16 6QN ☎(01625) 534400** 86 F5

Theatre Royal
Built in 1819 by William Wilkins, a rare example of a late Georgian playhouse with fine pit, boxes and gallery. A working theatre presenting a year-round programme of professional drama, comedy, dance, music, mime, pantomime and amateur work. **Westgate Street, Bury St Edmunds, Suffolk IP33 1QR ☎(01284) 769505** 56 C2

The Courts Garden
One of Wiltshire's best-kept secrets, this is the English garden style at its best, full of charm and variety. The garden includes topiary, water features and fine specimen trees underplanted with spring bulbs. A new kitchen garden is also being created around recently laid brick paths. **Holt, nr Trowbridge, Wiltshire BA14 6RR ☎(01225) 782340** 24 C3

The Fleece Inn
A medieval farmhouse in the centre of the village, containing family collection of furniture. It became a licensed house in 1848 and remains largely unaltered. **Bretforton, nr Evesham, Worcestershire WR11 5JE ☎(01386) 831173** 51 E5

The Greyfriars
Built in 1480 for a Worcester brewer on a site next to a Franciscan monastery. The Greyfriars remains a good example of a wealthy merchant's home of the late Middle Ages with early 17th- and late 18th-century additions. Interesting textiles and furnishings add character to the panelled rooms. An archway leads through to a delightful garden. **Friar Street, Worcester, Worcestershire WR1 2LZ ☎(01905) 23571** 50 D3

The Levant Steam Engine
Harvey's of Hayle built the machinery in 1840 for the Levant mine which visitors will discover just north of St Just, spectacularly housed in a building set on the edge of the cliffs. After 60 idle years, the famous engine is steaming again. **Trewellard, Pendeen, nr St Just, Cornwall ☎(01736) 796993** 2 C2

The Needles Old Battery
A Victorian coastal fort built in 1862, high above the sea. A tunnel leads to spectacular views of Needles Rocks, lighthouse and coastline. Two original gun barrels are mounted on carriages in the parade ground and the Laboratory, Searchlight Position and Poisition-Finding Cells have been restored. **West Highdown, Totland, Isle of Wight PO39 0JH ☎(01983) 754772 during opening hours** 14 F4

The Vyne
A house of comfortable charm drawing the visitor back to the time of Henry VIII. Now set in fine parkland dating from the mid 18th-century. Highlights include the pillared portico, a remarkable staircase, rich Tudor panelling and excellent 18th-century furnishings. **Sherborne St John, Basingstoke, Hampshire RG24 9HL ☎(01256) 881337** 26 D4

The Weir
Delightful riverside garden particularly spectacular in early spring, with fine views over the River Wye and Black Mountains. **Swainshill, nr Hereford, Herefordshire HR4 8BS ☎Regional Office (01981) 590509** 49 E6

Tintagel Old Post Office
One of the most distinctive buildings in Cornwall, and a house of great antiquity, this small 14th-century manor is full of charm and interest. Restored in the fashion of the Post Office it was for nearly 50 years. **Tintagel, Cornwall PL34 0DB ☎(01840) 770024 during opening hours only.** 8 F2

Tintinhull Garden
Tintinhull Garden is a delightful walled garden divided into separate areas by clipped hedges. Closer to the house stands the impressive cedar court. **Farm Street, Tintinhull, Yeovil, Somerset BA22 9PZ ☎(01935) 822545** 12 C3

Townend
Townend is one of the finest examples of vernacular domestic Lake District architecture. Its contents reflect a fascinating accumulation by a sheep-farming family gradually rising in society. In the unique little library are first editions of Milton and throughout the house an impressive range of carved oak furniture. **Troutbeck, Windermere, Cumbria LA23 1LB ☎(015394) 32628** 99 D6

Treasurer's House
In the shade of York Minster this elegant 17th-/18th-century town house is set in a peaceful garden. It has a medieval-style hall with a half-timbered gallery, fine Georgian features with handsomely decorated plasterwork, panelling and elaborate fireplaces, and an excellent collection of furniture. It is renowned for being the home of the oldest ghost in England. **Minster Yard, York YO1 7JL ☎(01904) 624247** 96 D2

Trelissick Garden
The garden is set in rolling parkland and has exotic flora in the summer. The park, with views down to Falmouth and the open sea, is never closed. Stables, harness room, converted barn restaurant, fairy-tale water tower and a new orchard featuring many old varieties of Cornish apples. **Feock, nr Truro, Cornwall TR3 6QL ☎(01872) 862090** 4 C7

Trengwainton
The garden of mainland Britain perhaps most favoured for the cultivation of exotic trees and shrubs. The walled garden shelters many tender plants. **Nr Penzance, Cornwall TR20 8RZ ☎(01736) 362297 (during opening hours)** 2 C3

Trerice
A delightful, secluded Elizabethan manor house, built in 1571 with an early gabled facade. A small museum in the barn traces the development of the lawn mower. **Nr Newquay, Cornwall TR8 4PG ☎(01637) 875404** 4 D3

Tudor Merchant's House
A late 15th-century example of domestic town architecture, characteristic of the stone building tradition found in south west Wales. Furnishings and fittings recreate the atmosphere of the house when a Tudor family was in residence. **Quay Hill, Tenby, Pembrokeshire SA70 7BX ☎(01834) 842279** 32 D2

Tyntesfield
Magnificent Gothic-Revival country house with original furnishings and decor, acquired by the National Trust in June 2002, following a public appeal. Access only by pre-booked guided tours via park-and-ride from Nailsea. **Tyntesfield, Wraxall, Somerset ☎0870 458 4500** 23 B7

Ty'n-y-Coed Uchaf
A smallholding with 19th-century farmhouse and outbuildings which provide a record of the Welsh traditional way of life. **Penmachno, Betws-y-coed LL24 0PS ☎(01690) 760229** 83 F8

Ty Mawr Wybrnant
Situated in the beautiful and secluded Wybrnant Valley. Ty Mawr was the birthplace of Bishop William Morgan (1545-1604), first translator of the entire Bible into Welsh. The house has been restored to its probable 16th-/17th-century appearance, with a display of Welsh bibles. **Penmachno, Betws-y-coed LL25 0HJ ☎(01690) 760213** 83 F7

Uppark
A fine late 17th-century house, recently re-opened after major restoration following the fire in 1989. There is also an important collection of paintings formed by members of the Fetherstonhaugh family. Below stairs attractions include extensive servants' rooms where the mother of H.G. Wells worked as housekeeper. **South Harting, Petersfield, West Sussex GU31 5QR ☎(01730) 825415** 15 C8

Upton House
The house, built of a mellow local stone, dates from 1695, but the outstanding collections it contains are the chief attraction. These include paintings by Old Masters, Brussels tapestries, Sevres porcelain, Chelsea figures and 18th-century furniture. The garden is also of great interest, with the National Collection of Asters, a large kitchen garden, a water garden and pools with ornamental fish. **Nr Banbury, Warwickshire OX15 6HT ☎(01295) 670266** 51 E8

Waddesdon Manor
Waddesdon Manor, designed in the style of a French Renaissance chateau, was built in the 1870s by Baron Ferdinand de Rothschild. The interior evokes 18th-century France and is furnished with panelling, furniture, carpets and porcelain, many of which have a royal French provenance. There is an important collection of English 18th-century portraits by Gainsborough and Reynolds, rooms devoted to Sevres porcelain and Baron Ferdinand's 18th-century panelling. In the garden a rococo-style aviary houses exotic birds. **Waddesdon, nr Aylesbury, Buckinghamshire HP18 0JH ☎(01296) 653226** 39 C7

Wakehurst Place
This magnificent garden is leased to the Royal Botanic Gardens, Kew who manage and fund it. Wakehurst Place offers a unique blend of education, conservation and science. Here you can see four comprehensive National Collections: birch, hypericum, southern beech and skimmia, and compare the many different species. Temperate trees from across the continents and several lakes and ponds. **Ardingly, nr Haywards Heath, West Sussex RH17 6TN ☎(01444) 894066** 28 F4

Wallington
In 1728 Sir Walter Calverley Blackett inherited the estate which he transformed, laying out the park and gardens. He also turned the house, as Arthur Young the agriculturalist wrote after his visit in 1766, into a 'piece of magnificence that cannot be too much praised'. Other things to see include the writing desk of George Trevelyan, the wonderful dolls' house collection, 19th-century gentleman's bathroom and coaches and carriages in the coach house. **Cambo, Morpeth, Northumberland NE61 4AR ☎(01670) 773600** 117 F6

Washington Old Hall
From 1183 this house was the home of George Washington's direct ancestors. Intriguing arched doorways and a 17th-century staircase take the visitor past a fan given to Martha Washington by General Lafayette. The Jacobean garden filled with Old English flowers and herbs with a pair of 18th-century gates, a gift from the Colonial Dames of America. **The Avenue, Washington Village, Tyne and Wear NE38 7LE ☎(0191) 416 6879** 111 D6

Watersmeet House
A fishing lodge, built c.1832 in a picturesque valley has been a tea-garden since 1901 and is the focal point for several beautiful walks. **Watersmeet Road, Lynmouth, Devon EX35 6NT ☎(01598) 753348** 21 E6

Westbury Court Garden
A formal water garden with canals and yew hedges, laid out between 1696 and 1705. It is the earliest of its kind remaining in England, restored in 1971 and planted with species dating from pre-1700, including apple, pear and plum trees. **Westbury-on-Severn, Gloucestershire GL14 1PD ☎(01452) 760461** 36 C4

Westwood Manor (tenanted)
A 15th-century stone manor house, altered in the early 17th century, with late Gothic and Jacobean windows and fine plaster-work.There is a modern topiary garden. **Bradford-on-Avon, Wiltshire BA15 2AF ☎(01225) 863374** 24 D3

West Wycombe Park
A Palladian house with frescos and painted ceilings, fashioned for Sir Francis Dashwood in the mid-18th century. Dashwood is now chiefly remembered for his connection with the notorious Hellfire Club which met in caves on the estate. The landscape garden and lake were laid out at the same time as the house, with various classical temples. **West Wycombe, Buckinghamshire HP14 3AJ ☎(01494) 513569** 39 E8

West Wycombe Village and Hill
For six centuries a principal route passed through West Wycombe, nurturing the creation of this Chilterns village. There are fine examples of buildings from the 16th to 18th centuries. The hill is part of the 18th-century landscape of West Wycombe Park. It is surmounted by an Iron Age hill fort, now the site of the church and Dashwood mausoleum, and commands fine views. **West Wycombe, Buckinghamshire ☎(Hughden Estate Office) 01494 755573** 39 E8

Wicken Fen National Nature Reserve
Britain's oldest nature reserve and a unique fragment of the wilderness that once covered East Anglia. A haven for birds, plants, insects and mammals alike, the Fen can be explored by the traditional wide droves and lush green paths, and there is a boardwalk nature trail giving access to several hides. **Lode Lane, Wicken, Ely, Cambridgeshire CB7 5XP ☎(01353) 720274** 55 B6

Wightwick Manor
Begun in 1887, the house is a notable example of the influence of William Morris, with many original Morris wallpapers and fabrics. Also of interest are Pre-Raphaelite pictures, Kempe glass and de Morgan ware. An attractive garden reflects the style and character of the house. **Wightwick Bank, Wolverhampton, West Midlands WV6 8EE ☎(01902) 761400** 62 E2

Wimpole Hall, Garden, Park and Home Farm
The largest house in Cambridgeshire, its facades date from the first half of the 18th century when visitors included Swift and Pope. There is an impressive library and also a Chapel with painted decorations. Home Farm presents a living museum of agriculture with ancient farm implements and many rare breeds, all housed in the thatched farm buildings. **Arrington, Royston, Cambridgeshire SG8 0BW ☎(01223) 207257 ⎙(01223) 207838** 54 D4

Winkworth Arboretum
Winkworth Arboretum was planned and planted as a woodland in the 1930s. It has two lakes and many rare trees and shrubs. The Arboretum is worth a visit at any time of the year. It is open daily from dawn to dusk. Wildlife abounds and there is an impressive show of butterflies and moths. **Hascombe Road, Godalming, Surrey GU8 4AD ☎(01483) 208477** 27 E7

Woodchester Park
This secret wooded valley, formerly an 18th-century park with five lakes, was first opened to the public in 1996. There are waymarked trails (steep and strenuous in places) through delightful scenery with spectacular views. **The Warden's Office, Old Ebworth Centre, Ebworth Estate, The Camp, Stroud, Gloucestershire GL6 7ES ☎(01452) 814213** 37 D5

Woolsthorpe Manor
Sir Isaac Newton grew up here (returning when plague closed Cambridge University in 1665). Upstairs is his study, hung with prints of other famous scientists of the day. In the orchard is a descendant of the famous apple tree. Also Science Discovery Centre. **23 Newton Way, Woolsthorpe-by-Colsterworth, Lincolnshire NG33 5NR ☎(01476) 860338** 65 B6

Wordsworth House
The birthplace of the poet Wordsworth. This Georgian house is preserved in an 18th-century style, and stands a stone's throw from one of Wordsworth's favourite subjects, the ruined castle of Cockermouth. The house includes many personal effects. The garden referred to in 'The Prelude' has a terrace walk overlooking the River Derwent. **Main Street, Cockermouth, Cumbria CA13 9RX ☎(01900) 824805** 107 F8

National Trust for Scotland properties

The following directory lists properties owned and managed by the National Trust for Scotland that are open to the public.

How to join the National Trust for Scotland

For immediate membership you can join at almost all of the Trust's properties or shops. Alternatively contact The National Trust for Scotland, 28 Charlotte Square, Edinburgh EH2 4ET
☎0131 243 9300 ☏0131 243 9301 wwww.nts.org.uk

Alloa Tower

On A907 in Alloa, Clackmannanshire 6m east of Stirling ● A fascinating view inside the ancestral home of the Earls of Mar, whose portraits still look down from the walls of the tower. Parts of the structure date back to medieval times and you can still see the original dungeon, well and roof-beams contrasting with the elegant staircase added in the 18th century. **Alloa Park, Alloa, Clackmannanshire FK10 1PP ☎(01259) 211701** 133 E7

Angus Folk Museum

Off A94, in Kirk Wynd, Glamis, 5m south-west of Forfar ● A fascinating glimpse into traditional Scottish rural life. House in a group of 18th-century buildings, the folk museum's collection offers an insight into the realities of living as a local land worker. It includes farming tools, domestic objects and the restored 19th-century Glenisla hearse.
Kirkwynd, Glamis, Forfar, Angus DD8 1RT ☎(01307) 840288 142 E3

Arduaine Garden

On A816, 20m south of Oban and 18m north of Lochgilphead. ● A favourite destination for gardeners all year round. The perennial borders at Arduaine are magnificent throughout the season, but in late spring and early summer the rhododendrons and azaleas really come into their own. Stroll through the woodland and enjoy the views from the coast, or relax in the water garden. **Arduaine, nr Oban, Argyll PA34 4XQ ☎(01852) 200366** 130 D3

Bachelors' Club

In Tarbolton, off A77 south of Kilmarnock and off A76 at Mauchline. 7½ m north-east of Ayr ● A chance to find out more about Scotland's most famous poet, Robert Burns. In this thatched 17th century house, Burns hotly debated the topics of the day before drinking their fill at the inn next door. **Sandgate Street, Tarbolton KA5 5RB ☎(01292) 541940** 112 B4

Balmacara Estate and Lochalsh Woodland Garden

A87, adjoining Kyle of Lochalsh.
● Wandering around this charming crofting estate reveals many delights. There are spectacular views across to Skye and Applecross. The beautiful village of Plockton is an Outstanding Conservation Area, and the old steadings in Balmacara Square have been restored to provide workshops for local crafts, a delicatessen and a interactive Visitor Centre. Enjoy quiet lochside walks at the Lochalsh Woodland Garden.
Lochalsh House (NTS), Balmacara, Kyle IV40 8DN ☎(01599) 566325 155 J3

Bannockburn

Off M80/M9 at junction 9, 2m south of Stirling. ● Here in 1314 King Robert the Bruce routed the English forces to win freedom for the Scots. In the Heritage Centre close to the Borestone, Bruce's command post, you can experience the epic encounter through an exciting audio-visual show and exhibition. You can even see the battle through Bruce's eyes by trying on a reproduction of his battle helmet. Shop and cafe. **Glasgow Road, Stirling FK7 0LJ ☎(01786) 812664** 133 E6

JM Barrie's Birthplace, Celebrating 100 years of Peter Pan

A90/A926, in Kirriemuir, 6m north-west of Forfar. ● A great afternoon out for children of all ages. JM Barrie, the creator of Peter Pan, was born here in 1860, one of ten children. Barrie established his first theatre in the outside wash-house. There's an imaginative exhibition about the author and 'Pirates' Workshop' for children. Look out for the crocodile in the garden! Self-service tearoom, picnic area. **9 Brechin Road, Kirriemuir, Angus DD8 4BX ☎(01575) 572646** 142 D3

Camera Obscura

Signposted from Kirriemuir town centre, A90/A926 ● This fascinating camera obscura, one of only three in the country, was a gift to the town from JM Barrie. From the top of Kirriemuir Hill you can enjoy superb views of the surrounding countryside.
The Barrie Pavilion, Kirriemuir Hill, Kirriemuir, Angus DD8 4BX ☎(01575) 572646 142 D3

Barry Water Mill

North of Barry village, between A92 and A930, 2m west of Carnoustie, 9m east of Dundee. ● Enjoy the splash of the waterwheel, the rumble of the machinery and the smell of the grinding corn in this 19th-century mill, working on a demonstration basis. There's an exhibition on the historical role of the mill, and a delightful walkway along the mill lade. Milling demonstrations normally take place on Sunday afternoons and for pre-booked parties. **Barry, Carnoustie, Angus DD7 7RJ ☎(01241) 856761** 143 F5

Ben Lawers National Nature Reserve

Mountain Visitor Centre, off A827, 6m north-east of Killin ● Climb to the summit of Ben Lawers, the central Highlands' highest mountain, on a clear day and it's possible to enjoy views of the Atlantic and the North Sea. For naturalists, its slopes are home to a rich variety of birds and mountain plants. The Trust is pioneering habitat restoration here and you can find out more from the Visitor Centre exhibition. Shop. **NTS Office, Lynedoch, Main Street, Killin FK21 8UW ☎(01567) 820397** 140 F3

Ben Lomond

B837, at Rowardennan, 11m beyond Drymen off A811 ● Rising from the east shore of Loch Lomond to a height of 3,193ft (974m), Ben Lomond offers exhilarating walking and spectacular views across the Loch Lomond and Trossachs National Park. Walking routes, including the low-level Ardess Hidden History Trail, are available from the Information Centre and it's also possible to arrange ranger guided walks.
Ardess Lodge, Rowardennan, by Drymen, Glasgow G63 0AR ☎(01360) 870224 132 D2

Branklyn Garden

A85, Perth. ● With its fine collection of rare and unusual plants, this enchanting little garden attracts gardeners and botanists from all over the world. Among the rhododendrons, alpines, herbaceous, and peat gardens, look out for the vivid blue Himalayan poppy. Shop and plant sales.
116 Dundee Road, Perth PH2 7BB ☎(01738) 625535 134 B3

Brodick Castle, Garden and Country Park

Isle of Arran, ferry from Ardrossan to Brodick (connecting bus to castle) and Claonaig, Kintyre to Lochranza (ferry enquiries 0870 565 0000) ● Brodick Castle, with origins in Viking times, has everything – heritage, horticulture and activity. For antique-spotters, the castle is packed with artefacts telling Brodick's story. Gardeners will love exploring the estate, with its famous rhododendron collection. Still in the mood for walking? Discover woodlands, waterfalls and wildlife along trails around the Country Park, or tackle the rugged clopes of Goatfell. Licensed terrace restaurant, coffee shop, shop, plant sales centre, picnic area, adventure playground. **Isle of Arran KA27 8HY ☎(01770) 302202** 119 C7

Brodie Castle

Off A96 4 1/2m west of Forres and 24m east of Inverness ● This 16th-century castle is packed with enough arts and antiques to keep connoisseurs happy all day. It houses a major art collection, as well as porcelain and fine furniture. In springtime the grounds are carpeted with daffodils, making for pleasant walking. Meanwhile the children can enjoy storming the play fort and special quizzes. Tearoom, shop, available for weddings/corporate events. **Brodie, Forres IV36 0TE ☎(01309) 641371** 158 D3

Broughton House and Garden

Off A711/A755 ● Broughton House, the home and studio of the artist EA Hornel from 1901-1933, is closed in 2004 for extensive conservation work, but the garden created by the artist remains open. See how the design and colours of the garden reflect the artist's vision through a series of charming 'outdoor rooms'.
12 High Street, Kirkcudbright DG6 4JX ☎(01557) 330437 106 D3

Bucinch and Ceardach

In Loch Lomond. ● These two small, uninhabited islands in the loch, between Luss and Balmaha, were presented by Col Charles L Spencer of Warmanbie, Dumfries, in 1943. 132 E2

Burg

Isle of Mull, Argyll and Bute. By footpath, 8 km (5 miles) W of Tiroran, off B8035 on N shore of Loch Scridain. ● These 1405 acres of Mull, with high cliffs known as 'The Wilderness', were bequeathed by Mr A Campbell Blair of Dolgelly in 1932. MacCulloch's Fossil Tree, possibly 50 million years old, is beyond Burg Farm and can be reached at low water with difficulty. A 11 km (7 mile) walk on a path which becomes very rough and precipitous culminates in a steep descent to the beach by an iron ladder. 137 F5

Caiy Stane

In Caiystane View, off B701, Oxgangs Road ● This 9ft (3m) tall prehistoric cup-marked stone, also known as General Kay's Monument, or the Kel Stone, traditionally marks the site of an ancient battle, perhaps between the Picts and the Romans. 122 C5

Cameronians' Regimental Memorial

Off A70, in Douglas. ● Statue of the Earl of Angus who was the first Colonel of the Cameronian Regiment which was raised at Douglas in 1689. The statue is situated at north edge of village. 121 F8

Canna

Highland. Cruises from Mallaig and Arisaig. ● The most westerly of the Small Isles, Canna is 8 km (5 miles) long and 2 km (1.25 miles) wide and is one of the most interesting islands in the Hebrides for scenic, agricultural, scientific and historical reasons. 144 C2

Thomas Carlyle's Birthplace

Off M74,5 1/2m south east of Lockerbie ● A fascinating view into the life and work of writer and historian Thomas Carlyle. He was born here in 1795 and the house is furnished in period style with an intriguing collection of portraits and Carlyle's personal belongings.
The Arched House, Ecclefechan, Lockerbie DG11 3DG ☎(01576) 300666 107 B8

Castle Fraser, Garden and Estate

Off A944, 4m north of Dunecht and 16m west of Aberdeen ● Approaching Castle Fraser, you're certain to be impressed by the magnificent tower with its distinctive turrets. Dating from 1636, this is one of the grandest of the 'Castles of Mar'. Inside the Great Hall, fine furniture. paintings and embroideries powerfully evoke the past. In the grounds, enjoy the secluded walled garden and woodland walks. Children will love the adventure playground. Courtyard tearoom, shop, plant sales.
Sauchen, Inverurie AB51 7LD ☎(01330) 833463 151 C6

28 Charlotte Square

Edinburgh, 2 mins from west end of Princes Street. ● Sample the best of Scotland's heritage in the New Town with a visit to the Trust gallery. There's a fine collection of 20th century works by the Scottish Colourists, and a wonderful display of Regency furniture. Temporary exhibitions are advertised separately. Relax in the coffee house and the courtyard garden, or enjoy light lunches in the restaurant. Licensed restaurant, coffee house, gift shop, New Interiors Collection shop.
28 Charlotte Square, Edinburgh EH2 4ET ☎(0131) 243 9300 122 B5

Corrieshalloch Gorge National Nature Reserve

A832/A835 at Braemore. ● This spectacular gorge, one of the finest examples in Britain of a box canyon, is 60 m (200 ft) deep. The river which carved this channel through hard metamorphic rock, plunges over the Falls of Measach. The suspension bridge, downstream from the falls, was built by John Fowler, joint designer of the Forth Railway Bridge. 156 B3

Craigower

1½m north of Pitlochry, off A924
● A bracing walk to the summit viewpoint (1,335 ft/405m) will reveal splendid views of Pitlochry and Loch Faskally below, along Lochs Tummel and Rannoch and across Rannoch Moor to Glencoe. 141 D6

Crarae Garden

On A83, 15m north of Lochgilphead and 10m south of Inveraray ● Crarae, on the banks of Loch Fyne, is a beautiful woodland glen with tumbling waterfalls. Trees and shrubs from all over the world thrive here throughout the year, and in the spring the rhododendrons burst into life. Shop, refreshments, picnic area. **Inveraray PA32 8YA ☎(01852) 200366 or (01546) 886614** 131 F5

Crathes Castle, Garden and Estate

On A93, 3m east of Banchory and 15m west of Aberdeen ● With its intriguing round towers and overhanging turrets, Crathes is a fine example of a 16th century tower house, home to the Burnett family for over four centuries. The magnificent gardens, with their massive yew hedges and colourful herbaceous borders, were recently judged one of the three best in Britain. Gardens and estate with fascinating waymarked trails, are ideal for a family day out. Circular Mill Restaurant, wildlife exhibition, shop, plant sales centre, picnic area, adventure playground.
Banchory AB31 3QJ ☎(01330) 844525 151 E6

Culloden Battlefield and Visitor Centre

On B9006, 5m east of Inverness ● Culloden is one of the most poignant and haunting battlegrounds in the British Isles. Here, on a sleet-filled April morning in 1746, Jacobite forces were brutally crushed by government troops, ending Bonnie Prince Charlie's dream of restoring the crown to the Stuarts. You can relive the battle through the Visitor Centre presentations or wander among evocative memorials on the battlefield itself. Restaurant, speciality Scottish bookshop, battlefield tours.
NTS Visitor Centre, Culloden Moor, Inverness IV2 5EU ☎(01463) 790607 157 E8

Royal Burgh of Culross

Off A985, 12m west of Forth Road Bridge and 6m west of Dunfermline ● Wandering among the old buildings and cobbled streets of this royal burgh on the river Forth is like stepping back into the 16th and 17th centuries. You can explore the splendid refurbished palace and gardens dating from 1597, and find out more about this historic town from the video in the palace. Shop and tearoom.
☎(01383) 880359 133 F8

Culzean Castle and Country Park

12m south of Ayr, on A719, 4m west of Maybole, off A77 ● Culzean Castle occupies a stunning location with spectacular views across the Firth of Clyde; it is surrounded by acres of ornamental gardens and parkland. Inside the castle, look out for the Oval Staircase, the Circular Saloon and the impressive armoury. Afterwards enjoy the delicious Scottish produce in the Home Farm restaurant or take home some plants from the Country Park shop. Ranger service, full events programme including special children's events, adventure playground, deer park, licensed restaurant.
Maybole KA19 8LE ☎(01655) 884455 112 D2

Cunninghame Graham Memorial

Stirling. Off A81, in Gartmore ● Cairn to the memory of R B Cunninghame Graham of Ardoch, distinguished Scottish author; erected in 1937, a year after his death, at Castlehill, Dumbarton. Moved to Gartmore in 1981. 132 E4

Dollar Glen

Clackmannanshire. Off A91, N of Dollar.
● This wooded glen provides a spectacular walk to Castle Campbell. Waymarked walks. During or after rain the path can be dangerous. Dogs must be kept strictly under control and on leads during lambing season. 133 E8

Drum Castle, Garden and Estate

Off A93, 3m west of Peterculter, 8m east of Banchoryand 10m west of Aberdeen ● A visit to Drum Castle is a little like striding across the centuries. It includes a 13th century keep, with adjoining Jacobean mansion house and several 'modern' additions by Victorian lairds. The castle holds a superb collection of paintings and furniture, and for keen gardeners there is a splendid collection of roses in the Garden of Historic Roses. For children there are woodland trails and a play area. Shop and tearoom. **Drumoak, nr Banchory AB31 3EY ☎(01330) 811204** 151 D6

Dunkeld and the Hermitage

12m north of Perth on A9 ● There's an air of timeless tranquility about the village of Dunkeld. Here you can wander among restored 17th century houses and drop into the Ell Shop, named after the weaver's measure fixed to the wall. At The Hermitage, one mile west, a woodland walk leads to Ossian's Hall, and 18th century folly overlooking the dramatic Falls of Braan.
Ell Shop, The Cross, Dunkeld PH8 0AN
☎The Hermitage: (01350) 728641 141 E7

Fair Isle

Accessible in summer by regular sailings of the mail boat from Grutness, on Shetland. Flights from Tingwall (Lerwick) airport and Kirkwall, Orkney. ● One of the most isolated inhabited islands in Britain. The Fair Isle Knitting Co-operative sells island knitwear world-wide. Important for the study of birds, flora and fauna, for its traditional crofting practices and for conservation of the environment. Additional crafts now include traditional wooden boatbuilding, fiddle making and the manufacture of stained glass windows. 175 L3

Falkland Palace and Garden

A912 in the village of Falkland, 11m north of Kirkcaldy, 10m from M90, junction 8 ● A landmark building in the life of Mary, Queen of Scots. Set in the gentle scenery of the Royal Burgh of Falkland in the Kingdom of Fife, Falkland Palace was the hunting lodge of the Royal Stuarts. It is a stunning example of Renaissance architecture and contains sumptuous interiors from the 16th century. Stroll around the beautiful gardens and visit the Real Tennis court built in 1539. Shop and plant sales centre.
Falkland, Cupar, Fife KY15 7BU ☎(01337) 857397; Shop: (01337) 857918 134 D4

Falls of Glomach

Highland. NE of A87. ● One of the highest waterfalls in Britain, set in a steep narrow cleft in remote country. The best approach is from the Dorusduain car park, by path allow 5 hours for round trip, or, for the very fit only, leave car by the Ling bridge, N end Loch Long, for a long walk along Glen Elchaig before making a steep climb to the Falls, allow 8 hours. 146 B3

Finavon Doocot

Angus. Off A90 ● Largest doocot in Scotland, with 2400 nesting boxes. Believed to have been built by the Earl of Crawford in the 16th century. 142 D4

Fyvie Castle

Off A947, 8m southeast of Turriff and 25m north of Aberdeen ● The appeal of Fyvie Castle spans the centuries. Some parts date from the 13th century, while the opulent interiors are Edwardian. Art lovers will recognise paintings by Raeburn and Gainsborough, and military enthusiasts will appreciate the impressive collection of arms and armour. Take a leisurely stroll around the lake, or visit the restored racquets court and bowling alley. Tearoom and shop. **Fyvie, Turriff AB53 8JS ☎(01651) 891266** 160 E4

Gatehouse of Fleet

Dumfries and Galloway. Off A75. ● Venniehill: a field with hilltop viewpoint at the west end of the main street. The Murray Isles: two small uninhabited islands in the Islands of Fleet, Wigtown Bay, off Carrick Point. 106 D3

Geilston Garden

Off A814 at west end of Cardross, 18m north-west of Glasgow ● A delight for garden enthusiasts. This 200 year old walled garden has shrub borders, lawns and a herbaceous border that bursts into spectacular colour in summer. There are enchanting woodland walks along Geilston burn. A wide range of market garden crops can be seen growing in the popular vegetable garden. This produce is also offered for sale to visitors. Produce sales and picnic area. **Cardross, Dumbarton G82 5HD ☎(01389) 849187** 120 B2

Gladstone's Land

On Edinburgh's Royal Mile, near the castle
● A window onto 17th century Edinburgh life. Antique lovers will be fascinated by this Old Town apartment, featuring authentic decoration and period furniture as well as a fine collection of Dutch paintings. Don't forget to look up and admire the remarkable painted ceilings. Experience the 17th century-style shopping in the reconstructed 'luckenbooth' cloth shop.**477B Lawnmarket, Edinburgh EH1 2NT ☎(0131) 226 5856** 122 B5

Glencoe

Off A82, 17m south of Fort William ● Glencoe is a dramatic location in every sense. This spectacular landscape was the setting for the notorious massacre of th MacDonalds by government soldiers in 1692. Find out about the glen's remarkable history, landscape and wildlife at the Trust's eco-friendly Visitor Centre. The glen is also a walker's paradise – from gentle strolls to challenging climbs for experienced mountaineers. Cafe, shop and picnic area. **NTS Visitor Centre, Glencoe, Ballachulish PA39 4HX ☎Ranger:(01855) 811729** 139 D5

Glenfinnan Monument

On A830, 18m west of Fort William • Set in superb scenery at the head of Loch Shiel, this monument to the Jacobite clansmen stands close to the spot where Bonnie Prince Charlie raised his standard in 1745. There's an exhibition and commentary on the Jacobite campaign, and from this spot you can see the viaduct that features in the Harry Potter films. Shop and restaurant. **NTS Information Centre, Glenfinnan PH37 4LT ☎(01397) 722250** 146 F2

Goatfell

Isle of Arran • Goatfell is the highest peak on the Isle of Arran, with impressive views. Trust property includes part of Glen Rosa and Cir Mhor; fine rock-climbing and ridge-walking. 119 B6

Greenbank Garden

Flenders Road off Mearns Road, Clarkston. Off M77 and A726, 6m south of Glasgow city centre • A source of inspiration for suburban gardeners, this unique walled garden has a fine collection of plants and design features, fountains and a woodland walk. Pick up practical advice from one of the gardening demonstrations or join us for other special events throughout the year. Tearoom, shop, plant sales centre, special disabled visitor centre. **Flenders Road, Clarkston, Glasgow G76 8RB ☎(0141) 616 5216** 121 D5

Grey Mare's Tail Nature Reserve

On A708, 10m northeast of Moffat • A magnificent upland area, reaching from the waterfall that cascades into the Moffat valley, up steep slopes to Loch Skeen and corries beyond. Home to rare upland plants and a variety of wildlife. This landscape, shaped by human activity since the Iron Age, offered refuge to the 17th century Covenanters. Guided walks are available in summer. Video link to peregrine falcon nest site. **☎(01556) 502575** 114 C4

Haddo House

Off B999, near Tarves, 19m north of Aberdeen • Imagine life amongst the Scottish nobility when you visit this elegant country house, once the home of the Earls and Marquesses of Aberdeen. The distinctive Georgian exterior leads into sumptuous Victorian interiors. You're also free to wander among the terrace gardens and country park beyond, with lakes, walks and monuments. Tearoom and shop. **Ellon AB41 7EQ ☎(01651) 851440** 161 E5

Harmony Garden

In Melrose, opposite the Abbey. • The name says it all, Harmony Garden, surrounded by high walls and screened by trees, has an unmistakable aura of peace and serenity. It's a special place to wander and enjoy the simple pleasures of the flowers, fruits and vegetables growing here. **St Mary's Road, Melrose TD6 9LJ. ☎(01721) 722502**123 F8

Hill of Tarvit Mansionhouse and Garden

Off A916, 2m south of Cupar • A fine early 20th century home and a treat for collectors and antique lovers. The house was rebuilt in 1906 by renowned Scottish architect Sir Robert Lorimer for a Dundee industrialist. It contains a superb collection of furniture, porcelain and paintings. Lorimer also designed the terrace gardens. The grounds contain one of the largest mixed borders in the country and some delightful woodland walks. Shop, tearoom, plant sales centre. **Cupar, Fife KY15 5PB ☎(01334) 653127** 135 C5

Holmwood House

Signposted from Clarkston Road, B767, 4m south of Glasgow city centre • The villa was the finest work of Glasgow architect, Alexander 'Greek' Thompson, and was completed in 1858. Inside, see conservation work bringing the original ornamentation and decoration back to life and discover more from the exhibition and audio tour. Attractive riverside grounds. Shop and refreshments. **61-63 Netherlee Road, Cathcart, Glasgow G44 3YG ☎(0141) 637 2129** 121 D5

House of Dun and Montrose Basin Nature Reserve

3m west of Montrose on the A935 • This handsome house, dating from 1730, was once the home of Lady Augusta FitzClarence, daughter of William IV and the actress Mrs Jordan. Don't miss her royal mementoes, or the superb plasterwork by Joseph Enzer in the saloon. The surrounding estate includes a woodland walk and a recreated Victorian walled garden. Visitors have access to the Montrose Basin Nature Reserve. Restaurant, shop and picnic area. **Montrose, Angus DD10 9LQ ☎(01674) 810264** 145 C6

House of the Binns

Off A904 4m east of Linlithgow. • Home of the Dalyell family since 1612, the house contains a fascinating collection of portraits, furniture and porcelain, revealing the family's lives and interests through the centuries. A walk around the grounds will reward you with panoramic views over the river Forth. **Linlithgow, West Lothian EH49 7NA ☎(01506) 834255** 122 B3

Hugh Miller's Cottage

Via Kessock Bridge and A832, in Cromarty, 22m northeast of Inverness • The Trust is proud to present an entirely new museum portraying every aspect of the great Cromarty writer and geologist, Hugh Miller. Situated in Miller House, a handsome Georgian villa, the museum features three floors of exhibitions covering Miller's life from harsh toil as a stonemason to national fame as a scientist, church reformer and campaigning editor. **Cromarty IV11 8XA ☎(01381) 600245** 157 C8

Hutchesons' Hall

Ingram Street, near southeast corner of George Square • A chance to look inside one of Glasgow city centre's landmark buildings. The Hall was completed in 1805 and remodelled 70 years later to create the elegant interior you can see today. The exhibition, Glasgow Style, contains work for sale by young designers from this vibrant city. Contemporary Design Shop, Interiors Collection Shop.**158 Ingram Street, Glasgow G1 1EJ ☎(0141) 552 8391** 121 C5

Inveresk Lodge Garden

A6124, south of Musselburgh • This attractive terraced garden and 17th-century lodge (which is not open to the public) were presented to the Trust in 1959 by Mrs Helen E Brunton. Fine Edwardian conservatory. **24 Inveresk Village, Musselburgh, East Lothian EH21 7TE** 123 B6

Inverewe Garden

On A832, by Poolewe, 6m northeast of Gairloch. • A mecca for garden enthusiasts, Inverewe is an oasis of exotic plants bursting with vibrant colour. Rhododendrons from the Himalayas, eucalypts from Tasmania, Olearia from New Zealand and other species from such far-flung places as Chile and South Africa all flourish here, in a display that changes with the seasons, so it's always worth a repeat visit. Licensed Woodside Restaurant, extensive shop, plant sales centre. **Poolewe IV22 2LQ ☎(01445) 781200** 162 F2

Iona

By ferry from Fionnphort, Isle of Mull (A 849) • In AD 563 Columba and his followers arrived here from Ireland to extend in Scotland and the north of England the gospel which had first been introduced by St Ninian at Whithorn in AD 397. 136 F3

Kellie Castle and Garden

On B9171, 3m north of Pittenweem • A truly atmospheric castle dating back more than six centuries. Kellie was restored by the Lorimer family in the late 19th century and today you can see furniture designed by Sir Robert Lorimer, magnificent plaster ceilings, painted panels and a mural by Phoebe Anna Traquair. Don't miss the exhibition on sculptor Hew Lorimer and the late-Victorian Organic Garden. Shop and tearoom. **Pittenweem, Fife KY10 2RF ☎(01333) 720271** 135 D7

Killiecrankie

3m north of Pitlochry on B8079 • Here, where the Highlands meet the Lowlands, you can enjoy this spectacular, deep fiver gorge, cloaked in ancient woodlands, and discover the story of the Jacobite victory at the Battle of Killiecrankie in 1689. The Visitor Centre features exhibitions and natural history displays. A camera link with the woodlands shows nesting or feeding birds. The Ranger Service offers guided walks in summer. Shop, snack bar, picnic area. **NTS Visitor Centre, Killiecrankie, Pitlochry PH16 5LG ☎(01796) 473233** 141 C6

Kintail and West Affric

North of A87, 16m east of Kyle of Lochalsh • This is magnificent territory for walking. There are ten Munroes in the area, which includes the Five Sisters of Kintail and the Falls of Glomach. Keen-eyed naturalists may be able to spot red deer, eagles and an amazing variety of other wildlife. 146 B2

Leith Hall, Garden and Estate

On B9002, 1m west of Kennethmont and 34m northwest of Aberdeen • This fine mansion house stands as a living monument to the Leith family who lived here for almost 300 years. You can find out more about how they lived when you wander through the elegantly furnished rooms. Outside you can explore the estate trails or lose yourself among the colourful herbaceous borders. Period tearoom, picnic area, bird hide. **Huntly AB54 4NQ ☎(01464) 831216** 150 B4

Linn of Tummel

2m northwest of Pitlochry on B8019 • Enjoy a quiet walk through the woodlands to the meeting place of the rivers Garry and Tummel. Here you can see a very early example of a fish-pass. Before the building of the hydro-electric scheme, this allowed salmon making their way upstream to bypass the Falls of Tummel. **☎(01350) 728641** 141 D6

Malleny Garden

In Balerno, near Edinburgh, off Lanark Road (A70). • The 17th-century house (not open to the public) was built for Sir James Murray of Kilbaberton about 1635, with two Georgian reception rooms added in 1823. The walled garden is dominated by four 400-year-old clipped yew trees and a large collection of old-fashioned roses. National Bonsai Collection for Scotland. Extensive woodland. **Balerno EH14 7AF ☎(0131) 449 2283** 122 C4

Mar Lodge Estate

Off A93, 6m west of Braemar via an unclassified road; parking at Linn of Dee • Located in the heart of the Cairngorms, Mar Lodge offers a wealth of interest for walkers and nature-lovers. The estate contains four of the five highest mountains in the UK as well as remnant Caledonian pine forest. There is a rich variety of wildlife and bird life including red deer, red squirrels and golden eagles, and walks to suit all abilities. Ranger-guided walks are also available. **Braemar, Ballater, Aberdeenshire AB35 5YJ ☎Ranger Service: (013397) 41669** 149 E6

Moirlanich Longhouse

Off A827, 1m northwest of Killin. • An outstanding example of traditional cruck frame cottage and byre, dating from the mid-19th century. Little altered and retaining many original features such as the box beds. A small shed adjacent displays a rare collection of working clothes found in the Longhouse, and an exhibition interprets the history and restoration of the building. **NTS Office, Lynedoch, Main Street, Killin FK21 8UW** 140 F2

Newhailes

Off Newhailes Road (A6095) • A mellow, untouched late 17th century house and designed landscape. The rococo interior has many original decorations and furnishings. It's easy to imagine famous figures from the Scottish Enlightenment gathered in the library with their hosts the Dalrymples, may of whom appear in the fine collection of portraits and paintings. The historic landscape surprises with unexpected features that inspire reflection. Shop and courtyard cafe. **Newhailes Road, Musselburgh, East Lothian EH21 6RY ☎(0131) 653 5599** 123 B6

Pitmedden Garden

On A920, 1m west of Pitmedden village and 14m north of Aberdeen • Gardeners will appreciate Pitmedden not only as a beautifully kept garden, but also as a unique historical recreation. The Great Garden follows elaborate 17th century parterre design with thousands of colourful bedding plants. There are also woodland walks, fine herbaceous borders, topiary and a herb garden. The Museum of Farming Life close by brings the agricultural past to life. Tearoom, shop, picnic area. **Ellon AB41 7PD ☎(01651) 842352** 151 B7

Pollok House

3m south of Glasgow city centre. Off M77 junction 1, follow signs for Burrell Collection • One of Glasgow's most elegant houses, home to the Maxwell family for nearly six centuries. The interiors are amazing, from the magnificent mahogany and marble hallway to the extensive servants' quarters. Collectors will love the famous paintings, silver and ceramics. Enjoy a stroll in the grounds, perhaps after a wonderful lunch in the Edwardian Kitchen restaurant! Varied events programme. Licensed Edwardian Kitchen restaurant, Servants' Hall Tearoom (weekends), gift shop, food shop. **Pollok Country Park, 2060 Pollokshaws Road, Glasgow G43 1AT ☎(0141) 616 6410** 121 C5

Preston Mill and Phantassie Doocot

East Lothian. Off A1, in East Linton. • There has been a mill on the site for centuries, and the present stone buildings date from the 18th century. The water-wheel and the grain milling machinery it powers are relatively modern and the mill continued in commercial use until 1959. The conical-roofed kiln, red pantiles and groupings of the buildings are popular with artists. **East Linton, East Lothian EH40 3DS ☎(01620) 860426** 123 B8

Priorwood Garden and Dried Flower Shop

Off A6091, in Melrose, adjacent to Abbey. • Priorwood is a centre for the unique craft of dried-flower arranging. The flowers used are grown in the gardens here and preserved using techniques from ancient Egypt. You can learn more about the craft, buy flowers from the shop, or simply relax in the sheltered gardens. Gift shop, dried-flower shop, food shop, picnic area. **Melrose TD6 9PX ☎(01896) 822493** 123 F8

Robert Smail's Printing Works

Innerleithen, 6m east of Peebles. • A living insight into the history of print. Robert Smail's is a working print shop preserved just as it was a century ago. You can still see the presses in action, try your hand at traditional typesetting amd pick up authentic replica Victorian prints from the shop. **7/9 High Street, Innerleithen EH44 6HA ☎(01896) 830206** 123 F6

Rockcliffe

Off A710, 7m south of Dalbeattie • A beautiful stretch of coastline for wandering and exploring. Includes a network of paths, among them the Jubilee path from Kippford to Rockcliffe, with guided walks available in summer. There's a huge variety of plants and flowers to see, as well as the Rough Island bird sanctuary and the Mote of Mark ancient hill fort. **☎(01556) 502575** 107 D5

St Abb's Head National Nature Reserve

Off A1107, 2m north of Coldingham • For birdwatchers and wildlife enthusiasts, St Abb's Head is a landmark site. This National Nature Reserve is home to thousands of cliff-nesting sea birds and offers a spectacular vantage point to watch them wheeling and diving into the North Sea. Find out more about the special exhibition or join a ranger-guided walk. **☎(018907) 71443** 124 C5

St Kilda National Nature Reserve

• Its main island of Hirta maintained its population until 1930, when the islanders were evacuated at their own request. Each year, Trust working parties using volunteer labour conserve and repair buildings and carry out archaeological work. 158 M8

Shieldaig Island

Highland. In Loch Torridon, off Shieldaig, A896. • This 32-acre island is almost entirely covered in Scots pine which once formed vast forests covering much of the Scottish Highlands. 155 F4

Souter Johnnie's Cottage

In Kirkoswald, A77, 4m southwest of Maybole • A visit to Souter Johnnie's cottage is like stepping into one of Burns' poems. The shoemaker who inspired the character Souter Johnnie in Burns' Tam O'Shanter lived and worked here. The much-loved poem comes to life in the garden, where life-sized stone figures of the characters sit in the restored ale-house. **Main Road, Kirkoswald KA19 8HY ☎(01655) 760603** 112 D2

Staffa

11 km (7 miles) northeast of Iona. • Romantic and uninhabited island, famous for its basaltic formations, the best known of which is Fingal's Cave. Immortalised by Mendelssohn in his celebrated Hebrides overture, its cluster columns and seemingly man-made symmetry give the cave a cathedral-like majesty. Visitors have included the artist J M W Turner, and poets and writers Keats, Wordsworth, Tennyson and Sir Walter Scott. 136 E4

Strome Castle

Highland. Off A896. • Ruined castle, romantically situated on a rocky promontory jutting into Loch Carron. First recorded in 1472 when it was a stronghold of the Lords of the Isles, it later belonged to the MacDonnells of Glengarry. Following a quarrel with Kenneth MacKenzie, Lord of Kintail, it fell in 1602 after a long siege and was blown up. 155 H4

The David Livingstone Centre

Leave the M74 at junction 5 – join A725 – take the A724 to Blantyre. • Scotland's most famous explorer was born in this one-room tenement in 1813. Today his birthplace commemorates his life with a fascinating exhibition including personal belongings and a new sculpture of Livingstone and the Lion. There's plenty to do for families – dressing up, jigsaws and even a lion hunt. Shop, cafe and adventure playground. **165 Station Road, Blantyre, Glasgow G72 9BT ☎(01698) 823140** 121 D6

The Georgian House

Charlotte Square, 2 mins from west end of Princes Street. • On the opposite side of Charlotte Square to No 28 Charlotte Square, home of the NTS, at No 7 is The Georgian House, a vivid recreation of life in late 18th century Edinburgh. Experience a real taste of high society and the fascinating 'below stairs' life of servants who made this elegant lifestyle possible. **7 Charlotte Square, Edinburgh EH2 4DR ☎(0131) 226 3318** 122 B5

The Hill House

Off B832, between A82 and A814, 23 m northwest of Glasgow • Anyone with a passion for design and architecture will love this house, commissioned in 1902 but still looking startlingly modern. Mackintosh and his wife Margaret also designed the interiors and fittings, including the exquisite writing cabinet recently acquired by the Trust and now in its original setting from April to July. Look out for the changing exhibitions of contemporary design. Mackintosh Shop and Contemporary Design Shop, tearoom. **Upper Colquhoun Street, Helensburgh G84 9AJ ☎(01463) 673900** 129 B7

The Tenement House

Buccleuch Street, Garnethill, three streets northwest of Sauchiehall Street, near Charing Cross. Restricted parking. • A fascinating view of turn-of-the-century tenement life fozen in time. This Victorian tenement was the home of a shorthand typist for more than 50 years. Little has changed in the flat since the early 20th century and many of the fittings are original, including the splendid kitchen range, along with the other family items on display. **145 Buccleuch Street, Glasgow G3 6QN ☎(0141) 333 0183** 121 C5

Threave House, Garden and Countryside Centre

Off A75, 1m west of Castle Douglas • A fascinating spot for garden enthusiasts. Wander around the rose garden and the walled garden with its splendid glasshouse collection. In spring, see the gardens come alive with nearly 200 varieties of daffodil. Meanwhile in Threave House discover past times with the Maxwelton Collection of household objects. Or see a live video link with the estate's bird life from the Countryside Centre. Licensed terrace restaurant, shop, plant sales centre. **Castle Douglas DG7 1RX ☎(01556) 502575** 106 C4

Tighnabruaich Viewpoint

On A8003, northeast of Tighnabruaich • The indicators, attributed to the Trust and the Scottish Civic Trust, were erected by a Trust supporter in memory of two brothers, who gave generously of their time to the work of the Trust. 128 C4

Torridon

A896, 9m southwest of Kinlochewe, Wester Ross • Climbers, geologists and naturalists are all drawn to the Torridon estate, which contains some of Scotland's most formidable scenery. Learn more about the area at the Countryside Centre and Deer Museum, and see herds of red deer and Highland cattle kept nearby. **☎(01445) 791221** 154 E5

Unst and Yell

Shetland. Ferry from Aberdeen to Lerwick, then (via two ferries) by hired car or bus. • The estate of Unst and Yell, at the northern tip of Shetland and Britain, extends to 3,830 acres. Most of the land is in agricultural use and there is a first-class Shetland pony stud. Scenically the three west coast areas of Woodwick, Collaster and Lund are outstanding, with undulating hills, low rocky coastline, beaches, cliffs and voes. The area is of geological, botanical and ornithological importance. There is an interesting wood – the only one on Unst – at Halligarth. **Shetland ZE2 9UT** 174 B8

Weaver's Cottage

M8 junction 28a, A737, follow signs for Kilbarchan, 12m southwest of Glasgow • Built in 1723, this cottage still has the atmosphere of a pre-Industrial Revolution home and workplace. See authentic domestic objects in their original settings, and watch weavers and spinners work on traditional looms and wheels. The cottage garden includes some interesting archaeological finds. There are costumed guides and activities for children too. **Shuttle Street at The Cross, Kilbarchan PA10 2JG ☎(01505) 705588** 120 C4

English Heritage properties

The properties in this directory are classified to make it easier to choose those of particular interest. Most categories are self-explanatory. Others include Humps and Bumps which are archaeological remains (many still remarkably intact), Pot Luck, which can be anything from a medieval bridge to a Georgian deer shelter, and Far from the crowd, remote sites that are mostly free but tend to be less easily accessible. Opening times vary so please telephone before visiting to avoid disappointment.

Become a member of English Heritage

Become a member of English Heritage and enjoy some of the best days out in history for as little as £34.00 a year. For further details call the membership department on 0870 333 1182 quoting Philip's or online at www.english-heritage.org.uk

Key to symbols

- ✝ Christian heritage
- ♜ Castle / fort
- ⌂ Historic house
- ♡ Romantic ruin
- △ Humps and bumps
- ⛑ Roman
- ✿ Garden / park
- ⚙ Industrial monument
- ⚱ Pot luck
- ✈ Far from the crowd
- Π Great antiquity

Abbotsbury Abbey Remains
Dorset
⚱ The remains of a cloister building of this Benedictine abbey, founded in 1044.
➲ **In Abbotsbury, off B3157, near churchyard.** 12 F3

Abingdon County Hall
Oxfordshire
⚱ This 17th-century public building was built to house the Assize Courts.
➲ **In Abingdon, 7m S of Oxford in Market Place.** ✆ **01235 523703** 38 E4

Acton Burnell Castle
Shropshire
✈ ♡ The warm red sandstone shell of a fortified 13th-century manor house.
➲ **In Acton Burnell, on unclassified road 8m S of Shrewsbury.** 60 D5

Aldborough Roman Town
North Yorkshire
⛑ The principal town of the Brigantes, the largest tribe in Roman Britain. The delightfully located remains include parts of the Roman defences and two mosaic pavements. A museum displays Roman mosaic designs. ➲ **0.75m SE of Boroughbridge, on minor road off B6265 within 1m of junction of A1 and A6055.** ✆ **01423 322768** 95 C7

Alexander Keiller Museum, Avebury
Wiltshire Alexander Keiller put together one of the most important prehistoric archaeological collections in Britain, and this can be seen in the Avebury Museum. ➲ **In Avebury 7m W of Marlborough.** ✆ **01672 539250** 25 C6

Ambleside Roman Fort
Cumbria
⛑ △ Remains of a 1st- and 2nd-century fort were built to guard the Roman road from Brougham to Ravenglass.
➲ **200 yds W of Waterhead car park, Ambleside.** 99 D5

Appuldurcombe House
Isle of Wight
♡ ✈ The fine 18th-century baroque-style house retains its elegant east front and stands in its own ornamental grounds, designed by 'Capability' Brown. ➲ **0.5 m W of Wroxall off B3327.** ✆ **01983 852484** 15 G6

Arbor Low Stone Circle and Gib Hill Barrow
Derbyshire
△ A fine Neolithic monument, this 'Stonehenge of Derbyshire' comprises many slabs of limestone. ➲ **0.5m W of A515 2m S of Monyash.** ✆ **01629 816200 (Site managed by Peak District National Park Authority)** 75 C8

Arthur's Stone
Dorstone, Herefordshire
△ Impressive prehistoric burial chamber formed of large blocks of stone.
➲ **7m E of Hay-on-Wye off B4348 near Dorstone.** 48 E5

Ashby de la Zouch Castle
Leicestershire
♡ The impressive ruins of this late-mediaeval castle are dominated by a magnificent 24-metre (80-foot) high tower, split in two during the Civil War, from which there are panoramic views of the surrounding countryside. ➲ **In Ashby de la Zouch, 12m S of Derby on A50.** ✆ **01530 413343** 63 C7

Auckland Castle Deer House
Bishop Auckland, County Durham
⚱ A charming building erected in 1760 in the park of the Bishops of Durham so that deer could shelter and find food.
➲ **In Auckland Park, Bishop Auckland, N of town centre on A68.** 110 F5

Audley End House and Gardens
Essex
⌂ ✿ Just a short drive from Cambridge, Audley End House is set within a magnificent eighteenth century park designed by "Capability" Brown. The interior of the mansion remains unaltered since the early 1700s, reflecting past generations of style. Highlights of Audley End are the Great Hall, reception rooms designed by Robert Adam and the Victorian appearance of Lady Braybrooke's Sitting Room. Works of art by Canaletto and Van Goyen can be seen. The newly restored laundry and kitchen give an insight into life below stairs. Outside, the organic kitchen garden is being restored to how it was during its Victorian hey-day, with box-edged paths, trained fruit and a magnificent 170-foot long vine house. An artificial lake created with water from the River Cam runs through the estate and there is a restored 19th century parterre, Robert Adam's elegant Tea Bridge and the classical Temple of Concord. There are two tearooms and a gift shop. ➲ **1m W of Saffron Walden, Essex on B1383 (M11 exits 8, 9 Northbound only, and 10).** 55 F6

Avebury
Wiltshire See: Avebury Stone Circles, The Sanctuary, Silbury Hill, West Kennet Avenue, West Kennet Long Barrow and Windmill Hill. 25 C6

Avebury Stone Circles
Wiltshire
Π Complex, gigantic and mysterious, the Circles were constructed 4,500 years ago, originally comprising more than 180 stones. ➲ **In Avebury 7m W of Marlborough.** 25 C6

Aydon Castle
Northumberland
♜ ♡ One of the finest fortified manor houses in England, built in the late 13th century. Situated in a position of great natural beauty, its remarkably intact state is due to its conversion to a farmhouse in the 17th century. ➲ **1m NE of Corbridge, on minor road off B6321 or A68.** ✆ **01434 632450** 110 C3

Baconsthorpe Castle
Norfolk
⚱ ✈ Remains of the gatehouses of a large 15th-century fortified manor house. ➲ **0.75m N of village of Baconsthorpe off unclassified road 3m E of Holt.** 81 D7

Ballowall Barrow
St Just, Cornwall
△ In a spectacular position, this is an unusual Bronze Age chambered tomb with a complex layout.
➲ **1m W of St Just, near Carn Gloose.** 2 C2

Bant's Carn Burial Chamber and Halangy Down Ancient Village
St Mary's, Isles of Scilly
✈ In a wonderful scenic location lies this Bronze Age burial mound with entrance passage and chamber.
➲ **1m N of Hugh Town.** 2 E4

Barnard Castle
County Durham
♜ The substantial remains of this large castle stand on a rugged escarpment overlooking the River Tees. You can still see parts of the 14th-century Great Hall and the cylindrical 12th-century tower.
✆ **01833 638212** 101 C5

1066 Battle of Hastings, Battlefield and Abbey
East Sussex
✝ It was here in 1066 that the Battle of Hastings took place and The Abbey was built by William the Conqueror in 1070 as penance for the slaughter – the high altar marks the spot where Harold fell. There is an interactive tour around the battlefield and a prelude to Battle Exhibition plus a gift shop.
➲ **In Battle, East Sussex, at S end of High St.** ✆ **01424 773792** 18 D4

Bayard's Cove Fort
Dartmouth, Devon
⚱ A small artillery fort built before 1534 to defend the harbour entrance.
➲ **In Dartmouth, on riverfront.** 7 D6

Bayham Old Abbey
East Sussex
✝ Ruins of a house of 'white' canons, founded in c.1208, in an 18th-century landscaped setting. The Georgian House (Dower House) is also open to the public.
➲ **1.75 m W of Lamberhurst off B2169.** ✆ **01892 890381** 18 B3

Beeston Castle
Cheshire
♜ ♡ Standing majestically on sheer, rocky crags which fall sharply away from the castle walls, Beeston has possibly the most stunning views of the surrounding countryside of any castle in England and the rock has a history which stretches back over 2,500 years. ➲ **11m SE of Chester on minor road off A49 or A41.** ✆ **01829 260464** 74 D2

Belas Knap Long Barrow
Gloucestershire
△ Neolithic long barrow surrounded by a stone wall. The chamber tombs, where the remains of 31 people were found, have been opened up so that visitors can see inside.
➲ **2m S of Winchcombe, near Charlton Abbots, 0.5 mile on Cotswold Way.** 37 B7

Belsay Hall, Castle and Gardens
Northumberland
⌂ ♜ ✿ ♡ The beautiful honey-coloured stone from which Belsay Hall is built came from its own quarries in the grounds. Those quarries have since become the unusual setting for one of a series of spectacular gardens. They are the property's finest feature, deservedly listed Grade I in the Register of Gardens. The house itself was innovative, when built between 1810 and 1817 in a style derived directly from Ancient Greece.
➲ **In Belsay, Northumberland, 14m NW of Newcastle on A696.** ✆ **01661 881636** 110 B3

Berkhamsted Castle
Hertfordshire
♜ The extensive remains of a large 11th-century motte and bailey castle. ➲ **By Berkhamsted station.** ✆ **01442 871737** 40 D2

Berry Pomeroy Castle
Devon
♜ ♡ ➲ **2.5m E of Totnes off A385.** ✆ **01803 866618** 7 C6

Berwick-upon-Tweed Barracks
Northumberland
♜ ➲ **On the Parade, off Church St, Berwick town centre.** ✆ **01289 304493** 125 D6

Berwick-upon-Tweed Castle
Northumberland
⚱ Remains of 12th-century castle
➲ **Adjacent to Berwick railway station, W of town centre, accessible also from river bank.** 125 D5

Berwick-upon-Tweed Main Guard
Northumberland
⚱ Georgian Guard House near the quay. An exhibition celebrates the 150th anniversary of the railway coming to Berwick-upon-Tweed. ➲ **Surrounding Berwick town centre on N bank of River Tweed.** 125 D5

Berwick-upon-Tweed Ramparts
Northumberland Remarkably complete, 16th-century town fortifications, with gateways and projecting bastions. ➲ **Surrounding Berwick town centre on N bank of River Tweed.** 125 D6

Bessie Surtees House
Tyne and Wear
⌂ Two 16th- and 17th-century merchants' houses. One is a remarkable and rare example of Jacobean domestic architecture.
➲ **41-44 Sandhill, Newcastle.** ✆ **0191 269 1200** 110 C5

Binham Priory
Norfolk
✝ Extensive remains of a Benedictine priory.
➲ **0.25m NW of village of Binham-on-Wells on road off B1388. G01328 830362 81 C5**

Binham Wayside Cross
Norfolk
⚱ Mediaeval cross marking the site of an annual fair held from the reign of Henry I until the 1950s.
➲ **On village green adjacent to Priory.** 81 D5

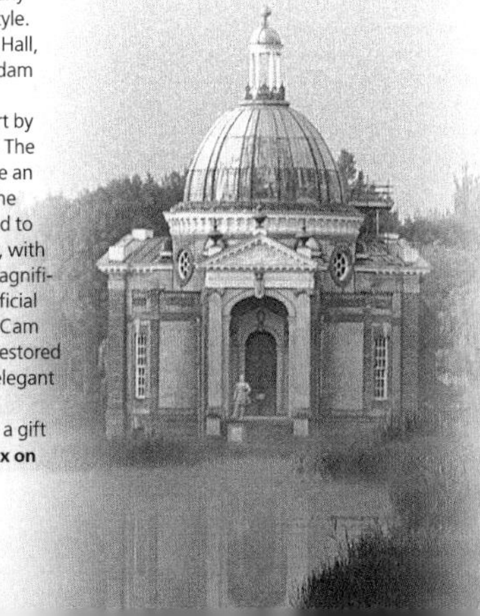

Wrest Park Gardens
English Heritage Photographic Library

Bishop's Waltham Palace
Hampshire
✝ This mediaeval seat of the Bishops of Winchester once stood in an enormous park. Wooded grounds still surround the mainly 12th- and 14th-century remains, including the Great Hall and three-storey tower, as well as the moat which once enclosed the palace.
➲ **In Bishop's Waltham 5m from junction 8 of M27.** ✆ **01489 892460** 15 C6

Blackbury Camp
Devon
△ An Iron Age hillfort, defended by a bank and ditch. ➲ **1.5m SW of Southleigh off B3174 / A3052.** 11 E6

Blackfriars
Gloucester, Gloucestershire
✝ A small Dominican priory churchwith original 13th-century scissor-braced roof.
➲ **In Ladybellegate Street off Southgate Street and Blackfriars Walk.**
✆ **0117 975 0700.** 37 C5

Black Middens Bastle House
Northumberland
✈ ⚱ A 16th-century two-storey defended farmhouse, set in splendid walking country. ➲ **200yds N of minor road 7m NW of Bellingham; access also along minor road from A68.** 116 E3

Blakeney Guildhall
Norfolk
⚱ The surviving basement of a large 14th-century building, probably a merchant's house. ➲ **In Blakeney off A149.** 81 C6

Bolingbroke Castle
Lincolnshire
⚱ ✈ ♜ Remains of a 13th-century hexagonal castle, birthplace of Henry IV in 1367 and besieged by Parliamentary forces in 1643. ➲ **In Old Bolingbroke, 16m N of Boston off A16.** ✆ **01529 461499 Site managed by Heritage Lincolnshire)** 79 C6

Bolsover Castle
Derbyshire
♡ ⌂ ✿ An enchanting and romantic spectacle, situated high on a wooded hilltop dominating the surrounding landscape. Built on the site of a Norman castle, this is largely an early 17th-century mansion. Explore the 'Little Castle' or 'keep', a unique celebration of Jacobean romanticism with its elaborate fireplaces, panelling and wall paintings. There is also an impressive 17th-century indoor Riding House, built by the Duke of Newcastle, and ruins of great state apartments. ➲ **Off M1 at junction 29, 6m from Mansfield. In Bolsover, 6m E of Chesterfield on A632.** ✆ **01246 822844** 76 B4

Boscobel House and the Royal Oak
Shropshire
⌂ ✿ Fully refurnished and restored, the panelled rooms, secret hiding places and pretty gardens lend this 17th-century timber-framed hunting lodge a truly romantic character. King Charles II hid in the house and the nearby Royal Oak after the Battle of Worcester in 1651 to avoid detection by Cromwell's troops. Today there is a farmhouse with dairy, farmyard and smithy, and an exhibition in the house. ➲ **On minor road from A41 to A5, 8m NW of Wolverhampton.** ✆ **01902 850244** 61 D8

Bow Bridge
Barrow-in-Furness, Cumbria
⚱ ✈ Late mediaeval stone bridge across Mill Beck, carrying a route to nearby Furness Abbey. ➲ **0.5m N of Barrow-in-Furness, on minor road off A590 near Furness Abbey.** 92 B2

Bowes Castle
County Durham
♜ ⚱ Massive ruins of Henry II's tower keep, three storeys high and set within the earthworks of a Roman fort.
➲ **In Bowes Village just off A66, 4m W of Barnard Castle.** 100 C4

Bowhill
Exeter, Devon
⌂ A mansion of considerable status built c.1500 by a member of the Holland family. ➲ **1.5m SW of Exeter on B3212.** ✆ **0117 975 0700.** 10 E4

Boxgrove Priory
West Sussex
✝ Remains of the Guest House, Chapter House and church of a 12th century priory. 16 D3

Bradford-on-Avon Tithe Barn
Wiltshire
⚱ A mediaeval stone-built barn with slate roof and wooden beamed interior.
➲ **0.25m S of town centre, off B3109.** 24 D2

Bramber Castle
West Sussex
⚱ The remains of a Norman castle gatehouse, walls and earthworks. ➲ **On W side of Bramber village off A283.** 17 C5

Bratton Camp and White Horse
Wiltshire
△ A large Iron Age hill fort. ➲ **2m E of Westbury off B3098, 1m SW of Bratton.** 24 D2

Brinkburn Priory
Northumberland
✝ This late 12th-century church is a fine example of early Gothic architecture.
➲ **4.5m SE of Rothbury off B6344.** ✆ **01665 570628** 117 E6

Brodsworth Hall
South Yorkshire
⌂ ✿ Brodsworth Hall offers a unique opportunity to see the faded grandeur of a Victorian country house with original interiors dating back to the 1860s. Much of the original decorating scheme survives – from the grand reception rooms and private quarters to the cluttered Victorian kitchen. Outside, the gardens have been undergoing a programme of restoration and now include one of the largest collections of ferns in the north of England. Tearoom and shop. ➲ **In Brodsworth, South Yorkshire, off A635 Barnsley Road, from junction 37 of A1(M).** ✆ **01302 722598** 89 D6

Brougham Castle
Cumbria
♜ These impressive ruins on the banks of the River Eamont include an early 13th-century keep and later buildings. Its one-time owner Lady Anne Clifford restored the castle in the 17th century. ➲ **1.5m SE of Penrith on minor road off A66.** ✆ **01768 862488** 99 B7

Brough Castle
Cumbria
♜ Dating from Roman times, the 12th-century keep replaced an earlier stronghold destroyed by the Scots in 1174.
➲ **8m SE of Appleby S of A66.** 100 C2

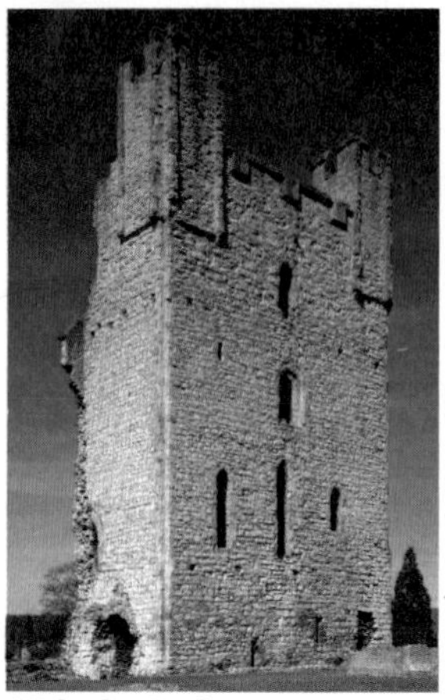

▲**Helmsley Castle**
English Heritage Photographic Library

Buildwas Abbey
Shropshire
Set beside the River Severn, against a backdrop of wooded grounds, are extensive remains of this Cistercian abbey begun in 1135. ➲ **On S bank of River Severn on B4378, 2m W of Iron Bridge. ✆01952 433274** 61 D6

Burgh Castle
Norfolk
A Roman fort built in the late 3rd century as one of a chain to defend the coast against Saxon raiders. ➲ **At far W end of Breydon Water, on unclassified road 3m W of Great Yarmouth.** 69 D7

Burton Agnes Manor House
East Riding of Yorkshire
Rare example of a Norman house, altered and encased in brick in the 17th and 18th centuries. ➲ **In Burton Agnes village, 5m SW of Bridlington on A166.** 97 C6

Bury St Edmunds Abbey
Suffolk
A Norman tower and 14th-century gatehouse of a ruined Benedictine abbey, church and precinct. ➲ **E end of town centre.** 56 C2

Butter Cross
Dunster, Somerset
A mediaeval stone cross. ➲ **Beside minor road to Alcombe, 350m (400 yds) NW of Dunster parish church.** 21 E8

Byland Abbey
North Yorkshire
A hauntingly lovely ruin set in peaceful meadows in the shadow of the Hambleton Hills. It illustrates the later development of Cistercian churches, including the beautiful floor tiles. ➲ **2m S of A170 between Thirsk and Helmsley, near Coxwold village. ✆01347 868614** 95 B8

Caister Roman Site
Norfolk
The remains of a Roman fort, including part of a defensive wall, a gateway and buildings along a main street. ➲ **Near Caister-on-Sea, 3m N of Great Yarmouth.** 69 C8

Calshot Castle
Hampshire
From the 20th century, the fort has been part of both an RN and an RAF base. Henry VIII built this coastal fort to command the sea passage to Southampton. ➲ **On spit 2m SE of Fawley off B3053. ✆023 8089 2023** 15 D5

Camber Castle
East Sussex
A rare example of an Henrician fort surviving in its original plan. (Site managed by Rye Harbour Nature Reserve.) ➲ **Access by a delightful 1m walk across fields, off the A259, 1m S of Rye off harbour road. ✆01797 223862 for further information.** 19 D6

Cantlop Bridge
Shropshire
Single-span cast-iron road bridge over the Cound Brook, designed by the great engineer Thomas Telford. ➲ **0.75m SW of Berrington on unclassified road off A458.** 60 D5

Carisbrooke Castle
Isle of Wight
From time immemorial, whosoever controlled Carisbrooke controlled the Isle of Wight. The castle sits at the very heart of the island, and has been a fixture since its foundation as a Saxon camp during the 8th century. ➲ **1.25m SW of Newport, Isle of Wight. ✆01983 522107** 15 F5

Carlisle Castle
Cumbria
Sitting proudly on the highest point above the River Eden, Carlisle Castle has guarded the western end of the Anglo-Scottish border for over nine centuries. It was first built after William II relieved Carlisle of two centuries of Scottish domination in 1092. Since then it has often been the scene of turbulent conflict between the two nations, being fought over fairly constantly until the union of the crowns in 1603. It then fell into Scottish hands again during the Civil War and the Jacobite Rising 100 years later. ➲ **In Carlisle, Cumbria ✆01228 591922** 108 D3

Carn Euny Ancient Village
Cornwall
The remains of an Iron Age settlement. ➲ **1.25m SW of Sancreed off A30.** 2 D3

Castle Acre: Bailey Gate
Norfolk
The north gateway to the mediaeval planned town of Acre with flint towers. ➲ **In Castle Acre, at E end of Stocks Green, 5m N of Swaffham.** 72 B5

Castle Acre Castle
Norfolk
The remains of a Norman manor house, which became a castle with earthworks, set by the side of the village. ➲ **At E end of Castle Acre, 5m N of Swaffham.** 80 F4

Castle Acre Priory
Norfolk
The great west front of the 12th-century church of this Cluniac priory still rises to its full height and is elaborately decorated, whilst the prior's lodgings and porch retain their roofs. The delightful herb garden, re-created to show herbs used in mediaeval times for both culinary and medicinal purposes, should not be missed. ➲ **0.25m W of village of Castle Acre, 5m N of Swaffham. ✆01760 755394** 80 F4

Castlerigg Stone Circle
Cumbria
Possibly one of the earliest Neolithic stone circles in Britain. ➲ **1.5m E of Keswick.** 98 B4

Castle Rising Castle
Norfolk
A fine mid 12th-century domestic keep, set in the centre of massive defensive earthworks, once palace and prison to Isabella, 'She-Wolf' dowager Queen of England. ➲ **4m NE of King's Lynn off A149. ✆01553 631330** 80 F4

Chester Castle: Agricola Tower and Castle Walls
Cheshire
Set in the angle of the city walls, this 12th-century tower contains a fine vaulted chapel. ➲ **Access via Assizes Court car park on Grosvenor St.** 73 C8

Chester Roman Amphitheatre
Cheshire
The largest Roman amphitheatre in Britain. Used for entertainment and military training by the 20th Legion, based at the fortress of Deva. ➲ **On Vicars Lane beyond Newgate, Chester.** 73 C8

Chichele College
Northamptonshire
Parts of a quadrangle remain of this college for secular canons, founded in 1422. ➲ **In Higham Ferrers, on A6. ✆01933 314157. (Site managed by East Northamptonshire Council.)** 53 C7

Chisbury Chapel
Wiltshire
A thatched 13th-century chapel rescued from use as a farm building. ➲ **On unclassified road 0.25m E of Chisbury off A4 6m E of Marlborough.** 25 C7

Chiswick House
Chiswick, Greater London
Close to the centre of London lies one of the first and finest English Palladian villas, surrounded by beautiful gardens. It was designed by the third Earl of Burlington, one of the foremost architects of his generation and a great promoter of the Palladian style first pioneered in England by Inigo Jones. Today you can enjoy the house and its lavish interiors before stepping outside into the classical gardens – a perfect complement to the house itself. ➲ **Burlington Lane, London W4. Tube: Turnham Green ✆020 8995 0508** 28 B3

Christchurch Castle and Norman House
Dorset
Early 12th-century Norman keep, and Constable's house, built c.1160. ➲ **In Christchurch, near Priory.** 14 E2

Church of the Holy Sepulchre
Thetford, Norfolk
The ruined nave of a priory church of the Canons of the Holy Sepulchre, the only surviving remains in England of a house of this order. ➲ **On W side of Thetford off B1107.** 67 F8

Chysauster Ancient Village
Cornwall
A deserted Romano-Cornish village with a 'street' of eight well-preserved houses, each comprising a number of rooms around an open court. ➲ **2.5m NW of Gulval off B3311. ✆07831 757934 for details.** 2 C3

Cirencester Amphitheatre
Gloucestershire
A large well-preserved Roman amphitheatre. ➲ **Next to bypass W of town – access from town or along Chesterton Lane from W end of bypass onto Cotswold Ave. Park next to obelisk.** 37 D7

Cleeve Abbey
Somerset
One of the few 13th-century monastic sites where you will see such a complete set of cloister buildings. ➲ **In Washford, 0.25m S of A39. ✆01984 640377** 22 E2

Clifford's Tower
York, City of York
Standing high on its mound in the city of York, Clifford's Tower is one of the few vestiges of the pair of castles built by William the Conqueror after his victory in 1066. ➲ **In Tower St. ✆01904 646940** 96 D2

Clifton Hall
Cumbria
The surviving tower block of a 15th-century manor house. ➲ **In Clifton next to Clifton Hall Farm, 2m S of Penrith on A6.** 99 B7

Clun Castle
Shropshire
The remains of a four-storey keep and other buildings of this border castle. ➲ **In Clun, off A488, 18m W of Ludlow.** 60 F2

Conduit House
Canterbury, Kent
The Conduit House is the monastic waterworks which supplied nearby St Augustine's Abbey. ➲ **Approximately 5-10 minutes' walk from St Augustine's Abbey. Situated within the new St Martin's Heights housing estate, St Martin's Avenue, Canterbury.** 30 D5

Conisbrough Castle
South Yorkshire
The spectacular white circular keep of a 12th-century castle. It is the oldest circular keep in England and one of the finest mediaeval buildings. There is also a visitor centre and exhibition. ➲ **NE of Conisbrough town centre off A630, 4.5m SW of Doncaster. ✆01709 863329** 89 E6

Coombe Conduit
Kingston-Upon-Thames, Greater London
Built by Henry VIII to supply water to Hampton Court Palace, three miles away, Coombe Conduit consists of two small buildings (one now a ruin) connected by an underground passage. ➲ **Coombe Lane, on the corner of Lord Chancellor's Walk. ✆020 8942 1296** 28 C2

Countess Pillar
Brougham, Cumbria
An unusual monument, bearing sundials and family crests, erected in 1656 by Lady Anne Clifford to commemorate her parting with her mother in 1616. 99 B7

Cow Tower
Norwich, Norfolk
A circular brick tower, which once formed part of the 14th-century city defences. ➲ **In Norwich, near cathedral. ✆01603 212343** 68 D5

Creake Abbey
Norfolk
The ruins of the church of an Augustinian abbey. ➲ **1m N of North Creake off B1355.** 80 D4

Cromwell's Castle
Tresco, Isles of Scilly
This 17th-century round tower was built to command the haven of New Grimsby. ➲ **On shoreline, 0.75m NW of New Grimsby.** 2 E3

Croxden Abbey
Staffordshire
Remains of a Cistercian abbey founded in 1176. ➲ **5m NW of Uttoxeter off A522.** 75 F7

Dartmouth Castle
Devon
This brilliantly positioned defensive castle juts out into the narrow entrance to the Dart estuary, with the sea lapping at its foot. It was one of the first castles constructed with artillery in mind and has seen 450 years of fortification and preparation for war. ➲ **1m SE of Dartmouth off B3205, narrow approach road. ✆01803 833588** 7 D6

Daws Castle
Somerset
The site where the people of the Saxon town of Watchet sought refuge against the threat of Viking attack. ➲ **0.5m W of Watchet off B3191 on cliff top.** 22 E2

Deal Castle
Kent
Crouching low and menacing, the huge, rounded bastions of this austere fort, built by Henry VIII, once carried 119 guns. It is a fascinating castle to explore, with long, dark passages, battlements, and a huge basement with an exhibition on England's coastal defences. ➲ **SW of Deal town centre. ✆01304 372762** 31 D7

Deddington Castle
Oxfordshire
Extensive earthworks conceal the remains of a 12th-century castle. ➲ **S of B4031 on E side of Deddington, 17m N of Oxford on A423.** 52 F2

De Grey Mausoleum
Flitton, Bedfordshire
A remarkable treasure-house of sculpted tombs and monuments from the 16th to 19th centuries, dedicated to the de Grey family of Wrest Park. ➲ **Flitton, attached to church, on unclassified road 1.5m W of A6 at Silsoe. ✆01525 860094. Access through Flitton Church.** 53 F8

Denny Abbey and the Farmland Museum
Cambridgeshire
Remains of a 12th-century Benedictine abbey founded by the Countess of Pembroke which, at different times, also housed the Knights Templar and Franciscan nuns. ➲ **6m N of Cambridge on A10. ✆01223 860489** 55 C5

Derwentcote Steel Furnace
County Durham
Built in the 18th century, the earliest and most complete steel-making furnace to have survived. Closed in the 1870s, it has now been restored and opened to the public. ➲ **10m SW of Newcastle on A694 between Rowland's Gill and Hamsterley. ✆01207 562573** 110 D4

Donnington Castle
Berkshire
Built in the late 14th century, the twin towered gatehouse of this castle survives amidst some impressive earthworks. ➲ **1m N of Newbury off B4494.** 26 C2

Dover Castle
Kent
Dover Castle's Secret Wartime Tunnels, running beneath the White Cliffs, show the cramped conditions in the 1940s underground military hospital, telecommunications station and barracks. In the Keep, a Henry VIII exhibition recreates preparations for a visit by the Tudor king in 1539 and a Siege of 1216 exhibition shows Dover Castle under siege from the French. Other attractions include the royal chapel and Princess of Wales' Royal Regiment Museum. Restaurant, coffee shop and tea bar, gift shops and a free Land Train. ➲ **On E side of Dover. ✆01304 211067.** 31 E7

Down House
Downe, Greater London
Charles Darwin was perhaps the most influential scientist of the 19th century. It was from his study at Down House that he worked on the scientific theories that first scandalized and then revolutionized the Victorian world, culminating in the publication of the most significant book of the century, 'On the Origin of Species by means of Natural Selection', in 1859. His home for forty years, Down House was the centre of his intellectual world and even now his study remains full of his notebooks and journals, and mementoes. The house has been restored so that you can visit Darwin's much-loved family home in the tranquil Kent countryside. ➲ **In Luxted Road, Downe, Kent, off A21 near Biggin Hill. ✆01689 859119** 28 C5

Dunstanburgh Castle
Northumberland
An easy coastal walk leads to the eerie skeleton of this wonderful 14th-century castle, which is sited on a basalt crag more than 30 metres (100 feet) high. ➲ **8m NE of Alnwick, on footpaths from Craster or Embleton. ✆01665 576231** 117 B8

Dupath Well
Callington, Cornwall
A charming granite-built well house set over a holy well of c.1500 and almost complete. ➲ **1m E of Callington off A388.** 5 C8

Duxford Chapel
Cambridgeshire
A mediaeval chapel once part of the Hospital of St John. ➲ **Adjacent to Whittlesford station off A505. ✆01223 443000** 55 E5

Dymchurch Martello Tower
Kent
One of many artillery towers which formed part of a chain of strongholds intended to resist invasion by Napoleon. ➲ **Access from High Street, not from seafront. ✆01304 211067** 19 C8

Easby Abbey
North Yorkshire
Substantial remains of the mediaeval abbey buildings stand in a beautiful setting by the River Swale near Richmond. The abbey can be reached by a pleasant riverside walk from Richmond Castle. ➲ **1m SE of Richmond off B6271.** 101 D6

Edlingham Castle
Northumberland
This complex ruin has defensive features spanning the 13th-15th centuries. ➲ **At E end of Edlingham village, on minor road off B6341 6m SW of Alnwick.** 117 D7

Edvin Loach Old Church
Herefordshire
Peaceful and isolated 11th-century church remains. ➲ **4m N of Bromyard on unclassified road off B4203.** 49 D8

Egglestone Abbey
County Durham
Picturesque remains of a 12th-century abbey. ➲ **1m S of Barnard Castle on minor road off B6277.** 101 C5

Eleanor Cross
Geddington, Northamptonshire
One of a series of famous crosses erected by Edward I to mark the resting places of the body of his wife, Eleanor. ➲ **In Geddington, off A43 between Kettering and Corby.** 65 F5

Eltham Palace
Eltham, Greater London
A fascinating blend of a mediaeval royal palace and a 1930s' Art Deco country house. Step from the 15th-century Great Hall, straight into the lost pre-War world with a suite of striking Modernist interiors. ➲ **0.75m N of A20 off Court Yard, SE9. ✆020 8294 2548** 28 B5

Etal Castle
Northumberland
A 14th-century border castle located in the picturesque village of Etal. There is a major award-winning exhibition about the castle, border warfare and the Battle of Flodden, which took place nearby in 1513. ➲ **In Etal village, 10m SW of Berwick. ✆01890 820332** 124 F5

Eynsford Castle
Kent
One of the first stone castles built by the Normans. ➲ **In Eynsford off A225.** 29 C6

Farleigh Hungerford Castle
Somerset
Ruins of a 14th-century castle with a chapel containing wall paintings, stained glass and the fine tomb of Sir Thomas Hungerford, the builder of the castle. ➲ **In Farleigh Hungerford 3.5m W of Trowbridge on A366. ✆01225 754026** 24 D2

Farnham Castle Keep
Surrey
A motte and bailey castle, once one of the seats of the Bishop of Winchester, which has been in continuous occupation since the 12th century. ➲ **0.5m N of Farnham town centre on A287. ✆01252 713393** 27 E6

Faversham: Stone Chapel
Kent
The remains of a small mediaeval church incorporating part of a 4th-century Romano-British pagan mausoleum. ➲ **1.25m W of Faversham on A2.** 30 C3

Fiddleford Manor
Dorset
⌂ Part of a mediaeval manor house, with a remarkable interior. ➡ **1m E of Sturminster Newton off A357.** 13 C6

Finchale Priory
County Durham
⛪ These beautiful priory ruins, dating from the 13th century, are in a wooded setting beside the River Wear. ➡ **3m NE of Durham, on minor road off A167. ✆0191 386 3828** 111 E5

Flowerdown Barrows
Hampshire
△ Round barrows of a Bronze Age burial site which were once part of a larger group. ➡ **In Littleton, 2.5m NW of Winchester off A272.** 26 F2

Fort Brockhurst
Hampshire
♜ This was a new type of fort, built in the 19th century to protect Portsmouth with formidable fire-power. Largely unaltered, the parade ground, gun ramps and moated keep can all be viewed. ➡ **Off A32, in Gunner's Way, Elson, on N side of Gosport. ✆023 9258 1059** 15 D6

Fort Cumberland
Hampshire
♜ Constructed in the shape of a wide pentagon by the Duke of Cumberland in 1746. Perhaps the most impressive piece of 18th-century defensive architecture remaining in England. Opens occasionally, pre-booked guided tours. Please telephone for details. ➡ **In the Eastney district of Portsmouth on the estuary approach via Henderson Road, a turning off Eastney Road, or from the Esplanade. ✆01483 252015** 15 E7

Framlingham Castle
Suffolk
♜ A superb 12th-century castle. From the continuous curtain wall, linking 13 towers, there are excellent views over Framlingham and the charming reed-fringed mere. At different times, the castle has been a fortress, an Elizabethan prison, a poor house and a school. ➡ **In Framlingham on B1116. ✆01728 724189** 57 C6

Furness Abbey
Cumbria
⛪ In a peaceful valley, the red sandstone remains of a wealthy abbey founded in 1123 by Stephen, later King of England, are at the end of an ancient route from Bow Bridge. There is an exhibition and a museum contains fine stone carvings. ➡ **1.5m N of Barrow-in-Furness, on minor road off A590. ✆01229 823420** 92 B2

Gainsborough Old Hall
Lincolnshire
⌂ A large mediaeval house with a magnificent Great Hall and suites of rooms. ➡ **In Gainsborough, opposite the Library. ✆01427 612669** 90 E2

Gainsthorpe Mediaeval Village
North Lincolnshire
⌂ △ This hidden village comprises earthworks of peasant houses, gardens and streets. ➡ **On minor road W of A15 S of Hibaldstow 5m SW of Brigg (no signs).** 90 D3

Gallox Bridge
Dunster, Somerset
∩ A stone packhorse bridge with two ribbed arches which spans the old mill stream. ➡ **Off A396 at S end of Dunster.** 21 E8

Garrison Walls
St Mary's, Isles of Scilly
♜ Take a pleasant walk along the ramparts of these well-preserved walls and earthworks, built as part of the island's defences. ➡ **Around the headland W of Hugh Town.** 2 F3

Geddington, Eleanor Cross
⛪ See Eleanor Cross. 65 F5

Glastonbury Tribunal
Somerset
⌂ A well-preserved mediaeval town house. ➡ **In Glastonbury High St. ✆01458 832954** 23 F7

Goodrich Castle
Herefordshire
♜ ♡ Remarkably complete, magnificent red sandstone castle with 12th-century keep and extensive remains from the 13th and 14th centuries. ➡ **5m S of Ross-on-Wye off A40. ✆01600 890538** 36 C2

Goodshaw Chapel
Lancashire
⛪ A restored 18th-century Baptist chapel with all its furnishings complete. ➡ **In Crawshawbooth, 2m N of Rawtenstall, in Goodshaw Avenue off A682. ✆0161 242 1400 for details.** 87 B6

Great Witcombe Roman Villa
Gloucestershire
∩ The remains of a large villa. Built around three sides of a courtyard. ➡ **5m SE of Gloucester, off A417, 0.5m S of reservoir in Witcombe Park. ✆0117 975 0700.** 37 C5

Greyfriars
Gloucester, Gloucestershire
⛪ Remains of a late 15th-early 16th-century Franciscan friary church. ➡ **On Greyfriars Walk, behind Eastgate Market off Southgate St.** 37 C5

Grime's Graves
Norfolk
△ ⌂ ∩ These remarkable Neolithic flint mines, unique in England, comprise over 300 pits and shafts. The visitor can descend some 10m (30ft) by ladder into one excavated shaft, and look along the radiating galleries, where the flint for making axes and knives was extracted. ➡ **7m NW of Thetford off A134. ✆01842 810656** 37 F8

Grimspound
Dartmoor, Devon
△ This late Bronze Age settlement displays the remains of 24 huts in an area of four acres enclosed by a stone wall. ➡ **6m SW of Moretonhampstead off B3212.** 6 A5

Guisborough Priory
Redcar and Cleveland
⛪ An Augustinian priory. The remains also include the gatehouse and the east end of an early 14th-century church. ➡ **In Guisborough town, next to parish church. ✆01287 633801** 102 C4

Hadleigh Castle
Essex
♜ The curtain wall and two towers of this 13th-century castle survive almost to their full height. ➡ **0.75m S of A13 at Hadleigh. ✆01760 755161** 42 F4

Hadrian's Wall
Cumbria, Northumberland
∩ Stretching across northern England from the Solway Firth in the west to the Tyne in the east, Hadrian's Wall divided the 'civilized' world of the Romans, from the northern tribes beyond. Emperor Hadrian, who came to Britain in 122, was unusual in that he believed consolidation to be more glorious than new conquest. The Wall was the physical manifestation of his strategy, a defensive barrier linking the existing system of forts and watchtowers along the Stanegate road ➡ **West of Hexham, the Wall runs roughly parallel to the A69 Carlisle-Newcastle-upon-Tyne road, lying between 1-4 miles North of it, close to the B6318.** 109 C7

Banks East Turret Well-preserved turret with adjoining stretches of Wall and fine views. ➡ **On minor road E of Banks village, 3.5m NE of Brampton.** 109 C5

Benwell Roman Temple Remains of small temple, surrounded by modern housing. ➡ **Immediately S off A69 at Benwell in Broomridge Ave.** 110 C5

Benwell Vallum Crossing The sole remaining example of an original stone-built causeway across the ditch of the Vallum earthwork that ran parallel to the Wall. ➡ **Immediately S off A69 at Benwell in Broomridge Ave.** 110 C5

Birdoswald Fort Almost on the edge of the Irthing escarpment, there is visible evidence of the granaries, the west gate and, most importantly, the east gate, which is among the best-preserved on the Wall. ➡ **2.75m W of Greenhead, on minor road off B6318. ✆01697 747602** 109 C2

Black Carts Turret A 460 metre (500 yard) length of Wall and turret foundations, with magnificent views to the north. ➡ **2m W of Chollerford on B6318.** 109 B8

Brunton Turret Well-preserved 2.5 metre (8 foot) high turret with a 20 metre (70 yard) stretch of Wall. ➡ **0.25m S of Low Brunton on A6079.** 110 C2

Cawfields Roman Wall A concentration of Roman sites – camps, turrets, a fortlet, and Milecastle 42 – along with a particularly fine, consolidated stretch of the Wall, and one of the best-preserved sections of the Vallum earthwork and ditch. ➡ **1.25m N of Haltwhistle off B6318.** 109 C2

Chesters Bridge Fragments of the bridge that carried Hadrian's Wall across the North Tyne are visible on each bank. The most impressive remains are on the east side, across from Chesters Fort, where a short stretch of the Wall itself leads from the broad splay of the bridge's east abutment, and ends at a gatehouse tower. ➡ **0.25m S of Low Brunton on A6079.** 110 C2

Chesters Roman Fort ➡ **1.5m W of Chollerford on B6318. ✆01434 681379** 110 B2

Corbridge Roman Site Originally the site of a fort on the former patrol road, Corbridge evolved into a principal town of the Roman era, flourishing until the 5th century. The large granaries, with their ingenious ventilation system, are among its most impressive remains. Corbridge is an excellent starting point to explore the Wall. ➡ **0.5m NW of Corbridge on minor road, signed Corbridge Roman Site. ✆01434 632349** 110 C2

Denton Hall Turret Foundations and 65 metre (70 yard) section of Wall. The turret retains the base of the platform on which rested the ladder to the upper floor. ➡ **4m W of Newcastle city centre on A69.** 110 C4

Hare Hill A short length of wall standing nine feet high. ➡ **0.75m NE of Lanercost, off minor road.** 109 C5

Harrow's Scar Milecastle Remains linked to Birdoswald Fort by probably the most instructive mile section on the whole length of Hadrian's Wall. ➡ **0.25m E of Birdoswald, on minor road off B6318.** 109 C6

Heddon-on-the-Wall A fine stretch of the Wall up to two metres (six feet) thick, with the remains of a mediaeval kiln near the west end. ➡ **Immediately E of Heddon village, S of A69.** 110 C4

Housesteads Roman Fort Housesteads occupies a commanding position on the basalt cliffs of the Whin Sill. One of the twelve permanent forts built by Hadrian c. 124, between milecastles 36 and 37, Housesteads is the most complete example of a Roman fort to be seen in Britain. To the east of Housesteads, Knag Burn Gate, constructed in the third century, was an alternative way through the wall when the north gate in the fort itself fell out of use. It is one of only two isolated gates – all the rest are found at forts and milecastles. This gate and some of the Wall have been partially reconstructed, and much has been consolidated, to give one of the most coherent pictures of the Romans and their great works in Britain. ➡ **2.75m NE of Bardon Mill on B6318. ✆01434 344363** 109 C7

Leahill Turret and Piper Sike Turret Turrets in the section of Wall west of Birdoswald, originally constucted for the turf wall. ➡ **On minor road 2m W of Birdoswald Fort.** 109 C5

Pike Hill Signal Tower Remains of a signal tower joined to the Wall at an angle of 45 degrees. ➡ **On minor road E of Banks village.** 109 C6

Planetrees Roman Wall A 15-metre (50-foot) length of narrow wall on broad foundations, showing extensive rebuilding in Roman times. ➡ **1m SE of Chollerford on B6318.** 110 C2

Poltross Burn Milecastle One of the best-preserved milecastles, with part of a flight of steps to the top of the Wall and the remains of the gates, enclosing walls and barrack blocks. ➡ **Immediately SW of Gilsland village by old railway station.** 109 C6

Sewingshields Wall Largely unexcavated section of Wall. Remains of Sewingshields Milecastle and Turret and Grindon and Coesike Turrets. ➡ **N of B6318, 1.5m E of Housesteads Fort.** 109 B8

Temple of Mithras, Carrawburgh Remains of a third-century temple and facsimiles of altars found during excavations. ➡ **3.75m W of Chollerford on B6318.** 109 B8

Vindolanda Fort A fort and well-excavated civil settlement. A museum there contains many unusual artefacts from everyday Roman life. ➡ **1.25m SE of Twice Brewed, on minor road off B6318. ✆01434 344277** 109 C7

Walltown Crags One of the best-preserved sections of the Wall, snaking over the crags to the turret on its summit. ➡ **1m NE of Greenhead off B6318.** 109 C6

Willowford Wall, Turrets and Bridge One thousand yards of Wall, including two turrets, leading to bridge abutment remains. ➡ **W of minor road 0.75m W of Gilsland.** 109 C6

Winshields Wall Very rugged section of the Wall, including the highest point at Winshields Crag. ➡ **W of Steel Rigg car park, on minor road off B6318.** 109 C7

Hailes Abbey
Gloucestershire
⛪ 13th-century Cistercian abbey, set in wooded pastureland, with examples of high quality sculpture in the site museum. ➡ **2m NE of Winchcombe off B4632. ✆01242 602398** 51 F5

Halesowen Abbey
West Midlands
⛪ Remains of an abbey founded by King John in the 13th century, now incorporated into a 19th-century farm. ➡ **Off A456 Kidderminster road, 6m W of Birmingham centre.** 62 F3

Halliggye Fogou
Cornwall
✕ One of several strange underground tunnels, associated with Iron Age villages, which are unique to Cornwall. ➡ **5m SE of Helston off B3293 E of Garras on Trelowarren estate.** 3 D6

Hardknott Roman Fort
Cumbria
∩ One of the most dramatic Roman sites in Britain. The fort, built between AD120 and 138, controlled the road from Ravenglass to Ambleside. There are visible remains of granaries, the head-quarters building and the commandant's house, with a bath house and parade ground outside the fort. ➡ **9m NE of Ravenglass, at W end of Hardknott Pass.** 98 D4

Hardwick Old Hall
Derbyshire
♡ ⌂ This large ruined house, finished in 1591, still displays Bess of Hardwick's innovative planning and interesting decorative plasterwork. ➡ **9.5m SE of Chesterfield, off A6175, from J 29 of M1. ✆01246 850431** 76 C4

Harry's Walls
St Mary's, Isles of Scilly
♜ An uncompleted 16th-century fort. ➡ **0.25m NE of Hugh Town.** 2 E4

Hatfield Earthworks
Wiltshire
△ Part of a Neolithic enclosure complex 3,500 years old. ➡ **5.5m SE of Devizes off A342 NE of village of Marden.** 25 D5

Haughmond Abbey
Shropshire
⛪ ➡ **3m NE of Shrewsbury off B5062. ✆01743 709661** 60 C5

Helmsley Castle
North Yorkshire
♜ This 12th-century castle lies close to the market square, with a view of the town. There is an exhibition on the history of the castle in Elizabethan buildings. **✆01439 770442** 102 F4

Hob Hurst's House
Derbyshire
△ ✕ A square prehistoric burial mound with an earthwork ditch and outer bank. ➡ **From unclassified road off B5057, 9m W of Chesterfield.** 76 C2

Horne's Place Chapel
Appledore, Kent
⛪ This 14th-century domestic chapel was once attached to the manor house. The house and chapel are privately owned. ➡ **1.5m N of Appledore. ✆01304 211067.** 19 B6

Houghton House
Bedfordshire
♡ ⌂ Reputedly the inspiration for 'House Beautiful' in Bunyan's Pilgrim's Progress, the remains of this early 17th-century mansion still convey elements that justify the description, including work attributed to Inigo Jones. ➡ **1m NE of Ampthill off A421, 8m S of Bedford.** 53 F8

Hound Tor Deserted Mediaeval Village
Dartmoor, Devon
✕ Remains of three or four mediaeval farmsteads, first occupied in the Bronze Age. ➡ **1.5m S of Manaton off The Ashburton Road. Park in Hound Tor car park, 0.5m walk.** 6 B5

Howden Minster
East Riding of Yorkshire
⛪ A large, cathedral-like church dating from the 14th century, which belonged to the Bishop of Durham. The ruined chancel and octagonal chapter house are in the care of English Heritage, and managed by Howden Minster Parochial Church Council. They may be viewed from the outside only. ➡ **In Howden, 23m W of Kingston Upon Hull, 25m SE of York, near junction of A63 and A614.** 89 B8

Hurlers Stone Circles
∩ These three Bronze Age stone circles in a line are some of the best examples of ceremonial standing stones in the South West. ➡ **0.5m NW of Minions off B3254.** 5 B7

Hurst Castle
Hampshire
♜ This was one of the most sophisticated fortresses built by Henry VIII, and later strengthened in the 19th and 20th centuries, to command the narrow entrance to the Solent. There are two exhibitions in the castle, and two huge 38-ton guns from the fort's armaments. ➡ **On Pebble Spit S of Keyhaven. Best approached by ferry from Keyhaven, telephone 01590 642500 (June-Sept, 9am-2pm) for ferry details. ✆01590 642344** 14 F4

Hylton Castle
Tyne and Wear
♜ A 15th-century keep-gatehouse, with a fine display of mediaeval heraldry adorning the facades. ➡ **3.75m W of Sunderland.** 111 D6

Innisidgen Lower and Upper Burial Chambers
St Mary's, Isles of Scilly
△ Two Bronze Age cairns, about 30 metres apart. ➡ **1.75m NE of Hugh Town.** 2 E4

Iron Bridge
Shropshire
∩ The world's first iron bridge and Britain's best-known industrial monument. Cast in Coalbrookdale by local ironmaster Abraham Darby, it was erected across the River Severn in 1779. ➡ **In Ironbridge, adjacent to A4169.** 61 D6

Isleham Priory Church
Cambridgeshire
⛪ Rare example of an early Norman church. It has survived little altered, despite being later converted to a barn. ➡ **In Isleham, 16m NE of Cambridge on B1104. ✆Regional office 01223 582700** 55 B7

Jewel Tower
Westminster, Greater London
♜ One of two surviving buildings of the original Palace of Westminster, the Jewel Tower was built c.1365 to house the personal treasure of Edward III. It was subsequently used as a storehouse and government office. The exhibition, 'Parliament Past and Present', and accompanying video provide a fascinating account of the Houses of Lords and Commons. ➡ **Opposite S end of Houses of Parliament (Victoria Tower). ✆020 7222 2219** 28 B3

Jewry Wall
Leicester, Leicestershire
∩ One of the largest surviving lengths of Roman wall in the country. Over 9 metres (30 ft) high, it formed one side of the civic baths' exercise hall. ➡ **In St Nicholas St W of Church of St Nicholas. ✆0116 225 4971 (Site managed by Jewry Wall Museum)** 64 D2

Jordan Hill Roman Temple
Weymouth, Dorset
∩ ∩ Foundations of a Romano-Celtic temple enclosing an area of about 22 square metres (240 square feet). 12 F4

Kenilworth Castle
Warwickshire
♡ ♜ England's largest castle ruin has been linked with many great names in history, including Henry V and Elizabeth I. Once one of the most important castles in the area, Kenilworth's key features include the Norman keep, reconstructed Tudor gardens and the remains of John of Gaunt's Great Hall. Tea room and gift shop. ➡ **In Kenilworth, Warwickshire ✆01926 852078** 55 H4

▼**Kenilworth Castle** English Heritage Photographic Library

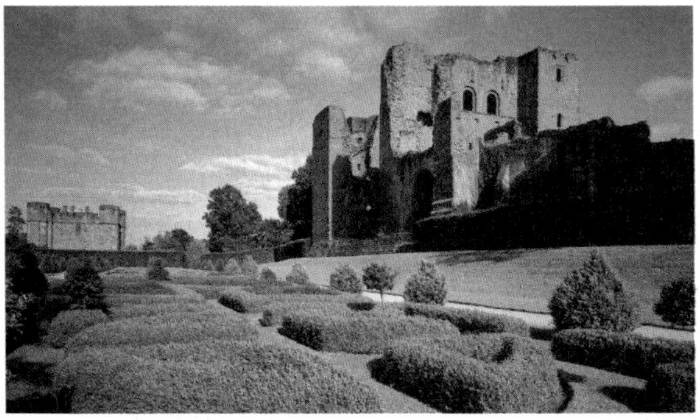

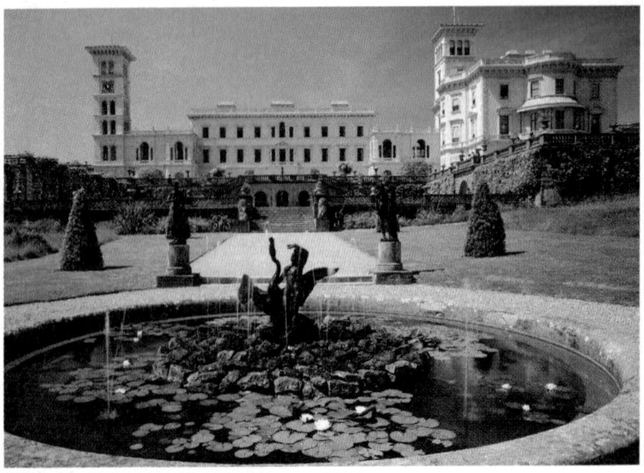

▲**Osborne House** English Heritage Photographic Library

Kenwood
Hampstead, Greater London
Standing in splendid, landscaped grounds on the edge of Hampstead Heath, Kenwood contains the most important private collection of paintings ever given to the nation, the Iveagh Bequest. Among the finest is the 'Self-Portrait' by Rembrandt and 'The Guitar Player' by Vermeer, and also other works by such eminent British artists as Gainsborough, Turner and Reynolds. The outstanding neoclassical house was remodelled by Robert Adam, 1764-79 and English Heritage has restored his original colour scheme in the Entrance Hall. Outside, the landscaped park forms the perfect setting for the concerts that are held here in summer. **➡ Hampstead Lane, London, NW3. ✆020 8348 1286** 41 F5

King Arthur's Round Table
Cumbria
A prehistoric circular earthwork bounded by a ditch and an outer bank. **➡ At Eamont Bridge, 1m S of Penrith.** 99 B7

King Charles's Castle
Tresco, Isles of Scilly
At the end of a bracing coastal walk to the northern end of Tresco you will find the remains of this castle built for coastal defence. **➡ 0.75 m NW of New Grimsby.** 2 E3

King Doniert's Stone
St Cleer, Cornwall
Two decorated pieces of a 9th-century cross with an inscription believed to commemorate Durngarth, King of Cornwall, who drowned c.875. **➡ 1m NW of St Cleer off B3254.** 5 C7

King James's and Landport Gates
Portsmouth, Hampshire
These gates were once part of the 17th-century defences of Portsmouth **➡ King James's Gate: forms entrance to United Services Recreation Ground (officers) on Park Rd; Landport Gate: as above, men's entrance on St George's Rd.** 15 E7

Kingston Russell Stone Circle
Dorset
A Bronze Age stone circle of 18 stones. **➡ 2m N of Abbotsbury, 1m along foot-path off minor road to Hardy Monument.** 12 F3

Kingswood Abbey Gatehouse
Gloucestershire
The 16th-century gatehouse, with a richly carved mullioned window. **➡ In Kingswood off B4060 1m SW of Wotton-under-Edge.** 36 E4

Kirby Hall
Northamptonshire
Outstanding example of a large, stone-built Elizabethan mansion, begun in 1570 with 17th-century alterations. The fine gardens are home to beautiful peacocks. **➡ On unclassified road off A43 4m NE of Corby. ✆01536 203230** 65 E6

Kirkham House
Paignton, Devon
A well preserved, mediaeval stone house, much restored and repaired. **➡ In Kirkham St, off Cecil Rd, Paignton. ✆0117 975 0700.** 7 C6

Kirkham Priory
North Yorkshire
The remains of this Augustinian priory, including a magnificent carved gatehouse, are set in a peaceful and secluded valley by the River Derwent. **➡ 5m SW of Malton on minor road off A64. ✆01653 618768** 96 C3

Kit's Coty House and Little Kit's Coty House
Kent
Ruins of two prehistoric burial chambers. **➡ W of A229 2m N of Maidstone.** 29 C8

Knights Templar Church
Dover, Kent
Standing across the valley from Dover Castle are the foundations of a small circular 12th-century church. **➡ On the Western Heights above Dover.** 51 B7

Knowlton Church and Earthworks
Dorset
The ruins of this Norman church stand in the middle of Neolithic earthworks, symbolizing the transition from pagan to Christian worship. **➡ 3m SW of Cranborne on B3078.** 13 C8

Landguard Fort
Felixstowe, Suffolk
An 18th-century fort, with later additions. There is a museum featuring displays of local history. **➡ 1m S of Felixstowe near docks. ✆01394 277767 (evenings)** 57 F6

Lanercost Priory
Cumbria
Augustinian priory founded c.1166. The church's nave contrasts with the ruined chancel, transepts and priory buildings. **➡ Off minor road S of Lanercost, 2m NE of Brampton. ✆01697 73030** 109 C5

Langley Chapel
Shropshire
This small chapel, standing alone in a field, contains a complete set of early 17th-century wooden fittings and furniture. **➡ 1.5m S of Acton Burnell, on unclassified road off A49, 9.5m S of Shrewsbury.** 60 D5

Launceston Castle
Cornwall
Set on the motte of a Norman castle and commanding the town and surrounding countryside, this mediaeval castle controlled the main route into Cornwall. The shell keep and tower survive. **➡ In Launceston. ✆01566 772365** 8 F5

Leicester Jewry Wall
See Jewry Wall. 64 D2

Leigh Court Barn
Worcestershire
Magnificent 14th-century timber-framed barn, built for the monks of Pershore Abbey. **➡ 5m W of Worcester on unclassified road off A4103.** 50 D2

Leiston Abbey
Suffolk
The remains of this abbey for Premonstratensian canons include a restored chapel. **➡ 1m N of Leiston off B1069.** 57 C8

Lexden Earthworks and Bluebottle Grove
Colchester, Essex
Parts of a series of earthworks, once encompassing 12 square miles, which protected Iron Age Colchester and were subsequently added to by the conquering Romans. **➡ 2m W of Colchester off A604. ✆01206 282931 (Site managed by Colchester Borough Council.)** 43 B5

Lilleshall Abbey
Shropshire
Extensive and evocative ruins of an abbey of Augustinian canons, including remains of the 12th- and 13th-century church and the cloister buildings. **➡ On unclassified road off A518, 4m N of Oakengates. ✆0121 625 6820 (Regional Office)** 61 C7

Lincoln Mediaeval Bishop's Palace
Lincoln, Lincolnshire
The remains of this mediaeval palace of the Bishops of Lincoln are in the shadow of Lincoln Cathedral. You can climb the stairs to the Alnwick Tower, explore the undercroft and see the recently established Contemporary Heritage Garden. **➡ S side of Lincoln Cathedral. ✆01522 527468** 78 B2

Lindisfarne Priory
Northumberland
➡ On Holy Island, Northumberland, only reached at low tide across causeway (tide tables at each end). ✆01289 389200 125 E7

Lindsey Chapel
Lindsey, Suffolk
A little 13th-century chapel with thatched roof and lancet windows. **➡ On unclassified road 0.5m E of Rose Green, 8m E of Sudbury.** 56 E3

London Wall
Tower Hill, Greater London
The best preserved piece of the Roman Wall, heightened in the Middle Ages, which formed part of the eastern defences of the City of London. **➡ Near Tower Hill Underground station EC3** 41 F6

Longtown Castle
Herefordshire
An unusual cylindrical keep built c.1200, with walls 4.5 metres (15 feet) thick. There are magnificent views to the Black Mountains. **➡ 4m WSW of Abbey Dore.** 35 B7

Ludgershall Castle and Cross
Wiltshire
Ruins of an early 12th-century royal hunting palace and a late-mediaeval cross. **➡ On N side of Ludgershall off A342.** 25 D7

Lullingstone Roman Villa
Kent
The villa, discovered in 1939, was one of the most exciting finds of the century. Dating from c.100 AD, but extended during 300 years of Roman occupation, much is visible today. **➡ 0.5m SW of Eynsford off A225 off junction 3 of M25. Follow A20 towards Brands Hatch. ✆01322 863467** 29 C6

Lulworth Castle
Dorset
An early 17th-century romantic hunting lodge, Lulworth Castle became a fashionable country house set in beautiful parkland during the 18th century. Gutted by fire in 1929, the exterior is now being restored by English Heritage. **➡ In east Lulworth off B3070, 3 miles NE of Lulworth Cove. ✆01929 400352** 13 F6

Lyddington Bede House
Rutland
➡ Next to church in Lyddington, 6m N of Corby, 1m E of A6003. ✆01572 822438 65 E5

Lydford Castles and Saxon Town
Devon
Standing above the gorge of the River Lyd, this 12th-century tower was notorious as a prison. The earthworks of the original Norman fort are to the south. **➡ In Lydford off A386 8m S of Okehampton.** 9 F7

Maiden Castle
Dorset
This is the finest Iron Age hill fort in Britain. The earthworks are enormous, with a series of ramparts and complicated entrances. **➡ 2m S of Dorchester. Access off A354, N of bypass.** 12 F4

Maison Dieu
Ospringe, Kent
Part of a mediaeval complex of Royal lodge, almshouses and hospital, it is much as it was 400 years ago. It contains an exhibition about Ospringe in Roman times. **➡ In Ospringe on A2, 0.5m W of Faversham. ✆01795 534542** 30 C3

Marble Hill House
Twickenham, Greater London A magnificent Thames-side Palladian villa built 1724-29 for Henrietta Howard, Countess of Suffolk, set in 66 acres of parkland. The Great Room has lavish gilded decoration and architectural paintings by Panini. The house also contains an important collection of early Georgian furniture, the Lazenby Bequest Chinoiserie collection and an 18th-century lacquer screen. **➡ Richmond Road, Twickenham. ✆020 8892 5115** 28 B2

Marmion Tower
North Yorkshire
A mediaeval gatehouse with a fine oriel window. **➡ N of Ripon on A6108 in West Tanfield.** 95 B5

Mattersey Priory
Nottinghamshire
Remains of a small Gilbertine monastery founded in 1185. **➡ Rough access down drive 0.75m long, 1m E of Mattersey off B6045, 7m N of East Retford.** 89 F8

Mayburgh Henge
Cumbria
An impressive prehistoric circular henge, with banks up to 4.5 metres (15 feet) high, enclosing a central area of one and a half acres containing a single large stone. **➡ At Eamont Bridge, 1m S of Penrith off A6.** 99 B7

Meare Fish House
Somerset
A simple, well-preserved stone dwelling. **➡ In Meare village on B3151.** 23 E6

Mediaeval Merchant's House
Southampton, Hampshire
Life in the Middle Ages is vividly evoked by the brightly painted cabinets and colourful wall hangings authentically re-created for this 13th-century town house, originally built as shop and home for a prosperous wine merchant. **➡ 58 French Street, 0.25m S of city centre just off Castle Way (between High St and Bugle St). ✆023 8022 1503** 14 C5

Merrivale Prehistoric Settlement
Dartmoor, Devon
Two rows of standing stones stretching up to 263 metres (864 feet) across the moors, together with the remains of an early Bronze Age village. **➡ 1m E of Merrivale.** 6 B3

Middleham Castle
North Yorkshire This childhood home of Richard III stands controlling the river that winds through Wensleydale. There is a massive 12th-century keep with splendid views of the surrounding countryside from the battlements. **➡ At Middleham, 2m S of Leyburn on A6108. ✆01969 623899** 101 F6

Milton Chantry
Gravesend, Kent
A small 14th-century building which housed the chapel of a leper hospital and a family chantry. It later became a tavern and, in 1780, part of a fort. **➡ In New Tavern Fort Gardens E of central Gravesend off A226. ✆01474 321520** 29 B7

Minster Lovell Hall and Dovecote
Oxfordshire
The handsome ruins of Lord Lovell's 15th-century manor house. **➡ Adjacent to Minster Lovell church, 3m W of Witney off A40.** 38 C3

Mistley Towers
Essex
The remains of a church designed by Robert Adam and built in 1776. It was unusual in having towers at both the east and west ends. **➡ On B1352, 1.5m E of A137 at Lawford, 9m E of Colchester. ✆01206 393884. (Site managed by Mistley Thorn Residents Association.)** 56 F5

Mitchell's Fold Stone Circle
Shropshire
Bronze Age stone circle, set on dramatic moorland and consisting of some 30 stones of which 15 are visible. **➡ 16m SW of Shrewsbury W of A488.** 60 E3

Monk Bretton Priory
South Yorkshire
Sandstone ruins of a Cluniac monastery founded in 1153. There are extensive remains of the fully restored 14th-century gatehouse. 88 D4

Moreton Corbet Castle
Shropshire
A ruined mediaeval castle with the substantial remains of a splendid Elizabethan mansion. **➡ In Moreton Corbet off B5063, 7m NE of Shrewsbury.** 61 B5

Mortimer's Cross Water Mill
Herefordshire
Intriguing 18th-century mill, still in working order, showing the process of corn milling. **➡ 7m NW of Leominster on B4362. ✆0121 625 6820** 49 C6

Moulton Packhorse Bridge
Suffolk
Mediaeval four-arched bridge spanning the River Kennett. **➡ In Moulton off B1085, 4m E of Newmarket.** 55 C7

Mount Grace Priory
North Yorkshire
➡ 12m N of Thirsk, 7m NE of Northallerton on A19. ✆01609 883494 102 E2

Muchelney Abbey
Somerset
The well-preserved remains of the cloisters and abbot's lodging of this Benedictine abbey **➡ In Muchelney 2m S of Langport. ✆01458 250664** 12 B2

Netheravon Dovecote
Wiltshire
A charming 18th-century brick dovecote with most of its 700 or more nesting boxes still present. **➡ In Netheravon, 4.5m N of Amesbury on A345.** 25 E6

Netley Abbey
Hampshire
A 13th-century Cistercian abbey converted in Tudor times for use as a house. **➡ In Netley, 4m SE of Southampton, facing Southampton Water. ✆023 9258 1059** 15 D5

Nine Ladies Stone Circle
Stanton Moor, Derbyshire
Once part of the burial site for 300-400 people, this Early Bronze Age circle is 15 metres (50 feet) across. **➡ From unclassified road off A6, 5m SE of Bakewell.** 76 C2

Norham Castle
Northumberland
Set on a promontory in a curve of the River Tweed, this was one of the strongest of the border castles, built c.1160. **➡ Norham village, 6.5m SW of Berwick-upon-Tweed on minor road off B6470 (from A698). ✆01289 382329** 124 E5

North Elmham Chapel
Norfolk
Remains of a Norman chapel converted into a fortified dwelling and enclosed by earthworks in the late 14th century by the notorious Bishop of Norwich, Hugh le Despencer. **➡ 6m N of East Dereham on B1110.** 81 E5

North Hinksey Conduit House
Oxfordshire
Roofed reservoir for Oxford's first water mains, built in the early 17th century. **➡ In North Hinksey off A34, 2.5m W of Oxford. Located off track leading from Harcourt Hill; use footpath from Ferry Hinksey Lane (near station).** 38 D4

Northington Grange
Hampshire
Magnificent neoclassical country house, built at the beginning of the 18th century. **➡ 4m N of New Alresford off B3046. ✆023 9258 1059** 26 F3

North Leigh Roman Villa
Oxfordshire
The remains of a large and well-built Roman courtyard villa. **➡ 2m N of North Leigh, 10m W of Oxford off A4095.** 43 F4

Notgrove Long Barrow
Gloucestershire
A Neolithic burial mound with chambers for human remains opening from a stone-built central passage. **➡ 1.5m NW of Notgrove on A436.** 38 C3

Nunney Castle
Somerset
A small 14th-century moated castle which is distinctly French in style. **➡ In Nunney 3.5m SW of Frome, off A361 (no coach access).** 24 E2

Nympsfield Long Barrow
Gloucestershire
A chambered Neolithic long barrow 30 metres (90 feet) in length. **➡ 1m NW of Nympsfield on B4066.** 37 D5

Odda's Chapel
Deerhurst, Gloucestershire
A rare Anglo-Saxon chapel attached, unusually, to a half-timbered farmhouse. **➡ In Deerhurst (off B4213) at Abbots Court SW of parish church.** 37 B5

Offa's Dyke
Gloucestershire
Three-mile section of the great earthwork built by Offa, King of Mercia 757-96, from the Severn estuary to the Welsh coast as a defensive boundary to his kingdom. **➡ 3m NE of Chepstow off B4228. Access via Forestry Commission Tidenham car park. 1m walk (way marked) down to Devil's Pulpit on Offa's Dyke. (Access suitable only for those wearing proper walking shoes; not suitable for very young, old or infirm).** 36 D2

Okehampton Castle
Devon
The ruins of the largest castle in Devon. There is a picnic area and

there are also lovely woodland walks. ➲ **1m SW of Okehampton town centre. ✆01837 52844** 9 E7

Old Blockhouse
Tresco, Isles of Scilly
The remains of a small 16th-century gun tower. ➲ **On Blockhouse Point, at S end of Old Grimsby harbour.** 2 E4

Old Gorhambury House
Hertfordshire
The remains of this Elizabethan mansion illustrate the impact of the Renaissance on English architecture. ➲ **0.25m W of Gorhambury House and accessible only through private drive from A4147 at St Albans (2m).** 40 D4

Old Oswestry Hill Fort
Shropshire
An impressive Iron Age fort of 68 acres defended by a series of five ramparts, with an elaborate western entrance and unusual earthwork cisterns. ➲ **1m N of Oswestry, accessible from unclassified road off A483.** 73 F6

Old Sarum
Wiltshire
Originally an Iron Age hillfort, the 56-acre site was once a major settlement in the area, occupied by the Romans, Saxons and Normans. It was one of William the Conqueror's great palaces and site of the first Salisbury Cathedral. Gift shop. ➲ **2m N of Salisbury, Wiltshire off A345. ✆01722 335398** 25 F6

Old Soar Manor
Plaxtol, Kent
The remains of a late 13th-century knight's manor house, comprising the two-storey solar and chapel. There is an exhibition to visit. ➲ **1m E of Plaxtol. ✆01732 810378** 29 D7

Old Wardour Castle
Wiltshire
The unusual hexagonal ruins of this 14th-century castle are on the edge of a beautiful lake, surrounded by landscaped grounds, which include an elaborate rockwork grotto. ➲ **Off A30 2m SW of Tisbury. ✆01747 870487** 13 B7

Orford Castle
Suffolk
A royal castle built for coastal defence in the 12th century. A magnificent keep survives almost intact with three immense towers reaching to 30m (90 feet). Inside a spiral stair leads to a maze of rooms and passageways. ➲ **In Orford on B1084 20m NE of Ipswich. ✆01394 450472** 57 E8

Osborne House
Isle of Wight
Osborne House was 'a place of one's own, quiet and retired', for Queen Victoria and Prince Albert. They found tranquillity on the Isle of Wight, far from the formality of court life at Buckingham Palace and Windsor Castle. The house they built was set among terraced gardens and filled with treasured mementoes. Victoria died at Osborne in 1901, still mourning her beloved Albert, who had died in middle age. Visit the newly refurbished Durbar Wing with its exquisite collection of Indian items. ➲ **1m SE of East Cowes, Isle of Wight. ✆01983 200022** 15 E6

Over Bridge
Gloucestershire
A single-arch masonry bridge spanning the River Severn, built by Thomas Telford 1825-27. ➲ **1m NW of Gloucester city centre at junction of A40 (Ross) and A419 (Ledbury).** 37 C5

Pendennis Castle
Cornwall
Henry VIII's fortress at the mouth of the Fal boasts Second World War secret underground defences. Attractions include the re-constructed Second World War Battery Observation Post housing range-finding equipment, a First World War Guard House, 16th-century keep with a recreated working gun-deck, plus a hands-on discovery centre, tearoom and gift shop. ➲ **On Pendennis Head, Cornwall, 1m SE of Falmouth. ✆01326 316594** 4 F3

Penhallam
Cornwall
Ruins of a mediaeval manor house surrounded by a protective moat. ➲ **1m NW of Week St Mary, off minor road off A39 from Treskinnick Cross (10 minute walk from car park).** 8 E4

Penrith Castle
Cumbria
A 14th-century castle set in a park on the edge of the town. ➲ **Opposite Penrith railway station.** 99 B7

Pevensey Castle
East Sussex
William the Conqueror landed at Pevensey on September 28, 1066. Today you can see the ruins of the mediaeval castle including remains of an unusual keep enclosed within its walls, originally dating back to the 4th-century Roman fort Anderida. ➲ **In Pevensey off A259. ✆01323 762604** 18 E3

Peveril Castle
Derbyshire
There are breathtaking views of the Peak District from this castle, perched high above the pretty village of Castleton. ➲ **On S side of Castleton, 15m W of Sheffield on A6187. ✆01433 620613** 88 F2

Pickering Castle
North Yorkshire
A splendid motte and bailey castle, once a royal hunting lodge. It is well preserved, with much of the original walls, towers and keep. There is an exhibition on the castle's history. ➲ **In Pickering 15m SW of Scarborough. ✆01751 474989** 103 F6

Piel Castle
Cumbria
The ruins of a 14th-century castle, accessible by boat from Roa Island. 92 C2

Piercebridge Roman Bridge
North Yorkshire
Remains of the stone piers and abutment of a Roman timber bridge over the River Tees. ➲ **At Piercebridge, 4m W of Darlington on B6275.** 101 C7

Portchester Castle
Hampshire
A residence for kings and a rallying point for troops, this grand castle has a history stretching back nearly 2,000 years. There are Roman walls, the most complete in Europe, substantial remains of the castle and an exhibition telling the story of Portchester. ➲ **On S side of Portchester off A27, Junction 11 on M27. ✆023 9237 8291** 15 E7

Porth Hellick Down Burial Chamber
St Mary's, Isles of Scilly
Probably the best-preserved Bronze Age burial mound on the Islands, with an entrance passage and chamber. ➲ **1.5 m E of Hugh Town.** 2 E4

Portland Castle
Dorset
One of Henry VIII's best-preserved coastal forts, Portland Castle was in use up to the Second World War. There are superb views over the harbour, a gift shop and tearoom. ➲ **Overlooking Portland harbour. ✆01305 820539** 12 G4

Prior's Hall Barn
Widdington, Essex
One of the finest surviving mediaeval barns in south-east England and representative of the aisled barns of NW Essex. ➲ **In Widdington, on unclassified road 2m SE of Newport, off B1383. ✆01799 522842** 55 F6

Prudhoe Castle
Northumberland
Set on a wooded hillside overlooking the River Tyne are the extensive remains of a 12th-century castle, with gatehouse, curtain wall and keep. ➲ **In Prudhoe, on minor road off A695. ✆01661 833459** 110 C4

Ravenglass Roman Bath House
Cumbria
The walls of the bathhouse are among the most complete Roman remains in Britain. ➲ **0.25m E of Ravenglass, off minor road leading to A595.** 98 E2

Reculver Towers and Roman Fort
Kent
Standing in a country park, a 12th-century landmark of twin towers and the walls of a Roman fort. ➲ **At Reculver 3m E of Herne Bay. ✆01227 740676** 31 C6

Restormel Castle
Cornwall
➲ **1.5m N of Lostwithiel off A390. ✆01208 872687** 5 C6

Richborough Castle, Roman Fort
Kent
This fort and township date back to the Roman landing in AD 43. The fortified walls and the massive foundations of a triumphal arch which stood 25 m (80 ft) high still survive. ➲ **1.5m N of Sandwich off A257. ✆01304 612013** 31 C7

Richborough Roman Amphitheatre
Kent
Ditch associated with the nearby 3rd-century castle. ➲ **1.25m N of Sandwich off A257, Junction 7 of M2, onto A2. ✆01304 612013 for details.** 31 D7

Richmond Castle
North Yorkshire
Hugely dramatic Norman fortress, built by William the Conqueror in his quest to quell the rebellious North. William's close ally, Alan of Brittany, chose the site for his principal castle and residence. The 11th-century remains of the curtain wall and domestic buildings are combined with the 100ft high keep, with its hugely thick walls, which was added in the 12th century. There are magnificent views over the River Swale from the keep. ➲ **In Richmond. ✆01748 822493** 101 D6

Rievaulx Abbey
North Yorkshire
Situated in the beautiful River Rye valley, Rievaulx's incomparable setting makes it one of the most atmospheric ruined abbeys of the north. It's site was carefully chosen and the course of the River Rye was diverted so that it could be built. Originally one of the wealthiest monasteries in medieval England, Rievaulx was home to Cistercian monks from the 12th to the 15th century, including St Aelred (famous in Christian heritage circles). Today most of the spectacular presbytery stands virtually to its full height, revealing the Abbey's former splendour. Within the abbey visitors can enjoy an exhibition on Cistercian life. There is a gift shop. ➲ **In Rievaulx, North Yorkshire 2.25m W of Helmsley on minor road off B1257. ✆01439 798228** 102 F3

Roche Abbey
South Yorkshire
A Cistercian monastery, founded in 1147. ➲ **1.5m S of Maltby off A634. ✆01709 812739** 89 F6

Rochester Castle
Kent
Built on the Roman city wall, this Norman bishop's castle was a vital royal stronghold. ➲ **By Rochester Bridge (A2), Junction 1 of M2 and Junction 2 of M25. ✆01634 402276** 29 C8

Rollright Stones
Oxfordshire
Three groups of stones, known as 'The King's Men', 'The Whispering Knights' and 'The King Stone', spanning nearly 2,000 years of the Neolithic and Bronze Ages. ➲ **Off unclassified road between A44 and A3400, 2m NW of Chipping Norton near villages of Little Rollright and Long Compton.** 51 F7

Roman Wall
St Albans, Hertfordshire
➲ **On S side of St Albans, 0.5m from centre off A4147.** 40 D4

Rotherwas Chapel
Hereford and Worcester
This Roman Catholic chapel dates from the 14th and 16th centuries and features an interesting mid-Victorian side chapel and High Altar. ➲ **1.5m SE of Hereford on B4399.** 49 F7

Row 111 House Old Merchant's House and Greyfriars' Cloisters
Norfolk
Two 17th-century Row Houses, a type of building unique to Great Yarmouth, containing original fixtures and displays of local architectural fittings salvaged from bombing in 1942-43. Nearby are the remains of a Franciscan friary, with rare early wall paintings, accidentally discovered during bomb damage repairs. ➲ **Great Yarmouth, head for South Quay along riverside and dock, 0.5m inland from beach. Follow signs to dock and south quay. ✆01493 857900** 69 D8

Royal Citadel
Plymouth, Devon
A dramatic 17th-century fortress, with walls up to 21 metres (70 feet) high. ➲ **At E end of Plymouth Hoe. ✆0117 975 0700** 6 D2

Royal Garrison Church
Portsmouth, Hampshire
Originally a hospice for pilgrims, this 16th-century chapel became the Garrison Church after the Dissolution. ➲ **On Grand Parade S of Portsmouth High St. ✆023 9237 8291** 15 E7

Rufford Abbey
Nottinghamshire
The remains of a 17th-century country house, built on the foundations of a 12th-century Cistercian abbey. ➲ **2m S of Ollerton off A614. ✆01623 822944** 77 C6

Rushton Triangular Lodge
Northamptonshire
Extraordinary building built by the Catholic Sir Thomas Tresham on his return from imprisonment for his religious beliefs. Completed in 1597, it symbolizes the Holy Trinity. It has three sides, three floors, trefoil windows and three triangular gables on each side. ➲ **1m W of Rushton, on unclassified road 3m from Desborough on A6. ✆01536 710761** 64 F5

Rycote Chapel
Oxfordshire
Lovely 15th-century chapel, with exquisitely carved and painted woodwork. ➲ **3m SW of Thame off A329. ✆01424 775705** 39 D6

St Augustine's Abbey
Canterbury, Kent
➲ **In Longport 0.25m E of Cathedral Close. ✆01227 767345** 31 D5

St Augustine's Cross
Ebbsfleet, Kent
19th-century cross, in Celtic design, marking the traditional site of St Augustine's landing in 597. ➲ **2m E of Minster off B29048.** 31 C7

St Botolph's Priory
Colchester, Essex
The nave, with an impressive arcaded west end, one of the first Augustinian priories in England. ➲ **Colchester, near Colchester Town station. ✆01206 282931 (Site managed by Colchester Borough Council)** 43 B5

St Breock Downs Monolith
Cornwall
A prehistoric standing stone, originally about 5 metres (16 feet) high, set in beautiful countryside. ➲ **On St Breock Downs, 3.75 m SW of Wadebridge off unclassified road to Rosenannon.** 4 C4

St Briavel's Castle
Gloucestershire
A splendid 12th-century castle now used as a youth hostel. ➲ **In St Briavel's, 7m NE of Chepstow off B4228.** 36 D2

St Catherine's Castle
Fowey, Cornwall
A small fort built by Henry VIII to defend Fowey Harbour. ➲ **0.75 m SW of Fowey along footpath off A3082.** 5 D6

St Catherine's Chapel
Abbotsbury, Dorset
A small stone chapel, set on a hilltop, with an unusual roof and small turret used as a lighthouse. ➲ **0.5m S of Abbotsbury by pedestrian track from village off B3157.** 12 F3

St Catherine's Oratory
Isle of Wight
Affectionately known as the Pepperpot, this 14th-century lighthouse stands on the highest point of the island. ➲ **0.75m NW of Niton.** 15 G5

St John's Abbey Gate
Colchester, Essex
This fine abbey gatehouse, in East Anglian flintwork, survives from the Benedictine abbey of St John. ➲ **On S side of central Colchester.** 43 B6

St John's Commandery
Swingfield, Kent
A mediaeval chapel, converted into a farmhouse in the 16th century. ➲ **2m NE of Densole off A260. ✆01304 211067 for details.** 31 E6

St Leonard's Tower
West Malling, Kent
An early and particularly fine example of a Norman tower keep, built c.1080 by Gundulf, Bishop of Rochester. ➲ **On unclassified road W of A228. ✆01732 870872** 29 D7

St Mary's Church
Kempley, Gloucestershire
A Norman church with superb wall paintings from the 12th-14th centuries. ➲ **1m N of Kempley off B4024, 6m NE of Ross-on-Wye.** 49 F8

St Mary's Church Studley Royal
Studley Royal, North Yorkshire
Magnificent Victorian church, designed by William Burges in the 1870s, with a highly decorated interior. ➲ **2.5m W of Ripon off B6265, in grounds of Studley Royal estate. ✆01765 608888** 95 C5

St Mawes Castle
Cornwall
Set in the wonderful location alongside the pretty fishing village of St Mawes, with delightful landscaped gardens and extensive views of the coastline.

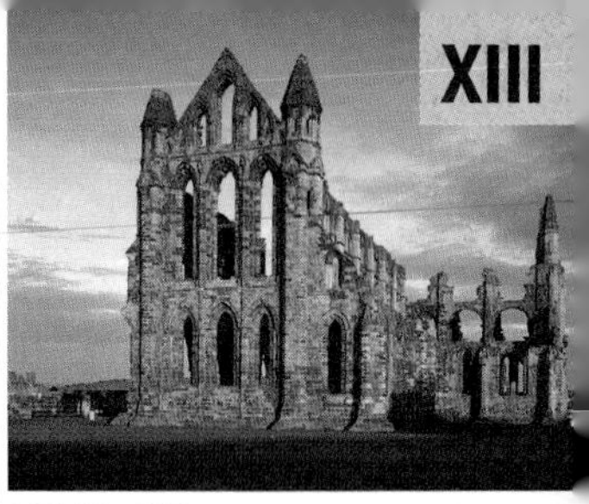

▲Whitby Abbey English Heritage Photographic Library

The castle is the most perfectly preserved of Henry VIII's coastal fortresses, complete with its commons. Gift shop. ➲ **In St Mawes on A3078. ✆01326 270526** 4 F3

St Olave's Priory
Norfolk
Remains of an Augustinian priory founded nearly 200 years after the death in 1030 of the patron saint of Norway, after whom it is named. ➲ **5.5m SW of Great Yarmouth on A143.** 69 D7

St Paul's Monastery and Bede's World Museum
Jarrow, Tyne and Wear
The home of the Venerable Bede, partly surviving as the chancel of the parish church. The monastery has become one of the best-understood Anglo-Saxon monastic sites. ➲ **In Jarrow, on minor road N of A185. ✆0191 489 7052** 111 C6

St Peter's Church
Barton-upon-Humber, North Lincolnshire
A fine 15th-century former parish church, with an Anglo-Saxon tower and baptistry. ➲ **In Barton-upon-Humber. ✆01652 632516** 90 B4

Sandbach Crosses
Cheshire
Rare Saxon stone crosses from the 9th century, carved with animals, dragons and biblical scenes, in the centre of the market square. ➲ **Market Square, Sandbach.** 74 C4

Saxtead Green Post Mill
Suffolk
A fine example of a post mill, where the superstructure turns on a great post to face the wind. The mill, which ceased production in 1947, is still in working order. ➲ **2.5m NW of Framlingham on A1120. ✆01728 685789** 57 C6

Scarborough Castle
North Yorkshire
There are spectacular coastal views from the walls of this enormous 12th-century castle. The buttressed castle walls stretch out along the cliff edge and the remains of the great rectangular stone keep still stand to over three storeys high. There is also the site of a 4th-century Roman signal station. The castle was often attacked, but despite being blasted by cannons of the Civil War and bombarded during World War I, it is still a spectacular place to visit. ➲ **Castle Rd, E of town centre. ✆01723 372451** 103 F8

Shap Abbey
Cumbria
The striking tower and other remains of this Premonstratensian abbey stand in a remote and isolated location. ➲ **1.5m W of Shap on bank of River Lowther.** 99 C7

Sherborne Old Castle
Dorset
The ruins of this early 12th-century castle are a testament to the 16 days Cromwell took to capture it during the Civil War. It was then abandoned. ➲ **0.5m E of Sherborne off B3145. ✆01935 812730** 12 C4

Sibsey Trader Windmill
Lincolnshire
An impressive tower mill built in 1877, with its machinery and six sails intact. Flour milled on the spot can be bought there. ➲ **0.5m W of village of Sibsey, off A16 5m N of Boston. ✆01205 750036** 79 D6

Silbury Hill
Wiltshire
An extraordinary artificial prehistoric mound, the largest Neolithic construction of its type in Europe. There is no access to the hill. ➲ **1m W of West Kennet on A4.** 25 C6

Silchester Roman City Walls and Amphitheatre
Hampshire
The best preserved Roman town walls in Britain, almost one-and-a-half miles around, with an impressive, recently restored amphitheatre. ➲ **On minor road 1m E of Silchester.** 26 C4

Sir Bevil Grenville's Monument
Lansdown, Bath and NE Somerset
◯ Commemorates the heroism of a Royalist commander and his Cornish pikemen at the Battle of Lansdown. **➲ 4m NW of Bath, on N edge of Lansdown Hill, near road to Wick.** 24 B2

Skipsea Castle
East Riding of Yorkshire
◯ The remaining earthworks of a Norman motte and bailey castle. **➲ 8m S of Bridlington, W of Skipsea village.** 97 D7

Spofforth Castle
North Yorkshire
◯ ◯ Manor house with fascinating features including an undercroft built into the rock. Once owned by the Percy family. **➲ 3.5m SE of Harrogate, off A661 at Spofforth.** 95 D6

Stanton Drew Circles and Cove
Bath and NE Somerset
△ A fascinating assembly of three stone circles, two avenues and a burial chamber makes this one of the finest Neolithic religious sites in the country. **➲ Circles: E of Stanton Drew village; Cove: in garden of Druid's Arms. ✆ 0117 975 0700 for details.** 23 C8

Stanwick Iron Age Fortifications
North Yorkshire
△ The tribal stronghold of the Brigantes, whose vast earthworks cover some 850 acres. **➲ On minor road off A6274 at Forcett Village.** 101 C6

Steeton Hall Gateway
North Yorkshire
◯ A fine example of a small, well-preserved 14th-century gatehouse. **➲ 4m NE of Castleford, on minor road off A162 at South Milford. ✆ Regional Office 0191 261 1585** 95 F7

Stokesay Castle
Shropshire
◯ ◯ ✿ The finest mediaeval manor house in England, situated in peaceful countryside. The castle now stands in a picturesque group with its own splendid timber-framed Jacobean gatehouse and the parish church. **➲ 7m NW of Ludlow off A49. ✆ 01588 672544** 60 F4

Stonehenge, World Heritage Site
Wiltshire
◯ Visitors from all over the globe are fascinated by the mystery surrounding the ancient stone circle of Stonehenge in Wiltshire, English Heritage's most visited historic attraction and a World Heritage Site. With the first phase built over 5,000 years ago, speculation still surrounds the purpose of the monument, which is aligned with the rising and the setting of the sun. As the focal point of a landscape filled with prehistoric ceremonial structures, it is generally acknowledged that only a sophisticated society would have the design and construction skills needed to build Stonehenge and its surrounding monuments. But whether Stonehenge was built by a sun-worshipping culture or as part of a huge astronomical calendar, remains unknown. An inclusive audio tour is available in nine languages and a gift shop and refreshments are available. **➲ 2m W of Amesbury, Wiltshire on junction A303 and A344/A360. ✆ 01980 624715 (information line)** 25 E6

Stoney Littleton Long Barrow
Bath and NE Somerset
△ This Neolithic burial mound is about 30 metres (100 feet) long and has chambers where human remains once lay. **➲ 1m S of Wellow off A367.** 24 D2

Stott Park Bobbin Mill
Cumbria
◯ Working mill, built in 1835. It is typical of the mills in the Lake District which supplied the spinning and weaving industry in Lancashire. **➲ 0.5m N of Finsthwaite near Newby Bridge. ✆ 01539 531087** 99 F5

Sutton Scarsdale Hall
Derbyshire
◯ ◯ The dramatic hilltop shell of a great early 18th-century baroque mansion. **➲ Between Chesterfield and Bolsover, 1.5m S of Arkwright Town. ✆ 01604 735400** 76 C4

Sutton Valence Castle
Kent
◯ ◯ The ruins of a 12th-century stone keep. **➲ 5m SE of Maidstone in Sutton Valence village on A274.** 30 E2

Tattershall College
Lincolnshire
✝ Remains of a grammar school for church choristers, built in the mid-15th century by Ralph, Lord Cromwell, the builder of nearby Tattershall Castle. **➲ In Tattershall (off Market Place) 14m NE of Sleaford on A153.** 78 D5

Temple Church
Bristol
✝ The handsome tower and walls of this 15th-century church defied the bombs of World War II. The graveyard is now a pleasant public garden. **➲ In Temple St off Victoria St.** 23 B7

Temple Manor
Rochester, Kent
◯ The 13th-century manor house of the Knights Templar. **➲ In Strood (Rochester) off A228.** 29 B8

The Nine Stones
Winterbourne Abbas, Dorset
△ Remains of a prehistoric circle of nine standing stones constructed about 4,000 years ago. **➲ 1.5 m W of Winterbourne Abbas, on A35.** 12 E4

The Sanctuary
Wiltshire
△ Possibly 5,000 years old, The Sanctuary consists of two concentric circles of stones and six of timber uprights. **➲ Beside A4, 0.5m E of West Kennet.** 25 C6

Thetford Priory
Norfolk
✝ The 14th-century gatehouse is the best preserved part of this Cluniac priory built in 1103. The extensive remains include the plan of the cloisters **➲ On W side of Thetford near station.** 67 F8

Thetford Warren Lodge
Norfolk
◯ The ruins of a small, two-storeyed mediaeval house. **➲ 2m W of Thetford off B1107.** 67 F8

The Wernher Collection at Ranger's House
Greenwich, Greater London
◯ One of the finest and most unusual 19th-century mixed art collections in the world, containing over 650 exhibits collected by millionaire diamond dealer Sir Julius Wernher. Highlights include Renaissance jewellery, carved medieval, Byzantine and Renaissance ivories, Limoges enamels and immaculate Sevres porcelain. **➲ Chesterfield Walk, Greenwich, SE10. ✆ 020 8853 0035** 28 B4

Thornton Abbey and Gatehouse
North Lincolnshire
✝ Ruined Augustinian priory with magnificent brick gatehouse. **➲ 18m NE of Scunthorpe on minor road N of A160; 7m SE of Humber Bridge on minor road E of A1077.** 90 C5

Tilbury Fort
Essex
◯ ◯ The largest and best preserved example of 17th-century military engineering in England, commanding the Thames and showing the development of fortifications over the following 200 years. Exhibitions, the powder magazine and the bunker-like 'casemates' demonstrate how the fort protected London from seaborne attack. There's even a chance to fire an anti-aircraft gun! **➲ 0.5m E of Tilbury off A126. ✆ 01375 858489** 29 B7

Tintagel Castle
Cornwall
◯ ◯ The mystical Tintagel Castle, renowned as the birthplace of the legendary warrior leader, King Arthur, is English Heritage's top Cornish site. A site of outstanding natural beauty, groups can explore the remains of the 13th century castle on the mainland and walk the narrow and rugged trail across the wild and windswept Tintagel Island for spectacular views. Remains of the castle, built by Richard, Earl of Cornwall, include steep stone steps and stout walls. Recent excavation works at the site resulted in a dramatic find: a 1500 year old piece of slate, bearing the name ?rtognou,' refuelling speculation about links with King Arthur. **➲ On Tintagel Head 0.5m along uneven track from Tintagel, no vehicles. ✆ 01840 770328** 8 F2

Titchfield Abbey
Hampshire
✝ Remains of a 13th-century abbey overshadowed by a grand Tudor gatehouse. **➲ 0.5m N of Titchfield off A27. ✆ 01329 842133** 15 D6

Totnes Castle
Devon
◯ ◯ A superb motte and bailey castle, a fine example of Norman fortification. **➲ In Totnes, on hill overlooking town. ✆ 01803 864406** 7 C6

Tregiffian Burial Chamber
St Buryan, Cornwall
△ A Neolithic or early Bronze Age chambered tomb by the side of a country road. **➲ 2m SE of St Buryan on B3315.** 2 D3

Trethevy Quoit
St Cleer, Cornwall
△ An ancient Neolithic burial chamber, consisting of five standing stones surmounted by a huge capstone. **➲ 1m NE of St Cleer near Darite off B3254.** 5 C7

Tynemouth Priory and Castle
Tyne and Wear
✝ The castle walls and gatehouse enclose the substantial remains of a Benedictine priory founded c.1090 on a Saxon monastic site. **➲ In Tynemouth, near North Pier. ✆ 0191 257 1090** 111 C6

Uffington Castle, White Horse and Dragon Hill
Oxfordshire
△ A group of sites lying along the Ridgeway, an old prehistoric route. There is a large Iron Age camp enclosed within ramparts, a natural mound known as Dragon Hill and the spectacular White Horse, cut from turf to reveal chalk. **➲ S of B4507, 7m W of Wantage.** 38 F3

Uley Long Barrow (Hetty Pegler's Tump)
Gloucestershire
△ Dating from around 3000 BC, this 55 metre- (180 foot-) long Neolithic chambered burial mound is unusual in that its mound is still intact. **➲ 3.5m NE of Dursley on B4066.** 36 E4

Upnor Castle
Kent
◯ ◯ Well preserved 17th-century castle, built to protect Queen Elizabeth I's warships. **➲ At Upnor, on unclassified road off A228. ✆ 01634 718742** 29 B8

Upper Plym Valley
Dartmoor, Devon
△ Scores of prehistoric and mediaeval sites covering six square miles of ancient landscape. **➲ 4m E of Yelverton.** 6 C3

Wall Roman Site (Letocetum)
Staffordshire
◯ The remains of a staging post, alongside Watling Street. Foundations of an inn and bath-house can be seen, and there is a display of finds in the site museum. **➲ Off A5 at Wall near Lichfield. ✆ 01543 480768** 62 D4

Walmer Castle and Gardens
Kent
◯ ✿ Walmer Castle is the official residence of the Lord Warden of the Cinque Ports, an ancient title previously held by Her Majesty, Queen Elizabeth the Queen Mother. Created for her is a garden featuring topiary, a 95-foot pond, an E-shaped box parterre and mixed borders. Other garden highlights are a working kitchen garden, herbaceous border, croquet lawn and woodland walk. Tea room and shop. **➲ On coast S of Walmer, Kent, on A258. Junction 13 off M20 or from M2 to Deal. ✆ 01304 364288** 31 E7

Waltham Abbey Gatehouse and Bridge
Essex
✝ A late 14th-century abbey gatehouse, part of the cloister and 'Harold's Bridge'. **➲ In Waltham Abbey off A112. ✆ 01992 702200** 41 D6

Warkworth Castle and Hermitage
Northumberland
◯ The magnificent eight-towered keep of Warkworth Castle stands on its hill above the River Coquet, dominating all around it. A large and complex stronghold, it was home to the Percy family who at times wielded more power in the North than the King himself. Most famous of them all was Harry Hotspur (Sir Henry Percy), immortalised in Northumbrian ballads and Shakespeare's Henry IV, several scenes of which were set at Warkworth. **➲ In Warkworth, Northumberland 7.5m S of Alnwick on A1068. ✆ 01665 711423** 117 D8

Warton Old Rectory
Lancashire
✝ Rare mediaeval stone house with remains of the hall, chambers and domestic offices. **➲ At Warton, 1m N of Carnforth on minor road off A6.** 92 B5

Waverley Abbey
Surrey
◯ First Cistercian house in England, founded in 1128. **➲ 2m SE of Farnham off B3001 and off junction 10 of M25.** 27 E6

Wayland's Smithy
Oxfordshire
△ Near to the Uffington White Horse lies this evocative Neolithic burial site, surrounded by a small circle of trees. **➲ On the Ridgeway 0.75m NE of B4000 Ashbury-Lambourn road.** 38 F2

Weeting Castle
Norfolk
◯ ◯ The ruins of an early mediaeval manor house within a shallow rectangular moat. **➲ 2m N of Brandon off B1106.** 67 F7

Wellington Arch
Hyde Park Corner, Greater London
◯ Step inside this splendid London landmark and take in spectacular views of the capital from the viewing platforms. Gaze over surrounding parks to the Houses of Parliament, Big Ben and the London Eye, and see the mounted Horse Guards as they ride through the Arch's majestic columns every day. Beneath the magnificent Quadriga – the largest bronze sculpture in England – Wellington Arch houses exhibitions on the monuments, statues and memorials of London. **➲ Hyde Park Corner. ✆ 020 7930 2726** 28 B3

Wenlock Priory
Shropshire
✝ The ruins of a large Cluniac priory in an attractive garden setting featuring delightful topiary. There are substantial remains of the early 13th-century church and Norman chapter house **➲ In Much Wenlock. ✆ 01952 727466** 61 D6

Western Heights
Dover, Kent
◯ Parts of moat of 19th-century fort built to fend off a French attack. **➲ Above Dover town on W side of Harbour. ✆ 01304 211067** 31 E7

West Kennet Avenue
Avebury, Wiltshire
△ An avenue of standing stones, which ran in a curve from Avebury Stone Circles to The Sanctuary, probably dating from the late Neolithic Age. **➲ Runs alongside B4003.** 25 C6

West Kennet Long Barrow
Wiltshire
△ A Neolithic chambered tomb, consisting of a long earthen mound containing a passage with side chambers, and with the entrance guarded by a large stone. **➲ 0.75m SW of West Kennet along footpath off A4.** 25 C6

Wetheral Priory Gatehouse
Cumbria
✝ A Benedictine priory gatehouse, preserved after the Dissolution by serving as the vicarage for the parish church. **➲ On minor road in Wetheral village, 6m E of Carlisle on B6263.** 108 D4

Whalley Abbey Gatehouse
Lancashire
✝ The outer gatehouse of the nearby Cistercian abbey. There was originally a chapel on the first floor. **➲ In Whalley, 6m NE of Blackburn on minor road off A59.** 93 F7

Wharram Percy Deserted Village
North Yorkshire
◯ One of over 3,000 deserted villages to have been identified from faint outlines of walls and foundations. The remains of the mediaeval church still stand. **➲ 6m SE of Malton, on minor road from B1248 0.5m S of Wharram le Street.** 96 C4

Wheeldale Roman Road
N. Yorkshire
◯ This mile-long stretch of Roman road, still with its hardcore and drainage ditches, runs across isolated moorland. **➲ S of Goathland, W of A169, 7m S of Whitby.** 103 E6

Whitby Abbey
North Yorkshire
✝ These moody and magnificent ruins offer dramatic views over the town and harbour. A superb new visitor centre and museum helps visitors discover key periods in the site's history – from the Synod of 644 who decided on the date of Easter to the inspiration behind Bram Stoker's fictional classic Dracula. **➲ On cliff top E of Whitby in North Yorkshire ✆ 01947 603568** 103 C7

White Ladies Priory
Shropshire
✝ The ruins of the late 12th-century church of a small priory of Augustinian canonesses. **➲ 1m SW of Boscobel House off unclassified road between A41 and A5, 8m NW of Wolverhampton.** 61 D8

Wigmore Castle
Herefordshire
◯ Fortified since the 1060s, the present ruins date from the 13th and 14th centuries. The castle was dismantled during the Civil War, and remains very much as it was left then. **➲ 11m NW of Leominster, 14m SW of Ludlow off W side of A4110.** 49 C6

Winchester Palace
Southwark, Greater London
✝ Remains of the Great Hall of this 13th-century town house of the Bishops of Winchester, damaged by fire in 1814. **➲ Near Southwark Cathedral, at corner of Clink St and Storey St, SE1.** 28 B4

Windmill Hill
Wiltshire
△ Neolithic remains of three concentric rings of ditches, enclosing an area of 21 acres. **➲ 1.5m NW of Avebury.** 25 B5

Wingfield Manor
Derbyshire
◯ ◯ ◯ Huge, ruined, country mansion built in mid-15th century. Mary Queen of Scots was imprisoned here in 1584 and 1585. The manor has been used as a film location for 'Peak Practice' and Zeffirelli's 'Jane Eyre'. **➲ 17m N of Derby, 11m S of Chesterfield on B5035 0.5m S of South Wingfield. From M1 – Junc. 28, W on A38, A615 (Matlock Road) at Alfreton and turn onto B5035 after 1.5m. ✆ 01773 832060** 76 D3

Winterbourne Poor Lot Barrows
Dorset
△ Part of an extensive 4,000-year-old Bronze Age cemetery. **➲ 2m W of Winterbourne Abbas, S of junction of A35 with minor road to Compton Valence. Access via Wellbottom Lodge – 180 metres (200 yards) E along A35 from junction.** 12 E3

Witley Court
Worcestershire
◯ ◯ In its heyday, the gardens and vast mansion (destroyed by fire in 1937) regularly hosted royalty and society. A parterre garden is also being created, as is a wilderness garden. Gift shop. **✆ 01299 896636** 50 C2

Wolvesey Castle (Old Bishop's Palace)
Winchester, Hampshire
◯ One of the greatest mediaeval buildings in England, the Palace was the chief residence of the Bishops of Winchester. Its extensive ruins still reflect their importance and wealth. The last great occasion was on 25th July, 1554 when Queen Mary and Philip of Spain held their wedding breakfast in the East Hall. **➲ 0.25m SE of Winchester Cathedral, next to the Bishop's Palace; access from College St. ✆ 01962 854766** 15 B5

Woodhenge
Wiltshire
△ Neolithic ceremonial monument of c. 2300 BC, consisting of a bank and ditch and six concentric rings of timber posts, now shown by concrete markers. **➲ 1.5m N of Amesbury, off A345 S of Durrington.** 25 E6

Wrest Park Gardens
Bedfordshire
◯ ✿ Over 90 acres of wonderful gardens originally laid out in the early 18th century, including the Great Garden, with charming buildings and ornaments, and the delightfully intricate French Garden, with statues and fountain. The house, once the home of the de Grey family whose Mausoleum at Flitton is nearby, was inspired by 18th-century French chateaux. **➲ 0.75m E of Silsoe off A6, 10m S of Bedford. ✆ 01525 860152** 53 F8

Wroxeter Roman City
Shropshire
◯ The excavated centre of the fourth largest city in Roman Britain, with impressive remains of the 2nd-century municipal baths. **➲ At Wroxeter, 5m E of Shrewsbury on B4380. ✆ 01743 761330** 61 D5

Yarmouth Castle
Isle of Wight
◯ This last addition to Henry VIII's coastal defences was completed in 1547. It houses exhibitions of paintings of the Isle of Wight and photographs of old Yarmouth. **➲ In Yarmouth adjacent to car ferry terminal. ✆ 01983 760678** 14 F4

Yarn Market
Dunster, Somerset
◯ A 17th-century octagonal market hall. **➲ In Dunster High St.** 21 E8

Historic Scotland properties

The following properties are in the care of Historic Scotland, Longmore House, Salisbury Place, Edinburgh EH9 1SH ℡0131 668 8800

Aberdour Castle
Fife • A 14th-century castle, extended in the 16th and 17th centuries with splendid residential accommodation and a terraced garden and bowling green. There is a fine circular dovecote. **In Aberdour. ℡01383 860519.** 134 F3

Arbroath Abbey
Angus • The substantial ruins of a Tironensian monastery, founded by William the Lion in 1178. Parts of the abbey church and domestic buildings remain. This was the scene of the Declaration of Arbroath of 1320, which asserted Scotland's independence from England. **In Arbroath. ℡01241 878756.** 143 E6

Balvenie Castle
Moray • A castle of enclosure first owned by the Comyns with a curtain wall of 13th-century date. Added to in the 15th and 16th centuries and visited by Mary Queen of Scots in 1562. **At Dufftown. ℡01340 820121** 159 E7

Bishop's and Earl's Palaces
Orkney • The Bishop's palace is a 12th-century hall-house, later much altered, with a round tower begun by Bishop Reid in 1541. A later addition was made by the notorious Patrick Stewart, Earl of Orkney, who built the adjacent Earl's Palace between 1600 and 1607 in a splendid Renaissance style.
In Kirkwall. ℡01856 875461. 176 E3

Black House
Western Isles • A traditional Lewis thatched house, with byre, attached barn and stackyard, complete and furnished. **In Arnol village, Lewis. ℡01851 710395.** 172 D6

Blackness Castle
Falkirk • Built in the 1440s, and massively strengthened in the 16th century as an artillery fortress, Blackness was an ammunition depot in the 1870s. It was restored by the Office of Works in the 1920s.
4m N of Linlithgow, on a promontory in the Forth estuary. ℡01506 834807. 134 F2

Bonawe Iron Furnace
Argyll and Bute • Founded in 1753 by a Lake District partnership, this is the most complete charcoal-fuelled ironworks in Britain. Displays illustrate how iron was made here. **Close to the village of Taynuilt. ℡01866 822432.** 131 B6

Bothwell Castle
South Lanarkshire • The largest and finest 13th- century stone castle in Scotland, much fought over during the Wars of Independence. Part of the original circular keep survives, but most of the castle dates from the 14th and 15th centuries. **In Bothwell, approached from Uddingston, off the B7071. ℡01698 816894.** 121 D6

Broch of Gurness
Orkney • Protected by three lines of ditch and rampart, the base of the broch is surrounded by a warren of Iron Age buildings.
At Aikerness, about 14m NW of Kirkwall. ℡01831 579478. 176 D2

Caerlaverock Castle
Dumfries and Galloway • One of the finest castles in Scotland, on a triangular site surrounded by moats. Its special features are the twin-towered gatehouse and the Nithsdale Lodging, a Renaissance range dating from 1638. **8m SE of Dumfries. ℡01387 770244.** 107 C7

Cardoness Castle
Dumfries and Galloway • The well-preserved ruin of a tower house of 15th-century date, the ancient home of the McCullochs. **1m SW of Gatehouse of Fleet. ℡01557 814427.** 106 D2

Castle Campbell
Clackmannanshire • Traditionally known as the 'Castle of Gloom'. The oldest part is a well-preserved 15th-century tower, around which other buildings were constructed, including an unusual loggia. **At the head of Dollar Glen. ℡01259 742408.** 133 E8

Corgarff Castle
Aberdeenshire • A 16th-century tower house converted into a barracks for Hanoverian troops in 1748. Its last military use was to control the smuggling of illicit whisky between 1827 and 1831. Still complete and with star-shaped fortification. **8m W of Strathdon village. ℡01975 651460.** 149 D8

Craigmillar Castle
City of Edinburgh • Built round an L-plan tower house of the early 15th century, Craigmillar was much expanded in the 15th and 16th centuries. It is a handsome ruin, and includes a range of private rooms. **2.5 m SE of central Edinburgh, to E of Edinburgh to Dalkeith Road. ℡0131 661 4445.** 123 B5

Craignethan Castle
South Lanarkshire • The oldest part is a tower house built by Sir James Hamilton of Finnart in the 16th century, defended by an outer wall pierced by gun ports, and by a wide and deep ditch with a most unusual 'caponier' – a stone vaulted chamber for artillery. **5.5m NW of Lanark. ℡01555 860364.** 121 E8

Crichton Castle
Midlothian • A large and sophisticated castle, of which the most spectacular part is the range erected by the Earl of Bothwell between 1581 and 1591. **2.5 m SW of Pathhead. ℡01875 320017.** 123 C6

Crossraguel Abbey
South Ayrshire • The 13th-century remains, which are remarkably complete and of high quality, include the church, cloister, chapter house and much of the domestic premises.
2m S of Maybole. ℡01655 883113. 112 D2

Dallas Dhu Distillery and Visitor Centre
Moray • A perfectly preserved time capsule of the distiller's art. Built in 1898 to supply malt whisky for Wright and Greig's 'Roderick Dhu' blend. Video presentation and a glass of whisky to end your visit.
About 1m S of Forres off the Grantown Road. ℡01309 676548. 158 D4

Dirleton Castle and Gardens
East Lothian • The oldest part of this romantic castle dates from the 13th century. It was rebuilt in the 14th century and extended in the 16th century, when the gardens were established. **In the village of Dirleton. ℡01620 850330.** 135 F7

Doune Castle
Stirling • A late 14th-century courtyard castle built for the Regent Albany. Its most striking feature is the combination of keep, gatehouse and hall, with its kitchen in a massive frontal block. **In Doune. ℡01786 841742.** 133 D6

Dryburgh Abbey
Scottish Borders • Both beautifully situated and of intrinsic quality, the ruins of Dryburgh Abbey are remarkably complete. Much of the work is of the 12th and 13th century. Sir Walter Scott and Field Marshal Earl Haig are buried in the abbey. **5m SE of Melrose, near St Boswells. ℡01835 822381.** 123 F8

Dumbarton Castle
West Dumbartonshire • Spectacularly sited on a volcanic rock, this was the site of the ancient capital of Strathclyde. The most interesting features are the 18th-century artillery fortifications, with 19th-century guns. **At Dumbarton. ℡01389 732167.** 120 B4

Dundonald Castle
South Ayrshire • A fine 13th-century tower built by Robert II incorporating part of an earlier building. The king used the castle as a summer residence until his death in 1390.
In Dundonald, off the A759. ℡01563 850201. 120 F3

Dundrennan Abbey
Dumfries and Galloway • The beautiful ruins of a Cistercian abbey founded by David I. Mary Queen of Scots spent her last night on Scottish soil here. **6.5m SE of Kirkcudbright. ℡01557 500262.** 106 E4

Dunfermline Abbey and Palace
Fife • The remains of a Benedictine abbey which was founded by Queen Margaret in the 11th century. The foundations of her church are under the superb, Romanesque nave, built in the 12th century. Robert the Bruce was buried in the choir, now the site of the present parish church.
In Dunfermline. ℡01383 739026. 134 F2

Dunstaffnage Castle and Chapel
Argyll and Bute • A very fine 13th-century castle enclosure, built on a rock, with nearby ruins of a chapel of exceptional architectural refinement. **By Loch Etive, 3.5m from Oban. ℡01631 562465.** 130 B4

Edinburgh Castle
City of Edinburgh • The most famous of Scottish castles has a complex history. The oldest part dates from the Norman period; there is a Great Hall built by the James IV; the Half Moon battery was built by Regent Morton in the late 16th century; the Scottish National War Memorial was formed after World War I. The castle also houses the crown jewels (Honours) of Scotland, the history of which is described in a new exhibition. Also see the famous 15th-century gun, Mons Meg. Attractive restaurant with spectacular views over the city. **In the centre of Edinburgh. ℡0131 225 9846.** 123 B5

Edzell Castle and Garden
Angus • Very beautiful complex with a late-medieval tower house incorporated into a 16th-century courtyard mansion. The carved decoration of the garden walls is unique in Britain. **At Edzell, 6m N of Brechin. ℡01356 648631.** 143 C5

Elgin Cathedral
Moray • The superb ruin of what many think was Scotland's most beautiful cathedral. Much of the work is in a rich late 13th century style, much modified after the burning of the church by the Wolf of Badenoch in 1390. The octagonal chapter house is the finest in Scotland. **In Elgin. ℡01343 547171.** 159 C6

Fort George
Highland • A vast site and one of the most outstanding artillery fortifications in Europe. It was planned in 1747 as a base for George II's army, and was completed in 1769. Since then it has served as a barracks. There are reconstructions of barrack rooms in different periods and a display of muskets and pikes.
11m NE of Inverness, by the village of Ardersier. ℡01667 460232 157 D8

Glenluce Abbey
Dumfries and Galloway • Cistercian abbey founded in 1192. The remains include a handsome early 16th-century chapter house. **2m N of Glenluce village. ℡01581 300541.** 105 D5

Hermitage Castle
Scottish Borders • A vast and eerie ruin in a lonely situation, of the 14th and 15th centuries. Mary Queen of Scots made her famous ride there to meet the Earl of Bothwell.
In Liddesdale, 5.5m NE of Newcastleton, off the B6399. ℡013873 76222. 115 E7

Huntingtower Castle
Perth and Kinross • Two fine and complete towers, of the 15th and 16th centuries, now linked by a 17th-century range. There are fine painted ceilings.
2m W of Perth. ℡01738 627231. 134 B2

Huntly Castle
Aberdeenshire • A magnificent ruin consisting mainly of a palace block erected in the 16th and 17th centuries by the Gordon family.
In Huntly. ℡01466 793191. 160 D2

Inchcolm Abbey
Fife • The best-preserved group of monastic buildings in Scotland, founded in about 1123, and including a 13th-century octagonal chapter house. **On an island on the Firth of Forth, opposite Aberdour. Ferries from South Queensferry and North Queensferry. ℡01383 823332.** 134 F3

Inchmahome Priory
Stirling • A beautifully situated Augustinian monastery founded in 1238, with much of the original 13th-century building surviving.
On an island in the Lake of Menteith, approached by boat from Port of Menteith. ℡01877 385294. 132 D4

Iona Abbey and Nunnery
Argyll and Bute • One of Scotland's most historic and sacred sites, Iona Abbey was founded by St Columba and his Irish followers in AD 563. A celebrated focus for Christian pilgrimage, Iona retains its spiritual atmosphere and remains an enduring symbol of worship. **On the Island of Iona, public ferry from Fionnphort, Mull. ℡01681 700512** 136 F3

Jarlshof Prehistoric and Norse Settlement
Shetland • An very important site with a complex of ancient settlements within three acres. The oldest is a Bronze Age village of oval stone huts. There is an Iron Age broch and an entire Viking settlement. The visitor centre has new displays on Iron Age life and a history of the site. **At Sumburgh Head, about 22m S of Lerwick. ℡01950 460112.** 175 M5

Jedburgh Abbey and Visitor Centre
Scottish Borders • One of the abbeys founded by David I and the Bishop of Glasgow in about 1138 for Augustinian canons. The church is mostly in Romanesque and early Gothic styles and is remarkably complete.
In Jedburgh. ℡01835 863925. 116 B2

Kildrummy Castle
Aberdeenshire • Though ruined, the best example in Scotland of a 13th-century castle, with a curtain wall, four round towers, hall and chapel. The seat of the Earls of Mar, it was dismantled after the 1715 Jacobite Rising.
10m W of Alford. ℡01975 571331. 150 C3

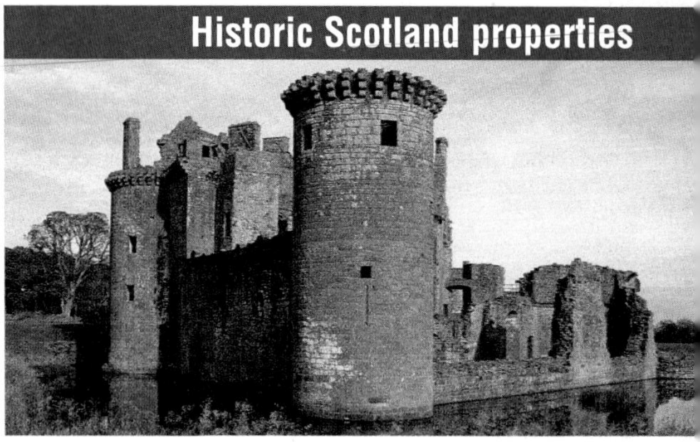

▲**Caerlaverock Castle** Historic Scotland

Kinnaird Head Lighthouse
Aberdeenshire • Built in 1787 within a 16th-century tower house, Kinnaird Head was the first lighthouse built by the Northern Lighthouse Company. **On a promontory in Fraserburgh. ℡01346 511022.** 161 B7

Linlithgow Palace
West Lothian • Magnificent ruin of a great royal palace, set in its own park. All the Stewart kings lived here, and work commissioned by James I, III, IV, V and VI can be seen. The great hall and the chapel are particularly fine. **In Linlithgow. ℡01506 842896.** 122 B3

Loch Leven Castle
Fife • Late 14th-century tower on one side of an irregular courtyard. Mary Queen of Scots was imprisoned here in 1567 and escaped in 1568. **On an island in Loch Leven, accessible by boat from Kinross. ℡07778 040483.** 134 D3

MacLellan's Castle
Dumfries and Galloway • A castellated town house built by the then provost of Kirkcudbright from 1577, with particularly good architectural details. **In the centre of Kirkcudbright. ℡01557 331856.** 106 D3

Maes Howe Chambered Cairn
Orkney • The finest megalithic tomb in the British Isles, with a large mound covering a stone-built passage and a large burial chamber with cells in the walls. Of Neolithic date, broken into during Viking times, with Viking runes carved on the walls. **About 9m W of Kirkwall. ℡01856 761606.** 176 E2

Meigle Sculptured Stone Museum
Perth and Kinross • A magnificent collection of 25 sculptured monuments of the Celtic Christian period, one of the finest collections of Dark Age sculpture in Western Europe.
In Meigle. ℡01828 640612. 142 E2

Melrose Abbey
Scottish Borders • Probably the most famous ruin in Scotland, founded around 1136 as a Cistercian abbey by David I, and repeatedly wrecked in the Wars of Independence. The surviving remains of the church are 15th century and of an elegance unique in Scotland. The Commendator's house contains displays relating to the abbey's history and to the Roman fort at Newstead.
In Melrose. ℡01896 822562. 123 F8

New Abbey Corn Mill
Dumfries and Galloway • A carefully renovated water-powered oatmeal mill, in working order, and demonstrated regularly to visitors in the summer.
In New Abbey village. ℡01387 850260. 107 C6

Newark Castle
Inverclyde • The oldest part of the castle is a tower built soon after 1478, with a detached gatehouse. The main part was added in 1597-9 by Patrick Maxwell.
In Port Glasgow. ℡01475 741858. 120 B3

Rothesay Castle
Argyll and Bute • A remarkable 13th-century, circular castle of enclosure. A favourite residence of the Stewart kings. **In Rothesay, Isle of Bute. ℡01700 502691.** 129 D5

St Andrews Castle and Visitor Centre
Fife • Ruins of the castle of the Archbishops of St Andrews, dating in part from the 13th century. Features include a 'bottle dungeon', and mine and counter-mine tunnelled during the siege that followed the murder of Cardinal Beaton in 1546. Visitor Centre with shop and major exhibition depicting the history of the castle and cathedral.
In St Andrews. ℡01334 477196. 135 C7

St Andrews Cathedral
Fife • Remains of the largest cathedral in Scotland, and of the priory's domestic ranges. The precinct walls are particularly well-preserved. **In St Andrews. ℡01334 472563.** 135 C7

Seton Collegiate Church
East Lothian • The chancel and apse of this lovely building date from the 15th century, and the transepts and steeple were built by the widow of Lord Seton, who was killed at Flodden in 1513. **1m SE of Cockenzie off Edinburgh – North Berwick Road. ℡01875 813334.** 123 B7

Skara Brae Prehistoric Village
Orkney • The best-preserved group of Stone Age houses in Western Europe. The houses contain hearths, stone furniture and drains, and give a remarkable picture of life in Neolithic times. **19m NW of Kirkwall. ℡01856 841815.** 176 E1

Smailholm Tower
Scottish Borders • A simple rectangular tower in a good state of preservation. It houses costume figures and tapestries relating to Sir Walter Scott's 'Minstrelsy of the Scottish Borders'. **Near Smailholm village, 6m NW of Kelso. ℡01573 460365.** 124 F2

Spynie Palace
Moray • Residence of the Bishops of Moray from the 14th century to 1686. The site is dominated by the massive tower built by Bishop David Stewart (1461-77). **2m N of Elgin, off the A941. ℡01343 546358.** 159 C6

Stirling Castle
Stirling • The grandest of all Scottish castles. The Great Hall and the Gatehouse of James IV, the marvellous Palace of James V, the Chapel Royal remodelled by James VI, and the artillery fortifications of the 16th and 18th centuries, are all of outstanding interest. Medieval kitchens and introductory display now open.
In Stirling. ℡01786 450000. 133 E6

Sweetheart Abbey
Dumfries and Galloway • Splendid ruin of a late 13th- and early 14th-century Cistercian abbey founded by Dervorgilla, Lady of Galloway. **In New Abbey village, 7m S of Dumfries. ℡01387 850397.** 107 C6

Tantallon Castle
East Lothian • Remarkable fortification with earthwork defences, and a massive 14th-century curtain wall with towers. Interpretative displays include replica guns. **3m E of North Berwick. ℡01620 892727.** 135 F7

Threave Castle
Dumfries and Galloway • Massive tower built in the late 14th century. Round its base is an artillery fortification built before 1455, when the castle was besieged by James II. It is on an island, approached by boat, followed by a long walk. **3m W of Castle Douglas. ℡07711 223101.** 106 C4

Tolquhon Castle
Aberdeenshire • Built for the Forbes family, Tolquhon has an early 15th-century tower. It is noted for its highly ornamented gatehouse.
15m from Aberdeen off the Pitmedden – Tarves Road. ℡01651 851286. 151 B7

Urquhart Castle
Highland • Standing above Loch Ness, this was one of the largest castles in Scotland, having fallen into decay after 1689. Most of the existing buildings date from after the 16th century. **On Loch Ness, near Drumnadrochit. ℡01456 450551.** 147 B8

Whithorn Priory and Museum
Dumfries and Galloway • Site of the first Christian church in Scotland, founded as 'Candida Casa' by St Ninian in the early 5th century. The priory was built over the church for remonstratensian canons in the 12th century and became the cathedral church of Galloway. In the museum is a fine collection of early Christian stones.
In Whithorn. ℡01988 500508. 105 E8

Historic Royal Palaces

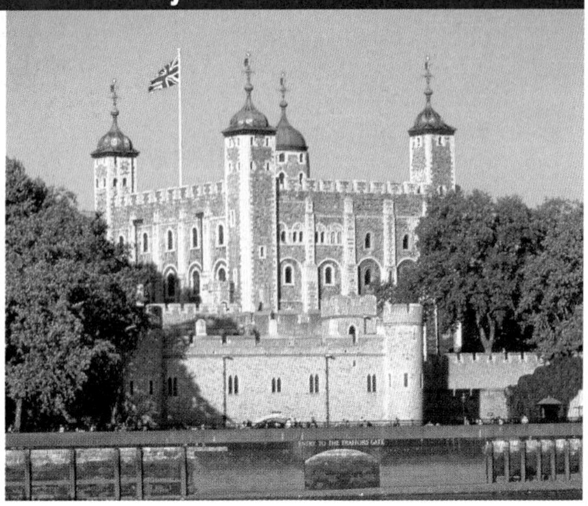

▲The Tower of London ©HRP 2004

The Banqueting House

The Banqueting House was built between 1619 and 1622 during the reign of James I. Designed by Inigo Jones, it is the only surviving building of the vast Whitehall Palace, destroyed by fire nearly 300 years ago. The palace has seen many significant royal events including the only execution of a British monarch – Charles I in 1649. The Banqueting House is a welcome retreat away from the bustle of the city, and a hidden treasure for anyone interested in art and architecture. Its Rubens ceiling paintings are stunning examples of the larger works of the Flemish master and its classical Palladian style sets the fashion for much of London's later architecture.

☎0870 751 5178

How to get there

⊖ Westminster (District, Circle and Jubilee lines), Embankment (Bakerloo, Northern, District and Circle Lines)

🚌 3, 11, 24, 53, 88, 112

⇄ Charing Cross

Hampton Court Palace

With its 500 years of royal history, Hampton Court Palace has something to offer everyone. Set in sixty acres of world-famous gardens, the Palace is a living tapestry of history from Henry VIII to George II. From the elegance of the recently restored 18th-Century Privy Garden to the domestic reality of the Tudor Kitchens, visitors are taken back through the centuries to experience the palace as it was when royalty was in residence. Costumed guides and audio tours provide inside information on life in the royal households, and free family trails encourage a closer look at the palace, with the chance of a prize at the end. In the summer months horse-drawn carriages offer a sedate trip around the stunning gardens. **☎020 8781 9500**

How to get there

🚗 The palace is on the A308 close to the A3, M3 and several exits of the M25

🚌 111, 216, 411, 416, 451, 461, 513, 726, 267 (Sundays) Green Line coach 415 and 718

⇄ Hampton Court station, 32 minutes from Waterloo via Clapham Junction

⊖ Wimbledon (District Line) for connecting train from Waterloo to Hampton Court, or Richmond (District Line) then R68 bus

⛴ River launch From Westminster, Richmond or Kingston upon Thames

Helpful hints

Wear comfortable shoes as the cobbles can be very hard on the feet. Drop in to the information centre when you arrive; staff there will help you to plan your visit. During the summer, gardeners, housekeepers, flower arrangers and the vine keeper all regularly give informal presentations of their work.

Timing your visit

Recommended visit time 4 hours	
Henry VIII's State Apartments	30 mins
Tudor Kitchens	40 mins
The King's Apartments	45 mins
The Queen's State Apartments	30 mins
The Georgian Rooms	30 mins
The Wolsey Rooms and Renaissance Picture Gallery	30 mins
The Palace Gardens	45 mins
The Maze	it depends...

HM Tower of London

A palace and fortress for over 900 years, the Tower's bloody legends and its renown worldwide as the repository of the Crown Jewels make it a 'must see' site on the visitor map. Once inside, free Yeoman Warder tours leave from the front entrance every half an hour, and there are costumed guides giving special presentations in the Medieval Palace. The original Tower of London, the White Tower, has recently been refurbished and is home to the Royal Armouries collection including Henry VIII's armour. New events and exhibitions take place throughout the year and for families, family trails take children on a special path through the Tower with a prize for all those who complete it. **☎0870 751 5177**

How to get there

⊖ Tower Hill station (District and Circle Lines)

🚌 15, 25, 42, 78, 100

⇄ Fenchurch Street station, London Bridge station Docklands Light Railway (DLR): Tower Gateway station

Timing your visit

Recommended visit time	3 hours
A Yeoman Warder tour 1 hour	
The Crown Jewels	35 mins
Crowns and Diamonds	20 mins
The Medieval Palace	25 mins
The Bloody Tower	10 mins
The Beauchamp Tower	20 mins
The White Tower and Royal Armouries	30 mins

Kensington Palace State Apartments

Situated in the peaceful surroundings of Kensington Gardens, Kensington Palace was the residence of William III and Mary II, and later the childhood home of Queen Victoria. The magnificent State Apartments include William Kent's elaborate trompe l'oeil ceilings and the Cupola Room where Queen Victoria was baptised. There is a stunning presentation of Royal Court and Ceremonial Dress dating from the 18th century, which allows visitors to participate in the excitement of dressing for court – from invitation to presentation, and also a dazzling selection of dresses owned and worn by HM Queen Elizabeth II. Multi-language sound guides are available.

☎020 7937 9561

How to get there

⊖ Queensway (Central Line), Notting Hill Gate (District, Circle and Central Lines), High Street Kensington (District and Circle Lines), Gloucester Road (District, Circle and Piccadilly Lines)

🚌 9, 12, 33, 49, 52, 52a, 88, C1

Kew Palace and Queen Charlotte's Cottage

Kew Palace, originally built in 1631, was the favourite residence of King George III and Queen Charlotte and is the country's smallest royal palace. Kew Palace is presently closed to the public. Queen Charlotte's Cottage was enjoyed by George III and his queen as a picnic place. Its pretty interiors are decorated with paintings, probably done by George's daughter Princess Elizabeth. Queen Charlotte's cottage is open on weekends only from May to September. Entry is free with usual admission to the Royal Botanical Gardens.

How to get there

⊖ Kew Gardens (District Line)

⇄ Kew Bridge station 25mins from Waterloo via Clapham Junction

The Royal Horticultural Society

Step into a world of inspirational gardens with the RHS

The RHS is the UK's leading gardening charity, dedicated to advancing horticulture and promoting good gardening. Membership is at the heart of the RHS, since without member support we would be unable to fulfill many of our charitable aims. These include providing expert advice and information, training the next generation of gardeners, helping school children learn about plants, and conducting research into plant pests and environmental issues affecting gardeners.

Join today and enjoy the privileges of RHS membership...

Free entry with a guest to RHS gardens Wisley in Surrey, Rosemoor in Devon, Hyde Hall in Essex and Harlow Carr in North Yorkshire

Free Access to partner gardens. There are over 100 inspirational gardens to visit throughout their opening season or at selected periods.

RHS flower shows. Privileged entry and reduced rate tickets for RHS shows; Chelsea, Hampton Court Palace, Tatton Park, plus free entry to London and Wisley Flower Shows.

Free monthly magazine. Receive monthly the RHS members' magazine for free (RRP £3.95). Full of practical advice, ideas and inspiration.

FREE advice. Invaluable support and answers to your gardening questions all year round.

FREE seeds. You can apply for seeds harvested from RHS gardens. (There is a small postage and packaging charge).

Flower shows. Reduced admission to BB Gardeners' World Live and the Malvern Spring and Autumn Garden and Country Shows.

RHS Plant Selector. Privileged information on over 4,500 plants at www.rhs.org.uk

Special events. Reduced price tickets to hundreds of lectures, tours workshops and events around the UK.

Support the RHS and secure a healthy future for gardening.

How to join the RHS

To join the RHS and enjoy all of the benefits of membership please call 0845 130 4646 and quote 1557. Lines open from 9am to 5pm, Monday to Friday or visit our website at **www.rhs.org.uk**

Hyde Hall

Rettendon, Chelmsford, Essex

☎ (01245) 400256

Hyde Hall is set on a hilltop amongst rolling hills of arable crops. This 28-acre garden combines environmental and sustainable practices with the high standards of horticulture for which the RHS gardens are renowned. Highlights include the widely acclaimed Dry Garden; the inspirational colour-themed Herbaceous Border, demonstrating the art of ornamental horticulture; the commemorative Queen Mother'≥ Garden and the model Garden for Wildlife. Hyde Hall'≥ long association with roses is very much in evidence, with the many varieties thriving in the heavy Essex clay soil and high light levels. A comprehensive range of courses, demonstrations and walks are held throughout the year. Contact the garden direct to receive a copy of the Events Programme.

Opening hours

Open all year, except Christmas Day, from 10am. Closes at 6pm Apr to Sept and 5pm or dusk Oct to Mar.

Directions

Seven miles southeast of Chelmsford and signposted from the A130.

Rosemoor

Great Torrington, North Devon

☎ (01805) 624067

Rosemoor is a garden acclaimed by gardeners throughout the world. You do not have to be a keen gardener to appreciate the beauty and diversity of Rosemoor. Whatever the season, the garden is a unique and enchanting place that people return to time and again for ideas, inspiration or simply to enjoy a marvellous day out. The Spiral, Square and Foliage andamp; Plantsman'≥ Gardens demonstrate the many contrasting forms, textures and colours that can be found in garden plants, providing plenty of ideas and inspiration to take away with you.

Opening hours

Open all year, except Christmas Day, from 10am. Closes at 6pm Apr to Sept and 5pm Oct to Mar.

Directions

One mile south of Great Torrington on the A3124.

Harlow Carr

Harlow Carr, Crag Lane, Harrogate

☎ (01423) 565418

For over 50 years Harlow Carr has provided a garden setting to assess the suitability of plants for growing in the north. Now, as the first northern RHS garden, and with exciting future developments planned, the garden is "Growing to inspire"Æ The woodland and arboretum are havens for wildlife, whilst the spectacular summer swathe of candelabra primulas along the famous streamside will delight adults and children alike. With scented, herb and foliage themed gardens, extensive vegetable and flower trials, contemporary grasses border and much more, both the keen gardener, and those just wanting a relaxing day out, will find Harlow Carr a place of magic and beauty.

Opening hours

Open all year from 9.30am to 6pm (or dusk if sooner).

Directions

Just off the B6162 (Otley Road) 1.5 miles from the centre of Harrogate.

Wisley

Wisley, Woking, Surrey

☎ (01483) 224234

Whatever the season, Wisley demostrates British gardening at its best with 240 acres of glorious garden. For 100 years the garden has been a centre of gardening excellence with visitors benefiting from the knowledge and experience of experts. Highlights of the garden include the Mixed Borders, the Country Garden, the magnificent Rock Garden, and the Alpine Houses. In addition you can visit the spectacular Piet Oudolf borders, with their modern approach to perennial planting, or Battleston Hill, alight with colour in spring, which leads on to the Trials Field with more than 50 trials each year. Everyone has their favourite area of Wisley, and the whole garden is a living encyclopaedia for all gardeners, however experienced they are.

Opening hours

Open all year, except for Christmas Day, from 10am to 6pm (opens 9am weekends, closes 4.30pm in winter).

Directions

20 miles southwest of London on the A3, junction 10 off the M25.

Gardens free to RHS Members

Please note, free access to RHS members may be limited to specific months. Please telephone to check opening times before visiting

Abbotsbury Sub-Tropical Gardens

Abbotsbury, Weymouth, DT3 4LA

☎ (01305) 871387

RHS Members: free Oct-Feb. Open: all year, daily, 10am-6pm (dusk in winter). Closed over Christmas and New Year.

Abriachan Gardens

Loch Ness Side, by Inverness, IV3 8LA

☎ (01463) 861 232

RHS Members: free throughout open period Open: Feb-Nov, daily, 9am-5pm.

Arley Hall and Gardens

Arley, Northwich, Cheshire CW9 6NA

☎ (01565) 777353

RHS Members: free throughout open period, excluding special event days. Open: 9th Apr-28th Sept, Tue-Sun and Bank Holidays, 11am-5pm, Oct – weekends only.

Barnsdale Gardens

The Avenue, Exton, Oakham, Rutland LE15 8AH ☎ (01572) 813200

RHS Members: free throughout open period Open: Mar-May and Sept-Oct, daily, 9am-5pm; Jun-Aug, daily, 9am-7pm; Nov-Feb, daily, 10am-4pm.

Batsford Arboretum

Batsford Park, Moreton-in-Marsh, Gloucestershire GL56 9QB ☎ (01386) 701441

RHS Members: free Jan-Sept and Nov-Dec. Open: 1st Feb-mid Nov, 10am-5pm. Mid Nov-1st Feb, 10am-4pm. Closed Christmas Day.

Bedgebury

The National Pinetum, Goudhurst, Cranbrook, Kent TN17 2SL

☎ (01580) 211781

RHS Members: free throughout open period. Open: all year, daily, 10am-5pm

Bide-a-Wee Cottage Gardens

Stanton, Netherwitton, Morpeth, Northumberland NE65 8PR

☎ (01670) 772262

RHS Members: free throughout open period (excluding group visits outside normal opening hours). Open: 24th Apr-28th Aug, Wed and Sat only, 1.30pm-5pm

Bluebell Arboretum and Nursery
Annwell Lane, Smisby, Ashby-de-la Zouch, Leicestershire LE65 2TA ☎ (01530) 413700
RHS Members: free throughout open period. Open: Mar-Oct, Mon-Sat, 9am-5pm, Sun, 10.30am-4.30pm, Nov-Feb, Mon-Sat, 9am-4pm (closed 24th Dec-4th Jan and Easter Sunday).

Bluebell Cottage Gardens and Lodge Lane Nursery
Bluebell Cottage, Lodge Lane, Dutton, nr Warrington, Cheshire WA4 4HP ☎ (01928) 713718
RHS Members: free throughout open period. Open: May-Aug, Sat-Sun and Bank Holidays, 12-5pm

Bodnant Garden
Tal-y-Cafn, nr Colwyn Bay, Conwy LL28 5RE ☎ (01492) 650460
RHS Members: free throughout open period. Open: 13th Mar-31st Oct, 10am-5pm, last admission 4.30pm.

Borde Hill Garden
Balcombe Road, Haywards Heath, West Sussex RH16 1XP ☎ (01444) 450326
RHS Members: free Jan, Feb, Nov, Dec. Open: all year, daily, 10am-6pm (or dusk if earlier).

Broadview Gardens
Hadlow, Tonbridge Kent, TN11 OAL ☎ (01732) 853211
RHS Members: free Sept, Oct. Open Apr-Oct, daily, 10am-5pm (4pm Sun).

Brogdale Horticultural Trust
Brogdale Road, Faversham, Kent ME13 8XZ ☎ (01795) 535286/535462
RHS Members: free Easter-Nov except festivals. Open: Mar-Nov, daily, 10am-5pm, Nov-Mar, daily, 10am-4pm.

Burnby Hall Museum and Gardens
The Balk, Pocklington, York YO42 2QE ☎ (01759) 302068
RHS Members: free Apr-Sept. Open: 29th Mar-28th Sept, daily, 10am-6pm.

Burton Agnes Gardens
Burton Agnes Hall, Burton Agnes, Driffield, East Yorkshire YO25 4NB ☎ (01262) 490324
RHS Members: free throughout open period. Open: Apr-Oct, daily, 11am-5pm.

Cawdor Castle Gardens
Cawdor Castle, Nairn, Highland, IV12 5RD ☎ (01667) 404401
RHS Members: free May, Jun, Sept, Oct. Open: 1st May-10th Oct, daily, 10am-5.30pm.

Chiffchaffs
Chaffeymoor, Bourton, Gillingham, Dorset, SP3 5BY ☎ (01747) 840841
RHS Members: free throughout open period. Open: Mar-Oct, Wed and Thur, 2-5pm. Also open some Sundays. Please call the garden for further details.

Cholmondeley Castle
Malpas, Cheshire SY14 8AH ☎ (01829) 720383
RHS Members: free Jun. Open: Apr-Sept, Wed, Thur, Sun and Bank Holidays, 11.30am-5pm.

Clovelly Court
Clovelly, nr Bideford, Devon EX39 5SZ ☎ (01237) 431200
RHS Members: free Mar and Oct. Open: Mar-Oct, daily, 10am-4pm

Cottesbrooke Hall Gardens
Cottesbrooke Hall, Cottesbrooke, Northamptonshire NN6 8PF ☎ (01604) 505808
RHS Members: free throughout open period. Open: 5th May-end Jun, Wed, Thur and Bank Holiday Mon, 2-5pm. Jul-Sept, Thur and Bank Holiday Mon, 2-5pm. For details of opening times of house, please contact Cottesbrooke Hall.

Corsham Court Gardens
Corsham Court, Corsham, Wiltshire SN13 0BZ ☎ (01249) 701610
RHS Members: free throughout open period. Open: 20th Mar-30th Sept, Tues-Thur and weekends, 2-5pm, 1st Oct-19th Mar, weekends only, 2-4pm. Closed Dec.

Cranborne Manor Garden
Cranborne, Wimborne, Dorset, BH21 5PP ☎ (01725) 517248
RHS Members: free throughout open period. Open: Mar-Sept, Wed only, 9am-5pm.

Dalemain Historic House and Gardens
Dalemain, Penrith, Cumbria CA11 0BH ☎ (01768) 486450
RHS Members: free 20th Apr-16th May. Open: 28th Mar-21st Oct, Sun-Thur, 10.30am-5pm (4pm Sept and Oct). House open 11am-4pm (3pm Sept and Oct).

Docton Mill and Gardens
Lymebridge, Hartland, Devon, EX29 6EA ☎ (01237) 441369
RHS Members: free Mar, Apr, Sept, Oct, and any Sat May-Aug. Open: Mar-Oct, daily, 10am-6pm

Duncombe Park
Helmsley, York, North Yorkshire, YO62 5EB ☎ (01439) 770213
RHS Members: free throughout open period (house and garden). Open: 13th Apr-24th Oct, Sun-Thur, please telephone for times.

Dundee University Botanic Garden
University of Dundee, Riverside Drive, Dundee DD2 1QH ☎ (01382) 647190
RHS Members: free throughout open period. Open: Mar-Oct, daily, 10am-4.30pm, Nov-Feb, daily, 10am-3.30pm

Dunrobin Castle Gardens
Golspie, Sutherland KW10 6SF ☎ (01408) 633177
RHS Members: free throughout open period. Open: Apr, May and 1st-15th Oct, daily, 10.30am-4.30pm, Jun-Sept, daily, 10.30am-5.30pm

East Ruston Old Vicarage
East Ruston, Norwich, NR12 9HN ☎ (01692) 650432
RHS Members: free Sept, Oct. Open: 28 Mar-30 Oct, Wed, Fri, Sat, Sun and Bank Holidays, 2-5.30pm.

Fairhaven Woodland and Water Garden
School Road, South Walsham, nr Norwich NR13 6DZ ☎ (01603) 270449
RHS Members: free Feb-Apr and Oct. Open: all year, daily, 10am-5pm (9pm, Wed and Thur, May-Aug). Closed Christmas Day

Felley Priory
Underwood, Nottinghamshire NG16 5FL ☎ (01773) 810230
RHS Members: free throughout open period. Open: all year, Tue, Wed and Fri, 9am-12.30pm. Mar-Oct, every 2nd and 4th Wed, 9am-4pm, every 3rd Sun 11am-4pm.

Forde Abbey Gardens
Chard, Somerset, TA20 4LU ☎ (01460) 221290
RHS Members: free Oct-Feb. Open: all year, daily, 10am-4.30pm.

Furzey Gardens
School Lane, Minstead, nr Lyndhurst, Hampshire SO43 7GL ☎ (023) 8081 2464
RHS Members: free Mar-Oct. Open: all year, daily (except Christmsa and Boxing Day), 10am-5pm (dusk in winter).

Geilston Gardens
(National Trust for Scotland) Cardross, Dumbarton G82 5EZ ☎ (01389) 849187
RHS Members: free throughout open period. Open: Apr-Oct, daily, 9.30am-5pm.

Glen Chantry
Ishams Chase, Wickham Bishops, nr Witham CM8 3LG ☎ (01621) 891342
RHS Members: free throughout open period. Open: 2 Apr-25 Sept, Fri and Sat, 10am-4pm.

Glenwhan Garden
Dunragit, by Stranraer, Wigtownshire DG9 8PH ☎ (01581) 400222
RHS Members: free 1 Aug-30 Oct. Open: all year, daily, 10am-5pm.

Goodnestone Park Gardens
Goodnestone Park, nr Wingham, Canterbury, Kent CT3 1PL ☎ (01304) 840107
RHS Members: free Apr, May, Sept, excluding special events. Open: 31 Mar-22 Sept, Mon, Wed, Thur, Fri, 11am-5pm. Sun 12-6pm.

Harmony Garden
(National Trust for Scotland) St Mary's Road, Melrose, Borders TD6 9LJ ☎ (01721) 722502
RHS Members: free throughout open period. Open: Easter, Jun-Sept, Mon-Sat, 10am-5pm, Sun 1-5pm.

Harewood House
Harewood, Leeds, West Yorkshire, LS17 9LQ ☎ (0113) 218 1010
RHS Members: free Mar-Jun, excluding weekends, Bank Holidays and special event days. Open: Feb-Oct, daily, 10am-6pm.

Hill of Tarvit Mansionhouse and Garden
(National Trust for Scotland) Cupar, Fife KY15 5PB ☎ (01334) 653127
RHS Members: free (garden) throughout open period. Open: all year, daily, 9.30am-sunset.

Holker Hall Garden
Cark-in-Cartmel, nr Grange-over-Sands, Cumbria LA11 7PL ☎ (01539) 558328
RHS Members: free Apr-Oct (excluding special event days). Open: 28 Mar-31 Oct, Sun-Fri, 10am-6pm (last entry 4.30pm), closed Sat.

Kellie Castle and Garden
(National Trust for Scotland) Pittenweem, Fife KT10 2RF ☎ (01333) 720271
RHS Members: free throughout open period. Open: all year, daily, 9.30am-sunset. Castle open Easter weekend and Jun-Sept, daily 1pm-5pm.

Kingston Maurward Gardens
Kingston Maurward, Dorchester, Dorset DT2 8PY ☎ (01305) 215003
RHS Members: free throughout open period. Open: 5 Jan-19 Dec, daily, 10am-5.30pm.

Knoll Gardens
Hampreston, nr Wimborne, Dorset BH21 7ND ☎ (01202) 873931
RHS Members: free Apr-Oct. Open: all year (except over Christmas and New Year), daily, 10am-5pm (or dusk if earlier).

Leith Hall and Garden
(National Trust for Scotland) Huntly, Aberdeenshire AB54 4NQ ☎ (01464) 831216
RHS Members: free throughout open period. Open: all year, daily, 9.30am-sunset. House open Easter weekend, May-Sept, Fri-Tue, 12pm-5pm.

Losely Park
Guildford, Surrey GU23 1HS ☎ (01483) 304440
RHS Members: free May and Sept (excluding special event days). Open: May-Sept, Wed-Sun, 11am-5pm. House open Jun-Aug.

Mapperton Gardens
Nr Beaminster, Dorset DT8 3NR ☎ (01308) 862645
RHS Members: free throughout open period. Open: Mar-Oct, daily, 2-6pm.

Mill Dene Garden
Blockley, Moreton-in-Marsh, Gloucestershire GL56 9HU ☎ (01386) 700457
RHS Members: free Apr and Oct. Open: Apr-Oct, Tue-Fri and Bank Holidays, 10am-5.30pm, Sundays 2pm-5.30pm for June sculpture exhibitions.

Millgate House
Richmond, North Yorkshire DL10 4JN ☎ (01748) 823571
RHS Members: free Apr-Oct. Open: 16 Feb-30 Mar, Sun, 12pm-4pm (weather permitting or by appointment). Apr-Oct, daily, 10am-5.30pm.

Muncaster Castle
Ravenglass, Cumbria CA18 1RQ ☎ (01229) 717614
RHS Members: free 1 Jul-7 Nov. Open: all year, daily, 10.30am-6pm.

Middleton, National Botanic Garden of Wales
Llanarthne, Carmarthenshire SA32 8HG ☎ (01558) 668768
RHS members: free Jan-Mar, Oct-Dec. Open: 25 Oct-31 Mar, daily, 10am-4.30pm, 1 Apr-24 Oct, daily, 10am-6pm. Closed Christmas Day.

Newby Hall and Gardens
Ripon, North Yorkshire HG4 5AE ☎ (0845) 450 4068
RHS Members: free throughout open period (except special event days). Open: 1 Apr-26 Sept, Tue-Sun and Bank Holidays, 11am-5.30pm.

Normanby Hall Victorian Walled Garden
Normanby Hall Country Park, Normanby, Scunthorpe, North Lincolnshire DN15 9HU ☎ (01724) 720588
RHS Members: free throughout open period. Open: all year, daily, 10.30am-5pm (4.30 in winter). Closed Christmas Day, Boxing Day, New Year's Day.

Nymans Garden
Handcross, nr Haywards Heath, West Sussex RH17 6EB ☎ (01444) 400321
RHS Members: free throughout open period. Open: 18 Feb-31 Oct, Wed-Sun and Bank Holidays, 11am-6pm (or dusk). Nov-Feb, Sat and Sun only, 11am-4pm. Closed 1 and 2 Jan 2005.

Parcevall Hall Gardens
Skyreholme, Skipton, North Yorkshire BD23 6DE ☎ (01756) 720311
RHS Members: May-Aug. Open: Apr-Oct: daily, 10am-6pm.

Penshurst Place and Gardens
Penshurst, Nr Tonbridge, Kent, TN11 8DG ☎ (01892) 870307
RHS Members: Apr, Sept, Oct. Open: 6-27 Mar, weekends, 10.30am-6pm, 28 Mar-31 Oct, daily, 10.30am-6pm.

Picton Castle and Woodland Gardens
Haverfordwest, Pembrokeshire SA62 4AS ☎ (01437) 751326
RHS Members: free Apr-Sept (gardens and gallery only, excluding event dys). Open: Apr-Oct, Tue-Sun and Bank Holidays, 10.30am-5pm.

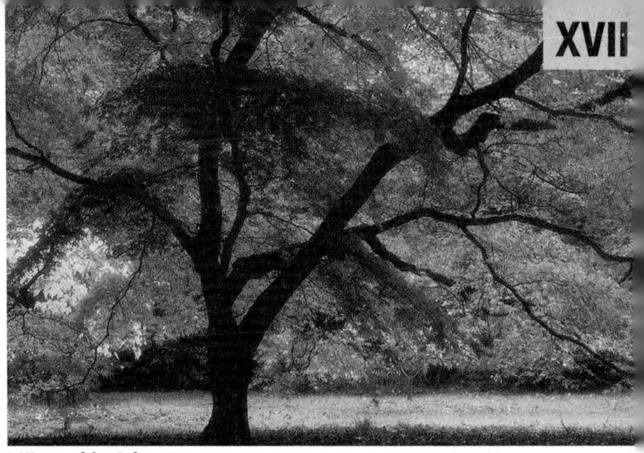
▲ **Westonbirt Arboretum** Robert Harding Picture Library Ltd / Alamy

Pound Hill Garden
Pound Hill, West Kington, nr Chippenham, Wiltshire SN14 7JG ☎ (01249) 783880
Nursery: Feb-Dec, daily, 10am-5pm.

Probus Gardens
Probus, Truro, TR2 4HQ ☎ (01726) 882597
RHS Members: free Aug-Oct. Open:3 Nov-28 Feb, 1-24 Dec, Mon-Fri, 10am-4pm (or dusk if earlier), 3 Mar-31 Oct, daily, 10am-5pm (or dusk if earlier).

Raby Castle Gardens
Staindrop, Darlington, County Durham DL2 3AH ☎ (01833) 660202
RHS Members: free throughout open period (excluding special event days). Open: May and Sept, Wed and Sun, 11am-5.30pm, Jun-Aug, Sun-Fri, 11am-5.30pm and Bank Holidays (Sat to following Wed, 11am-5.30pm).

Ripley Castle Gardens
Ripley, nr Harrogate, North Yorkshire HG3 3AY ☎ (01423) 770152
RHS Members: free throughout open period. Open: all year, daily, 9am-5pm (4.30pm during winter).

Rode Hall Gardens
Church Lane, Scholar Green, Cheshire ST7 3QP ☎ (01270) 882961/873237
RHS Members: free throughout open period. Open: 7-22 Feb, daily, 12pm-4pm. Apr-Sept, Tue-Thu and Bank Holidays, 2-5pm.

Ryton Organic Gardens
Ryton-on-Dunsmore, Coventry CV8 3LG ☎ (024) 7630 3517
RHS Members: free throughout open period. Open: all year (closed Christmas week), 9am-5pm.

St Andrews Botanic Garden
Canongate, St Andrews KY16 8RT ☎ (01334) 477178
RHS Members: free throughout open period. Open: all year, daily, 10am-7pm (Oct-Apr, gardens close at 4pm).

Scone Palace
Perth, Perthshire PY2 6BD ☎ (01738) 552300
RHS Members: free Sept, Oct. Open: Apr-Oct, daily, 9.30am-5.45pm.

Sheffield Park Garden
Sheffield Park, East Sussex TN22 3QX ☎ (01825) 790231
RHS Members: free throughout open period. Open: Jan, Feb, weekends, 10.30am-4pm (or dusk), Mar-Dec, Tue-Sun and Bank Holidays, 10.30am-6pm (4pm or dusk Nov, Dec).

Stillingfleet Lodge Nurseries
Stewart Lane, York, North Yorkshire YO19 6HP ☎ (01904) 728506
RHS Members: free throughout open period. Open: May-Sept, Wed and Fri, 1-4pm.

Tapeley Park
Instow, nr Bideford, Devon EX39 4NT ☎ (01271) 342558
RHS Members: free 8 Jun-8 Jul. Open: 18 Mar-1 Nov, Sun-Fri, 10am-5pm.

Tatton Park Gardens
Tatton Park, Knutsford, Cheshire WA16 6QN ☎ (01625) 534400
RHS Members: free throughout open period (gardens only). Open: 27 Mar-3 Oct, Tue-Sun, 10am-6pm, 4 Oct-25 Mar, Tue-Sun, 11am-4pm.

The Beth Chatto Gardens
Elmstead Market, Colchester, Essex CO7 7DB ☎ (01206) 822007
RHS Members: free Feb-Mar. Open: Mar-Oct, Mon-Sat, 9am-5pm, Nov-Feb, Mon-Fri, 9am-4pm.

The Dorothy Clive Garden
Willoughbridge, Market Drayton, Shropshire TF9 4EU ☎ (01630) 647237
RHS Members: free Jul-Aug. Open: 14 Mar-31 Oct, daily, 10am-5.30pm.

The Quinta Arboretum and Nature Reserve
Swettenham Village, nr Congleton, Cheshire CW12 2LD ☎ (01477) 537698
RHS Members: free throughout open period. Open: all year during daylight hours, except Christmas Day.

Torosay Castle and Gardens
Torosay Castle, Craignure, Isle of Mull PA65 6AY ☎ (01680) 812421
RHS Members: free Apr-Jun and Sept-Oct. Open: all year, daily, 9am-sunset.

Thorp Perrow Arboretum and Woodland Garden
Bedale, North Yorkshire DL8 2PR ☎ (01677) 425323
RHS Members: free Mon-Fri (excluding Bank Holidays and event days) throughout open period. Open: Mar-mid-Nov, daily, dawn-dusk.

Threave Garden and Estate
(National Trust for Scotland), Castle Douglas, Dumfries and Galloway DG7 1RX ☎ (01556) 502575
RHS Members: free Apr, May, Sept, Oct. Open: all year, daily, 9am-sunset. Visitor Centre open Feb, Mar and Nov, Dec, daily 10am-4pm; Apr-Oct, daily, 9.30am-5.30pm.

Trebah Garden
Mawnan Smith, nr Falmouth, Cornwall TR11 5JZ ☎ (01326) 250448
RHS Members: free throughout open period. Open: all year, daily, 10.30am-5pm.

Trevarno Estate Gardens and the National Museum of Gardening
Trevarno Manor, Helston, Cornwall TR13 0RU ☎ (01326) 574274
RHS Members: free 1 Jan-8 Apr, 1 Nov-31 Dec. Open: all year, daily, 10.30am-5pm. Closed Christmas and Boxing Day.

Trewithen Gardens
Grampound Road, Truro, Cornwall TR2 4DD ☎ (01726) 883647
RHS Members: free Jul-Sept. Open: Mar-Sept, daily (Sun only Apr, May), 10am-4.30pm.

Waddesdon Manor
Nr Aylesbury, Buckinghamshire HP18 0JH ☎ (01296) 653226
RHS Members: free Mar, Sept, Oct. Open: 3 Mar-31 Oct, Wed-Sun and Bank Holiday, 10am-5pm. 3 Nov-23 Dec, Wed-Sun 11am-5pm.

Waterperry Gardens
Wheatley, Oxford OX33 1JZ ☎ (01844) 339254 (office), (01844) 339226 (shop)
RHS Members: free Sept. Open: all year, daily, 9am-5pm.

Westonbirt The National Arboretum
Westonbirt, Tetbury, Gloucestershire GL8 8QS ☎ (01666) 880220
RHS Members: throughout open period. Open: all year, daily, 10am-8pm (dusk if earlier).

Wollerton Old Hall Garden
Wollerton, Market Drayton, Shropshire TF9 3NA ☎ (01630) 685760
RHS Members: free Apr, May, Sept. Open: Easter-Aug, Fri, Sun and Bank Holidays, 12-5pm, Sept, Sun only, 12pm-5pm.

Yalding Organic Gardens
Benover Road, Yalding, Maidstone, Kent, ME18 6EX ☎ (01622) 814650
RHS Members: free throughout open period. Open: May-Sept, Wed-Sun, 10am-5pm, Apr and Oct, weekends and Bank Holidays, 10am-5pm.

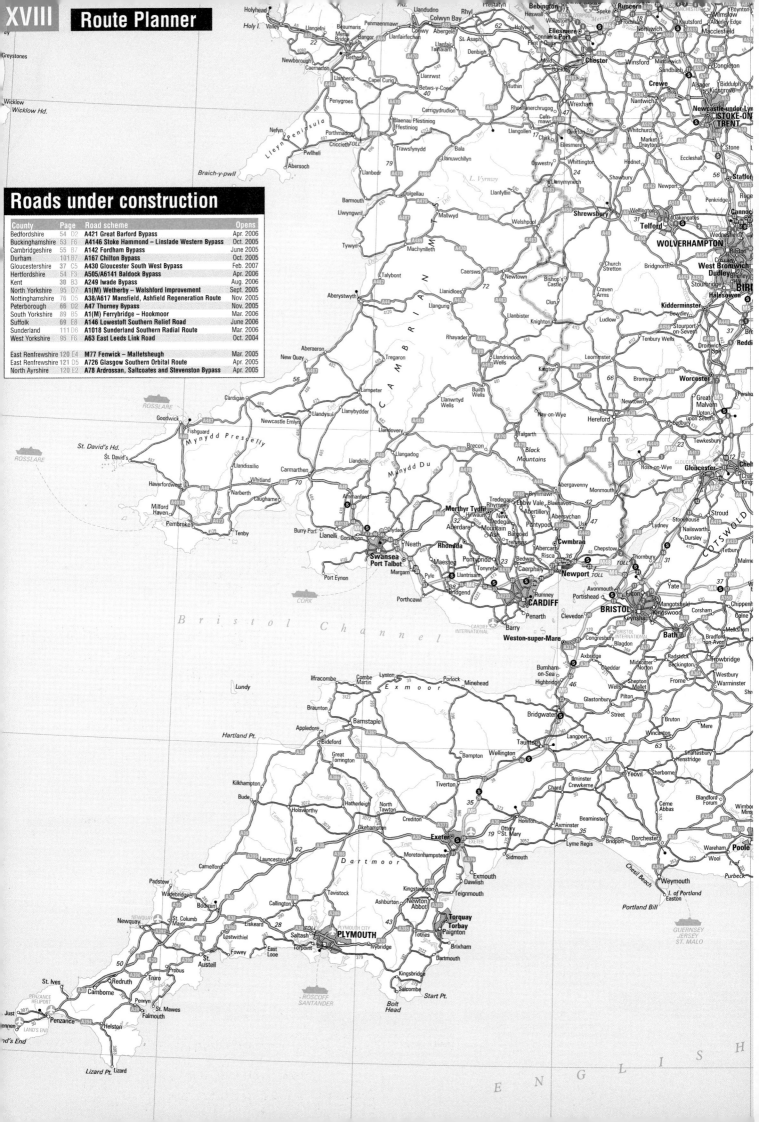

Roads under construction

County	Page	Road scheme	Opens
Bedfordshire	54 D2	A421 Great Barford Bypass	Apr. 2006
Buckinghamshire	53 F6	A4146 Stoke Hammond – Linslade Western Bypass	Oct. 2005
Cambridgeshire	55 B7	A142 Fordham Bypass	June 2005
Durham	101 B7	A167 Chilton Bypass	Oct. 2005
Gloucestershire	37 C5	A430 Gloucester South West Bypass	Feb. 2007
Hertfordshire	54 F3	A505/A6141 Baldock Bypass	Apr. 2006
Kent	30 B3	A249 Iwade Bypass	Aug. 2006
North Yorkshire	95 D7	A1(M) Wetherby – Walshford Improvement	Sept. 2005
Nottinghamshire	76 D5	A38/A617 Mansfield, Ashfield Regeneration Route	Nov. 2005
Peterborough	66 D2	A47 Thorney Bypass	Nov. 2005
South Yorkshire	89 B5	A1(M) Ferrybridge – Hookmoor	Mar. 2006
Suffolk	69 E8	A146 Lowestoft Southern Relief Road	June 2006
Sunderland	111 D6	A1018 Sunderland Southern Radial Route	Mar. 2006
West Yorkshire	95 F6	A63 East Leeds Link Road	Oct. 2004
East Renfrewshire	120 E4	M77 Fenwick – Malletsheugh	Mar. 2005
East Renfrewshire	121 D5	A726 Glasgow Southern Orbital Route	Apr. 2005
North Ayrshire	120 E2	A78 Ardrossan, Saltcoates and Stevenston Bypass	Apr. 2005

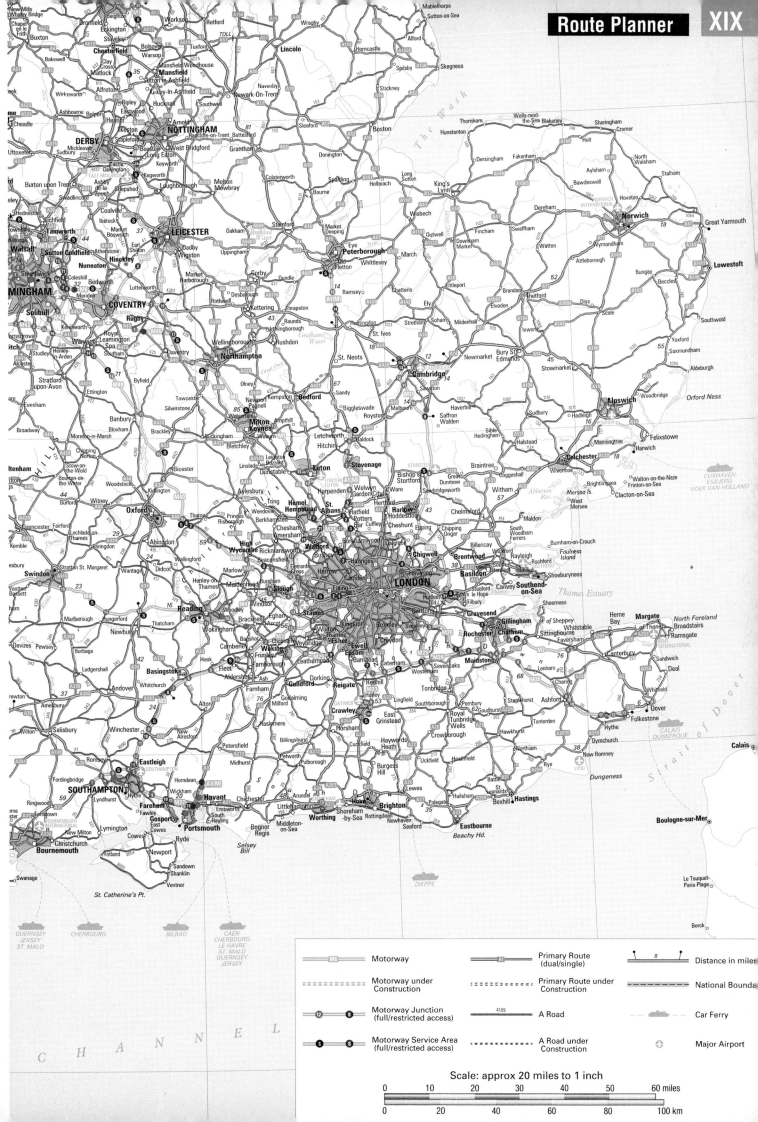

Scale: approx 20 miles to 1 inch

Motorway		Primary Route (dual/single)		Distance in miles
Motorway under Construction		Primary Route under Construction		National Boundary
Motorway Junction (full/restricted access)		A Road		Car Ferry
Motorway Service Area (full/restricted access)		A Road under Construction		Major Airport

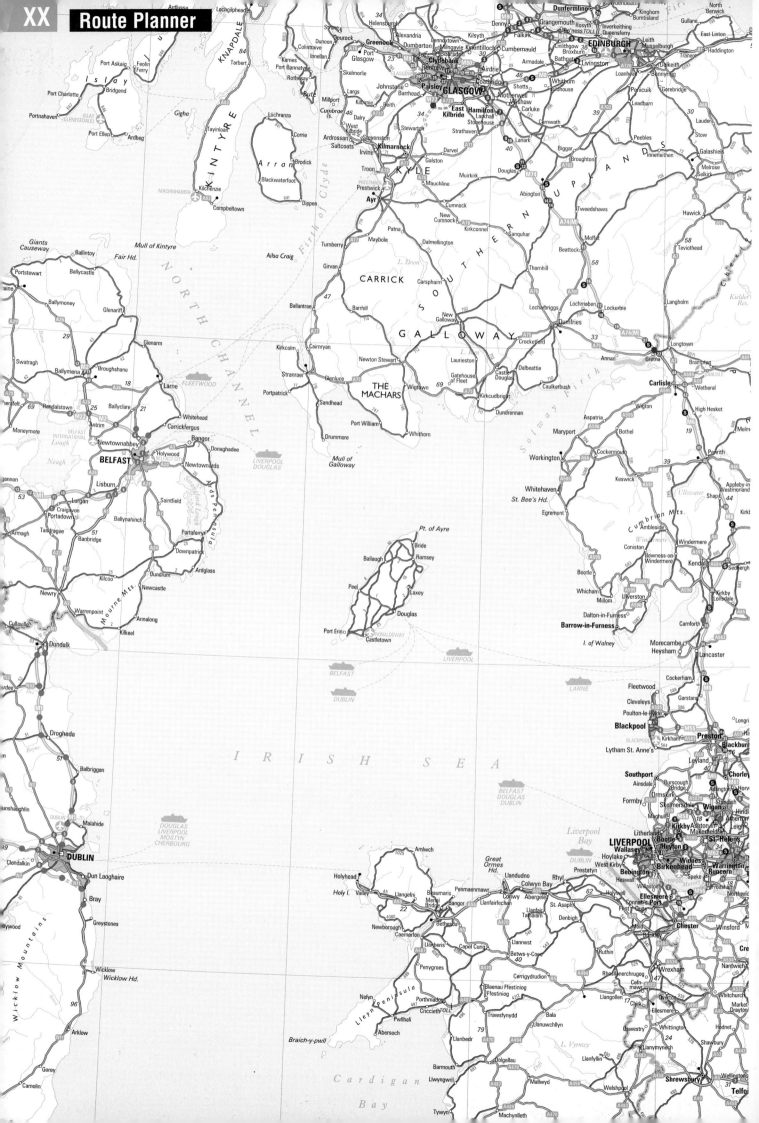

Restricted motorway junctions

M1	Northbound	Southbound
2	No exit	No access
4	No exit	No access
6a	No exit	No access
	Access from M25 only	Exit to M25 only
7	No exit	No access
	Access from M10 only	Exit to M10 only
17	No access	No exit
	Exit to M45 only	Access from M45 only
19	No exit to A14	No access from A14
21a	No access	No exit
23a	Exit to A42 only	
24a	No access	No access
35a	No access	No exit
43	No exit to M621 northbound	
48	No exit to A1 southbound	

M2	Eastbound	Westbound
1	Access from A2 eastbound only	Exit to A2 westbound only

M3	Eastbound	Westbound
8	No exit	No access
10	No access	No exit
13	No access to M27 eastbound	
14	No exit	No access

M4	Eastbound	Westbound
1	Exit to A4 eastbound only	Access from A4 westbound only
2	Access to A4 eastbound only	Access to A4 westbound only
21	No exit	No access
23	No access	No exit
25	No exit	No access
25a	No exit	No access
29	No exit	No access

M4	Eastbound	Westbound
38		No access
39	No exit or access	No exit
41	No access	No exit
41a	No exit	No access
42		Exit to A483 only

M5	Northbound	Southbound
10	No exit	No access
11a	No access from A417 eastbound	No exit to A417 westbound

M6	Northbound	Southbound
4a	No exit	No access
	Access from M42 southbound only	Exit to M42 only
5	No access	No exit
10a	No access	No exit
	Exit to M54 only	Access from M54 only
11a	No exit / access	No access / exit
	No access to M6 Toll	
20	No exit to M56 eastbound	No access from M56 westbound
22	No access	No exit
24	No exit	No access
25	No access	No access
30	No exit	No access
	Access from M61 northbound only	Exit to M61 southbound
31a	No access	No access

M6 Toll	Northbound	Southbound
T1		No exit
T2	No exit / access	No access
T5	No exit	No access
T7	No access	No access
T8	No acess	No access

M8	Eastbound	Westbound
8	No exit to M73 northbound	No access from M73 southbound
9	No access	No exit
13	No exit southbound	No access
14	No access	No exit
16	No exit	No access
17	No exit	No access
18		No exit
19	No exit to A814 eastbound	No access from A814 westbound
20	No exit	No access
21	No access	No exit
22	No exit	No access
	Access from M77 only	Exit to M77 only
23	No exit	No access
25	Exit to A739 northbound only	Exit to A739 northbound only
	Access from A739 southbound only	Access from A739 southbound only
25a	No exit	No access
28	No exit	No access
28a	No exit	No access

M9	Eastbound	Westbound
1a	No exit	No access
2	No access	No exit
3	No exit	No access
6	No access	No exit
8	No exit	No access

M11	Northbound	Southbound
4	No exit	No access
5	No access	No exit
9	No access	No exit
13	No access	No exit
14	No exit to A428 westbound	No exit
		Access from A14 westbound only

Continued on page XXIII

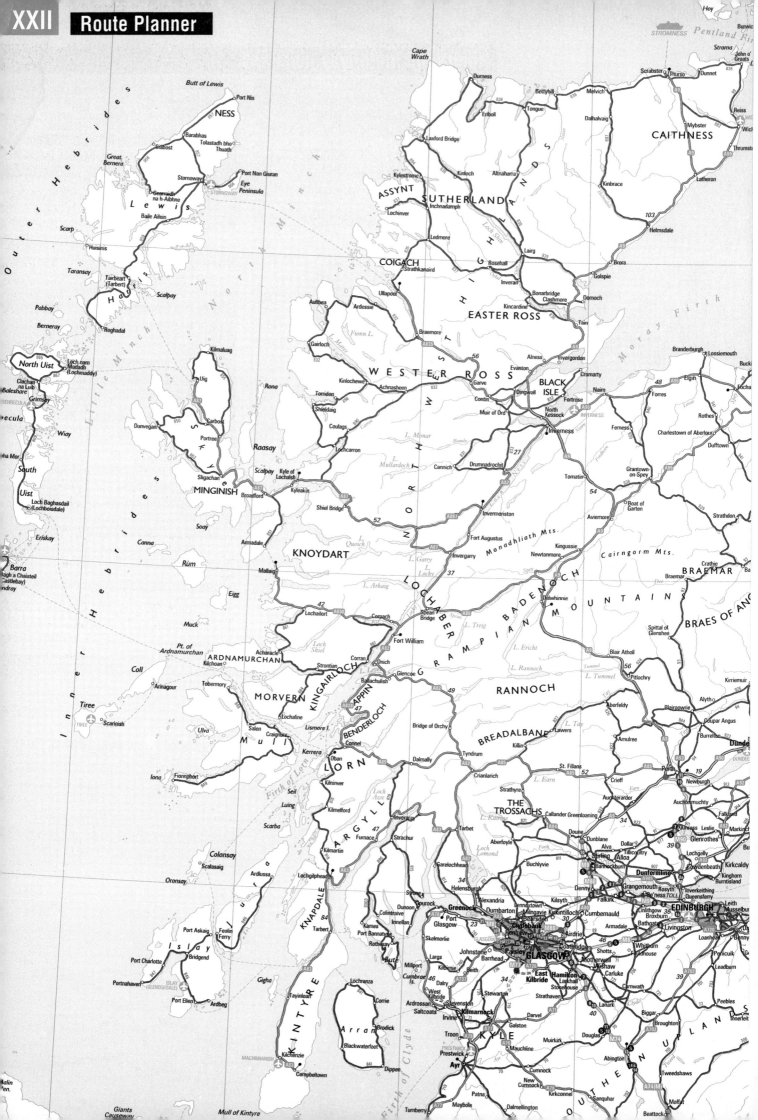

Restricted motorway junctions

Continuation from page XXI

M20	Eastbound	Westbound
2	No access	No exit
3	No exit	No access
	Access from M26 eastbound only	Exit to M26 westbound only
11a	No access	No exit

M23	Northbound	Southbound
7	No exit to A23 southbound	No access from A23 northbound
10a	No exit	No access

M25	Clockwise	Anticlockwise
5	No exit to M26 eastbound	No access from M26 westbound
19	No access	No exit
21	No exit to M1 southbound	No exit to M1 southbound
	Access from M1 southbound only	Access from M1 southbound only
31	No exit	No access

M27	Eastbound	Westbound
10	No exit	No access
12	No access	No exit

M40	Eastbound	Westbound
3	No exit	No access
7	No exit	No access
7a	No exit	No access
13	No exit	No access
14	No access	No exit
16	No access	No exit

M42	Northbound	Southbound
1	No exit	No access
7	No access	No exit
	Exit to M6 northbound only	Access from M6 northbound only
7a	No access	No exit
	Exit to M6 only	Access from M6 northbound only
8	No exit	Exit to M6 northbound
	Access from M6 southbound only	Access from M6 southbound only

M45	Eastbound	Westbound
M1 junc 17	Access to M1 southbound only	No access from M1 southbound
With A45 (Dunchurch)	No access	No exit

M49	Southbound	
18a	No exit to M5 northbound	

M53	Northbound	Southbound
11	Exit to M56 eastbound only	Exit to M56 eastbound only
	Access from M56 westbound only	Access from M56 westbound only

M56	Eastbound	Westbound
2	No exit	No access
4	No exit	No access
7		No access
8	No exit or access	
9	No access from M6 northbound	No access to M6 southbound
15	No exit to M53	No access from M53 northbound

M57	Northbound	Southbound
3	No exit	No access
5	No exit	No access

M58	Eastbound	Westbound
1	No exit	No access

M60	Clockwise	Anticlockwise
2	No exit	No access
3	No exit to A34 northbound	No exit to A34 northbound
4	No access to M56	No exit to M56
5	No exit to A5103 southbound	No exit to A5103 northbound
7	No access	No exit (Exit from J8 only)
14	No exit to A580	No access from A580
16	No exit	No access
25	No access	
26		No exit or access
27	No exit	No access

M61	Northbound	Southbound
2	No access from A580 eastbound	No exit from A580 westbound
3	No access from A580 eastbound	No exit from A580 westbound
M6 junc 30	No exit to M6 southbound	No access from M6 northbound

M62	Eastbound	Westbound
23	No access	No exit

M65	Eastbound	Westbound
9	No access	No exit
11	No exit	No access

M67	Eastbound	Westbound
1a	No access	No exit
2	No exit	No access

M69	Northbound	Southbound
2	No exit	No access

M73	Northbound	Southbound
2	No access from M8 or A89 eastbound	No exit to M8 or A89 westbound
	No exit to A89	No access from A89
3	Exit to A80 northbound only	Access from A80 southbound only

M74	Northbound	Southbound
2	No access	No exit
3	No exit	No access
7	No exit	No access
9	No exit or access	No access
10		No access
11	No exit	No access
12	No access	No exit

M77	Northbound	Southbound
4	No exit	No access
M8 junc 22	Exit to M8 eastbound only	Access from M8 westbound only

M80	Northbound	Southbound
3	No access	No exit
5	No access from M876	No exit to M876

M90	Northbound	Southbound
2a	No access	No exit
7	No exit	No access
8	No access	No exit
10	No access from A912	No exit to A912

M180	Northbound	Southbound
1	No access	No exit

M621	Eastbound	Westbound
2a	No exit	No access
4	No exit or access	
5	No exit	No access
6	No access	No exit

M876	Northbound	Southbound
2	No access	No access

A1(M)	Northbound	Southbound
2	No access	No exit
3		No access
5	No exit	No access
44	No exit, access from M1 only	Exit to M1 only
57	No access	No exit
65	No access	No exit

A3(M)	Northbound	Southbound
1		No access
4	No access	No exit

A38(M)	Northbound	Southbound
With Victoria Road (Park Circus) Birmingham	No exit	No access

A48(M)	Northbound	Southbound
M4 Junc 29	Exit to M4 eastbound only	Access from M4 westbound only
29a	Access from A48 eastbound only	Exit to A48 westbound only

A57(M)	Eastbound	Westbound
With A5103	No access	No exit
With A34	No access	No exit

A58(M)	Southbound	
With Park Lane and Westgate, Leeds	No access	

A64(M)	Eastbound	Westbound
With A58 Clay Pit Lane, Leeds	No access	No exit
With Regent Street, Leeds	No access	No access

A74(M)	Northbound	Southbound
18	No access	No exit
22	No access	No exit

A167(M)	Northbound	Southbound
With Camden St, Newcastle	No exit	No exit or access

A194(M)	Northbound	Southbound
A1(M) junc 65 Gateshead Western Bypass	Access from A1(M) northbound only	Exit to A1(M) southbound only

Road map symbols

M6 Motorway, toll motorway

4 5 Motorway junction – full, restricted access

S S Motorway service area – full, restricted access

Motorway under construction

A453 Primary route – dual, single carriageway

S Service area, roundabout, multi-level junction

4 5 Numbered primary route junction – access, restricted access

Primary route under construction

Narrow primary route

Derby Primary destination

A34

A road – dual, single carriageway

A road under construction

Narrow A road

B2135

B road – dual, single carriageway

B road under construction

Narrow B road

Minor road – over 4 metres wide, under 4 metres wide

Minor road with restricted access

2 Distance in miles

Tunnel

TOLL Toll, steep gradient – arrow points downhill

National trail – England and Wales

Long distance footpath – Scotland

Railway with station

Level crossing, tunnel

Preserved railway with station

National boundary

County or unitary authority boundary

Car ferry, catamaran

Passenger ferry, catamaran

Hovercraft, freight ferry

CALAIS 1:15 Ferry destination, journey time – hrs : mins

Ferry Car ferry – river crossing

Principal airport, other airport

National park

Area of Outstanding Natural Beauty – England and Wales
National Scenic Area – Scotland / forest park / regional park / national forest

Woodland

Beach

Linear antiquity

Roman road

Hillfort, battlefield – with date

1066

Viewpoint, national nature reserve, spot height – in metres

795

Golf course, youth hostel, national sporting venue

Camp site, caravan site, camping and caravan site

P&R Shopping village, park and ride

29 Adjoining page number – road maps

Road map scale: 1: 200000, 3·15 miles to 1 inch

0 1 2 3 4 5 6 7 8 9 miles

0 1 2 3 4 5 6 7 8 9 10 11 12 13 14 15km

Tourist information

✠ Abbey, cathedral or priory

🏛 Ancient monument

🐟 Aquarium

🏛 Art gallery

🦅 Bird collection or aviary

🏰 Castle

⛪ Church

Country park
🎪 England and Wales
🦌 Scotland

🐄 Farm park

✿ Garden

⚓ Historic ship

🏠 House

🏠 House and garden

▨ Motor racing circuit

🏛 Museum

Ⓐ Picnic area

🚂 Preserved railway

🏇 Race course

🏺 Roman antiquity

Safari park

🎡 Theme park

Tourist information centre
ℹ open all year
ℹ open seasonally

🐗 Zoo

✦ Other place of interest

Relief

Feet	metres
3000	914
2600	792
2200	671
1800	549
1400	427
1000	305
0	0

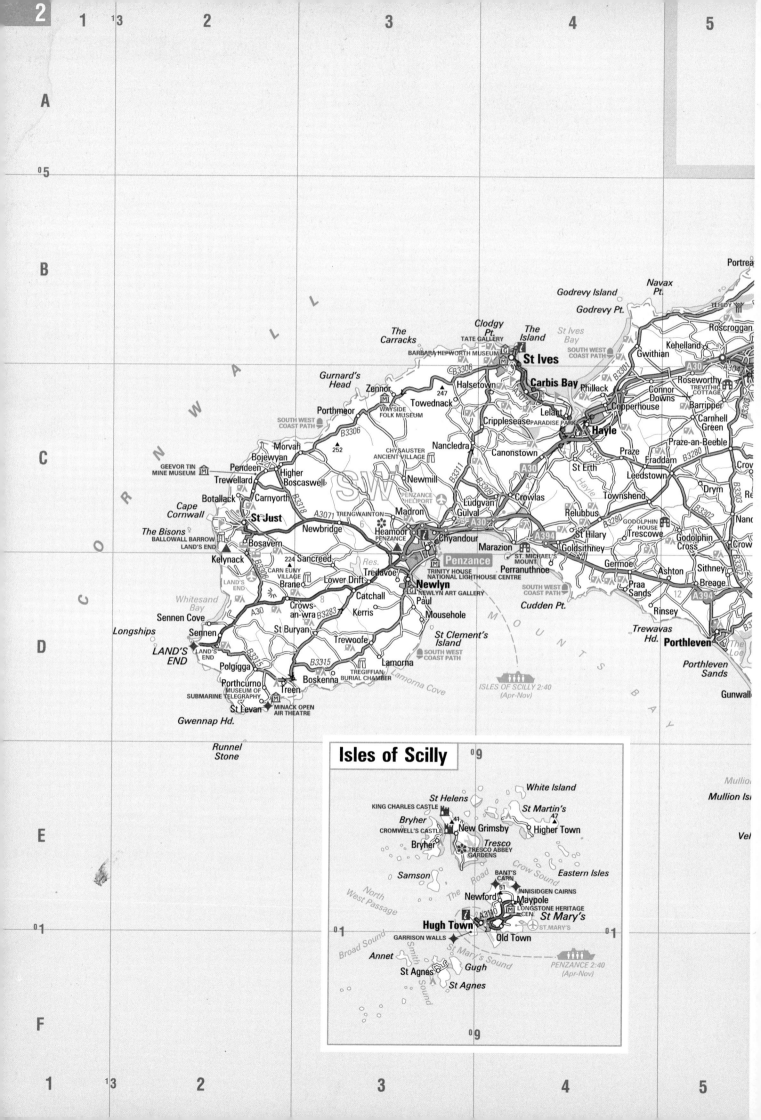

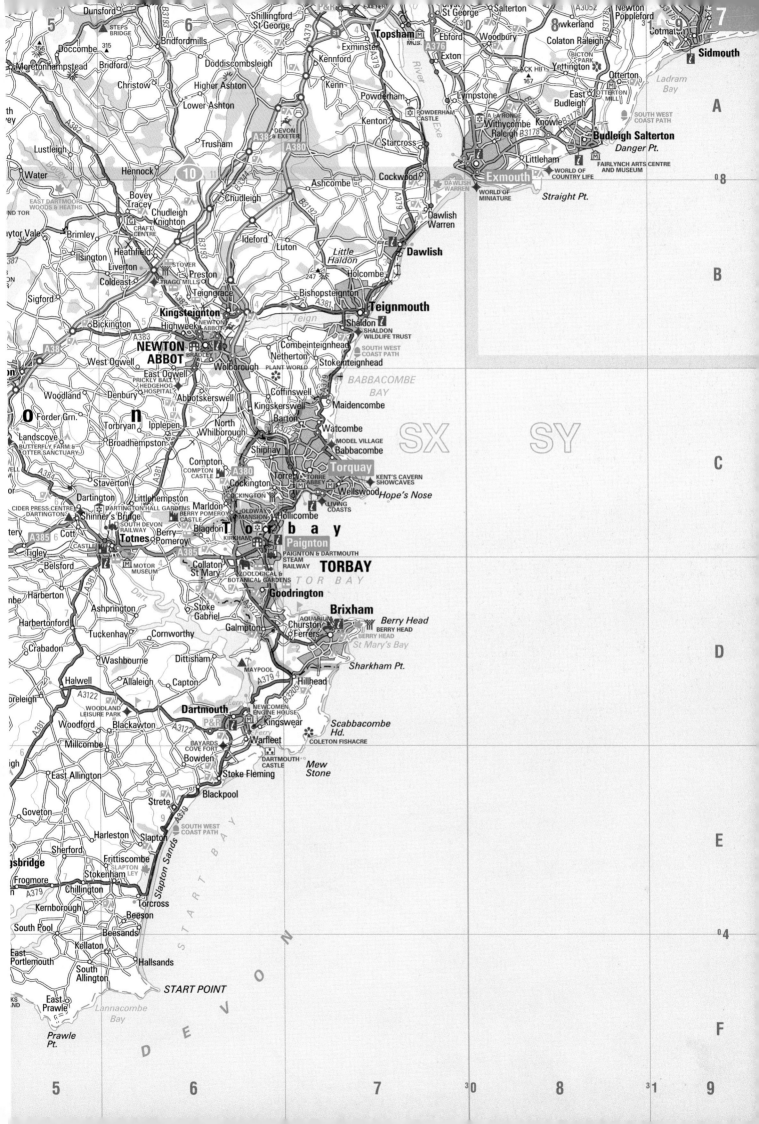

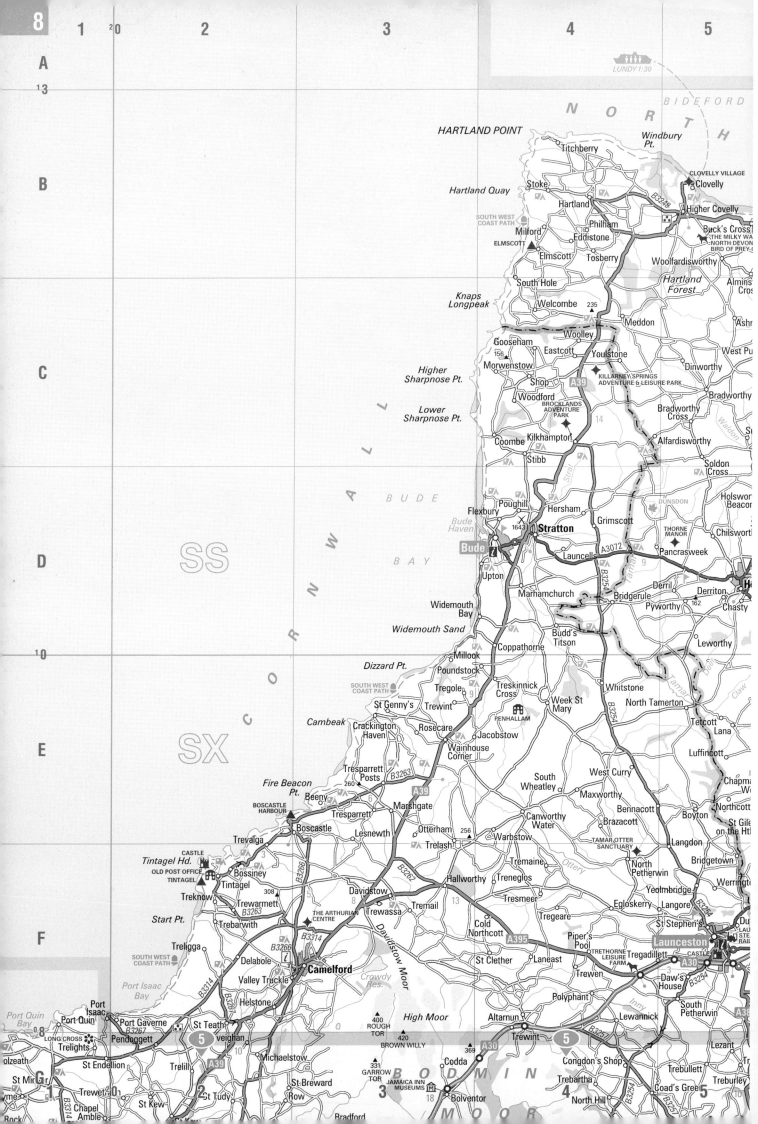

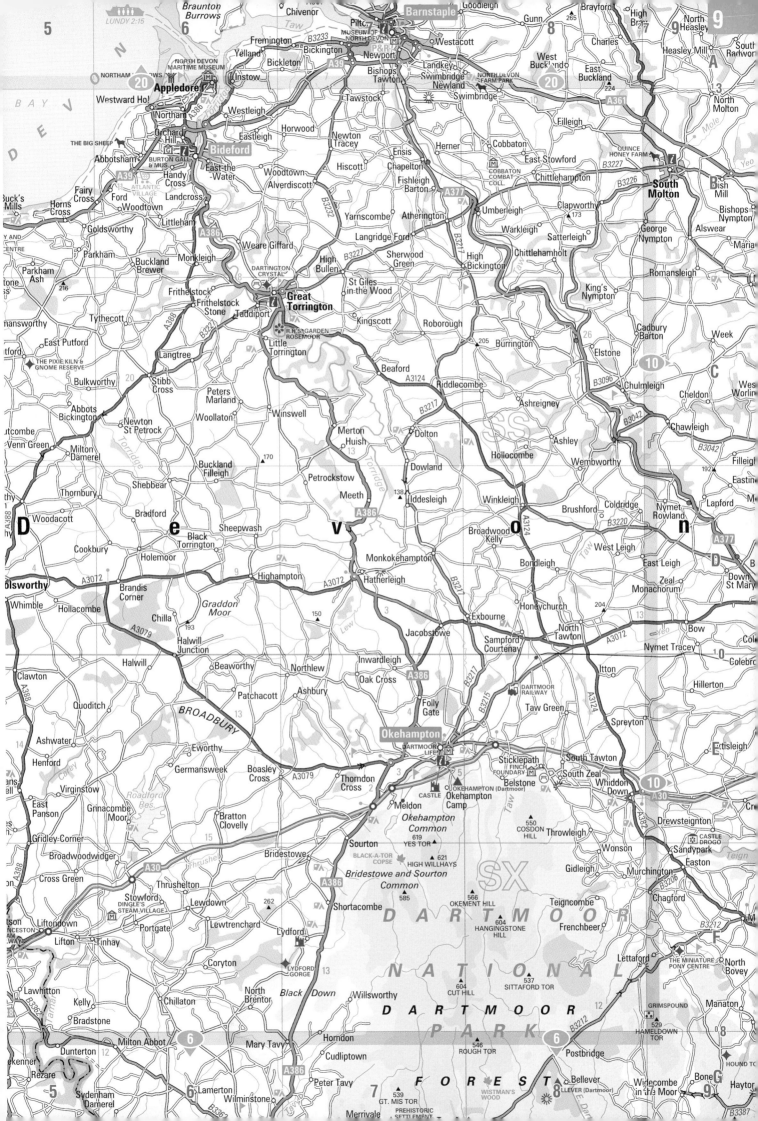

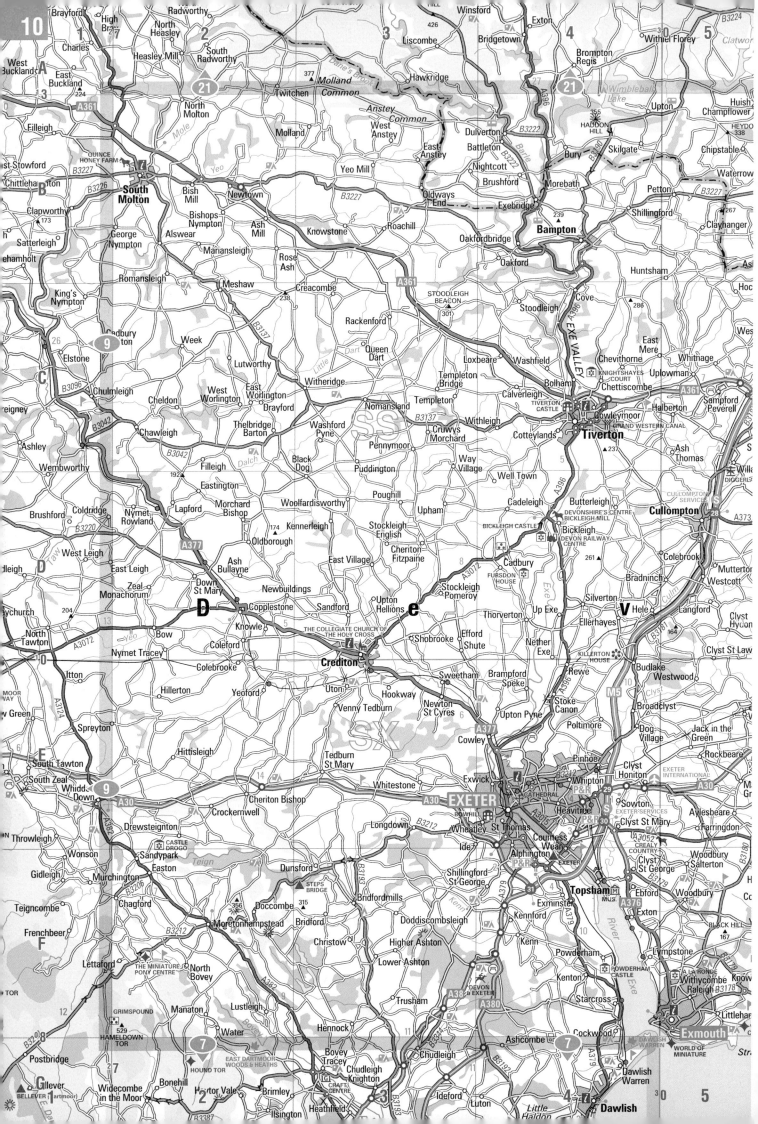

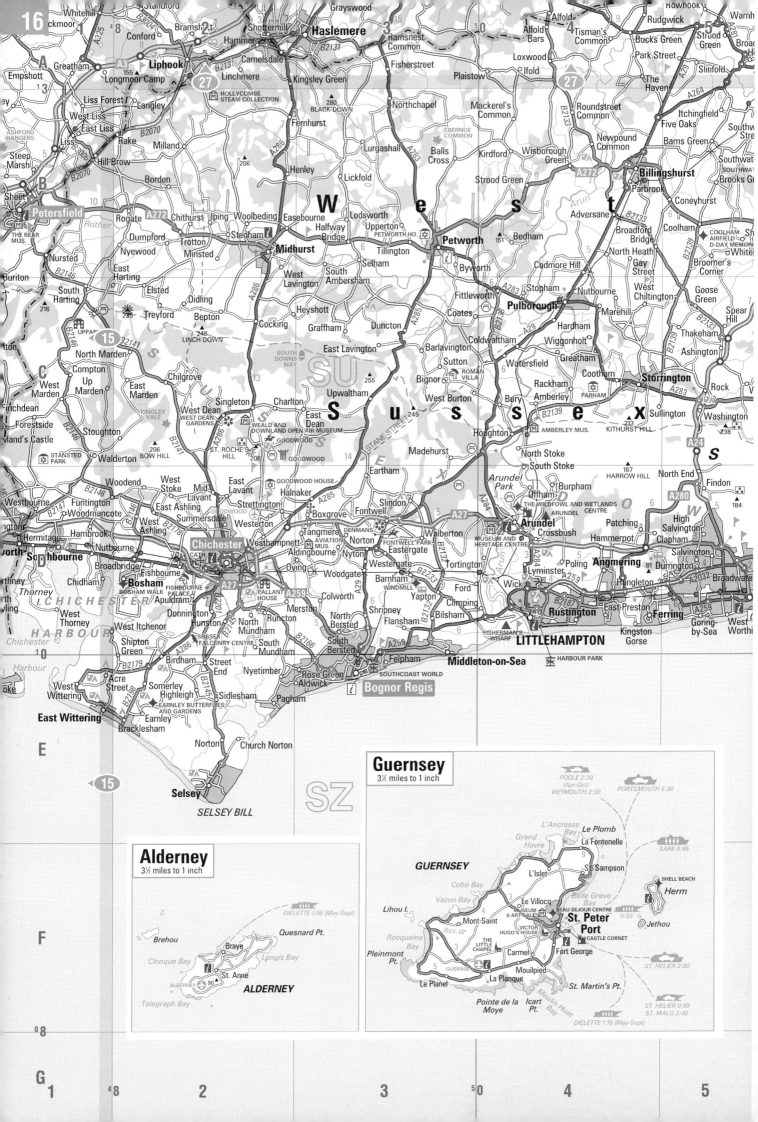

ENGLISH CHANNEL

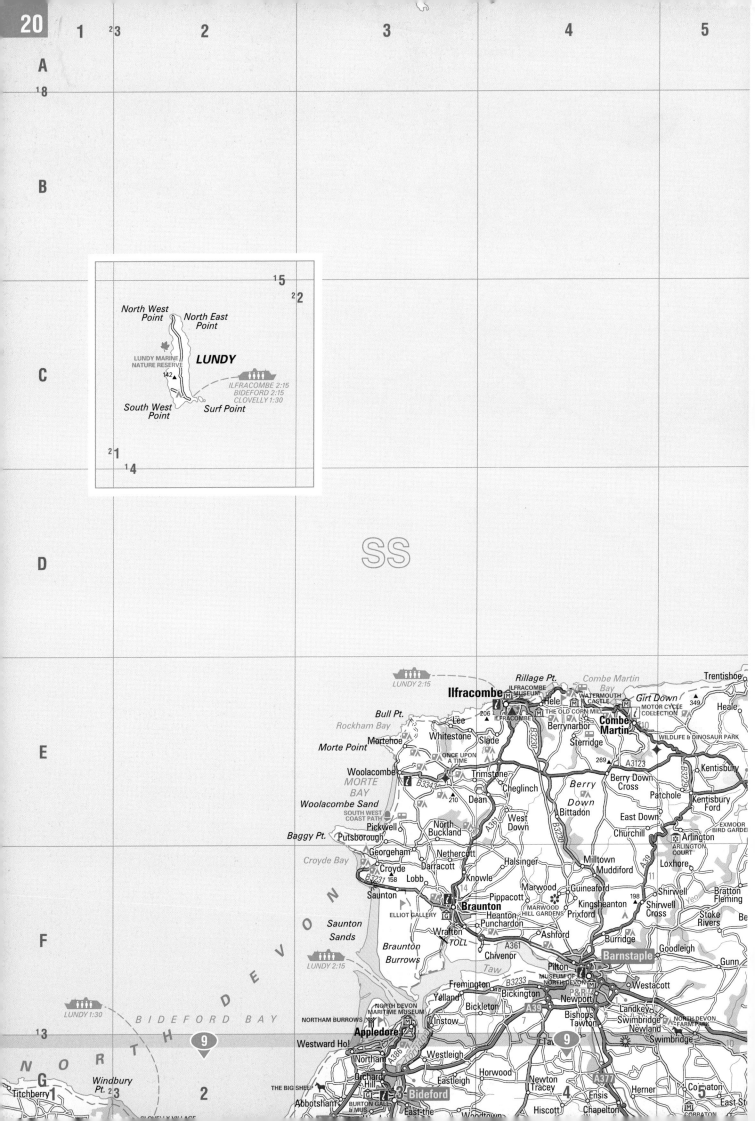

1   23   2   3   4   5

A

18

B

15
22

North West
Point   North East
Point

LUNDY

LUNDY MARINE
NATURE RESERVE

142

ILFRACOMBE 2:15
BIDEFORD 2:15
CLOVELLY 1:30

C

South West
Point   Surf Point

21
14

D

SS

LUNDY 2:15

Rillage Pt.   Combe Martin
Bay   Trentishoe

Ilfracombe   ILFRACOMBE   WATERMOUTH
                              MUSEUM   Hele   CASTLE   Girt Down

Bull Pt.   206   THE OLD CORN MILL   Combe   MOTOR CYCLE
                              ILFRACOMBE   Berrynarbor   Martin   COLLECTION   349   Heale

Rockham Bay   Lee   Berrynarbor   510
                    Whitestone   Slade   Sterridge   WILDLIFE & DINOSAUR PARK

Mortehoe   ONCE UPON   Berry   Kentisbury
Morte Point   A TIME   Trimstone   Down   Berry Down
                                                            Cross   Kentisbury

E   Woolacombe   269   A3123   Patchole   Ford

MORTE   B3343   Cheglinch   Bittadon   East Down
BAY   210   Dean

Woolacombe Sand   West   Churchill   Arlington
                    North   Down   ARLINGTON   EXMOOR
SOUTH WEST   Buckland   A361   Milltown   COURT   BIRD GARDEN
Pickwell   COAST PATH   Muddiford   Loxhore

Baggy Pt.   Putsborough   Nethercott   Halsinger   Marwood   Guineaford   198   Shirwell   Bratton
                    Georgeham   Darracott   MARWOOD   Kingsheanton   Shirwell   Fleming
Croyde Bay   Croyde   Knowle   HILL GARDENS   Prixford   Cross   Stoke
                    B3231   158   Lobb   Pippacott   Rivers

Saunton   14   Heanton   Ashford   Burridge
ELLIOT GALLERY   Braunton   Punchardon

F   Saunton   Wrafton   Chivenor   A361   Pilton   Barnstaple   Goodleigh   Gunn
Sands   TOLL   Taw   MUSEUM OF   Westacott
Braunton   Fremington   B3233   NORTH DEVON   Newport
Burrows   LUNDY 2:15   Yelland   Bickington   P&R   Landkey
                                        A39   Bishops   NORTH DEVON
                    NORTH DEVON   Instow   Tawton   Swimbridge   FARM PARK
                    MARITIME MUSEUM   7   Newland
LUNDY 1:30   NORTHAM BURROWS   Taw   9   Swimbridge   10

BIDEFORD BAY   13   Appledore   Westward Ho!
9   Northam   A386   Westleigh   Newton   A377
                    Orchard   Horwood   Tracey   Herner   Co
Titchberry   Windbury   THE BIG SHEEP   Hill   Ensis   East
G   Pt.   23   Bideford   Hiscott   Chapelton
NORTH DEVON   Abbotsham   Woodtown   CORRATON
                    1   2   East-the   3   4   5

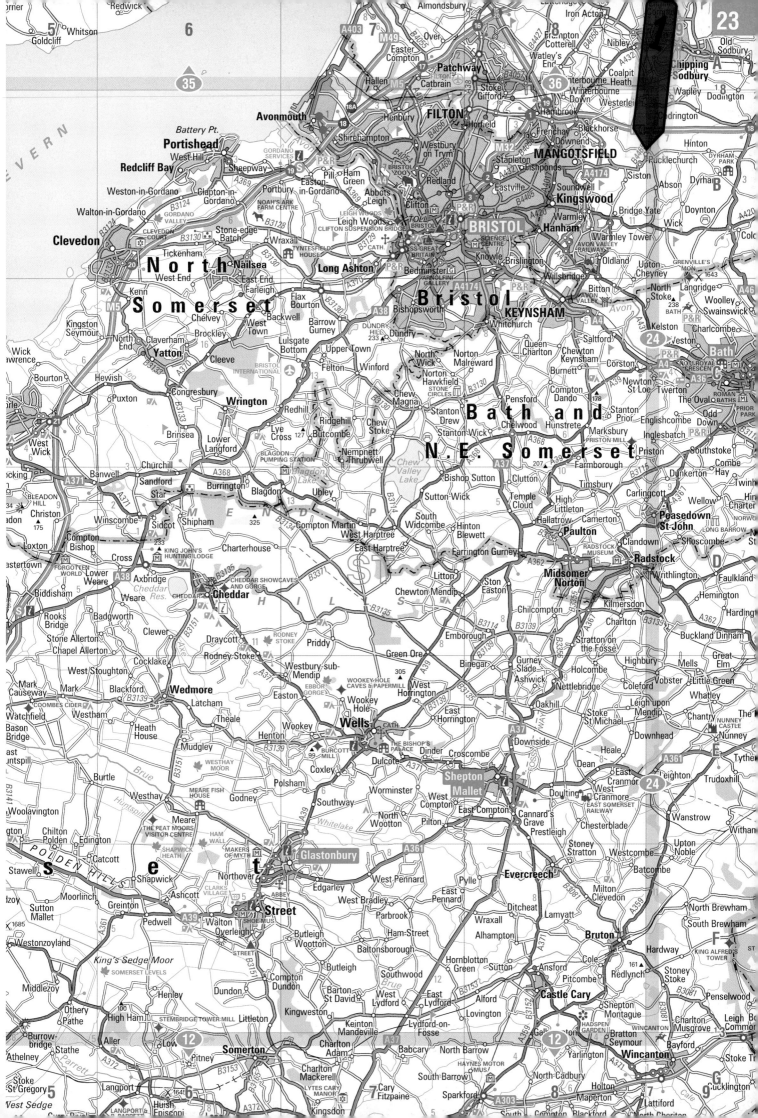

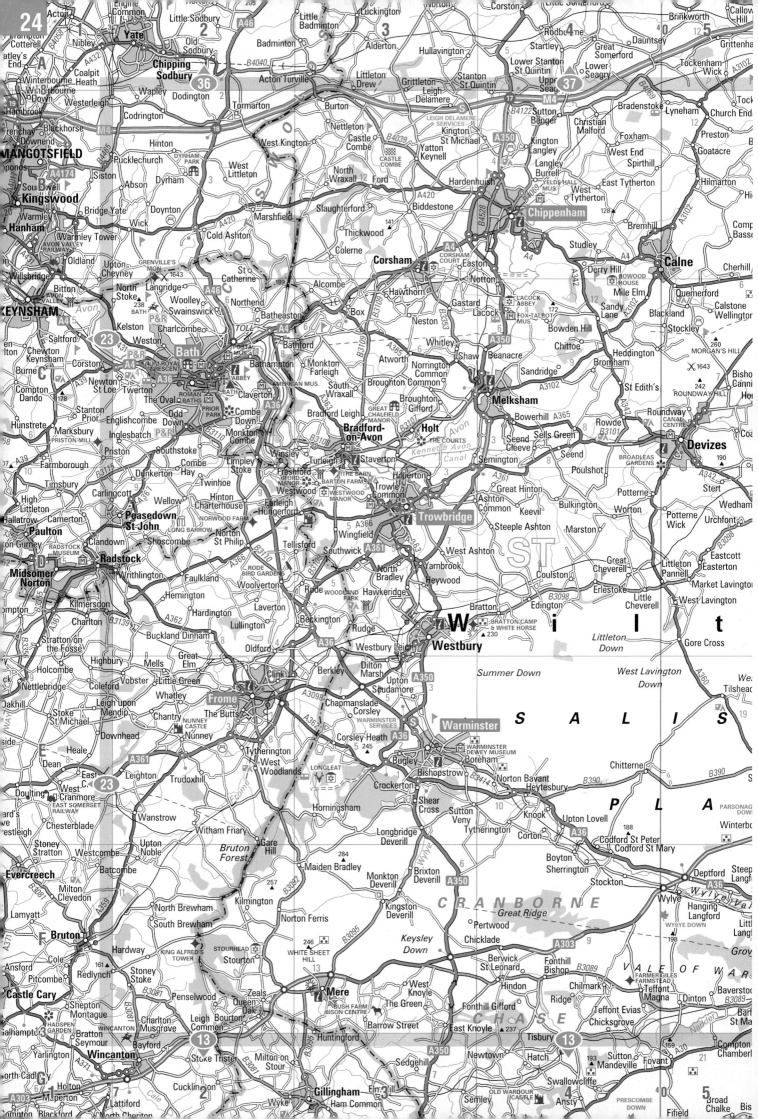

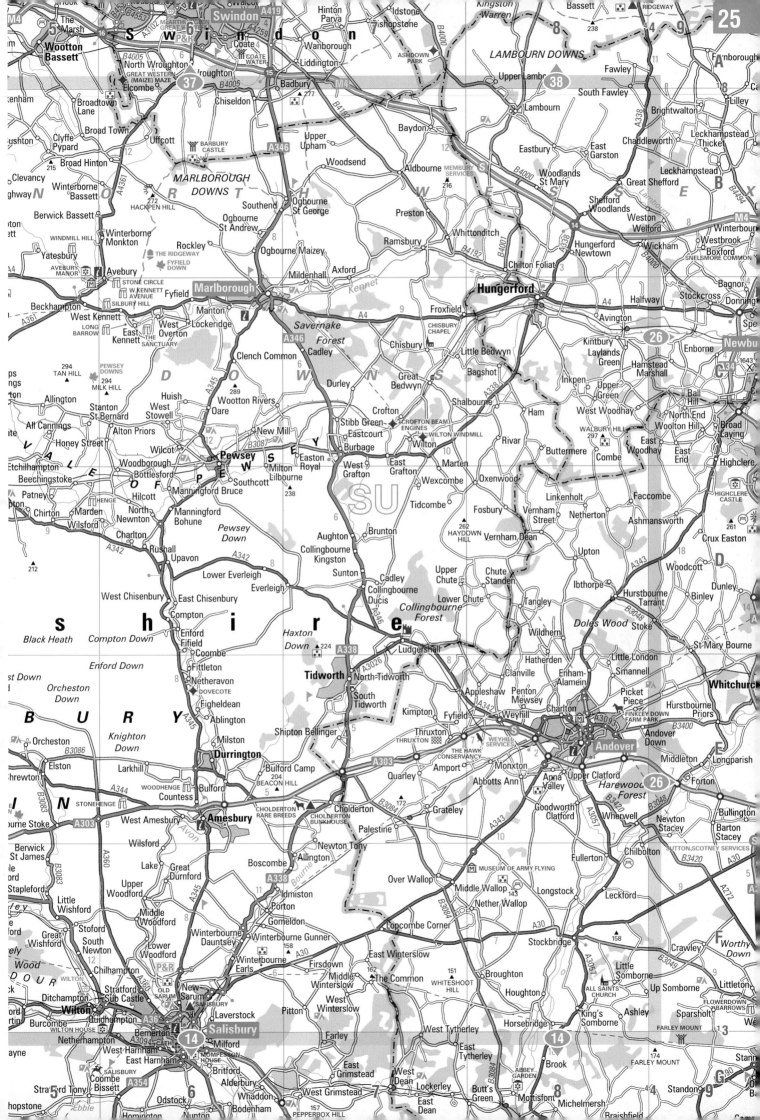

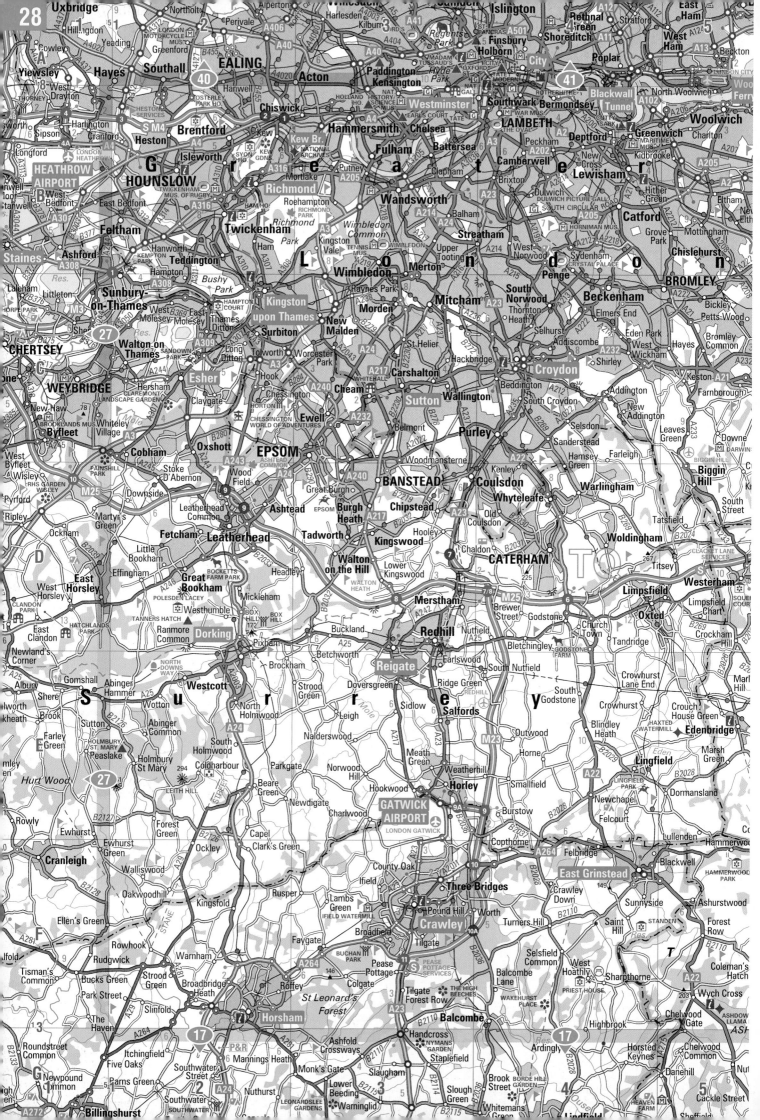

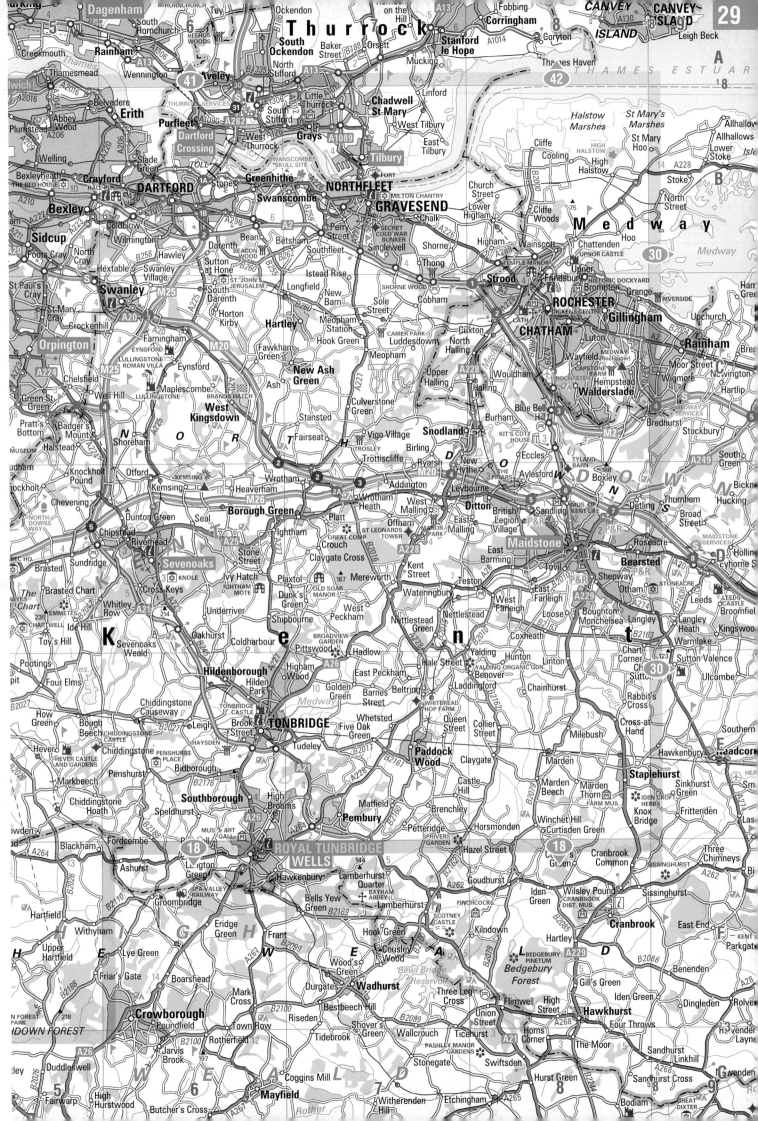

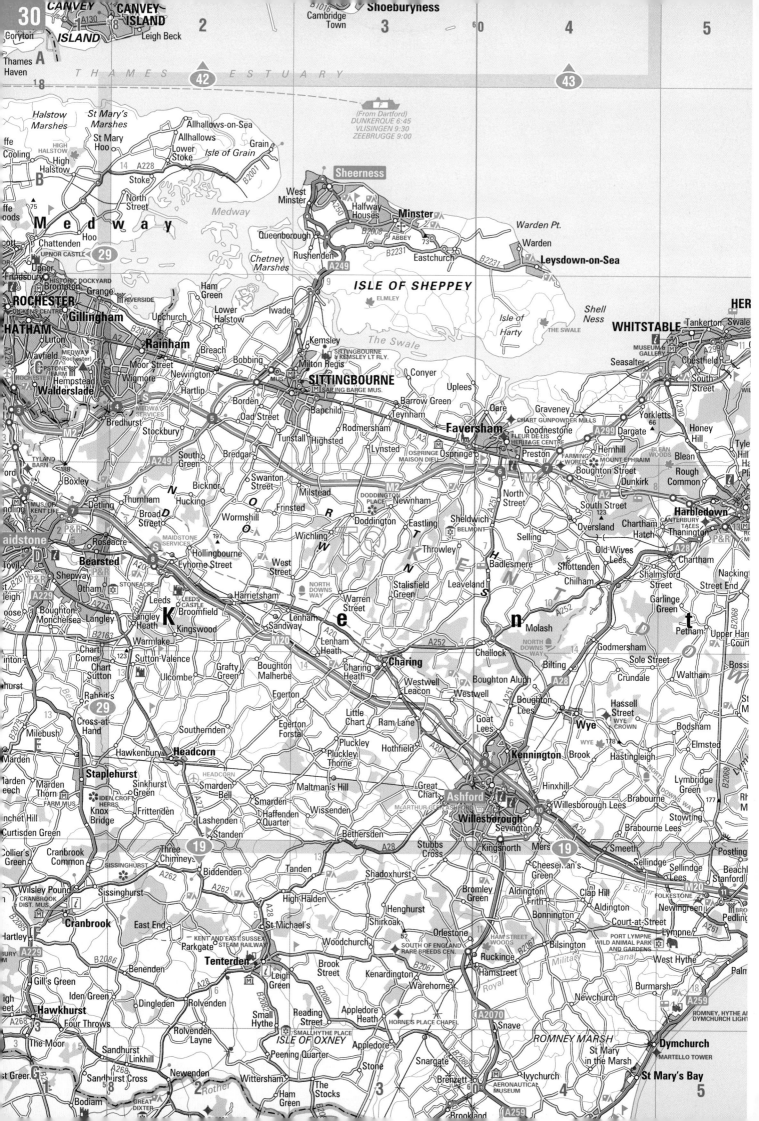

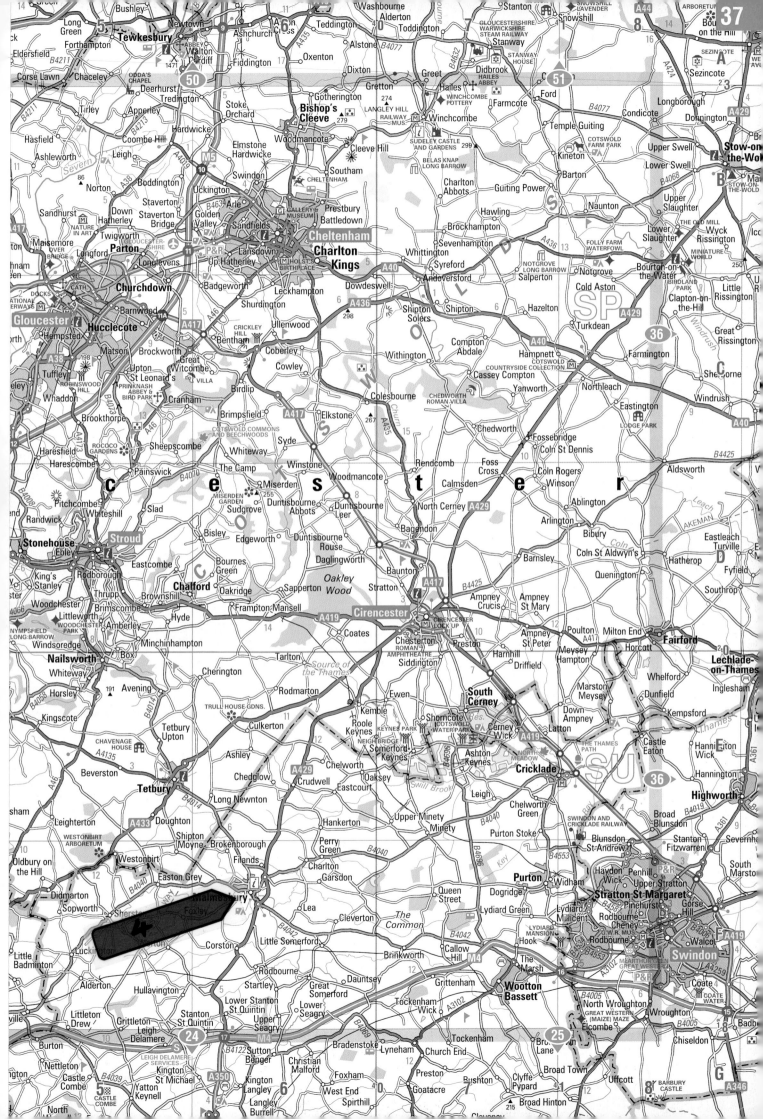

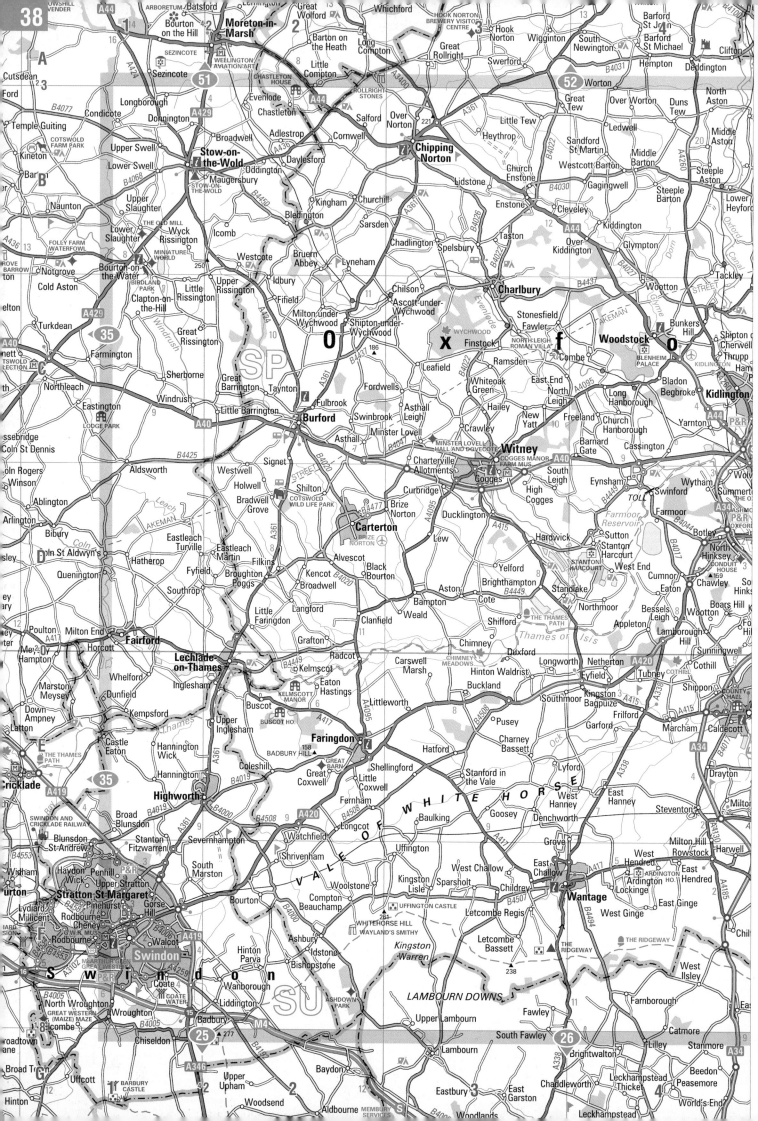

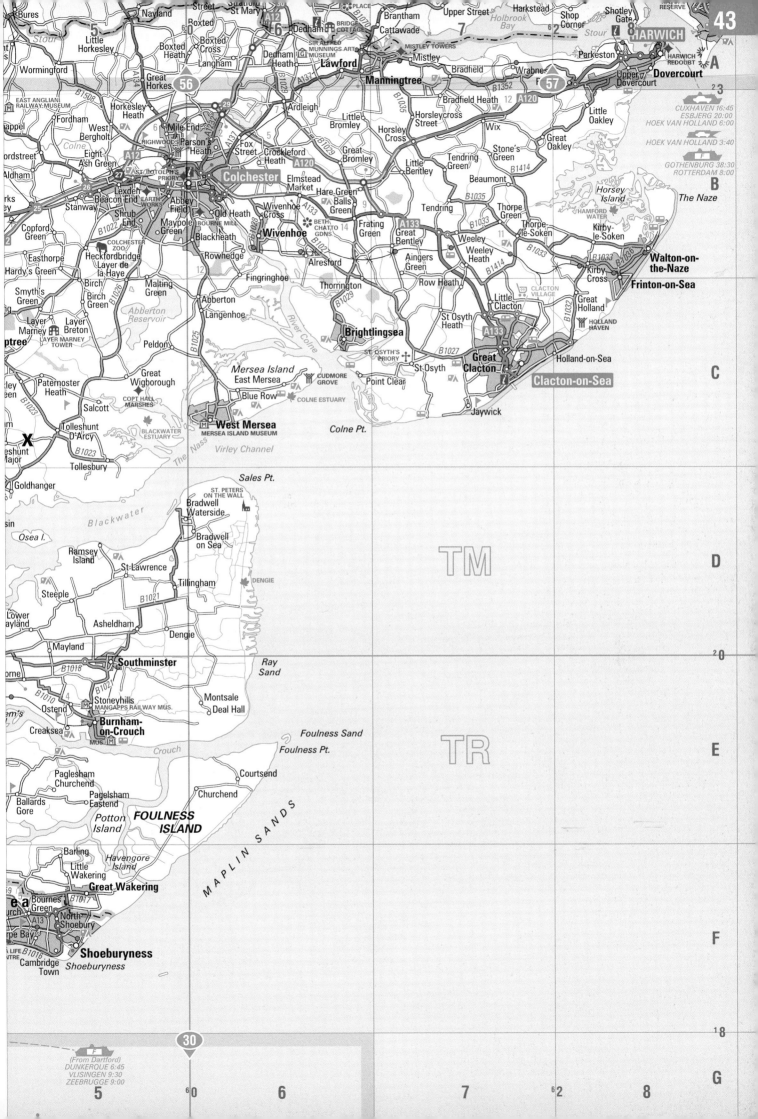

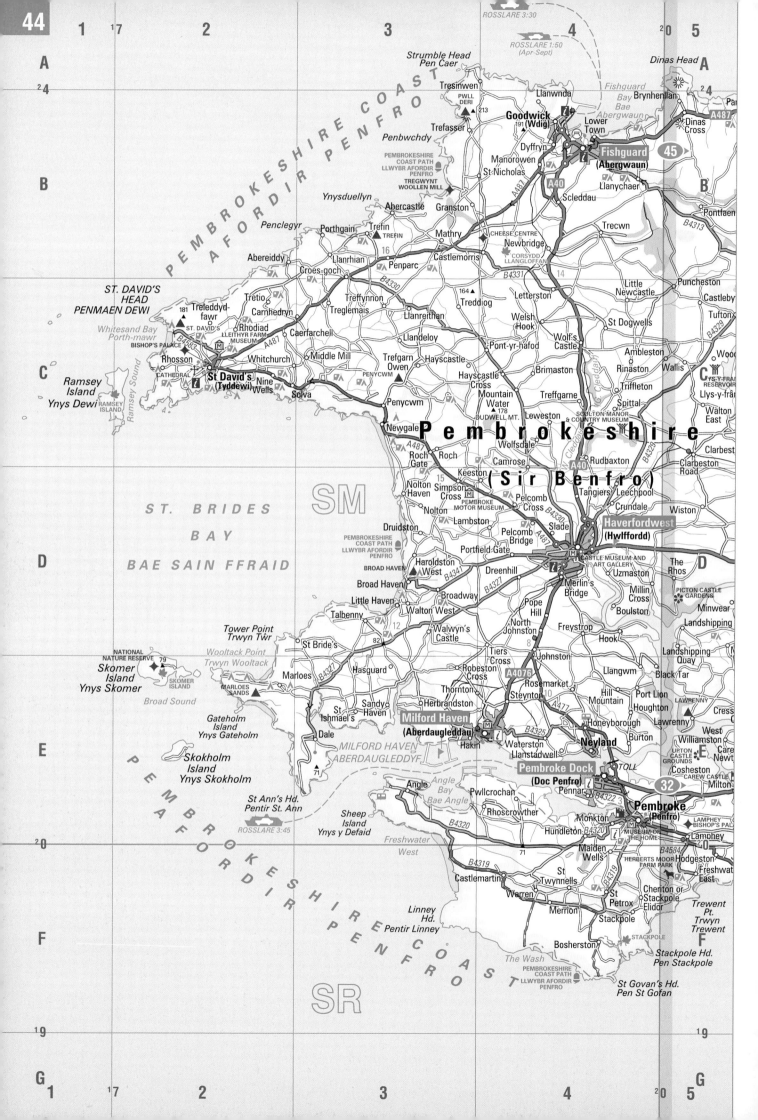

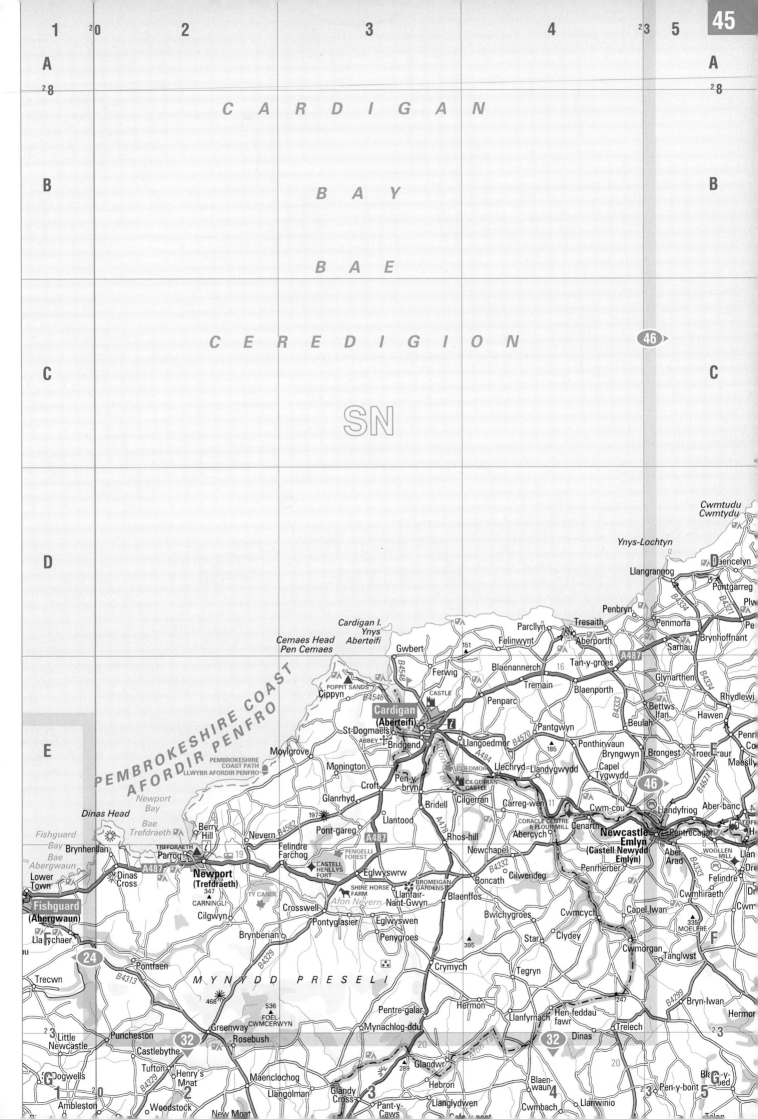

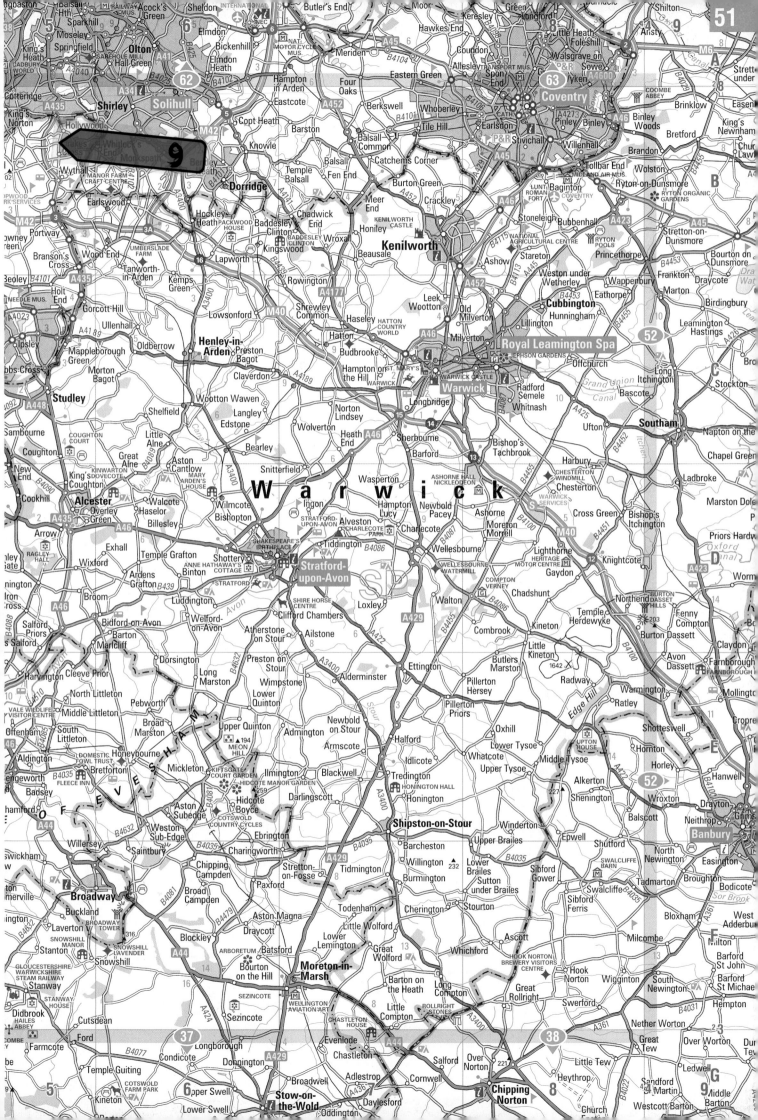

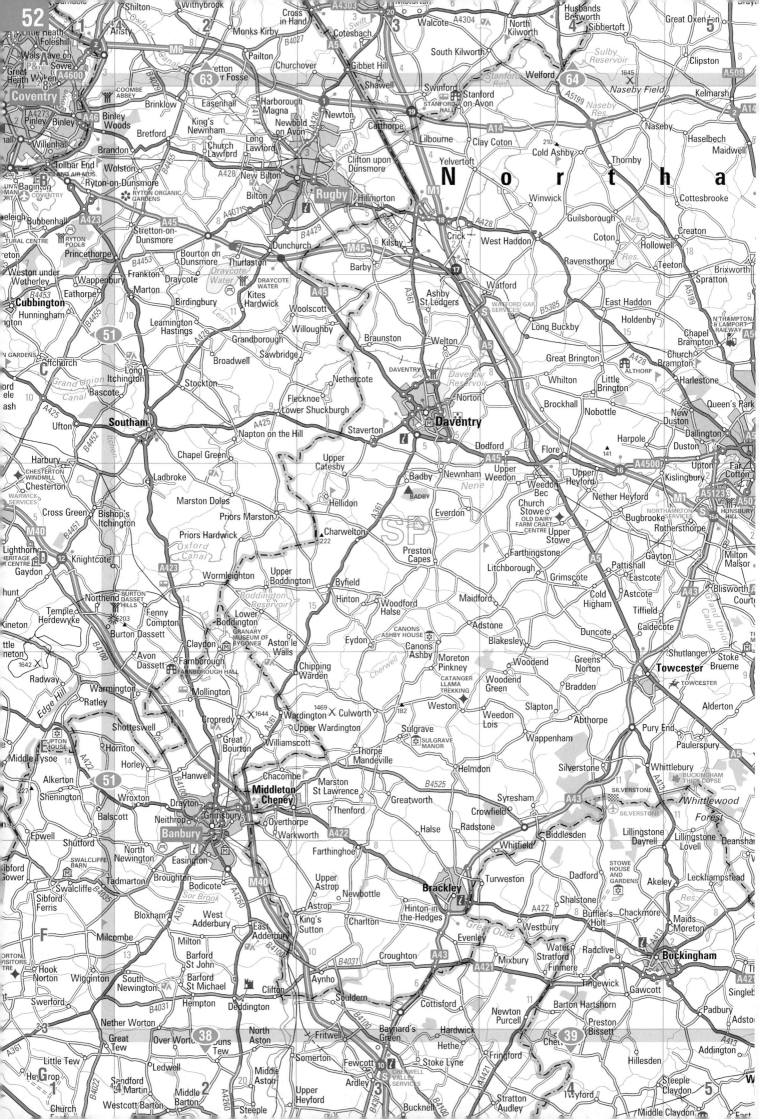

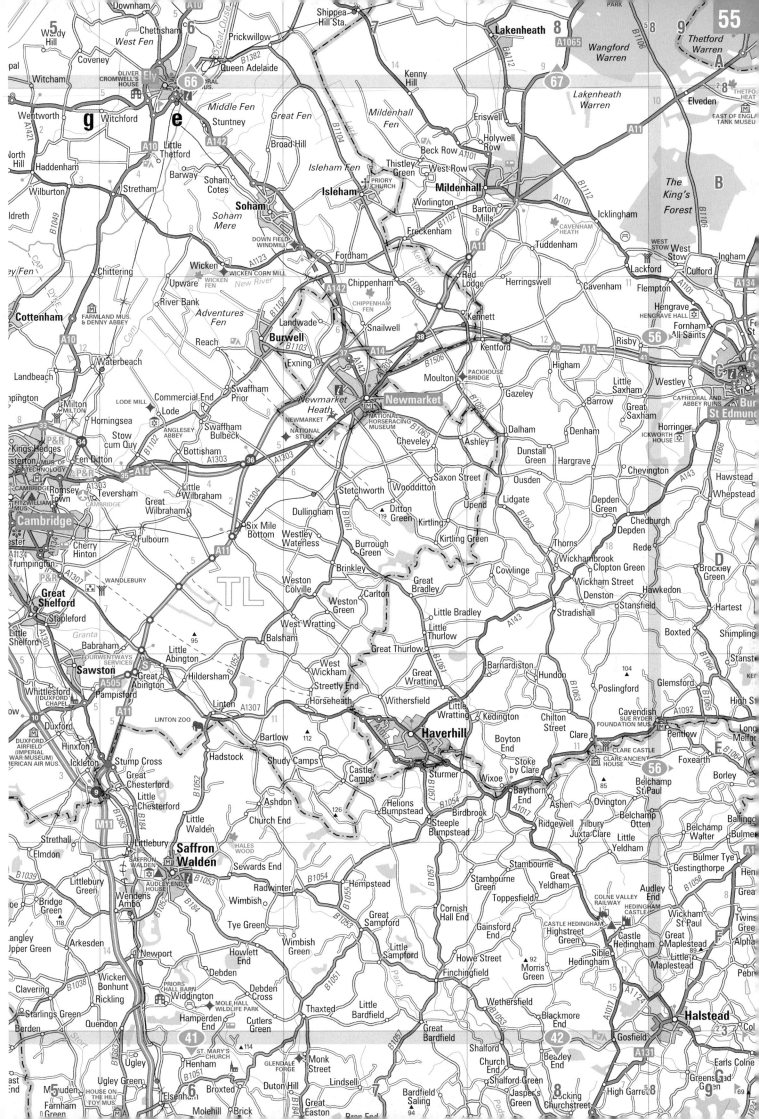

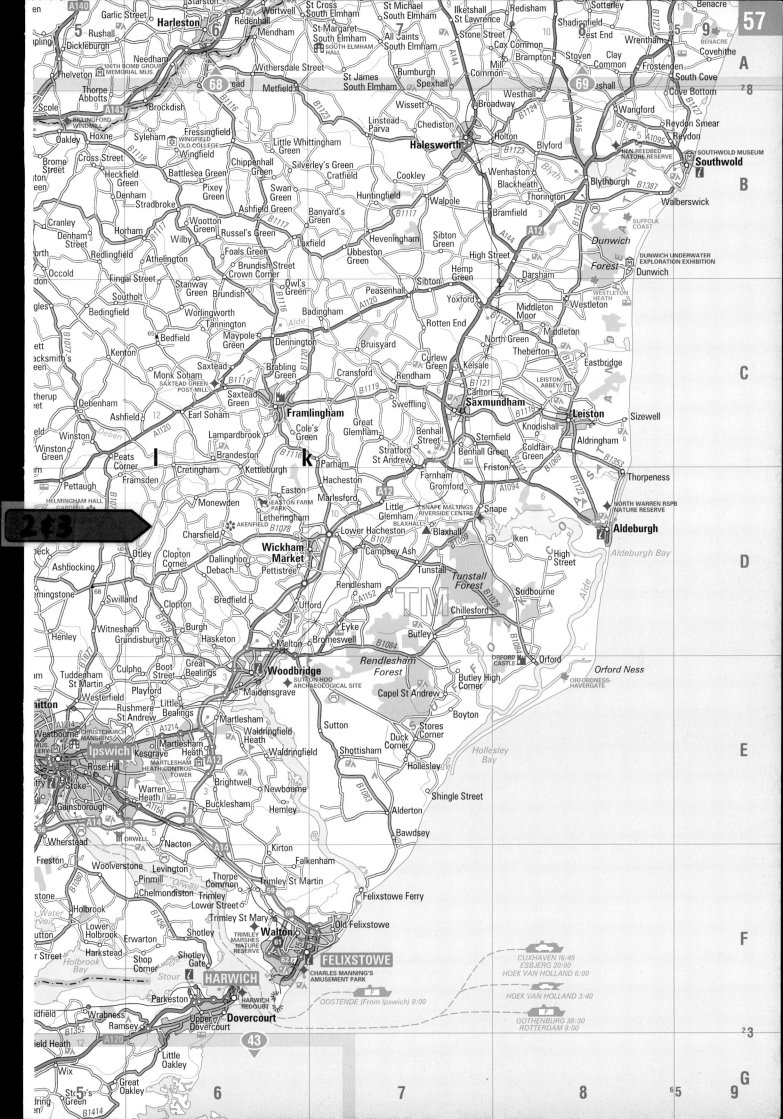

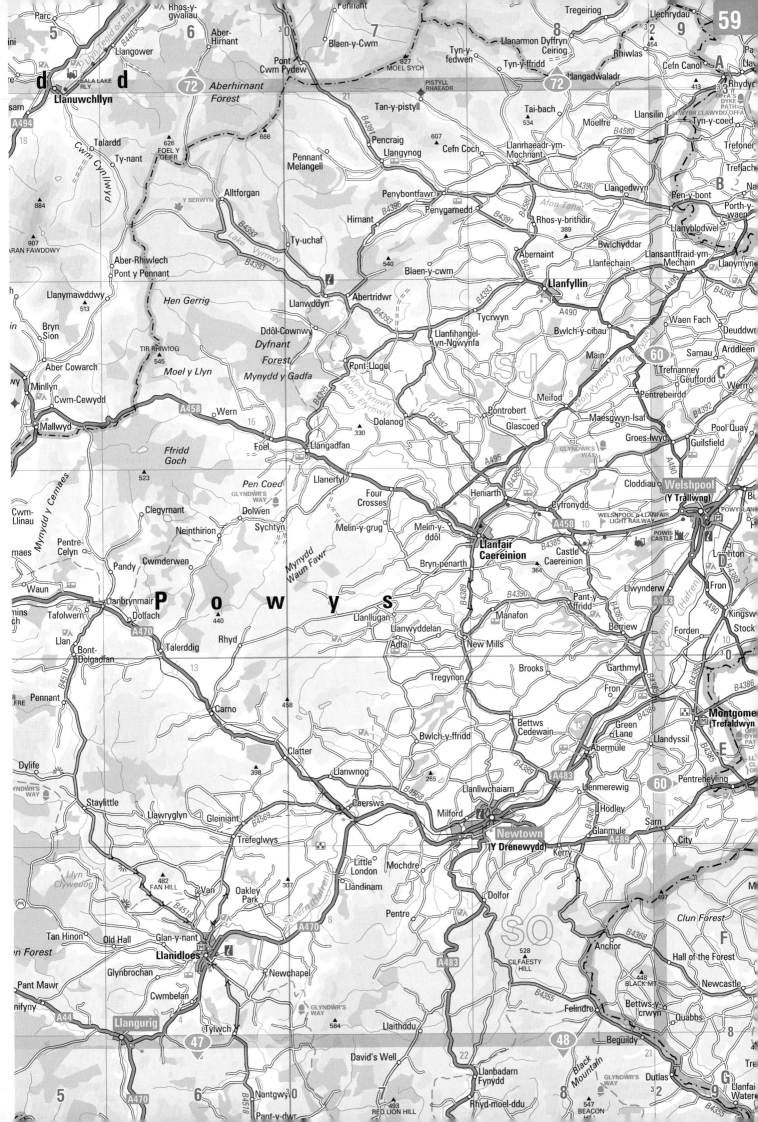

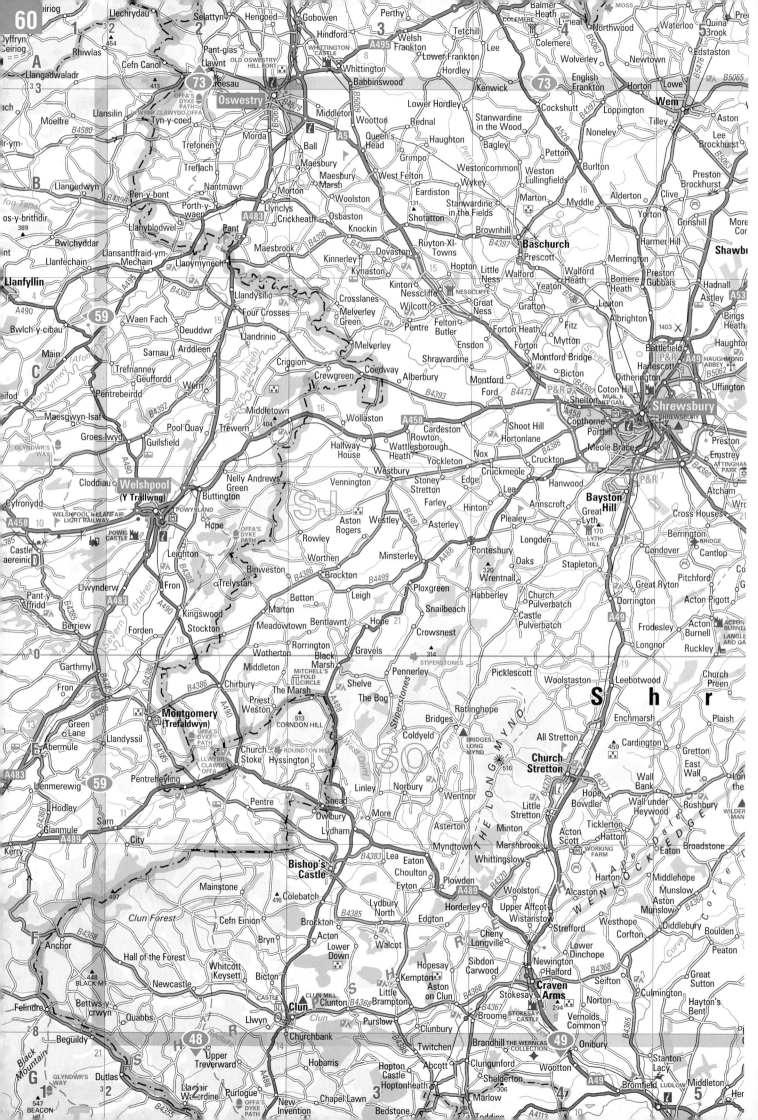

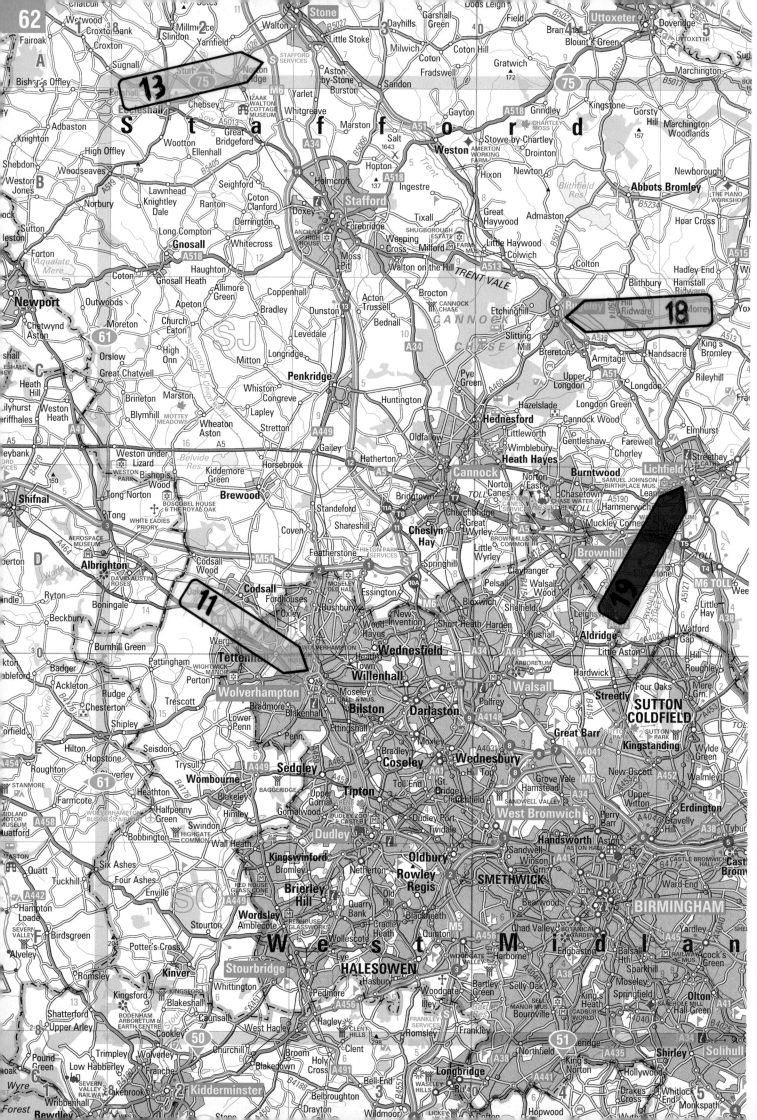

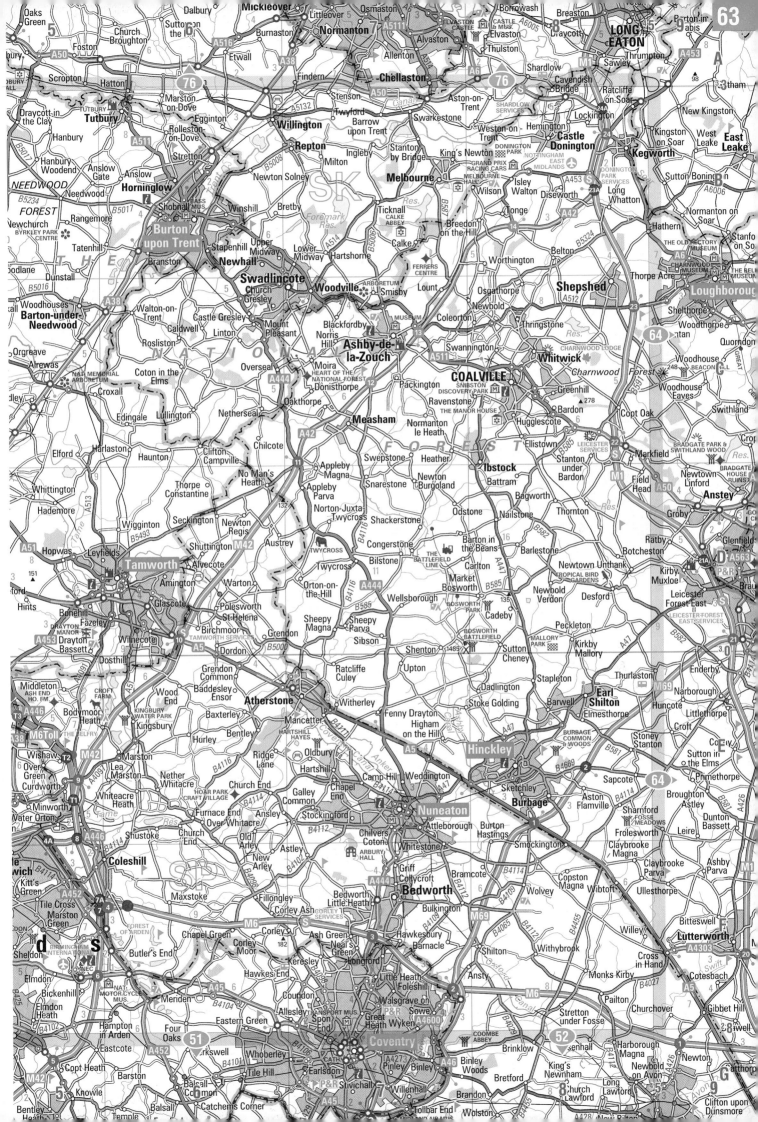

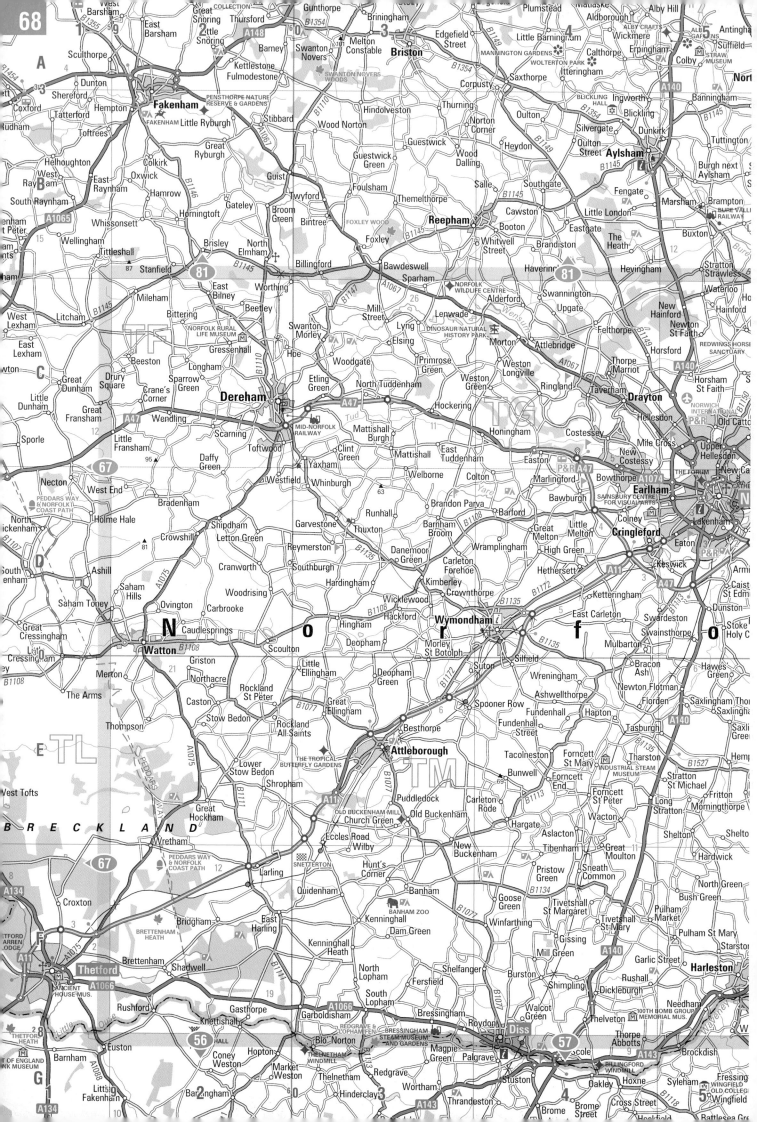

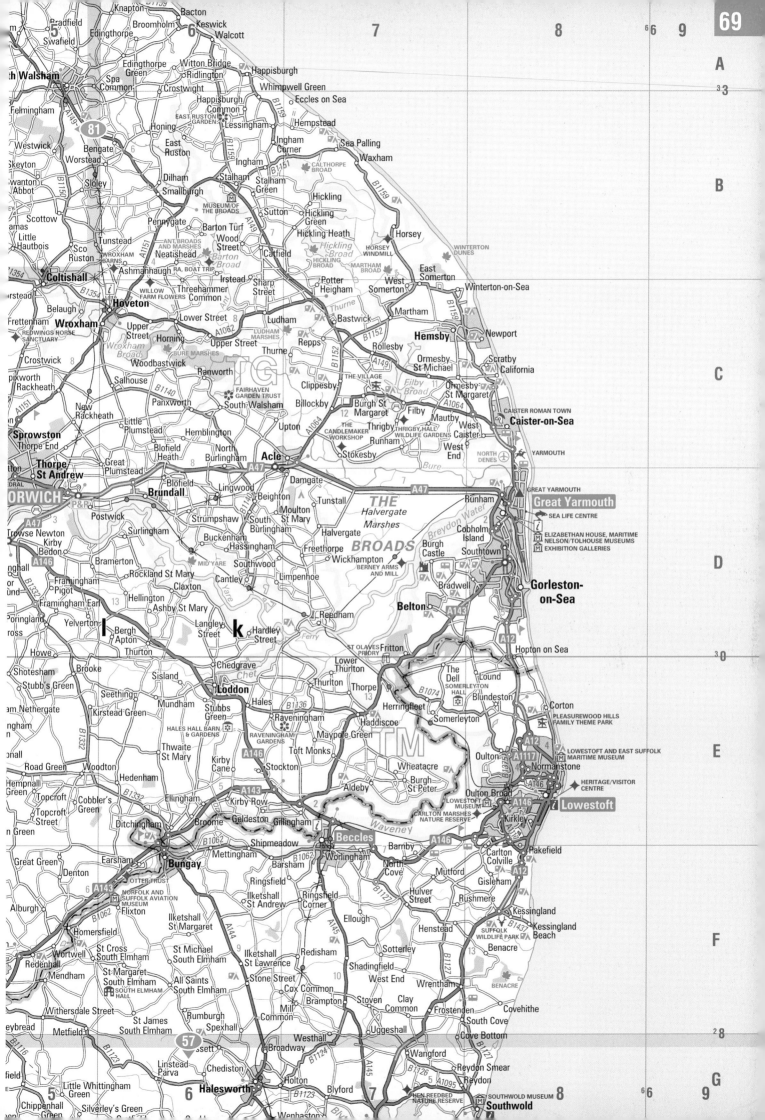

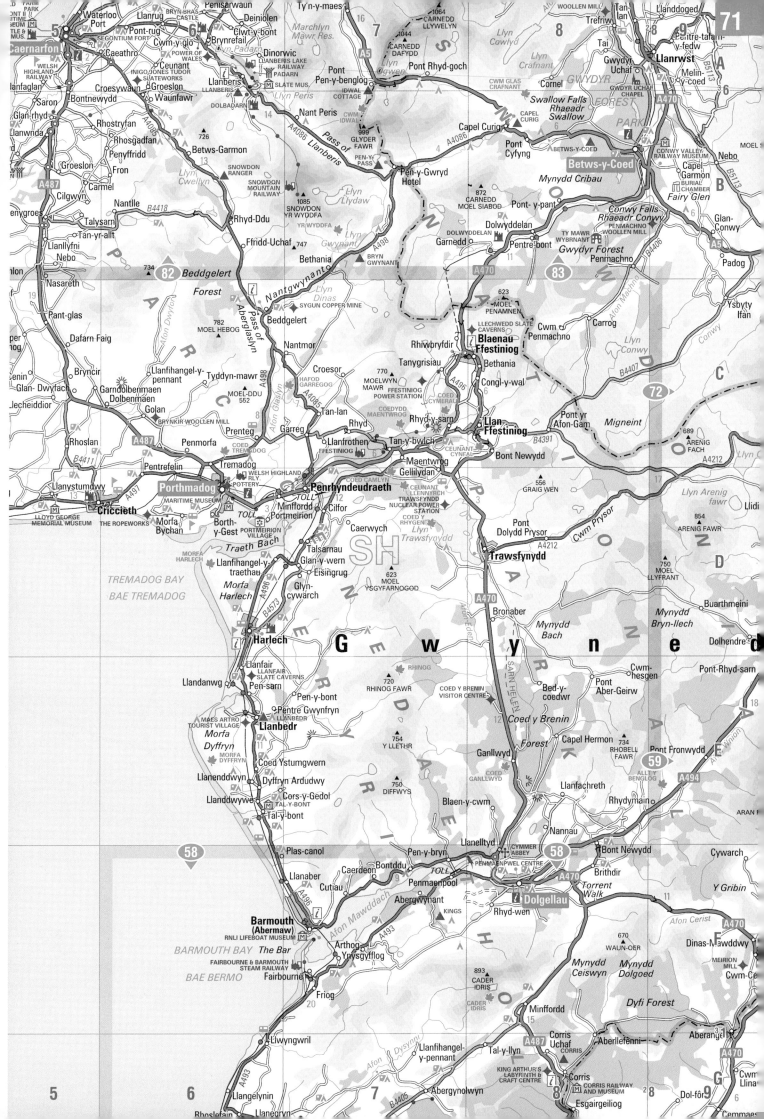

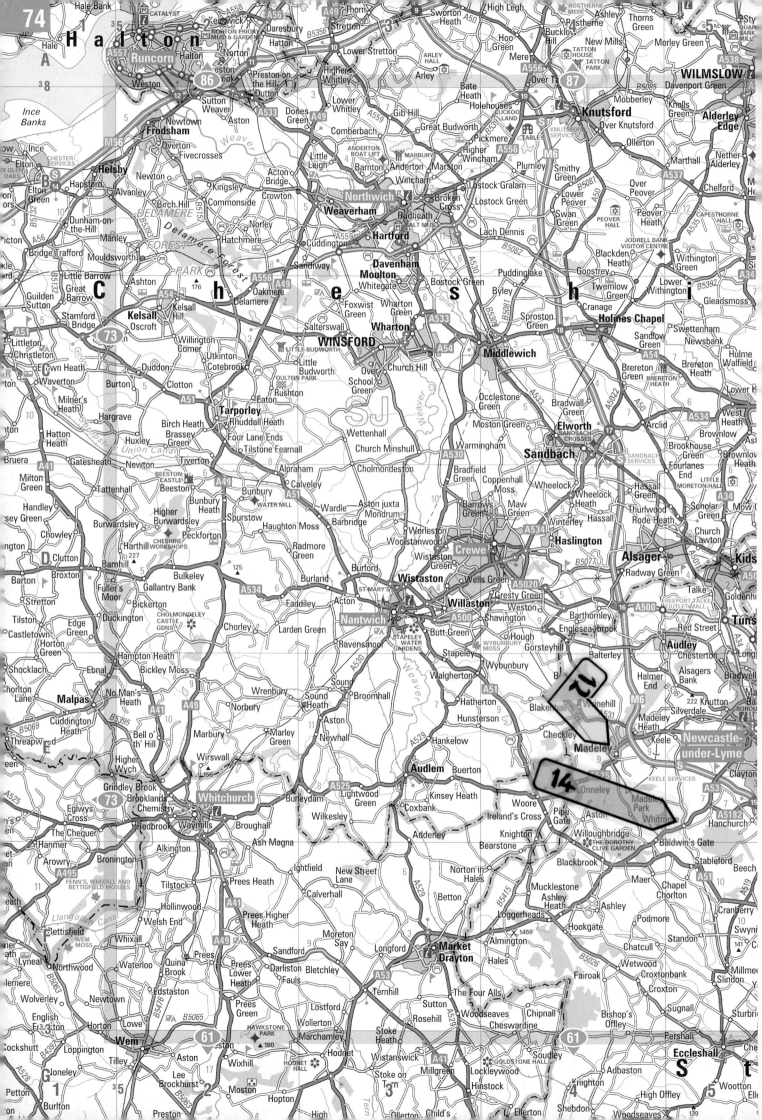

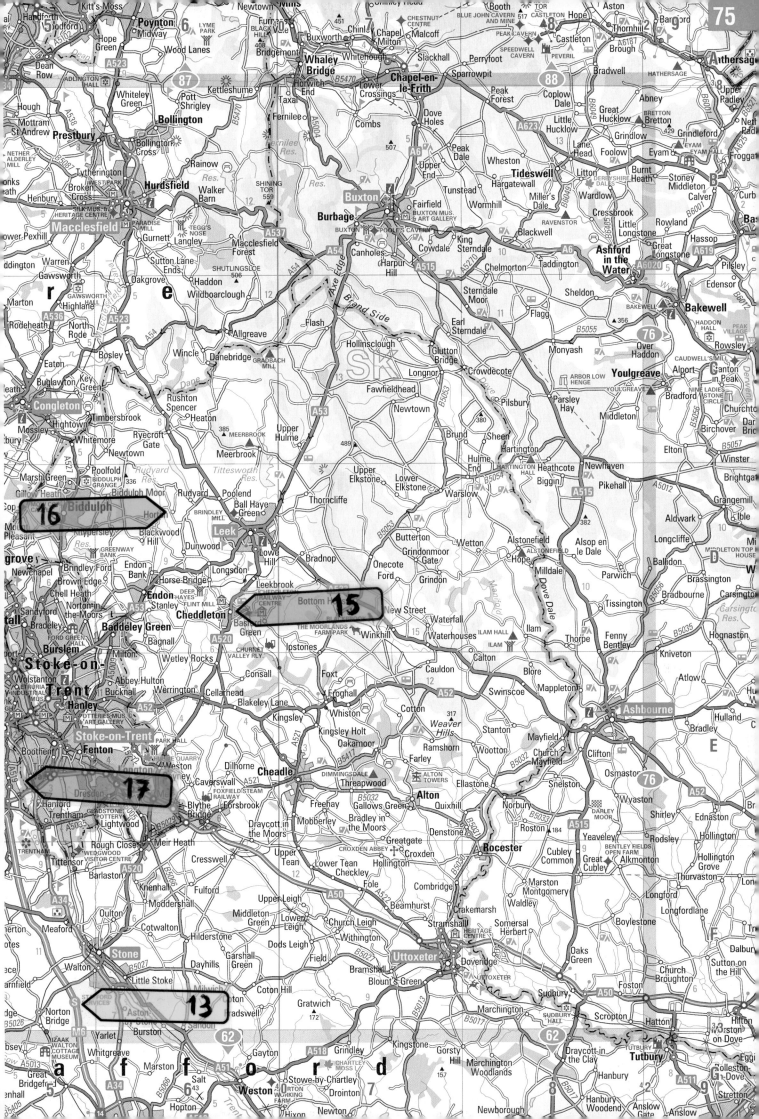

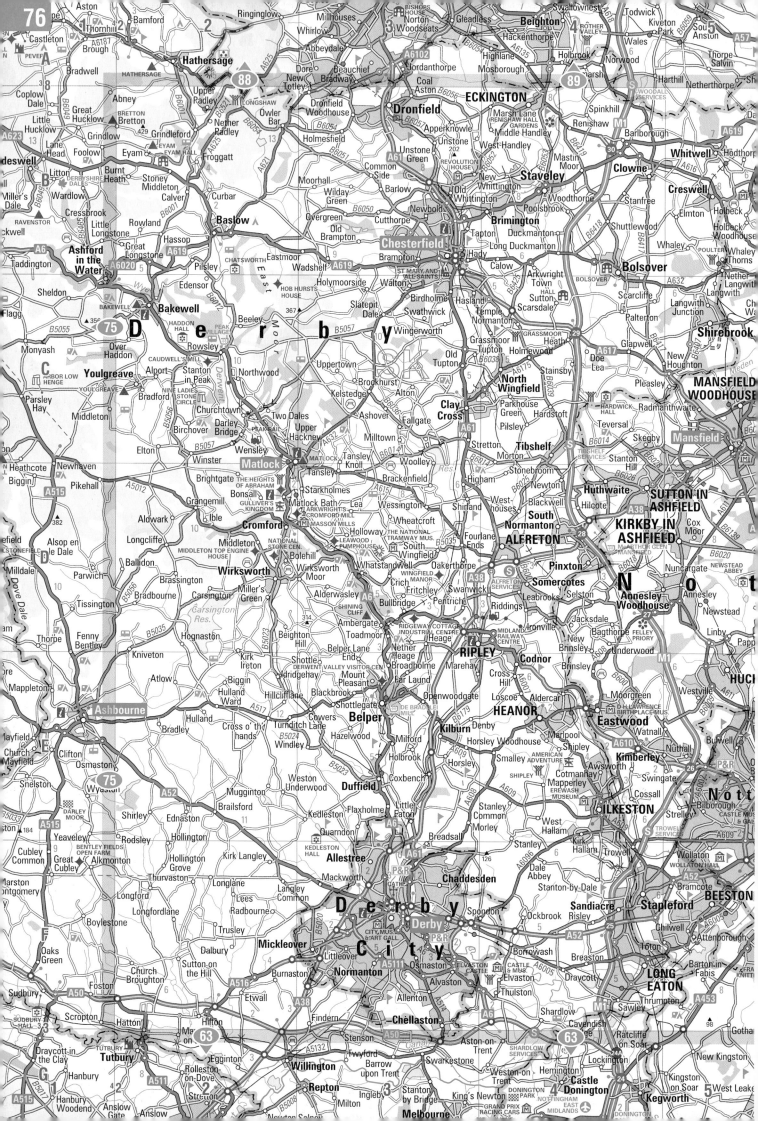

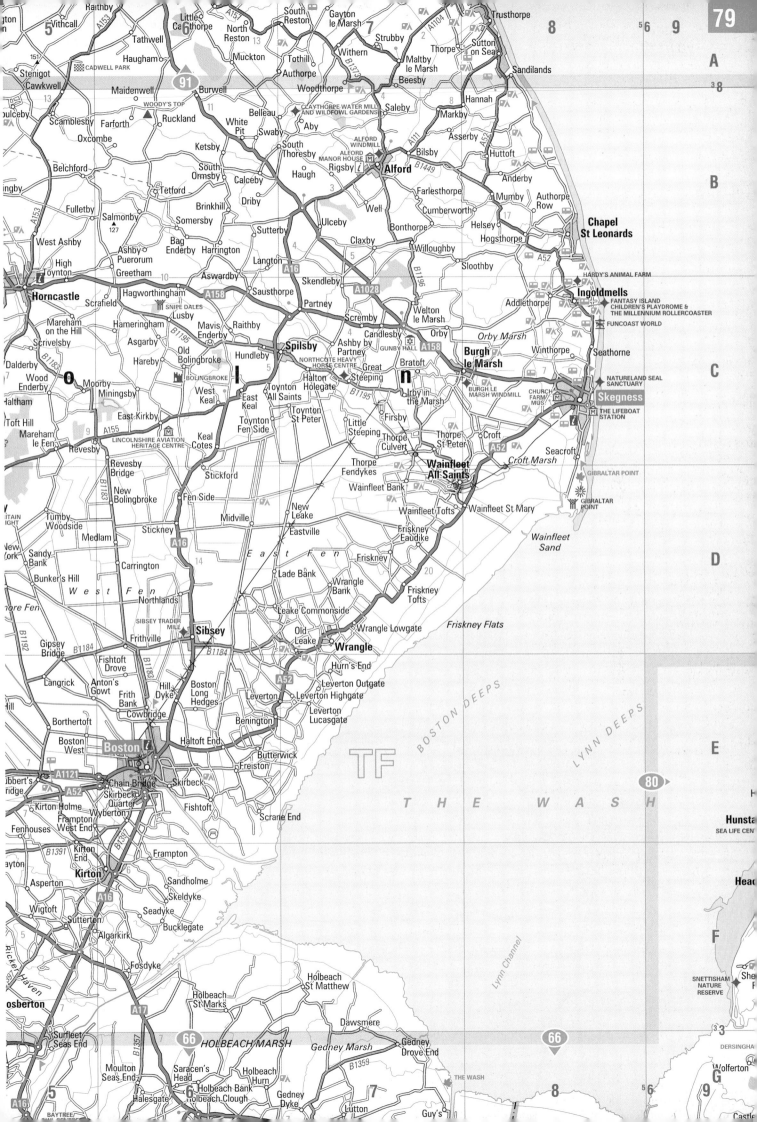

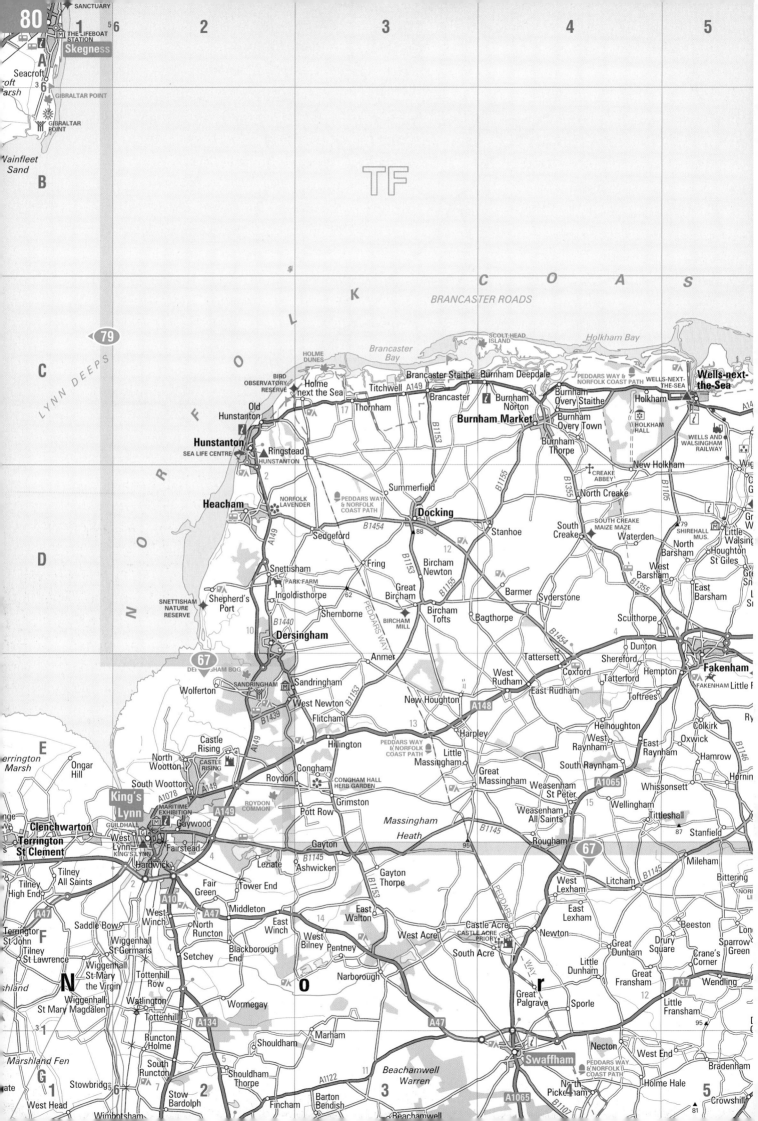

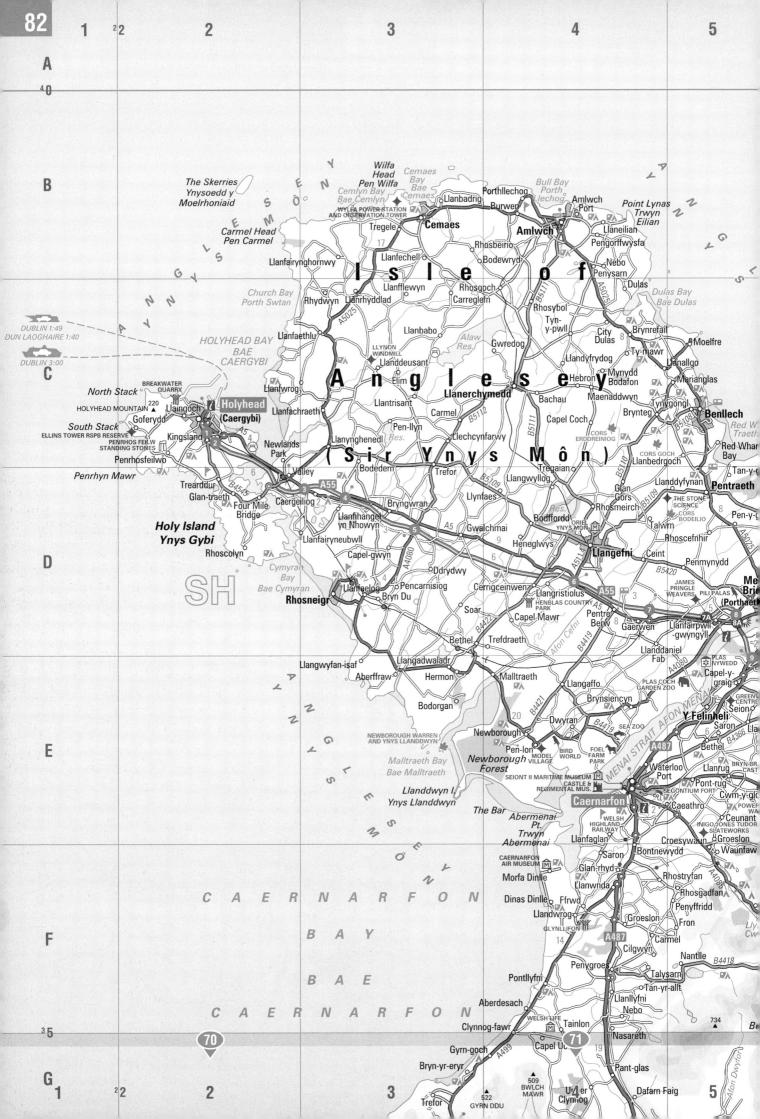

A B C D E F G

1 2 3 4 5

Isle of Anglesey (Sir Ynys Môn)

The Skerries
Ynysoedd y Moelrhoniaid

Carmel Head
Pen Carmel

Wilfa Head
Pen Wilfa
WYLFA POWER STATION
AND OBSERVATION TOWER

Cemaes Bay
Bae Cemaes
Cemlyn Bay
Bae Cemlyn

Tregele
Cemaes
Llanbadrig
Burwen
Porthllechog
Bull Bay
Porth Llechog
Amlwch Port
Amlwch

Point Lynas
Trwyn Eilian

Llanfairynghornwy
Llanfechell
Rhosbeirio
Bodewryd
Llaneilian
Pengorffwysfa

Church Bay
Porth Swtan

Rhydwyn
Llanrhyddlad
Rhosgoch
Carreglefn
Nebo
Penysarn
Dulas

Llanfaethlu
Llanbabo
Rhosybol
Tyn-y-pwll
Dulas Bay
Bae Dulas

LLYNON WINDMILL

Llanddeusant
Elim
Alaw Res.
Gwredog
City Dulas
Brynrefail
Moelfre

HOLYHEAD BAY
BAE CAERGYBI

Llantwrog
Hebron
Llandyfrydog
Mynydd Bodafon
Ty-mawr
Llanallgo
Marianglas

DUBLIN 1:49
DUN LAOGHAIRE 1:40

DUBLIN 3:00

Llantrisant
Llanerchymedd
Bachau
Maenaddwyn
Tynygongl
Benllech

NORTH STACK
BREAKWATER QUARRY

HOLYHEAD MOUNTAIN 220

Llaingoch
Holyhead
(Caergybi)

Llanfachraeth
Carmel
Capel Coch
Brynteg
Red W. Traeth

South Stack
Goferydd
Kingsland

Pen-llyn Res.
Llechcynfarwy

CORS ERDDREINIOG
Llanbedrgoch
Red Wharf Bay

ELLINS TOWER RSPB RESERVE
PENRHOS FEILW STANDING STONES

Penrhosfeilw

Llanynghenedl
Bodedern
Trefor
Tregaian
Glan Gors
Rhosmeirch
Llanddyfnan
Pentraeth
Tan-y-...

Penrhyn Mawr

Valley
Bryngwran
Llangwyllog
Llynfaes
Bodffordd

CORS BODEILIO
THE STONE SCIENCE
Pen-y-...

Trearddur
Glan-traeth

B4545
A55
Caergeiliog

Gwalchmai
ORIEL YNYS MÔN
Talwrn
Rhoscefnhir

Four Mile Bridge

Llanfihangel yn Nhowyn
Heneglwys
Llangefni
Ceint
Penmynydd

Holy Island
Ynys Gybi

Llanfairyneubwll
Ddrydwy
Cerrigceinwen
JAMES PRINGLE WEAVERS
PILI PALAS
B5420

Rhoscolyn

SH

Cymyran Bay
Bae Cymyran

Llanfaelog
Bryn Du
Pencarnisiog
Soar
Llangristiolus
HENBLAS COUNTRY PARK
Pentre Berw
Gaerwen
A55
Llanfairpwll-gwyngyll

Rhosneigr

Bethel
Trefdraeth
Capel Mawr
Llanddaniel Fab
PLAS NEWYDD

Capel-y-graig

Llangwyfan-isaf
Llangadwaladr
Hermon
Malltraeth
Llangaffo
PLAS COCH GARDEN ZOO

GREEN CENTRE

Aberffraw
Bodorgan
Brynsiencyn
SEA ZOO
Seion

NEWBOROUGH WARREN AND YNYS LLANDDWYN

Newborough
Dwyran
FOEL FARM PARK
BIRD WORLD
Y Felinheli
Saron

CAERNARFON BAY

Malltraeth Bay
Bae Malltraeth

Newborough Forest
Pen-lon
MODEL VILLAGE
Bethel
Llanrug
Waterloo Port
Pont-rug
Cwm-y-glo

Llanddwyn I.
Ynys Llanddwyn

SEIONT II MARITIME MUSEUM
CASTLE & REGIMENTAL MUS.
Caernarfon
Caeathro
Ceunant

The Bar
Abermenai Pt.
Trwyn Abermenai

WELSH HIGHLAND RAILWAY
SEGONTIUM FORT
INIGO JONES TUDOR SLATEWORKS

BAY

CAERNARFON AIR MUSEUM
Llanfaglan
Saron
Bontnewydd
Croesywaun
Groeslon
Waunfawr

BAE

Morfa Dinlle
Glan-rhyd
Rhostryfan

Dinas Dinlle
Ffrwd
Penyffridd
Groeslon
Fron

CAERNARFON

Llandwrog
GLYNLLIFON
Carmel

Cilgwyn
Nantlle
B4418

Penygroes
Talysarn
Tan-yr-allt

Pontllyfni
Llanllyfni
Nebo

Aberdesach

WELSH LIFE
Tainlon
Nasareth

Clynnog-fawr
Capel Uch...

Gyrn-goch
Pant-glas

Bryn-yr-eryr

Trefor
BWLCH MAWR
GYRN DDU
U...er Clynnog
Dafarn Faig

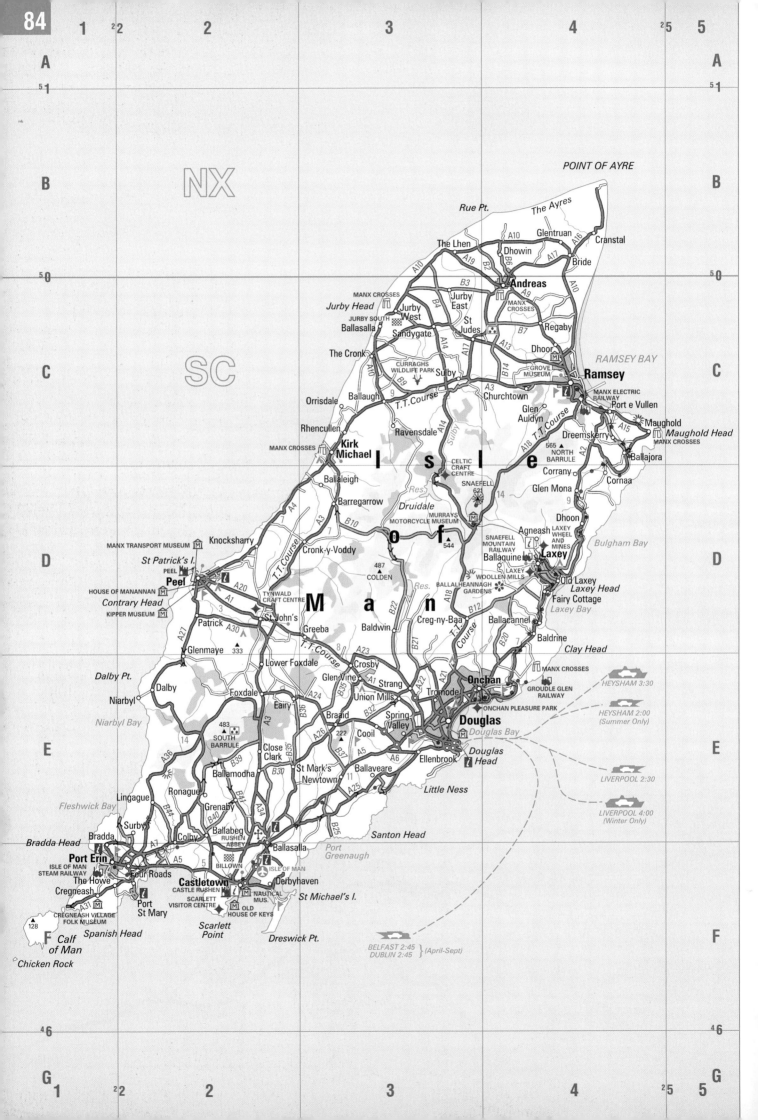

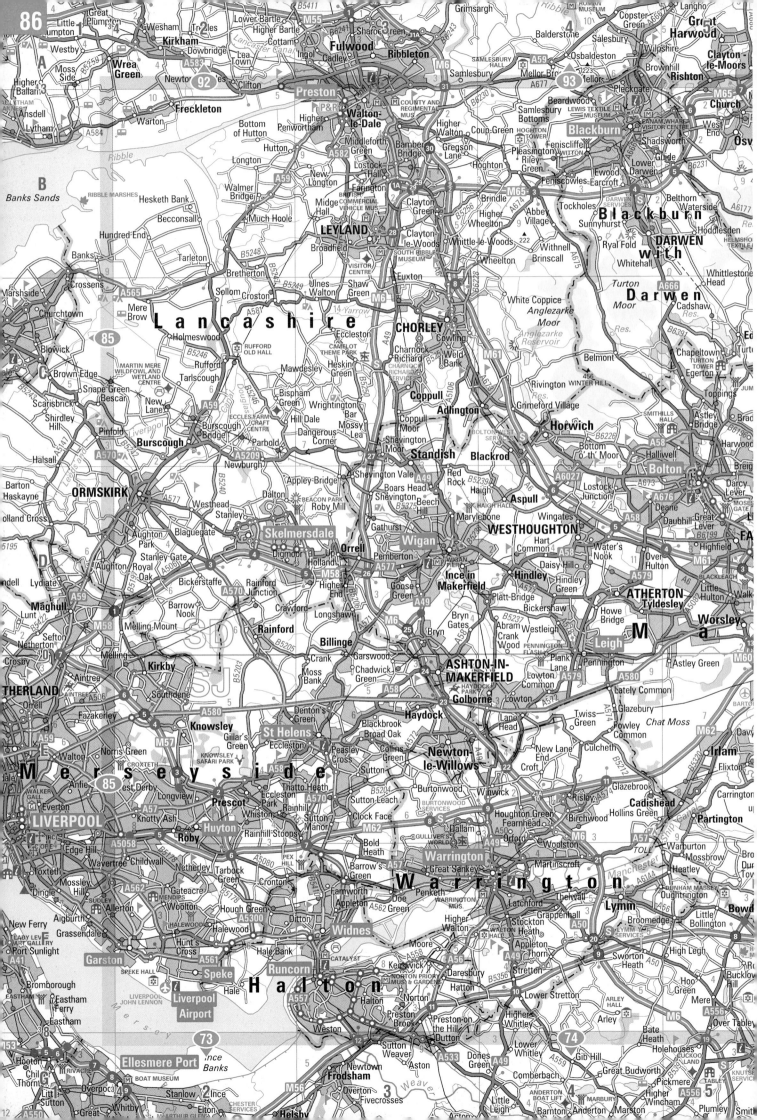

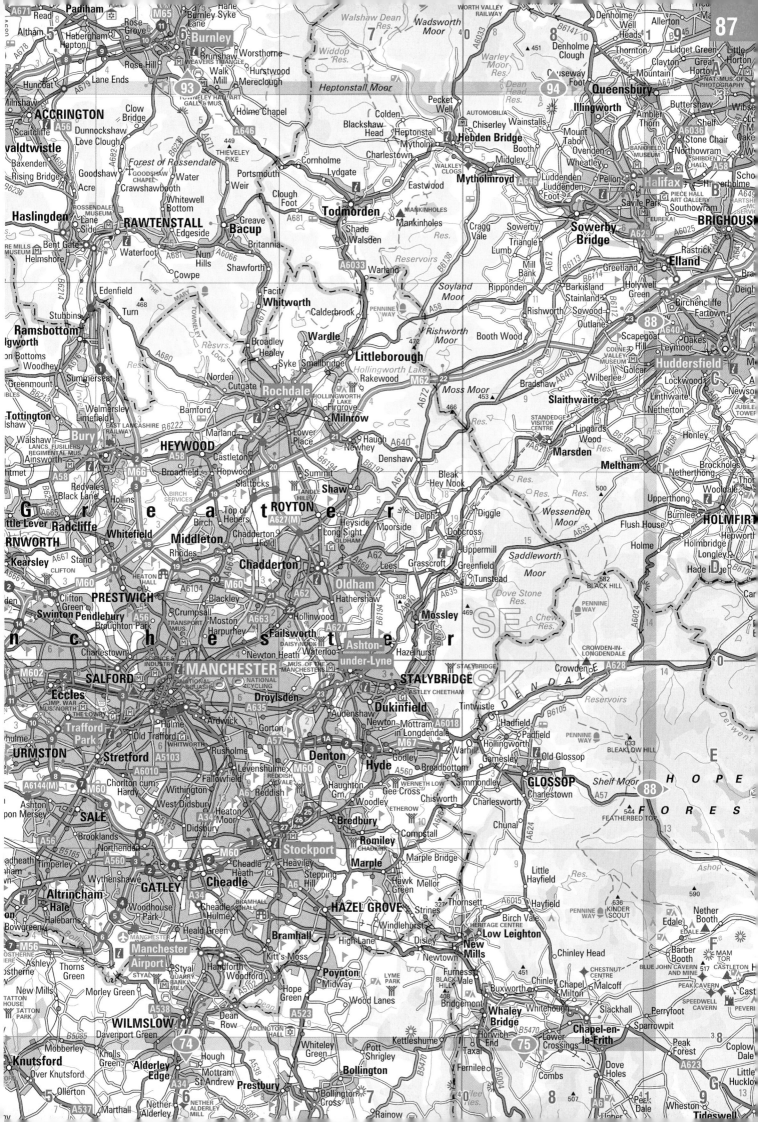

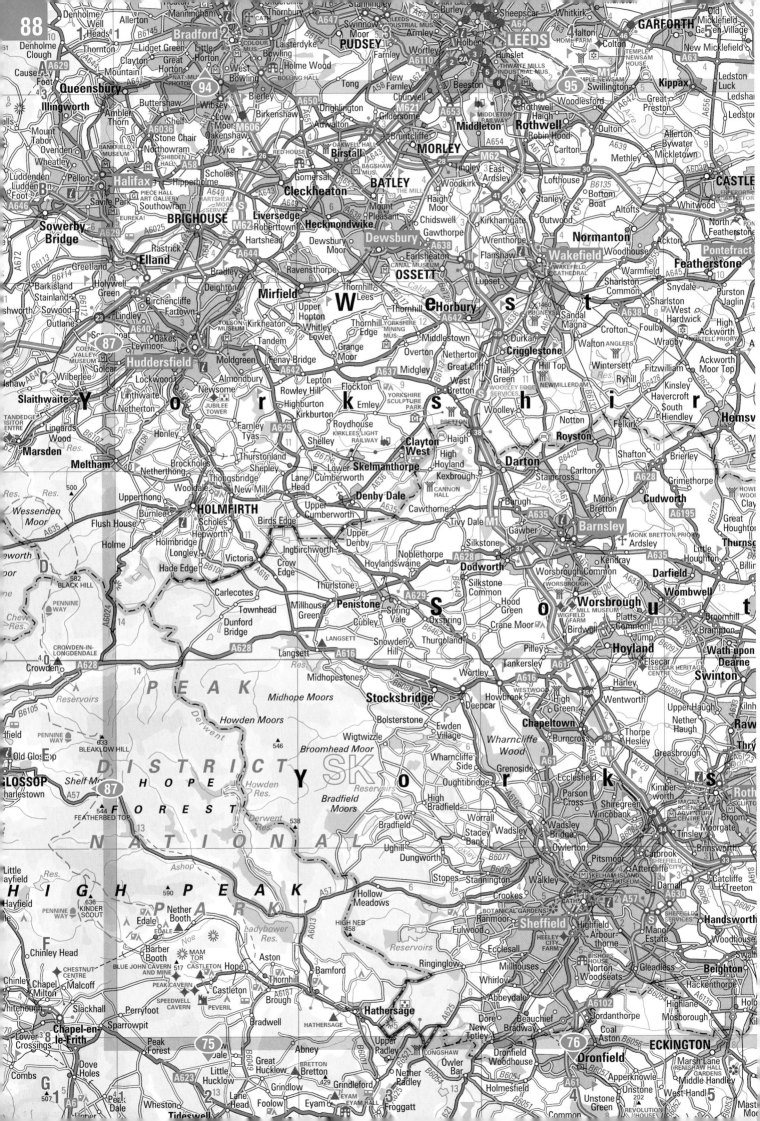

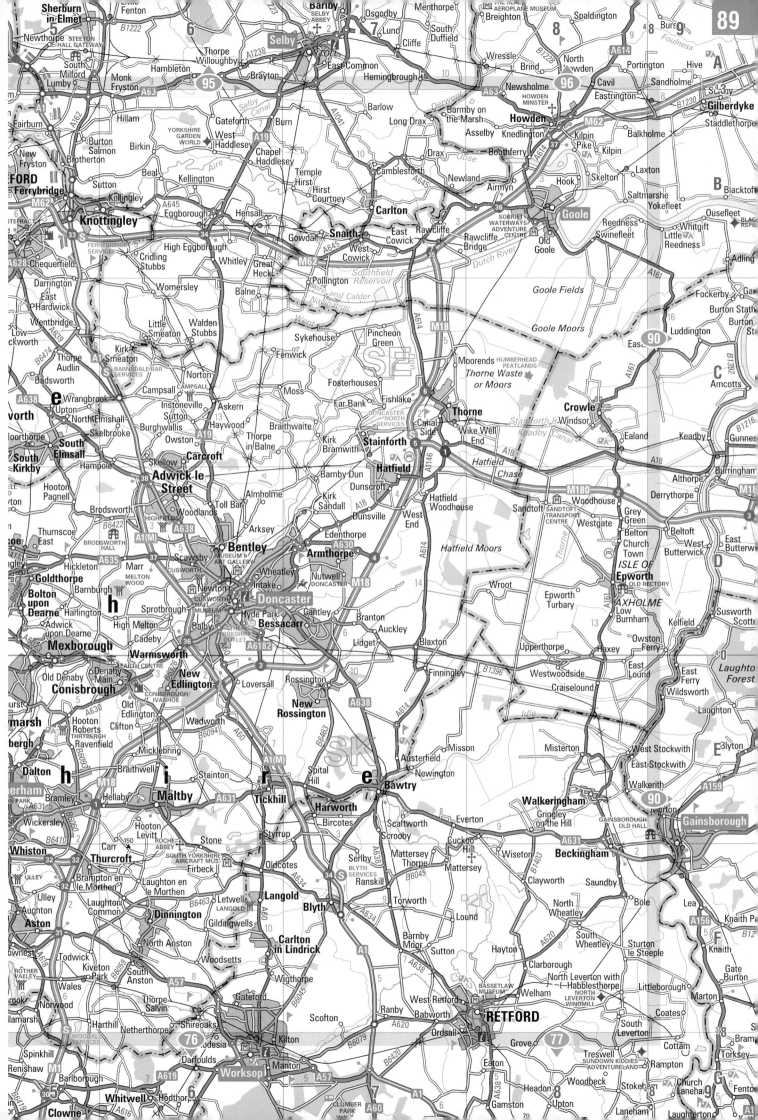

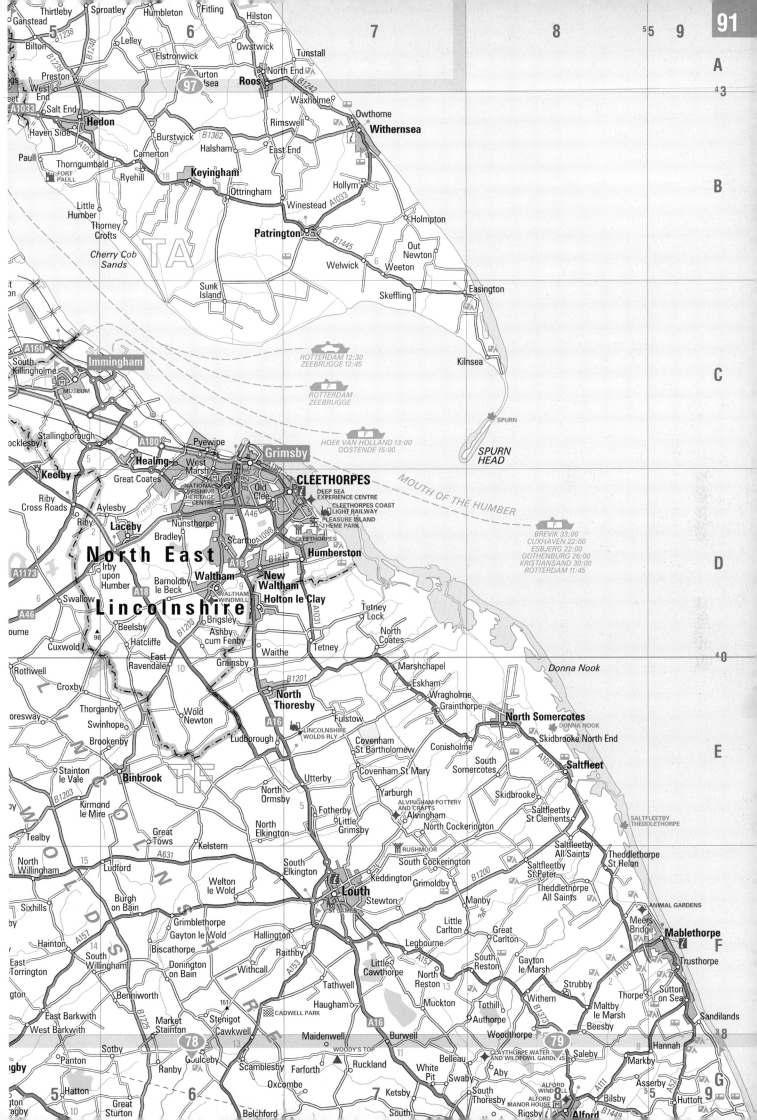

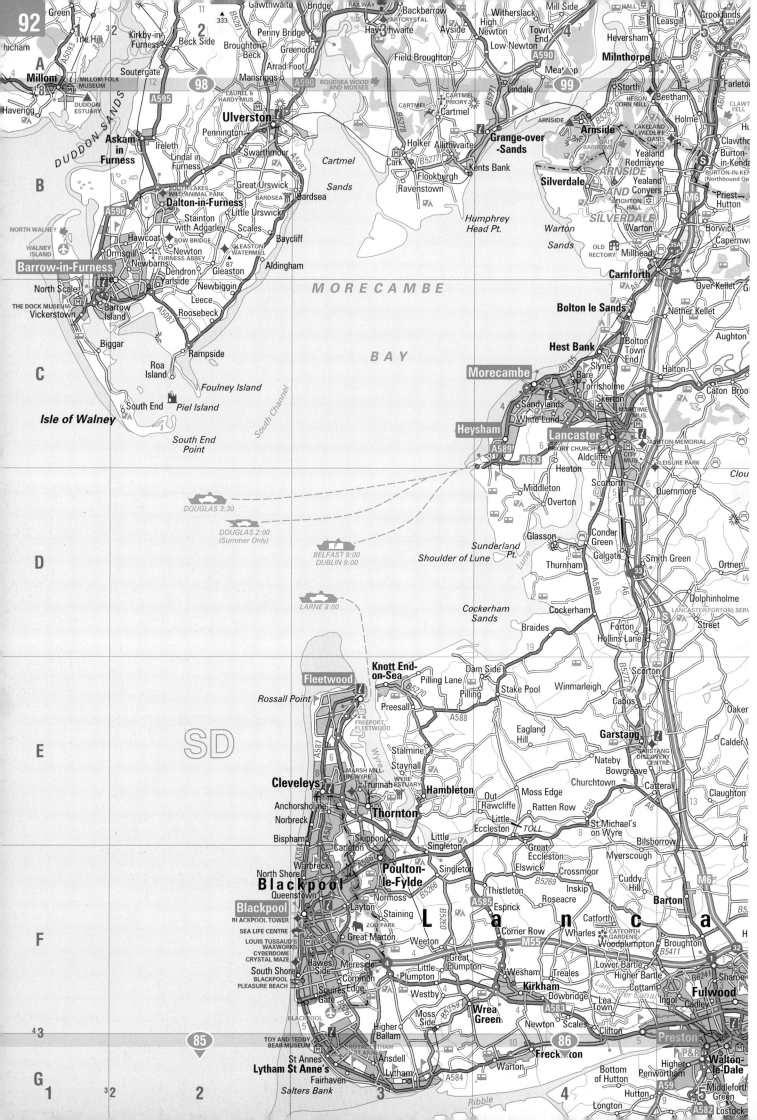

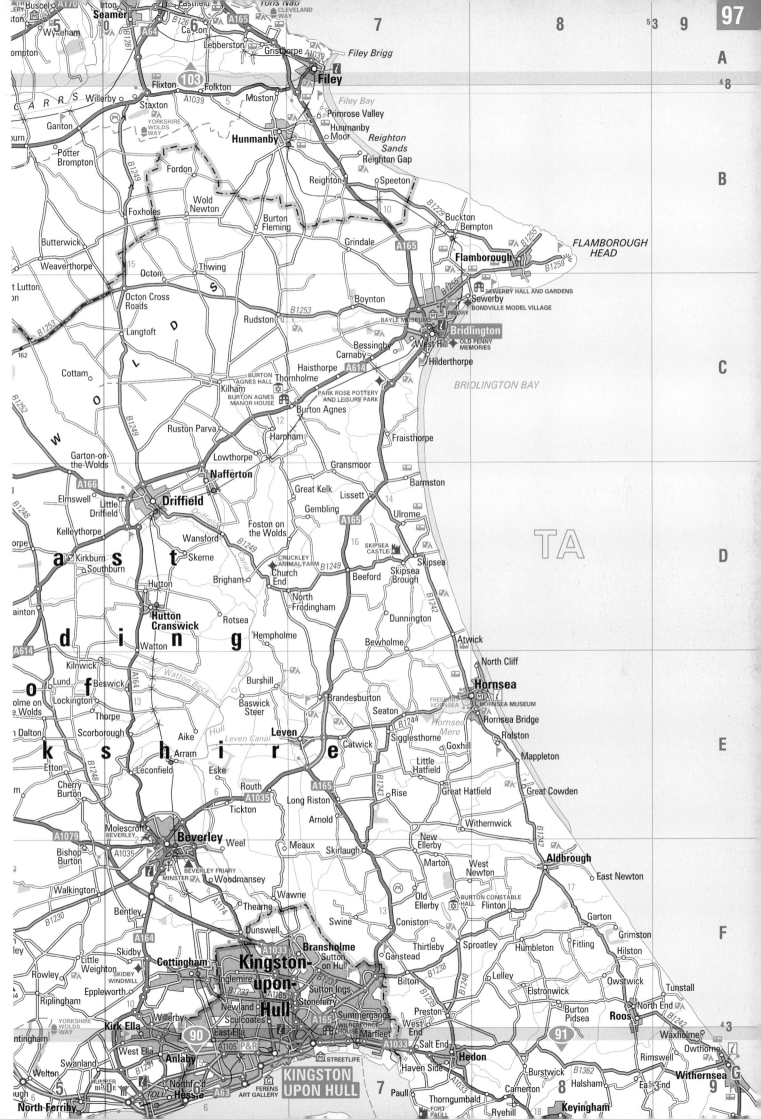

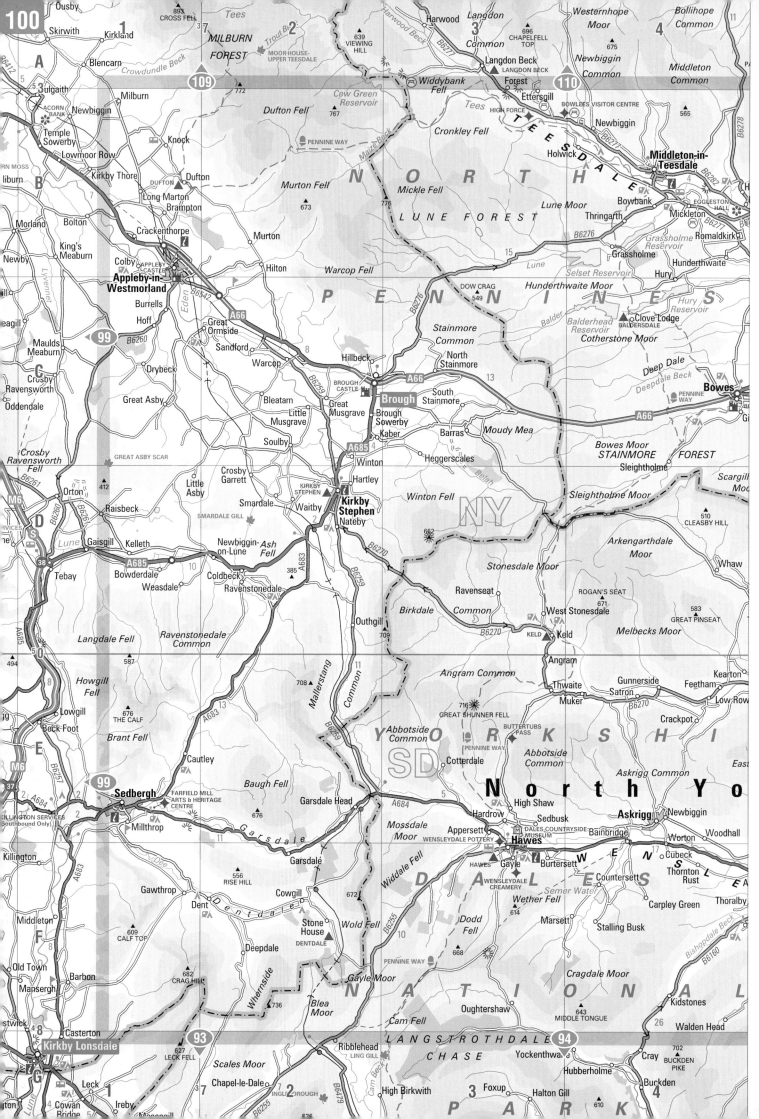

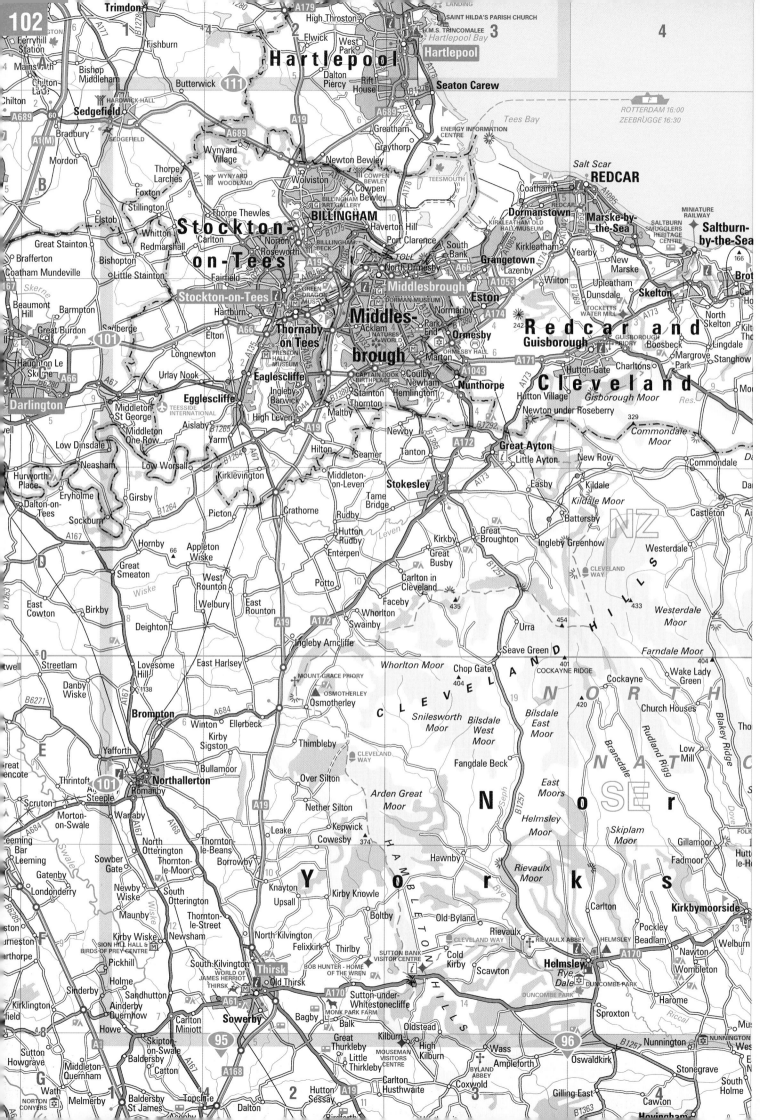

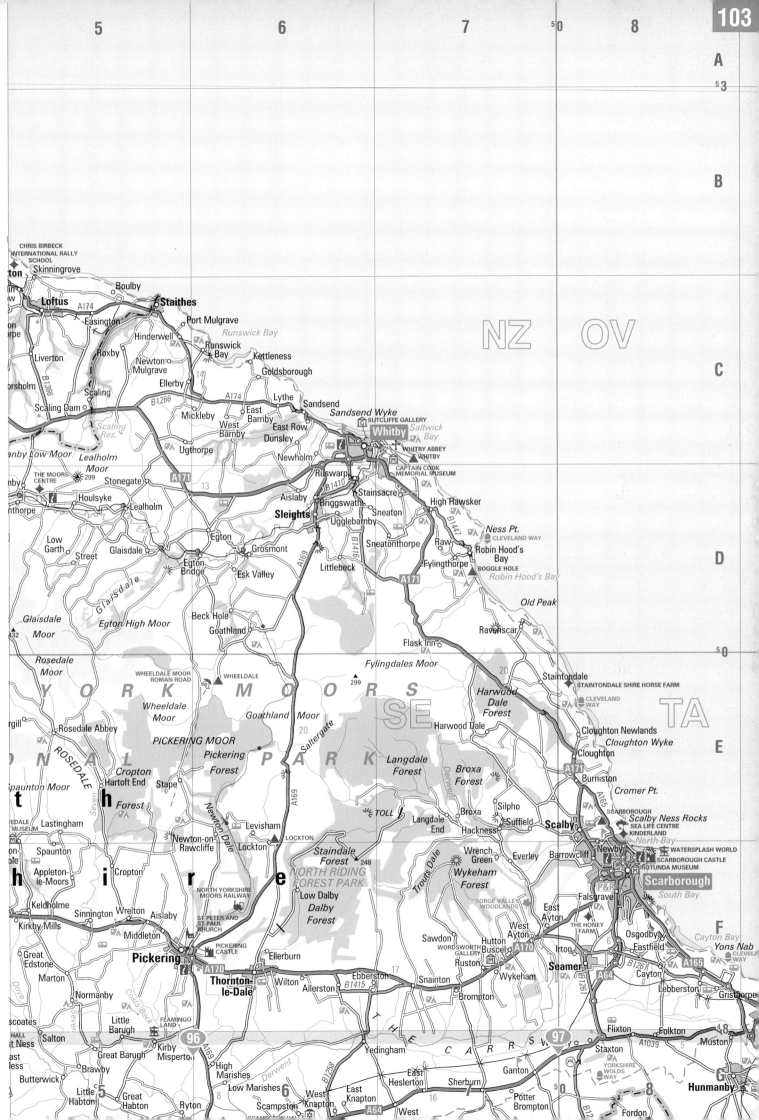

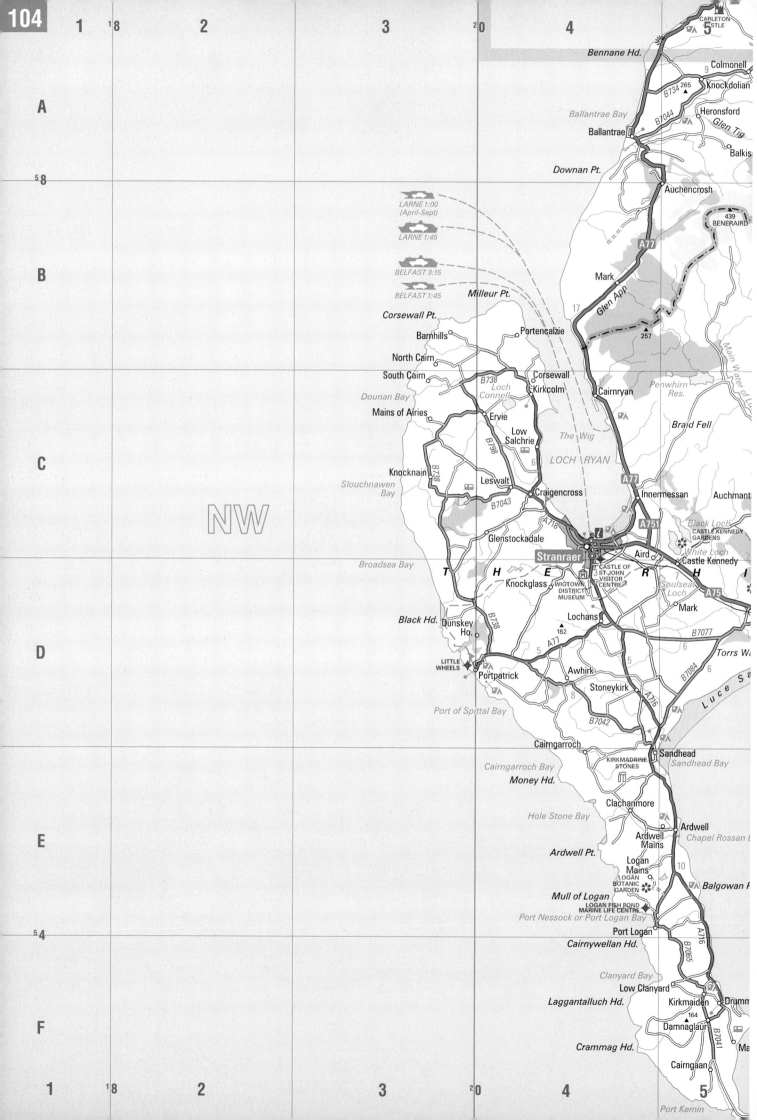

NW

LARNE 1:00
(April-Sept)

LARNE 1:45

BELFAST 3:15

BELFAST 1:45

Bennane Hd.

CARLETON CASTLE

Colmonell

B734 265

Knockdolian

Heronsford

B7044

Glen Tig

Ballantrae Bay

Balkis

Ballantrae

Downan Pt.

Auchencrosh

439
BENERAIRD

A77

Mark

Glen App

17

257

Milleur Pt.

Corsewall Pt.

Barnhills

Portencalzie

North Cairn

Corsewall

South Cairn

B738

Loch
Connell

Kirkcolm

Cairnryan

Penwhirn
Res.

Braid Fell

Dounan Bay

Mains of Airies

Ervie

B798

Low
Salchrie

The Wig

LOCH RYAN

Slouchnawen
Bay

Knocknain

B738

Leswalt

6

Craigencross

A77

Innermessan

Auchmant

B7043

A718

Black Loch

CASTLE KENNEDY
GARDENS

A751

Glenstockadale

A718

White Loch

Stranraer

Castle Kennedy

Broadsea Bay

T   H   E   E   M1   R   H   I

Knockglass

WIGTOWN
DISTRICT
MUSEUM

CASTLE OF
ST JOHN
VISITOR
CENTRE

Aird

Soulseat
Loch

7

A75

Black Hd.

Dunskey
Ho.

B738

Lochans

182

Mark

B7077

Torrs W

LITTLE
WHEELS

A77

5

5

6

Portpatrick

Awhirk

Stoneykirk

B7084

6

Port of Spittal Bay

8

A716

B7042

Cairngarroch

KIRKMADRINE
STONES

Sandhead

Luce Sa

Cairngarroch Bay

Sandhead Bay

Money Hd.

Clachanmore

Hole Stone Bay

Ardwell

Ardwell
Mains

Chapel Rossan

Ardwell Pt.

Logan
Mains

10

LOGAN
BOTANIC
GARDEN

Balgowan

Mull of Logan

LOGAN FISH POND
MARINE LIFE CENTRE

Port Nessock or Port Logan Bay

Port Logan

A716

Cairnywellan Hd.

B7065

Clanyard Bay

Low Clanyard

Laggantalluch Hd.

Kirkmaiden

Drumm

164

B7041

Damnaglaur

Crammag Hd.

Ma

Cairngaan

Port Kemin

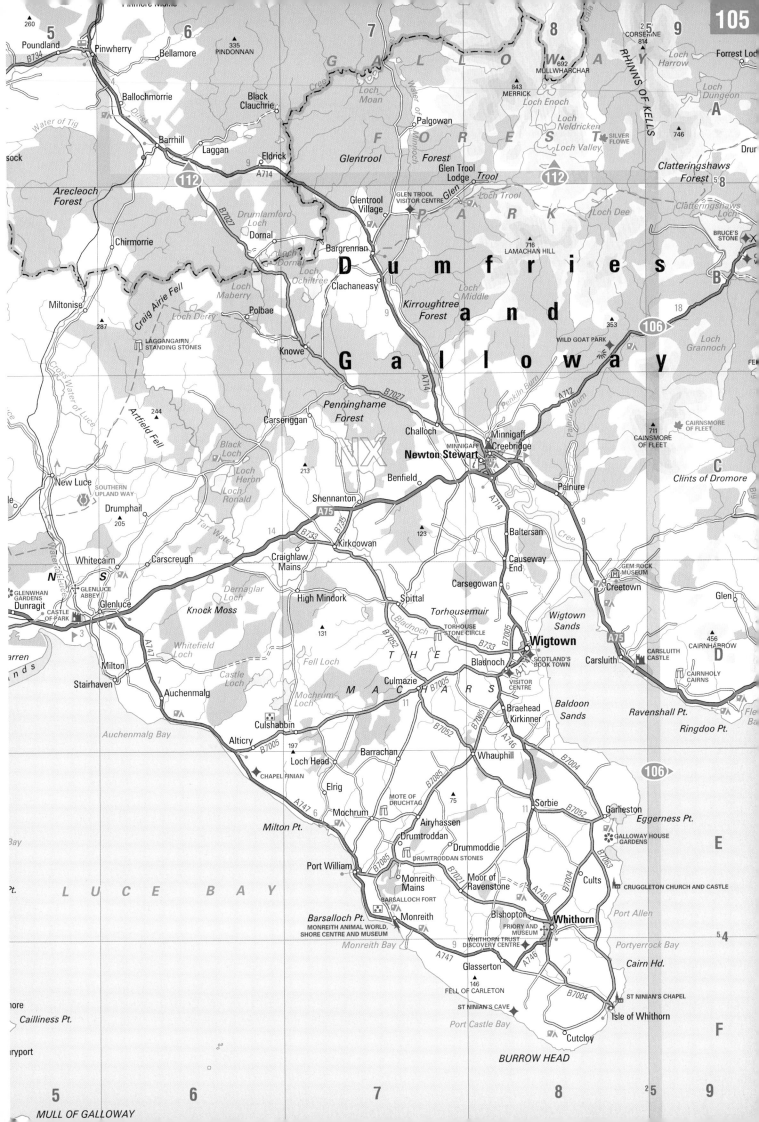

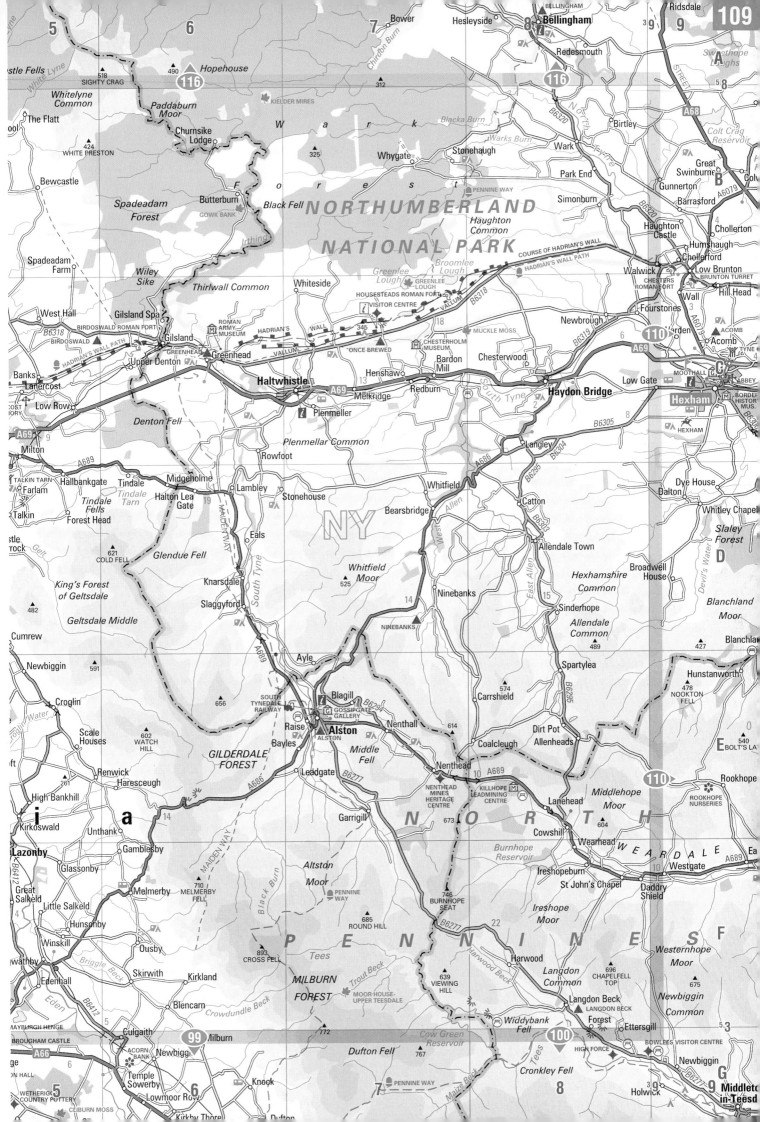

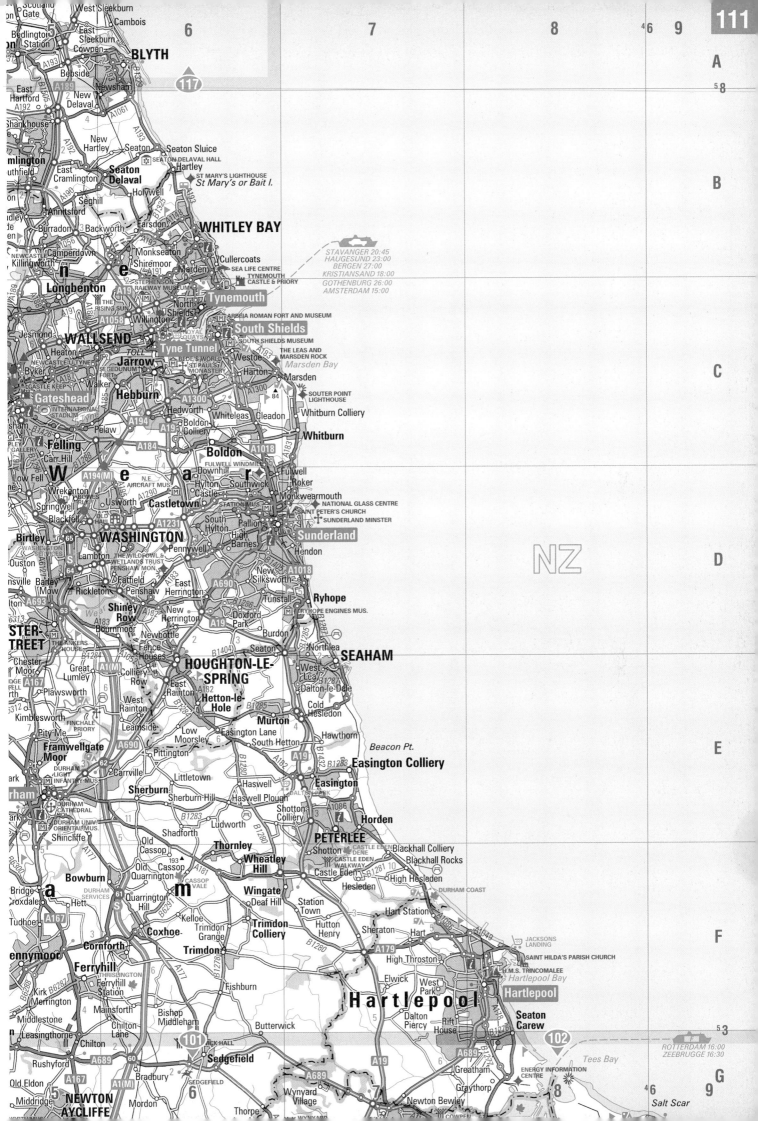

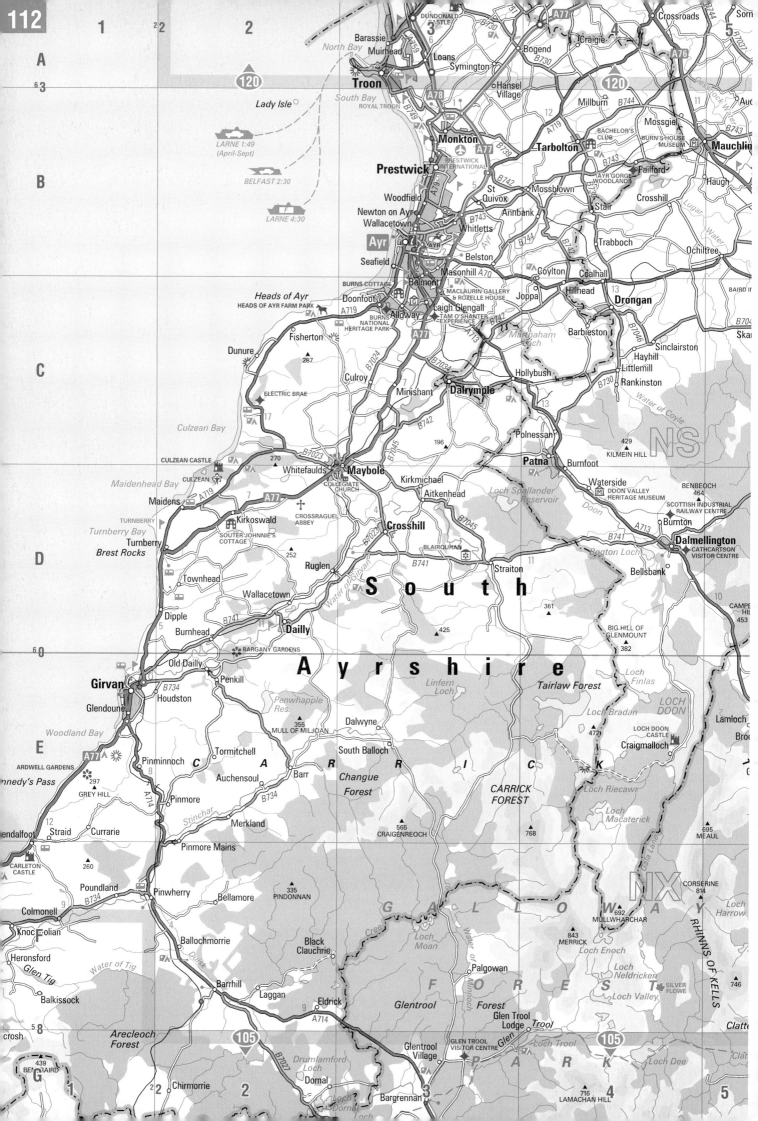

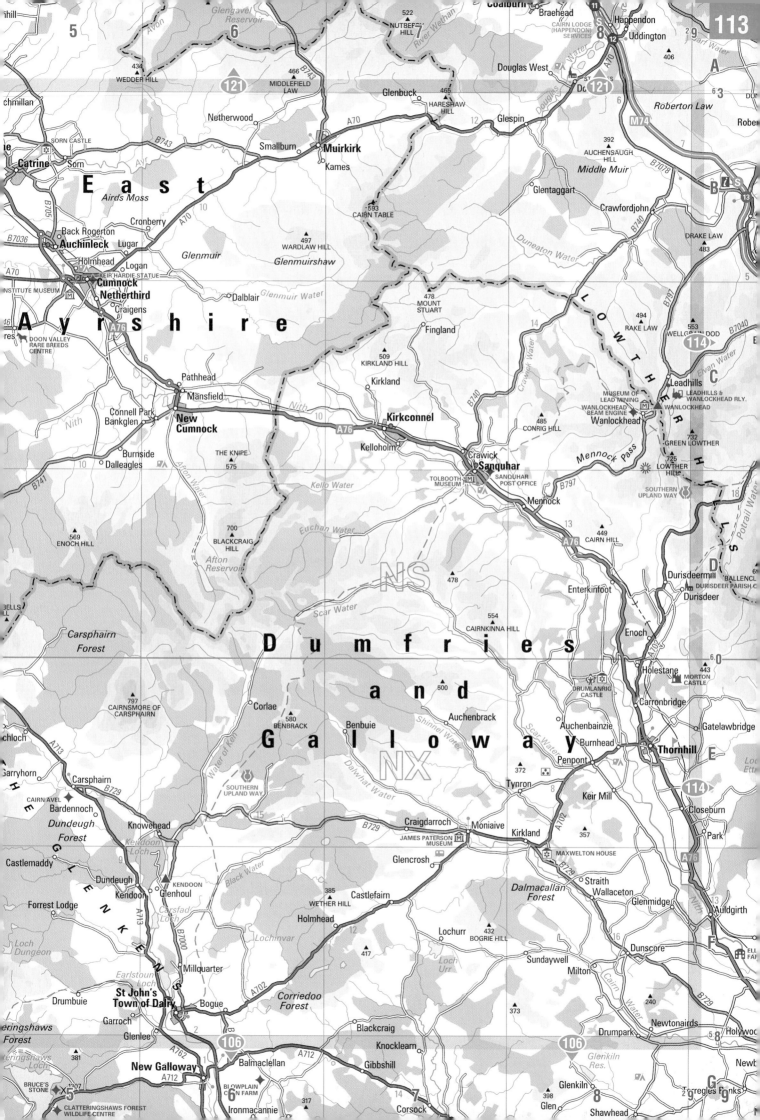

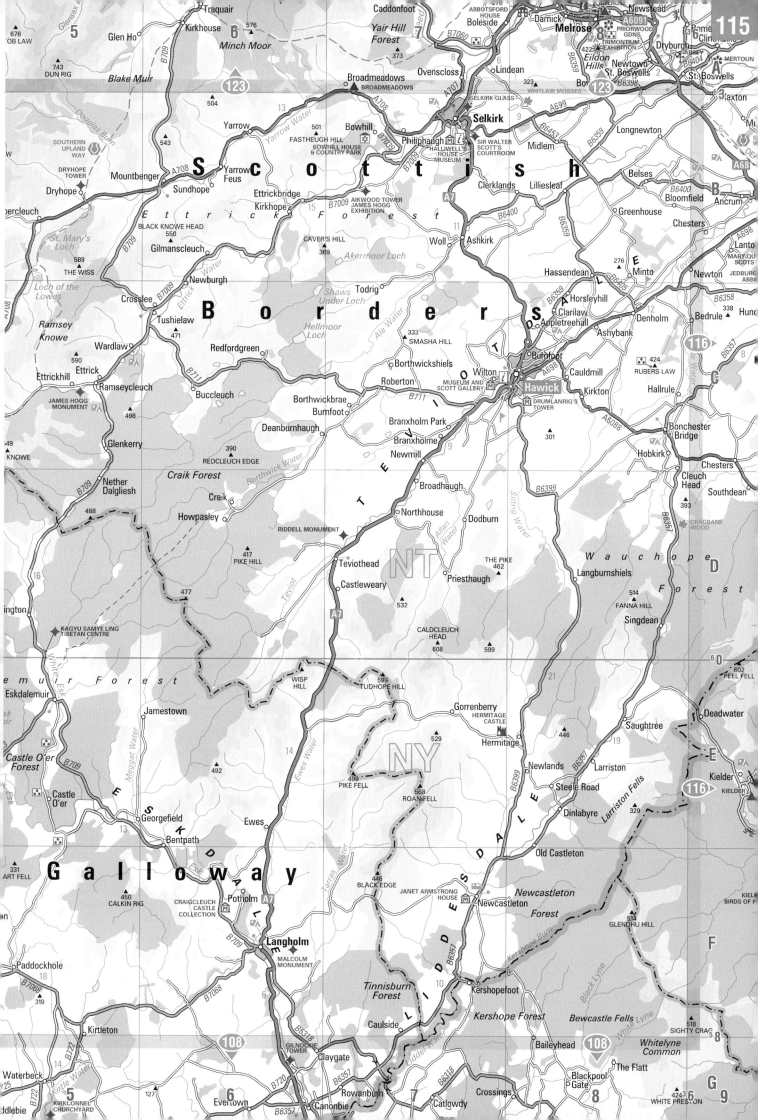

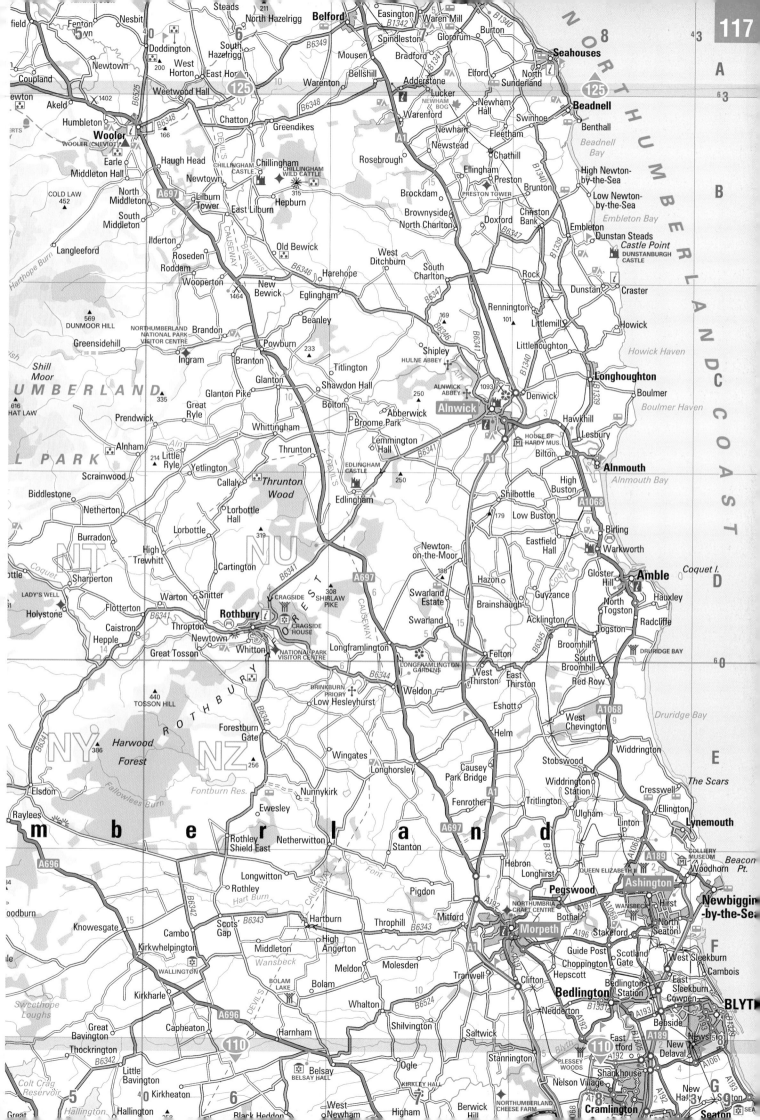

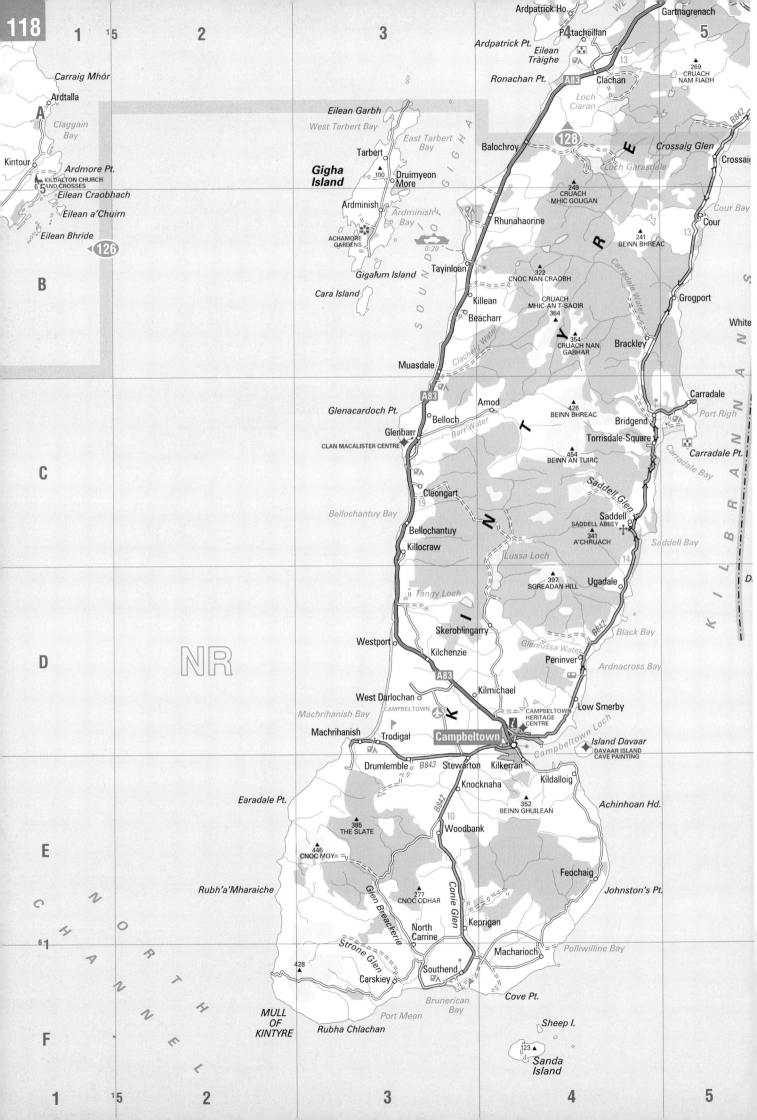

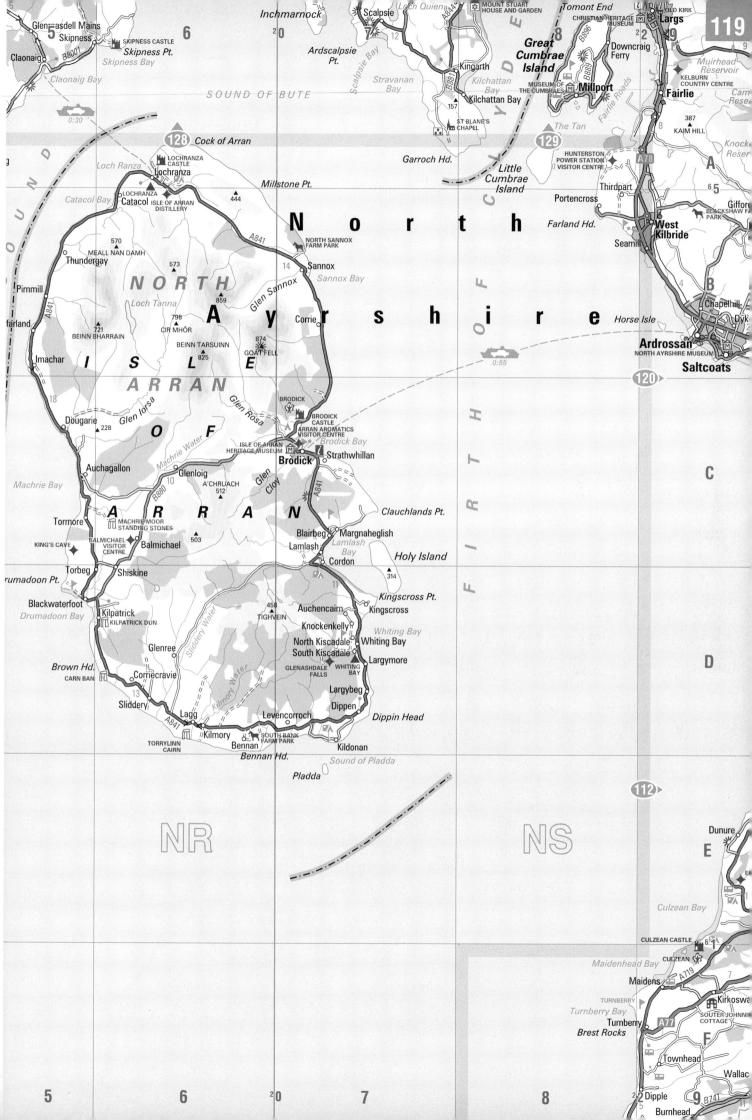

Scalpsie
Inchmarnock
Loch Quien
MOUNT STUART HOUSE AND GARDEN
Tomont End
OLD KIRK
CHRISTIAN HERITAGE MUSEUM
Largs
Downcraig Ferry
Muirhead Reservoir
KELBURN COUNTRY CENTRE

Ardscalpsie Pt.
Kingarth
Great Cumbrae Island
Millport
MUSEUM OF THE CUMBRAES
Fairlie
Kaim Hill
387
KAIM HILL

Stravanan Bay
Kilchattan Bay
Kilchattan Bay

SOUND OF BUTE
157
St Blane's Chapel
The Tan
129
HUNTERSTON POWER STATION VISITOR CENTRE
A78
Thirdpart

128 Cock of Arran
LOCHRANZA CASTLE
Garroch Hd.
Little Cumbrae Island
Portencross
West Kilbride

Loch Ranza
Lochranza
Millstone Pt.
Farland Hd.
Seamill

Catacol Bay
LOCHRANZA
Catacol ISLE OF ARRAN DISTILLERY
444
A841
North
Chapelhill

Pirnmill
MEALL NAN DAMH 570
NORTH SANNOX FARM PARK
Ardrossan
NORTH AYRSHIRE MUSEUM

Thundergay
573
A
y
r
s
h
i
r
e
Horse Isle
Saltcoats

farland
Loch Tanna 859
Glen Sannox
14
Sannox
Sannox Bay
120

721 BEINN BHARRAIN
798 CIR MHÒR
Corrie
0:55

Imachar
ISLE
825 BEINN TARSUINN
874 GOAT FELL

18
OF
Glen Rosa

Dougarie
228
Glen Iorsa
BRODICK
BRODICK CASTLE
ARRAN AROMATICS VISITOR CENTRE
Brodick Bay

ARRAN
Machrie Water
ISLE OF ARRAN HERITAGE MUSEUM
Brodick
Strathwhillan

Auchagallon
Glenloig
A'CHRUACH 512
Glen Cloy
Clauchlands Pt.

Machrie Bay
B880 10
503
A841

Tormore
MACHRIE MOOR STANDING STONES
Blairbeg
Margnaheglish
Lamlash Bay
Holy Island

KING'S CAVE
BALMICHAEL VISITOR CENTRE
Balmichael
Lamlash
Cordon

Torbeg
Shiskine
Sliddery Water
314

rumadoon Pt.
458 TIGHVEIN
Kingscross Pt.

Blackwaterfoot
Kilpatrick
KILPATRICK DUN
11
Auchencairn
Kingscross

Drumadoon Bay
Glenree
Knockenkelly

Brown Hd.
CARN BAN
Glenree
Kilmory Water
North Kiscadale
South Kiscadale
Whiting Bay
Largymore

Corriecravie
GLENASHDALE FALLS
WHITING BAY

13
Sliddery
Lagg
Largybeg
Dippen

Kilmory
Levencorroch
Dippin Head

TORRYLINN CAIRN
Bennan
SOUTH BANK FARM PARK
Kildonan

Bennan Hd.
Sound of Pladda

Pladda

NR
NS

Dunure

Culzean Bay

CULZEAN CASTLE
CULZEAN
Maidenhead Bay

Maidens

TURNBERRY
Turnberry Bay
Kirkoswald
SOUTER JOHNNIE'S COTTAGE

Turnberry
Brest Rocks
A77
Townhead

Dipple
Burnhead

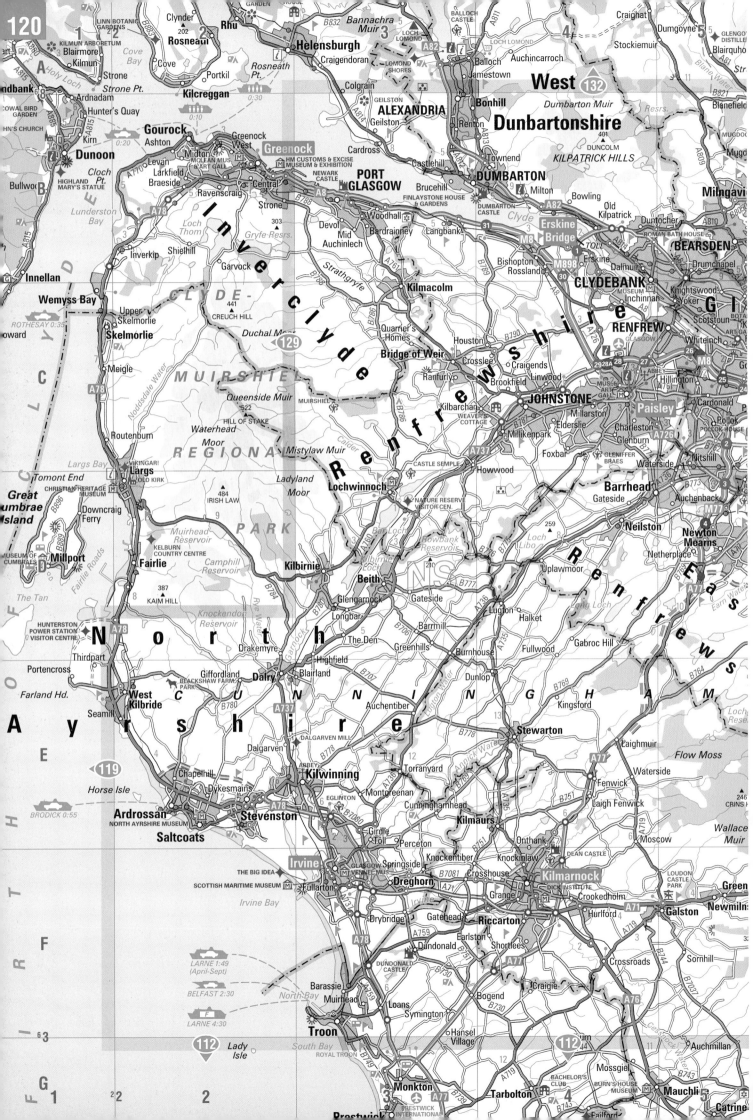

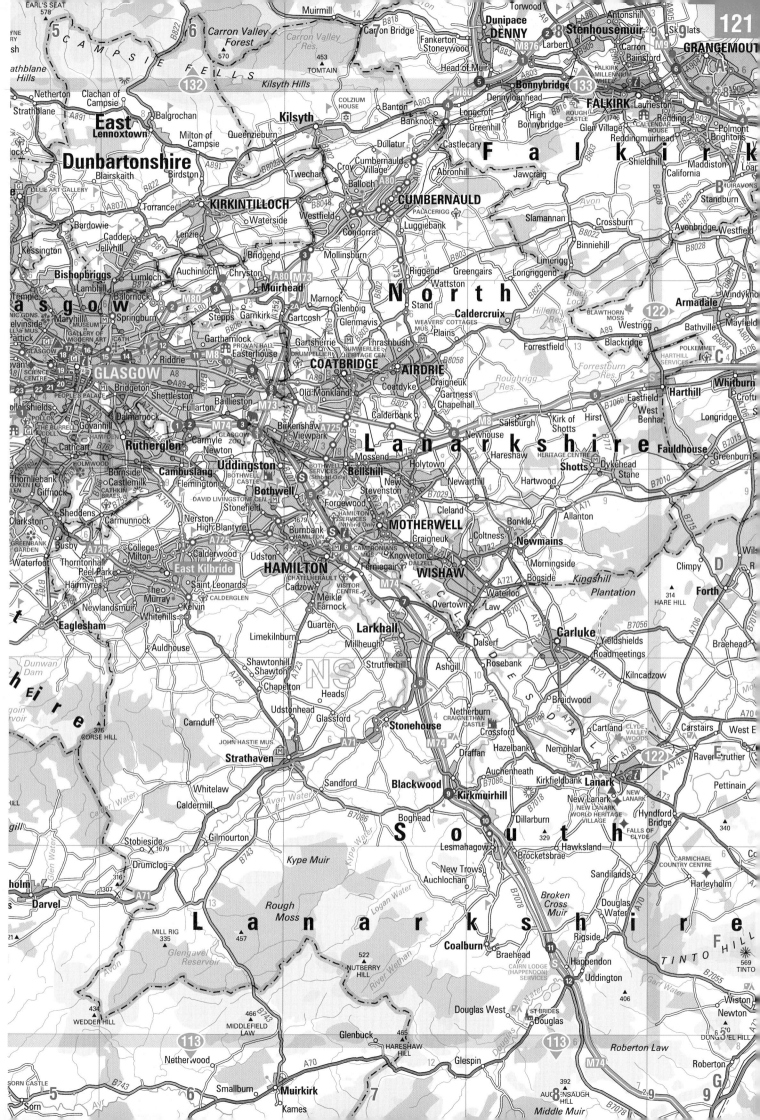

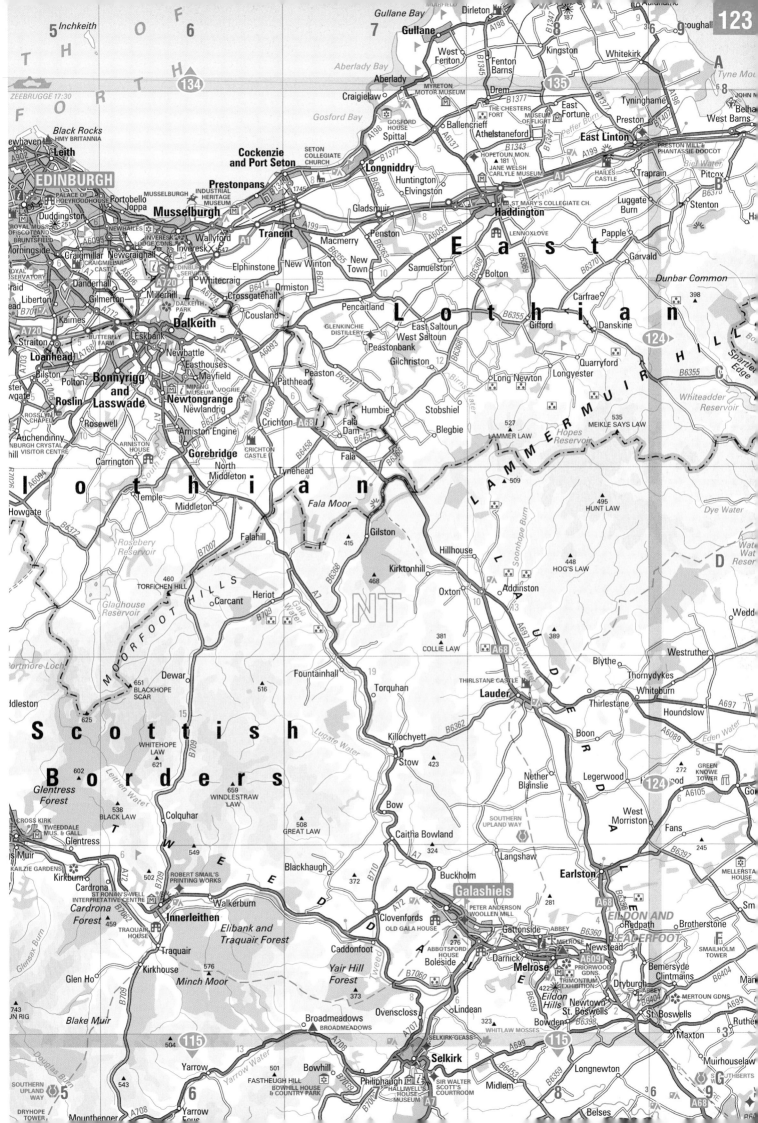

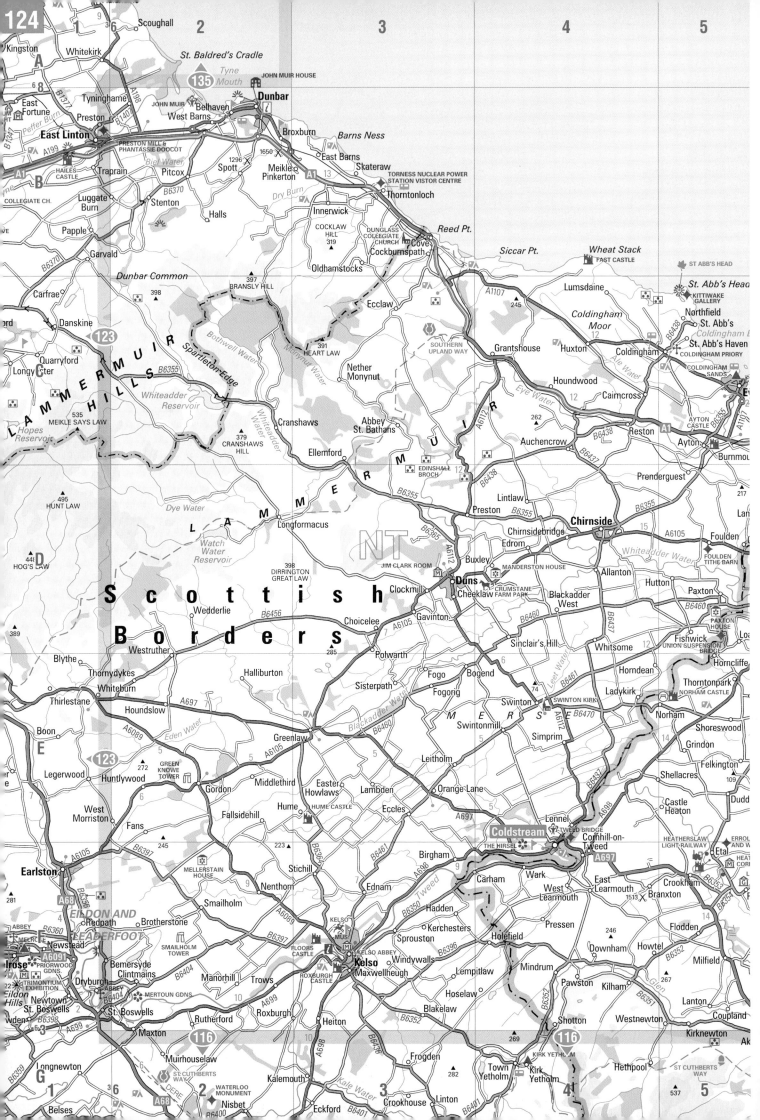

5 ⁴0 6 7 8 ⁴3 9

A

⁶8

B

C

D

Bay

Lamberton Beach

EYEMOUTH MUSEUM
yemouth

mberton

Clappers

5

1333 ✕

Highfields

Berwick-upon-Tweed

B6461

BARRACKS MUSEUM
& RAMPARTS

East
Ord

Tweedmouth

TOWER HOUSE POTTERY

Spittal

Tweed

anend

A698

Prior
Park

Redshin Cove

108 ▲

Scremerston

Murton
Thornton

West Allerdean

Shoresdean

Ancroft

North Low

Cheswick

Goswick

NU

E

NORTHUMBERLAND

Berrington

South Low

Haggerston

Beal

LINDISFARNE

Emmanuel Hd.

**Holy Island
(Lindisfarne)**

Bowsden

82

12

B6353

Barmoor
Lane End

Causeway
Holy
Island
Sands

Holy
Island

LINDISFARNE CASTLE

Castle Pt.

Fenham

HERITAGE
CENTRE

LINDISFARNE
PRIORY

*Farne
Islands*

HUT SMITHY
OOD WORKSHOP

Barmoor
Castle

West
Kyloe

Fenwick

*Guile
Pt.*

Staple Sound

THERSLAW
NMILL

B6353

Lowick

*Kyloe
Hills*

East
Kyloe

Buckton

Elwick

Ross

*Budle
Bay*

BAMBURGH
CASTLE

FARNE ISLANDS

Inner Sound

DY WATERFORD HALL

ST CUTHBERTS
WAY

Holburn

Detchant

Middleton

Budle

Bamburgh

F

ord

157

Hetton
Steads

211 ▲

North Hazelrigg

Belford

Easington

Spindlestone

Glororum

Burton

Kimmerston

Nesbit

Doddington

South
Hazelrigg

Mousen

Bradford

Elford

North
Sunderland

Seahouses

Fenton
Town

200

West
Horton

East Horton

Warenton

Bellshill

B6349

B1341

Newtown

1402 ✕

B6625

Weetwood Hall

117

10

Chatton

Warenford

Adderstone

Lucker

B6348

Newham
Hall

Bea

117

⁴3

A697

Humbleton

B6348

166

Greendikes

Warenford

A1

NEWHAM
BOG

Newham

Swinhoe

Benthall

Wooler

WOOLER (CHEVIOT)

5 ⁴0

Haugh Head

6

CHILLINGHAM
CASTLE

CHILLINGHAM
WILD CATTLE

Newton

Rosebrough

7

Fleetham

Newstead

Chathill

*Beadnell
Bay*

8

⁴3

9

High Newton-
by-the-Sea

Earle

Middleton Hall

Bradford

Ellingham

Preston

G

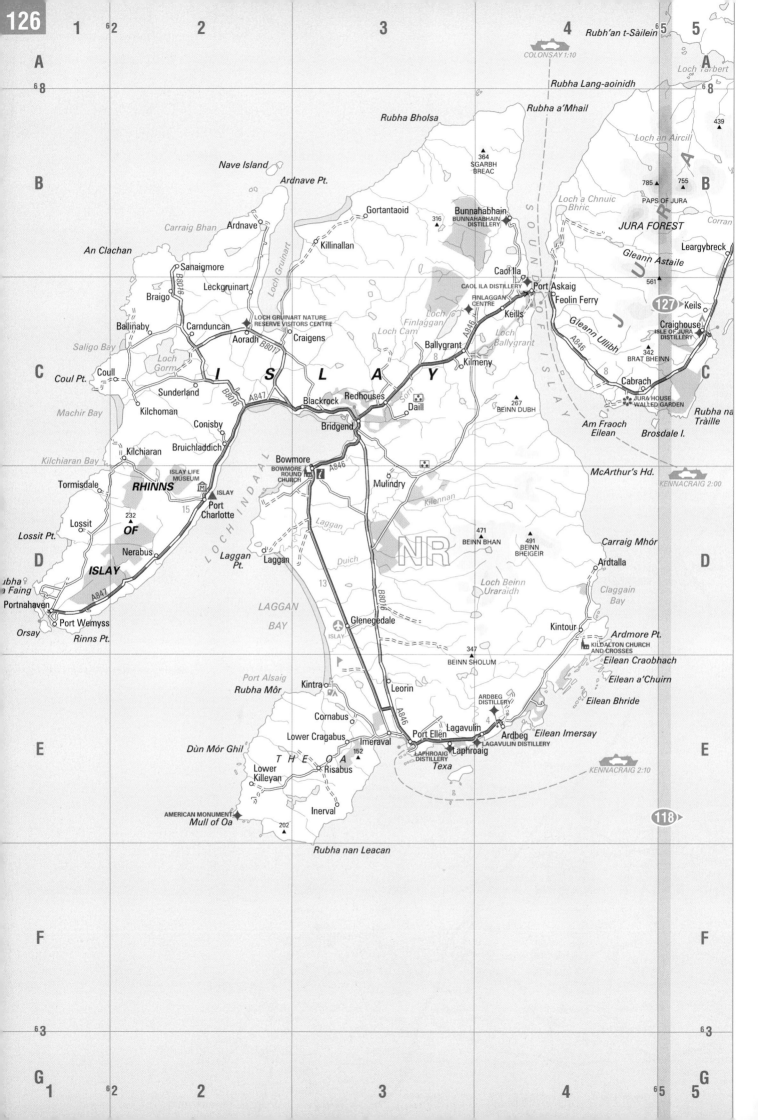

A B C D E F G

1 2 3 4 5

COLONSAY 1:10

Rubh'an t-Sàilein

Loch Tarbert

Rubha Lang-aoinidh

Rubha a'Mhail

Rubha Bholsa

Loch an Aircill

439

Nave Island

Ardnave Pt.

364
SGARBH
BREAC

785 755

PAPS OF JURA

Loch a Chnuic
Bhric

Gortantaoid

Bunnahabhain
BUNNAHABHAIN
DISTILLERY

JURA FOREST

Corran

Carraig Bhan

Ardnave

Killinallan

316

Leargybreck

An Clachan

Sanaigmore

Leckgruinart

Caol Ila

CAOL ILA DISTILLERY

Port Askaig

Gleann Astaile

561

Braigo

Loch Gruinart

FINLAGGAN
CENTRE

Feolin Ferry

127 Keils

Ballinaby

Carnduncan

LOCH GRUINART NATURE
RESERVE VISITORS CENTRE

Aoradh

Craigens

Loch
Finlaggan

Keills'

Loch Cam

Ballygrant

Loch
Ballygrant

Kilmeny

Gleann Ullibh

A846

Craighouse
ISLE OF JURA
DISTILLERY

342
BRAT BHEINN

Saligo Bay

Coul Pt. Coull

I S L A Y

8

Cabrach

JURA HOUSE
WALLED GARDEN

Loch
Gorm

B8018

Sunderland

A847

Blackrock

Redhouses

Sorn

Daill

267
BEINN DUBH

Am Fraoch
Eilean

Rubha na
Tràille

Brosdale I.

Machir Bay

Kilchoman

Conisby

Bridgend

Tormisdale

Kilchiaran

Bruichladdich

ISLAY LIFE
MUSEUM

Bowmore
BOWMORE
ROUND
CHURCH

A846

Mulindry

McArthur's Hd.

KENNACRAIG 2:00

Kilchiaran Bay

RHINNS

ISLAY

Port
Charlotte

Kilennan

Carraig Mhór

Lossit

232

15

OF

Nerabus

Laggan
Pt.

Laggan

Duich

NR

471
BEINN BHAN

491
BEINN
BHEIGEIR

Ardtalla

Lossit Pt.

ISLAY

Laggan

Loch Beinn
Uraraidh

Claggain
Bay

ubha
a Faing

ISLAY

A847

LAGGAN
BAY

13

B8016

Kintour

Ardmore Pt.

Portnahaven

Port Wemyss

Glenegedale

ISLAY

347
BEINN SHOLUM

KILDALTON CHURCH
AND CROSSES

Orsay

Rinns Pt.

Leorin

Eilean Craobhach

Port Alsaig

Rubha Mór

Kintra

A846

Eilean a'Chuirn

Cornabus

ARDBEG
DISTILLERY

4

Eilean Bhride

Dùn Mór Ghil

Lower Cragabus

Imeraval

Port Ellen

Lagavulin

Ardbeg

Eilean Imersay

T H E   O A

152

LAPHROAIG
DISTILLERY

Laphroaig

LAGAVULIN DISTILLERY

Lower
Killeyan

Risabus

Texa

KENNACRAIG 2:10

AMERICAN MONUMENT

Mull of Oa

Inerval

202

118

Rubha nan Leacan

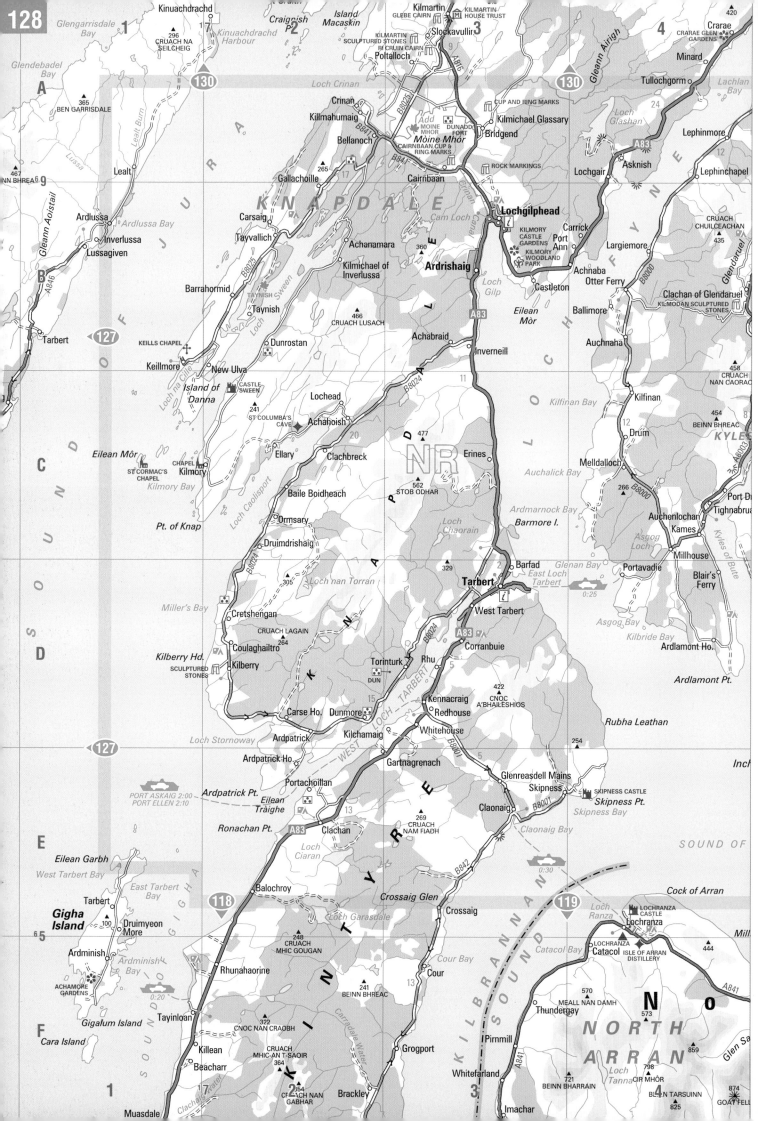

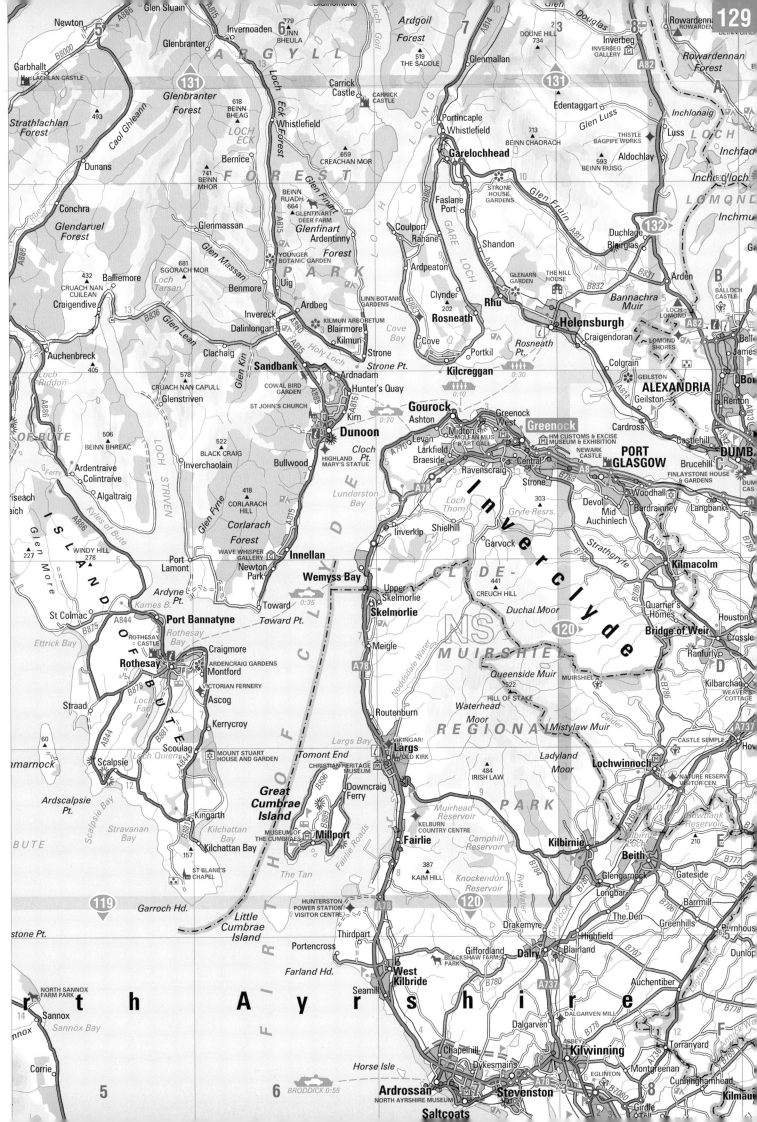

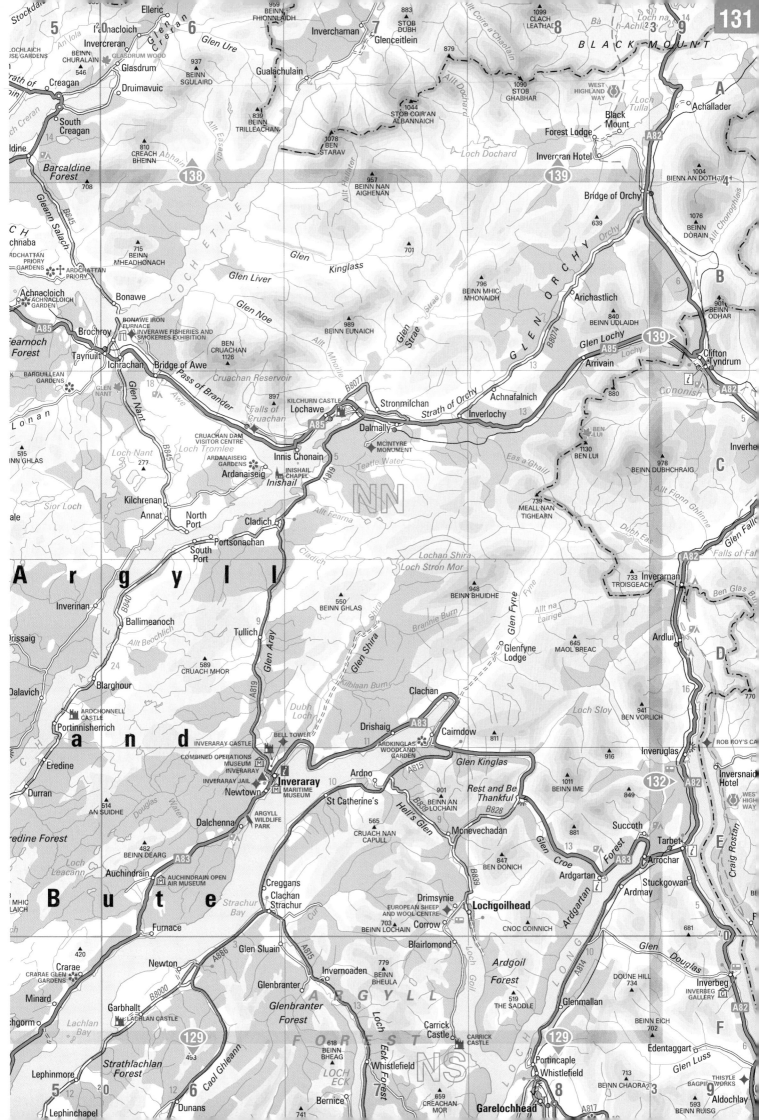

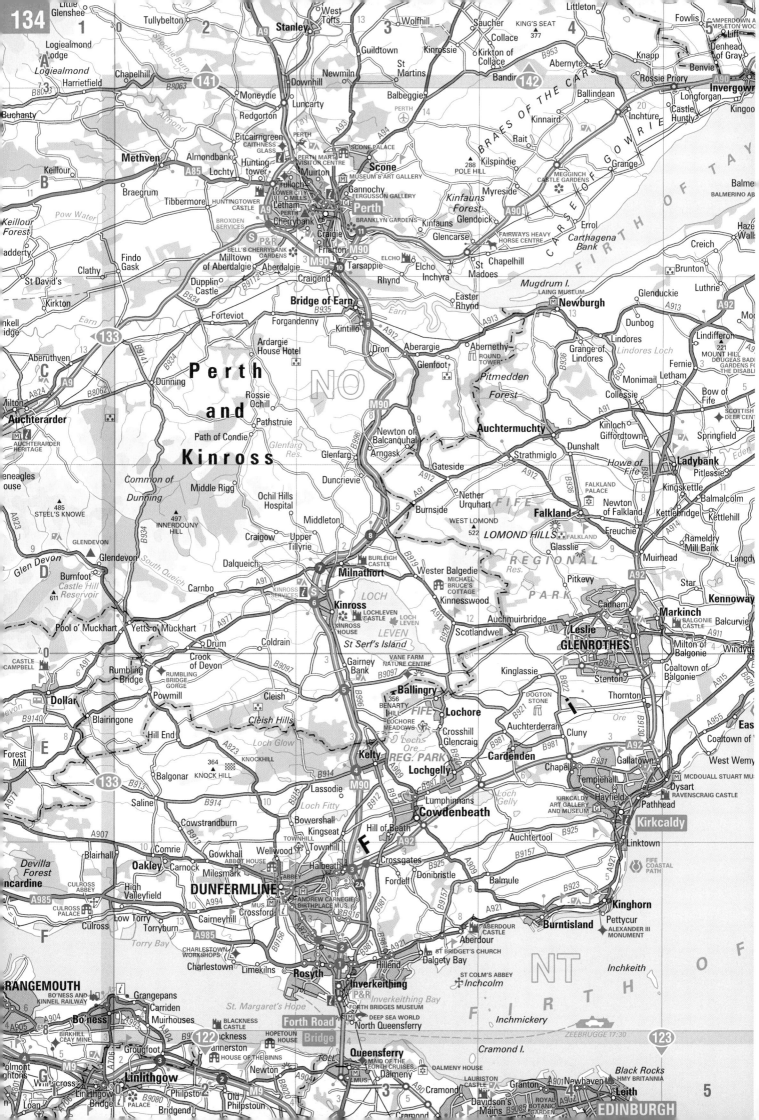

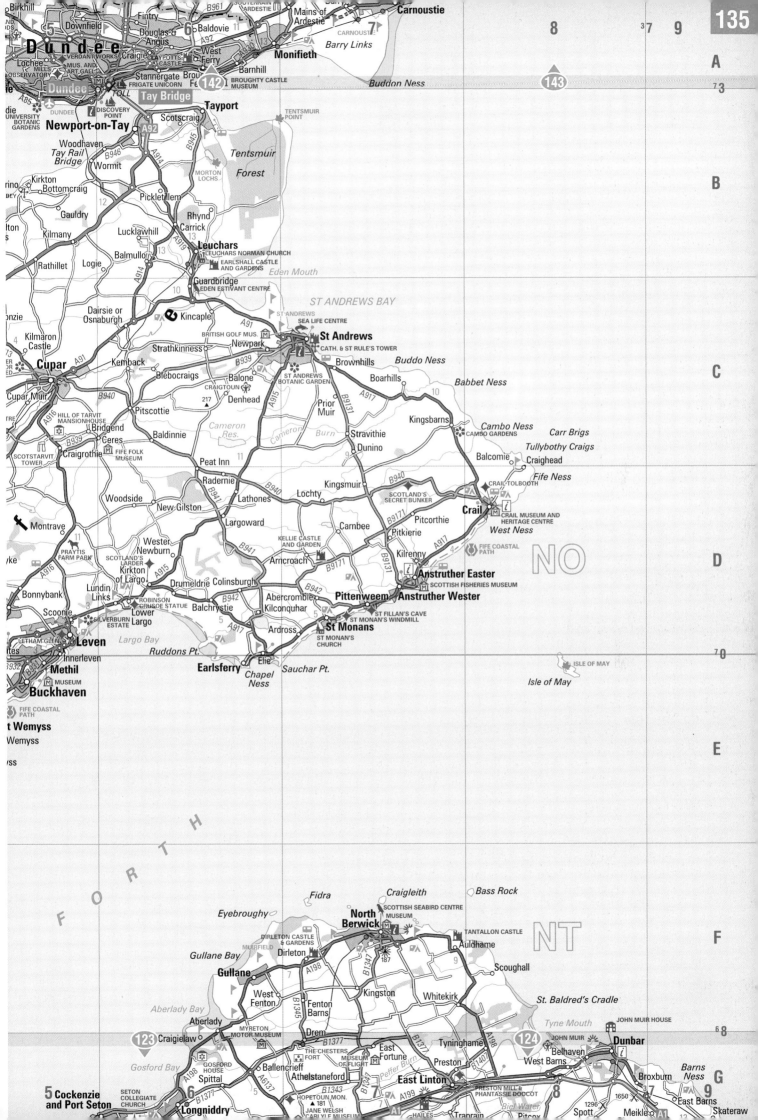

A

7

1

1

2

3

144

4

Cairns of Coll

Po.
Ardnamu
ARDNAMURCHAN LIG

B

Rubha Mor

Eilean Mor

Sorisdale

Bousd

Cliad Bay

B8072

Arnabost   Gallanach

Grishipoll

B8071

COLL

OBAN 2:40

Quinish

Ballyhaugh

B8071

Loch
Cliad

73

104

Rubha
an Aird

Hogh Bay

B8070

Arinagour

Caliach Pt.

Sunipol

M o r n i s h

C

Totronald

Penmore
Mil

Feall
Bay

Arileod

Acha

Eilean
Ornsay

Calgary

Calgary Pt.

Breachacha
Castle

Friesland

Loch Eatharna

Calgary Bay

Gunna

Soa

Loch Breachacha

Ensay

Treshnish Pt.

34
CARN

Crossapol
Bay

Treshnish Isles

Rubh a'Chaoil

Haunn

B8073

Burg

Balephetrish
Bay

Vaul
Bay

Caolas

T I R E E

Salum

Rubha Dubh

LOCH

Vaul

B8069

Ruaig

Fladda

Eilean Dioghlum

Gometra

Bearnus

D

Kenovay

B8068

Scarinish

Soa

0:55

Lunga

U

B8065

Heanish

NM

Bac Mor

Crossapol

Rubha Traigh
an Duin

Hynish Bay

alemartine

Little
Colonsay

Mannal

Staffa   STAFFA

Staffa

FINGAL'S CAVE

E

A r g y l l

0

1

Erisgeir

5

(April-Oct)
0:45

T I R E E

Vaul
Bay

Salum

Caolas

NL

Balephetrish
Bay

Vaul

B8069

Hough
Skerries

Balevullin

Kenovay

Ruaig

Soa

Eilean
Annraidh

MACLEAN'S CROSS

Rubha nan Cearc

R. Chraiginis

B8068

Gott Bay

IONA ABBEY AND
CATHEDRAL

Loch
na
Lathaich

F

Kilkenneth

TIREE

Scarinish

100

Kintra

IONA HERITAGE CENTRE

ST COLUMBA EXHIBITION
& WELCOME CENTRE

Middleton

Moss

B8068

Heylipol

B8065

Crossapol

Heanish

COLL 0:55

Iona

Baile Mor

Aridhglas

Eorabus

Port Mor

Barrapol

Rubha Traigh
an Duin

Stac an
Aoineidh

Fionnphort

A849

Tiraghoil

Bunessan

Rinn
Thorbhais

B8067

Balemartine

Hynish Bay

Loch
a'Phuill

Balephuil

141

B8068

Mannal

Fidden

Loch
Assapol

Balephuil
Bay

Hynish

NM

Erraid

Soa I.

R O S S O F

Ardalanish   Ardchiavaig

G

1

0

2

Eilean a'Chalmain

3

125

Uisk

4

Port Snoig

Rubh Ardalanish

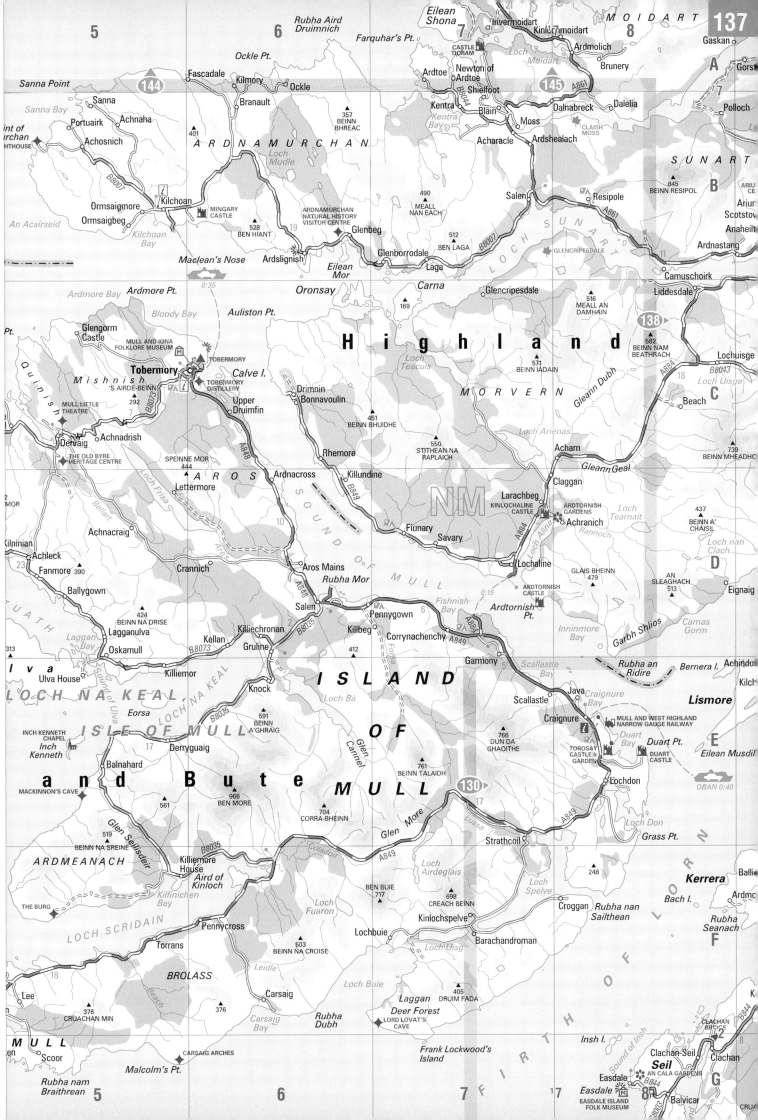

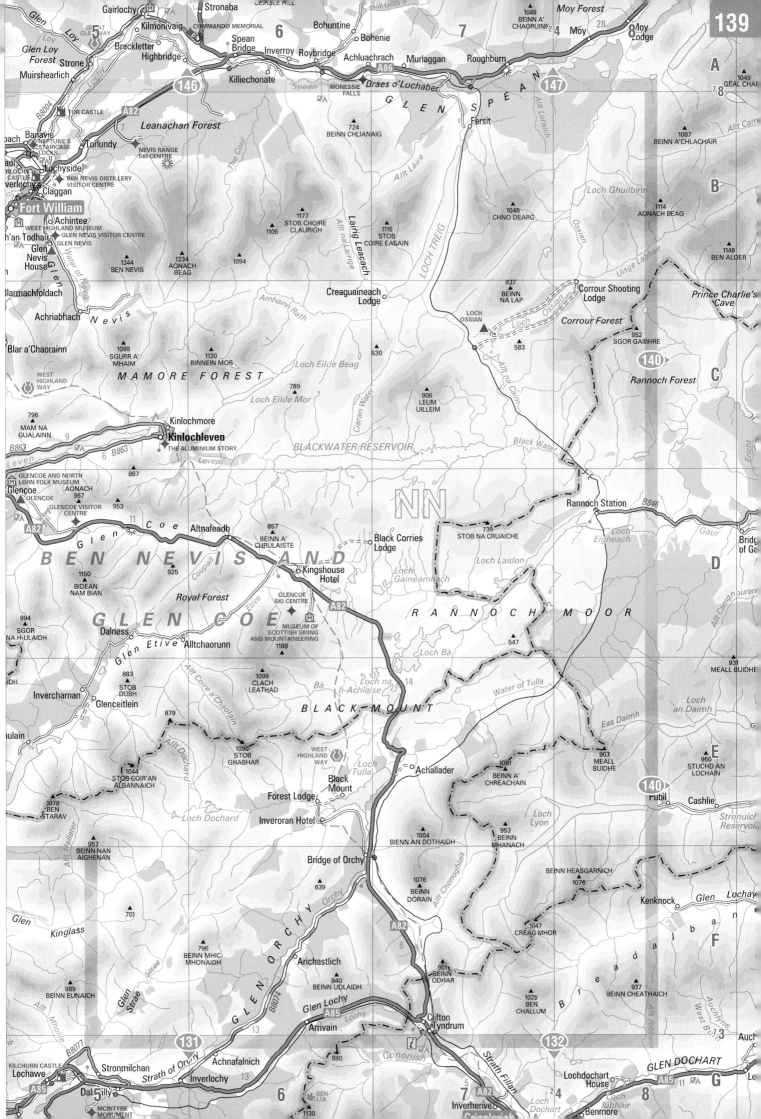

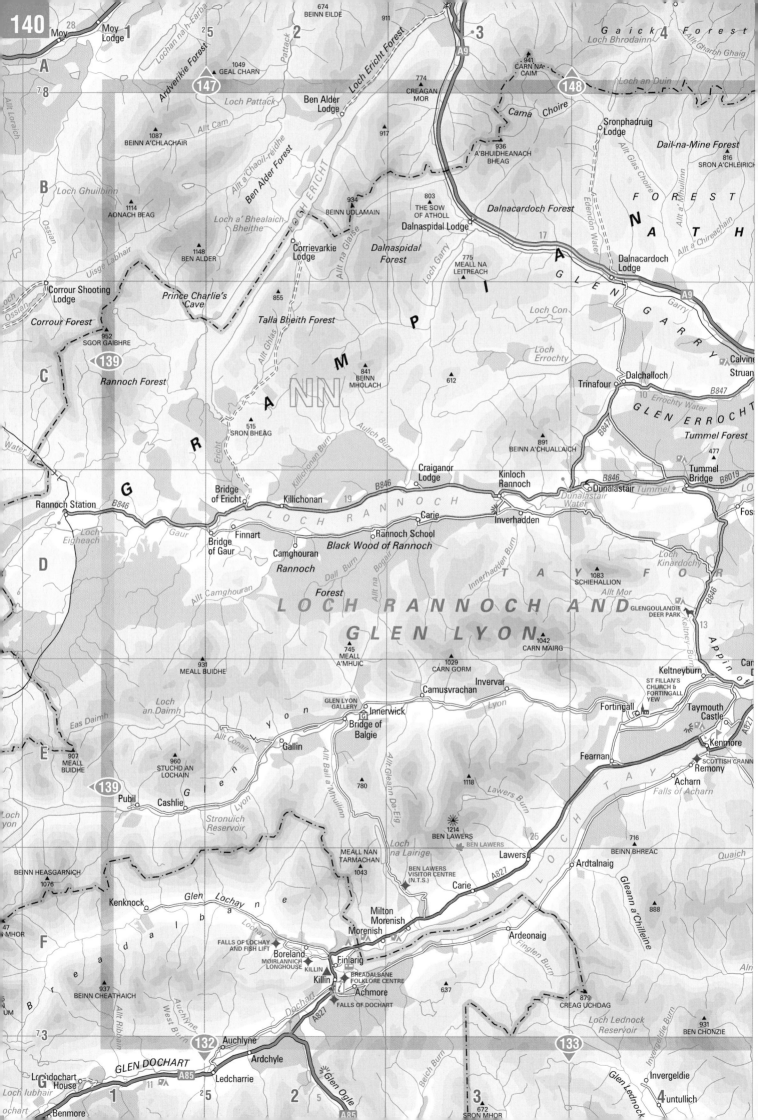

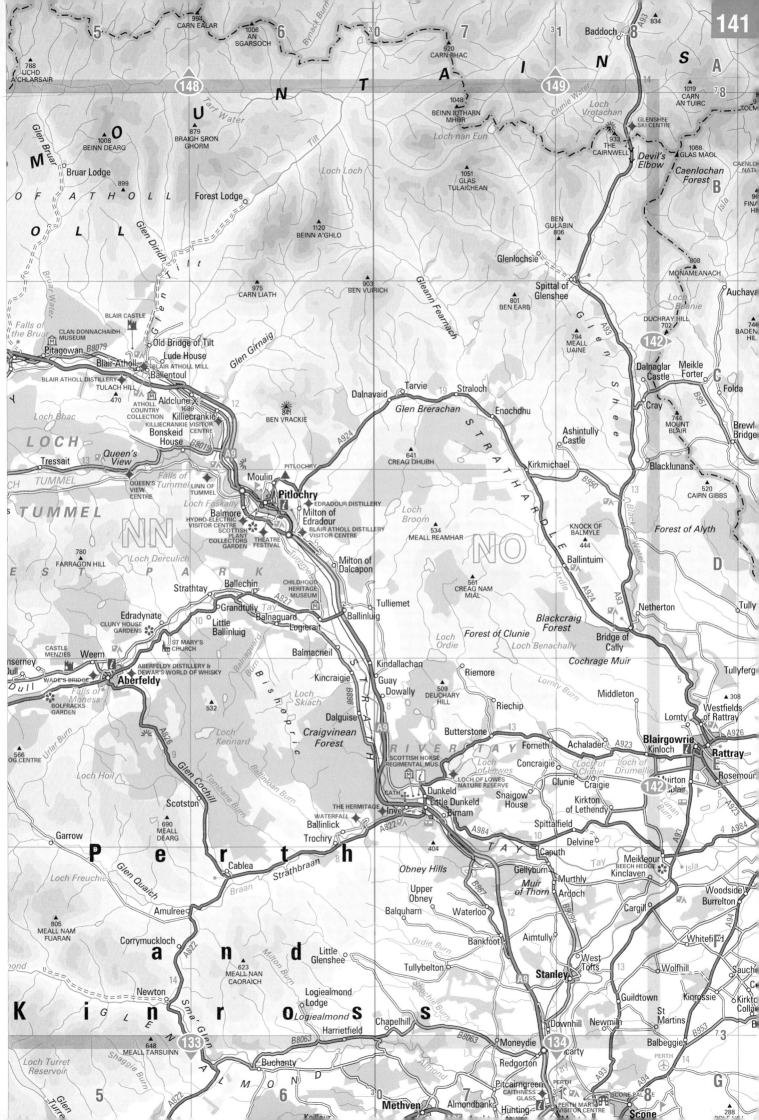

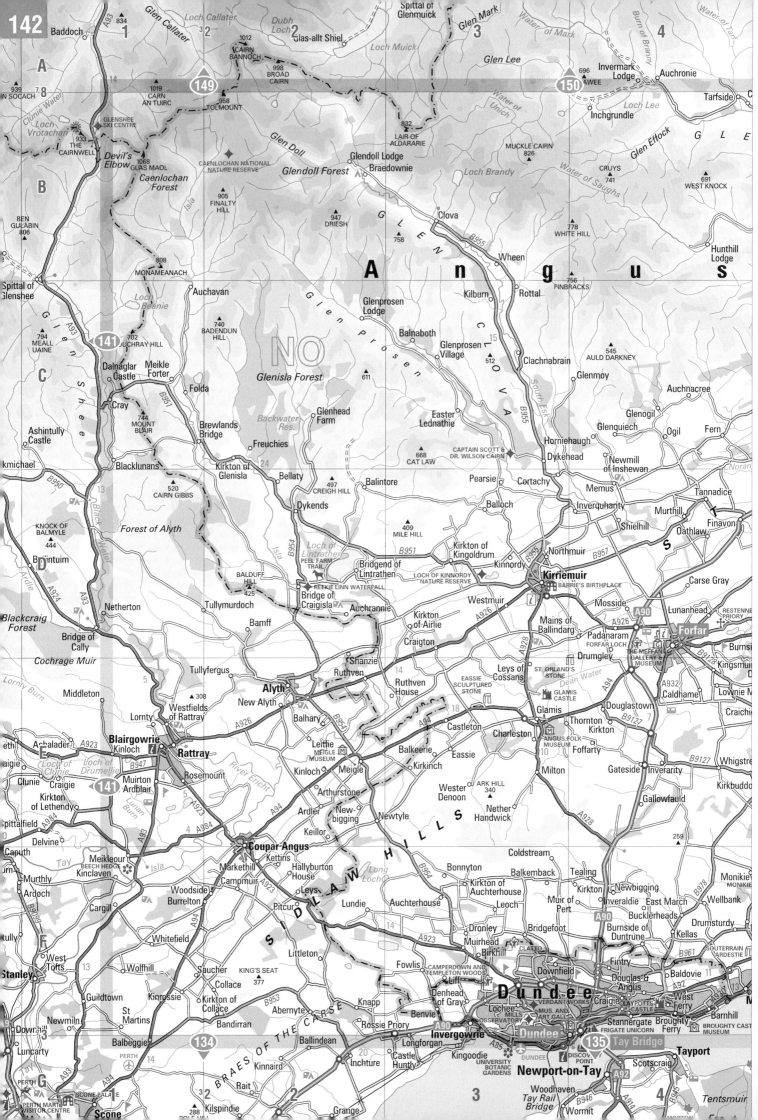

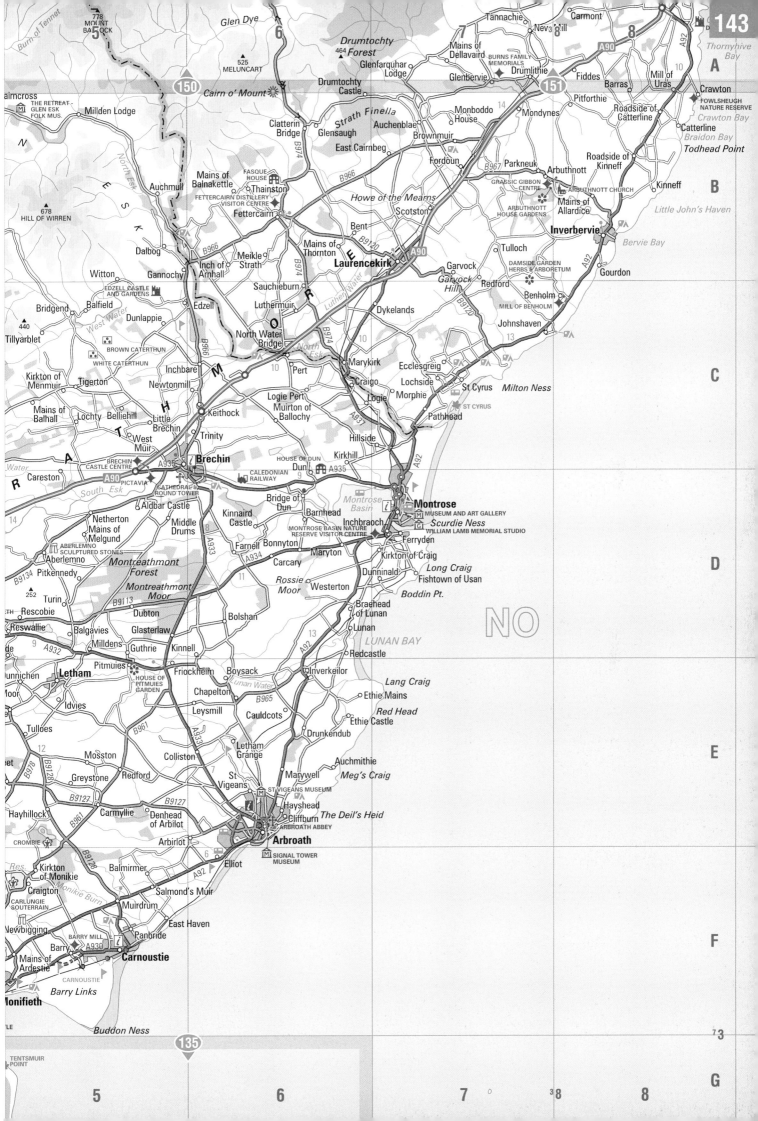

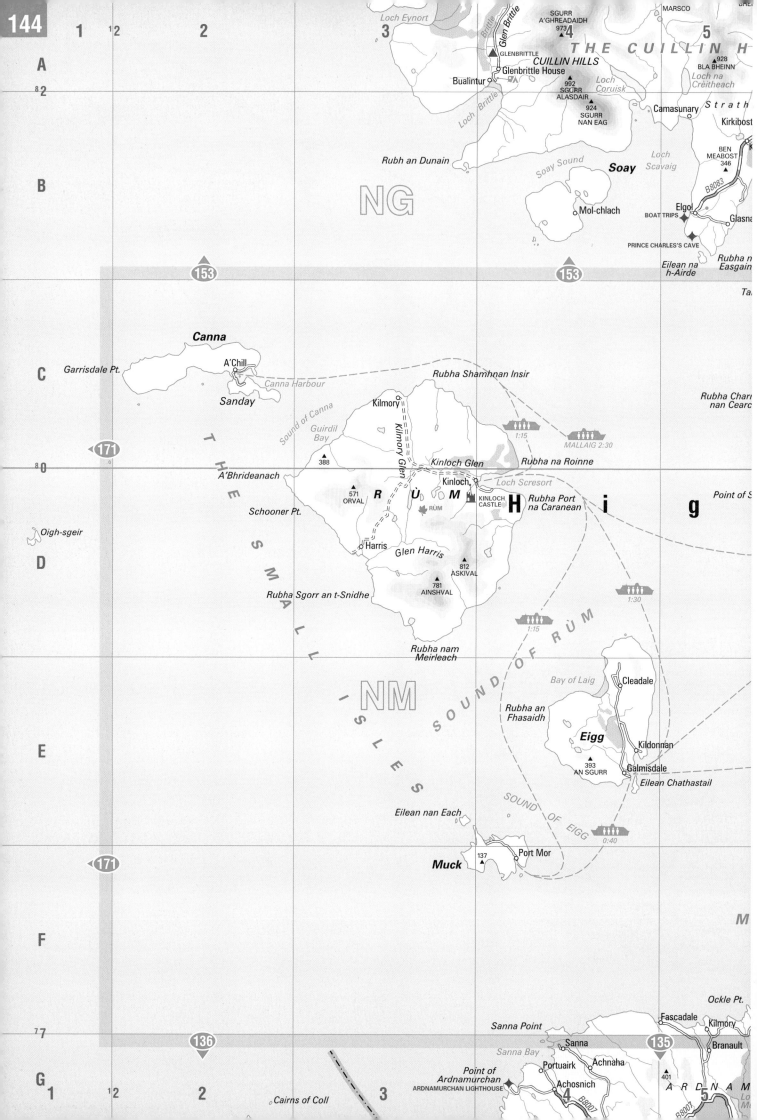

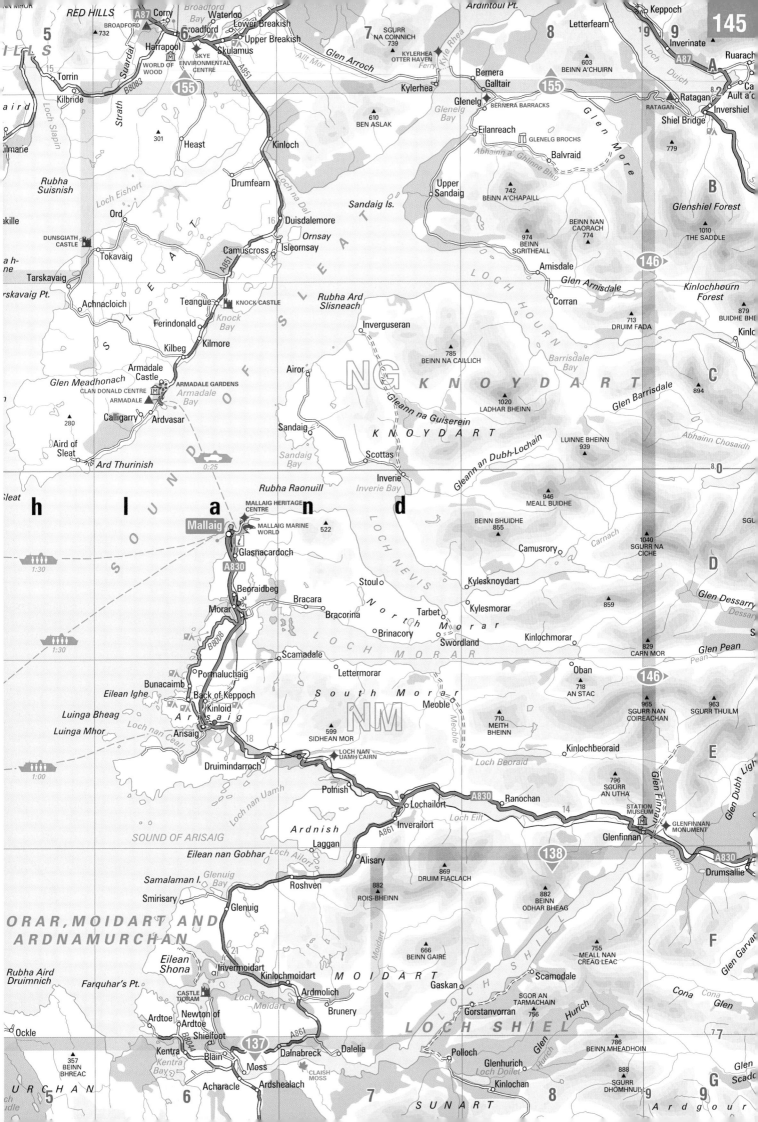

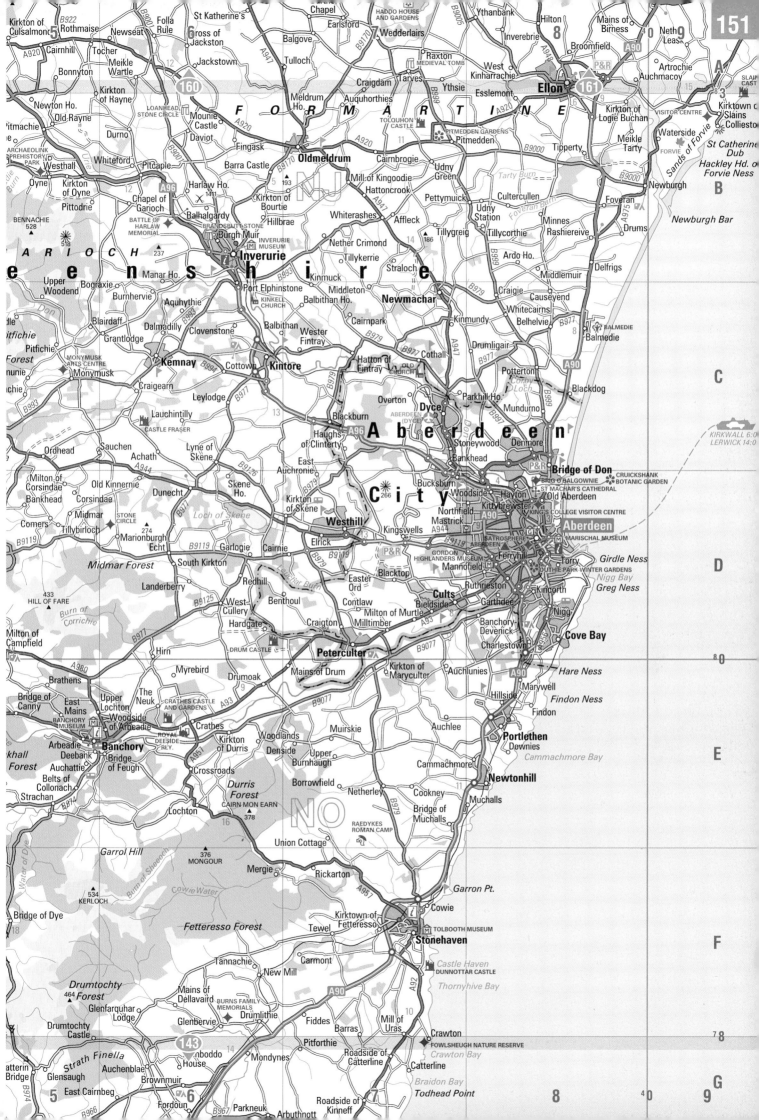

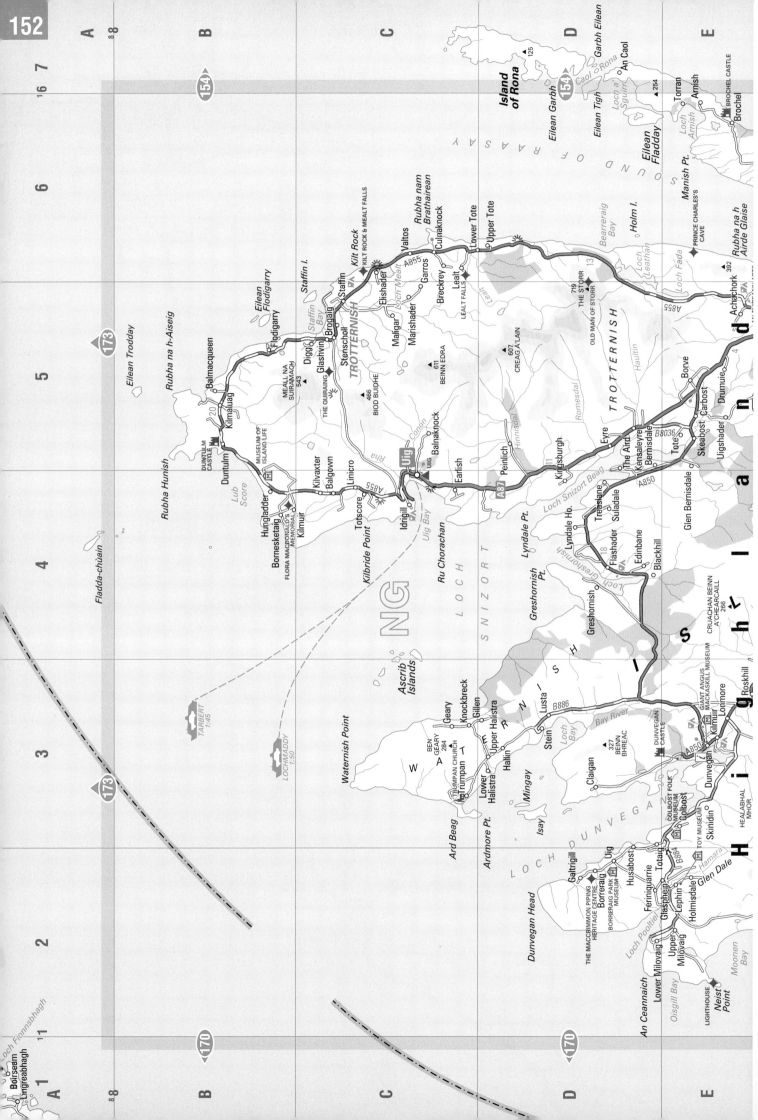

Boirseam
Lingreabhagh
Loch Fhionnsbhagh

Fladda-chuain

Rubha Hunish
Eilean Trodday
Rubha na h-Aiseig

Balmacqueen
Kilmaluag
Duntulm
DUNTULM CASTLE
MUSEUM OF ISLAND LIFE
Hungladder
Bornesketaig
Kilmuir
FLORA MACDONALD'S MEMORIAL
Kilvaxter
Balgown
Linicro
Totscore
Kilbride Point
Idrigill

Eilean Flodigarry
Flodigarry
Digg
Glashvin
MEALL NA SUIRAMACH
543
THE QUIRAING
BIOD BUIDHE
466
Staffin I.
Staffin Bay
Brogaig
Stenscholl
Staffin
TROTTERNISH
Elishader
Maligar
Marishader
Garros
Loch Mealt
611
BEINN EDRA
Balnaknock
Conon
Rha
Earlish
Peinlich

KILT ROCK & MEALT FALLS
Kilt Rock
Valtos
Breckrey
Lealt
LEALT FALLS
Culnaknock
Rubha nam Brathairean
Lower Tote
Upper Tote
607
CREAG A'LAIN
719 THE STORR
OLD MAN OF STORR
Haultin
Romesdal
13
Hinnisdal
Kingsburgh

Island of Rona
Eilean Garbh
Caol na Rona
125
Loch a Sguirr
254
Eilean Tigh
Holm I.
Bearreraig Bay
Loch Leathan
Loch Fada
392
Achachork

An Caol
Torran
Arnish
BROCHEL CASTLE
Brochel
Eilean Fladday
Manish Pt.
PRINCE CHARLES'S CAVE
Rubha na h Airde Glaise

SOUND OF RAASAY

TROTTERNISH

A855

A87
Uig
Uig Bay
Ru Chorachan
Ascrib Islands
Waternish Point

Kilbride Point

NG

TARBERT 1:45
LOCHMADDY 1:50

Loch Snizort Beag
Lyndale Pt.
Lyndale Ho.
Greshornish Pt.
Greshornish
Loch Greshornish

LOCH SNIZORT

Eyre
The Aird
Treaslane
Suladale
Flashader
Edinbane
Blackhill

Borve
Carbost
Skeabost
B8036
Tote
Kensaleyre
Bernisdale
A850
Uigshader
Drumuie
Glen Bernisdale

Skye

Highland

Ard Beag
Ardmore Pt.
Isay
Mingay
Dunvegan Head
LOCH DUNVEGAN

WATERNISH
BEN GEARY 284
Geary
Knockbreck
Gillen
TRUMPAN CHURCH
Trumpan
Lower Halistra
Upper Halistra
Hallin
Stein
Lusta
Loch Bay
B886
Bay River
Claigan
327 BEINN BHREAC
DUNVEGAN CASTLE
Colbost
COLBOST FOLK MUSEUM
Skinidin
Husabost
TOY MUSEUM
Borreraig
BORRERAIG PARK MUSEUM
THE MACCRIMMON PIPING HERITAGE CENTRE
Galtrigill
Uig
Feriniquarrie
Totaig
Glasphein
Holmisdale
Glen Dale
Hamara
Lephin
Loch Pooltiel
Upper Milovaig
Lower Milovaig
An Ceannaich
Oisgill Bay
LIGHTHOUSE
Neist Point
Moonen Bay

GIANT ANGUS MACASKILL MUSEUM
CRUACHAN BEINN A'CHEARCAILL 266
Kilmuir
Lonmore
Roskhill
Dunvegan
HEALABHAL MHOR

154
173
170

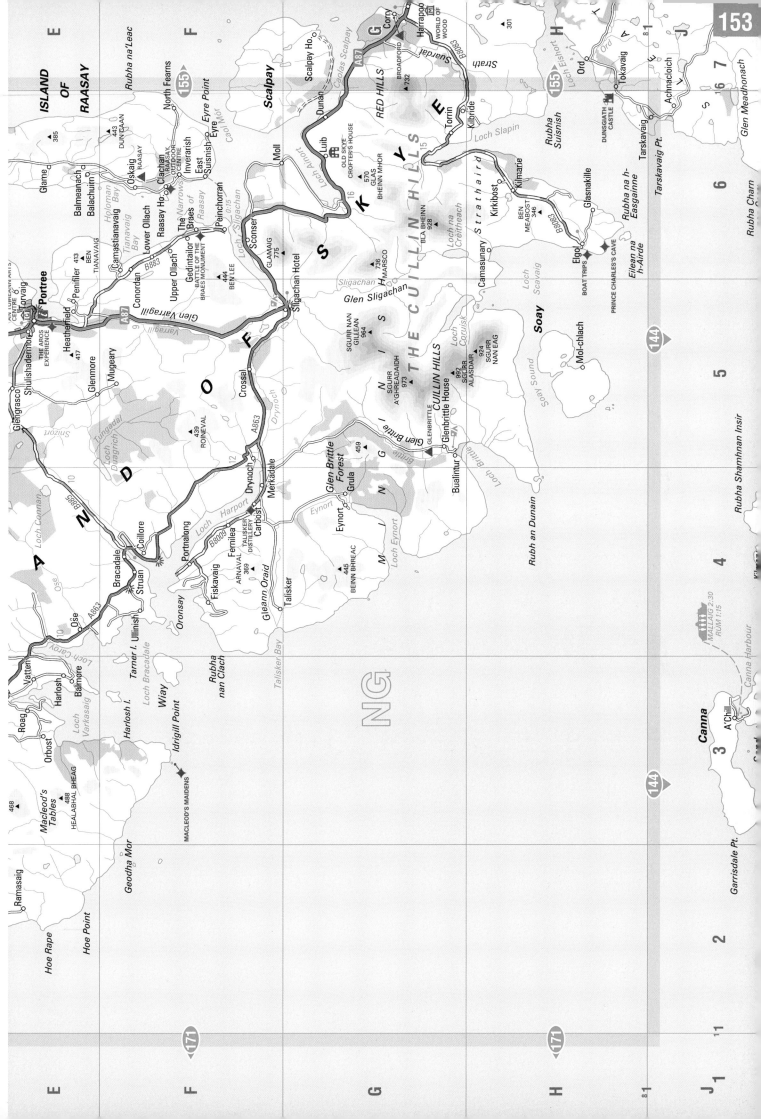

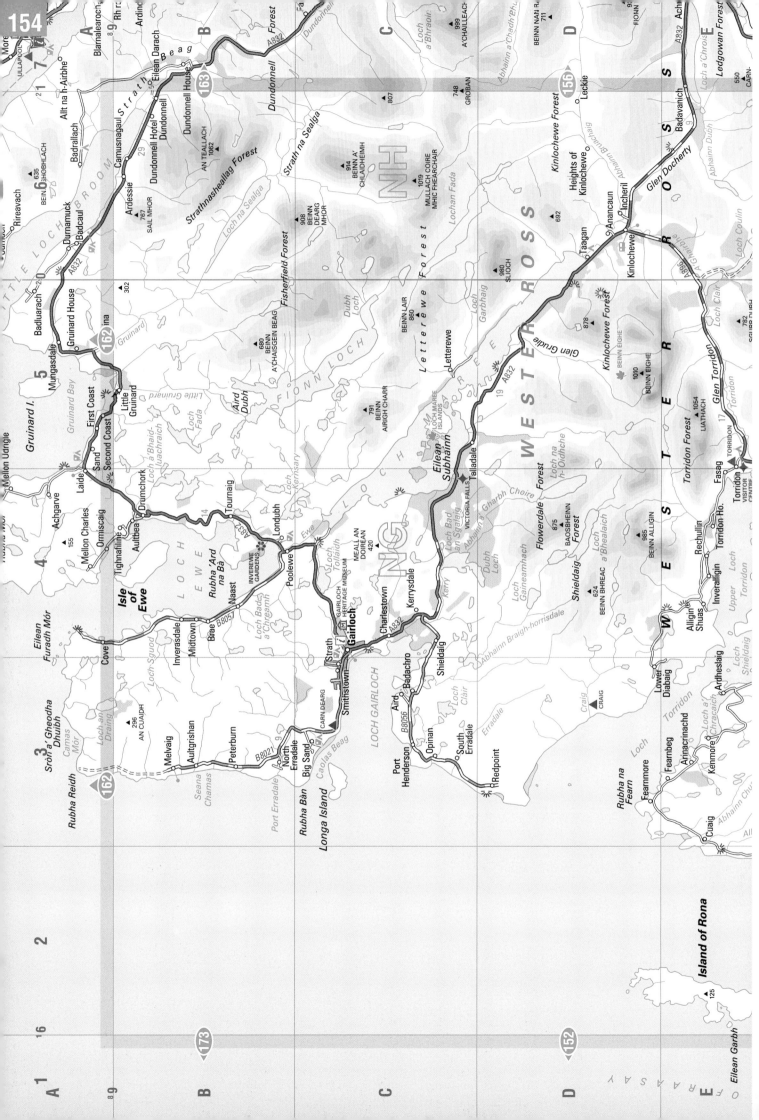

163
156
162
162
173
152

ULLAPOOL

Blarnalearoch
Ardindrean
Rhiroy
More
Dundonnell

A832
Dundonnell Forest
LOCH BROOM

Allt na h-Airbhe
Eilean Darach

Beag
Camusnagaul
Dundonnell House
Dundonnell Hotel
Dundonnell

AN TEALLACH 1062
Strath

Strath na Sealga

Loch a'Bhraoin
A'CHAILLEACH
BEINN NAN RAMH 711
FIONN
999

Badrallach
A832
Ardessie
29

SAIL MHOR 767
Strathnasheallag Forest
Loch na Sealga

BEINN A' CHLAIDHEIMH 914
MULLACH COIRE MHIC FHEARCHAIR 1019
GROBAN 748
807

Kinlochewe Forest
Heights of Kinlochewe
Leckie

BEINN DEARG MHOR 908
BEINN 6 SHOBHLACH 635
Badcaul
Durnamuck
Badcaul
A832
20

Loch a' Chroisg
Loch Coulin
550
CARN-
Badavanich
LOCH A' BHRAOIN

Rireavach
Fisherfield Forest
Abhainn Dubh
Mungasdale
Badluarach
Gruinard House
A832

ina
162
Gruinard
302

Loch Fada
Dubh Loch
692
Letterewe Forest

Glen Docherty
A832
Incheril
Anancaun
Taagan
Kinlochewe

BEINN LAIR 860
Letterewe
SLIOCH 980

Garbhaig
Lochan Fada
878

A832
19
Glen Grudie

BEINN EIGHE
1010
BEINN EIGHE
Kinlochewe Forest

782
SGURR DUBH

First Coast
Gruinard I.
5
Mungasdale
Second Coast
Little Gruinard
Sand
Laide
First Coast

Loch a'Bhaid-luachraich
Little Gruinard
Aird Dubh
BEINN A'CHAISGEIN BEAG
680 BEINN A'CHAISGEIN BEAG

Eilean Subhainn
Loch na h-Oidhche
875
BAOSBHEINN
875

1054 LIATHACH
Glen Torridon
A896
17
Torridon
TORRIDON

Mellon Udrigle
Achgarve
Mellon Charles
Ormiscaig
155
Drumchork
Aultbea
Tournaig

Isle of Ewe
Tighnafiline
INVEREWE GARDENS
Londubh
Poolewe

A832
14
Loch Ewe
Rubha 'Ard na Bà
Naast

MEALL AN DOIREAN 420
Loch Maree
Kerry
VICTORIA FALLS
Talladale

Flowerdale Forest
Shieldaig
624 BEINN BHREAC
BEINN ALLIGIN 985

Rechullin
Torridon Ho.
Fasag
TORRIDON VISITOR CENTRE

Eilean Furadh Mòr
Cove
Inverasdale
Midtown
Brae
B8057

GAIRLOCH HERITAGE MUSEUM
Strath
Gairloch
Charlestown
Kerrysdale
A832

Badachro
Shieldaig
Inveralligin
Alligin Shuas
W

Sròn a' Gheodha Dhuibh
Rubha Reidh
Camas Mór
Loch an Draing
AN CUAIDH 296
Melvaig
Aultgrishan
Peterburn
B8021

CARN DEARG
Smithstown
North Erradale
Big Sand
Longa Island
Rubha Bàn

Aird
LOCH GAIRLOCH
Opinan
South Erradale
Port Henderson

B8056
Loch Clair
CRAIG
Craig

Lower Diabaig
Torridon
Kenmore
Arinacrinachd
Fearnbeg
Fearnmore
Rubha na Fearn

Loch a' Chracaich
Ardheslaig

Seana Chamas
Port Erradale
Redpoint

Island of Rona
125

Eilean Garbh

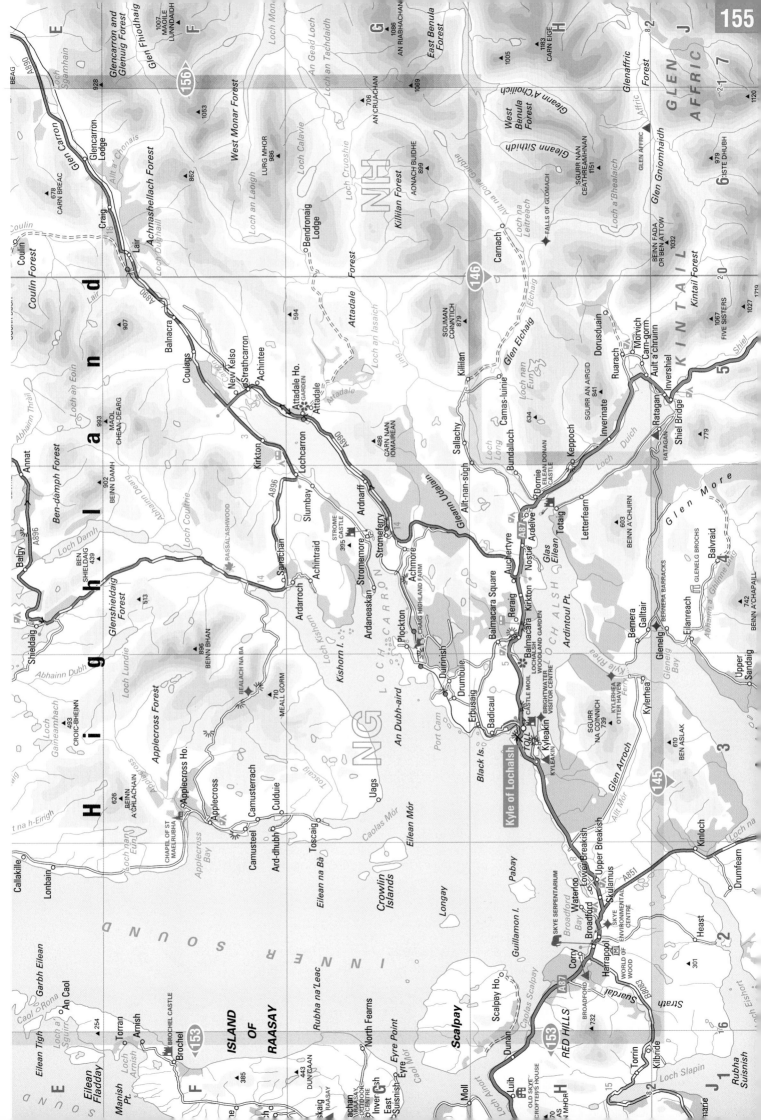

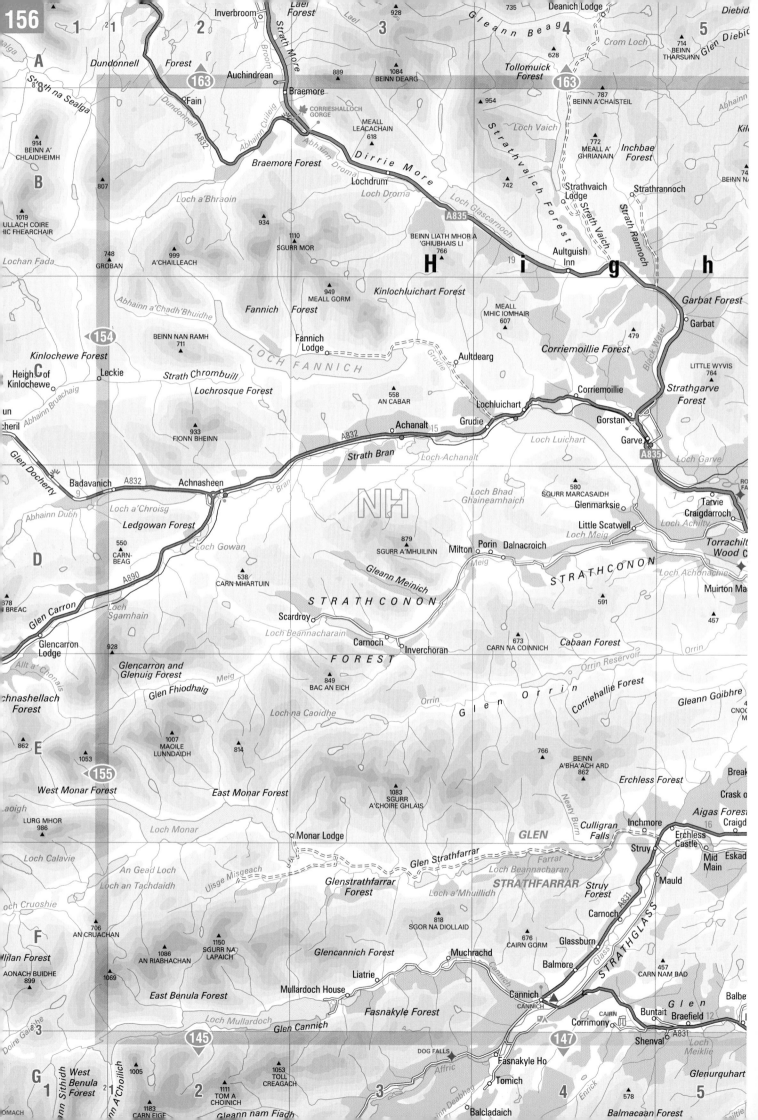

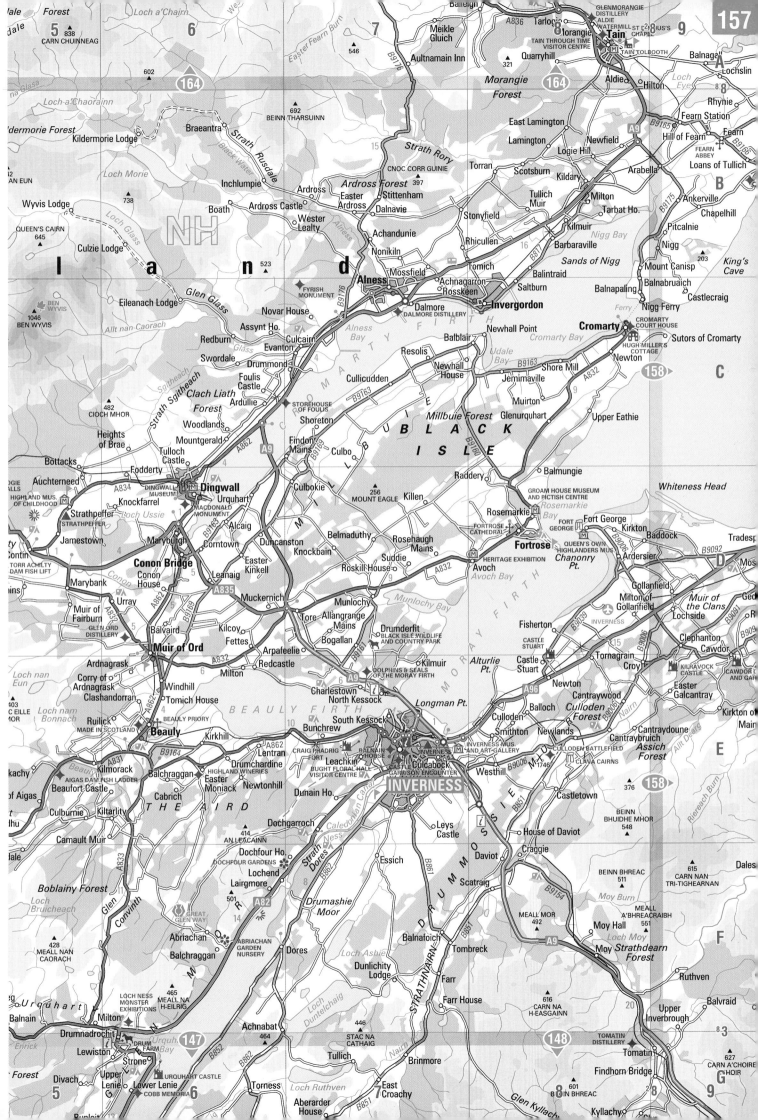

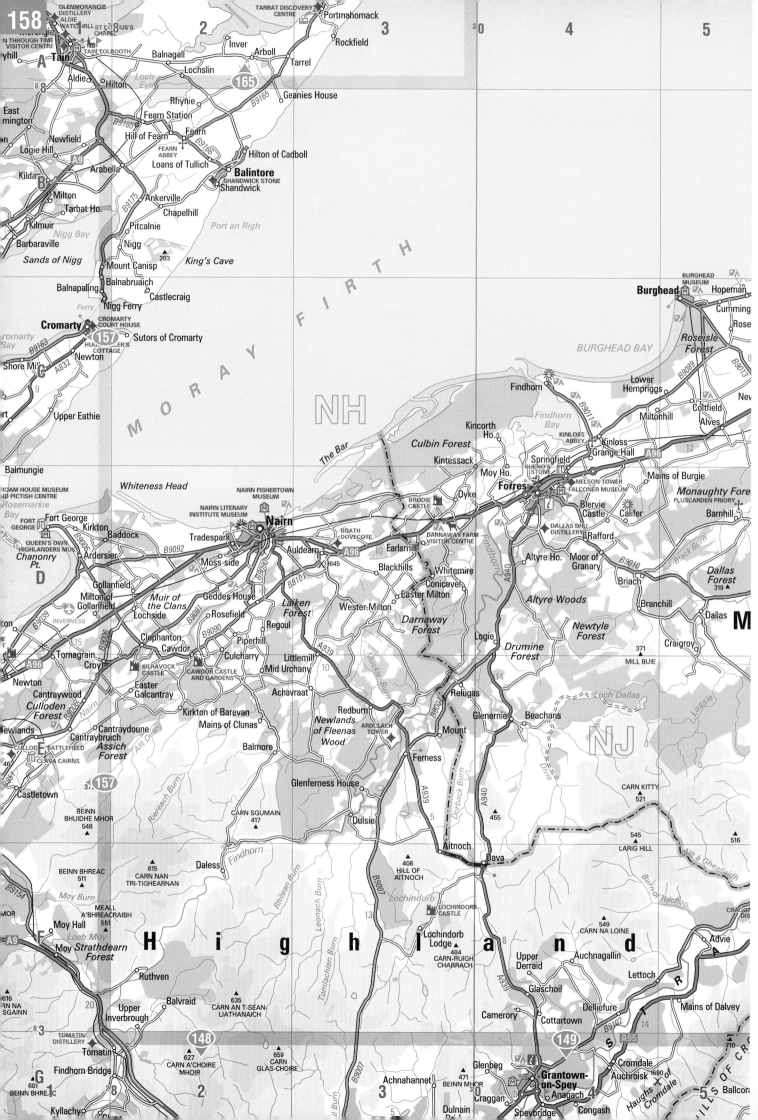

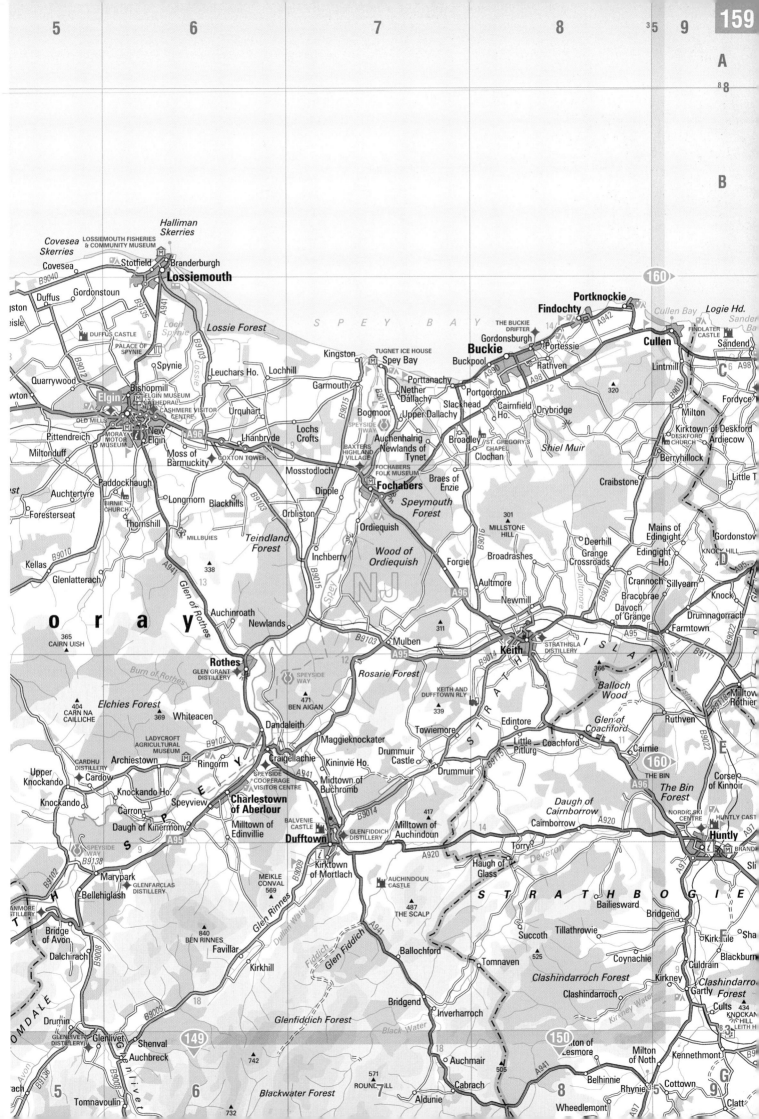

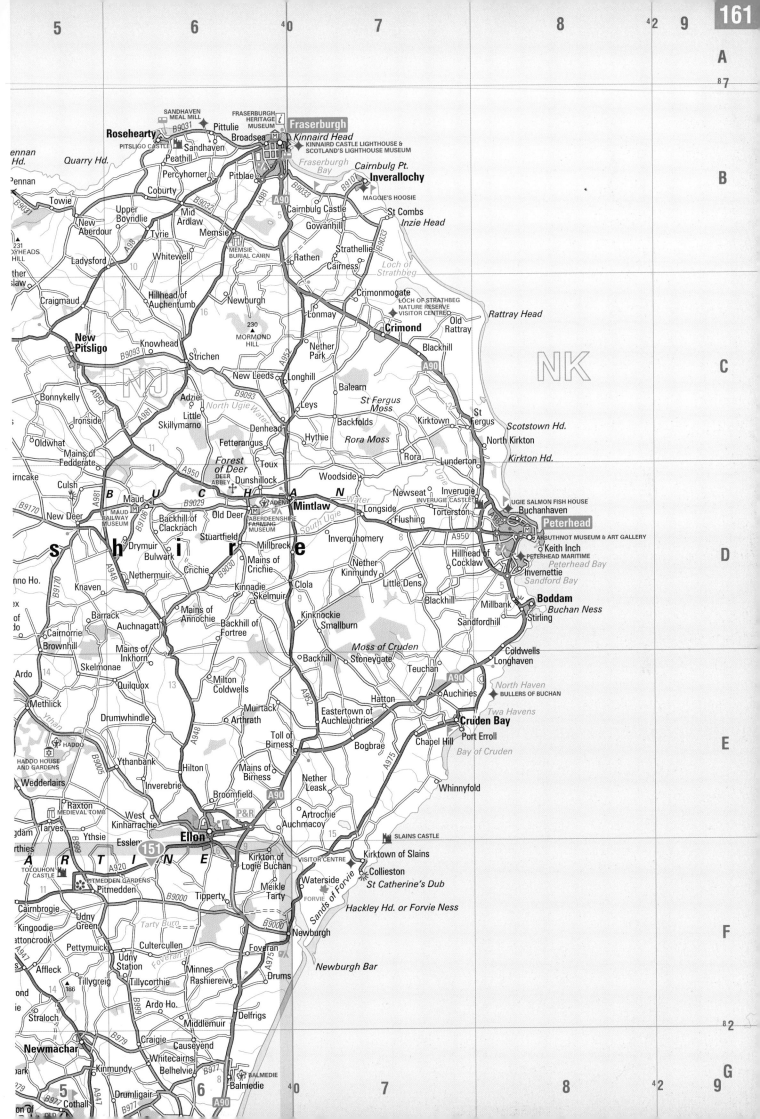

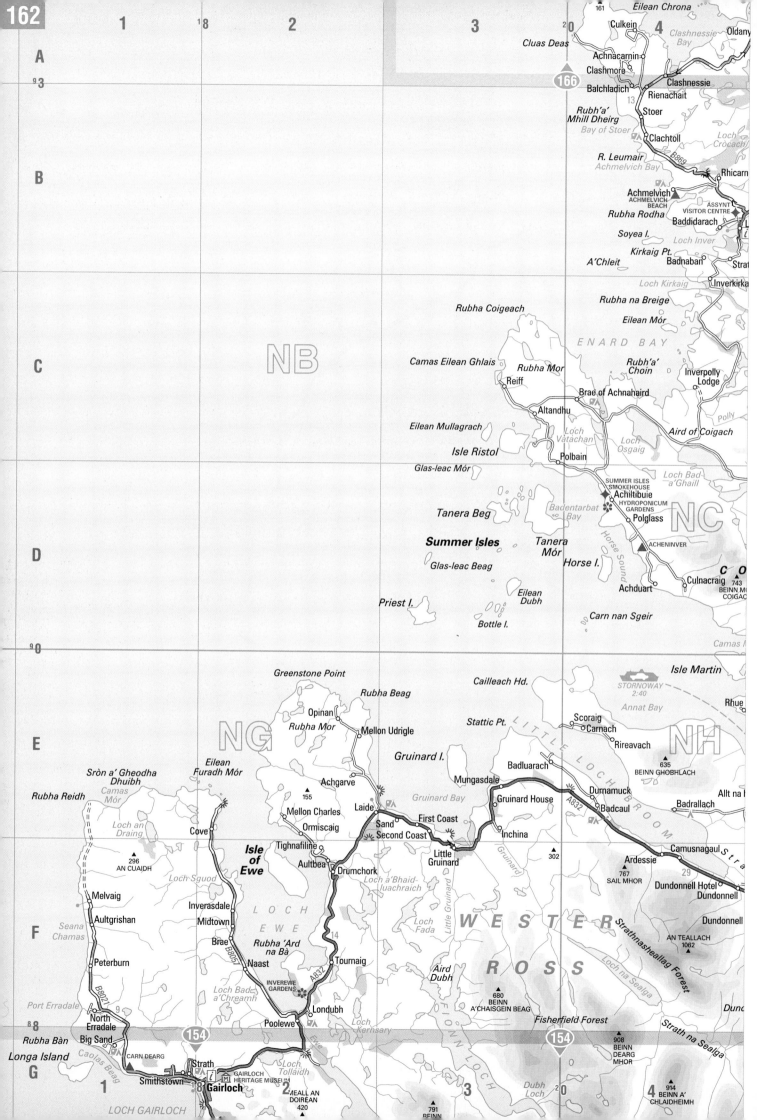

Eilean Chrona
Culkein
Cluas Deas
Achnacarnin
Clashnessie Bay
Oldany
Clashmore
166
Clashnessie
Balchladich
Rienachait
Stoer
13
Rubh 'a'
Mhill Dheirg
Bay of Stoer
Clachtoll
B869
R. Leumair
Rubha Rodha
Rhicarn
Achmelvich Bay
Achmelvich
ACHMELVICH BEACH
ASSYNT
VISITOR CENTRE
Soyea I.
Baddidarach
Loch Inver
Kirkaig Pt.
A'Chleit
Badnaban
Strath
Loch Kirkaig
Inverkirkaig

NB

Rubha Coigeach
Rubha na Breige
Eilean Mór
ENARD BAY
Camas Eilean Ghlais
Rubha Mor
Rubh 'a'
Choin
Inverpolly
Lodge
Reiff
Brae of Achnahaird
Altandhu
Eilean Mullagrach
Loch
Vatachan
Loch
Osgaig
Aird of Coigach
Isle Ristol
Polbain
polly
Glas-leac Mór
Loch Bad
a'Ghaill
SUMMER ISLES
SMOKEHOUSE
Achiltibuie
NC
HYDROPONICUM
GARDENS
Tanera Beg
Badentarbat
Bay
Polglass
Tanera
Mór
Horse Sound
ACHENINVER
Summer Isles
Horse I.
Glas-leac Beag
C O
Culnacraig
743
Priest I.
Eilean
Dubh
BEINN MO
COIGAC
Bottle I.
Carn nan Sgeir
Camas M

Greenstone Point
Cailleach Hd.
Isle Martin
Rubha Beag
STORNOWAY
2:40
Rhue
NG
Opinan
Annat Bay
Rubha Mor
Mellon Udrigle
Stattic Pt.
Scoraig
NH
Gruinard I.
Carnach
Rireavach
Sròn a' Gheodha
Dhuibh
Eilean
Furadh Mór
Achgarve
Badluarach
BEINN GHOBHLACH
635
Rubha Reidh
Camas
Mór
155
Gruinard Bay
Mungasdale
Gruinard House
Durnamuck
Mellon Charles
Laide
Badcaul
Badrallach
Loch an
Draing
Ormiscaig
Sand
First Coast
Inchina
A832
Cove
Second Coast
Allt na
Tighnafiline
Little
Gruinard
Camusnagaul
Stra
Isle
of
Ewe
Aultbea
302
Ardessie
296
AN CUAIDH
Drumchork
767
29
Melvaig
Loch-Sguod
Loch a'Bhaid-
luachraich
SAIL MHOR
Dundonnell Hotel
Dundonnell
Inverasdale
L O C H
Loch
Fada
W E S T E R
Aultgrishan
Midtown
Dundonnell
Seana
Chamas
E W E
14
AN TEALLACH
1062
Brae
Rubha 'Ard
na Bà
Naast
Tournaig
R O S S
Peterburn
B8021
A832
Aird
Dubh
680
Strathnasheallag Forest
BEINN
A'CHAISGEIN BEAG
INVEREWE
GARDENS
Loch Bad
a'Chreamh
Londubh
Fisherfield Forest
Strath na Sealga
North
Erradale
154
Poolewe
154
908
Big Sand
CARN DEARG
Loch
Tolláidh
BEINN
DEARG
MHOR
Rubha Bàn
Longa Island
Caolas Beag
Strath
GAIRLOCH
HERITAGE MUSEUM
914
BEINN A'
CHLAIDHEIMH
Smithstown
Gairloch
MEALL AN
DOIREAN
420
LOCH GAIRLOCH
791
BEINN
Dubh
Loch
FIONN LOCH

A
B
C
D
E
F
G

1
18
2
3
20
4

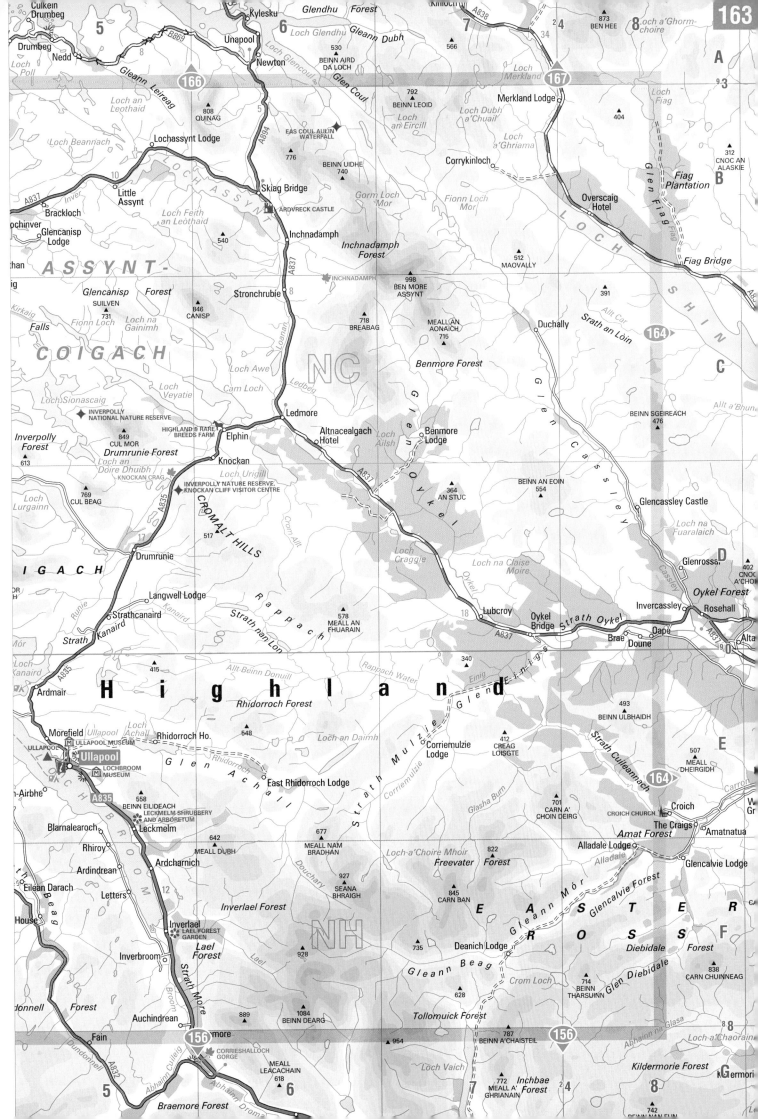

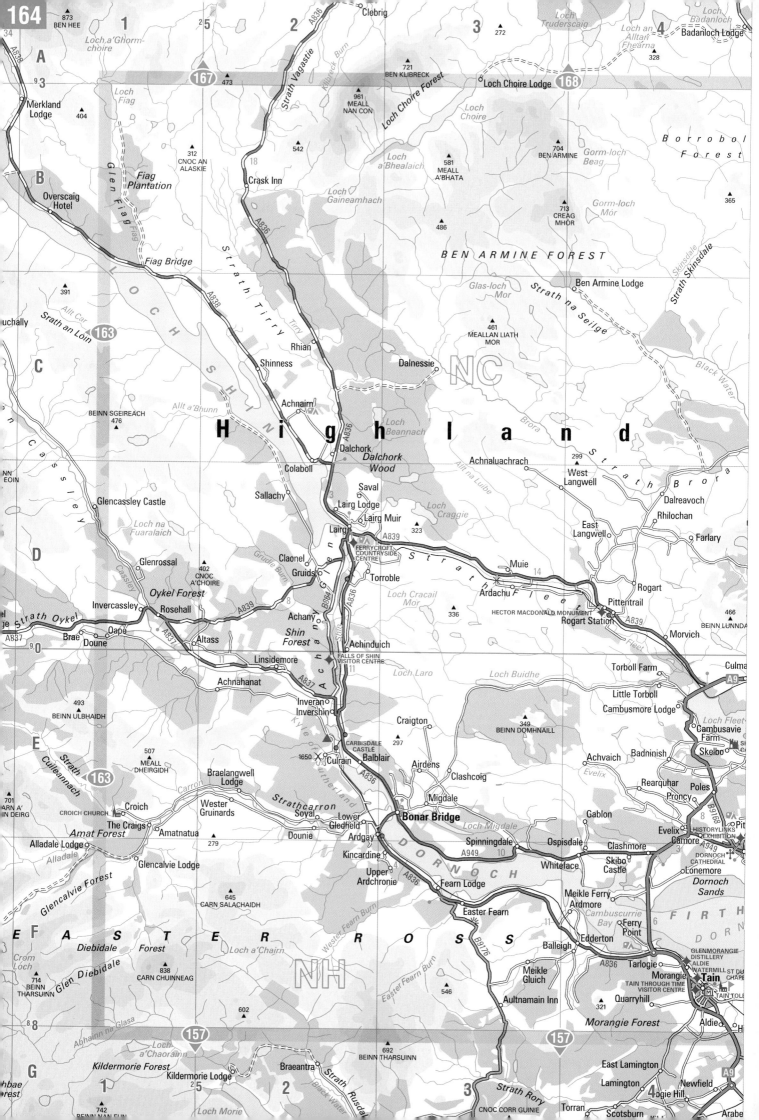

Loch Arichlinie
B871
Strath Beg
Helmsdale
A897
Achentoul
Kinbrace
Knockfin Heights
168
Kinbrace Burn
Smerral
Latheronwheel Ho.
Latheronw
A
Laidhay Crof MUSEUM
Dunbeath Water
Berriedale Water
Braem
169
283
Balnabruich
Dunbeath
Dunbeath Heritage Centre
Dunbeath Bay
DUNBEATH CASTLE
Knockally

318 CNOC LOCH MHADADH
438 CNOC COIRE NA PEARNA
705 MORVEN
Wag
626 SCARABEN
Langwell Forest
Ramscraigs
Newport
Borgue
B

Abhainn na Frithe
Altanduin
Borrobol Lodge
A897
17
387 CREAG NAM FIADH
555 CREAG SCALABSDALE
Aultibea
Langwell Ho.
19
Ceann Leathad nam Bò
Berriedale
Badbea Clearance Village

STRATH
Craggie
Craggie Burn
Kildonan Lodge
Baile An Òr Goldrush Site
Beinn Dubhain
414
422
A9
Ousdale

Tuarie Burn
OF
Helmsdale
Torrish
Kilphedir
A897

345
KILDONAN
628 BEINN DHORAIN
592
Eldrable Hill
417
Marrel
West Helmsdale
Gartymore
Helmsdale
Navidale
Ord Point
TIMESPAN HERITAGE CENTRE
NC
ND
C

Balnacoil
538 COL-BHEINN
Glen Sletdale
Glen Loth
Lothmore
11
Portgower
Gordonbush
Lothbeg
Lothbeg Pt.
Loch Brora
A9

GLEN HORN
521
Loch Horn
377 CAGAR FEOSAIG
Backies
9
Achrimsdale
East Clyne
West Clyne
Clynelish
CLYNELISH DISTILLERY
Dalchalm
Doll
Brora
D

Dunrobin Castle Museum & Gardens
Golspie
90

ily
Kirkton
LOCH FLEET
Littleferry
KELBO ASTLE
Fourpenny
Embo
Embo Street
grudy
WITCHES STONE
OLD POST OFFICE
VISITOR CENTRE
Dornoch
E

THUS'S
FIRTH
NH
Tarbat Ness
TARBAT NESS LIGHTHOUSE
Wilkhaven
NJ
F

Whiteness Sands
Tarbat Discovery Centre
Bindal
Portmahomack
LOCH

la
Inver
Arboll
Rockfield
Balnagall
Tarrel
Lochslin
B9165
Loch Eye
158
Geanies House
88

ilton
FEARN ABBEY
Rhynie
Fearn Station
Hill of Fearn
Fearn
B9165
5
Loans of Tullich
Hilton of Cadboll
Balintore
G

5
6
30
7
31
8

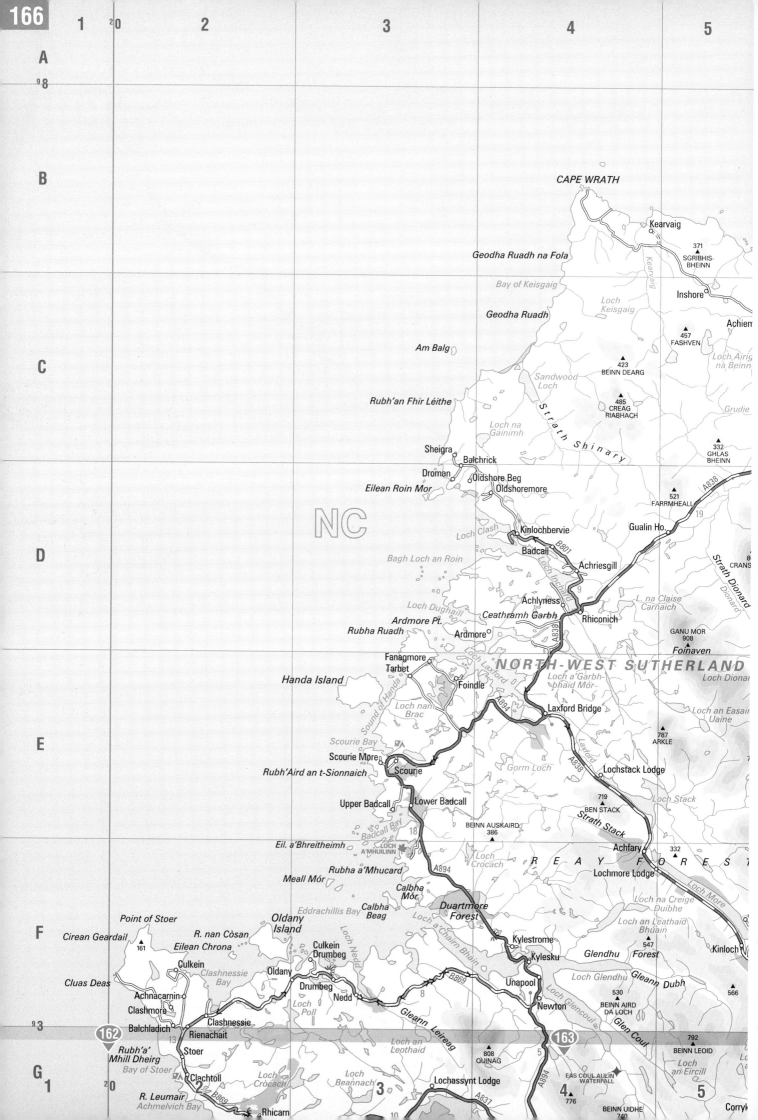

1 20 2 3 4 5

A 98

B

CAPE WRATH

Kearvaig

Geodha Ruadh na Fola

371
SGRIBHIS-
BHEINN

Bay of Keisgaig

Loch
Keisgaig

Inshore

Achie

Geodha Ruadh

457
FASHVEN

Loch Airig
nà Beinn

Am Balg

C

423
BEINN DEARG

Sandwood
Loch

Strath Shinary

Rubh'an Fhir Léithe

485
CREAG
RIABHACH

Grudie

Loch na
Gáinimh

332
GHLAS
BHEINN

Sheigra

Balchrick

Droman Oldshore Beg

Eilean Roin Mor Oldshoremore

521
FARRMHEALL

A838

19

NC

Loch Clash

Kinlochbervie

Gualin Ho.

D

Badcall

B801

Achriesgill

Strath Dionard

CRANS

Bagh Loch an Roin

Loch Inchard

9

L. na Claise
Carnaich

Loch Dughaill

Achlyness

Ardmore Pt.

Ceathramh Garbh

Rhiconich

Rubha Ruadh

Ardmore

A838

GANU MOR
908

Foinaven

Fanagmore
Tarbet

NORTH-WEST SUTHERLAND

Loch Dionar

Handa Island

Foindle

Loch a'Garbh-
bhaid Mór

Loch Laxford

Loch nam
Brac

A894

Laxford Bridge

Loch an Easair
Uaine

Sound of Handa

787
ARKLE

E

Scourie Bay

Gorm Loch

A838

Lochstack Lodge

Loch Stack

Scourie More

Scourie

Rubh'Aird an t-Sionnaich

Laxford

719
BEN STACK

Upper Badcall Lower Badcall

Strath Stack

Badcall Bay

18

BEINN AUSKAIRD
386

Achfary

332

Eil. a'Breitheimh

LOCH
A'MHUILINN

Lochmore Lodge

Rubha a'Mhucard

Loch
Crocach

R E A Y F O R E S T

Meall Mór

Calbha Mór

Loch na Creige
Duibhe

Loch More

Eddrachillis Bay

Calbha
Beag

Loch a'Chairn Bhàin

Duartmore
Forest

Loch an Leathaid
Bhúain

F

Point of Stoer

Oldany
Island

547

Cirean Geardail

R. nan Còsan

Kylestrome

Glendhu Forest

Kinloch

161

Eilean Chrona

Culkein
Drumbeg

Kylesku

Gleann Dubh

Cluas Deas

Culkein

Oldany

Loch Glendhu

566

Clashnessie Bay

Drumbeg

Loch Nedd

Unapool

530
BEINN AIRD
DA LOCH

Achnacarnin

Gleann Leireag

8

Loch Glencoul

Clashmore

Loch
Poll

Nedd

Newton

B869

Balchladich

Clashnessie

162

Rienachait

13

163

792
BEINN LEOID

Rubh'a'
Mhill Dheirg

Stoer

Loch an
Leothaid

808
QUINAG

A894

5

EAS COUL AULIN
WATERFALL

Loch
an Eircill

G 1 20 2 3 4 5

Bay of Stoer

Clachtoll

Loch
Cròcach

Loch
Beannach

Lochassynt Lodge

A837

776

Corryk

R. Leumair

B869

Rhicarn

BEINN UIDHE
740

Achmelvich Bay

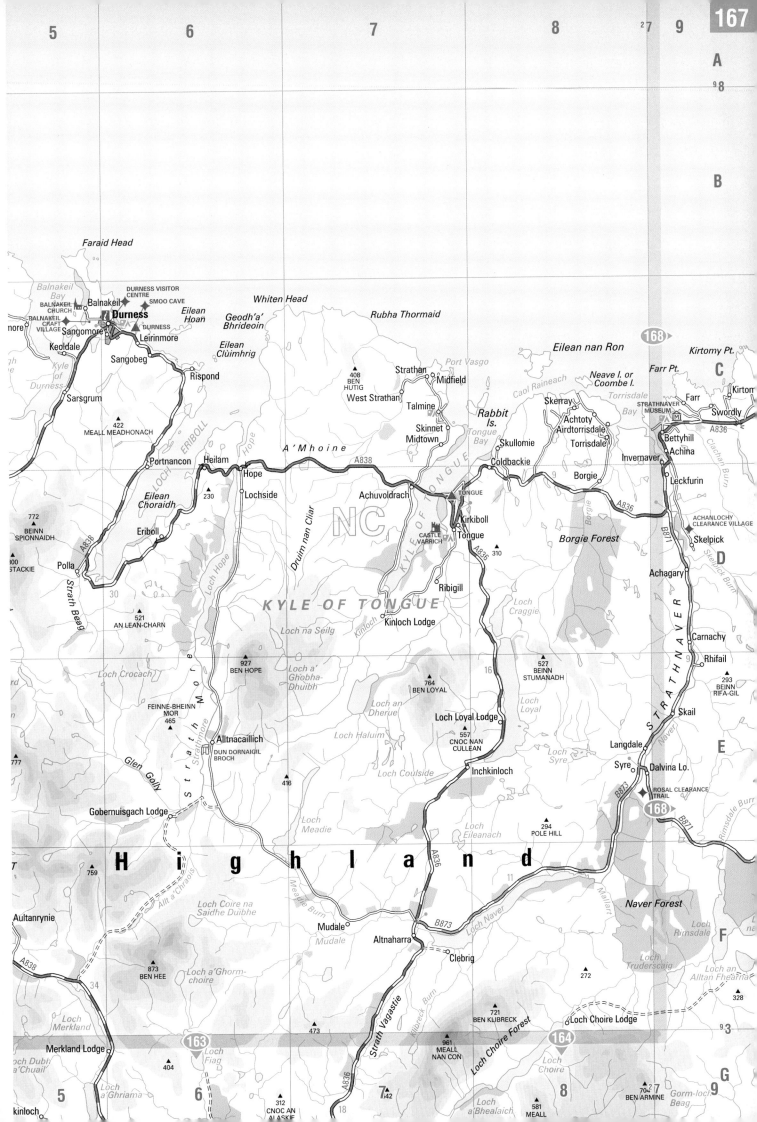

A B C D E F G

5 6 7 8 9

Faraid Head

Balnakeil Bay
Balnakeil Church
BALNAKEIL CRAFT VILLAGE
Balnakeil
DURNESS VISITOR CENTRE
SMOO CAVE
Durness
DURNESS
Sangomore
Eilean Hoan
Leirinmore
Keoldale
Sangobeg
Durness
Sarsgrum
Rispond
Kyle of Durness

Whiten Head

Geodh' a' Bhrideoin
Eilean Clùimhrig
Eilean Choraidh

Rubha Thormaid

Port Vasgo
Eilean nan Ron
Neave I. or Coombe I.
Farr Pt.

168

Kirtomy Pt.
Kirton
Farr
Swordly
Kirton

408 BEN HUTIG
Strathan
Midfield
West Strathan
Talmine
Skinnet
Midtown

Rabbit Is.
Tongue Bay
Skerray
Achtoty
Airdtorrisdale
Torrisdale
Skullomie
Coldbackie
Borgie

Caol Raineach
Torrisdale Bay
STRATHNAVER MUSEUM
Bettyhill
Invernaver
Achina
Leckfurin

A836

422 MEALL MEADHONACH
Portnancon
Heilam
Hope
230
Lochside
Polla
Eribol
Eilean Choraidh
LOCH ERIBOLL

A'Mhoine
A838

NC

Achuvoldrach
CASTLE VARRICH
Kirkiboll
Tongue
310

Borgie Forest

9

A836

B871

ACHANLOCHY CLEARANCE VILLAGE
Skelpick
Achagary
Carnachy
Rhifail

293 BEINN RIFA-GIL

772 BEINN SPIONNAIDH
STACKIE
Strath Beag
Loch Hope

521 AN LEAN-CHARN

Druim nan Cliar

KYLE OF TONGUE

Ribigill

Loch na Seilg
Kinloch
Kinloch Lodge

Loch Craggie

Loch Loyal

STRATHNAVER
Skail

927 BEN HOPE

FEINNE-BHEINN MOR
465

Strath More

Loch Crocach

Loch a' Ghobha-Dhuibh

764 BEN LOYAL

527 BEINN STUMANADH

16

Loch Loyal

Loch an Dherue

Loch Haluim

Loch Loyal Lodge

557 CNOC NAN CULLEAN

Loch Syre

Langdale
Syre
Dalvina Lo.

ROSAL CLEARANCE TRAIL
168

777
Glen Golly
416
Loch Coulside
Inchkinloch
B873

DUN DORNAIGIL BROCH
Alltnacaillich

Gobernuisgach Lodge

Loch Meadie

Loch Eileanach

294 POLE HILL

B871

Rimsdale Burn

H i g h l a n d
759

Allt a'Chraois

Loch Coire na Saidhe Duibhe

Meadie Burn

A836

B873

Loch Naver

11

Mallart

Naver Forest

Loch Rimsdale

Loch an Alltan Fhearna

Aultanrynie

Mudale
Mudale
Altnaharra

328

A838

873 BEN HEE

Loch a'Ghorm-choire

34

Strath Vagastie

Clebrig

Klibreck Burn

272

Loch Truderscaig

Loch Merkland

9 3

Merkland Lodge
163
Loch Fiag

473

721 BEN KLIBRECK

Loch Choire Lodge
164

Loch Choire Forest

Loch Dubh a'Chuail
404

961 MEALL NAN CON

Loch Choire

9 2 7
BEN ARMINE

kinloch
312 CNOC AN ALASKIE

18

7 42

581 MEALL

Gorm-loch Beag

5 6 7 8 9

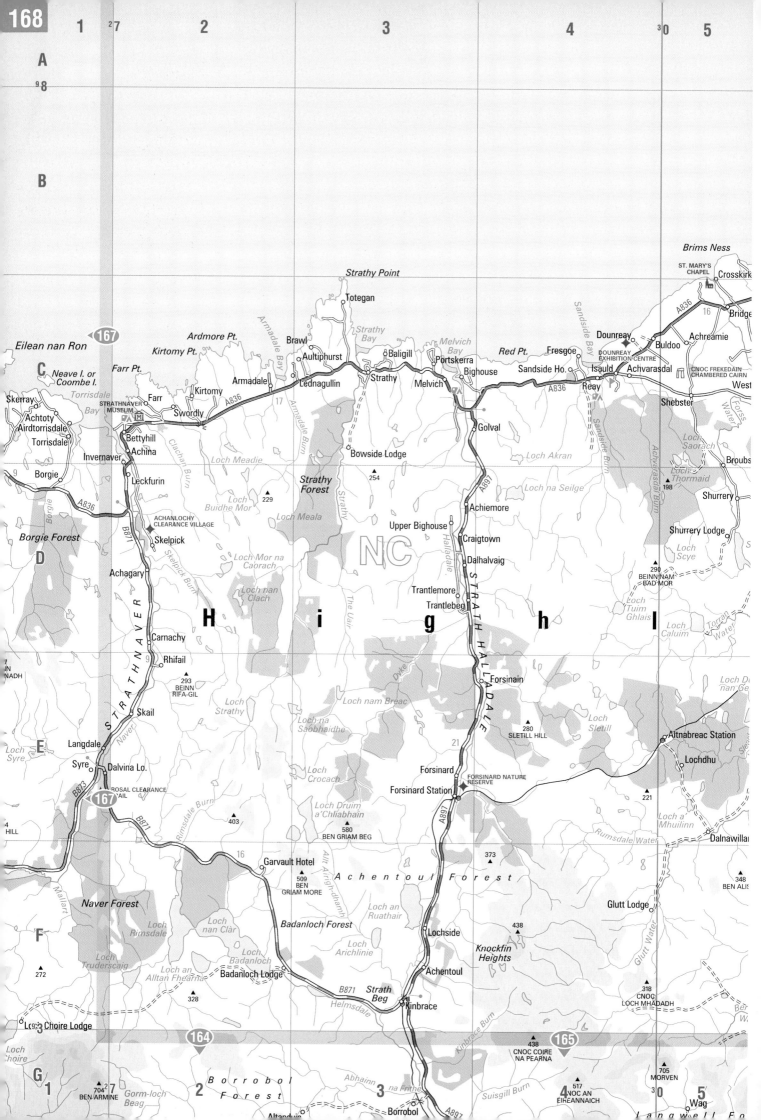

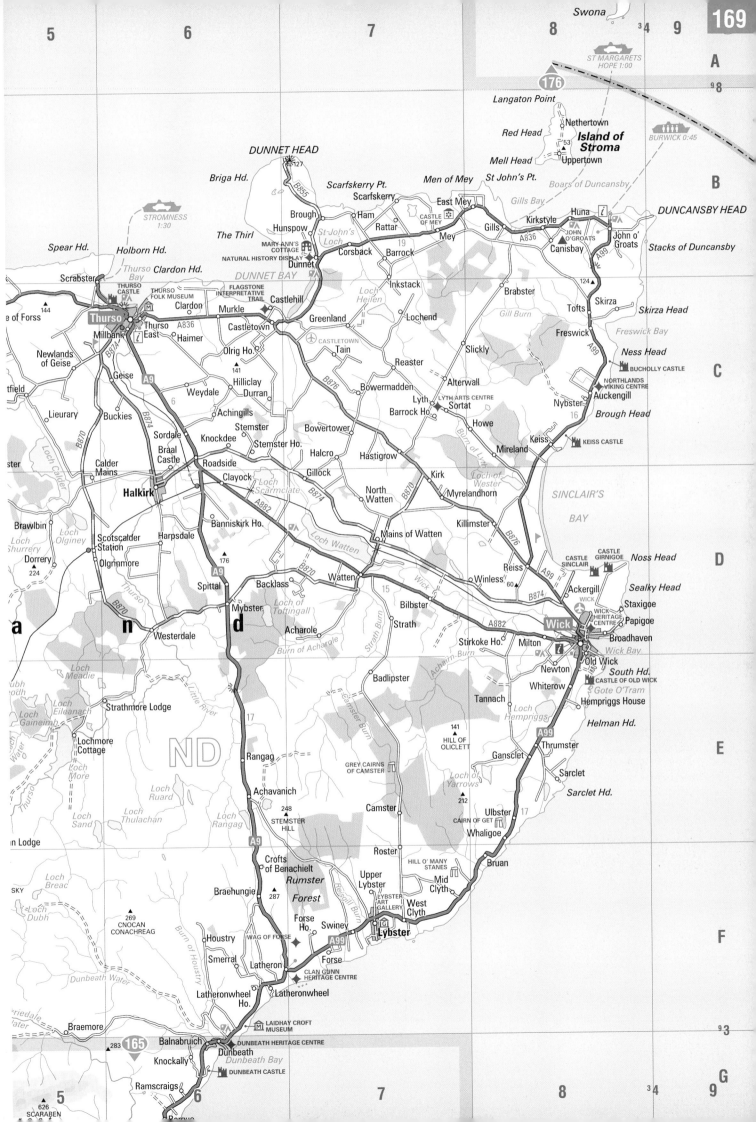

Swona

St Margarets Hope 1:00
176
Burwick 0:45

Langaton Point

Red Head · Nethertown

Island of Stroma
53
Mell Head
Uppertown

Men of Mey · *St John's Pt.*
Boars of Duncansby

DUNNET HEAD
127

Briga Hd.

Scarfskerry Pt. · Scarfskerry
Brough · Ham · Rattar
CASTLE OF MEY
East Mey
Gills Bay
Huna
i
DUNCANSBY HEAD

Hunspow
Mey · Gills
A836
Kirkstyle
JOHN O'GROATS
John o' Groats
Stacks of Duncansby

The Thirl
MARY-ANN'S COTTAGE
NATURAL HISTORY DISPLAY
Dunnet
Corsback · Barrock
Canisbay

STROMNESS 1:30

Spear Hd. · *Holborn Hd.*
FLAGSTONE INTERPRETATIVE TRAIL
Castlehill
Inkstack
Brabster
124

Clardon Hd.
DUNNET BAY
Greenland
Loch Heilen
Lochend
Skirza
Tofts
Skirza Head

Scrabster
THURSO CASTLE
Clardon
Castletown
Tain
Reaster
Slickly
Freswick
Freswick Bay

Thurso
144
THURSO FOLK MUSEUM
Murkle
Haimer
Castletown
CASTLETOWN
Ness Head
BUCHOLLY CASTLE

Millbank
Thurso East
A836
Olrig Ho.
141
Hilliclay
Durran
Bowermadden
Lyth
LYTH ARTS CENTRE
Sortat
Howe
NORTHLANDS VIKING CENTRE
Auckengill

Newlands of Geise
Geise
Weydale
Achingills
Reaster
Nybster
16
Brough Head

Lieurary
Buckies
Sordale
Stemster
Bowertower
Hastigrow
Keiss
KEISS CASTLE

Calder Mains
Braal Castle
Knockdee
Stemster Ho.
Halcro
Kirk
Mireland

-field
Roadside
Clayock
Gillock
North Watten
Myrelandhorn
Loch of Wester

Brawlbin
Loch Olginey
Halkirk
Loch Scarmclate
B874
B870
Killimster
SINCLAIR'S BAY

Scotscalder Station
Harpsdale
Banniskirk Ho.
A882
Mains of Watten
Reiss
CASTLE GIRNIGOE
CASTLE SINCLAIR
Noss Head

Dorrery
224
Olgrinmore
176
Loch of Toftingall
Watten
15
Winless
60
Ackergill
Sealky Head

Spittal
Backlass
Bilbster
WICK
Staxigoe

Westerdale
Mybster
Acharole
Strath
Stirkoke Ho.
Milton
Wick
WICK HERITAGE CENTRE
Papigoe

Burn of Acharole
Strath Burn
Broadhaven

Loch Meadie
Badlipster
Tannach
Newton
Old Wick
Wick Bay
South Hd.

Strathmore Lodge
Loch Eileanach
Whiterow
CASTLE OF OLD WICK
Gote O'Tram

Loch Gaineimh
Lochmore Cottage
Loch More
HILL OF OLICLETT
141
Loch Hempriggs
Hempriggs House
Helman Hd.

ND
Rangag
GREY CAIRNS OF CAMSTER
Gansclet
Thrumster
A99

Loch Ruard
Achavanich
212
Loch of Yarrows
Sarclet

Loch Sand
Loch Thulachan
248
STEMSTER HILL
Camster
CAIRN OF GET
Ulbster
17
Sarclet Hd.

Loch Rangag
Roster
HILL O' MANY STANES
Whaligoe

Loch Breac
Crofts of Benachielt
Rumster Forest
287
Upper Lybster
Mid Clyth
Bruan

-SKY
Loch Dubh
269
CNOCAN CONACHREAG
Braehungie
LYBSTER ART GALLERY
West Clyth
Forse Ho.
Swiney
Lybster

Houstry
WAG OF FORSE
Forse

Smerral
Latheron
CLAN GUNN HERITAGE CENTRE

Dunbeath Water
Latheronwheel Ho.
Latheronwheel

Friedale Water
Braemore
LAIDHAY CROFT MUSEUM

283
165
Balnabruich
DUNBEATH HERITAGE CENTRE
Knockally
Dunbeath
Dunbeath Bay
DUNBEATH CASTLE

Ramscraigs

626
SCARABEN

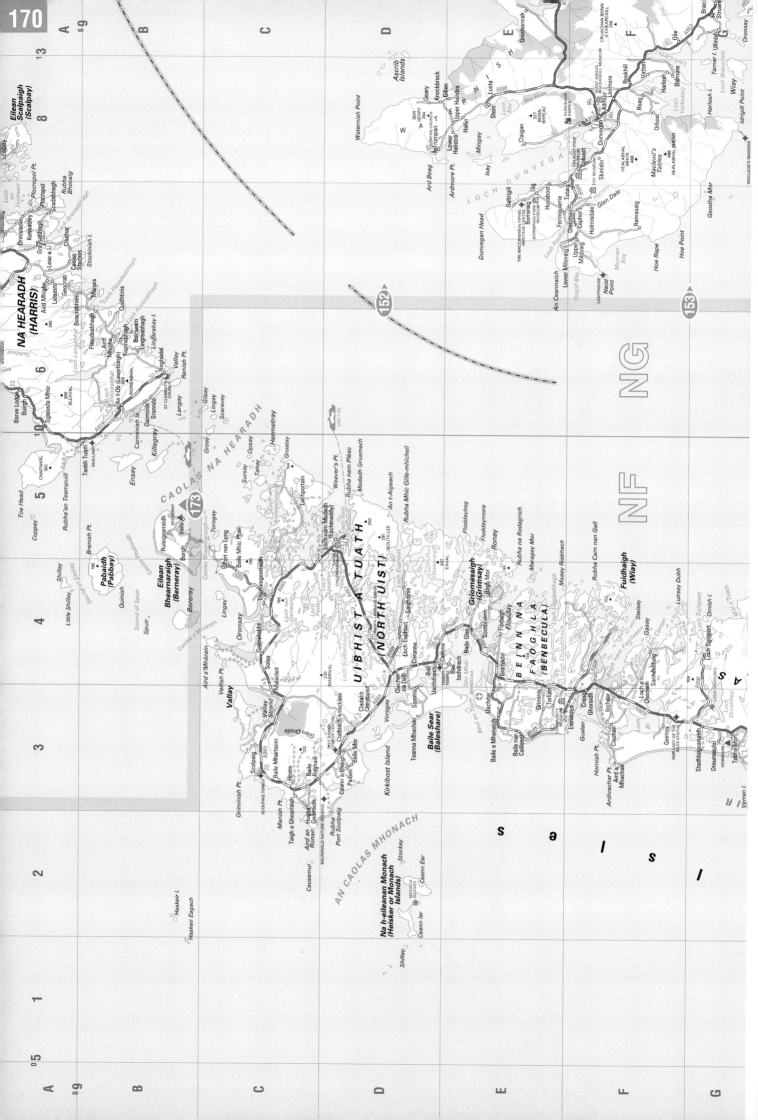

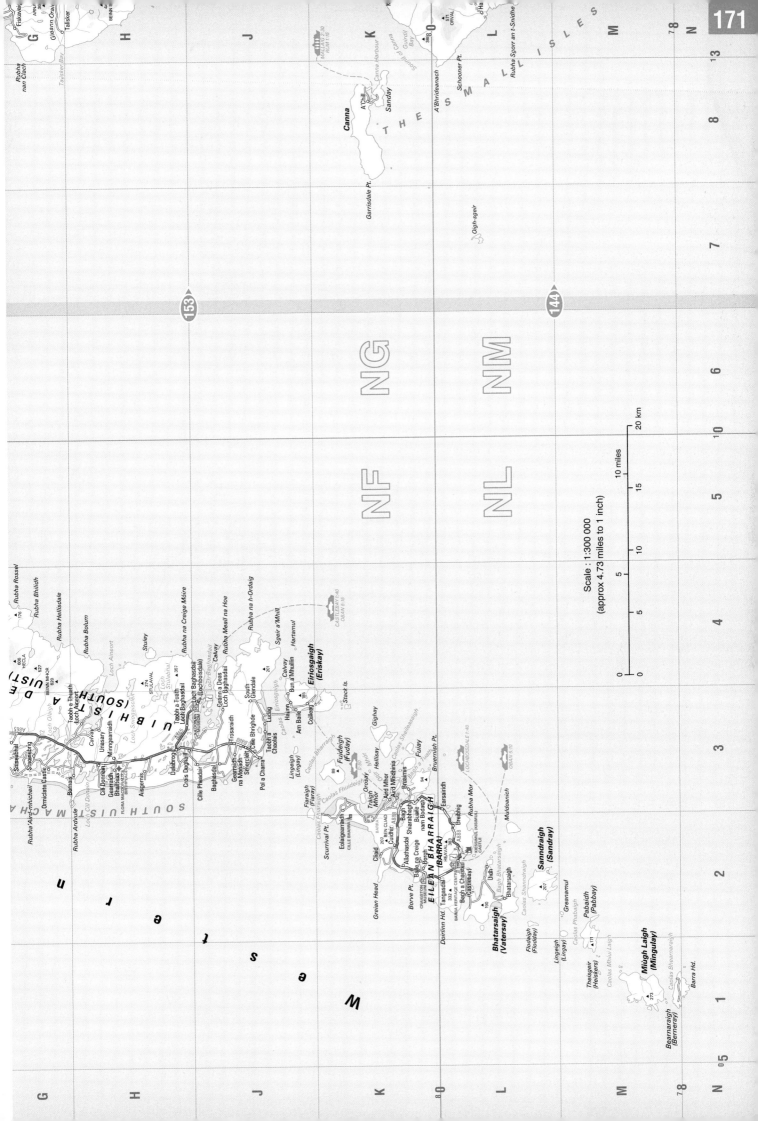

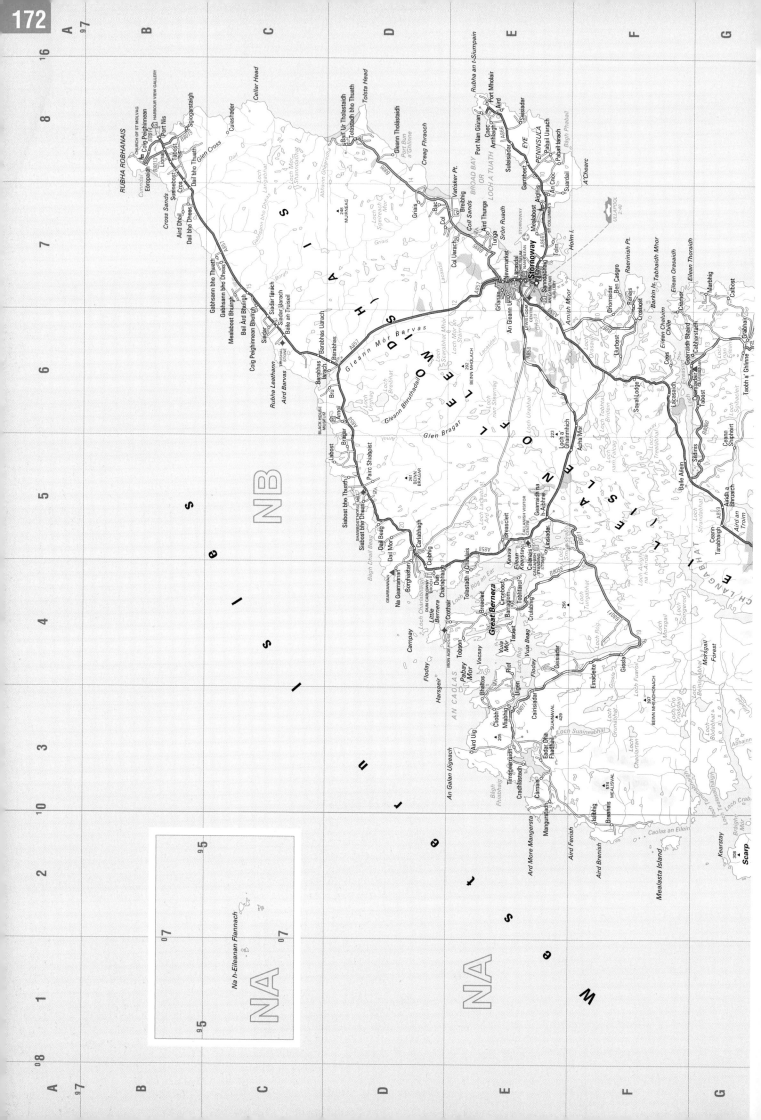

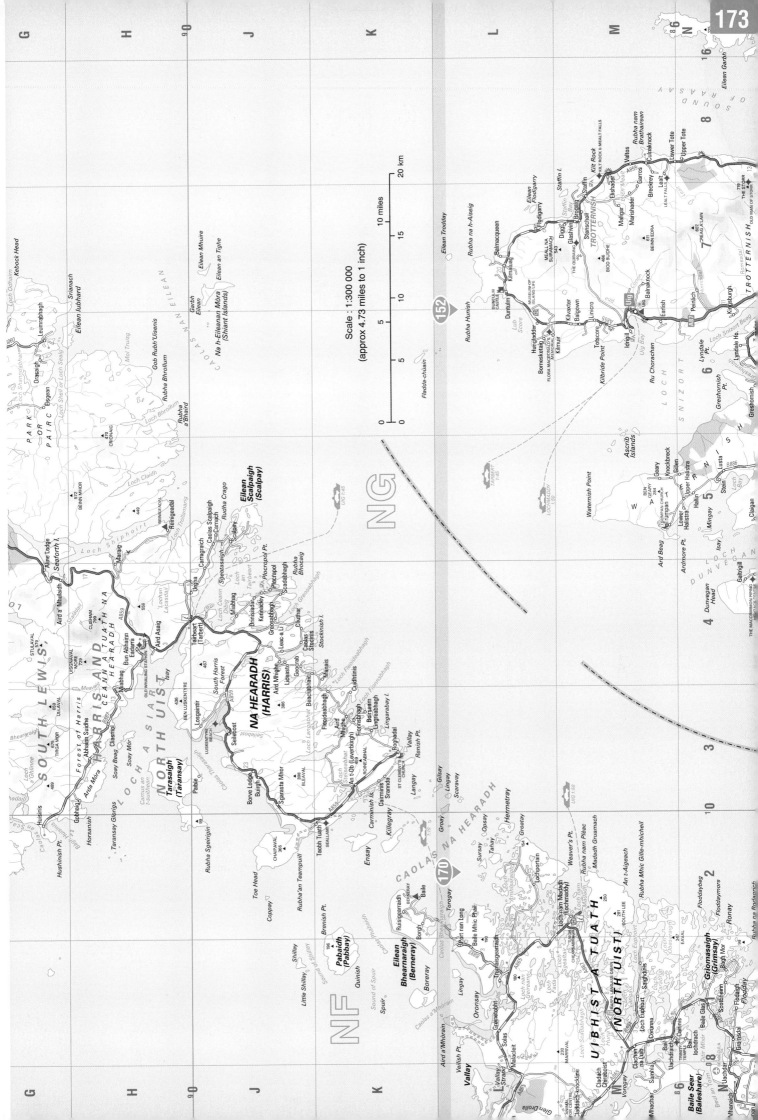

Scale : 1:300 000

(approx 4.73 miles to 1 inch)

0   5   10   15   20 km

0   5   10 miles

SOUTH LEWIS,
Kebock Head
Leumrabhagh
Loch Odhairn
Orasaigh
Loch Sealg or Loch Seaforth
Eilean Iubhard
Espean
Srianach
Mol Truisg
Gob Rubh'Uisenis
Rubha Bhrollum
Loch Bhrollum
Rubha a'Bhaird

Garbh Eilean
Eilean Mhuire
Eilean an Tighe
Na h-Eileanan Móra
(Shiant Islands)

CAOLAS NAN EILEAN

Aline Lodge
Seaforth I.
PARK OR PÁIRC
Loch Shell or Loch Seilig
CRONAIG

Loch Shiphoirt

Loch Claidh

Reinigeadal
BEINIGEADAL
Maraig
Loch Trollamarig

HARRIS AND
CEANN A TUATH NA HEARADH
572 BEINN MHOR
Loch Lacasdail
Loch Ceann Dibig

Eilean Scalpaigh
(Scalpay)
Caolas Scalpaigh
Rudha Cró
Camach
Scalpay

Ùithaig
Carragraich
Sgeatasaigh
Loch an Tairbeart
Kennavay
Plocrapol
Procrapol
Rubha Plocrapol Pt.
Scadabhagh
Rubha
Bhocaig
Loch Greosabhagh
Cliuthar

NF
NG

UIG 145

Tarbert (Tarbert)
Tairbeart
Brinisiadar
Miabhag
Aird Mhighe
Loch Fleodeabhagh
Stockinish I.
Caolas Stocinis
Stocinis
Leac a Lì
Geocrab
Manais

449
Reinigeadal

Cliasmol
Soay Beag
Soay Mór
TIRGA MOR
676
Forest of Harris
ULUAVAL
729
Meavaig
A859
Clisham
Aird Asaig
Bun Abhainn
Eadarra
OLD WHALING STATION
Isay

NORTH UIST
LOCH A SIAR
Abhainn Suidhe
Arda Móra
Aird a' Mhuladaidh

489
Bhearraigh
659 ULAVAL
OLAVAL
Hushinish
Hushinish Pt.
Horsanish
Gobhaig

STULAVAL
579

436
BEN LUSKENTYRE
386
South Harris Forest
A859
LUSKENTYRE BEACH
Losgaintir
467
Seilebost
Borve Lodge
Buirgh
Sgarasta Mhor
388 BLEAVAL

NA HEARADH
(HARRIS)
Aird Mhighe
Beacrabhaic
Fleodeabhagh
Bodraoim
Boilseam
Aird Mhighe
Loch Langabhat
Loch Fionnsbhagh
Lingarabay I.
An t-Ob (Leverburgh)
RONEABHAL
ST CLEMENT'S CHURCH
Strannda
Carminish Is.
Carminish I.
Taobh Tuath
SEALLAM!

Boghadal
Renish Pt.
Valley
Langay
Gilsay
Groay
Lingay
Scaravay

CAOLAS NA HEARADH

UIG 170

Tarasaigh
(Taransay)
Paible
Taransay Glorigs
Rubha Sgeirigin
CHAPAVAL
366
Toe Head
Rubha'an Teampuill

Ensay
Killegray
Coppay

Shillay
Little Shillay

Pabaidh
(Pabbay)
196
Quinish
Caolas Shilldinis

Eilean
Bhearnaraigh
(Berneray)
Ruisigearraidh
Borgh
BERNERAY
Baile

Sound of Spuir
Spuir

Aird a'Mhorain
Vellish Pt.
Valley
Vallay Strand
Solas
Malaclet

Borve Mhic Phail
Port nan Long
Torogay

Sursay
Tahay
Opsay
Groatay

Hermetray

Lingay
Oronsay
Geireann
Loch nan Geireann
A865
A867
Loch Scadavay

Flodaybeg
Flodaydmore
An t-Aigeach
Rubha Mhic Gille-mhicheil

UIBHIST A TUATH
(NORTH UIST)
Lochmaddy
(Lochmadaidh)
Lochmaddy
250
SOUTH-LEE
281
Weaver's Pt.
Rubha nam Pleac
Madadh Gruamach

Eilean Troddaay

152

Rubha na h-Aiseig
Rubha Hunish
Eilean Trodday
Balmacqueen
Kilmaluag
Duntulm
DUNTULM CASTLE
MUSEUM OF ISLAND LIFE
Kilmuir
FLORA MACDONALD'S MONUMENT
Hungladder
Bornesketaig
Lub Score
Kilvaxter
Balgown
Linicro
Totscore
Idrigill
Uig
MR
A855

Eilean Fladigarry
Flodigarry
Staffin I.
Digg
241
Brogaig
Staffin
KILT ROCK & MEALT FALLS
MEALL NA SURAMACH
543
THE QUIRAING
Glashvin
Stenscholl
Garros
Maligar
Marishader
Ellishader
Brockrey

Rubha nam
Brathairean
Lower Tote
Upper Tote
Culnaknock
Lealt
LEALT FALLS
607
BEINN EDRA
611
PEINGOWN
Earlish
Kingsburgh
Loch Snizort Beag

TROTTERNISH

BIOD BUIDHE
BINN EDRA

Kilmaluag
Balnaknock
Peinlich

Hinnisdal
779
THE STORR
719
OLD MAN OF STORR

Balmeanach
Glashvin

NG

TARBERT 145

Ascrib Islands
Waternish Point
Ard Beag
Ardmore Pt.
Isay
4 Dunvegan Head

W
BEN GEARY
284
Geary
Knockbreck
Gillen
TRUMPAN CHURCH
Trumpan
Lower Halistra
Upper Halistra
Hallin
Stein
Lusta
Loch Bay
Claigan

Mingay
B886

Greshornish Pt.
Greshornish
Ru Chorachan
Lyndale Pt.
Lyndale Ho.
Kilbride Point

THE MACCRIMMON PIPING
MEMORIAL
GALTRIGILL
Gatrigill

LOCH SNIZORT
LOCH DUNVEGAN

Lyndale

UIG 150

Tabost
A865
Tigharry
190
Hougharry
Baleshare
Bayhead
Clachan
Kyles Paible
Cladach Chirceboist
An t-Aigeach
Carinish
TEAMPULL
Claddach-kirkibost

Grimsay
Griomasaigh
(Grimsay)
Baghasdal
Baghmor
347
EAVAL
Flodaigh
Flodday

Ronay
Rubha na Rodaich

Vorogay
Loch Euphort
Saighdinis
Ceallan
Kallin

Baile Sear
(Baleshare)

Lochportain

230
MARRIVAL

Uachdar
BENBECULA
Gramsdal
Grimsdal
Glen Dròlla

Beul an Toilm
Sollas
Malaclet
Strome
Vallaquie

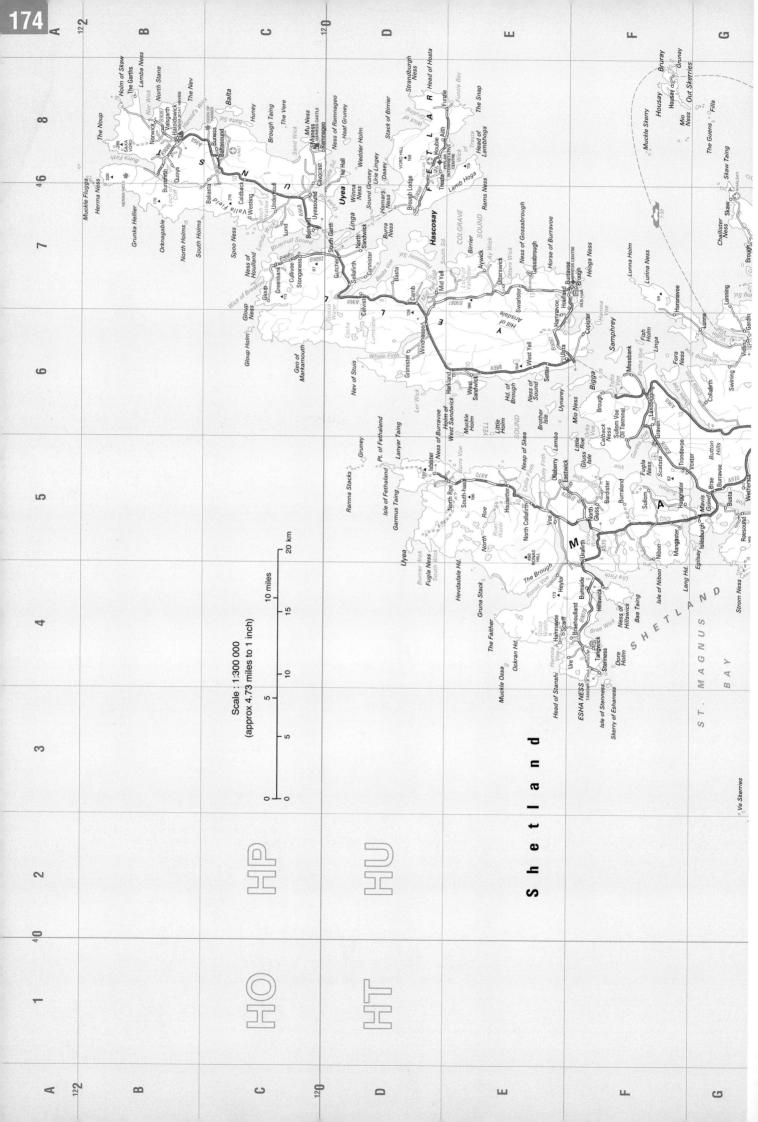

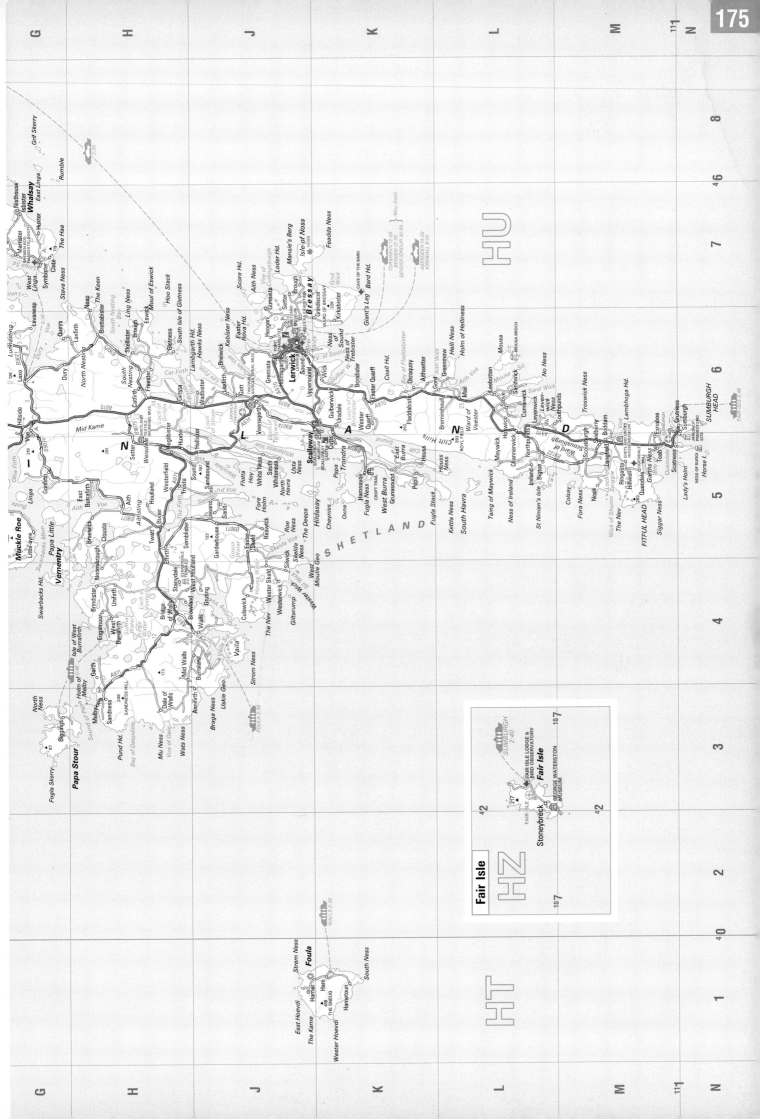

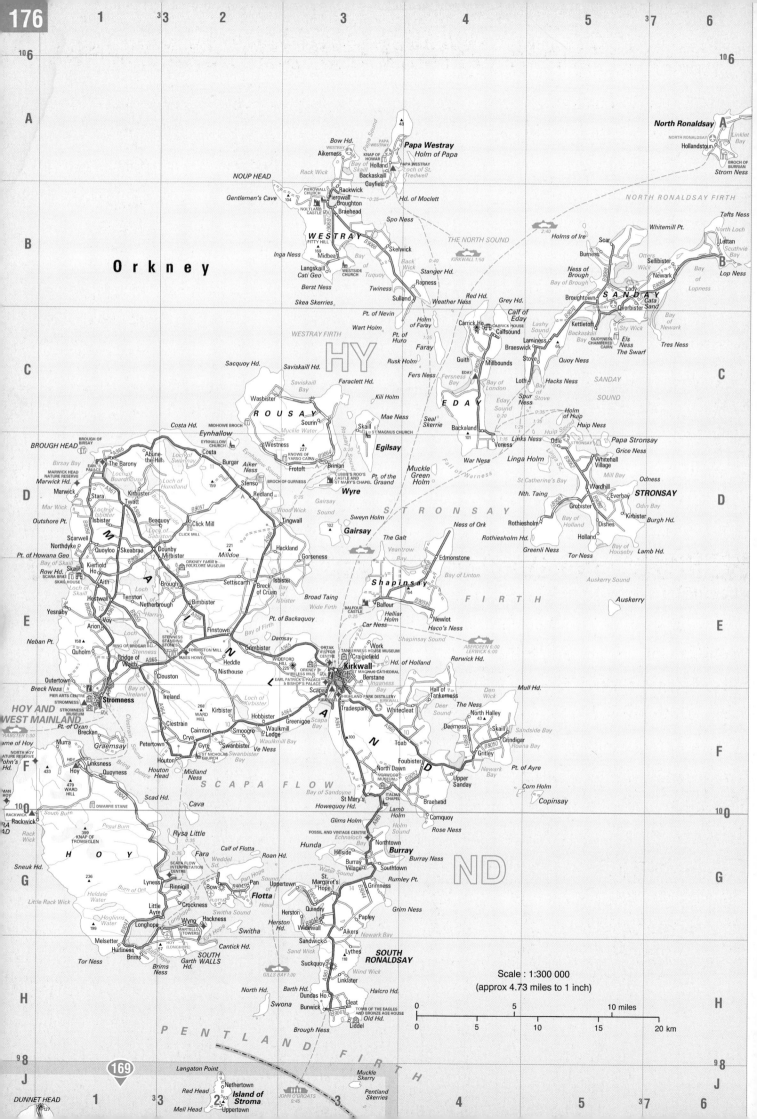

Key to Town Plan Symbols

Motorway	Shopping Streets
Primary Route Dual/Single	Railway
Main Road Dual/Single	Tramway with Station
Secondary Road Dual/Single	Railway/ Bus Station
Minor Through Road/ One Way Street	Shopping Precinct/ Retail Park
Pedestrian Roads	Park

✝ Abbey/Cathedral	⛛ Railway Station
Ancient Monument	Roman Antiquity
Aquarium	Safari Park
Art Gallery	Shopmobility
Bird Garden	Theatre
Building of Public Interest	ℹ Tourist Information Centre (open all year)
Castle	ℹ Tourist Information Centre (open summer only)
Church of Interest	Zoo
Cinema	✦ Other Place of Interest
Garden	Underground/ Metro Station
Historic Ship	Ⓗ Hospital
House	Ⓟ Parking
House & Garden	Police
Museum	PO Post Office
Preserved Railway	▲ Youth Hostel

Key to Approach Mapping Symbols

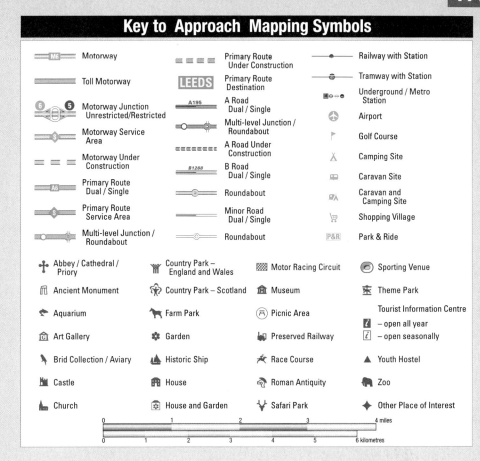

M6 Motorway	Primary Route Under Construction
Toll Motorway	LEEDS Primary Route Destination
Motorway Junction Unrestricted/Restricted	A195 A Road Dual / Single
Motorway Service Area	Multi-level Junction / Roundabout
Motorway Under Construction	A Road Under Construction
A6 Primary Route Dual / Single	B1288 B Road Dual / Single
Primary Route Service Area	Roundabout
Multi-level Junction / Roundabout	Minor Road Dual / Single
	Roundabout

Railway with Station	
Tramway with Station	
Underground / Metro Station	
Airport	
Golf Course	
Camping Site	
Caravan Site	
Caravan and Camping Site	
Shopping Village	
P&R Park & Ride	

✝ Abbey / Cathedral / Priory	Country Park – England and Wales	Motor Racing Circuit	Sporting Venue
Ancient Monument	Country Park – Scotland	Museum	Theme Park
Aquarium	Farm Park	Picnic Area	Tourist Information Centre
Art Gallery	Garden	Preserved Railway	ℹ – open all year
Brid Collection / Aviary	Historic Ship	Race Course	ℹ – open seasonally
Castle	House	Roman Antiquity	▲ Youth Hostel
Church	House and Garden	Safari Park	Zoo
			✦ Other Place of Interest

Scale: 0 – 4 miles / 0 – 6 kilometres

Aberdeen

0 — Miles — ¼

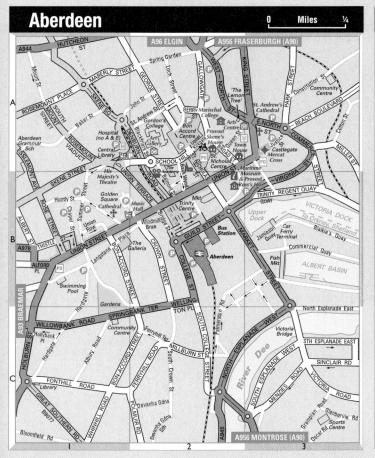

Bath

0 — Miles — ¼

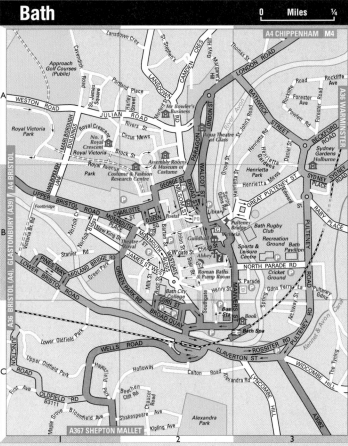

Birmingham

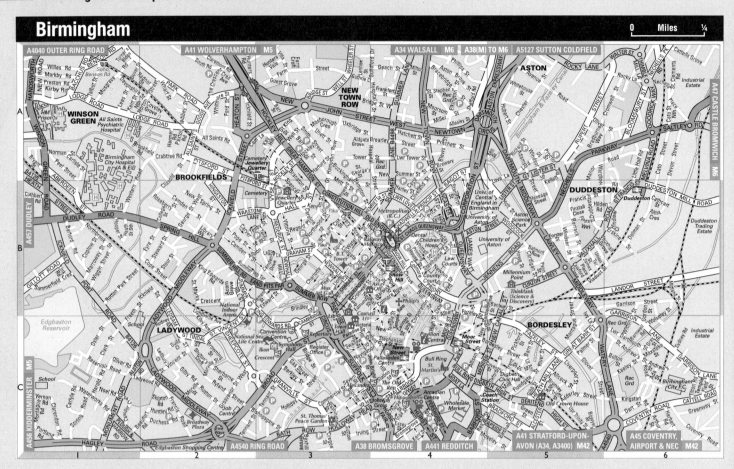

0 Miles ¼

Blackpool

0 Miles ¼

Bournemouth

0 Miles ¼

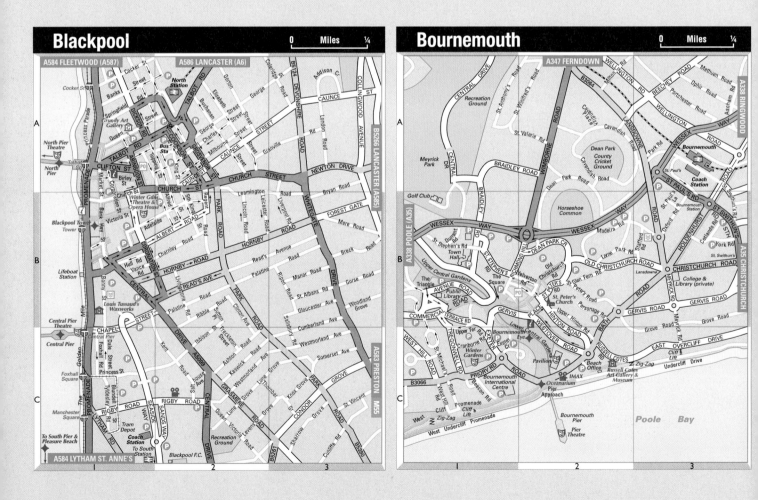

Bradford

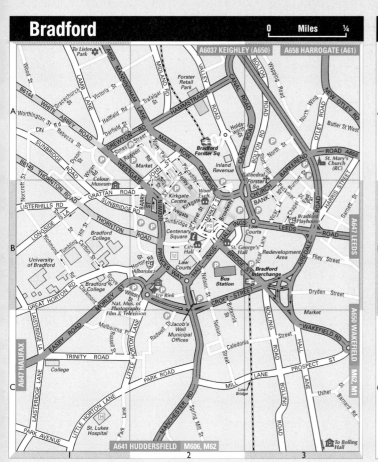

Brighton

Bristol

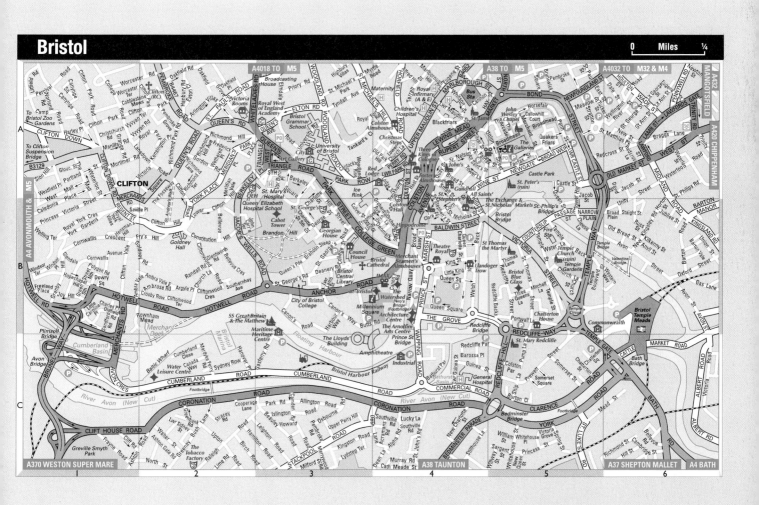

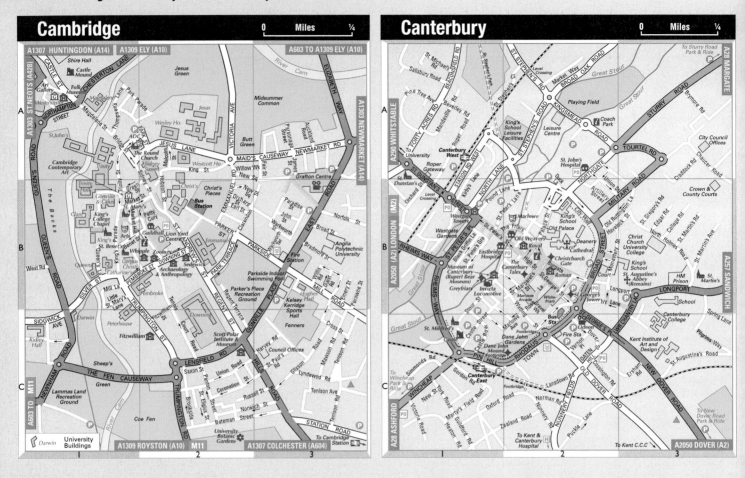

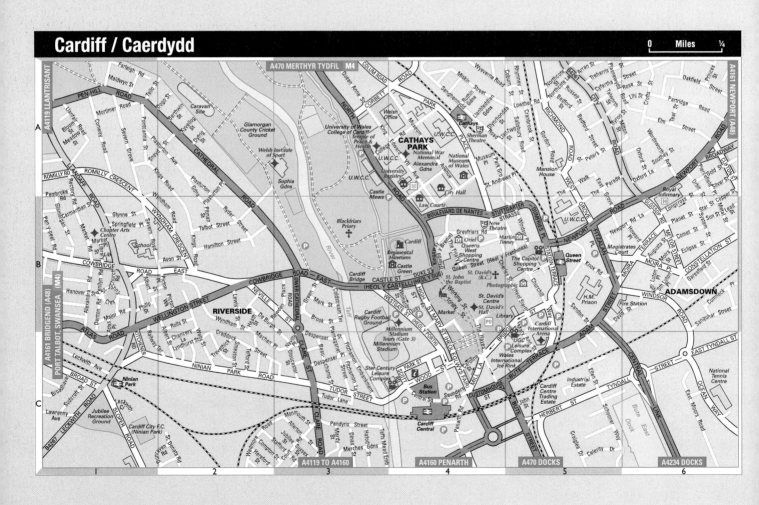

Cheltenham

0 Miles ¼

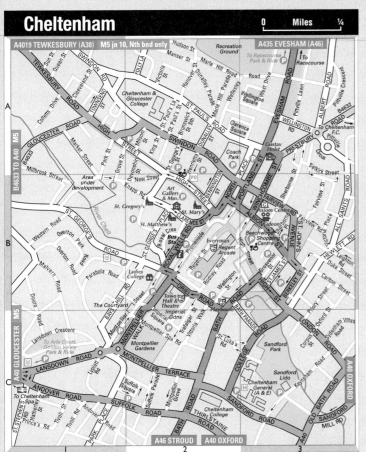

Chester

0 Miles ¼

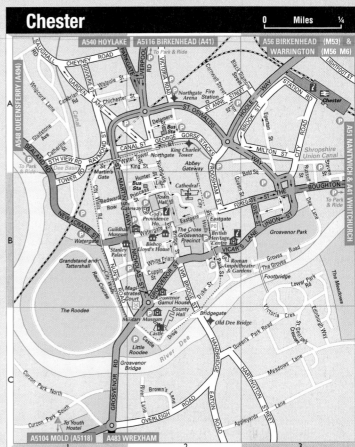

Colchester

0 Miles ¼

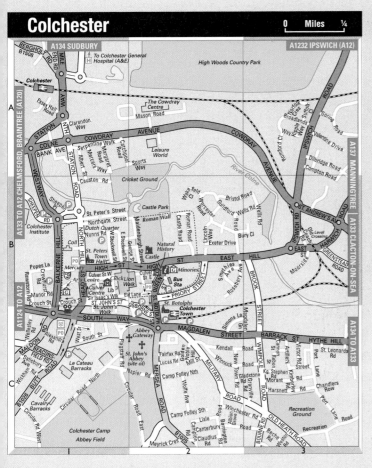

Coventry

0 Miles ¼

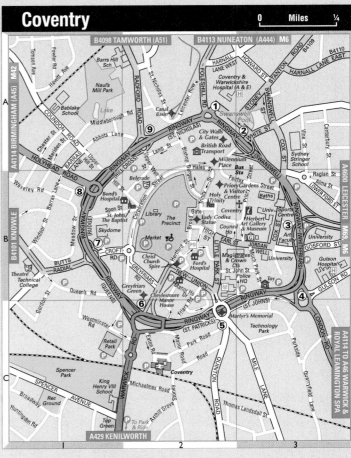

Derby

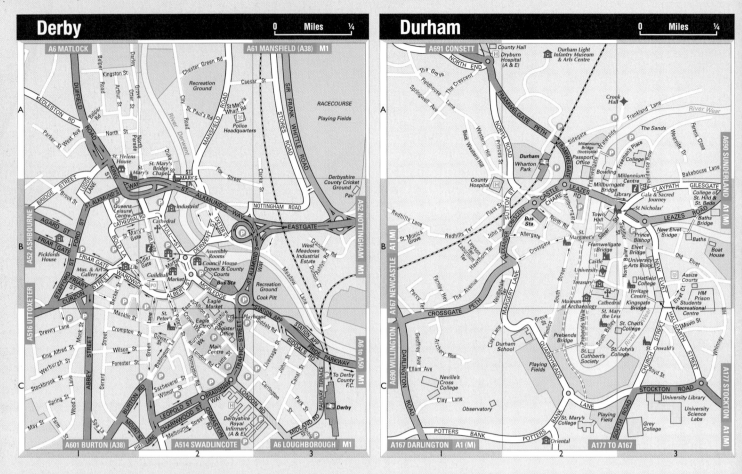

Durham

Edinburgh

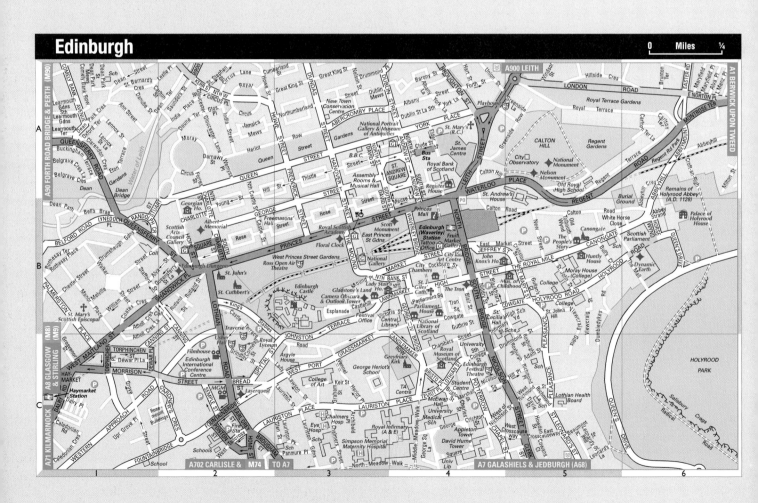

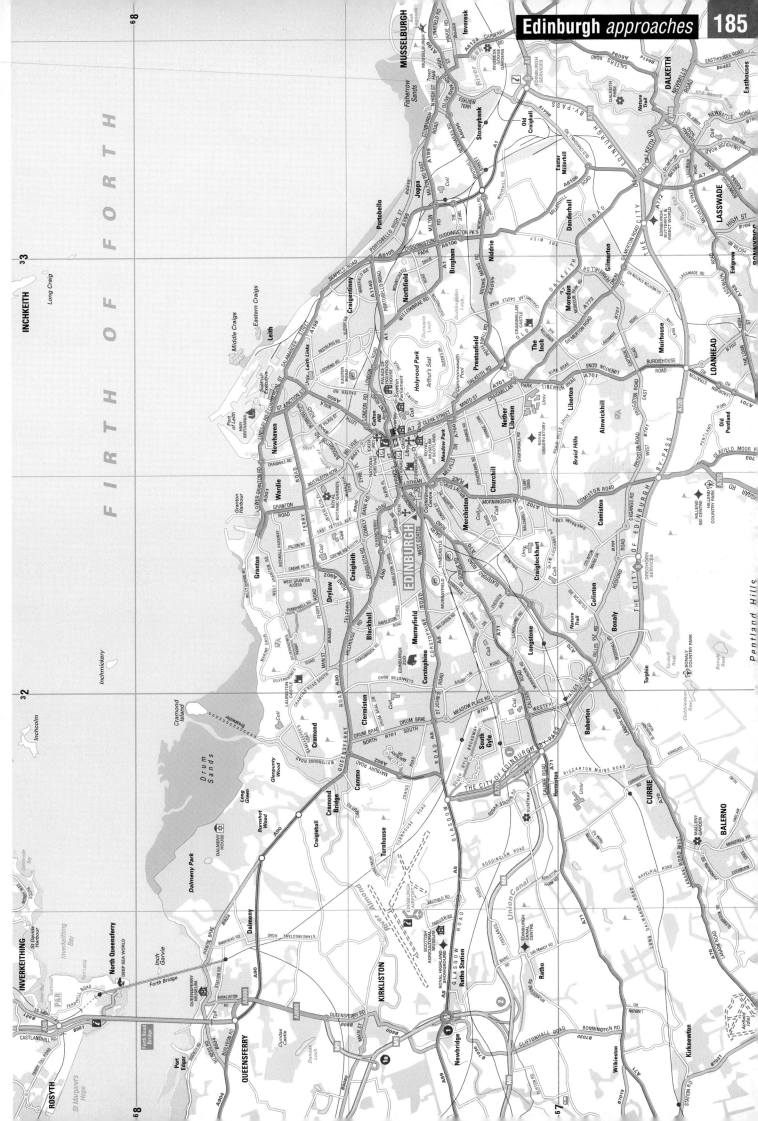

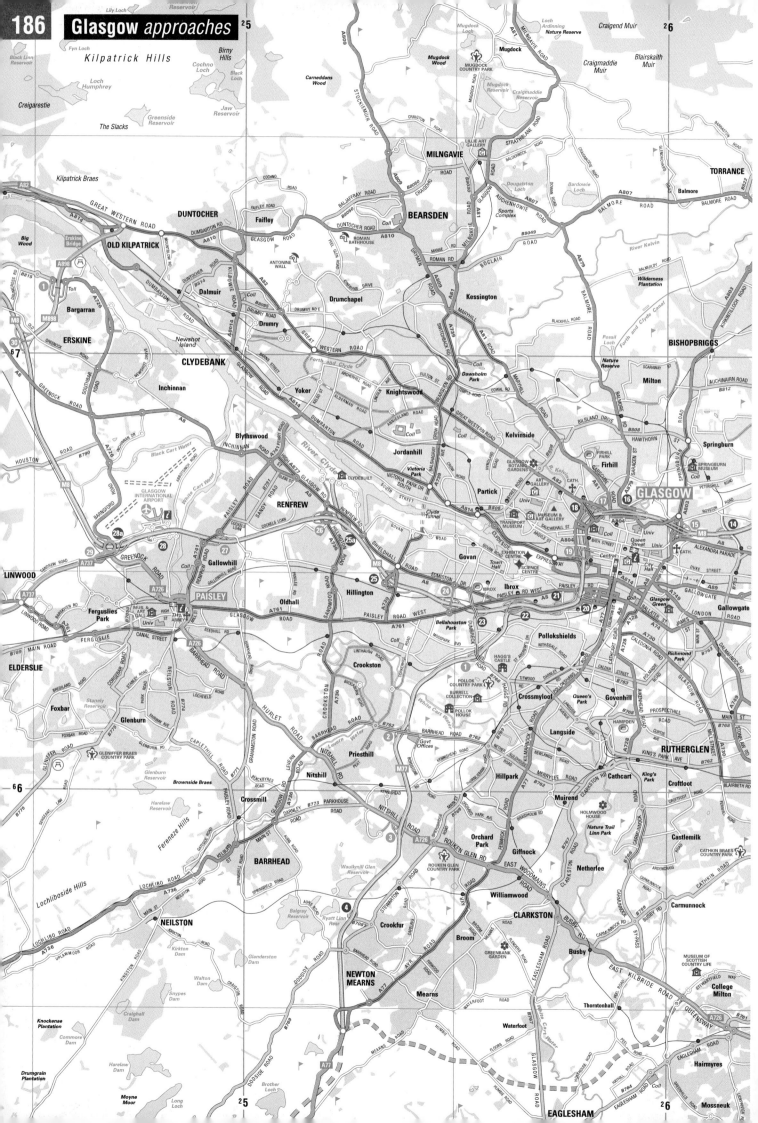

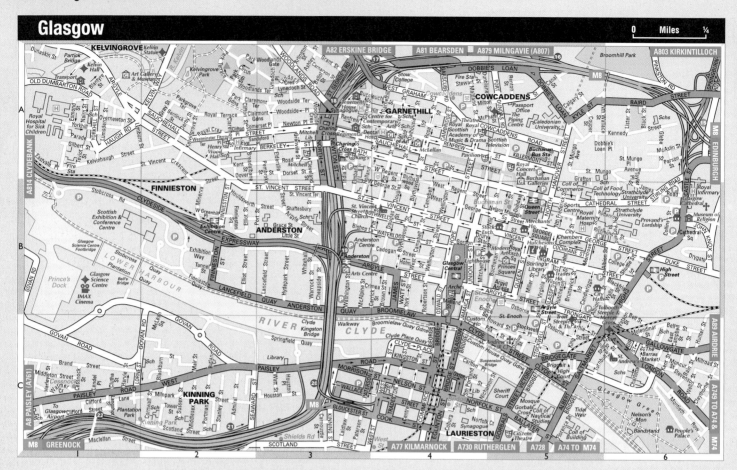

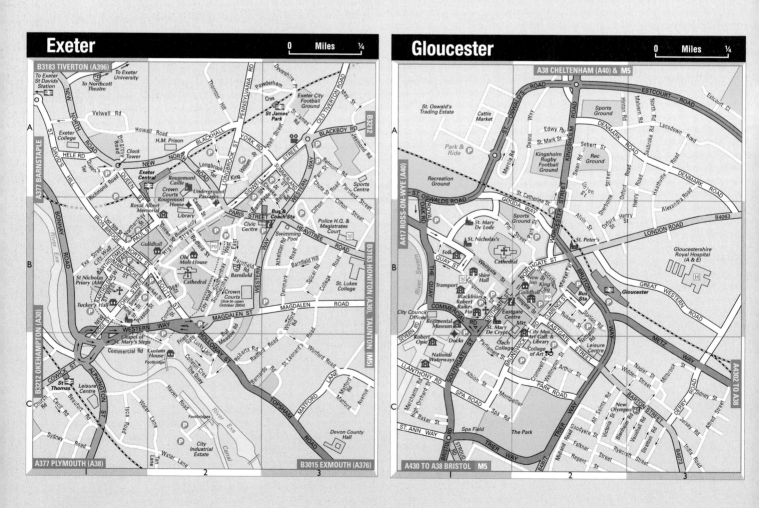

Hull

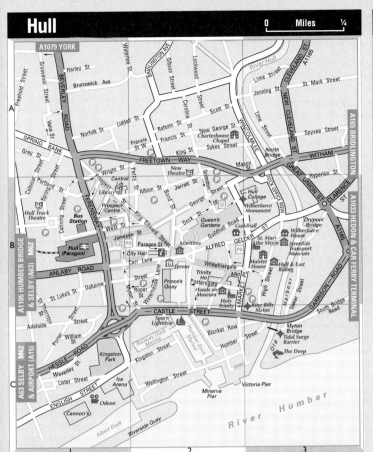

Ipswich

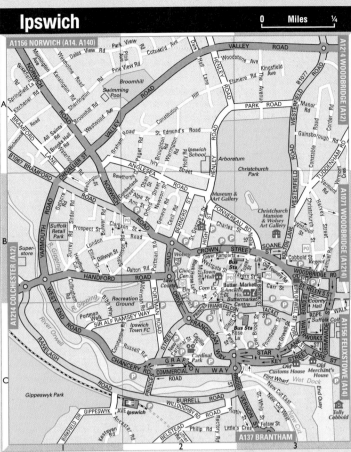

Leeds

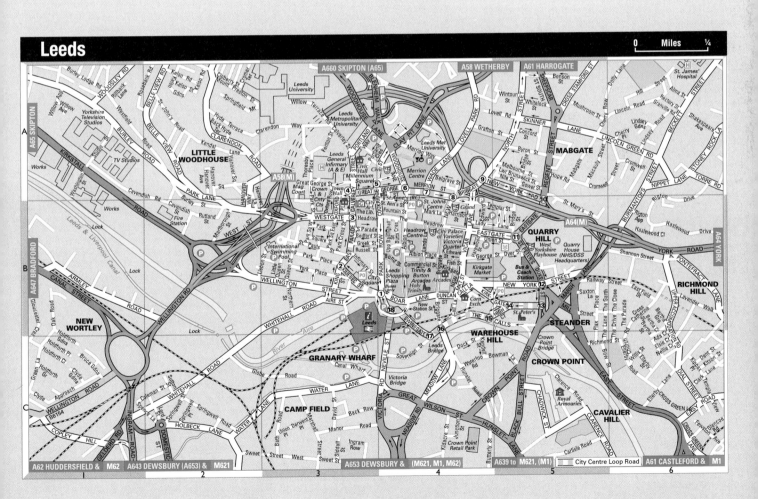

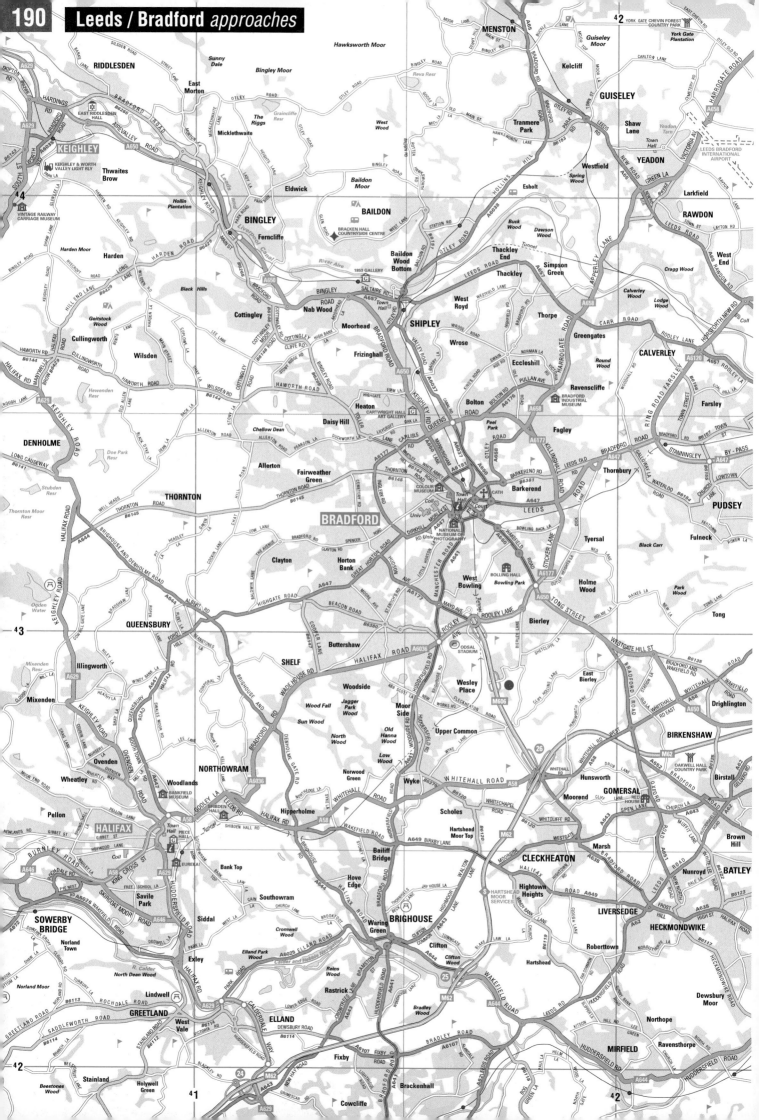

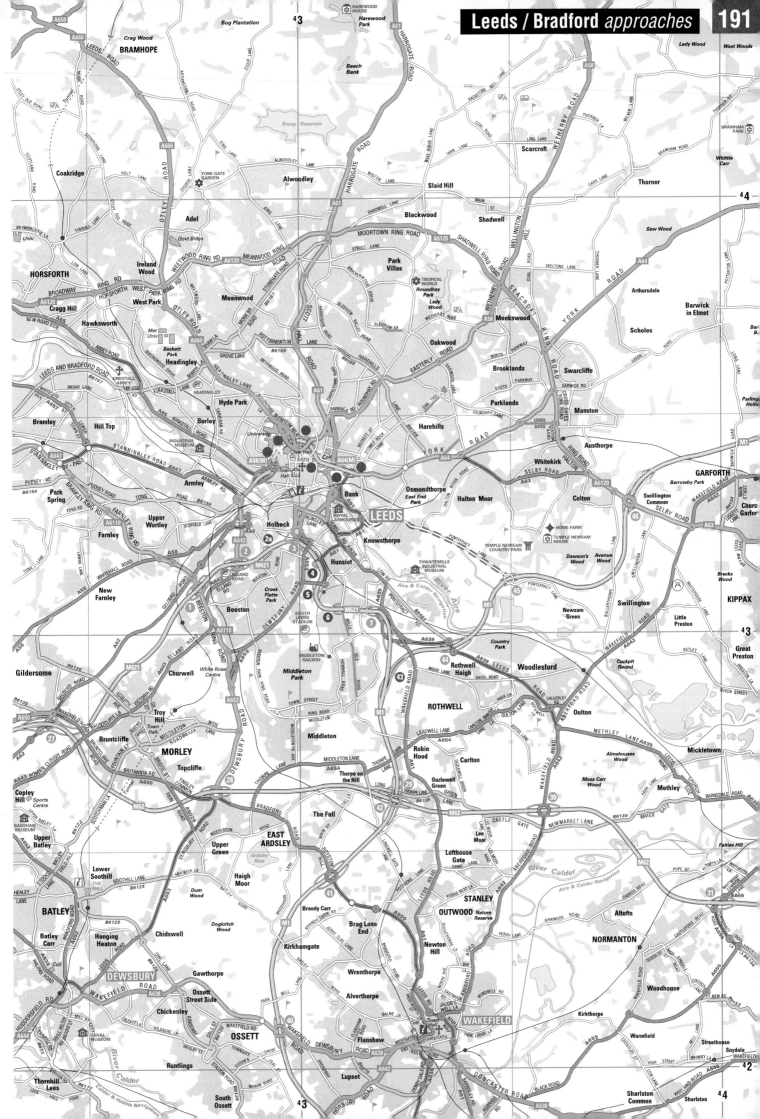

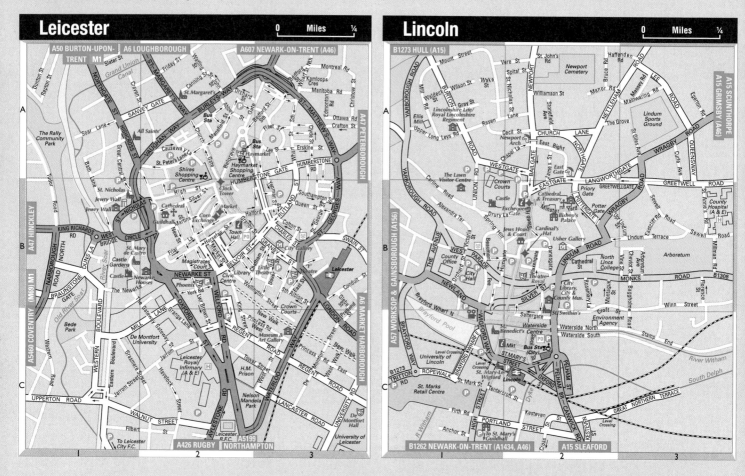

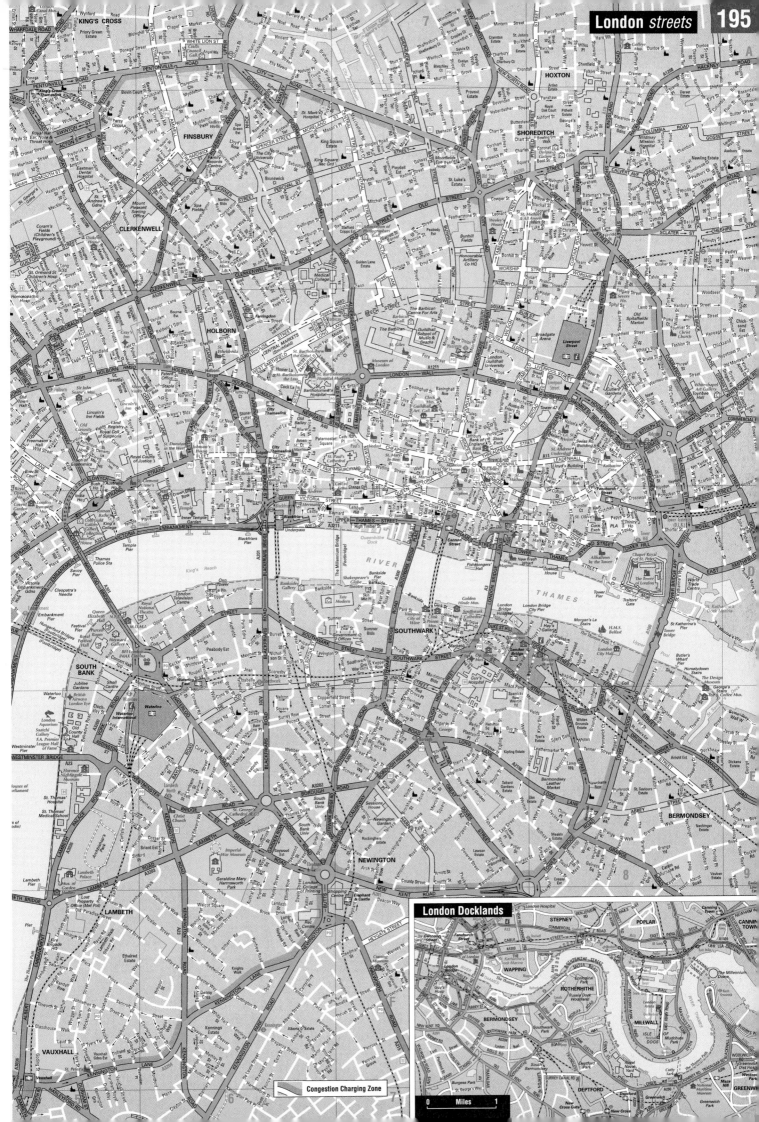

KING'S CROSS
WHARFDALE ROAD
WHITE LION ST
FINSBURY
HOXTON
SHOREDITCH
CLERKENWELL
HOLBORN
The Barbican
Liverpool Street
FINSBURY
St. Bartholomew's Hospital
Museum of London
London Wall
St. Paul's Cathedral
Cheapside
Bank of England
Lloyd's Building
Royal Courts of Justice
STRAND
FLEET STREET
LUDGATE HILL
CANNON STREET
Fenchurch Street
Tower Hill
The Tower of London
EMBANKMENT
QUEEN VICTORIA STREET
UPPER THAMES STREET
LOWER THAMES STREET
Tower Bridge
Blackfriars Pier
RIVER THAMES
World Trade Centre
St Katharine's Way
Tower Bridge
Cleopatra's Needle
Blackfriars Bridge
The Millennium Bridge
Tate Modern
Shakespeare's Globe Theatre
SOUTHWARK
London Bridge
Butler's Wharf
SOUTH BANK
Royal National Theatre
BFI London IMAX Cinema
Waterloo
London Eye
London Aquarium
Westminster Bridge
St. Thomas' Hospital
Houses of Parliament
SOUTHWARK STREET
UNION STREET
BERMONDSEY
Imperial War Museum
Guy's Hospital
NEWINGTON
Lambeth Palace
LAMBETH
BOROUGH ROAD
South Bank Univ
NEW KENT ROAD
Elephant & Castle
VAUXHALL
KENNINGTON

London Docklands
STEPNEY
POPLAR
CANNING TOWN
WAPPING
ROTHERHITHE
BERMONDSEY
MILLWALL
ISLE OF DOGS
The Millennium Dome
DEPTFORD
GREENWICH

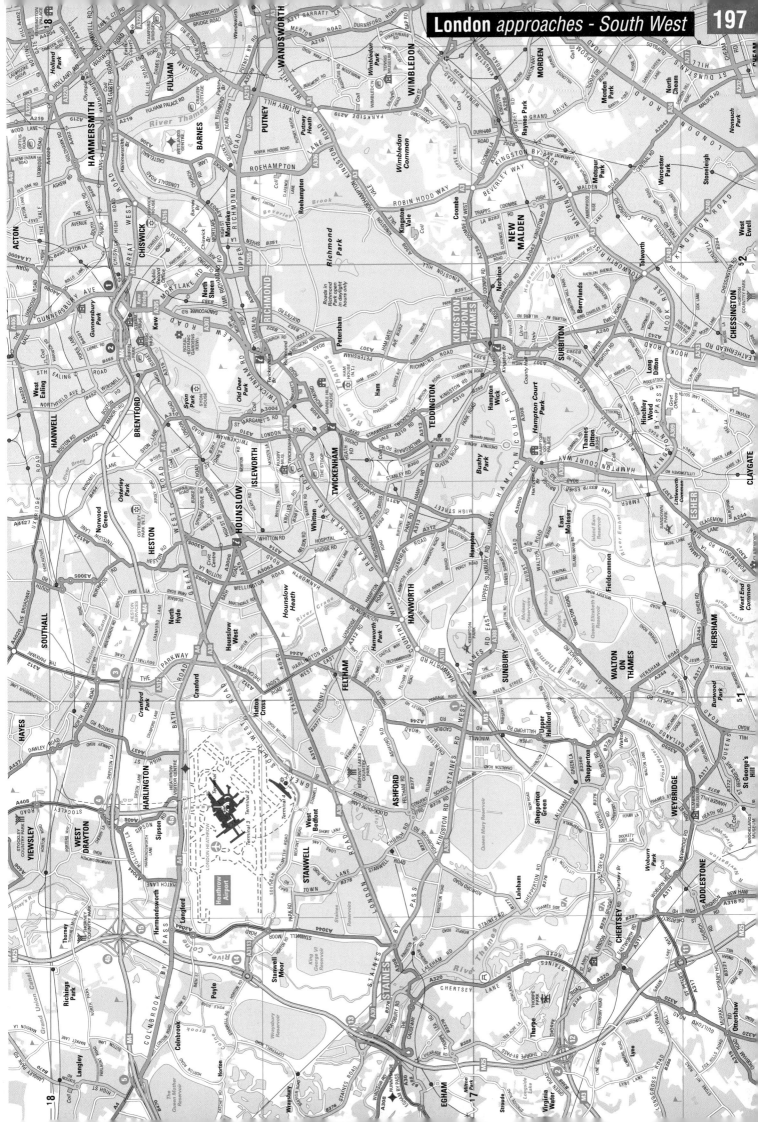

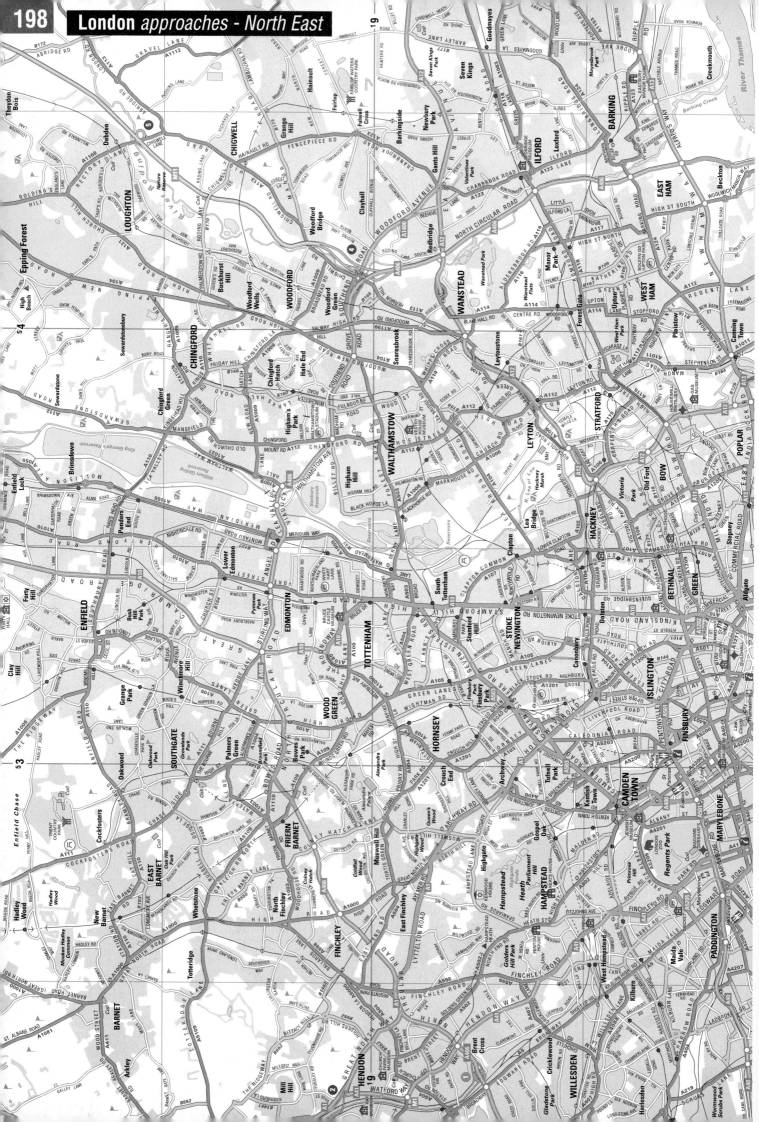

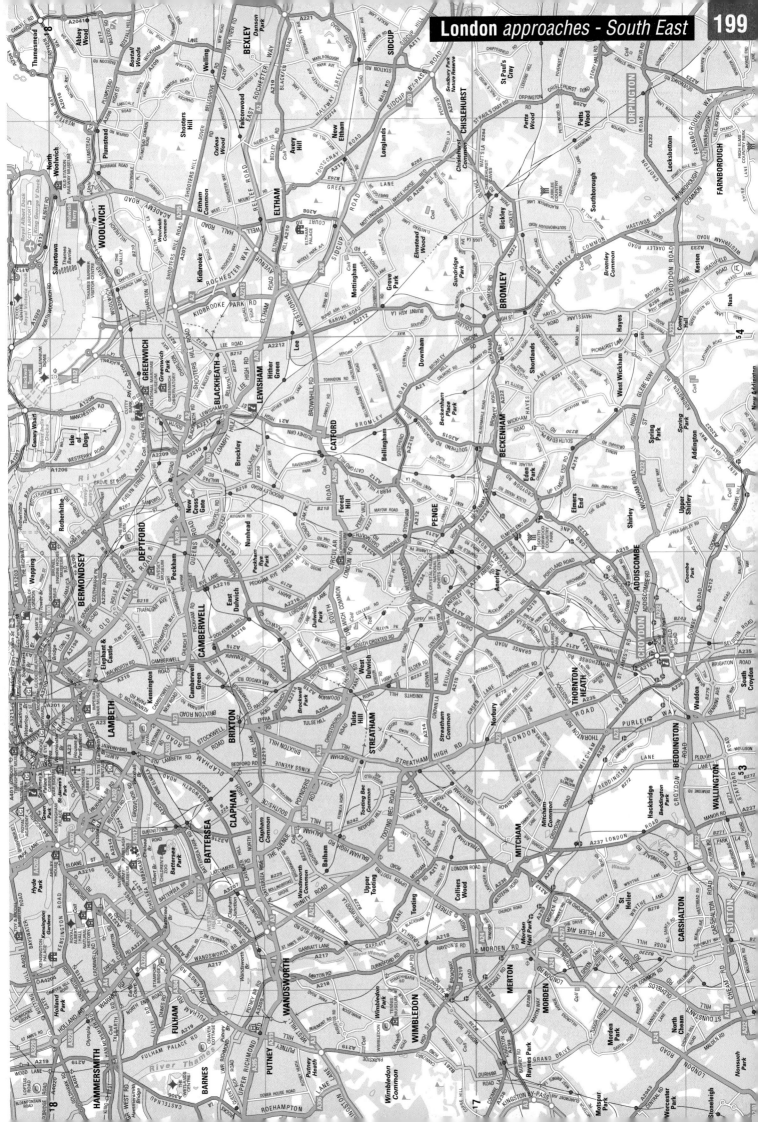

Middlesbrough

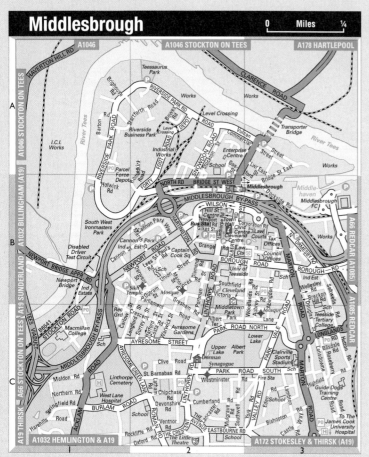

Milton Keynes

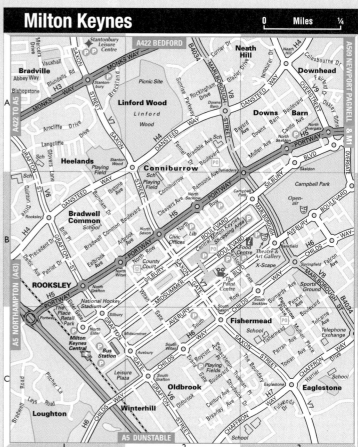

Manchester

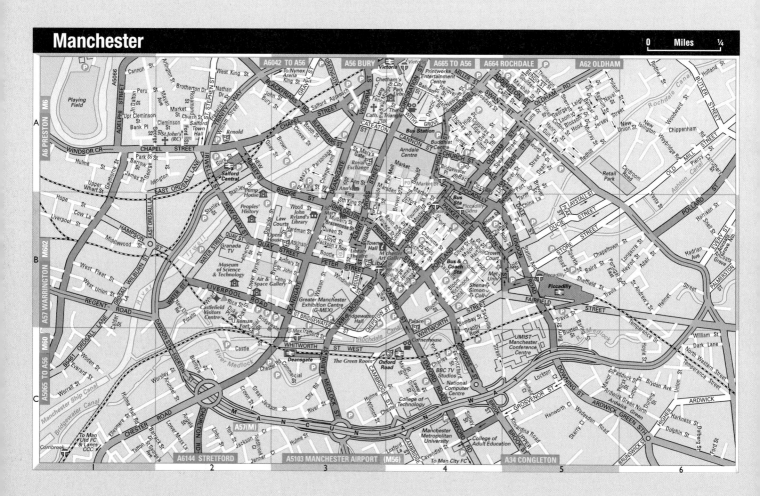

Newcastle-upon-Tyne

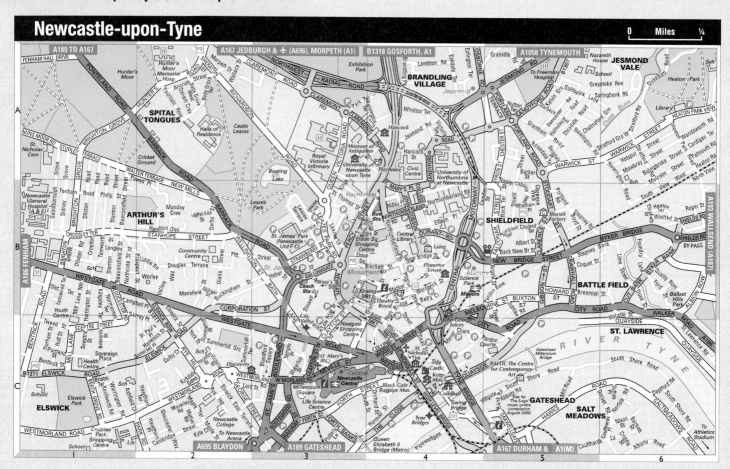

Northampton

Norwich

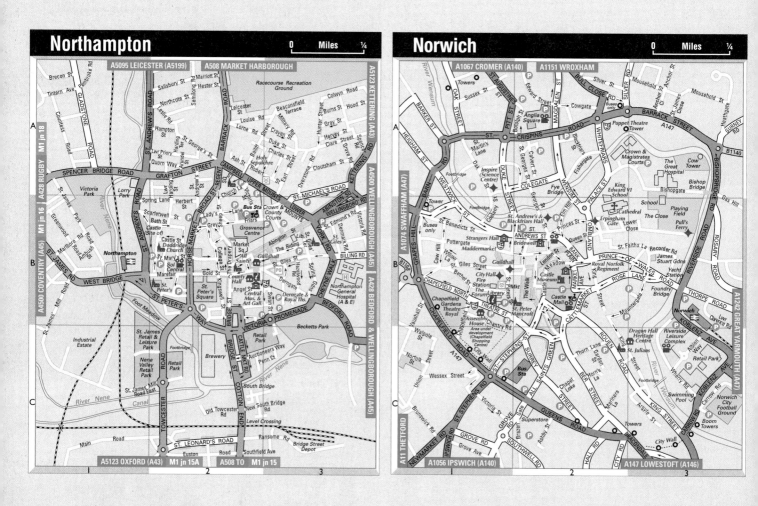

Nottingham

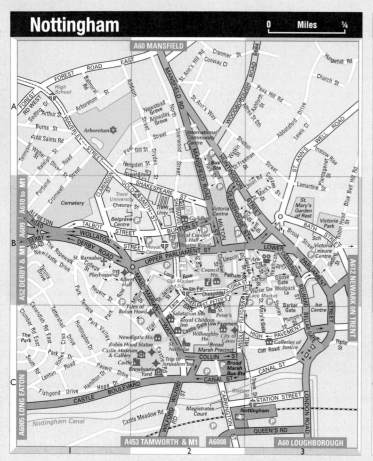

Oxford

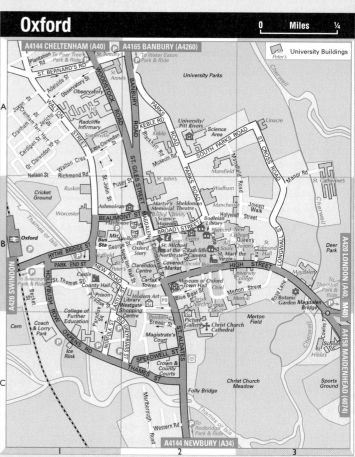

Plymouth

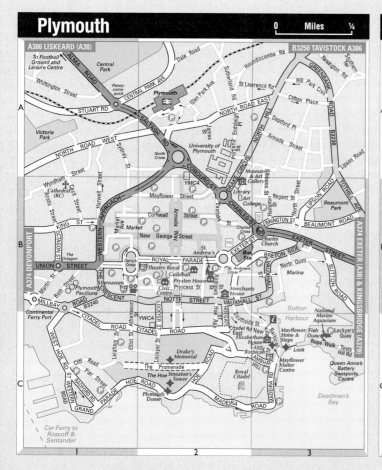

Portsmouth

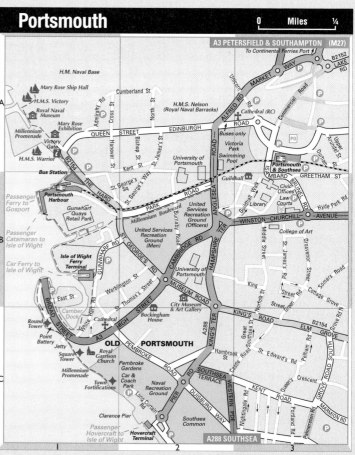

Reading

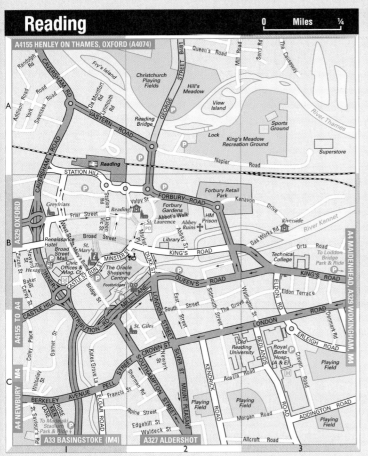

Salisbury

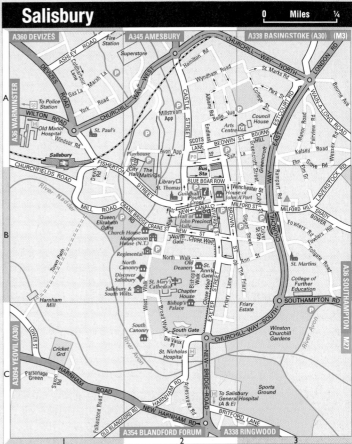

Scarborough

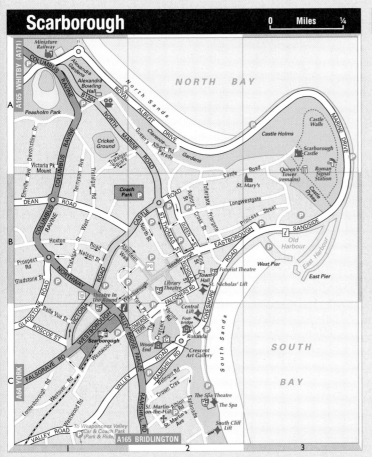

Southampton

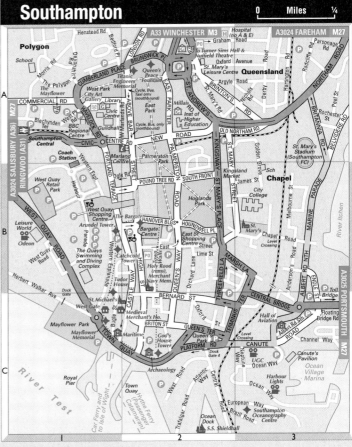

Sheffield

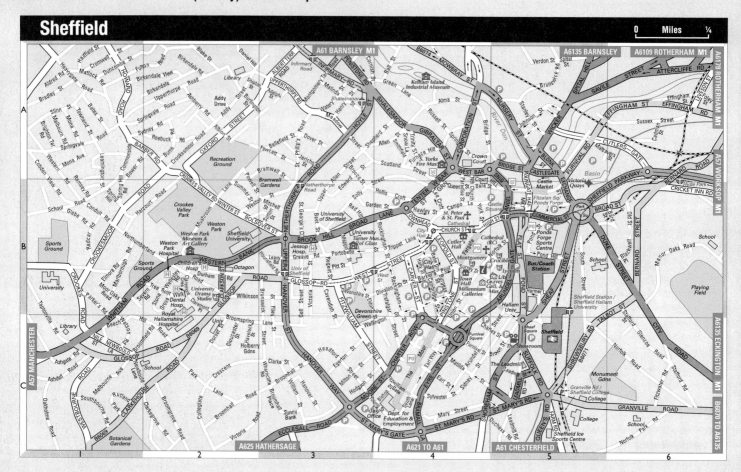

Stoke-on-Trent (Hanley)

Stratford-upon-Avon

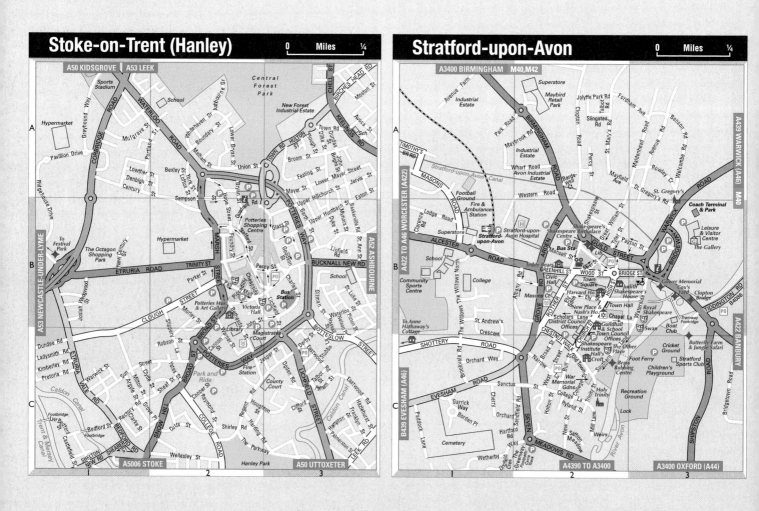

Sunderland

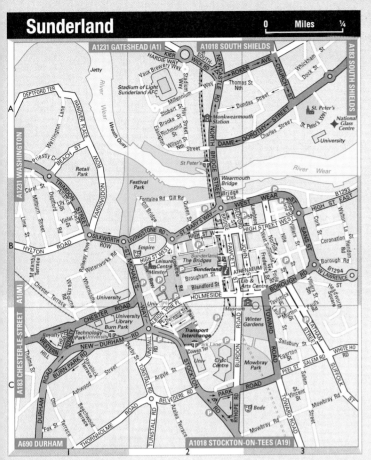

Swansea / Abertawe

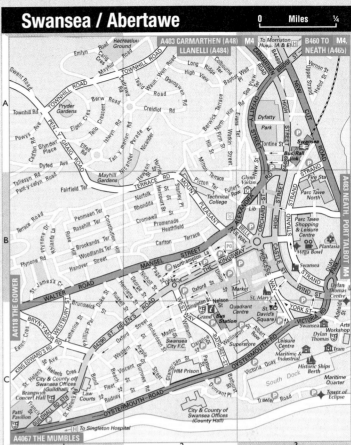

Telford

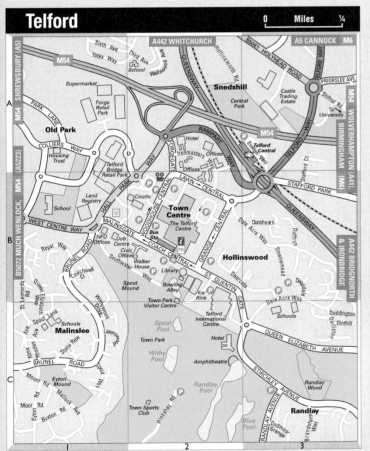

Torquay

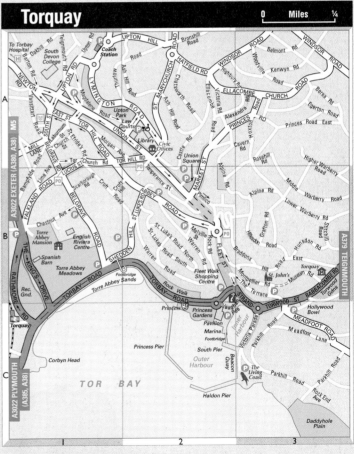

Winchester

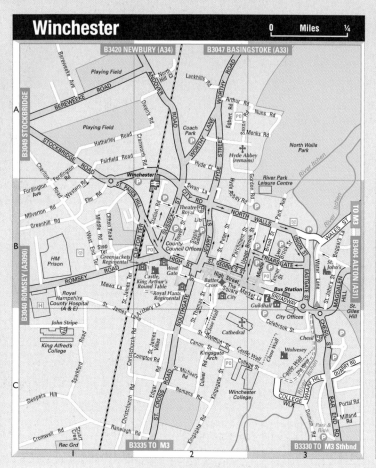

Windsor

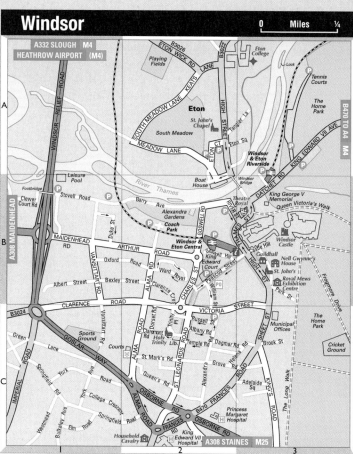

Worcester

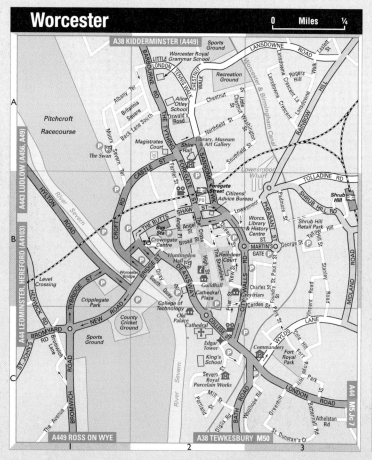

York

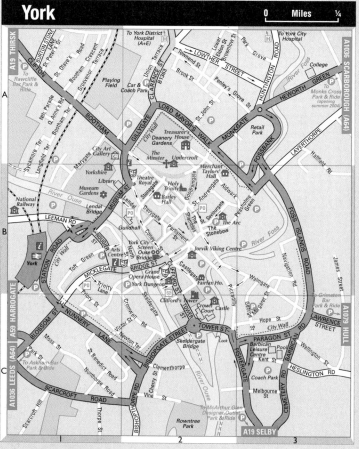

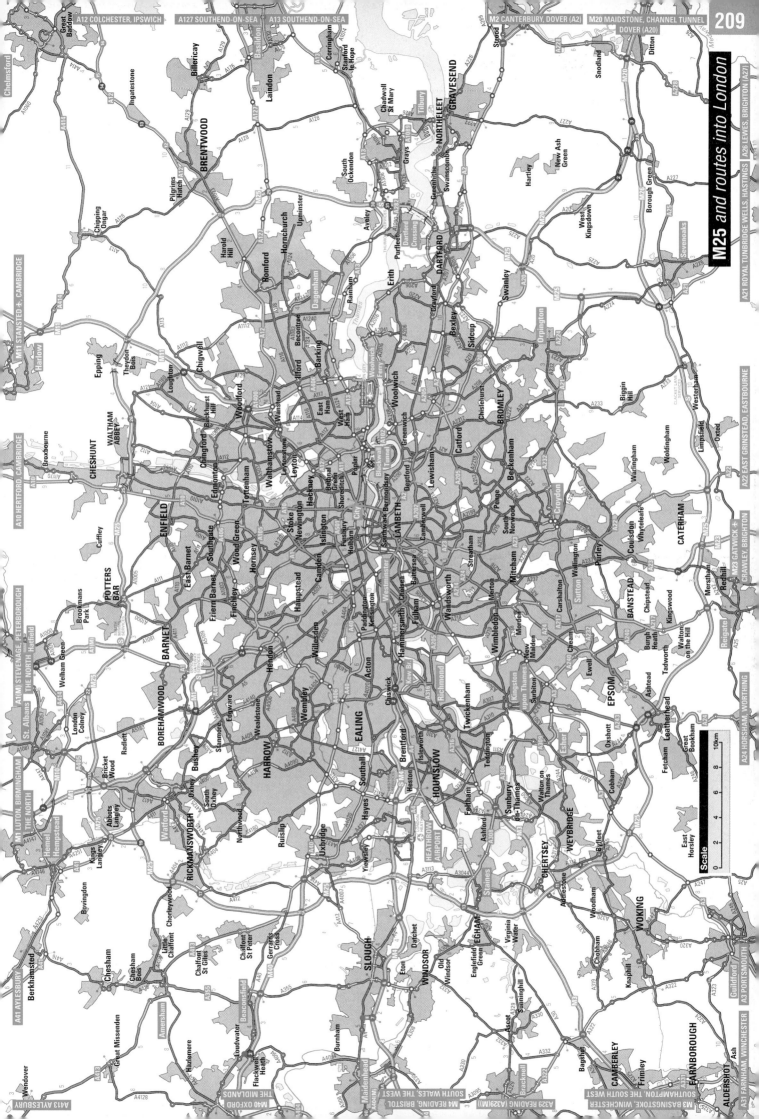

Heathrow Airport (London)

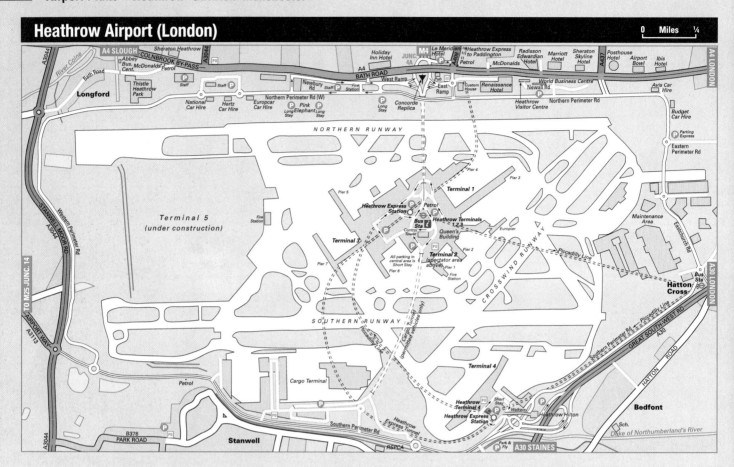

Gatwick Airport (London)

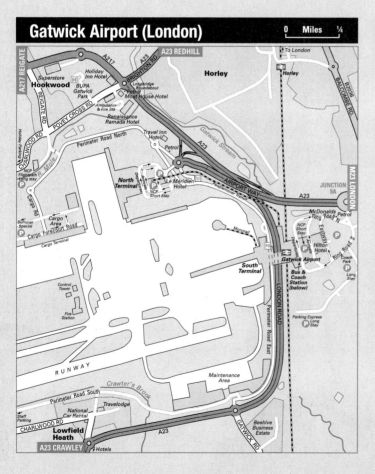

Manchester Airport

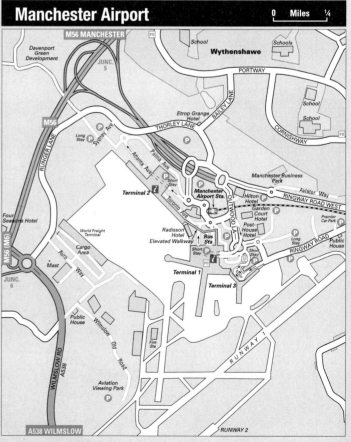

Port of Dover

0 Miles ¼

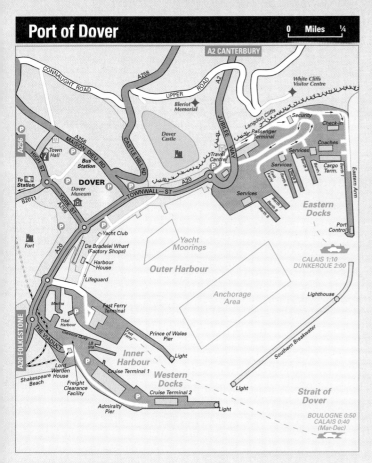

Port of Felixstowe

0 Miles ¼

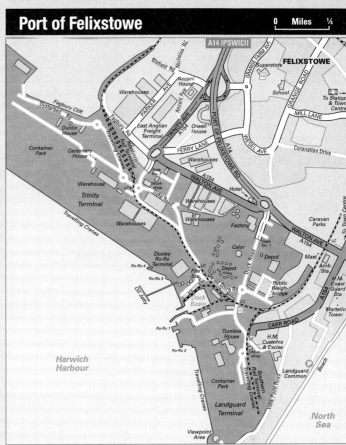

Portsmouth Continental Ferry Port

0 Miles ¼

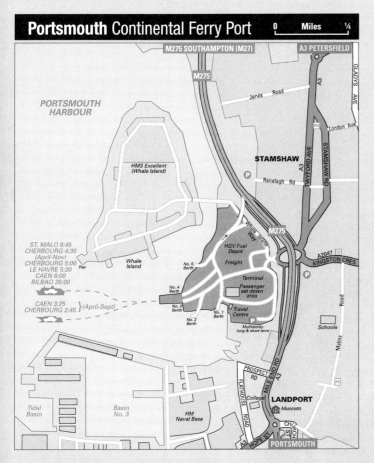

Port of Southampton

0 Miles 1

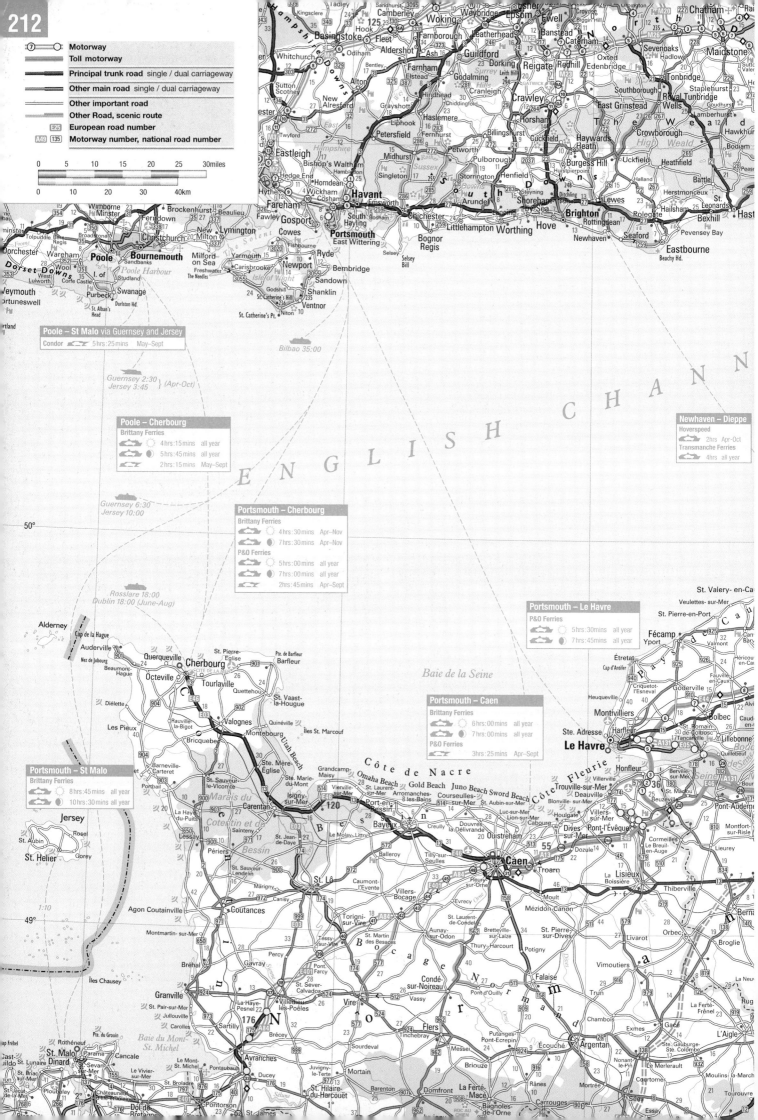

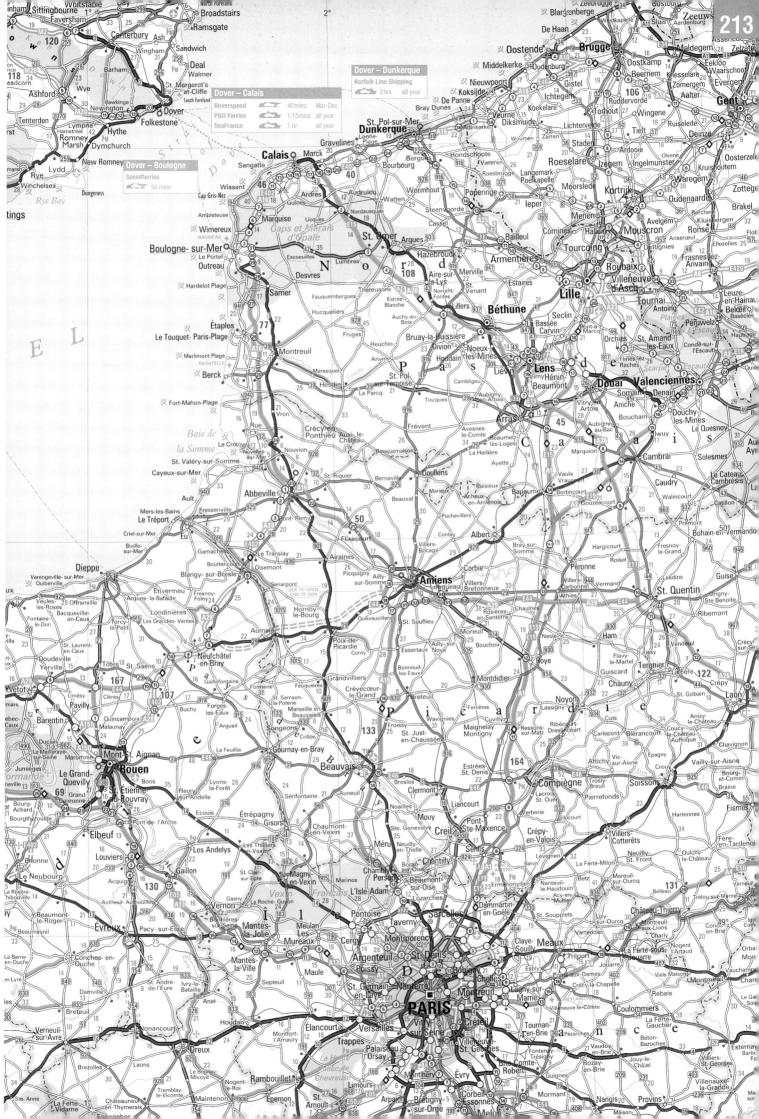

Boulogne

0 Miles ¼

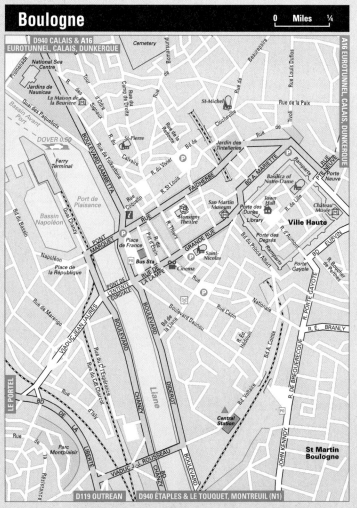

Calais

0 Miles ¼

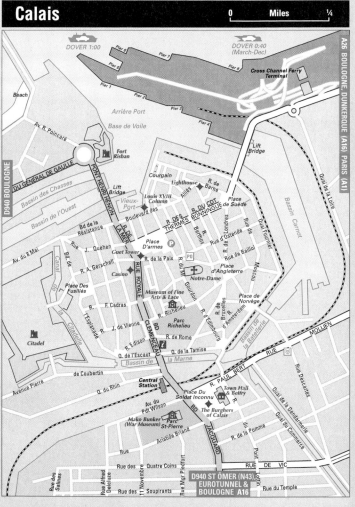

How to use the index

Example: Alvingham *Lincs* **91** F7

- grid square
- page number
- county or unitary authority

Places of special interest are highlighted in red

Abbreviations

Aberd C	**Aberdeen City**
Aberds	**Aberdeenshire**
Angl	**Isle of Anglesey**
Arg/Bute	**Argyll & Bute**
Bath/NE Som'set	**Bath & North East Somerset**
Beds	**Bedfordshire**
Bl Gwent	**Blaenau Gwent**
Blackb'n	**Blackburn with Darwen**
Blackp'l	**Blackpool**
Bournem'th	**Bournemouth**
Brackn'l	**Bracknell Forest**
Bridg	**Bridgend**
Brighton/Hove	**City of Brighton and Hove**
Bristol	**City and County of Bristol**
Bucks	**Buckinghamshire**
C/Edinb	**City of Edinburgh**
C/Glasg	**Glasgow City**
C/York	**City of York**
Caerph	**Caerphilly**
Cambs	**Cambridgeshire**
Card	**Cardiff**
Carms	**Carmarthenshire**
Ceredig'n	**Ceredigion**
Ches	**Cheshire**
Clack	**Clackmannanshire**
Cornw'l	**Cornwall**
Cumb	**Cumbria**
D'lington	**Darlington**
Denbs	**Denbighshire**
Derby	**Derbyshire**
Derby C	**Derby City**
Dumf/Gal	**Dumfries & Galloway**
Dundee C	**Dundee City**
E Ayrs	**East Ayrshire**
E Dunb	**East Dunbartonshire**
E Loth	**East Lothian**
E Renf	**East Renfrewshire**
ER Yorks	**East Riding of Yorkshire**
E Sussex	**East Sussex**
Falk	**Falkirk**
Flints	**Flintshire**
Glos	**Gloucestershire**
Gtr Man	**Greater Manchester**
Gwyn	**Gwynedd**
H'land	**Highland**
Hants	**Hampshire**
Hartlep'l	**Hartlepool**
Heref'd	**Herefordshire**
Herts	**Hertfordshire**
I/Man	**Isle of Man**
I/Scilly	**Isles of Scilly**
I/Wight	**Isle of Wight**
Invercl	**Inverclyde**
Kingston/Hull	**Kingston upon Hull**
Lancs	**Lancashire**
Leics	**Leicestershire**
Leics C	**Leicester City**
Lincs	**Lincolnshire**
London	**Greater London**
M/Keynes	**Milton Keynes**
Mersey	**Merseyside**
Merth Tyd	**Merthyr Tydfil**
Middlesbro	**Middlesbrough**
Midloth	**Midlothian**
Monmouths	**Monmouthshire**
N Ayrs	**North Ayrshire**
N Lanarks	**North Lanarkshire**
N Lincs	**North Lincolnshire**
N Som'set	**North Somerset**
N Yorks	**North Yorkshire**
NE Lincs	**North East Lincolnshire**
Neath P Talb	**Neath Port Talbot**
Newp	**City and County of Newport**
Northants	**Northamptonshire**
Northum	**Northumberland**
Nott'ham	**City of Nottingham**
Notts	**Nottinghamshire**
Oxon	**Oxfordshire**
Pembs	**Pembrokeshire**
Perth/Kinr	**Perth and Kinross**
Peterbro	**Peterborough**
Plym'th	**Plymouth**
Portsm'th	**Portsmouth**
Redcar/Clevel'd	**Redcar and Cleveland**
Renf	**Renfrewshire**
Rh Cyn Taff	**Rhondda Cynon Taff**
Rutl'd	**Rutland**
S'thampton	**Southampton**
S Ayrs	**South Ayrshire**
S Gloucs	**South Gloucestershire**
S Lanarks	**South Lanarkshire**
S Yorks	**South Yorkshire**
Scot Borders	**Scottish Borders**
Shetl'd	**Shetland**
Shrops	**Shropshire**
Som'set	**Somerset**
Southend	**Southend-on-Sea**
Staffs	**Staffordshire**
Stirl	**Stirling**
Stockton	**Stockton on Tees**
Stoke	**Stoke-on-Trent**
Swan	**Swansea**
Telford	**Telford and Wrekin**
Thurr'k	**Thurrock**
Torf	**Torfaen**
Tyne/Wear	**Tyne and Wear**
V/Glam	**Vale of Glamorgan**
W Berks	**West Berkshire**
W Dunb	**West Dunbartonshire**
W Isles	**Western Isles**
W Loth	**West Lothian**
W Midlands	**West Midlands**
W Sussex	**West Sussex**
W Yorks	**West Yorkshire**
Warwick	**Warwickshire**
Wilts	**Wiltshire**
Windsor	**Windsor and Maidenhead**
Worcs	**Worcestershire**
Wrex	**Wrexham**

A

Ab Kettleby *Leics* **64** B4
Ab Lench *Worcs* **50** D5
Abbas Combe *Som'set* **12** B5
Abberley *Worcs* **50** C2
Abberton *Essex* **43** C6
Abberton *Worcs* **50** D4
Abberwick *Northum* **117** C7
Abbess Roding *Essex* **42** C1
Abbey *Devon* **11** C6
Abbey-cwm-hir *Powys* **48** B2
Abbey Dore *Heref'd* **49** F5
Abbey Field *Essex* **43** B5
Abbey Hulton *Stoke* **75** E6
Abbey St Bathans *Scot Borders* **124** C3
Abbey Village *Lancs* **86** B4
Abbey Wood *London* **29** B5
Abbeydale *S Yorks* **88** F4
Abbeystead *Lancs* **93** D5
Abbeytown *Cumb* **107** D8
Abbots Bickington *Devon* **9** C5
Abbots Bromley *Staffs* **62** B4
Abbots Langley *Herts* **40** D3
Abbots Leigh *N Som'set* **23** B7
Abbots Morton *Worcs* **50** D5
Abbots Ripton *Cambs* **54** B3
Abbots Salford *Warwick* **51** D5
Abbotsbury *Dorset* **12** F3
Abbotsbury Sub Tropical Gardens *Dorset* 12 F3
Abbotsford House *Scot Borders* 123 F8
Abbotsham *Devon* **9** B6
Abbotskerswell *Devon* **7** C6
Abbotsley *Cambs* **54** D3
Abbotswood *Hants* **14** B4
Abbotts Ann *Hants* **25** E8
Abcott *Shrops* **49** B5
Abdon *Shrops* **61** F5
Aber *Ceredig'n* **46** E3
Aber-Arad *Carms* **46** F2
Aber-banc *Ceredig'n* **46** E2
Aber Cowarch *Gwyn* **59** C5
Aber-Giâr *Carms* **46** E4
Aber-gwynfi *Neath P Talb* **34** E2
Aber-Hirnant *Gwyn* **72** F3
Aber-nant *Rh Cyn Taff* **34** D4
Aber-Rhiwlech *Gwyn* **59** B6
Aber-Village *Powys* **35** B5
Aberaeron *Ceredig'n* **46** C3
Aberaman *Rh Cyn Taff* **34** D4
Aberangell *Gwyn* **58** C5
Aberarder *H'land* **147** F7
Aberarder House *H'land* **148** B2
Aberarder Lodge *H'land* **147** F8
Aberargie *Perth/Kinr* **134** C3
Aberarth *Ceredig'n* **46** C3
Aberavon *Neath P Talb* **33** E8
Aberbeeg *Bl Gwent* **35** D6
Abercanaid *Merth Tyd* **34** D4
Abercarn *Caerph* **35** E6
Abercastle *Pembs* **44** B3
Abercegir *Powys* **58** D5
Aberchirder *Aberds* **160** C3
Aberconwy House, Conwy *Conwy* 83 D7
Abercraf *Powys* **34** C2
Abercrombie *Fife* **135** D7
Abercych *Pembs* **45** E4
Abercynafon *Powys* **34** C4
Abercynon *Rh Cyn Taff* **34** E4
Aberdalgie *Perth/Kinr* **134** B2
Aberdâr = Aberdare *Rh Cyn Taff* **34** D3
Aberdare = Aberdâr *Rh Cyn Taff* **34** D3
Aberdaron *Gwyn* **70** E2
Aberdaugleddau = Milford Haven *Pembs* **44** E4
Aberdeen *Aberd C* **151** D8
Aberdesach *Gwyn* **82** F4
Aberdour *Fife* **134** F3
Aberdovey *Gwyn* **58** E3
Aberdulais *Neath P Talb* **34** D1
Aberedw *Powys* **48** E2
Abereiddy *Pembs* **44** B2
Abererch *Gwyn* **70** D4
Aberfan *Merth Tyd* **34** D4
Aberfeldy *Perth/Kinr* **141** E5
Aberffraw *Angl* **82** E3
Aberffrwd *Ceredig'n* **47** B5
Aberford *W Yorks* **95** F7
Aberfoyle *Stirl* **132** D4
Abergavenny = Y Fenni *Monmouths* **35** C6
Abergele *Conwy* **72** B3
Abergorlech *Carms* **46** F4
Abergwaun = Fishguard *Pembs* **44** B4
Abergwesyn *Powys* **47** D7
Abergwili *Carms* **33** B5
Abergwynant *Gwyn* **58** C3
Abergwyngregyn *Gwyn* **83** D6
Abergynolwyn *Gwyn* **58** D3
Aberhonddu = Brecon *Powys* **34** B4
Aberhosan *Powys* **58** E5
Aberkenfig *Bridg* **34** F2
Aberlady *E Loth* **135** F6
Aberlemno *Angus* **143** D5
Aberllefenni *Gwyn* **58** D4
Abermagwr *Ceredig'n* **47** B5
Abermaw = Barmouth *Gwyn* **58** C3
Abermeurig *Ceredig'n* **46** D4
Abermule *Powys* **59** E8
Abernaint *Powys* **59** B8
Abernant *Carms* **32** B4
Abernethy *Perth/Kinr* **134** C3
Abernyte *Perth/Kinr* **142** F2
Aberpennar = Mountain Ash *Rh Cyn Taff* **34** E4
Aberporth *Ceredig'n* **45** D4
Abersoch *Gwyn* **70** E4
Abersychan *Torf* **35** D6
Abertawe = Swansea *Swan* **33** E7
Aberteifi = Cardigan *Ceredig'n* **45** E3
Aberthin *V/Glam* **22** B2
Abertillery = Abertyleri *Bl Gwent* **35** D6
Abertridwr *Caerph* **35** F5
Abertridwr *Powys* **59** C7
Abertyleri = Abertillery *Bl Gwent* **35** D6
Abertysswg *Caerph* **35** D5
Aberuthven *Perth/Kinr* **133** C8
Aberyscir *Powys* **34** B3
Aberystwyth *Ceredig'n* **58** F2
Abhainn Suidhe *W Isles* **173** H3
Abingdon *Oxon* **38** E4
Abinger Common *Surrey* **28** E2
Abinger Hammer *Surrey* **27** E8
Abington *S Lanarks* **114** B2
Abington Piggotts *Cambs* **54** E4
Ablington *Glos* **37** D8
Ablington *Wilts* **25** E6
Abney *Derby* **75** B8
Aboyne *Aberds* **150** E4
Abram *Gtr Man* **86** D4
Abriachan *H'land* **157** F6
Abridge *Essex* **41** E7
Abronhill *N Lanarks* **121** B7
Abson *S Gloucs* **24** B2
Abthorpe *Northants* **52** E4
Abune-the-Hill *Orkney* **176** D1
Aby *Lincs* **79** B7
Acaster Malbis *C/York* **95** E8
Acaster Selby *N Yorks* **95** E8
Accrington *Lancs* **87** B5
Acha *Arg/Bute* **136** C2
Acha Mor *W Isles* **172** F6
Achabraid *Arg/Bute* **128** B3
Achachork *H'land* **152** E5
Achafolla *Arg/Bute* **130** D3
Achagary *H'land* **168** D2
Achahoish *Arg/Bute* **128** C2
Achalader *Perth/Kinr* **141** E8
Achallader *Arg/Bute* **139** E7
Ach'an Todhair *H'land* **138** B4
Achanalt *H'land* **156** C3
Achanamara *Arg/Bute* **128** B2
Achandunie *H'land* **157** B7
Achany *H'land* **164** D2
Achaphubuil *H'land* **138** B4
Acharacle *H'land* **137** B7
Acharn *H'land* **137** C8
Acharn *Perth/Kinr* **140** E4
Acharole *H'land* **169** D7
Achath *Aberds* **151** C6
Achavanich *H'land* **169** E6
Achavraat *H'land* **158** E3
Achddu *Carms* **33** D5
Achduart *H'land* **162** D4
Achentoul *H'land* **168** F3
Achfary *H'land* **166** F4
Achgarve *H'land* **162** E2
Achiemore *H'land* **167** C5
Achiemore *H'land* **168** D3
A'Chill *H'land* **144** C2
Achiltibuie *H'land* **162** D4
Achina *H'land* **168** C2
Achinduich *H'land* **164** D2
Achinduin *Arg/Bute* **130** B4
Achingills *H'land* **169** C6
Achintee *H'land* **139** B5
Achintee *H'land* **155** F5
Achintraid *H'land* **155** G4
Achlean *H'land* **148** E4
Achleck *Arg/Bute* **137** D5
Achluachrach *H'land* **147** F5
Achlyness *H'land* **166** D4
Achmelvich *H'land* **162** B4
Achmore *H'land* **155** G4
Achmore *Stirl* **140** F2
Achnaba *Arg/Bute* **130** B5
Achnaba *Arg/Bute* **128** B4
Achnabat *H'land* **157** F6
Achnacarnin *H'land* **166** F2
Achnacarry *H'land* **146** F4
Achnacloich *Arg/Bute* **131** B5
Achnacloich *H'land* **145** C5
Achnaconeran *H'land* **147** C7
Achnacraig *Arg/Bute* **137** D5
Achnacroish *Arg/Bute* **138** E2
Achnadrish *Arg/Bute* **137** C5
Achnafalnich *Arg/Bute* **131** C8
Achnagarron *H'land* **157** C7
Achnaha *H'land* **137** B5
Achnahanat *H'land* **164** E2
Achnahannet *H'land* **149** B5
Achnairn *H'land* **164** C2
Achnaluachrach *H'land* **164** D3
Achnasaul *H'land* **146** F4
Achnasheen *H'land* **156** D2
Achosnich *H'land* **137** B5
Achranich *H'land* **137** D8
Achreamie *H'land* **168** C5
Achriabhach *H'land* **139** C5
Achriesgill *H'land* **166** D4
Achrimsdale *H'land* **165** D6
Achtoty *H'land* **167** C8
Achurch *Northants* **65** F7
Achuvoldrach *H'land* **167** D7
Achvaich *H'land* **164** E4
Achvarasdal *H'land* **168** C4
Ackergill *H'land* **169** D8
Acklam *Middlesbro* **102** C2
Acklam *N Yorks* **96** C3
Ackleton *Shrops* **61** E7
Acklington *Northum* **117** D8
Ackton *W Yorks* **88** B5
Ackworth Moor Top *W Yorks* **88** C5
Acle *Norfolk* **69** C7
Acock's Green *W Midlands* **62** F5
Acol *Kent* **31** C7
Acomb *Northum* **110** C2
Acomb *C/York* **95** D8
Aconbury *Heref'd* **49** F7
Acre *Lancs* **87** B5
Acre Street *W Sussex* **15** E8
Acrefair *Wrex* **73** E6
Acton *Ches* **74** D3
Acton *Dorset* **13** G7
Acton *London* **41** F5
Acton *Shrops* **60** F3
Acton *Suffolk* **56** E2
Acton *Wrex* **73** D7
Acton Beauchamp *Heref'd* **49** D8
Acton Bridge *Ches* **74** B2
Acton Burnell *Shrops* **60** D5
Acton Green *Heref'd* **49** D8
Acton Pigott *Shrops* **60** D5
Acton Round *Shrops* **61** E6
Acton Scott *Shrops* **60** F4
Acton Trussell *Staffs* **62** C3
Acton Turville *S Gloucs* **37** F5
Adbaston *Staffs* **61** B7
Adber *Dorset* **12** B3
Adderley *Shrops* **74** E3
Adderstone *Northum* **125** F7
Addiewell *W Loth* **122** C2
Addingham *W Yorks* **94** E3
Addington *Bucks* **39** B7
Addington *London* **28** C4
Addington *Kent* **29** D7
Addinston *Scot Borders* **123** D8
Addiscombe *London* **28** C4
Addlestone *Surrey* **27** C8
Addlethorpe *Lincs* **79** C8
Adel *W Yorks* **95** F5
Adeney *Telford* **61** C7
Adfa *Powys* **59** D7
Adforton *Heref'd* **49** B6
Adisham *Kent* **31** D6
Adlestrop *Glos* **38** B2
Adlingfleet *ER Yorks* **90** B2
Adlington *Lancs* **86** C4
Admaston *Staffs* **62** B4
Admaston *Telford* **61** C6
Admington *Warwick* **51** E7
Adstock *Bucks* **52** F5
Adstone *Northants* **52** D3
Adversane *W Sussex* **16** B4
Advie *H'land* **158** F5
Adwalton *W Yorks* **88** B3
Adwell *Oxon* **39** E6
Adwick le Street *S Yorks* **89** D6
Adwick upon Dearne *S Yorks* **89** D5
Adziel *Aberds* **161** C6
Ae Village *Dumf/Gal* **114** F2
Aerospace Museum, Cosford *Shrops* 61 D7
Affleck *Aberds* **151** B7
Affpuddle *Dorset* **13** E6
Affric Lodge *H'land* **146** B4
Afon-wen *Flints* **72** B5
Afton *I/Wight* **14** F4
Agglethorpe *N Yorks* **101** F5
Agneash *I/Man* **84** D4
Aigburth *Mersey* **85** F4
Aiginis *W Isles* **172** E7
Aike *ER Yorks* **97** E6
Aikerness *Orkney* **176** A3
Aikers *Orkney* **176** G3
Aiketgate *Cumb* **108** E4
Aikton *Cumb* **108** D2
Ailey *Heref'd* **48** E5
Ailstone *Warwick* **51** D7
Ailsworth *Peterbro* **65** E8
Ainderby Quernhow *N Yorks* **102** F1
Ainderby Steeple *N Yorks* **101** E8
Aingers Green *Essex* **43** B7
Ainsdale *Mersey* **85** C4
Ainsdale-on-Sea *Mersey* **85** C4
Ainstable *Cumb* **108** E5
Ainsworth *Gtr Man* **87** C5
Ainthorpe *N Yorks* **103** D5
Aintree *Mersey* **85** E4
Aintree Racecourse *Mersey* 85 E8
Aird *Arg/Bute* **130** E3
Aird *Dumf/Gal* **104** C4
Aird *H'land* **154** C3
Aird *W Isles* **172** E8
Aird a Mhachair *W Isles* **170** F3
Aird a'Mhulaidh *W Isles* **173** G4
Aird Asaig *W Isles* **173** H4
Aird Dhail *W Isles* **172** B7
Aird Mhidhinis *W Isles* **171** K3
Aird Mhighe *W Isles* **173** J4
Aird Mhighe *W Isles* **173** K3
Aird Mhor *W Isles* **171** K3
Aird of Sleat *H'land* **145** C5
Aird Thunga *W Isles* **172** E7
Aird Uig *W Isles* **172** E3
Airdens *H'land* **164** E3
Airdrie *N Lanarks* **121** C7
Airdtorrisdale *H'land* **167** C8
Airidh a Bhruaich *W Isles* **172** G5
Airieland *Dumf/Gal* **106** D4
Airmyn *ER Yorks* **89** B8
Airntully *Perth/Kinr* **141** F7
Airor *H'land* **145** C7
Airth *Falk* **133** F7
Airton *N Yorks* **94** D2
Airyhassen *Dumf/Gal* **105** E7
Aisby *Lincs* **90** E2
Aisby *Lincs* **78** F3
Aisgernis *W Isles* **171** H3
Aiskew *N Yorks* **101** F7
Aislaby *N Yorks* **103** F5
Aislaby *N Yorks* **103** D6
Aislaby *Stockton* **102** C2
Aisthorpe *Lincs* **78** A2
Aith *Orkney* **176** E1
Aith *Shetl'd* **175** H5
Aith *Shetl'd* **174** D8
Aithsetter *Shetl'd* **175** K6
Aitkenhead *S Ayrs* **112** D3
Aitnoch *H'land* **158** F3
Akeld *Northum* **117** B5
Akeley *Bucks* **52** F5
Akenham *Suffolk* **56** E5
Albaston *Cornw'l* **6** B2
Alberbury *Shrops* **60** C3
Albert Dock, Liverpool *Mersey* 85 F8
Albourne *W Sussex* **17** C6
Albrighton *Shrops* **60** C4
Albrighton *Shrops* **62** D2
Alburgh *Norfolk* **69** F5
Albury *Herts* **41** B7
Albury *Surrey* **27** E8
Albury End *Herts* **41** B7
Alby Hill *Norfolk* **81** D7
Alcaig *H'land* **157** D6
Alcaston *Shrops* **60** F4
Alcester *Warwick* **51** D5
Alciston *E Sussex* **18** E2
Alcombe *Som'set* **21** E8
Alcombe *Wilts* **24** C3
Alconbury *Cambs* **54** B2
Alconbury Weston *Cambs* **54** B2
Aldbar Castle *Angus* **143** D5
Aldborough *Norfolk* **81** D7
Aldborough *N Yorks* **95** C7
Aldbourne *Wilts* **25** B7
Aldbrough *ER Yorks* **97** F8
Aldbrough St John *N Yorks* **101** C7
Aldbury *Herts* **40** C2
Aldcliffe *Lancs* **92** C4
Aldclune *Perth/Kinr* **141** C6
Aldeburgh *Suffolk* **57** D8
Aldeby *Norfolk* **69** E7
Aldenham *Herts* **40** E4
Alderbury *Wilts* **14** B2
Aldercar *Derby* **76** E4
Alderford *Norfolk* **68** C4
Alderholt *Dorset* **14** C2
Alderley *Glos* **36** E4
Alderley Edge *Ches* **74** B5
Aldermaston *W Berks* **26** C3
Aldermaston Wharf *W Berks* **26** C4
Alderminster *Warwick* **51** E7
Alder's End *Heref'd* **49** E8
Aldersey Green *Ches* **73** D8
Aldershot *Hants* **27** D6
Alderton *Glos* **50** F5
Alderton *Northants* **52** E5
Alderton *Shrops* **60** B4
Alderton *Suffolk* **57** E7
Alderton *Wilts* **37** F5
Alderwasley *Derby* **76** D3
Aldfield *N Yorks* **95** C5
Aldford *Ches* **73** D8
Aldham *Essex* **43** B5
Aldham *Suffolk* **56** E4
Aldie *H'land* **164** F4
Aldingbourne *W Sussex* **16** D3
Aldingham *Cumb* **92** B2
Aldington *Kent* **19** B7
Aldington *Worcs* **51** E5
Aldington Frith *Kent* **19** B7
Aldochlay *Arg/Bute* **132** E2
Aldreth *Cambs* **54** B5
Aldridge *W Midlands* **62** D4
Aldringham *Suffolk* **57** C8
Aldsworth *Glos* **38** C1
Aldunie *Moray* **150** B2
Aldwark *Derby* **76** D2
Aldwark *N Yorks* **95** C7
Aldwick *W Sussex* **16** E3
Aldwincle *Northants* **65** F7
Aldworth *W Berks* **26** B3
Alexandria *W Dunb* **120** B3
Alfardisworthy *Devon* **8** C4
Alfington *Devon* **11** E6
Alfold *Surrey* **27** F8
Alfold Bars *W Sussex* **27** F8
Alfold Crossways *Surrey* **27** F8
Alford *Aberds* **150** C4
Alford *Lincs* **79** B7
Alford *Som'set* **23** F8
Alfreton *Derby* **76** D4
Alfrick *Worcs* **50** D2
Alfrick Pound *Worcs* **50** D2
Alfriston *E Sussex* **18** E2
Algaltraig *Arg/Bute* **129** C5
Algarkirk *Lincs* **79** F5
Alhampton *Som'set* **23** F8
Aline Lodge *W Isles* **173** G4
Alisary *H'land* **145** F7
Alkborough *N Lincs* **90** B2
Alkerton *Oxon* **51** E8
Alkham *Kent* **31** E6
Alkington *Shrops* **74** F2
Alkmonton *Derby* **75** F8
All Cannings *Wilts* **25** C5
All Saints Church, Godshill *I/Wight* 15 F6
All Saints South Elmham *Suffolk* **69** F6
All Stretton *Shrops* **60** E4
Alladale Lodge *H'land* **163** F8
Allaleigh *Devon* **7** D6
Allanaquoich *Aberds* **149** E7
Allangrange Mains *H'land* **157** D7
Allanton *Scot Borders* **124** D4
Allanton *N Lanarks* **121** D8
Allathasdal *W Isles* **171** K2
Allendale Town *Northum* **109** D8
Allenheads *Northum* **109** E8
Allens Green *Herts* **41** C7
Allensford *Durham* **110** D3
Allensmore *Heref'd* **49** F6
Allenton *Derby C* **76** F3
Aller *Som'set* **12** B2
Allerby *Cumb* **107** F7
Allerford *Som'set* **21** E8
Allerston *N Yorks* **103** F6
Allerthorpe *ER Yorks* **96** E3
Allerton *Mersey* **86** F2
Allerton *W Yorks* **94** F4
Allerton Bywater *W Yorks* **88** B5
Allerton Mauleverer *N Yorks* **95** D7
Allesley *W Midlands* **63** F7
Allestree *Derby C* **76** F3
Allet *Cornw'l* **3** B6
Allexton *Leics* **64** D5
Allgreave *Ches* **75** C6
Allhallows *Medway* **30** B2
Allhallows-on-Sea *Medway* **30** B2
Alligin Shuas *H'land* **154** E4
Allimore Green *Staffs* **62** C2
Allington *Lincs* **77** E8
Allington *Wilts* **25** F7
Allington *Wilts* **25** C5
Allithwaite *Cumb* **92** B3
Alloa *Clack* **133** E7
Allonby *Cumb* **107** E7
Alloway *S Ayrs* **112** C3
Allt *Carms* **33** D6
Allt na h-Airbhe *H'land* **163** E5
Allt-nan-sùgh *H'land* **146** B2
Alltchaorunn *H'land* **139** D5
Alltforgan *Powys* **59** B6
Alltmawr *Powys* **48** E2
Alltnacaillich *H'land* **167** E6
Alltsigh *H'land* **147** C7
Alltwalis *Carms* **46** F3
Alltwen *Neath P Talb* **33** D8
Alltyblaca *Ceredig'n* **46** E4
Allwood Green *Suffolk* **56** B4
Almeley *Heref'd* **48** D5
Almer *Dorset* **13** E7
Almholme *S Yorks* **89** D6
Almington *Staffs* **74** F4
Alminstone Cross *Devon* **8** B5
Almondbank *Perth/Kinr* **134** B2
Almondbury *W Yorks* **88** C2
Almondsbury *S Gloucs* **36** F3
Alne *N Yorks* **95** C7
Alness *H'land* **157** C7
Alnham *Northum* **117** C5
Alnmouth *Northum* **117** C8
Alnwick *Northum* **117** C7
Alperton *London* **40** F4
Alphamstone *Essex* **56** F2
Alpheton *Suffolk* **56** D2
Alphington *Devon* **10** E4
Alport *Derby* **76** C2
Alpraham *Ches* **74** D2
Alresford *Essex* **43** B6
Alrewas *Staffs* **63** C5
Alsager *Ches* **74** D4
Alsagers Bank *Staffs* **74** E5
Alsop en le Dale *Derby* **75** D8
Alston *Cumb* **109** E7
Alston *Devon* **11** D8
Alstone *Glos* **50** F4
Alstonefield *Staffs* **75** D8
Alswear *Devon* **10** B2
Altandhu *H'land* **162** C3
Altanduin *H'land* **165** B5
Altarnun *Cornw'l* **8** F4
Altass *H'land* **164** D1
Alterwall *H'land* **169** C7
Altham *Lancs* **93** F7
Althorne *Essex* **43** E5
Althorp House, Great Brington *Northants* 52 C4
Althorpe *N Lincs* **90** D2
Alticry *Dumf/Gal* **105** D6
Altnabreac Station *H'land* **168** E5
Altnacealgach Hotel *H'land* **163** C6
Altnacraig *Arg/Bute* **130** C4
Altnafeadh *H'land* **139** D6
Altnaharra *H'land* **167** F7
Altofts *W Yorks* **88** B4
Alton *Derby* **76** C3
Alton *Hants* **26** F5
Alton *Staffs* **75** E7
Alton Pancras *Dorset* **12** D5
Alton Priors *Wilts* **25** C6
Alton Towers *Staffs* 75 E7
Altrincham *Gtr Man* **87** F5
Altrua *H'land* **146** F5
Altskeith *Stirl* **132** D3
Altyre Ho. *Moray* **158** D4
Alva *Clack* **133** E7
Alvanley *Ches* **73** B8
Alvaston *Derby C* **76** F3
Alvechurch *Worcs* **50** B5
Alvecote *Warwick* **63** D6
Alvediston *Wilts* **13** B7
Alveley *Shrops* **61** F7
Alverdiscott *Devon* **9** B7
Alverstoke *Hants* **15** E7
Alverstone *I/Wight* **15** F6
Alverton *Notts* **77** E7
Alves *Moray* **158** C5
Alvescot *Oxon* **38** D2
Alveston *S Gloucs* **36** F3
Alveston *Warwick* **51** D7
Alvie *H'land* **148** D4
Alvingham *Lincs* **91** E7
Alvington *Glos* **36** D3
Alwalton *Cambs* **65** E8
Alweston *Dorset* **12** C4
Alwinton *Northum* **116** D5
Alwoodley *W Yorks* **95** E5
Alyth *Perth/Kinr* **142** E2
Am Baile *W Isles* **171** J3
Am Buth *Arg/Bute* **130** C4
Amatnatua *H'land* **164** E1
Amber Hill *Lincs* **78** E5
Ambergate *Derby* **76** D3
Amberley *Glos* **37** D5
Amberley *W Sussex* **16** C4
Amble *Northum* **117** D8
Amblecote *W Midlands* **62** F2
Ambler Thorn *W Yorks* **87** B8
Ambleside *Cumb* **99** D5
Ambleston *Pembs* **44** C5
Ambrosden *Oxon* **39** C6
Amcotts *N Lincs* **90** C2
American Adventure, Ilkeston *Derby* 76 E4
American Air Museum, Duxford *Cambs* 55 E5
Amersham *Bucks* **40** E2
Amerton Working Farm, Stowe-by-Chartley *Staffs* 62 B3
Amesbury *Wilts* **25** E6
Amington *Staffs* **63** D6
Amisfield *Dumf/Gal* **114** F2
Amlwch *Angl* **82** B4
Amlwch Port *Angl* **82** B4
Ammanford = Rhydaman *Carms* **33** C7
Amod *Arg/Bute* **118** C4
Amotherby *N Yorks* **96** B3
Ampfield *Hants* **14** B5
Ampleforth *N Yorks* **95** B8
Ampney Crucis *Glos* **37** D7
Ampney St Mary *Glos* **37** D7
Ampney St Peter *Glos* **37** D7
Amport *Hants* **25** E7
Ampthill *Beds* **53** F8
Ampton *Suffolk* **56** B2
Amroth *Pembs* **32** D2
Amulree *Perth/Kinr* **141** F5
An Caol *H'land* **155** E2
An Cnoc *W Isles* **172** E7
An Gleann Ur *W Isles* **172** E7
An t-Ob = Leverburgh *W Isles* **173** K3
Anagach *H'land* **149** B6
Anaheilt *H'land* **138** C2
Anancaun *H'land* **154** D6
Ancaster *Lincs* **78** E2
Anchor *Shrops* **59** F8
Anchorsholme *Blackp'l* **92** E3
Ancroft *Northum* **125** E5
Ancrum *Scot Borders* **116** B2
Anderby *Lincs* **79** B8
Anderson *Dorset* **13** E6
Anderton *Ches* **74** B3
Andover *Hants* **25** E8
Andover Down *Hants* **25** E8
Andoversford *Glos* **37** C7
Andreas *I/Man* **84** C4
Anfield *Mersey* **85** E4
Angersleigh *Som'set* **11** C6
Angle *Pembs* **44** E3
Angmering *W Sussex* **16** D4
Angram *N Yorks* **95** E8
Angram *N Yorks* **100** E3
Anie *Stirl* **132** C4
Ankerville *H'land* **158** B2
Anlaby *ER Yorks* **90** B4
Anmer *Norfolk* **80** E3
Anna Valley *Hants* **25** E8
Annan *Dumf/Gal* **107** C8
Annat *Arg/Bute* **131** C6
Annat *H'land* **155** E4
Annbank *S Ayrs* **112** B4
Anne Hathaway's Cottage, Stratford-upon-Avon *Warwick* 51 D6
Annesley *Notts* **76** D5
Annesley Woodhouse *Notts* **76** D4
Annfield Plain *Durham* **110** D4
Annifirth *Shetl'd* **175** J3
Annitsford *Tyne/Wear* **111** B5
Annscroft *Shrops* **60** D4
Ansdell *Lancs* **85** B4
Ansford *Som'set* **23** F8
Ansley *Warwick* **63** E6
Anslow *Staffs* **63** B6
Anslow Gate *Staffs* **63** B5
Anstey *Herts* **54** F5
Anstey *Leics* **64** D2
Anstruther Easter *Fife* **135** D7
Anstruther Wester *Fife* **135** D7
Ansty *Hants* **26** E5
Ansty *Warwick* **63** F7
Ansty *Wilts* **13** B7
Ansty *W Sussex* **17** B6
Anthill Common *Hants* **15** C7
Anthorn *Cumb* **107** D8
Antingham *Norfolk* **81** D8
Anton's Gowt *Lincs* **79** E5
Antonshill *Falk* **133** F7
Antony *Cornw'l* **5** D8
Anwick *Lincs* **78** D4
Anwoth *Dumf/Gal* **106** D2
Aoradh *Arg/Bute* **126** C2
Apes Hall *Cambs* **67** E5
Apethorpe *Northants* **65** E7
Apeton *Staffs* **62** C2
Apley *Lincs* **78** B4
Apperknowle *Derby* **76** B3
Apperley *Glos* **37** B5
Apperley Bridge *W Yorks* **94** F4
Appersett *N Yorks* **100** E3
Appin *Arg/Bute* **138** E3
Appin House *Arg/Bute* **138** E3
Appleby *N Lincs* **90** C3
Appleby-in-Westmorland *Cumb* **100** B1
Appleby Magna *Leics* **63** D7
Appleby Parva *Leics* **63** D7
Applecross *H'land* **155** F3
Applecross Ho. *H'land* **155** F3
Appledore *Devon* **20** F3
Appledore *Devon* **11** C5
Appledore *Kent* **19** C6
Appledore Heath *Kent* **19** B6
Appleford *Oxon* **39** E5
Applegarthtown *Dumf/Gal* **114** F4
Appleshaw *Hants* **25** E8
Applethwaite *Cumb* **98** B4
Appleton *Halton* **86** F3
Appleton *Oxon* **38** D4
Appleton-le-Moors *N Yorks* **103** F5
Appleton-le-Street *N Yorks* **96** B3
Appleton Roebuck *N Yorks* **95** E8
Appleton Thorn *Warrington* **86** F4
Appleton Wiske *N Yorks* **102** D1
Appletreehall *Scot Borders* **115** C8
Appletreewick *N Yorks* **94** C3
Appley *Som'set* **11** B5
Appley Bridge *Lancs* **86** D3
Apse Heath *I/Wight* **15** F6
Apsley End *Beds* **54** F2
Apuldram *W Sussex* **16** D2
Aquhythie *Aberds* **151** C6
Arabella *H'land* **158** B2
Arbeadie *Aberds* **151** E5
Arbeia Roman Fort and Museum *Tyne/Wear* 111 C6
Arberth = Narberth *Pembs* **32** C2
Arbirlot *Angus* **143** E6
Arboll *H'land* **165** F5
Arborfield *Wokingham* **27** C5
Arborfield Cross *Wokingham* **27** C5
Arborfield Garrison *Wokingham* **27** C5
Arbour-thorne *S Yorks* **88** F4
Arbroath *Angus* **143** E6
Arbuthnott *Aberds* **143** B7
Archiestown *Moray* **159** E6
Arclid *Ches* **74** C4
Ard-dhubh *H'land* **155** F3
Ardachu *H'land* **164** D3
Ardalanish *Arg/Bute* **136** G4
Ardanaiseig *Arg/Bute* **131** C6
Ardaneaskan *H'land* **155** G4
Ardanstur *Arg/Bute* **130** D4
Ardargie House Hotel *Perth/Kinr* **134** C2
Ardarroch *H'land* **155** G4
Ardbeg *Arg/Bute* **126** E4
Ardbeg *Arg/Bute* **129** B6
Ardbeg Distillery, Port Ellen *Arg/Bute* 126 E4
Ardcharnich *H'land* **163** F5
Ardchiavaig *Arg/Bute* **136** G4
Ardchullarie More *Stirl* **132** C4
Ardchyle *Stirl* **132** B4
Arddleen *Powys* **60** C2
Ardechvie *H'land* **146** E4
Ardeley *Herts* **41** B6
Ardelve *H'land* **155** H4
Arden *Arg/Bute* **132** F2
Ardens Grafton *Warwick* **51** D6
Ardentinny *Arg/Bute* **129** B6
Ardentraive *Arg/Bute* **129** C5
Ardeonaig *Stirl* **140** F3
Ardersier *H'land* **157** D8
Ardessie *H'land* **162** F4
Ardfern *Arg/Bute* **130** E4
Ardgartan *Arg/Bute* **131** E8
Ardgay *H'land* **164** E2
Ardgour *H'land* **138** C4
Ardheslaig *H'land* **154** E3
Ardiecow *Moray* **160** B2
Ardindrean *H'land* **163** F5
Ardingly *W Sussex* **17** B7
Ardington *Oxon* **38** F4
Ardlair *Aberds* **150** B4
Ardlamont Ho. *Arg/Bute* **128** D4
Ardleigh *Essex* **43** B6
Ardler *Perth/Kinr* **142** E2
Ardley *Oxon* **39** B5
Ardlui *Arg/Bute* **132** C2
Ardlussa *Arg/Bute* **127** D4
Ardmair *H'land* **163** E5
Ardmay *Arg/Bute* **131** E8
Ardminish *Arg/Bute* **118** B3
Ardmolich *H'land* **145** F7
Ardmore *Arg/Bute* **130** C3
Ardmore *H'land* **166** D4
Ardmore *H'land* **164** F4
Ardnacross *Arg/Bute* **137** D6
Ardnadam *Arg/Bute* **129** C6
Ardnagrask *H'land* **157** E6
Ardnarff *H'land* **155** G4
Ardnastang *H'land* **138** C2
Ardnave *Arg/Bute* **126** B2
Ardno *Arg/Bute* **131** E7
Ardo *Aberds* **160** E5
Ardo Ho. *Aberds* **151** B8
Ardoch *Perth/Kinr* **141** F7
Ardochy House *H'land* **146** D5
Ardoyne *Aberds* **151** B5
Ardpatrick *Arg/Bute* **128** D2
Ardpatrick Ho. *Arg/Bute* **128** E2
Ardpeaton *Arg/Bute* **129** B7
Ardrishaig *Arg/Bute* **128** B3
Ardross *Fife* **135** D7
Ardross *H'land* **157** B7
Ardross Castle *H'land* **157** B7
Ardrossan *N Ayrs* **120** E2
Ardshealach *H'land* **137** B7
Ardsley *S Yorks* **88** D4
Ardslignish *H'land* **137** B6
Ardtalla *Arg/Bute* **126** D4
Ardtalnaig *Perth/Kinr* **140** F4
Ardtoe *H'land* **145** F6
Ardtrostan *Perth/Kinr* **133** B5
Arduaine *Arg/Bute* **130** D3
Ardullie *H'land* **157** C6
Ardvasar *H'land* **145** C6
Ardvorlich *Perth/Kinr* **132** B5
Ardwell *Dumf/Gal* **104** E5
Ardwell Mains *Dumf/Gal* **104** E5
Ardwick *Gtr Man* **87** E6
Areley Kings *Worcs* **50** B3
Arford *Hants* **27** F6
Argoed *Caerph* **35** E5
Argoed Mill *Powys* **47** C8
Argyll & Sutherland Highlanders Museum (See Stirling Castle) *Stirl* 133 E6
Arichamish *Arg/Bute* **130** E5
Arichastlich *Arg/Bute* **131** B8
Aridhglas *Arg/Bute* **136** F4
Arileod *Arg/Bute* **136** C2
Arinacrinachd *H'land* **154** E3
Arinagour *Arg/Bute* **136** C3
Arion *Orkney* **176** E1
Arisaig *H'land* **145** E6
Ariundle *H'land* **138** C2
Arkendale *N Yorks* **95** C6
Arkesden *Essex* **55** F5
Arkholme *Lancs* **93** B5
Arkle Town *N Yorks* **101** D5
Arkley *London* **41** E5
Arksey *S Yorks* **89** D6
Arkwright Town *Derby* **76** B4
Arle *Glos* **37** B6
Arlecdon *Cumb* **98** C2
Arlesey *Beds* **54** F2
Arleston *Telford* **61** C6
Arley *Ches* **86** F4
Arlingham *Glos* **36** C4
Arlington *Devon* **20** E5
Arlington *E Sussex* **18** E2
Arlington *Glos* **37** D8
Arlington Court *Devon* 20 E5
Armadale *H'land* **168** C2
Armadale *W Loth* **122** C2
Armadale Castle *H'land* **145** C6
Armathwaite *Cumb* **108** E5
Arminghall *Norfolk* **69** D5
Armitage *Staffs* **62** C4
Armley *W Yorks* **95** F5
Armscote *Warwick* **51** E7
Armthorpe *S Yorks* **89** D7
Arnabost *Arg/Bute* **136** C3
Arncliffe *N Yorks* **94** B2
Arncroach *Fife* **135** D7
Arne *Dorset* **13** F7
Arnesby *Leics* **64** E3
Arngask *Perth/Kinr* **134** C3
Arnisdale *H'land* **145** B8
Arnish *H'land* **152** E6
Arniston Engine *Midloth* **123** C6
Arnol *W Isles* **172** D6
Arnold *ER Yorks* **97** E7
Arnold *Notts* **77** E5
Arnolfini Gallery *Bristol* 23 B7
Arnprior *Stirl* **132** E5
Arnside *Cumb* **92** B4
Aros Mains *Arg/Bute* **137** D6
Arowry *Wrex* **73** F8
Arpafeelie *H'land* **157** D7
Arrad Foot *Cumb* **99** F5
Arram *ER Yorks* **97** E6
Arrathorne *N Yorks* **101** E7
Arreton *I/Wight* **15** F6
Arrington *Cambs* **54** D4
Arrivain *Arg/Bute* **131** B8
Arrochar *Arg/Bute* **131** E8
Arrow *Warwick* **51** D5
Arthington *W Yorks* **95** E5
Arthingworth *Northants* **64** F4
Arthog *Gwyn* **58** C3
Arthrath *Aberds* **161** E6
Arthurstone *Perth/Kinr* **142** E2
Artrochie *Aberds* **161** E7
Arundel *W Sussex* **16** D4
Arundel Castle *W Sussex* 16 D4
Aryhoulan *H'land* **138** C4
Asby *Cumb* **98** B2
Ascog *Arg/Bute* **129** D6
Ascot *Windsor* **27** C7
Ascot Racecourse *Windsor* 27 C7
Ascott *Warwick* **51** F8

Beltring Kent 29 E7
Belts of Collonach Aberds 151 E5
Belvedere London 29 B5
Belvoir Leics 77 F8
Belvoir Leics 77 F8
Bembridge I/Wight 15 F7
Bemersyde Scot Borders 123 F8
Bemerton Wilts 25 F6
Bempton ER Yorks 97 B7
Ben Alder Lodge H'land 140 B2
Ben Armine Lodge H'land 164 C4
Ben Casgro W Isles 172 F7
Benacre Suffolk 69 F8
Benbuie Dumf/Gal 113 E7
Benderloch Arg/Bute 130 B5
Bendronaig Lodge H'land 155 G6
Benenden Kent 18 B5
Benfield Dumf/Gal 105 C7
Bengate Norfolk 69 B6
Bengeworth Worcs 50 E5
Benhall Green Suffolk 57 C7
Benhall Street Suffolk 57 C7
Benholm Aberds 143 C8
Beningbrough N Yorks 95 D8
Beningbrough Hall N Yorks 95 D8
Benington Herts 41 B5
Benington Lincs 79 E6
Benllech Angl 82 C5
Benmore Arg/Bute 129 B6
Benmore Stirl 132 B3
Benmore Lodge H'land 163 C7
Bennacott Cornw'l 8 E4
Bennan N Ayrs 119 D6
Benniworth Lincs 91 F6
Benover Kent 29 E8
Bensham Tyne/Wear 110 C5
Benson Oxon 39 E6
Bent Aberds 143 B6
Bent Gate Lancs 87 B5
Benthall Northum 117 B8
Benthall Shrops 61 D6
Bentham Glos 37 C6
Benthoul Aberd C 151 D7
Bentlawnt Shrops 60 D3
Bentley ER Yorks 97 F6
Bentley Hants 27 E5
Bentley Suffolk 56 F5
Bentley S Yorks 89 D6
Bentley Warwick 63 E6
Bentley Worcs 50 C4
Bentley Heath W Midlands 51 B6
Benton Devon 21 F5
Bentpath Dumf/Gal 115 E6
Bents W Loth 122 C2
Bentworth Hants 26 E4
Benvie Dundee C 142 F3
Benwick Cambs 66 E3
Beoley Worcs 51 C5
Beoraidbeg H'land 145 D6
Bepton W Sussex 16 C2
Berden Essex 41 B7
Bere Alston Devon 6 C2
Bere Ferrers Devon 6 C2
Bere Regis Dorset 13 E6
Berepper Cornw'l 3 D5
Bergh Apton Norfolk 69 D6
Berinsfield Oxon 39 E5
Berkeley Glos 36 E3
Berkhamsted Herts 40 D2
Berkley Som'set 24 E3
Berkswell W Midlands 51 B7
Bermondsey London 28 B4
Bernera H'land 155 H4
Bernice Arg/Bute 129 A6
Bernisdale H'land 152 D5
Berrick Salome Oxon 39 E6
Berriedale H'land 165 B8
Berrier Cumb 99 B5
Berriew Powys 59 D8
Berrington Northum 125 E6
Berrington Shrops 60 D5
Berrow Som'set 22 D5
Berrow Green Worcs 50 D2
Berry Down Cross Devon 20 E4
Berry Hill Glos 36 C2
Berry Hill Pembs 45 E2
Berry Pomeroy Devon 7 C6
Berryhillock Moray 160 B2
Berrynarbor Devon 20 E4
Bersham Wrex 73 E7
Berstane Orkney 176 E3
Berwick E Sussex 18 E2
Berwick Bassett Wilts 25 B5
Berwick Hill Northum 110 B4
Berwick St James Wilts 25 F5
Berwick St John Wilts 13 B7
Berwick St Leonard Wilts 24 F4
Berwick-upon-Tweed Northum 125 D5
Bescar Lancs 85 C4
Besford Worcs 50 E4
Bessacarr S Yorks 89 D7
Bessels Leigh Oxon 38 D4
Bessingby ER Yorks 97 C7
Bessingham Norfolk 81 D7
Bestbeech Hill E Sussex 18 B3
Besthorpe Norfolk 68 E3
Besthorpe Notts 77 C8
Bestwood Nott'ham 77 E5
Bestwood Village Notts 77 E5
Beswick ER Yorks 97 E6
Betchworth Surrey 28 E3
Beth Shalom Holocaust Centre, Laxton Notts 77 C7
Bethania Ceredig'n 46 C4
Bethania Gwyn 83 F6
Bethania Gwyn 71 C8
Bethel Angl 82 D3
Bethel Gwyn 82 E5
Bethel Gwyn 72 F3
Bethersden Kent 30 E3
Bethesda Gwyn 83 E6
Bethesda Pembs 32 C1
Bethlehem Carms 33 B7
Bethnal Green London 41 F6
Betley Staffs 74 E4
Betsham Kent 29 B7
Betteshanger Kent 31 D7
Bettiscombe Dorset 11 E8
Bettisfield Wrex 73 F8
Betton Shrops 60 D3
Betton Shrops 74 F3
Bettws Bridg 33 D8
Bettws Newp 35 E6
Bettws Cedewain Powys 59 E8
Bettws Gwerfil Goch Denbs 72 E4
Bettws Ifan Ceredig'n 46 E2
Bettws Newydd Monmouths 35 D7
Bettws-y-crwyn Shrops 60 F2
Bettyhill H'land 168 C2
Betws Carms 33 C7
Betws Bledrws Ceredig'n 46 D4
Betws-Garmon Gwyn 82 F5
Betws-y-Coed Conwy 83 F7
Betws-yn-Rhos Conwy 72 B3
Beulah Ceredig'n 45 E4
Beulah Powys 47 D8
Bevendean Brighton/Hove 17 D7
Bevercotes Notts 77 B6
Beverley ER Yorks 97 F6
Beverley Minster ER Yorks 97 F6
Beverley Racecourse ER Yorks 97 E6
Beverston Glos 37 E5
Bevington Glos 36 E3
Bewaldeth Cumb 108 F2
Bewcastle Cumb 109 B5
Bewdley Worcs 50 B2
Bewerley N Yorks 94 C4
Bewholme ER Yorks 97 D7
Bexhill E Sussex 18 E4
Bexley London 29 B5
Bexleyheath London 29 B5
Bexwell Norfolk 67 D6
Beyton Suffolk 56 C3
Bhaltos W Isles 172 E3
Bhatarsaigh W Isles 171 L2
Bibury Glos 37 D8
Bicester Oxon 39 B5
Bickenhall Som'set 11 C7
Bickenhill W Midlands 63 F5
Bicker Lincs 78 F5
Bickershaw Gtr Man 86 D4
Bickerstaffe Lancs 86 D2
Bickerton Ches 74 D2
Bickerton N Yorks 95 D7
Bickington Devon 7 B5
Bickington Devon 20 F4
Bickleigh Devon 10 D4
Bickleigh Devon 6 C3
Bickleton Devon 20 F4
Bickley London 28 C5
Bickley Moss Ches 74 E2
Bicknacre Essex 42 D3
Bicknoller Som'set 22 F3
Bicknor Kent 30 D2
Bickton Hants 14 C2
Bicton Shrops 60 C4
Bicton Shrops 60 F2
Bicton Park Gardens Devon 11 F5
Bidborough Kent 29 E6
Biddenden Kent 19 B5
Biddenham Beds 53 E8
Biddestone Wilts 24 B3
Biddisham Som'set 23 D5
Biddlesden Bucks 52 E4
Biddlestone Northum 117 D5
Biddulph Staffs 75 D5
Biddulph Moor Staffs 75 D6
Bideford Devon 9 B6
Bidford-on-Avon Warwick 51 D6
Bidston Mersey 85 E3
Bielby ER Yorks 96 E3
Bieldside Aberd C 151 D7
Bierley I/Wight 15 G6
Bierley W Yorks 94 F4
Bierton Bucks 39 C8
Big Pit National Mining Museum, Blaenavon Torf 35 D6
Big Sand H'land 154 C3
Bigbury Devon 6 E4
Bigbury on Sea Devon 6 E4
Bigby Lincs 90 D4
Biggar Cumb 92 C1
Biggar S Lanarks 122 F3
Biggin Derby 75 D8
Biggin Derby 76 E2
Biggin N Yorks 95 F8
Biggin Hill London 28 D5
Biggings Shetl'd 175 G3
Biggleswade Beds 54 E2
Bighouse H'land 168 C3
Bighton Hants 26 F4
Bignor W Sussex 16 C3
Bigton Shetl'd 175 L5
Bilberry Cornw'l 4 C5
Bilborough Nott'ham 76 E5
Bilbrook Som'set 22 E2
Bilbrough N Yorks 95 E8
Bilbster H'land 169 D7
Bildershaw Durham 101 B7
Bildeston Suffolk 56 E3
Billericay Essex 42 E2
Billesdon Leics 64 D4
Billesley Warwick 51 D6
Billingborough Lincs 78 F4
Billinge Mersey 86 D3
Billingford Norfolk 81 E6
Billingham Stockton 102 B2
Billinghay Lincs 78 D4
Billingley S Yorks 88 D5
Billingshurst W Sussex 16 B4
Billingsley Shrops 61 F7
Billington Beds 40 B2
Billington Lancs 93 F7
Billockby Norfolk 69 C7
Billy Row Durham 110 F4
Bilsborrow Lancs 92 F5
Bilsby Lincs 79 B7
Bilsham W Sussex 16 D3
Bilsington Kent 19 B7
Bilson Green Glos 36 C3
Bilsthorpe Notts 77 C6
Bilsthorpe Moor Notts 77 D6
Bilston Midloth 123 C5
Bilston W Midlands 62 E3
Bilstone Leics 63 D7
Bilting Kent 30 E4
Bilton ER Yorks 97 F7
Bilton Northum 117 C8
Bilton Warwick 52 B2
Bilton in Ainsty N Yorks 95 E7
Bimbister Orkney 176 E2
Binbrook Lincs 91 E6
Binchester Blocks Durham 110 F5
Bincombe Dorset 12 F4
Bindal H'land 165 F6
Binegar Som'set 23 E8
Binfield Brackn'l 27 B6
Binfield Hth Oxon 26 B5
Bingfield Northum 110 B2
Bingham Notts 77 F7
Bingley W Yorks 94 F4
Bings Heath Shrops 60 C5
Binham Norfolk 81 D5
Binley Hants 26 D2
Binley W Midlands 51 B8
Binley Woods Warwick 51 B8
Binniehill Falk 121 B8
Binsoe N Yorks 94 B5
Binstead I/Wight 15 E6
Binsted Hants 27 E5
Binton Warwick 51 D6
Bintree Norfolk 81 E6
Binweston Shrops 60 D3
Birch Essex 43 C5
Birch Gtr Man 87 D6
Birch Green Essex 43 C5
Birch Heath Ches 74 C2
Birch Hill Ches 74 B2
Birch Vale Derby 87 F8
Bircham Newton Norfolk 80 D3
Bircham Tofts Norfolk 80 D3
Birchanger Essex 41 B8
Birchencliffe W Yorks 88 C2
Bircher Heref'd 49 C6
Birchfield H'land 149 B5
Birchgrove Card 22 B3
Birchgrove Swan 33 E8
Birchington Kent 31 C6
Birchmoor Warwick 63 D6
Birchover Derby 76 C2
Birchwood Lincs 78 C2
Birchwood Warrington 86 E4
Bircotes Notts 89 E7
Birdbrook Essex 55 E8
Birdforth N Yorks 95 B7
Birdham W Sussex 16 E2
Birdholme Derby 76 C3
Birdingbury Warwick 52 C2
Birdland Park, Bourton-on-the-Water Glos 38 B1
Birdlip Glos 37 C6
Birds Edge W Yorks 88 D3
Birdsall N Yorks 96 C4
Birdsgreen Shrops 61 F7
Birdsmoor Gate Dorset 11 D8
Birdston E Dunb 121 B6
Birdwell S Yorks 88 D4
Birdwood Glos 36 C4
Birdworld and Underwaterworld, Farnham Hants 27 E6
Birgham Scot Borders 124 F3
Birkby N Yorks 101 D8
Birkdale Mersey 85 C4
Birkenhead Mersey 85 F4
Birkenhills Aberds 160 D4
Birkenshaw N Lanarks 121 C6
Birkenshaw W Yorks 88 B3
Birkhall Aberds 150 E2
Birkhill Angus 142 F3
Birkhill Dumf/Gal 114 C5
Birkholme Lincs 65 B6
Birkin N Yorks 89 B6
Birley Heref'd 49 D6
Birling Kent 29 C7
Birling Northum 117 D8
Birling Gap E Sussex 18 F2
Birlingham Worcs 50 E4
Birmingham W Midlands 62 F4
Birmingham Botanical Gardens W Midlands 62 F4
Birmingham Museum and Art Gallery W Midlands 62 F4
Birmingham Museum of Science and Technology W Midlands 62 F4
Birnam Perth/Kinr 141 E7
Birse Aberds 150 E4
Birsemore Aberds 150 E4
Birstall Leics 64 D2
Birstall W Yorks 88 B3
Birstwith N Yorks 94 D5
Birthorpe Lincs 78 F4
Birtley Heref'd 49 C5
Birtley Northum 109 B8
Birtley Tyne/Wear 111 D5
Birts Street Worcs 50 F2
Bisbrooke Rutl'd 65 E5
Biscathorpe Lincs 91 F6
Biscot Luton 40 B3
Bish Mill Devon 10 B2
Bisham Windsor 39 F8
Bishampton Worcs 50 D4
Bishop Auckland Durham 101 B7
Bishop Burton ER Yorks 97 F5
Bishop Middleham Durham 111 F6
Bishop Monkton N Yorks 95 C6
Bishop Norton Lincs 90 E3
Bishop Sutton Bath/NE Som'set 23 D7
Bishop Thornton N Yorks 95 C5
Bishop Wilton ER Yorks 96 D3
Bishopbridge Lincs 90 E4
Bishopbriggs E Dunb 121 C6
Bishopmill Moray 159 C6
Bishops Cannings Wilts 24 C5
Bishop's Castle Shrops 60 F3
Bishop's Caundle Dorset 12 C4
Bishop's Cleeve Glos 37 B6
Bishops Frome Heref'd 49 E8
Bishop's Green Essex 42 C2
Bishop's Hull Som'set 11 B7
Bishop's Itchington Warwick 51 D8
Bishops Lydeard Som'set 11 B6
Bishops Nympton Devon 10 B2
Bishop's Offley Staffs 61 B7
Bishop's Stortford Herts 41 B7
Bishop's Sutton Hants 26 F4
Bishop's Tachbrook Warwick 51 C8
Bishops Tawton Devon 20 F4
Bishop's Waltham Hants 15 C6
Bishop's Wood Staffs 62 D2
Bishopsbourne Kent 31 D5
Bishopsteignton Devon 7 B7
Bishopstoke Hants 15 C5
Bishopston Swan 33 F6
Bishopstone Bucks 39 C8
Bishopstone E Sussex 17 D8
Bishopstone Heref'd 49 E6
Bishopstone Swindon 38 F2
Bishopstone Wilts 13 B8
Bishopstrow Wilts 24 E3
Bishopswood Som'set 11 C7
Bishopsworth Bristol 23 C7
Bishopthorpe C/York 95 E8
Bishopton D'lington 102 B1
Bishopton Dumf/Gal 105 E8
Bishopton N Yorks 95 B6
Bishopton Renf 120 B4
Bishopton Warwick 51 D6
Bishton Newp 35 F7
Bisley Glos 37 D6
Bisley Surrey 27 D7
Bispham Blackp'l 92 E3
Bispham Green Lancs 86 C2
Bissoe Cornw'l 3 B6
Bisterne Close Hants 14 D3
Bitchfield Lincs 65 B6
Bittadon Devon 20 E4
Bittaford Devon 6 D4
Bittering Norfolk 68 C2
Bitterley Shrops 49 B7
Bitterne S'hampton 15 C5
Bitteswell Leics 64 F2
Bitton S Glouc 23 C8
Bix Oxon 39 F7
Bixter Shetl'd 175 H5
Blaby Leics 64 E2
Black Bourton Oxon 38 D2
Black Callerton Tyne/Wear 110 C4
Black Clauchrie S Ayrs 112 F2
Black Corries Lodge H'land 139 D6
Black Crofts Arg/Bute 130 B5
Black Dog Devon 10 D3
Black Heddon Northum 110 B3
Black Lane Gtr Man 87 D5
Black Marsh Shrops 60 E3
Black Mount Arg/Bute 139 E6
Black Notley Essex 42 B3
Black Pill Swan 33 E7
Black Tar Pembs 44 E4
Black Torrington Devon 9 D6
Blackacre Dumf/Gal 114 E3
Blackadder West Scot Borders 124 D4
Blackawton Devon 7 D6
Blackborough Devon 11 D5
Blackborough End Norfolk 67 C6
Blackboys E Sussex 18 C2
Blackbrook Derby 76 E3
Blackbrook Mersey 86 E3
Blackbrook Staffs 74 F4
Blackburn Aberds 160 E2
Blackburn Aberds 151 C7
Blackburn Blackb'n 86 B4
Blackburn W Loth 122 C2
Blackcraig Dumf/Gal 113 F7
Blackden Heath Ches 74 B4
Blackdog Aberds 151 C8
Blackfell Tyne/Wear 111 D5
Blackfield Hants 14 D5
Blackford Cumb 108 C3
Blackford Perth/Kinr 133 D7
Blackford Som'set 23 E6
Blackford Som'set 12 B4
Blackfordby Leics 63 C7
Blackgang I/Wight 15 G5
Blackgang Chine Fantasy I/Wight 15 G5
Blackhall Colliery Durham 111 F7
Blackhall Mill Tyne/Wear 110 D4
Blackhall Rocks Durham 111 F7
Blackham E Sussex 29 F5
Blackhaugh Scot Borders 123 F7
Blackheath Essex 43 B6
Blackheath Suffolk 57 B8
Blackheath Surrey 27 E8
Blackheath W Midlands 62 F3
Blackhill Aberds 161 D7
Blackhill Aberds 161 C7
Blackhill H'land 152 D4
Blackhills H'land 158 D3
Blackhills Moray 159 D6
Blackhorse S Glouc 23 B8
Blackland Wilts 24 C5
Blacklaw Aberds 160 C3
Blackley Gtr Man 87 D6
Blacklunans Perth/Kinr 142 C1
Blackmill Bridg 34 F3
Blackmoor Hants 27 F5
Blackmoor Gate Devon 21 E5
Blackmore Essex 42 D2
Blackmore End Essex 55 F8
Blackmore End Herts 40 C4
Blackness Falk 122 B3
Blacknest Hants 27 E5
Blacko Lancs 93 E8
Blackpool Blackp'l 92 F3
Blackpool Devon 7 E6
Blackpool Pembs 32 C1
Blackpool Gate Cumb 108 B5
Blackpool Pleasure Beach Blackp'l 92 F3
Blackpool Sea Life Centre Blackp'l 92 F3
Blackpool Tower Blackp'l 92 F3
Blackpool Zoo Park Blackp'l 92 F3
Blackridge W Loth 121 C8
Blackrock Arg/Bute 126 C3
Blackrock Monmouths 35 C6
Blackrod Gtr Man 86 C4
Blackshaw Dumf/Gal 107 C7
Blackshaw Head W Yorks 87 B7
Blacksmith's Green Suffolk 56 C5
Blackstone W Sussex 17 C6
Blackthorn Oxon 39 C6
Blackthorpe Suffolk 56 C3
Blacktoft ER Yorks 90 B2
Blacktop Aberd C 151 D7
Blacktown Newp 35 F6
Blackwall Tunnel London 41 F6
Blackwater Cornw'l 3 B6
Blackwater Hants 27 D6
Blackwater I/Wight 15 F6
Blackwaterfoot N Ayrs 119 D5
Blackwell Cumb 108 D4
Blackwell D'lington 101 C7
Blackwell Derby 75 B8
Blackwell Derby 76 D4
Blackwell Warwick 51 E7
Blackwell Worcs 50 B4
Blackwell W Sussex 28 F4
Blackwood S Lanarks 121 E7
Blackwood = Coed Duon Caerph 35 E5
Blackwood Hill Staffs 75 D6
Blacon Ches 73 C7
Bladnoch Dumf/Gal 105 D8
Bladon Oxon 38 C4
Blaen-gwynfi Neath P Talb 34 E2
Blaen-waun Carms 32 B3
Blaen-y-coed Carms 32 B4
Blaen-y-Cwm Denbs 72 F4
Blaen-y-cwm Gwyn 71 E8
Blaen-y-cwm Powys 59 B7
Blaenannerch Ceredig'n 45 E4
Blaenau Ffestiniog Gwyn 71 C8
Blaenavon Torf 35 D6
Blaenawey Monmouths 35 C6
Blaencelyn Ceredig'n 46 D2
Blaendyryn Powys 47 F8
Blaenffos Pembs 45 F3
Blaengarw Bridg 34 E3
Blaengwrach Neath P Talb 34 D2
Blaenpennal Ceredig'n 46 C5
Blaenplwyf Ceredig'n 46 B4
Blaenporth Ceredig'n 45 E4
Blaenrhondda Rh Cyn Taff 34 D3
Blaenycwm Ceredig'n 47 B7
Blagdon N Som'set 23 D7
Blagdon Torbay 7 C6
Blagdon Hill Som'set 11 C7
Blagill Cumb 109 E7
Blaguegate Lancs 86 D2
Blaich H'land 138 B4
Blain H'land 137 B7
Blaina Bl Gwent 35 D6
Blair Atholl Perth/Kinr 141 C5
Blair Castle, Blair Atholl Perth/Kinr 141 C5
Blair Drummond Stirl 133 E6
Blair Drummond Safari Park, Dunblane Stirl 133 E6
Blairbeg N Ayrs 119 C7
Blairdaff Aberds 151 C5
Blairglas Arg/Bute 129 B8
Blairgowrie Perth/Kinr 142 E1
Blairhall Fife 134 F2
Blairingone Perth/Kinr 133 E8
Blairland N Ayrs 120 E3
Blairlogie Stirl 133 E7
Blairlomond Arg/Bute 131 F7
Blairmore Arg/Bute 129 B6
Blairnamarrow Moray 149 C8
Blairquhosh Stirl 132 F4
Blair's Ferry Arg/Bute 128 D4
Blairskaith E Dunb 121 B5
Blaisdon Glos 36 C4
Blakebrook Worcs 50 B3
Blakedown Worcs 50 B3
Blakelaw Scot Borders 124 F3
Blakeley Staffs 62 E2
Blakeley Lane Staffs 75 E6
Blakemere Heref'd 49 E5
Blakeney Glos 36 D3
Blakeney Norfolk 81 C6
Blakeney Point NNR Norfolk 81 C6
Blakenhall Ches 74 E4
Blakenhall W Midlands 62 E3
Blakeshall Worcs 62 F2
Blakesley Northants 52 D4
Blanchland Northum 110 D2
Bland Hill N Yorks 94 D5
Blandford Forum Dorset 13 D6
Blandford St Mary Dorset 13 D6
Blanefield Stirl 121 B5
Blankney Lincs 78 C3
Blar a'Chaorainn H'land 139 C5
Blaran Arg/Bute 130 D4
Blarghour Arg/Bute 131 D5
Blarmachfoldach H'land 138 C4
Blarnalearoch H'land 163 E5
Blashford Hants 14 D2
Blaston Leics 64 E5
Blatherwycke Northants 65 E6
Blawith Cumb 98 F4
Blaxhall Suffolk 57 D7
Blaxton S Yorks 89 D7
Blaydon Tyne/Wear 110 C4
Bleadon N Som'set 22 D5
Bleak Hey Nook Gtr Man 87 D8
Blean Kent 30 C5
Bleasby Lincs 90 F5
Bleasby Notts 77 E7
Bleasdale Lancs 93 E5
Bleatarn Cumb 100 C2
Blebocraigs Fife 135 C6
Bleddfa Powys 48 C4
Bledington Glos 38 B2
Bledlow Bucks 39 D7
Bledlow Ridge Bucks 39 E7
Blegbie E Loth 123 C7
Blencarn Cumb 109 F6
Blencogo Cumb 107 E8
Blendworth Hants 15 C8
Blenheim Palace, Woodstock Oxon 38 C4
Blennerhasset Cumb 107 E8
Blervie Castle Moray 158 D4
Bletchingdon Oxon 39 C5
Bletchingley Surrey 28 D4
Bletchley M/Keynes 53 F6
Bletchley Shrops 74 F3
Bletherston Pembs 32 B1
Bletsoe Beds 53 D8
Blewbury Oxon 39 F5
Blickling Norfolk 81 E7
Blickling Hall, Aylsham Norfolk 81 E7
Blidworth Notts 77 D5
Blindburn Northum 116 C4
Blindcrake Cumb 107 F8
Blindley Heath Surrey 28 E4
Blisland Cornw'l 5 B6
Bliss Gate Worcs 50 B2
Blissford Hants 14 C2
Blisworth Northants 52 D5
Blithbury Staffs 62 B4
Blitterlees Cumb 107 D8
Blockley Glos 51 F6
Blofield Norfolk 69 D6
Blofield Heath Norfolk 69 C6
Blo'Norton Norfolk 56 B4
Bloomfield Scot Borders 115 B8
Blore Staffs 75 E8
Blount's Green Staffs 75 F7
Blowick Mersey 85 C4
Bloxham Oxon 52 F2
Bloxholm Lincs 78 D3
Bloxwich W Midlands 62 D3
Bloxworth Dorset 13 E6
Blubberhouses N Yorks 94 D4
Blue Anchor Som'set 22 E2
Blue Anchor Swan 33 E6
Blue Planet Aquarium Ches 73 B8
Blue Row Essex 43 C6
Blundeston Suffolk 69 E8
Blunham Beds 54 D2
Blunsdon St Andrew Swindon 37 F8
Bluntington Worcs 50 B3
Bluntisham Cambs 54 B4
Blunts Cornw'l 5 C8
Blyborough Lincs 90 E3
Blyford Suffolk 57 B8
Blymhill Staffs 62 C2
Blyth Notts 89 F7
Blyth Northum 117 F9
Blyth Bridge Scot Borders 122 E4
Blythburgh Suffolk 57 B8
Blythe Scot Borders 123 E8
Blythe Bridge Staffs 75 E6
Blyton Lincs 90 E2
Boarhills Fife 135 C7
Boarhunt Hants 15 D7
Boars Head Gtr Man 86 D3
Boars Hill Oxon 38 D4
Boarshead E Sussex 18 B2
Boarstall Bucks 39 C6
Boasley Cross Devon 9 E6
Boat of Garten H'land 148 C5
Boath H'land 157 B6
Bobbing Kent 30 C2
Bobbington Staffs 62 E2
Bobbingworth Essex 41 D8
Bocaddon Cornw'l 5 D6
Bochastle Stirl 132 D5
Bocking Essex 42 B3
Bocking Churchstreet Essex 42 B3
Boddam Aberds 161 D8
Boddam Shetl'd 175 M5
Boddington Glos 37 B5
Bodedern Angl 82 C3
Bodelwyddan Denbs 72 B4
Bodenham Heref'd 49 D7
Bodenham Wilts 14 B2
Bodenham Arboretum and Earth Centre Worcs 62 F2
Bodenham Moor Heref'd 49 D7
Bodermid Gwyn 70 E2
Bodewryd Angl 82 B3
Bodfari Denbs 72 B4
Bodffordd Angl 82 D4
Bodham Norfolk 81 C7
Bodiam E Sussex 18 C4
Bodiam Castle E Sussex 18 C4
Bodicote Oxon 52 F2
Bodieve Cornw'l 4 B4
Bodinnick Cornw'l 5 D6
Bodle Street Green E Sussex 18 D3
Bodmin Cornw'l 5 C5
Bodnant Garden, Colwyn Bay Conwy 83 D8
Bodney Norfolk 67 E8
Bodorgan Angl 82 E3
Bodsham Kent 30 E5
Boduan Gwyn 70 D4
Bodymoor Heath Warwick 63 E5
Bogallan H'land 157 D7
Bogbrae Aberds 161 E7
Bogend Scot Borders 124 E3
Bogend S Ayrs 120 F3
Boghall W Loth 122 C2
Boghead S Lanarks 121 E7
Bogmoor Moray 159 C7
Bogniebrae Aberds 160 D2
Bognor Regis W Sussex 16 E3
Bograxie Aberds 151 C6
Bogside N Lanarks 121 D8
Bogton Aberds 160 C3
Bogue Dumf/Gal 113 F6
Bohenie H'land 147 F5
Bohortha Cornw'l 3 C7
Bohuntine H'land 147 F5
Boirseam W Isles 173 K3
Bojewyan Cornw'l 2 C2
Bolam Durham 101 B6
Bolam Northum 117 F6
Bolberry Devon 6 F4
Bold Heath Mersey 86 F3
Boldon Tyne/Wear 111 C6
Boldon Colliery Tyne/Wear 111 C6
Boldre Hants 14 E4
Boldron Durham 101 C5
Bole Notts 89 F8
Bolehill Derby 76 D2
Boleside Scot Borders 123 F7
Bolham Devon 10 C4
Bolham Water Devon 11 C6
Bolingey Cornw'l 4 D2
Bollington Ches 75 B6
Bollington Cross Ches 75 B6
Bolney W Sussex 17 B6
Bolnhurst Beds 53 D8
Bolshan Angus 143 D6
Bolsover Derby 76 B4
Bolsterstone S Yorks 88 E3
Bolstone Heref'd 49 F7
Boltby N Yorks 102 F2
Bolter End Bucks 39 E7
Bolton Cumb 99 B8
Bolton E Loth 123 B8
Bolton ER Yorks 96 D3
Bolton Gtr Man 86 D5
Bolton Northum 117 C7
Bolton Abbey N Yorks 94 D3
Bolton Abbey, Skipton N Yorks 94 D3
Bolton Bridge N Yorks 94 D3
Bolton-by-Bowland Lancs 93 E7
Bolton Castle, Leyburn N Yorks 101 E5
Bolton le Sands Lancs 92 C4
Bolton Low Houses Cumb 108 E2
Bolton-on-Swale N Yorks 101 E7
Bolton Percy N Yorks 95 E8
Bolton Town End Lancs 92 C4
Bolton upon Dearne S Yorks 89 D5
Boltonfellend Cumb 108 C4
Boltongate Cumb 108 E2
Bolventor Cornw'l 5 B6
Bomere Heath Shrops 60 C4
Bon-y-maen Swan 33 E7
Bonar Bridge H'land 164 E3
Bonawe Arg/Bute 131 B6
Bonby N Lincs 90 C4
Boncath Pembs 45 F4
Bonchester Bridge Scot Borders 115 C8
Bonchurch I/Wight 15 G6
Bondleigh Devon 9 D8
Bonehill Devon 6 B5
Bonehill Staffs 63 D5
Bo'ness Falk 133 F8
Bonhill W Dunb 120 B3
Boningale Shrops 62 D2
Bonjedward Scot Borders 116 B2
Bonkle N Lanarks 121 D8
Bonnavoulin H'land 137 C6
Bonnington C/Edinb 122 C4
Bonnington Kent 19 B7
Bonnybank Fife 135 D5
Bonnybridge Falk 133 F7
Bonnykelly Aberds 161 C5
Bonnyrigg and Lasswade Midloth 123 C6
Bonnyton Aberds 160 E3
Bonnyton Angus 142 F3
Bonnyton Angus 143 D6
Bonsall Derby 76 D2
Bonskeid House Perth/Kinr 141 C5
Bont Monmouths 35 C7
Bont-Dolgadfan Powys 59 D5
Bont-goch Ceredig'n 58 F3
Bont-newydd Conwy 72 B4
Bont Newydd Gwyn 71 C8
Bont Newydd Gwyn 71 E8
Bontddu Gwyn 58 C3
Bonthorpe Lincs 79 B7
Bontnewydd Ceredig'n 46 C5
Bontnewydd Gwyn 82 F4
Bontuchel Denbs 72 D4
Bonvilston V/Glam 22 B2
Booker Bucks 39 E8
Boon Scot Borders 123 E8
Boosbeck Redcar/Clevel'd 102 C4
Boot Cumb 98 D3
Boot Street Suffolk 57 E6
Booth W Yorks 87 B8
Booth Wood W Yorks 87 C8
Boothby Graffoe Lincs 78 D2
Boothby Pagnell Lincs 78 F2
Boothen Stoke 75 E5
Boothferry ER Yorks 89 B8
Boothville Northants 53 C5
Bootle Cumb 98 F3
Bootle Mersey 85 E4
Booton Norfolk 81 E7
Boquhan Stirl 132 F4
Boraston Shrops 49 C8
Borden Kent 30 C2
Borden W Sussex 16 B2
Bordley N Yorks 94 C2
Bordon Hants 27 F6
Bordon Camp Hants 27 F5
Boreham Essex 42 D3
Boreham Wilts 24 E3
Boreham Street E Sussex 18 D3
Borehamwood Herts 40 E4
Boreland Dumf/Gal 114 E4
Boreland Stirl 140 F2
Borgh W Isles 171 K2
Borgh W Isles 173 K2
Borghastan W Isles 172 D5
Borgie H'land 167 D8
Borgue Dumf/Gal 106 E3
Borgue H'land 165 B8
Borley Essex 56 E2
Bornais W Isles 171 H3
Bornesketaig H'land 152 B4
Borness Dumf/Gal 106 E3
Borough Green Kent 29 D7
Boroughbridge N Yorks 95 C6
Borras Head Wrex 73 D7
Borreraig H'land 152 D2
Borrobol Lodge H'land 165 B5
Borrowash Derby 76 F4
Borrowby N Yorks 102 F2
Borrowdale Cumb 98 C4
Borrowfield Aberds 151 E7
Borth Ceredig'n 58 E3
Borth-y-Gest Gwyn 71 D6
Borthertoft Lincs 79 E5
Borthwickbrae Scot Borders 115 C7
Borthwickshiels Scot Borders 115 C7
Borve H'land 152 E5
Borve Lodge W Isles 173 J3
Borwick Lancs 92 B5
Bosavern Cornw'l 2 C2
Bosbury Heref'd 49 E8
Boscastle Cornw'l 8 E3
Boscombe Bournem'th 14 E2
Boscombe Wilts 25 F7
Boscoppa Cornw'l 4 D5
Bosham W Sussex 16 D2
Bosherston Pembs 44 F4
Boskenna Cornw'l 2 D3
Bosley Ches 75 C6
Bossall N Yorks 96 C3
Bossiney Cornw'l 8 F2
Bossingham Kent 31 E5
Bossington Som'set 21 E7
Bostock Green Ches 74 C3
Boston Lincs 79 E6
Boston Long Hedges Lincs 79 E6
Boston Spa W Yorks 95 E7
Boston West Lincs 79 E5
Boswinger Cornw'l 3 B8
Botallack Cornw'l 2 C2
Botany Bay London 41 E5
Botcherby Cumb 108 D4
Botcheston Leics 63 D8
Botesdale Suffolk 56 B4
Bothal Northum 117 F8
Bothamsall Notts 77 B6
Bothel Cumb 107 F8
Bothenhampton Dorset 12 E2
Bothwell S Lanarks 121 D7
Botley Bucks 40 D2
Botley Hants 15 C6
Botley Oxon 38 D4
Botolph Claydon Bucks 39 B7
Botolphs W Sussex 17 D5
Bottacks H'land 157 C5
Bottesford Leics 77 F8
Bottesford N Lincs 90 D2
Bottisham Cambs 55 C6
Bottlesford Wilts 25 D6
Bottom Boat W Yorks 88 B4
Bottom House Staffs 75 D7
Bottom of Hutton Lancs 86 B2
Bottom o'th'Moor Gtr Man 86 C4
Bottomcraig Fife 135 B5
Botusfleming Cornw'l 6 C2
Botwnnog Gwyn 70 D3
Bough Beech Kent 29 E5
Boughrood Powys 48 F3
Boughspring Glos 36 E2
Boughton Norfolk 67 D6
Boughton Notts 77 C6
Boughton Northants 53 C5
Boughton Aluph Kent 30 E4
Boughton Lees Kent 30 E4
Boughton Malherbe Kent 30 E2
Boughton Monchelsea Kent 29 D8
Boughton Street Kent 30 D4
Boulby Redcar/Clevel'd 103 C5
Boulden Shrops 60 F5
Boulmer Northum 117 C8
Boulston Pembs 44 D4
Boultenstone Aberds 150 C3
Boultham Lincs 78 C2
Bourn Cambs 54 D4
Bourne Lincs 65 B7
Bourne End Beds 53 E7
Bourne End Bucks 40 F1
Bourne End Herts 40 D3
Bournemouth Bournem'th 13 E8
Bournes Green Glos 37 D6
Bournes Green Southend 43 F5
Bournheath Worcs 50 B4
Bournmoor Durham 111 D6
Bournville W Midlands 62 F4
Bourton Dorset 24 F2
Bourton N Som'set 23 C5
Bourton Oxon 38 F2
Bourton Shrops 61 E5
Bourton on Dunsmore Warwick 52 B2
Bourton on the Hill Glos 51 F6
Bourton-on-the-Water Glos 38 B1
Bousd Arg/Bute 136 B3
Boustead Hill Cumb 108 D2
Bouth Cumb 99 F5
Bouthwaite N Yorks 94 B4
Boveney Bucks 27 B7
Boverton V/Glam 21 C8
Bovey Tracey Devon 7 B6
Bovingdon Herts 40 D3
Bovingdon Green Bucks 39 F8
Bovingdon Green Herts 40 D3
Bovinger Essex 41 D8
Bovington Camp Dorset 13 F6
Bow Scot Borders 123 E7
Bow Devon 10 D2
Bow Orkney 176 G2
Bow Brickhill M/Keynes 53 F7
Bow of Fife Fife 134 C5
Bow Street Ceredig'n 58 F3
Bowbank Durham 100 B4
Bowburn Durham 111 F6
Bowcombe I/Wight 15 F5
Bowd Devon 11 E6
Bowden Scot Borders 123 F8
Bowden Devon 7 E6
Bowden Hill Wilts 24 C4
Bowderdale Cumb 100 D1
Bowdon Gtr Man 87 F5
Bower Northum 116 F3
Bower Hinton Som'set 12 C2
Bowerchalke Wilts 13 B8
Bowerhill Wilts 24 C4
Bowermadden H'land 169 C7
Bowers Gifford Essex 42 F3
Bowershall Fife 134 E2
Bowertower H'land 169 C7
Bowes Durham 100 C4
Bowgreave Lancs 92 E4
Bowgreen Gtr Man 87 F5
Bowhill Scot Borders 115 B7
Bowhouse Dumf/Gal 107 C7
Bowland Bridge Cumb 99 F6
Bowley Heref'd 49 D7
Bowlhead Green Surrey 27 F7
Bowling W Dunb 120 B4
Bowling W Yorks 94 F4
Bowling Bank Wrex 73 E7
Bowling Green Worcs 50 D3
Bowmanstead Cumb 99 E5
Bowmore Arg/Bute 126 D3
Bowness-on-Solway Cumb 108 C2
Bowness-on-Windermere Cumb 99 E6
Bowood House and Gardens, Calne Wilts 24 C4
Bowsden Northum 125 E5
Bowside Lodge H'land 168 C3
Bowston Cumb 99 E6
Bowthorpe Norfolk 68 D4
Box Glos 37 D5
Box Wilts 24 C3
Box End Beds 53 E8
Boxbush Glos 36 C4
Boxford Suffolk 56 E3
Boxford W Berks 26 B2
Boxgrove W Sussex 16 D3
Boxley Kent 29 D8
Boxmoor Herts 40 D3
Boxted Essex 56 F4
Boxted Suffolk 56 D2
Boxted Cross Essex 56 F4
Boxted Heath Essex 56 F4
Boxworth Cambs 54 C4
Boxworth End Cambs 54 C4
Boyden Gate Kent 31 C6
Boylestone Derby 75 F8
Boyndie Aberds 160 B3
Boynton ER Yorks 97 C7
Boysack Angus 143 E6
Boyton Cornw'l 8 E5
Boyton Suffolk 57 E7
Boyton Wilts 24 F4
Boyton Cross Essex 42 D2
Boyton End Suffolk 55 E8
Bozeat Northants 53 D7
Braaid I/Man 84 E3
Braal Castle H'land 169 C6
Brabling Green Suffolk 57 C6
Brabourne Kent 30 E4
Brabourne Lees Kent 30 E4
Brabster H'land 169 C8
Bracadale H'land 153 F4
Bracara H'land 145 D7
Braceborough Lincs 65 C7
Bracebridge Lincs 78 C2
Bracebridge Heath Lincs 78 C2
Bracebridge Low Fields Lincs 78 C2
Braceby Lincs 78 F3
Bracewell Lancs 93 E8
Brackenfield Derby 76 D3
Brackenthwaite Cumb 108 E2
Brackenthwaite N Yorks 95 D5
Brackletsham W Sussex 16 E2
Brackletter H'land 146 F4
Brackley Arg/Bute 118 B4
Brackley Northants 52 F3
Brackloch H'land 163 B5
Bracknell Brackn'l 27 C6
Braco Perth/Kinr 133 D7
Bracobrae Moray 160 C2
Bracon Ash Norfolk 68 E4
Bracorina H'land 145 D7
Bradbourne Derby 76 D2
Bradbury Durham 101 B8
Bradda I/Man 84 F1
Bradden Northants 52 E4
Braddock Cornw'l 5 C6
Bradeley Stoke 75 D5
Bradenham Bucks 39 E8
Bradenham Norfolk 68 D2
Bradenstoke Wilts 24 B5
Bradfield Essex 56 F5
Bradfield Norfolk 81 D8
Bradfield W Berks 26 B4
Bradfield Combust Suffolk 56 D2
Bradfield Green Ches 74 D3
Bradfield Heath Essex 43 B7
Bradfield St Clare Suffolk 56 D3
Bradfield St George Suffolk 56 C3
Bradford Cornw'l 5 B6
Bradford Derby 76 C2
Bradford Devon 9 D6
Bradford Northum 125 F7
Bradford W Yorks 94 F4
Bradford Abbas Dorset 12 C3
Bradford Cathedral W Yorks 94 F4
Bradford Industrial Museum W Yorks 94 F4
Bradford Leigh Wilts 24 C3
Bradford-on-Avon Wilts 24 C3
Bradford on Tone Som'set 11 B6
Bradford Peverell Dorset 12 E4
Brading I/Wight 15 F7
Bradley Derby 76 E2
Bradley Hants 26 E4
Bradley NE Lincs 91 D6
Bradley Staffs 62 C2
Bradley W Midlands 62 E3
Bradley W Yorks 88 B2
Bradley Green Worcs 50 C4
Bradley in the Moors Staffs 75 E7
Bradlow Heref'd 50 F2
Bradmore Notts 77 F5
Bradmore W Midlands 62 E2
Bradninch Devon 10 D5
Bradnop Staffs 75 D7
Bradpole Dorset 12 E2
Bradshaw Gtr Man 86 C5
Bradshaw W Yorks 87 C8
Bradstone Devon 9 F5
Bradwall Green Ches 74 C4
Bradway S Yorks 88 F4
Bradwell Derby 88 F2
Bradwell Essex 42 B4
Bradwell M/Keynes 53 F6
Bradwell Norfolk 69 D8
Bradwell Staffs 74 E5
Bradwell Grove Oxon 38 D2
Bradwell on Sea Essex 43 D6
Bradwell Waterside Essex 43 D5
Bradworthy Devon 8 C5
Bradworthy Cross Devon 8 C5
Brae Dumf/Gal 107 B5
Brae H'land 154 B4
Brae H'land 163 D8
Brae Shetl'd 174 G5
Brae of Achnahaird H'land 162 C4
Brae Roy Lodge H'land 147 E6
Braeantra H'land 157 B6
Braedownie Angus 142 B2
Braefield H'land 156 F5
Braegrum Perth/Kinr 134 B2
Braehead Dumf/Gal 105 D8
Braehead Orkney 176 F4
Braehead Orkney 176 B3
Braehead S Lanarks 121 F8
Braehead S Lanarks 122 D2
Braehead of Lunan Angus 143 D6
Braehoulland Shetl'd 174 F4
Braehungie H'land 169 F6
Braelangwell Lodge H'land 164 E2
Braemar Aberds 149 E7
Braemore H'land 169 F5
Braemore H'land 156 B2
Braes of Enzie Moray 159 D7
Braeside Invercl 129 C7
Braeswick Orkney 176 C5
Braewick Shetl'd 175 H5
Brafferton D'lington 101 B7
Brafferton N Yorks 95 B7
Brafield-on-the-Green Northants 53 D6
Bragar W Isles 172 D5
Bragbury End Herts 41 B5
Bragleenmore Arg/Bute 130 C5
Braichmelyn Gwyn 83 E6
Braid C/Edinb 122 C5
Braides Lancs 92 D4
Braidley N Yorks 101 F5
Braidwood S Lanarks 121 E8
Braigo Arg/Bute 126 C2
Brailsford Derby 76 E2
Brainshaugh Northum 117 D8
Braintree Essex 42 B3
Braiseworth Suffolk 56 B5
Braishfield Hants 14 B4
Braithwaite Cumb 98 B4
Braithwaite S Yorks 89 C7
Braithwaite W Yorks 94 E3
Braithwell S Yorks 89 E6
Bramber W Sussex 17 C5
Bramcote Notts 76 F5
Bramcote Warwick 63 F8
Bramdean Hants 15 B7
Bramerton Norfolk 69 D5
Bramfield Herts 41 C5
Bramfield Suffolk 57 B7
Bramford Suffolk 56 E5
Bramhall Gtr Man 87 F6
Bramham W Yorks 95 E7
Bramhope W Yorks 95 E5
Bramley Hants 26 D4
Bramley Surrey 27 E8
Bramley S Yorks 89 E5
Bramley W Yorks 94 F5
Bramling Kent 31 D6
Brampford Speke Devon 10 E4
Brampton Cambs 54 B3
Brampton Cumb 100 B1
Brampton Cumb 108 C5
Brampton Derby 76 B3
Brampton Heref'd 49 F6
Brampton Lincs 77 B8
Brampton Norfolk 81 E8
Brampton Suffolk 69 F7
Brampton S Yorks 88 D5
Brampton Abbotts Heref'd 36 B3
Brampton Ash Northants 64 F4
Brampton Bryan Heref'd 49 B5
Brampton en le Morthen S Yorks 89 F5
Bramshall Staffs 75 F7
Bramshaw Hants 14 C3

Bramshill Hants 26 C5
Bramshott Hants 27 F6
Bran End Essex 42 B2
Branault H'land 137 B6
Brancaster Norfolk 80 C3
Brancaster Staithe Norfolk 80 C3
Brancepeth Durham 110 F5
Branch End Northum 110 C3
Branchill Moray 158 D4
Brand Green Glos 36 B4
Branderburgh Moray 159 B6
Brandesburton ER Yorks 97 E7
Brandeston Suffolk 57 C6
Brandhill Shrops 49 B6
Brandis Corner Devon 9 D6
Brandiston Norfolk 81 E7
Brandon Durham 110 F5
Brandon Lincs 78 E2
Brandon Northum 117 C6
Brandon Suffolk 67 F7
Brandon Warwick 52 B2
Brandon Bank Norfolk 67 F6
Brandon Creek Norfolk 67 E6
Brandon Parva Norfolk 68 D3
Brandsby N Yorks 95 B8
Brandy Wharf Lincs 90 E4
Brane Cornw'l 2 D3
Branksome Poole 13 E8
Branksome Park Poole 13 E8
Bransby Lincs 77 B8
Branscombe Devon 11 F6
Bransford Worcs 50 D2
Bransgore Hants 14 E2
Branshill Clack 133 E7
Bransholme Kingston/Hull 97 F7
Branson's Cross Worcs 51 B5
Branston Leics 64 B5
Branston Lincs 78 C3
Branston Staffs 63 B6
Branston Booths Lincs 78 C3
Branstone I/Wight 15 F6
Bransty Cumb 98 C1
Brant Broughton Lincs 78 D2
Brantham Suffolk 56 F5
Branthwaite Cumb 98 B2
Branthwaite Cumb 108 F2
Brantingham ER Yorks 90 B3
Branton Northum 117 C6
Branton S Yorks 89 D7
Branxholm Park Scot Borders 115 C7
Branxholme Scot Borders 115 C7
Branxton Northum 124 F4
Brassey Green Ches 74 C2
Brassington Derby 76 D2
Brasted Kent 29 D5
Brasted Chart Kent 29 D5
Brathens Aberds 151 E5
Bratoft Lincs 79 C7
Brattleby Lincs 90 F3
Bratton Telford 61 C6
Bratton Wilts 24 D4
Bratton Clovelly Devon 9 E6
Bratton Fleming Devon 20 F5
Bratton Seymour Som'set 12 B4
Braughing Herts 41 B6
Braunston Northants 52 C3
Braunston-in-Rutland Rutl'd 64 D5
Braunstone Town Leics 64 D2
Braunton Devon 20 F3
Brawby N Yorks 96 B3
Brawl H'land 168 C3
Brawlbin H'land 169 D5
Bray Windsor 27 B7
Bray Shop Cornw'l 5 B8
Bray Wick Windsor 27 B6
Braybrooke Northants 64 F4
Braye Alderney 16
Brayford Devon 21 F5
Braystones Cumb 98 D2
Braythorn N Yorks 94 E5
Brayton N Yorks 95 F9
Brazacott Cornw'l 8 E4
Breach Kent 30 C2
Breachacha Castle Arg/Bute 136 C2
Breachwood Green Herts 40 B4
Breaclete W Isles 172 E4
Breaden Heath Shrops 73 F8
Breadsall Derby 76 F3
Breadstone Glos 36 D4
Breage Cornw'l 2 D5
Breakachy H'land 157 E5
Bream Glos 36 D3
Breamore Hants 14 C2
Brean Som'set 22 D4
Breanais W Isles 172 F2
Brearton N Yorks 95 C6
Breascleit W Isles 172 E5
Breaston Derby 76 F4
Brechfa Carms 46 F4
Brechin Angus 143 C5
Breck of Cruan Orkney 176 E2
Breckan Orkney 176 F1
Breckrey H'land 152 C6
Brecon = Aberhonddu Powys 34 B4
Brecon Beacons Mountain Centre Powys 34 B3
Bredbury Gtr Man 87 E7
Brede E Sussex 18 D5
Bredenbury Heref'd 49 D8
Bredfield Suffolk 57 D6
Bredgar Kent 30 C2
Bredhurst Kent 29 C8
Bredicot Worcs 50 D4
Bredon Worcs 50 F4
Bredon's Norton Worcs 50 F4
Bredwardine Heref'd 48 E5
Breedon on the Hill Leics 63 B8
Breibhig W Isles 171 L2
Breibhig W Isles 172 E7
Breich W Loth 122 C2
Breightmet Gtr Man 86 D5
Breighton ER Yorks 96 F3
Breinton Heref'd 49 F6
Breinton Common Heref'd 49 E6
Breiwick Shetl'd 175 J6
Bremhill Wilts 24 B4
Bremirehoull Shetl'd 175 L6
Brenchley Kent 29 E7
Brendon Devon 21 E6
Brenkley Tyne/Wear 110 B5
Brent Eleigh Suffolk 56 E3
Brent Knoll Som'set 22 D5
Brent Pelham Herts 54 F5
Brentford London 28 B2
Brentingby Leics 64 C4
Brentwood Essex 42 E1
Brenzett Kent 19 C7
Brereton Staffs 62 C4
Brereton Green Ches 74 C4
Brereton Heath Ches 74 C5
Bressingham Norfolk 68 F3
Bretby Derby 63 B6
Bretford Warwick 52 B2
Bretforton Worcs 51 E5
Bretherdale Head Cumb 99 D7
Bretherton Lancs 86 B2
Brettabister Shetl'd 175 H6
Brettenham Norfolk 68 F2
Brettenham Suffolk 56 D3
Bretton Derby 76 B2
Bretton Flints 73 C7
Brewer Street Surrey 28 D4
Brewlands Bridge Angus 142 C1
Brewood Staffs 62 D2
Briach Moray 158 D4
Briants Puddle Dorset 13 E6
Brick End Essex 42 B1
Brickendon Herts 41 D6
Bricket Wood Herts 40 D4
Bricklehampton Worcs 50 E4
Bride I/Man 84 B4
Bridekirk Cumb 107 F8
Bridell Pembs 45 E3
Bridestowe Devon 9 F7
Brideswell Aberds 160 E2
Bridford Devon 10 F3
Bridfordmills Devon 10 F3
Bridge Kent 31 D5
Bridge End Lincs 78 F4
Bridge Green Essex 55 F5
Bridge Hewick N Yorks 95 B6
Bridge of Alford Aberds 150 C4
Bridge of Allan Stirl 133 E6
Bridge of Avon Moray 159 F5
Bridge of Awe Arg/Bute 131 C6
Bridge of Balgie Perth/Kinr 140 E2
Bridge of Cally Perth/Kinr 141 D8
Bridge of Canny Aberds 151 E5
Bridge of Craigisla Angus 142 D2
Bridge of Dee Dumf/Gal 106 D4
Bridge of Don Aberd C 151 C8
Bridge of Dun Angus 143 D6
Bridge of Dye Aberds 151 F5
Bridge of Earn Perth/Kinr 134 C3
Bridge of Ericht Perth/Kinr 140 D2
Bridge of Feugh Aberds 151 E6
Bridge of Forss H'land 168 C5
Bridge of Gairn Aberds 150 E2
Bridge of Gaur Perth/Kinr 140 D2
Bridge of Muchalls Aberds 151 E7
Bridge of Oich H'land 147 D6
Bridge of Orchy Arg/Bute 131 B8
Bridge of Waith Orkney 176 E1
Bridge of Walls Shetl'd 175 H4
Bridge of Weir Renf 120 C3
Bridge Sollers Heref'd 49 E6
Bridge Street Suffolk 56 E2
Bridge Trafford Ches 73 B8
Bridge Yate S Glos 23 B8
Bridgefoot Angus 142 F3
Bridgefoot Cumb 98 B2
Bridgehampton Som'set 12 B3
Bridgehill Durham 110 D3
Bridgemary Hants 15 D6
Bridgemont Derby 87 F8
Bridgend Aberds 160 E2
Bridgend Aberds 150 C4
Bridgend Angus 143 C5
Bridgend Arg/Bute 128 A3
Bridgend Arg/Bute 126 C3
Bridgend Arg/Bute 118 C4
Bridgend Cumb 99 C5
Bridgend Fife 135 C5
Bridgend Moray 159 F7
Bridgend N Lanarks 121 B6
Bridgend Pembs 45 E3
Bridgend W Loth 122 B3
Bridgend = Pen-y-Bont Ar Ogwr Bridg 21 B8
Bridgend of Lintrathen Angus 142 D2
Bridgerule Devon 8 D4
Bridges Shrops 60 E3
Bridgeton Glasg C 121 C6
Bridgetown Cornw'l 8 F5
Bridgetown Som'set 21 F8
Bridgham Norfolk 68 F2
Bridgnorth Shrops 61 E7
Bridgnorth Cliff Railway Shrops 61 E7
Bridgtown Staffs 62 D3
Bridgwater Som'set 22 F5
Bridlington ER Yorks 97 C7
Bridport Dorset 12 E2
Bridstow Heref'd 36 B2
Brierfield Lancs 93 F8
Brierley Glos 36 C3
Brierley Heref'd 49 D6
Brierley S Yorks 88 C5
Brierley Hill W Midlands 62 F3
Briery Hill Bl Gwent 35 D5
Brig o'Turk Stirl 132 D4
Brigg N Lincs 90 D4
Briggswath N Yorks 103 D6
Brigham Cumb 107 F7
Brigham ER Yorks 97 D6
Brighouse W Yorks 88 B2
Brighstone I/Wight 14 F5
Brightgate Derby 76 D2
Brighthampton Oxon 38 D3
Brightling E Sussex 18 C3
Brightlingsea Essex 43 C6
Brighton Brighton/Hove 17 D7
Brighton Cornw'l 3 B8
Brighton Hill Hants 26 E4
Brighton Museum and Art Gallery Brighton/Hove 17 D7
Brighton Racecourse Brighton/Hove 17 D7
Brighton Sea Life Centre Brighton/Hove 17 D7
Brightons Falk 122 B2
Brightwalton W Berks 26 B2
Brightwell Suffolk 57 E6
Brightwell Baldwin Oxon 39 E6
Brightwell cum Sotwell Oxon 39 E5
Brignall Durham 101 C5
Brigsley NE Lincs 91 D6
Brigsteer Cumb 99 F6
Brigstock Northants 65 F6
Brill Bucks 39 C6
Brilley Heref'd 48 E4
Brimaston Pembs 44 C4
Brimfield Heref'd 49 C7
Brimington Derby 76 B4
Brimley Devon 7 B5
Brimpsfield Glos 37 C6
Brimpton W Berks 26 C3
Brims Orkney 176 H1
Brimscombe Glos 37 D5
Brimstage Mersey 85 F4
Brinacory H'land 145 D7
Brind ER Yorks 96 F3
Brindister Shetl'd 175 H4
Brindister Shetl'd 175 K6
Brindle Lancs 86 B4
Brindley Ford Staffs 75 D5
Brineton Staffs 62 C2
Bringhurst Leics 64 E5
Brington Cambs 53 B8
Brinian Orkney 176 D3
Briningham Norfolk 81 D6
Brinkhill Lincs 79 B6
Brinkley Cambs 55 D7
Brinklow Warwick 52 B2
Brinkworth Wilts 37 F7
Brinmore H'land 148 B2
Brinscall Lancs 86 B4
Brinsea N Som'set 23 C6
Brinsley Notts 76 E4
Brinsop Heref'd 49 E6
Brinsworth S Yorks 88 F5
Brinton Norfolk 81 D6
Brisco Cumb 108 D4
Brisley Norfolk 80 E5
Brislington Bristol 23 B8
Bristol Bristol 23 B7
Bristol City Museum and Art Gallery Bristol 23 B7
Bristol Zoo Bristol 23 B7
Briston Norfolk 81 D6
Britannia Lancs 87 B7
Britford Wilts 14 B2
Brithdir Gwyn 58 C4
British Legion Village Kent 29 D8
British Museum London 41 F5
Briton Ferry Neath P Talb 33 E8
Britwell Salome Oxon 39 E6
Brixham Torbay 7 D7
Brixton Devon 6 D3
Brixton London 28 B4
Brixton Deverill Wilts 24 F3
Brixworth Northants 52 B5
Brize Norton Oxon 38 D3
Broad Blunsdon Swindon 38 E1
Broad Campden Glos 51 F6
Broad Chalke Wilts 13 B8
Broad Green Beds 53 E7
Broad Green Essex 42 B4
Broad Green Worcs 50 D2
Broad Haven Pembs 44 D3
Broad Heath Worcs 49 C8
Broad Hill Cambs 55 B6
Broad Hinton Wilts 25 B6
Broad Laying Hants 26 C2
Broad Marston Worcs 51 E6
Broad Oak Carms 33 B6
Broad Oak Cumb 98 E3
Broad Oak Dorset 12 E2
Broad Oak Dorset 13 C5
Broad Oak E Sussex 18 D5
Broad Oak E Sussex 18 C3
Broad Oak Heref'd 36 B1
Broad Oak Mersey 86 E3
Broad Street Kent 30 D2
Broad Street Green Essex 42 D4
Broad Town Wilts 25 B5
Broadbottom Gtr Man 87 E7
Broadbridge W Sussex 16 D2
Broadbridge Heath W Sussex 28 F2
Broadclyst Devon 10 E4
Broadfield Gtr Man 87 C6
Broadfield Lancs 86 B3
Broadfield Pembs 32 D2
Broadfield W Sussex 28 F3
Broadford H'land 155 H2
Broadford Bridge W Sussex 16 B4
Broadhaugh Scot Borders 115 D7
Broadhaven H'land 169 D8
Broadheath Gtr Man 87 F5
Broadhembury Devon 11 D6
Broadhempston Devon 7 C6
Broadholme Derby 76 E3
Broadholme Lincs 77 B8
Broadland Row E Sussex 18 D5
Broadlay Carms 32 D4
Broadley Lancs 87 C6
Broadley Moray 159 C7
Broadley Common Essex 41 D7
Broadmayne Dorset 12 F5
Broadmeadows Scot Borders 123 F7
Broadmere Hants 26 E4
Broadmoor Pembs 32 D1
Broadoak Kent 31 C5
Broadrashes Moray 159 D8
Broadsea Aberds 161 B6
Broadstairs Kent 31 C7
Broadstone Poole 13 E8
Broadstone Shrops 60 F5
Broadtown Lane Wilts 25 B5
Broadwater Gardens, Hadlow Kent 29 E7
Broadwas Worcs 50 D2
Broadwater Herts 41 B5
Broadwater W Sussex 17 D5
Broadway Carms 32 D3
Broadway Pembs 44 D3
Broadway Som'set 11 C8
Broadway Suffolk 57 B7
Broadway Worcs 51 F5
Broadwell Glos 36 C2
Broadwell Glos 38 B2
Broadwell Oxon 38 D2
Broadwell Warwick 52 C2
Broadwell House Northum 110 D2
Broadwey Dorset 12 F4
Broadwindsor Dorset 12 D2
Broadwood Kelly Devon 9 D8
Broadwoodwidger Devon 9 F6
Brobury Heref'd 48 E5
Brochel H'land 152 E6
Brochloch Dumf/Gal 113 E5
Brochroy Arg/Bute 131 B6
Brockamin Worcs 50 D2
Brockbridge Hants 15 C7
Brockdam Northum 117 B7
Brockdish Norfolk 57 B6
Brockenhurst Hants 14 D4
Brocketsbrae S Lanarks 121 F8
Brockford Street Suffolk 56 C5
Brockhall Northants 52 C4
Brockham Surrey 28 E2
Brockhampton Glos 37 B7
Brockhampton Heref'd 49 F7
Brockhole -National Park Visitor Centre, Windermere Cumb 99 D5
Brockholes W Yorks 88 C2
Brockhurst Derby 76 C3
Brockhurst Hants 15 D7
Brocklebank Cumb 108 E3
Brocklesby Lincs 90 C5
Brockley N Som'set 23 C6
Brockley Green Suffolk 56 D2
Brockleymoor Cumb 108 F4
Brockton Shrops 60 F3
Brockton Shrops 60 D3
Brockton Shrops 61 E5
Brockton Shrops 61 D7
Brockton Telford 61 C7
Brockweir Glos 36 D2
Brockwood Hants 15 B7
Brockworth Glos 37 C5
Brocton Staffs 62 C3
Brodick N Ayrs 119 C7
Brodick Castle N Ayrs 119 C7
Brodsworth S Yorks 89 D6
Brogaig H'land 152 C5
Brogborough Beds 53 F7
Broken Cross Ches 74 B3
Broken Cross Ches 75 B5
Brokenborough Wilts 37 F6
Bromborough Mersey 85 F4
Brome Suffolk 56 B5
Brome Street Suffolk 57 B5
Bromeswell Suffolk 57 D7
Bromfield Cumb 107 E8
Bromfield Shrops 49 B6
Bromham Beds 53 D8
Bromham Wilts 24 C4
Bromley London 28 C5
Bromley W Midlands 62 F3
Bromley Common London 28 C5
Bromley Green Kent 19 B6
Brompton Medway 29 C8
Brompton N Yorks 102 E1
Brompton N Yorks 103 F7
Brompton-on-Swale N Yorks 101 E7
Brompton Ralph Som'set 22 F2
Brompton Regis Som'set 21 F8
Bromsash Heref'd 36 B3
Bromsberrow Hth Glos 50 F2
Bromsgrove Worcs 50 B4
Bromyard Heref'd 49 D8
Bromyard Downs Heref'd 49 D8
Bronaber Gwyn 71 D8
Brongest Ceredig'n 46 E2
Bronington Wrex 73 F8
Bronllys Powys 48 F3
Bronnant Ceredig'n 46 C5
Bronte Parsonage Museum, Keighley W Yorks 94 F3
Bronwydd Arms Carms 33 B5
Bronydd Powys 48 E4
Bronygarth Shrops 73 F6
Brook Carms 32 D3
Brook Hants 14 C3
Brook Hants 14 B4
Brook I/Wight 14 F4
Brook Kent 30 E4
Brook Surrey 27 F7
Brook Surrey 27 E8
Brook End Beds 53 C8
Brook Hill Hants 14 C3
Brook Street Kent 29 E6
Brook Street Kent 19 B6
Brook Street W Sussex 17 B7
Brooke Norfolk 69 E5
Brooke Rutl'd 64 D5
Brookenby Lincs 91 E6
Brookend Glos 36 E2
Brookfield Renf 120 C4
Brookhouse Lancs 92 C5
Brookhouse Green Ches 74 C5
Brookland Kent 19 C6
Brooklands Dumf/Gal 106 B5
Brooklands Gtr Man 87 E5
Brooklands Shrops 74 E2
Brookmans Park Herts 41 D5
Brooks Powys 59 E8
Brooks Green W Sussex 16 B5
Brookthorpe Glos 37 C5
Brookville Norfolk 67 E7
Brookwood Surrey 27 D7
Broom Beds 54 E2
Broom S Yorks 88 E5
Broom Warwick 51 D5
Broom Worcs 50 B4
Broom Green Norfolk 81 E5
Broom Hill Dorset 13 D8
Broome Norfolk 69 E6
Broome Shrops 60 F4
Broome Park Northum 117 C7
Broomedge Warrington 86 F5
Broomer's Corner W Sussex 16 B5
Broomfield Aberds 161 E6
Broomfield Essex 42 C3
Broomfield Kent 30 D2
Broomfield Kent 31 C5
Broomfield Som'set 22 F4
Broomfleet ER Yorks 90 B2
Broomhall Ches 74 E3
Broomhall Windsor 27 C7
Broomhaugh Northum 110 C3
Broomhill Norfolk 67 D6
Broomhill Northum 117 D8
Broomhill S Yorks 88 D5
Broomholm Norfolk 81 D9
Broompark Durham 110 E5
Broom's Green Heref'd 50 F2
Broomy Lodge Hants 14 C3
Brora H'land 165 D6
Broseley Shrops 61 D6
Brotherhouse Bar Lincs 66 C2
Brotherstone Scot Borders 124 F2
Brotherton N Yorks 89 B5
Brotton Redcar/Clevel'd 102 C4
Broubster H'land 168 C5
Brough Cumb 100 C2
Brough Derby 88 F2
Brough ER Yorks 90 B3
Brough H'land 169 B7
Brough Notts 77 D8
Brough Orkney 176 E2
Brough Shetl'd 174 F6
Brough Shetl'd 174 G7
Brough Shetl'd 175 H6
Brough Shetl'd 175 J7
Brough Shetl'd 175 H6
Brough Lodge Shetl'd 174 D7
Brough Sowerby Cumb 100 C2
Broughall Shrops 74 E2
Broughton Scot Borders 122 F4
Broughton Cambs 54 B3
Broughton Flints 73 C7
Broughton Hants 25 F8
Broughton Lancs 92 F5
Broughton M/Keynes 53 E6
Broughton N Lincs 90 D3
Broughton Northants 53 B6
Broughton N Yorks 94 D2
Broughton N Yorks 96 B3
Broughton Orkney 176 B3
Broughton Oxon 52 F2
Broughton V/Glam 21 B8
Broughton Astley Leics 64 E2
Broughton Beck Cumb 98 F4
Broughton Common Wilts 24 C3
Broughton Gifford Wilts 24 C3
Broughton Hackett Worcs 50 D4
Broughton in Furness Cumb 98 F4
Broughton Mills Cumb 98 E4
Broughton Moor Cumb 107 F7
Broughton Park Gtr Man 87 D6
Broughton Poggs Oxon 38 D2
Broughtown Orkney 176 B5
Broughty Ferry Dundee C 142 F4
Browhouses Dumf/Gal 108 C2
Browland Shetl'd 175 H4
Brown Candover Hants 26 F3
Brown Edge Lancs 85 C4
Brown Edge Staffs 75 D6
Brown Heath Ches 73 C8
Brownhill Aberds 161 D5
Brownhill Aberds 160 B3
Brownhill Blackb'n 93 F6
Brownhill Shrops 60 B4
Brownhills Fife 135 C7
Brownhills W Midlands 62 D4
Brownlow Ches 74 C5
Brownlow Heath Ches 74 C5
Brownmuir Aberds 143 B7
Brown's End Glos 50 F2
Brownshill Glos 37 D5
Brownston Devon 6 D4
Brownyside Northum 117 B7
Broxa N Yorks 103 E7
Broxbourne Herts 41 D6
Broxburn E Loth 124 B2
Broxburn W Loth 122 B3
Broxholme Lincs 78 B2
Broxted Essex 42 B1
Broxton Ches 73 D8
Broxwood Heref'd 49 D5
Broyle Side E Sussex 17 C8
Brù W Isles 172 D6
Bruairnis W Isles 171 K3
Bruan H'land 169 F8
Bruar Lodge Perth/Kinr 141 B5
Brucehill W Dunb 120 B3
Bruera Ches 73 C8
Bruern Abbey Oxon 38 B2
Bruichladdich Arg/Bute 126 C2
Bruisyard Suffolk 57 C7
Brumby N Lincs 90 D2
Brund Staffs 75 C8
Brundall Norfolk 69 D6
Brundish Suffolk 57 C6
Brundish Street Suffolk 57 B6
Brunery H'land 145 F7
Brunshaw Lancs 93 F8
Brunswick Village Tyne/Wear 110 B5
Bruntcliffe W Yorks 88 B3
Bruntingthorpe Leics 64 E3
Brunton Fife 134 B5
Brunton Northum 117 B8
Brunton Wilts 25 D7
Brushford Devon 9 D8
Brushford Som'set 10 B4
Bruton Som'set 23 F8
Bryanston Dorset 13 D6
Brydekirk Dumf/Gal 107 B8
Bryher I/Scilly 2 C2
Brymbo Wrex 73 D6
Brympton Som'set 12 C3
Bryn Carms 33 D6
Bryn Gtr Man 86 D3
Bryn Neath P Talb 34 E2
Bryn Shrops 60 F2
Bryn-coch Neath P Talb 33 E8
Bryn Du Angl 82 D3
Bryn Gates Gtr Man 86 D3
Bryn-glas Conwy 83 E8
Bryn Golau Rh Cyn Taff 34 F3
Bryn-Iwan Carms 46 F2
Bryn-mawr Gwyn 70 D3
Bryn-nantllech Conwy 72 C3
Bryn-penarth Powys 59 D8
Bryn Rhyd-yr-Arian Conwy 72 C3
Bryn Saith Marchog Denbs 72 D4
Bryn Sion Gwyn 59 C5
Bryn-y-gwenin Monmouths 35 C7
Bryn-y-maen Conwy 83 D8
Bryn-yr-eryr Gwyn 70 C4
Brynamman Carms 33 C8
Brynberian Pembs 45 F3
Brynbryddan Neath P Talb 34 E1
Brynbuga = Usk Monmouths 35 D7
Bryncae Rh Cyn Taff 34 F3
Bryncethin Bridg 34 F3
Bryncir Gwyn 71 C5
Bryncroes Gwyn 70 D3
Bryncrug Gwyn 58 D3
Bryneglwys Denbs 72 E5
Brynford Flints 73 B5
Bryngwran Angl 82 D3
Bryngwyn Ceredig'n 45 E4
Bryngwyn Monmouths 35 D7
Bryngwyn Powys 48 E3
Brynhenllan Pembs 45 F2
Brynhoffnant Ceredig'n 46 D2
Brynithel Bl Gwent 35 D6
Brynmenyn Bridg 34 F3
Brynmill Swan 33 E7
Brynna Rh Cyn Taff 34 F3
Brynrefail Angl 82 C4
Brynrefail Gwyn 83 E5
Brynsadler Rh Cyn Taff 34 F4
Brynsiencyn Angl 82 E4
Brynteg Angl 82 C4
Brynteg Ceredig'n 46 E3
Buaile nam Bodach W Isles 171 K3
Bualintur H'land 153 G5
Buarthmeini Gwyn 72 F2
Bubbenhall Warwick 51 B8
Bubwith ER Yorks 96 F3
Buccleuch Scot Borders 115 C6
Buchanhaven Aberds 161 D8
Buchanty Perth/Kinr 133 B8
Buchlyvie Stirl 132 E4
Buckabank Cumb 108 E3
Buckden Cambs 54 C2
Buckden N Yorks 94 B2
Buckenham Norfolk 69 D6
Buckerell Devon 11 D6
Buckfast Devon 6 C5
Buckfast Abbey, Buckfastleigh Devon 6 C5
Buckfastleigh Devon 6 C5
Buckhaven Fife 135 E5
Buckholm Scot Borders 123 F7
Buckholt Monmouths 36 C2
Buckhorn Weston Dorset 13 B5
Buckhurst Hill Essex 41 E7
Buckie Moray 159 C8
Buckies H'land 169 C6
Buckingham Bucks 52 F4
Buckingham Palace London 28 B3
Buckland Bucks 40 C1
Buckland Devon 6 E4
Buckland Glos 51 F5
Buckland Hants 14 E4
Buckland Herts 54 F4
Buckland Kent 31 E7
Buckland Oxon 38 E3
Buckland Surrey 28 D3
Buckland Abbey Devon 6 C2
Buckland Brewer Devon 9 B6
Buckland Common Bucks 40 D2
Buckland Dinham Som'set 24 D2
Buckland Filleigh Devon 9 D6
Buckland in the Moor Devon 6 B5
Buckland Monachorum Devon 6 C2
Buckland Newton Dorset 12 D4
Buckland St Mary Som'set 11 C7
Bucklebury W Berks 26 B3
Bucklegate Lincs 79 F6
Bucklerheads Angus 142 F4
Bucklers Hard Hants 14 E5
Bucklesham Suffolk 57 E6
Buckley = Bwcle Flints 73 C6
Bucklow Hill Ches 86 F5
Buckminster Leics 65 B5
Bucknall Lincs 78 C4
Bucknall Stoke 75 E6
Bucknell Oxon 39 B5
Bucknell Shrops 49 B5
Buckpool Moray 159 C8
Buck's Cross Devon 8 B5
Bucks Green W Sussex 27 F8
Bucks Horn Oak Hants 27 E6
Buck's Mills Devon 8 B5
Bucksburn Aberd C 151 D7
Buckskin Hants 26 D4
Buckton ER Yorks 97 B7
Buckton Heref'd 49 B5
Buckton Northum 125 F6
Buckworth Cambs 54 B2
Budbrooke Warwick 51 C7
Budby Notts 77 C6
Budd's Titson Cornw'l 8 D4
Bude Cornw'l 8 D4
Budlake Devon 10 E4
Budle Northum 125 F7
Budleigh Salterton Devon 11 F5
Budock Water Cornw'l 3 C6
Buerton Ches 74 E3
Buffler's Holt Bucks 52 F4
Bugbrooke Northants 52 D4
Buglawton Ches 75 C5
Bugle Cornw'l 4 D5
Bugley Wilts 24 E3
Bugthorpe ER Yorks 96 D3
Buildwas Shrops 61 D6
Builth Road Powys 48 D2
Builth Wells = Llanfair-Ym-Muallt Powys 48 D2
Buirgh W Isles 173 J3
Bulby Lincs 65 B7
Bulcote Notts 77 E6
Buldoo H'land 168 C4
Bulford Wilts 25 E6
Bulford Camp Wilts 25 E6
Bulkeley Ches 74 D2
Bulkington Warwick 63 F7
Bulkington Wilts 24 D4
Bulkworthy Devon 9 C5
Bull Hill Hants 14 E4
Bullamoor N Yorks 102 E1
Bullbridge Derby 76 D3
Bullbrook Brackn'l 27 C6
Bulley Glos 36 C4
Bullgill Cumb 107 F7
Bullington Hants 26 E2
Bullington Lincs 78 B3
Bull's Green Herts 41 C5
Bullwood Arg/Bute 129 C6
Bulmer Essex 56 E2
Bulmer N Yorks 96 C2
Bulmer Tye Essex 56 F2
Bulphan Thurr'k 42 F2
Bulverhythe E Sussex 18 E4
Bulwark Aberds 161 D6
Bulwell Nott'ham 76 E5
Bulwick Northants 65 E6
Bumble's Green Essex 41 D7
Bun Abhainn Eadarra W Isles 173 H4
Bun a'Mhuillin W Isles 171 J3
Bun Loyne H'land 146 D5
Bunacaimb H'land 145 E6
Bunarkaig H'land 146 F4
Bunbury Ches 74 D2
Bunbury Heath Ches 74 D2
Bunchrew H'land 157 E7
Bundalloch H'land 155 H4
Buness Shetl'd 174 C8
Bunessan Arg/Bute 136 F4
Bungay Suffolk 69 F6
Bunker's Hill Lincs 78 B2
Bunker's Hill Lincs 79 D5
Bunkers Hill Oxon 38 C4
Bunloit H'land 147 B8
Bunnahabhain Arg/Bute 126 B4
Bunny Notts 64 B2
Buntait H'land 156 F4
Buntingford Herts 41 B6
Bunwell Norfolk 68 E4
Burbage Derby 75 B7
Burbage Leics 63 E8
Burbage Wilts 25 C7
Burchett's Green Windsor 39 F8
Burcombe Wilts 25 F5
Burcot Oxon 39 E5
Burcott Bucks 40 B1
Burdon Tyne/Wear 111 D6
Bures Suffolk 56 F3
Bures Green Suffolk 56 F3
Burford Ches 74 D3
Burford Oxon 38 C2
Burford Shrops 49 C7
Burg Arg/Bute 136 D4
Burgar Orkney 176 D2
Burgate Hants 14 C2
Burgate Suffolk 56 B4
Burgess Hill W Sussex 17 C7
Burgh Suffolk 57 D6
Burgh-by-Sands Cumb 108 D3
Burgh Castle Norfolk 69 D7
Burgh Heath Surrey 28 D3
Burgh le Marsh Lincs 79 C8
Burgh Muir Aberds 151 B6
Burgh next Aylsham Norfolk 81 E8
Burgh on Bain Lincs 91 F6
Burgh St Margaret Norfolk 69 C7
Burgh St Peter Norfolk 69 E8
Burghclere Hants 26 C2
Burghead Moray 158 C5
Burghfield W Berks 26 C4
Burghfield Common W Berks 26 C4
Burghfield Hill W Berks 26 C4
Burghill Heref'd 49 E6
Burghwallis S Yorks 89 C6
Burham Kent 29 C8
Buriton Hants 15 B8
Burland Ches 74 D3
Burlawn Cornw'l 4 B4
Burleigh Brackn'l 27 C6
Burlescombe Devon 11 C5
Burleston Dorset 13 E5
Burley Hants 14 D3
Burley Rutl'd 65 C5
Burley W Yorks 95 F5
Burley Gate Heref'd 49 E7
Burley in Wharfedale W Yorks 94 E4
Burley Lodge Hants 14 D3
Burley Street Hants 14 D3
Burleydam Ches 74 E3
Burlingjobb Powys 48 D4
Burlow E Sussex 18 D2
Burlton Shrops 60 B4
Burmarsh Kent 19 B7
Burmington Warwick 51 F7
Burn N Yorks 89 B6
Burn of Cambus Stirl 133 D6
Burnaston Derby 76 F2
Burnbank S Lanarks 121 D7
Burnby ER Yorks 96 E4
Burncross S Yorks 88 E4
Burneside Cumb 99 E7
Burness Orkney 176 B5
Burneston N Yorks 101 F8
Burnett Bath/NE Som'set 23 C8
Burnfoot Scot Borders 115 C7
Burnfoot Scot Borders 115 C8
Burnfoot E Ayrs 112 D4
Burnfoot Perth/Kinr 133 D8
Burnham Bucks 40 F2
Burnham N Lincs 90 C4
Burnham Deepdale Norfolk 80 C4
Burnham Green Herts 41 C5
Burnham Market Norfolk 80 C4
Burnham Norton Norfolk 80 C4
Burnham-on-Crouch Essex 43 E5
Burnham-on-Sea Som'set 22 E5
Burnham Overy Staithe Norfolk 80 C4
Burnham Overy Town Norfolk 80 C4
Burnham Thorpe Norfolk 80 C4
Burnhead Dumf/Gal 113 E8
Burnhead S Ayrs 112 D2
Burnhervie Aberds 151 C6
Burnhill Green Staffs 61 D7
Burnhope Durham 110 E4
Burnhouse N Ayrs 120 D3
Burniston N Yorks 103 E8
Burnlee W Yorks 88 D2
Burnley Lancs 93 F8
Burnley Lane Lancs 93 F8
Burnmouth Scot Borders 125 C5
Burnopfield Durham 110 D4
Burnsall N Yorks 94 C3
Burnside Angus 143 D5
Burnside E Ayrs 113 C5
Burnside Fife 134 D3
Burnside Shetl'd 174 F4
Burnside S Lanarks 121 C6
Burnside W Loth 122 B3
Burnside of Duntrune Angus 142 F4
Burnswark Dumf/Gal 107 B8
Burnt Heath Derby 76 B2
Burnt Houses Durham 101 B6
Burnt Yates N Yorks 95 C5
Burntcommon Surrey 27 D8
Burnthouse Cornw'l 3 C6
Burntisland Fife 134 F4
Burnton E Ayrs 112 D4
Burntwood Staffs 62 D4
Burnwynd C/Edinb 122 C4
Burpham Surrey 27 D8
Burpham W Sussex 16 D4
Burradon Northum 117 D5
Burradon Tyne/Wear 111 B5
Burrafirth Shetl'd 174 B8
Burraland Shetl'd 174 F5
Burraland Shetl'd 175 J4
Burras Cornw'l 3 C5
Burravoe Shetl'd 174 G5
Burravoe Shetl'd 174 F7
Burray Village Orkney 176 G3
Burrells Cumb 100 C1
Burrelton Perth/Kinr 142 F2
Burridge Devon 20 F4
Burridge Hants 15 C6
Burrill N Yorks 101 F7
Burringham N Lincs 90 D2
Burrington Devon 9 C8
Burrington Heref'd 49 B6
Burrington N Som'set 23 D6
Burrough Green Cambs 55 D7
Burrough on the Hill Leics 64 C4
Burrow-bridge Som'set 11 B8
Burrowhill Surrey 27 C7
Burry Swan 33 E5
Burry Green Swan 33 E5
Burry Port = Porth Tywyn Carms 33 D5
Burscough Lancs 86 C2
Burscough Bridge Lancs 86 C2
Bursea ER Yorks 96 F4
Burshill ER Yorks 97 E6
Bursledon Hants 15 D5
Burslem Stoke 75 E5
Burstall Suffolk 56 E4
Burstock Dorset 12 D2
Burston Norfolk 68 F4
Burston Staffs 75 F6
Burstow Surrey 28 E4
Burstwick ER Yorks 91 B6
Burtersett N Yorks 100 F3
Burtle Som'set 23 E5
Burton Ches 73 B7
Burton Ches 74 C2
Burton Dorset 14 E2
Burton Lincs 78 B2
Burton Northum 125 F7
Burton Pembs 44 E4
Burton Som'set 22 E3
Burton Wilts 24 B3
Burton Agnes ER Yorks 97 C7
Burton Bradstock Dorset 12 F2
Burton Dassett Warwick 51 D8
Burton Fleming ER Yorks 97 B6
Burton Green W Midlands 51 B7
Burton Green Wrex 73 D7
Burton Hastings Warwick 63 E8
Burton-in-Kendal Cumb 92 B5
Burton in Lonsdale N Yorks 93 B6
Burton Joyce Notts 77 E6
Burton Latimer Northants 53 B7
Burton Lazars Leics 64 C4
Burton-le-Coggles Lincs 65 B6
Burton Leonard N Yorks 95 C6
Burton on the Wolds Leics 64 B2
Burton Overy Leics 64 E3
Burton Pedwardine Lincs 78 E4
Burton Pidsea ER Yorks 97 F8
Burton Salmon N Yorks 89 B5
Burton Stather N Lincs 90 C2
Burton upon Stather N Lincs 90 C2
Burton upon Trent Staffs 63 B6
Burtonwood Warrington 86 E3
Burwardsley Ches 74 D2
Burwarton Shrops 61 F6
Burwash E Sussex 18 C3
Burwash Common E Sussex 18 C3
Burwash Weald E Sussex 18 C3
Burwell Cambs 55 C6
Burwell Lincs 79 B6
Burwen Angl 82 B4
Burwick Orkney 176 H3
Bury Cambs 66 F2
Bury Gtr Man 87 C6
Bury Som'set 10 B4
Bury W Sussex 16 C4
Bury Green Herts 41 B7
Bury St Edmunds Suffolk 56 C2
Burythorpe N Yorks 96 C3
Busby E Renf 121 D5
Buscot Oxon 38 E2
Bush Bank Heref'd 49 D6
Bush Crathie Aberds 149 E8
Bush Green Norfolk 68 F5
Bushbury W Midlands 62 D3
Bushby Leics 64 D3
Bushey Herts 40 E4
Bushey Heath Herts 40 E4
Bushley Worcs 50 F3
Bushton Wilts 25 B5
Buslingthorpe Lincs 90 F4
Busta Shetl'd 174 G5
Butcher's Cross E Sussex 18 C2
Butcher's Pasture Essex 42 B2
Butcombe N Som'set 23 C7
Butetown Card 22 B3
Butleigh Som'set 23 F7
Butleigh Wootton Som'set 23 F7
Butler's Cross Bucks 39 D8
Butler's End Warwick 63 F6
Butlers Marston Warwick 51 E8
Butley Suffolk 57 D7
Butley High Corner Suffolk 57 E7
Butt Green Ches 74 D3
Butterburn Cumb 109 B6
Buttercrambe N Yorks 96 D3
Butterknowle Durham 101 B6
Butterleigh Devon 10 D4
Buttermere Cumb 98 C3
Buttermere Wilts 25 C8
Buttershaw W Yorks 88 B2
Butterstone Perth/Kinr 141 E7
Butterton Staffs 75 D7
Butterwick Durham 102 B1
Butterwick Lincs 79 E6
Butterwick N Yorks 96 B3
Butterwick N Yorks 97 B5
Buttington Powys 60 D2
Buttonoak Shrops 50 B2
Butt's Green Hants 14 B4
Buttsash Hants 14 D5
Buxhall Suffolk 56 D4
Buxhall Fen Street Suffolk 56 D4
Buxley Scot Borders 124 D4
Buxted E Sussex 17 B8
Buxton Derby 75 B7
Buxton Norfolk 81 E8
Buxworth Derby 87 F8
Bwcle = Buckley Flints 73 C6
Bwlch Powys 35 B5
Bwlch-Llan Ceredig'n 46 D4
Bwlch-y-cibau Powys 59 C8
Bwlch-y-fadfa Ceredig'n 46 E3
Bwlch-y-ffridd Powys 59 E7
Bwlch-y-sarnau Powys 48 B2
Bwlchgwyn Wrex 73 D6
Bwlchnewydd Carms 32 B4
Bwlchtocyn Gwyn 70 E4
Bwlchyddar Powys 59 B8
Bwlchygroes Pembs 45 F4
Byermoor Tyne/Wear 110 D4
Byers Green Durham 110 F5
Byfield Northants 52 D3
Byfleet Surrey 27 C8
Byford Heref'd 49 E5
Bygrave Herts 54 F3
Byker Tyne/Wear 111 C5
Bylchau Conwy 72 C3
Byley Ches 74 C4
Bynea Carms 33 E6
Byrness Northum 116 D3
Bythorn Cambs 53 B8
Byton Heref'd 49 C5
Byworth W Sussex 16 B3

C

Cabharstadh W Isles 172 F6
Cablea Perth/Kinr 141 F6
Cabourne Lincs 90 D5
Cabrach Arg/Bute 127 F2
Cabrach Moray 150 B2
Cabrich H'land 157 E6
Cabus Lancs 92 E4
Cackle Street E Sussex 17 B8
Cadbury Devon 10 D4
Cadbury Barton Devon 9 C8
Cadbury World, Bournville W Midlands 62 F4
Cadder E Dunb 121 B6
Caddington Beds 40 C3
Caddonfoot Scot Borders 123 F7
Cade Street E Sussex 18 C3
Cadeby Leics 63 D8
Cadeby S Yorks 89 D6
Cadeleigh Devon 10 D4
Cadgwith Cornw'l 3 E6
Cadham Fife 134 D4
Cadishead Gtr Man 86 E5
Cadle Swan 33 E7
Cadley Lancs 92 F5
Cadley Wilts 25 D7
Cadley Wilts 25 C7
Cadmore End Bucks 39 E7
Cadnam Hants 14 C3
Cadney N Lincs 90 D4
Cadole Flints 73 C6
Cadoxton V/Glam 22 C3
Cadoxton-Juxta-Neath Neath P Talb 34 E1
Cadshaw Blackb'n 86 C5
Cadzow S Lanarks 121 D7
Caeathro Gwyn 82 E4
Caehopkin Powys 34 C2
Caenby Lincs 90 F4
Caenby Corner Lincs 90 F3
Caer-bryn Carms 33 C6
Caer Llan Monmouths 36 D1
Caerau Bridg 34 E2
Caerau Card 22 B3
Caerdeon Gwyn 58 C3
Caerdydd = Cardiff Card 22 B3
Caerfarchell Pembs 44 C2
Caerffili = Caerphilly Caerph 35 F5
Caerfyrddin = Carmarthen Carms 33 B5
Caergeiliog Angl 82 D3
Caergwrle Flints 73 D7
Caergybi = Holyhead Angl 82 C2
Caerleon = Caerllion Newp 35 E7
Caerllion = Caerleon Newp 35 E7
Caernarfon Gwyn 82 E4
Caernarfon Castle Gwyn 82 E4
Caerphilly = Caerffili Caerph 35 F5
Caersws Powys 59 E7
Caerwedros Ceredig'n 46 D2
Caerwent Monmouths 36 E1
Caerwych Gwyn 71 D7
Caerwys Flints 72 B5
Caethle Gwyn 58 E3
Caim Angl 83 C6
Caio Carms 47 F5
Cairinis W Isles 170 D4
Cairisiadar W Isles 172 E3
Cairminis W Isles 173 K3
Cairnbaan Arg/Bute 128 A3
Cairnbanno Ho. Aberds 160 D5
Cairnborrow Aberds 159 E8
Cairnbrogie Aberds 151 B7
Cairnbulg Castle Aberds 161 B7
Cairncross Angus 142 B4
Cairncross Scot Borders 124 C4
Cairndow Arg/Bute 131 D7
Cairness Aberds 161 B7
Cairneyhill Fife 134 F2
Cairnfield Ho. Moray 159 C8
Cairngaan Dumf/Gal 104 F5
Cairngarroch Dumf/Gal 104 E4
Cairnhill Aberds 160 E3
Cairnie Aberds 159 E8
Cairnie Aberds 151 D7
Cairnorrie Aberds 161 D5
Cairnpark Aberds 151 C7
Cairnryan Dumf/Gal 104 C4
Cairnton Orkney 176 F2
Caister-on-Sea Norfolk 69 C8
Caistor Lincs 90 D5
Caistor St Edmund Norfolk 68 D5
Caistron Northum 117 D5
Caitha Bowland Scot Borders 123 E7
Caithness Glass, Perth Perth/Kinr 134 B2
Calais Street Suffolk 56 F3
Calanais W Isles 172 E5
Calbost W Isles 172 G7
Calbourne I/Wight 14 F5
Calceby Lincs 79 B6
Calcot Row W Berks 26 B4
Calcott Kent 31 C5
Caldback Shetl'd 174 C8
Caldbeck Cumb 108 F3
Caldbergh N Yorks 101 F5
Caldecote Cambs 54 D4
Caldecote Cambs 65 F8
Caldecote Herts 54 F3
Caldecote Northants 52 D4
Caldecott Northants 53 C7
Caldecott Oxon 38 E4
Caldecott Rutl'd 65 E5
Calder Bridge Cumb 98 D2
Calder Hall Cumb 98 D2
Calder Mains H'land 169 D5
Calder Vale Lancs 92 E5
Calderbank N Lanarks 121 C7
Calderbrook Gtr Man 87 C7
Caldercruix N Lanarks 121 C8

Caldermill S Lanarks 121 E6
Calderwood S Lanarks 121 E6
Caldhame Angus 142 E4
Caldicot Monmouths 36 F1
Caldwell Derby 63 C6
Caldwell N Yorks 101 C6
Caldy Mersey 85 F3
Caledrhydiau Ceredig'n 46 D3
Calfsound Orkney 176 C4
Calgary Arg/Bute 136 C4
Califer Moray 158 D4
California Falk 122 B2
California Norfolk 69 C8
Calke Derby 63 B7
Callakille H'land 155 E2
Callaly Northum 117 D6
Callander Stirl 132 D5
Callaughton Shrops 61 E6
Callestick Cornw'l 4 D2
Callestock Cider Farm, Truro Cornw'l 4 D2
Calligarry H'land 145 C6
Callington Cornw'l 5 C8
Callow Heref'd 49 F6
Callow End Worcs 50 E3
Callow Hill Wilts 37 F7
Callow Hill Worcs 50 B2
Callows Grave Worcs 49 C7
Calmore Hants 14 C4
Calmsden Glos 37 D7
Calne Wilts 24 B5
Calow Derby 76 B4
Calshot Hants 15 D5
Calstock Cornw'l 6 C2
Calstone Wellington Wilts 24 C5
Calthorpe Norfolk 81 D7
Calthwaite Cumb 108 E4
Calton N Yorks 94 D2
Calton Staffs 75 D8
Calveley Ches 74 D2
Calver Derby 76 B2
Calver Hill Heref'd 49 E5
Calverhall Shrops 74 F3
Calverleigh Devon 10 C4
Calverley W Yorks 94 F5
Calvert Bucks 39 B6
Calverton M/Keynes 53 F5
Calverton Notts 77 E6
Calvine Perth/Kinr 140 C4
Calvo Cumb 107 D8
Cam Glos 36 E4
Camas-luinie H'land 146 B2
Camasnacroise H'land 138 D2
Camastianavaig H'land 153 F6
Camasunary H'land 153 H6
Camault Muir H'land 157 E6
Camb Shetl'd 174 D7
Camber E Sussex 19 D6
Camberley Surrey 27 C6
Camberwell London 28 B4
Camblesforth N Yorks 89 B7
Cambo Northum 117 F6
Cambois Northum 117 F9
Camborne Cornw'l 3 B5
Cambourne Cambs 54 D4
Cambridge Cambs 55 D5
Cambridge Glos 36 D4
Cambridge Town Southend 43 F5
Cambus Clack 133 E7
Cambusavie Farm H'land 164 E4
Cambusbarron Stirl 133 E6
Cambuskenneth Stirl 133 E7
Cambuslang S Lanarks 121 C6
Cambusmore Lodge H'land 164 E4
Camden London 41 F5
Camelford Cornw'l 8 F3
Camelot Theme Park, Chorley Lancs 86 C3
Camelsdale W Sussex 27 F6
Camerory H'land 158 F4
Camer's Green Worcs 50 F2
Camerton Bath/NE Som'set 23 D8
Camerton Cumb 107 F7
Camerton ER Yorks 91 B6
Camghouran Perth/Kinr 140 D2
Cammachmore Aberds 151 E8
Cammeringham Lincs 90 F3
Camore H'land 164 E4
Camp Hill Warwick 63 E7
Campbeltown Arg/Bute 118 D4
Camperdown Tyne/Wear 111 B5
Campmuir Perth/Kinr 142 F2
Campsall S Yorks 89 C6
Campsey Ash Suffolk 57 D7
Campton Beds 54 F2
Camptown Scot Borders 116 C2
Camrose Pembs 44 C4
Camserney Perth/Kinr 141 E5
Camster H'land 169 E7
Camuschoirk H'land 138 C1
Camuscross H'land 145 B6
Camusnagaul H'land 138 B4
Camusnagaul H'land 162 F4
Camusrory H'land 145 D8
Camusteel H'land 155 F3
Camusterrach H'land 155 F3
Camusvrachan Perth/Kinr 140 E3
Canada Hants 14 C3
Canadia E Sussex 18 D4
Canal Side S Yorks 89 C7
Candacraig Ho. Aberds 150 C2
Candlesby Lincs 79 C7
Candy Mill S Lanarks 122 E3
Cane End Oxon 26 B4
Canewdon Essex 42 E4
Canford Bottom Dorset 13 D8
Canford Cliffs Poole 13 F8
Canford Magna Poole 13 E8
Canham's Green Suffolk 56 C4
Canholes Derby 75 B7
Canisbay H'land 169 B8
Cann Dorset 13 B6
Cann Common Dorset 13 B6
Cannard's Grave Som'set 23 E8
Cannich H'land 156 F4
Cannington Som'set 22 F4
Cannock Staffs 62 D3
Cannock Wood Staffs 62 C4
Canon Bridge Heref'd 49 E6
Canon Frome Heref'd 49 E8
Canon Pyon Heref'd 49 E6
Canonbie Dumf/Gal 108 B3
Canons Ashby Northants 52 D3
Canonstown Cornw'l 2 C4
Canterbury Kent 30 D5
Canterbury Cathedral Kent 30 D5
Canterbury Tales Kent 30 D5
Cantley Norfolk 69 D6
Cantley S Yorks 89 D7
Cantlop Shrops 60 D5
Canton Card 22 B3
Cantraybruich H'land 157 E8
Cantraydoune H'land 157 E8
Cantraywood H'land 157 E8
Cantsfield Lancs 93 B6
Canvey Island Essex 42 F3
Canwick Lincs 78 C2
Canworthy Water Cornw'l 8 E4
Caol H'land 139 B5
Caol Ila Arg/Bute 126 B4
Caolas Arg/Bute 136 F2
Caolas Scalpaigh W Isles 173 J5
Caolas Stocinis W Isles 173 J4
Capel Surrey 28 E2
Capel Bangor Ceredig'n 58 F3
Capel Betws Lleucu Ceredig'n 46 D5
Capel Carmel Gwyn 70 E2
Capel Coch Angl 82 C4
Capel Curig Conwy 83 F7
Capel Cynon Ceredig'n 46 E2
Capel Dewi Ceredig'n 46 E3
Capel Dewi Ceredig'n 58 F3
Capel Dewi Carms 33 B5
Capel Garmon Conwy 83 F8
Capel-gwyn Angl 82 D3
Capel Gwyn Carms 33 B5
Capel Gwynfe Carms 33 B8
Capel Hendre Carms 33 C6
Capel Hermon Gwyn 71 E8
Capel Isaac Carms 33 B6
Capel Iwan Carms 45 F4
Capel le Ferne Kent 31 E6
Capel Llanilltern Card 34 F4
Capel Mawr Angl 82 D4
Capel St Andrew Suffolk 57 E7
Capel St Mary Suffolk 56 F4
Capel Seion Ceredig'n 46 B5
Capel Tygwydd Ceredig'n 45 E4
Capel Uchaf Gwyn 70 C5
Capel-y-graig Gwyn 82 E5
Capelulo Conwy 83 D7
Capenhurst Ches 73 B7
Capernwray Lancs 92 B5
Capheaton Northum 117 F6
Cappercleuch Scot Borders 115 B5
Capplegill Dumf/Gal 114 D4
Capton Devon 7 D6
Caputh Perth/Kinr 141 F7
Car Colston Notts 77 E7
Carbis Bay Cornw'l 2 C4
Carbost H'land 153 F4
Carbost H'land 152 E5
Carbrook S Yorks 88 F4
Carbrooke Norfolk 68 D2
Carburton Notts 77 B6
Carcant Scot Borders 123 D6
Carcary Angus 143 D6
Carclaze Cornw'l 4 D5
Carcroft S Yorks 89 C6
Cardenden Fife 134 E4
Cardeston Shrops 60 C3
Cardiff = Caerdydd Card 22 B3
Cardiff Bay Barrage Card 22 B3
Cardiff Castle Card 22 B3
Cardigan = Aberteifi Ceredig'n 45 E3
Cardington Beds 53 E8
Cardington Shrops 60 E5
Cardinham Cornw'l 5 C6
Cardonald Glasg C 120 C5
Cardow Moray 159 E5
Cardrona Scot Borders 123 F6
Cardross Arg/Bute 120 B3
Cardurnock Cumb 107 D8
Careby Lincs 65 C7
Careston Angus 143 D5
Carew Pembs 32 D1
Carew Cheriton Pembs 32 D1
Carew Newton Pembs 32 D1
Carey Heref'd 49 F7
Carfrae E Loth 123 C8
Cargenbridge Dumf/Gal 107 B6
Cargill Perth/Kinr 142 F1
Cargo Cumb 108 D3
Cargreen Cornw'l 6 C2
Carham Northum 124 F4
Carhampton Som'set 22 E2
Carharrack Cornw'l 3 B6
Carie Perth/Kinr 140 F3
Carie Perth/Kinr 140 D3
Carines Cornw'l 4 D2
Carisbrooke I/Wight 15 F5
Carisbrooke Castle I/Wight 15 F5
Cark Cumb 92 B3
Carlabhagh W Isles 172 D5
Carland Cross Cornw'l 4 D3
Carlby Lincs 65 C7
Carlecotes S Yorks 88 D2
Carlesmoor N Yorks 94 B4
Carleton Cumb 99 B7
Carleton Cumb 108 E4
Carleton Lancs 92 F3
Carleton N Yorks 94 E2
Carleton Forehoe Norfolk 68 D3
Carleton Rode Norfolk 68 E4
Carlin How Redcar/Clevel'd 103 C5
Carlingcott Bath/NE Som'set 23 D8
Carlisle Cumb 108 D4
Carlisle Cathedral Cumb 108 D3
Carlisle Racecourse Cumb 108 D3
Carlops Scot Borders 122 D4
Carlton Beds 53 D7
Carlton Cambs 55 D7
Carlton Leics 63 D7
Carlton Notts 77 E6
Carlton N Yorks 102 F4
Carlton N Yorks 89 B7
Carlton N Yorks 101 F5
Carlton N Yorks 101 C6
Carlton Stockton 102 B1
Carlton Suffolk 57 C7
Carlton S Yorks 88 C4
Carlton W Yorks 88 B4
Carlton Colville Suffolk 69 F8
Carlton Curlieu Leics 64 E3
Carlton Husthwaite N Yorks 95 B7
Carlton in Cleveland N Yorks 102 D3
Carlton in Lindrick Notts 89 F6
Carlton le Moorland Lincs 78 D2
Carlton Miniott N Yorks 102 F1
Carlton on Trent Notts 77 C7
Carlton Scroop Lincs 78 E2
Carluke S Lanarks 121 D8
Carmarthen = Caerfyrddin Carms 33 B5
Carmel Angl 82 C3
Carmel Carms 33 C6
Carmel Flints 73 B5
Carmel Guernsey 16
Carmel Gwyn 82 F4
Carmont Aberds 151 F7
Carmunnock Glasg C 121 D6
Carmyle Glasg C 121 C6
Carmyllie Angus 143 E5
Carn-gorm H'land 146 B2
Carnaby ER Yorks 97 C7
Carnach H'land 162 E4
Carnach H'land 146 B3
Carnach W Isles 173 J5
Carnachy H'land 168 D2
Càrnais W Isles 172 E3
Carnbee Fife 135 D7
Carnbo Perth/Kinr 134 D2
Carnbrea Cornw'l 3 B5
Carnduff S Lanarks 121 E6
Carnduncan Arg/Bute 126 C2
Carne Cornw'l 3 C8
Carnforth Lancs 92 B4
Carnhedryn Pembs 44 C3
Carnhell Green Cornw'l 2 C5
Carnkie Cornw'l 3 C6
Carnkie Cornw'l 3 C5
Carno Powys 59 E6
Carnoch H'land 156 F4
Carnoch H'land 156 D3
Carnock Fife 134 F2
Carnon Downs Cornw'l 3 B6
Carnousie Aberds 160 C3
Carnoustie Angus 143 F5
Carnwath S Lanarks 122 E2
Carnyorth Cornw'l 2 C2
Carperby N Yorks 101 F5
Carpley Green N Yorks 100 F4
Carr S Yorks 89 E6
Carr Hill Tyne/Wear 111 C5
Carradale Arg/Bute 118 C5
Carragraich W Isles 173 J4
Carrbridge H'land 148 B5
Carrefour Selous Jersey 17
Carreg-wen Pembs 45 E4
Carreglefn Angl 82 C3
Carrick Arg/Bute 128 B4
Carrick Fife 135 B6
Carrick Castle Arg/Bute 129 A6
Carrick Ho. Orkney 176 C4
Carriden Falk 134 F2
Carrington Gtr Man 86 E5
Carrington Lincs 79 D6
Carrington Midloth 123 C6
Carrog Conwy 71 C8
Carrog Denbs 72 E5
Carron Falk 133 F7
Carron Moray 159 E6
Carron Bridge N Lanarks 133 F6
Carronbridge Dumf/Gal 113 E8
Carrshield Northum 109 E8
Carrutherstown Dumf/Gal 107 B8
Carrville Durham 111 E6
Carsaig Arg/Bute 137 F6
Carsaig Arg/Bute 128 B2
Carscreugh Dumf/Gal 105 D6
Carse Gray Angus 142 D4
Carse Ho. Arg/Bute 128 D2
Carsegowan Dumf/Gal 105 D8
Carseriggan Dumf/Gal 105 C7
Carsethorn Dumf/Gal 107 D6
Carshalton London 28 C3
Carsington Derby 76 D2
Carskiey Arg/Bute 118 F3
Carsluith Dumf/Gal 105 D8
Carsphairn Dumf/Gal 113 E5
Carstairs S Lanarks 122 E2
Carstairs Junction S Lanarks 122 E2
Carswell Marsh Oxon 38 E3
Carter's Clay Hants 14 B4
Carterton Oxon 38 D2
Carterway Heads Northum 110 D3
Carthew Cornw'l 4 D5
Carthorpe N Yorks 101 F8
Cartington Northum 117 D6
Cartland S Lanarks 121 E8
Cartmel Cumb 92 B3
Cartmel Fell Cumb 99 F6
Cartmel Racecourse Cumb 92 B3
Carway Carms 33 D5
Cary Fitzpaine Som'set 12 B3
Cas-Gwent = Chepstow Monmouths 36 E2
Cascob Powys 48 C4
Cashlie Perth/Kinr 140 E1
Cashmere Visitor Centre, Elgin Moray 159 E6
Cashmoor Dorset 13 C7
Casnewydd = Newport Newp 35 F7
Cassey Compton Glos 37 C7
Cassington Oxon 38 C4
Cassop Durham 111 F6
Castell Denbs 72 C5
Castell Coch Card 35 F5
Castell-Howell Ceredig'n 46 E3
Castell-Nedd = Neath Neath P Talb 33 E8
Castell Newydd Emlyn = Newcastle Emlyn Carms 46 E2
Castell-y-bwch Torf 35 E6
Castellau Rh Cyn Taff 34 F4
Casterton Cumb 93 B6
Castle Acre Norfolk 67 C8
Castle Ashby Northants 53 D6
Castle Bolton N Yorks 101 E5
Castle Bromwich W Midlands 62 F5
Castle Bytham Lincs 65 C6
Castle Caereinion Powys 59 D8
Castle Camps Cambs 55 E7
Castle Carrock Cumb 108 D5
Castle Cary Som'set 23 F8
Castle Combe Wilts 24 B3
Castle Donington Leics 63 B8
Castle Douglas Dumf/Gal 106 C4
Castle Drogo, Exeter Devon 10 E2
Castle Eaton Swindon 37 E8
Castle Eden Durham 111 F7
Castle Forbes Aberds 150 C5
Castle Frome Heref'd 49 E8
Castle Green Surrey 27 C7
Castle Gresley Derby 63 C6
Castle Heaton Northum 124 E5
Castle Hedingham Essex 55 F8
Castle Hill Kent 29 E7
Castle Howard, Malton N Yorks 96 B3
Castle Huntly Perth/Kinr 134 B5
Castle Kennedy Dumf/Gal 104 D5
Castle O'er Dumf/Gal 115 E5
Castle Pulverbatch Shrops 60 D4
Castle Rising Norfolk 67 B6
Castle Stuart H'land 157 E8
Castlebay = Bagh a Chaisteil W Isles 171 L2
Castlebythe Pembs 32 B1
Castlecary N Lanarks 121 B7
Castlecraig H'land 158 C2
Castlefairn Dumf/Gal 113 F7
Castleford W Yorks 88 B5
Castlehill Scot Borders 122 F5
Castlehill H'land 169 C6
Castlehill W Dunb 120 B3
Castlemaddy Dumf/Gal 113 F5
Castlemartin Pembs 44 F4
Castlemilk Dumf/Gal 107 B8
Castlemilk Glasg C 121 D6
Castlemorris Pembs 44 B4
Castlemorton Worcs 50 F2
Castleside Durham 110 E3
Castlethorpe M/Keynes 53 E6
Castleton Angus 142 E3
Castleton Arg/Bute 128 B3
Castleton Derby 88 F2
Castleton Gtr Man 87 C6
Castleton Newp 35 F6
Castleton N Yorks 102 D4
Castletown Ches 73 D8
Castletown H'land 169 C6
Castletown H'land 157 E8
Castletown I/Man 84 F2
Castletown Tyne/Wear 111 D6
Castleweary Scot Borders 115 D7
Castley N Yorks 95 E5
Caston Norfolk 68 E2
Castor Peterbro 65 E8
Catacol N Ayrs 119 B6
Catbrain S Gloucs 36 F2
Catbrook Monmouths 36 D2
Catchall Cornw'l 2 D3
Catchems Corner W Midlands 51 B7
Catchgate Durham 110 D4
Catcleugh Northum 116 D3
Catcliffe S Yorks 88 F5
Catcott Som'set 23 F5
Caterham Surrey 28 D4
Catfield Norfolk 69 B6
Catfirth Shetl'd 175 H6
Catford London 28 B4
Catforth Lancs 92 F4
Cathays Card 22 B3
Cathcart Glasg C 121 C5
Cathedine Powys 35 B5
Catherington Hants 15 C7
Catherton Shrops 49 B8
Catlodge H'land 148 E2
Catlowdy Cumb 108 B4
Catmore W Berks 38 F4
Caton Lancs 92 C5
Caton Green Lancs 92 C5
Catrine E Ayrs 113 B5
Cat's Ash Newp 35 E7
Catsfield E Sussex 18 D4
Catshill Worcs 50 B4
Cattal N Yorks 95 D7
Cattawade Suffolk 56 F5
Catterall Lancs 92 E4
Catterick N Yorks 101 E7
Catterick Bridge N Yorks 101 E7
Catterick Garrison N Yorks 101 E6
Catterick Racecourse N Yorks 101 E7
Catterlen Cumb 108 F4
Catterline Aberds 143 B8
Catterton N Yorks 95 E8
Catthorpe Leics 52 B3
Cattistock Dorset 12 E3
Catton Northum 109 D8
Catton N Yorks 95 B6
Catwick ER Yorks 97 E7
Catworth Cambs 53 B8
Caudlesprings Norfolk 68 D2
Caudwell's Mill, Matlock Derby 76 C2
Caulcott Oxon 39 B5
Cauldcots Angus 143 E6
Cauldhame Stirl 132 E5
Cauldmill Scot Borders 115 C8
Cauldon Staffs 75 E7
Caulkerbush Dumf/Gal 107 D6
Caulside Dumf/Gal 115 F7
Caunsall Worcs 62 F2
Caunton Notts 77 D7
Causeway End Dumf/Gal 105 C8
Causeway Foot W Yorks 94 F3
Causeway-head Stirl 133 E6
Causewayend S Lanarks 122 F3
Causewayhead Cumb 107 D8
Causey Park Bridge Northum 117 E7
Causeyend Aberds 151 C8
Cautley Cumb 100 E1
Cavendish Suffolk 56 E2
Cavendish Bridge Leics 63 B8
Cavenham Suffolk 55 C8
Caversfield Oxon 39 B5
Caversham Reading 26 B5
Caverswall Staffs 75 E6
Cavil ER Yorks 96 F3
Cawdor H'land 158 D2
Cawdor Castle and Gardens H'land 158 E2
Cawkwell Lincs 79 B5
Cawood N Yorks 95 F8
Cawsand Cornw'l 6 D2
Cawston Norfolk 81 E7
Cawthorne S Yorks 88 D3
Cawthorpe Lincs 65 B7
Cawton N Yorks 96 B2
Caxton Cambs 54 D4
Caynham Shrops 49 B7
Caythorpe Lincs 78 E2
Caythorpe Notts 77 E6
Cayton N Yorks 103 F8
Ceann a Bhaigh W Isles 170 D3
Ceann a Deas Loch Baghasdail W Isles 171 J3
Ceann Shiphoirt W Isles 172 G5
Ceann Tarabhaigh W Isles 172 G5
Ceannacroc Lodge H'land 146 C5
Cearsiadair W Isles 172 F6
Cefn Berain Conwy 72 C3
Cefn-brith Conwy 72 D3
Cefn Canol Powys 73 F6
Cefn-coch Conwy 83 E8
Cefn Coch Powys 59 B8
Cefn-coed-y-cymmer Merth Tyd 34 D4
Cefn Cribbwr Bridg 34 F2
Cefn Cross Bridg 34 F2
Cefn-ddwysarn Gwyn 72 F3
Cefn Einion Shrops 60 F2
Cefn-gorwydd Powys 47 E8
Cefn-mawr Wrex 73 E6
Cefn-y-bedd Flints 73 D7
Cefn-y-pant Carms 32 B2
Cefneithin Carms 33 C6
Cei-bach Ceredig'n 46 D3
Ceinewydd = New Quay Ceredig'n 46 D2
Ceint Angl 82 D4
Cellan Ceredig'n 46 E5
Cellarhead Staffs 75 E6
Cemaes Angl 82 B3
Cemmaes Powys 58 D5
Cemmaes Road Powys 58 D5
Cenarth Carms 45 E4
Cenin Gwyn 71 C5
Central Invercl 129 C7
Ceos W Isles 172 F6
Ceres Fife 135 C6
Cerne Abbas Dorset 12 D4
Cerney Wick Glos 37 E7
Cerrigceinwen Angl 82 D4
Cerrigydrudion Conwy 72 E3
Cessford Scot Borders 116 B3
Ceunant Gwyn 82 E5
Chaceley Glos 50 F3
Chacewater Cornw'l 3 B6
Chackmore Bucks 52 F4
Chacombe Northants 52 E2
Chad Valley W Midlands 62 F4
Chadderton Gtr Man 87 D7
Chadderton Fold Gtr Man 87 D6
Chaddesden Derby C 76 F3
Chaddesley Corbett Worcs 50 B3
Chaddleworth W Berks 26 B2
Chadlington Oxon 38 B3
Chadshunt Warwick 51 D8
Chadwell Leics 64 B4
Chadwell St Mary Thurr'k 29 B7
Chadwick End W Midlands 51 B7
Chadwick Green Mersey 86 E3
Chaffcombe Som'set 11 C8
Chagford Devon 10 F2
Chailey E Sussex 17 C7
Chain Bridge Lincs 79 E6
Chainbridge Cambs 66 D4
Chainhurst Kent 29 E8
Chalbury Dorset 13 D8
Chalbury Common Dorset 13 D8
Chaldon Surrey 28 D4
Chaldon Herring or Dorset 13 F5
Chale I/Wight 15 G5
Chale Green I/Wight 15 G5
Chalfont Common Bucks 40 E3
Chalfont St Giles Bucks 40 E2
Chalfont St Peter Bucks 40 E3
Chalford Glos 37 D5
Chalgrove Oxon 39 E6
Chalk Kent 29 B7
Challacombe Devon 21 E5
Challoch Dumf/Gal 105 C7
Challock Kent 30 D4
Chalton Beds 40 B3
Chalton Hants 15 C8
Chalvington E Sussex 18 E2
Chancery Ceredig'n 46 B4
Chandler's Ford Hants 14 B5
Channel Tunnel Kent 19 B8
Channerwick Shetl'd 175 L6
Chantry Som'set 24 E2
Chantry Suffolk 56 E5
Chapel Fife 134 E4
Chapel Allerton Som'set 23 D6
Chapel Allerton W Yorks 95 F6
Chapel Amble Cornw'l 4 B4
Chapel Brampton Northants 52 C5
Chapel Chorlton Staffs 74 F5
Chapel-en-le-Frith Derby 87 F8
Chapel End Warwick 63 E7
Chapel Green Warwick 63 F6
Chapel Green Warwick 52 C2
Chapel Haddlesey N Yorks 89 B6
Chapel Head Cambs 66 F3
Chapel Hill Aberds 161 E7
Chapel Hill Lincs 78 D5
Chapel Hill Monmouths 36 E2
Chapel Hill N Yorks 95 E6
Chapel Lawn Shrops 48 B5
Chapel-le-Dale N Yorks 93 B7
Chapel Milton Derby 87 F8
Chapel of Garioch Aberds 151 B6
Chapel Row W Berks 26 C3
Chapel St Leonards Lincs 79 B8
Chapel Stile Cumb 99 D5
Chapelgate Lincs 66 B4
Chapelhall N Lanarks 121 C7
Chapelhill Dumf/Gal 114 E3
Chapelhill H'land 158 B2
Chapelhill N Ayrs 120 E2
Chapelhill Perth/Kinr 134 B4
Chapelhill Perth/Kinr 141 F7
Chapelknowe Dumf/Gal 108 B3
Chapelton Angus 143 E6
Chapelton Devon 9 B7
Chapelton H'land 148 C5
Chapelton S Lanarks 121 E6
Chapeltown Blackb'n 86 C5
Chapeltown Moray 149 B8
Chapeltown S Yorks 88 E4
Chapmans Well Devon 9 E5
Chapmanslade Wilts 24 E3
Chapmore End Herts 41 C6
Chappel Essex 42 B4
Chard Som'set 11 D8
Chardstock Devon 11 D8
Charfield S Gloucs 36 E4
Charford Worcs 50 C4
Charing Kent 30 E3
Charing Cross Dorset 14 C2
Charing Heath Kent 30 E3
Charingworth Glos 51 F7
Charlbury Oxon 38 C3
Charlcombe Bath/NE Som'set 24 C2
Charlecote Warwick 51 D7
Charlecote Park, Wellesbourne Warwick 51 D7
Charles Devon 21 F5
Charles Manning's Amusement Park, Felixstowe Suffolk 57 F6
Charles Tye Suffolk 56 D4
Charlesfield Dumf/Gal 107 C8
Charleston Angus 142 E3
Charleston Renf 120 C4
Charlestown Aberd C 151 D8
Charlestown Cornw'l 4 D5
Charlestown Derby 87 E8
Charlestown Dorset 12 G4
Charlestown Fife 134 F2
Charlestown Gtr Man 87 D6
Charlestown H'land 157 E7
Charlestown H'land 154 C4
Charlestown W Yorks 87 B7
Charlestown of Aberlour Moray 159 E6
Charlesworth Derby 87 E8
Charleton Devon 7 E5
Charlton London 28 B5
Charlton Hants 25 E8
Charlton Herts 40 B4
Charlton Northants 52 F3
Charlton Northum 116 F4
Charlton Som'set 23 D8
Charlton Telford 61 C5
Charlton Wilts 13 B7
Charlton Wilts 25 D6
Charlton Wilts 37 F6
Charlton Worcs 50 E5
Charlton W Sussex 16 C2
Charlton Abbots Glos 37 B7
Charlton Adam Som'set 12 B3
Charlton-All-Saints Wilts 14 B2
Charlton Horethorne Som'set 12 B4
Charlton Kings Glos 37 B6
Charlton Mackerell Som'set 12 B3
Charlton Marshall Dorset 13 D6
Charlton Musgrove Som'set 12 B5
Charlton on Otmoor Oxon 39 C5
Charltons Redcar/Clevel'd 102 C4
Charlwood Surrey 28 E3
Charlynch Som'set 22 F4
Charminster Dorset 12 E4
Charmouth Dorset 11 E8
Charndon Bucks 39 B6
Charney Bassett Oxon 38 E3
Charnock Richard Lancs 86 C3
Charsfield Suffolk 57 D6
Chart Corner Kent 29 D8
Chart Sutton Kent 30 E2
Charter Alley Hants 26 D3
Charterhouse Som'set 23 D6
Charterville Allotments Oxon 38 C3
Chartham Kent 30 D5
Chartham Hatch Kent 30 D5
Chartridge Bucks 40 D2
Chartwell, Westerham Kent 29 D5
Charvil Wokingham 27 B5
Charwelton Northants 52 D3
Chasetown Staffs 62 D4
Chastleton Oxon 38 B2
Chasty Devon 8 D5
Chatburn Lancs 93 E7
Chatcull Staffs 74 F4
Chatham Medway 29 C8
Chathill Northum 117 B7
Chatsworth, Bakewell Derby 76 B2
Chattenden Medway 29 B8
Chatteris Cambs 66 F3
Chattisham Suffolk 56 E4
Chatto Scot Borders 116 C3
Chatton Northum 117 B6
Chawleigh Devon 10 C2
Chawley Oxon 38 D4
Chawston Beds 54 D2
Chawton Hants 26 F5
Cheadle Gtr Man 87 F6
Cheadle Staffs 75 E7
Cheadle Heath Gtr Man 87 F6
Cheadle Hulme Gtr Man 87 F6
Cheam London 28 C3
Cheapside Surrey 27 D8
Chearsley Bucks 39 C7
Chebsey Staffs 62 B2
Checkendon Oxon 39 F6
Checkley Ches 74 E4
Checkley Heref'd 49 F7
Checkley Staffs 75 F7
Chedburgh Suffolk 55 D8
Cheddar Som'set 23 D6
Cheddar Showcaves and Gorge Som'set 23 D6
Cheddington Bucks 40 C2
Cheddleton Staffs 75 D6
Cheddon Fitzpaine Som'set 11 B7
Chedglow Wilts 37 E6
Chedgrave Norfolk 69 E6
Chedington Dorset 12 D2
Chediston Suffolk 57 B7
Chedworth Glos 37 C7
Chedworth Roman Villa Glos 37 C7
Chedzoy Som'set 22 F5
Cheeklaw Scot Borders 124 D3
Cheeseman's Green Kent 19 B7
Cheglinch Devon 20 E4
Cheldon Devon 10 C2
Chelford Ches 75 B5
Chell Heath Stoke 75 D5
Chellaston Derby C 76 F3
Chellington Beds 53 D7
Chelmarsh Shrops 61 F7
Chelmer Village Essex 42 D3
Chelmondiston Suffolk 57 F6
Chelmorton Derby 75 C8
Chelmsford Essex 42 D3
Chelsea London 28 B3
Chelsfield London 29 C5
Chelsworth Suffolk 56 E3
Cheltenham Glos 37 B6
Cheltenham Racecourse Glos 37 B6
Chelveston Northants 53 C7
Chelvey N Som'set 23 C6
Chelwood Bath/NE Som'set 23 C8
Chelwood Common E Sussex 17 B8
Chelwood Gate E Sussex 17 B8
Chelworth Wilts 37 E6
Chelworth Green Wilts 37 E7
Chemistry Shrops 74 E2
Chenies Bucks 40 E3
Cheny Longville Shrops 60 F4
Chepstow = Cas-Gwent Monmouths 36 E2
Chepstow Racecourse Monmouths 36 E2
Chequerfield W Yorks 89 B5
Cherhill Wilts 24 B5
Cherington Glos 37 E6
Cherington Warwick 51 F7
Cheriton Devon 21 E6
Cheriton Hants 15 B6
Cheriton Kent 31 F5
Cheriton Swan 33 E5
Cheriton Bishop Devon 10 E2
Cheriton Fitzpaine Devon 10 D3
Cheriton or Stackpole Elidor Pembs 44 F4
Cherrington Telford 61 B6
Cherry Burton ER Yorks 97 E5
Cherry Hinton Cambs 55 D5
Cherry Orchard Worcs 50 D3
Cherry Willingham Lincs 78 B3
Cherrybank Perth/Kinr 134 B3
Chertsey Surrey 27 C8
Cheselbourne Dorset 13 E5
Chesham Bucks 40 D2
Chesham Bois Bucks 40 E2
Cheshire Candle Workshops, Burwardsley Ches 74 D2
Cheshunt Herts 41 D6
Cheslyn Hay Staffs 62 D3
Chessington London 28 C2
Chessington World of Adventures London 28 C2
Chester Ches 73 C8
Chester Cathedral Ches 73 C7
Chester-Le-Street Durham 111 D5
Chester Moor Durham 111 E5
Chester Racecourse Ches 73 C7
Chester Zoo Ches 73 B8
Chesterblade Som'set 23 E8
Chesterfield Derby 76 B3
Chesters Scot Borders 116 C2
Chesters Scot Borders 116 B2
Chesters Roman Fort Northum 110 B2
Chesterton Cambs 65 E8
Chesterton Cambs 55 C5
Chesterton Glos 37 D7
Chesterton Oxon 39 B5
Chesterton Shrops 61 E7
Chesterton Staffs 74 E5
Chesterton Warwick 51 D8
Chesterwood Northum 109 C8
Chestfield Kent 30 C5
Cheston Devon 6 D4
Cheswardine Shrops 61 B7
Cheswick Northum 125 E6
Chetnole Dorset 12 D4
Chettiscombe Devon 10 C4
Chettisham Cambs 66 F5
Chettle Dorset 13 C7
Chetton Shrops 61 E6
Chetwode Bucks 39 B6
Chetwynd Aston Telford 61 C7
Cheveley Cambs 55 C7
Chevening Kent 29 D5
Chevington Suffolk 55 D8
Chevithorne Devon 10 C4
Chew Magna Bath/NE Som'set 23 C7
Chew Stoke Bath/NE Som'set 23 C7
Chewton Keynsham Bath/NE Som'set 23 C8
Chewton Mendip Som'set 23 D7
Chicheley M/Keynes 53 E7
Chichester W Sussex 16 D2
Chichester Cathedral W Sussex 16 D2
Chickerell Dorset 12 F4
Chicklade Wilts 24 F4
Chicksgrove Wilts 24 F4
Chidden Hants 15 C7
Chiddingfold Surrey 27 F7
Chiddingly E Sussex 18 D2
Chiddingstone Kent 29 E5
Chiddingstone Causeway Kent 29 E6
Chiddingstone Hoath Kent 29 E5
Chideock Dorset 12 E2
Chidham W Sussex 15 D8
Chidswell W Yorks 88 B3
Chieveley W Berks 26 B2
Chignall St James Essex 42 D2
Chignall Smealy Essex 42 C2
Chigwell Essex 41 E7
Chigwell Row Essex 41 E7
Chilbolton Hants 25 F8
Chilcomb Hants 15 B6
Chilcombe Dorset 12 E3
Chilcompton Som'set 23 D8
Chilcote Leics 63 C6
Child Okeford Dorset 13 C6
Childer Thornton Ches 73 B7
Childrey Oxon 38 F3
Child's Ercall Shrops 61 B6
Childswickham Worcs 51 F5
Childwall Mersey 86 F2
Childwick Green Herts 40 C4
Chilfrome Dorset 12 E3
Chilgrove W Sussex 16 C2
Chilham Kent 30 D4
Chilhampton Wilts 25 F5
Chilla Devon 9 D6
Chillaton Devon 9 F6
Chillenden Kent 31 D6
Chillerton I/Wight 15 F5
Chillesford Suffolk 57 D7
Chillingham Northum 117 B6
Chillington Devon 7 E5
Chillington Som'set 11 C8
Chilmark Wilts 24 F4
Chilson Oxon 38 C3
Chilsworthy Cornw'l 6 B2
Chilsworthy Devon 8 D5
Chilthorne Domer Som'set 12 C3
Chiltington E Sussex 17 C7
Chilton Bucks 39 C6
Chilton Durham 101 B7
Chilton Oxon 38 F4
Chilton Cantelo Som'set 12 B3
Chilton Foliat Wilts 25 B8
Chilton Lane Durham 111 F6
Chilton Polden Som'set 23 F5
Chilton Street Suffolk 55 E8
Chilton Trinity Som'set 22 F4
Chilvers Coton Warwick 63 E7
Chilwell Notts 76 F5
Chilworth Hants 14 C5
Chilworth Surrey 27 E8
Chimney Oxon 38 D3
Chineham Hants 26 D4
Chingford London 41 E6
Chinley Derby 87 F8
Chinley Head Derby 87 F8
Chinnor Oxon 39 D7
Chipnall Shrops 74 F4
Chippenhall Green Suffolk 57 B6
Chippenham Cambs 55 C7
Chippenham Wilts 24 B4
Chipperfield Herts 40 D3
Chipping Herts 54 F4
Chipping Lancs 93 E6
Chipping Campden Glos 51 F6
Chipping Hill Essex 42 C4
Chipping Norton Oxon 38 B3
Chipping Ongar Essex 42 D1
Chipping Sodbury S Gloucs 36 F4
Chipping Warden Northants 52 E2
Chipstable Som'set 10 B5
Chipstead Kent 29 D5
Chipstead Surrey 28 D3
Chirbury Shrops 60 E2
Chirk = Y Waun Wrex 73 F6
Chirk Bank Shrops 73 F6
Chirk Castle Wrex 73 F6
Chirmorrie S Ayrs 105 B6
Chirnside Scot Borders 124 D4
Chirnsidebridge Scot Borders 124 D4
Chirton Wilts 25 D5
Chisbury Wilts 25 C7
Chiselborough Som'set 12 C2
Chiseldon Swindon 25 B6
Chiserley W Yorks 87 B8
Chislehampton Oxon 39 E5
Chislehurst London 28 B5
Chislet Kent 31 C6
Chiswell Green Herts 40 D4
Chiswick London 28 B3
Chiswick End Cambs 54 E4
Chisworth Derby 87 E7
Chithurst W Sussex 16 B2
Chittering Cambs 55 B5
Chitterne Wilts 24 E4
Chittlehamholt Devon 9 B8
Chittlehampton Devon 9 B8
Chittoe Wilts 24 C4
Chivenor Devon 20 F4
Chobham Surrey 27 C7
Choicelee Scot Borders 124 D3
Cholderton Wilts 25 E7
Cholesbury Bucks 40 D2
Chollerford Northum 110 B2
Chollerton Northum 110 B2
Cholmondeston Ches 74 C3
Cholsey Oxon 39 F5
Cholstrey Heref'd 49 D6
Chop Gate N Yorks 102 E3
Choppington Northum 117 F8
Chopwell Tyne/Wear 110 D4
Chorley Ches 74 D2
Chorley Lancs 86 C3
Chorley Shrops 61 F6
Chorley Staffs 62 C4
Chorleywood Herts 40 E3
Chorlton cum Hardy Gtr Man 87 E6
Chorlton Lane Ches 73 E8
Choulton Shrops 60 F3
Chowdene Tyne/Wear 111 D5
Chowley Ches 73 D8
Chrishall Essex 54 F5
Christ Church Oxford Oxon 39 D5
Christchurch Cambs 66 E4
Christchurch Dorset 14 E2
Christchurch Glos 36 C2
Christchurch Newp 35 F7
Christchurch Priory Dorset 14 E2
Christian Malford Wilts 24 B4
Christleton Ches 73 C8
Christmas Common Oxon 39 E7
Christon N Som'set 23 D5
Christon Bank Northum 117 B8
Christow Devon 10 F3
Chryston N Lanarks 121 B6
Chudleigh Devon 7 B6
Chudleigh Knighton Devon 7 B6
Chulmleigh Devon 9 C8
Chunal Derby 87 E8
Church Lancs 86 B5
Church Aston Telford 61 C7
Church Brampton Northants 52 C5
Church Broughton Derby 76 F2
Church Crookham Hants 27 D6
Church Eaton Staffs 62 C2
Church End Beds 40 B2
Church End Beds 54 F2
Church End Beds 53 F7
Church End Cambs 66 F2
Church End Cambs 66 D3
Church End ER Yorks 97 D6
Church End Essex 55 E6
Church End Essex 42 B3
Church End Hants 26 D4
Church End Lincs 78 F5
Church End Warwick 63 E6
Church End Warwick 63 E6
Church End Wilts 24 B5
Church Enstone Oxon 38 B3
Church Fenton N Yorks 95 F8
Church Green Devon 11 E6
Church Green Norfolk 68 E3
Church Gresley Derby 63 C6
Church Hanborough Oxon 38 C4
Church Hill Ches 74 C3
Church Houses N Yorks 102 E4
Church Knowle Dorset 13 F7
Church Laneham Notts 77 B8
Church Langton Leics 64 E4
Church Lawford Warwick 52 B2
Church Lawton Ches 74 D5
Church Leigh Staffs 75 F7
Church Lench Worcs 50 D5
Church Mayfield Staffs 75 E8
Church Minshull Ches 74 C3
Church Norton W Sussex 16 E2
Church Preen Shrops 60 E5
Church Pulverbatch Shrops 60 D4
Church Stoke Powys 60 E2
Church Stowe Northants 52 D4
Church Street Kent 29 B8
Church Stretton Shrops 60 E4
Church Town N Lincs 89 D8
Church Town Surrey 28 D4
Church Village Rh Cyn Taff 34 F4
Church Warsop Notts 77 C5
Churcham Glos 36 C4
Churchbank Shrops 48 B4
Churchbridge Staffs 62 D3
Churchdown Glos 37 C5
Churchend Essex 42 B2
Churchend Essex 43 E6
Churchend S Gloucs 36 E4
Churchfield W Midlands 62 E4
Churchgate Street Essex 41 C7
Churchill Devon 20 E4
Churchill Devon 11 D8
Churchill N Som'set 23 D6
Churchill Oxon 38 B2
Churchill Worcs 50 B3
Churchill Worcs 50 D4
Churchinford Som'set 11 C7
Churchover Warwick 64 F2
Churchstanton Som'set 11 C6
Churchstow Devon 6 E5
Churchtown Derby 76 C2
Churchtown I/Man 84 C4
Churchtown Lancs 92 E4
Churchtown Mersey 85 C4
Churnsike Lodge Northum 109 B6
Churston Ferrers Torbay 7 D7
Churt Surrey 27 F6
Churton Ches 73 D8
Churwell W Yorks 88 B3
Chute Standen Wilts 25 D8
Chwilog Gwyn 70 D5
Chyandour Cornw'l 2 C3
Cilan Uchaf Gwyn 70 E3
Cilcain Flints 73 C5
Cilcennin Ceredig'n 46 C4
Cilfor Gwyn 71 D7
Cilfrew Neath P Talb 34 D1
Cilfynydd Rh Cyn Taff 34 E4
Cilgerran Pembs 45 E3
Cilgwyn Carms 33 B8
Cilgwyn Gwyn 82 F4
Cilgwyn Pembs 45 F2
Ciliau Aeron Ceredig'n 46 D3
Cill Donnain W Isles 171 H3
Cille Bhrighde W Isles 171 J3
Cille Pheadair W Isles 171 J3
Cilmery Powys 48 D2
Cilsan Carms 33 B6
Ciltalgarth Gwyn 72 E2
Cilwendeg Pembs 45 F4
Cilybebyll Neath P Talb 33 D8
Cilycwm Carms 47 F6
Cimla Neath P Talb 34 E1
Cinderford Glos 36 C3
Cippyn Pembs 45 E3
Circebost W Isles 172 E4
Cirencester Glos 37 D7
Ciribhig W Isles 172 D4
City London 41 F6
City Powys 60 F2
City Dulas Angl 82 C4
Clachaig Arg/Bute 129 B6
Clachan Arg/Bute 128 E2
Clachan Arg/Bute 130 D3
Clachan Arg/Bute 138 E2
Clachan Arg/Bute 131 D7
Clachan H'land 153 F6
Clachan W Isles 170 F3
Clachan na Luib W Isles 170 D4
Clachan of Campsie E Dunb 121 B6
Clachan of Glendaruel Arg/Bute 128 B4
Clachan-Seil Arg/Bute 130 D3
Clachan Strachur Arg/Bute 131 E6
Clachaneasy Dumf/Gal 105 B7
Clachanmore Dumf/Gal 104 E4
Clachbreck Arg/Bute 128 C2
Clachnabrain Angus 142 C3
Clachtoll H'land 162 B4
Clackmannan Clack 133 E8
Clacton-on-Sea Essex 43 C7
Cladach Chireboist W Isles 170 D3
Claddach-knockline W Isles 170 D3
Cladich Arg/Bute 131 C6
Claggan H'land 137 D7
Claggan H'land 139 B5
Claigan H'land 152 D3
Claines Worcs 50 D3
Clandown Bath/NE Som'set 23 D8
Clanfield Hants 15 C7
Clanfield Oxon 38 D2
Clanville Hants 25 E8
Claonaig Arg/Bute 128 E3
Claonel H'land 164 D2
Clap Hill Kent 19 B7
Clapgate Dorset 13 D8
Clapgate Herts 41 B7
Clapham Beds 53 D8
Clapham London 28 B3
Clapham N Yorks 93 C7
Clapham W Sussex 16 D4
Clappers Scot Borders 124 D5
Clappersgate Cumb 99 D5
Clapton Som'set 12 D2
Clapton-in-Gordano N Som'set 23 B6
Clapton-on-the-Hill Glos 38 C1
Clapworthy Devon 9 B8
Clara Vale Tyne/Wear 110 C4
Clarach Ceredig'n 58 F3
Clarbeston Pembs 32 B1
Clarbeston Road Pembs 32 B1
Clarborough Notts 89 F8
Clardon H'land 169 C6
Clare Suffolk 55 E8
Clarebrand Dumf/Gal 106 C4
Claremont Landscape Garden, Esher Surrey 28 C2
Clarencefield Dumf/Gal 107 C8
Clarilaw Scot Borders 115 C8
Clark's Green Surrey 28 F2
Clarkston E Renf 121 D5
Clashandorran H'land 157 E6
Clashcoig H'land 164 E3
Clashindarroch Aberds 159 F8
Clashmore H'land 166 F2
Clashmore H'land 164 F4
Clashnessie H'land 166 F2
Clashnoir Moray 149 B8
Clate Shetl'd 175 G7
Clathy Perth/Kinr 133 C8
Clatt Aberds 150 B4

Crosskeys Caerph 35 E6
Crosskirk H'land 168 B5
Crosslanes Shrops 60 C3
Crosslee Scot Borders 115 C6
Crosslee Renf 120 C4
Crossmichael Dumf/Gal 100 C4
Crossmoor Lancs 92 F4
Crossroads Aberds 151 E6
Crossroads E Ayrs 120 F4
Crossway Heref'd 49 F8
Crossway Monmouths 35 C8
Crossway Powys 48 D2
Crossway Green Worcs 50 C3
Crossways Dorset 13 F5
Crosswell Pembs 45 F3
Crosswood Ceredig'n 47 B5
Crosthwaite Cumb 99 E6
Croston Lancs 86 C2
Crostwick Norfolk 69 C5
Crostwight Norfolk 69 B6
Crothair W Isles 172 E4
Crouch Kent 29 D7
Crouch Hill Dorset 12 C5
Crouch House Green Kent 28 E5
Croucheston Wilts 13 B8
Croughton Northants 52 F3
Crovie Aberds 160 B5
Crow Edge S Yorks 88 D2
Crow Hill Heref'd 36 B3
Crowan Cornw'l 2 C5
Crowborough E Sussex 18 B2
Crowcombe Som'set 22 F3
Crowdecote Derby 75 C8
Crowden Derby 87 E8
Crowell Oxon 39 E7
Crowfield Northants 52 E4
Crowfield Suffolk 56 D5
Crowhurst E Sussex 18 D4
Crowhurst Surrey 28 E4
Crowhurst Lane End Surrey 28 E4
Crowland Lincs 66 C2
Crowlas Cornw'l 2 C4
Crowle N Lincs 89 C8
Crowle Worcs 50 D4
Crowmarsh Gifford Oxon 39 F6
Crown Corner Suffolk 57 B6
Crownhill Plym'th 6 D2
Crownland Suffolk 56 C4
Crownthorpe Norfolk 68 D3
Crowntown Cornw'l 2 C5
Crows-an-wra Cornw'l 2 D2
Crowshill Norfolk 68 D2
Crowsnest Shrops 60 D3
Crowthorne Brackn'l 27 C6
Crowton Ches 74 B2
Croxall Staffs 63 C5
Croxby Lincs 91 E5
Croxdale Durham 111 F5
Croxden Staffs 75 F7
Croxley Green Herts 40 E3
Croxton Cambs 54 C3
Croxton N Lincs 90 C4
Croxton Norfolk 67 F8
Croxton Staffs 74 F4
Croxton Kerrial Leics 64 B5
Croxtonbank Staffs 74 F4
Croy H'land 157 E8
Croy N Lanarks 121 B7
Croyde Devon 20 F3
Croydon Cambs 54 E4
Croydon London 28 C4
Crubenmore Lodge H'land 148 E2
Cruckmeole Shrops 60 D4
Cruckton Shrops 60 C4
Cruden Bay Aberds 161 E7
Crudgington Telford 61 C6
Crudwell Wilts 37 E6
Crug Powys 48 B3
Crugmeer Cornw'l 4 B4
Crugybar Carms 47 F5
Crulabhig W Isles 172 E4
Crumlin = Crymlyn Caerph 35 E6
Crumpsall Gtr Man 87 D6
Crundale Kent 30 E4
Crundale Pembs 44 D4
Cruwys Morchard Devon 10 C3
Crux Easton Hants 26 D2
Crwbin Carms 33 C5
Crya Orkney 176 F2
Cryers Hill Bucks 40 E1
Crymlyn Gwyn 83 D6
Crymlyn = Crumlin Caerph 35 E6
Crymych Pembs 45 F3
Crynant Neath P Talb 34 D1
Crynfryn Ceredig'n 46 C4
Crystal Palace National Sports Centre London 28 B4
Cuaig H'land 154 E3
Cuan Arg/Bute 130 D3
Cubbington Warwick 51 C8
Cubeck N Yorks 100 F4
Cubert Cornw'l 4 D2
Cubley S Yorks 88 D3
Cubley Common Derby 75 F8
Cublington Bucks 39 B8
Cublington Heref'd 49 F6
Cuckfield W Sussex 17 B7
Cucklington Som'set 13 B5
Cuckney Notts 77 B5
Cuckoo Hill Notts 89 E8
Cuddesdon Oxon 39 D6
Cuddington Bucks 39 C7
Cuddington Ches 74 B3
Cuddington Heath Ches 73 E8
Cuddy Hill Lancs 92 F4
Cudham London 28 D5
Cudliptown Devon 6 B3
Cudworth Som'set 11 C8
Cudworth S Yorks 88 D4
Cuffley Herts 41 D6
Cuiashader W Isles 172 C8
Cuidhir W Isles 171 K2
Cuidhtinis W Isles 173 K3
Culbo H'land 157 C7
Culbokie H'land 157 D7
Culburnie H'land 157 E5
Culcabock H'land 157 E7
Culcairn H'land 157 C7
Culcharry H'land 158 D2
Culcheth Warrington 86 E4
Culdrain Aberds 160 E2
Culduie H'land 155 F3
Culford Suffolk 56 B2
Culgaith Cumb 99 B8
Culham Oxon 39 E5
Culkein H'land 166 F2
Culkein Drumbeg H'land 166 F3
Culkerton Glos 37 E6
Cullachie H'land 149 B5
Cullen Moray 160 B2
Cullercoats Tyne/Wear 111 B6
Cullicudden H'land 157 C7
Cullingworth W Yorks 94 F3
Cullipool Arg/Bute 130 D3
Cullivoe Shetl'd 175 C7
Culloch Perth/Kinr 133 C6
Culloden H'land 157 E8
Culloden Battlefield, Inverness H'land 157 E8
Cullompton Devon 10 D5
Culmaily H'land 165 E5
Culmazie Dumf/Gal 105 D7
Culmington Shrops 60 F4
Culmstock Devon 11 C6
Culnacraig H'land 162 D4
Culnaknock H'land 152 C6
Culpho Suffolk 57 E6
Culrain H'land 164 E2
Culross Fife 133 F8
Culroy S Ayrs 112 C3
Culsh Aberds 161 D5
Culsh Aberds 150 E2
Culshabbin Dumf/Gal 105 D7
Culswick Shetl'd 175 J4
Cultercullen Aberds 151 B8
Cults Aberd C 151 D7
Cults Aberds 160 E2
Cults Dumf/Gal 105 E8
Culverstone Green Kent 29 C7
Culverthorpe Lincs 78 E3
Culworth Northants 52 E3
Culzean Castle, Maybole S Ayrs 112 D2
Culzie Lodge H'land 157 B6
Cumbernauld N Lanarks 121 B7
Cumbernauld Village N Lanarks 121 B7
Cumberworth Lincs 79 B8
Cuminestown Aberds 160 C5
Cumlewick Shetl'd 175 L6
Cummersdale Cumb 108 D3
Cummertrees Dumf/Gal 107 C8
Cummingston Moray 158 C5
Cumnock E Ayrs 113 B5
Cumnor Oxon 38 D4
Cumrew Cumb 108 D5
Cumwhinton Cumb 108 D4
Cumwhitton Cumb 108 D5
Cundall N Yorks 95 B7
Cunninghamhead N Ayrs 120 E3
Cunnister Shetl'd 174 D7
Cupar Fife 135 C5
Cupar Muir Fife 135 C5
Cupernham Hants 14 B4
Curbar Derby 76 B2
Curbridge Hants 15 C6
Curbridge Oxon 38 D3
Curdridge Hants 15 C6
Curdworth Warwick 63 E5
Curland Som'set 11 C7
Curlew Green Suffolk 57 C7
Currarie S Ayrs 112 E1
Curridge W Berks 26 B2
Currie C/Edinb 122 C4
Curry Mallet Som'set 11 B8
Curry Rivel Som'set 11 B8
Curtisden Green Kent 29 E8
Curtisknowle Devon 6 D5
Cury Cornw'l 3 D5
Cushnie Aberds 160 B4
Cushuish Som'set 22 F3
Cusop Heref'd 48 E4
Cutcloy Dumf/Gal 105 F8
Cutcombe Som'set 21 F8
Cutgate Gtr Man 87 C6
Cutiau Gwyn 58 C3
Cutlers Green Essex 55 F6
Cutnall Green Worcs 50 C3
Cutsdean Glos 51 F5
Cutthorpe Derby 76 B3
Cutts Shetl'd 175 K6
Cutty Sark, Greenwich London 28 B4
Cuxham Oxon 39 E6
Cuxton Medway 29 C8
Cuxwold Lincs 91 D5
Cwm Bl Gwent 35 D5
Cwm Denbs 72 B4
Cwm Swan 33 E7
Cwm-byr Carms 46 F5
Cwm-Cewydd Gwyn 59 C5
Cwm-cou Ceredig'n 45 E4
Cwm-Dulais Swan 33 D7
Cwm-felin-fach Caerph 35 E5
Cwm Ffrwd-oer Torf 35 D6
Cwm-hesgen Gwyn 71 E8
Cwm-hwnt Rh Cyn Taff 34 D3
Cwm Irfon Powys 47 E7
Cwm-Llinau Powys 58 D5
Cwm-mawr Carms 33 C6
Cwm-parc Rh Cyn Taff 34 E3
Cwm Penmachno Conwy 71 C8
Cwm-y-glo Carms 33 C6
Cwm-y-glo Gwyn 82 E5
Cwmafan Neath P Talb 34 E1
Cwmaman Rh Cyn Taff 34 E4
Cwmann Carms 46 E4
Cwmavon Torf 35 D6
Cwmbach Carms 32 B3
Cwmbach Carms 33 D5
Cwmbach Powys 48 D2
Cwmbach Powys 48 F3
Cwmbâch Rh Cyn Taff 34 D4
Cwmbelan Powys 59 F6
Cwmbran = Cwmbrân Torf 35 E6
Cwmbrân = Cwmbran Torf 35 E6
Cwmbrwyno Ceredig'n 58 F4
Cwmcarn Caerph 35 E6
Cwmcarvan Monmouths 36 D1
Cwmcych Pembs 45 F4
Cwmdare Rh Cyn Taff 34 D3
Cwmderwen Powys 59 D6
Cwmdu Carms 46 F5
Cwmdu Powys 35 B5
Cwmdu Swan 33 E7
Cwmduad Carms 46 F2
Cwmdwr Carms 47 F6
Cwmfelin Bridg 34 F2
Cwmfelin Merth Tyd 34 D4
Cwmfelin Boeth Carms 32 C2
Cwmfelin Mynach Carms 32 B3
Cwmffrwd Carms 33 C5
Cwmgiedd Powys 34 C1
Cwmgors Neath P Talb 33 C8
Cwmgwili Carms 33 C6
Cwmgwrach Neath P Talb 34 D2
Cwmhiraeth Carms 46 F2
Cwmifor Carms 33 B7
Cwmisfael Carms 33 C5
Cwmllynfell Neath P Talb 33 C8
Cwmorgan Carms 45 F5
Cwmpengraig Carms 46 F2
Cwmrhos Powys 35 B5
Cwmsychpant Ceredig'n 46 E3
Cwmtillery Bl Gwent 35 D6
Cwmwysg Powys 34 B2
Cwmyoy Monmouths 35 B6
Cwmystwyth Ceredig'n 47 B6
Cwrt Gwyn 58 D3
Cwrt-newydd Ceredig'n 46 E3
Cwrt-y-cadno Carms 47 E5
Cwrt-y-gollen Powys 35 C6
Cydweli = Kidwelly Carms 33 D5
Cyffordd Llandudno = Llandudno Junction Conwy 83 D7
Cyffylliog Denbs 72 D4
Cyfronydd Powys 59 D8
Cymer Neath P Talb 34 E2
Cyncoed Card 35 F5
Cynghordy Carms 47 E7
Cynheidre Carms 33 D5
Cynwyd Denbs 72 E4
Cynwyl Elfed Carms 32 B4
Cywarch Gwyn 59 C5

D

Dacre Cumb 99 B6
Dacre N Yorks 94 C4
Dacre Banks N Yorks 94 C4
Daddry Shield Durham 109 F8
Dadford Bucks 52 F4
Dadlington Leics 63 E8
Dafarn Faig Gwyn 71 C5
Dafen Carms 33 D6
Daffy Green Norfolk 68 D2
Dagenham London 41 F7
Daglingworth Glos 37 D6
Dagnall Bucks 40 C2
Dail Beag W Isles 172 D5
Dail bho Dheas W Isles 172 B7
Dail bho Thuath W Isles 172 B7
Dail Mor W Isles 172 D5
Daill Arg/Bute 126 C3
Dailly S Ayrs 112 D2
Dairsie or Osnaburgh Fife 135 C6
Daisy Hill Gtr Man 86 D4
Dalabrog W Isles 171 H3
Dalavich Arg/Bute 131 D5
Dalbeattie Dumf/Gal 106 C5
Dalblair E Ayrs 113 C6
Dalbog Angus 143 B5
Dalbury Derby 76 F2
Dalby I/Man 84 E2
Dalby N Yorks 96 B2
Dalchalloch Perth/Kinr 140 C4
Dalchalm H'land 165 D6
Dalchenna Arg/Bute 131 E6
Dalchirach Moray 159 F5
Dalchork H'land 164 C2
Dalchreichart H'land 147 C5
Dalchruin Perth/Kinr 133 C6
Dalderby Lincs 78 C5
Dale Pembs 44 E3
Dale Abbey Derby 76 F4
Dale Head Cumb 99 C6
Dale of Walls Shetl'd 175 H3
Dalelia H'land 137 B8
Daless H'land 158 F2
Dalfaber H'land 148 C5
Dalgarven N Ayrs 120 E2
Dalgety Bay Fife 134 F3
Dalginross Perth/Kinr 133 B6
Dalguise Perth/Kinr 141 E6
Dalhalvaig H'land 168 D3
Dalham Suffolk 55 C8
Dalinlongart Arg/Bute 129 B6
Dalkeith Midloth 123 C6
Dallam Warrington 86 E3
Dallas Moray 158 D5
Dalleagles E Ayrs 113 C5
Dallinghoo Suffolk 57 D6
Dallington E Sussex 18 D3
Dallington Northants 52 C5
Dallow N Yorks 94 B4
Dalmadilly Aberds 151 C6
Dalmally Arg/Bute 131 C7
Dalmarnock Glasg C 121 C6
Dalmary Stirl 132 E4
Dalmellington E Ayrs 112 D4
Dalmeny C/Edinb 122 B4
Dalmigavie H'land 148 C3
Dalmigavie Lodge H'land 148 B3
Dalmore H'land 157 C7
Dalmuir W Dunb 120 B4
Dalnabreck H'land 137 B7
Dalnacardoch Lodge Perth/Kinr 140 B4
Dalnacroich H'land 156 D4
Dalnaglar Castle Perth/Kinr 141 C8
Dalnahaitnach H'land 148 B4
Dalnaspidal Lodge Perth/Kinr 140 B3
Dalnavaid Perth/Kinr 141 C7
Dalnavie H'land 157 B7
Dalnawillan Lodge H'land 168 E5
Dalness H'land 139 D5
Dalnessie H'land 164 C3
Dalqueich Perth/Kinr 134 D2
Dalreavoch H'land 164 D4
Dalry N Ayrs 120 E2
Dalrymple E Ayrs 112 C3
Dalserf S Lanarks 121 D8
Dalston Cumb 108 D3
Dalswinton Dumf/Gal 114 F2
Dalton Dumf/Gal 107 B8
Dalton Lancs 86 D2
Dalton Northum 110 D2
Dalton Northum 110 B4
Dalton N Yorks 95 B7
Dalton N Yorks 101 D6
Dalton S Yorks 89 E5
Dalton-in-Furness Cumb 92 B2
Dalton-le-Dale Durham 111 E7
Dalton-on-Tees N Yorks 101 D7
Dalton Piercy Hartlep'l 111 F7
Dalveich Stirl 132 B5
Dalvina Lo H'land 167 E8
Dalwhinnie H'land 148 F2
Dalwood Devon 11 D7
Dalwyne S Ayrs 112 E3
Dam Green Norfolk 68 F3
Dam Side Lancs 92 E4
Damerham Hants 14 C2
Damgate Norfolk 69 D7
Damnaglaur Dumf/Gal 104 F5
Damside Scot Borders 122 E4
Danbury Essex 42 D3
Danby N Yorks 103 D5
Danby Wiske N Yorks 101 E8
Dandaleith Moray 159 E6
Danderhall Midloth 123 C6
Dane End Herts 41 B6
Danebridge Ches 75 C6
Danehill E Sussex 17 B8
Danemoor Green Norfolk 68 D3
Danesford Shrops 61 E7
Daneshill Hants 26 D4
Dangerous Corner Lancs 86 C3
Danskine E Loth 123 C8
Darcy Lever Gtr Man 86 D5
Darenth Kent 29 B6
Daresbury Halton 86 F3
Darfield S Yorks 88 D5
Darfoulds Notts 77 B5
Dargate Kent 30 C4
Darite Cornw'l 5 C7
Darlaston W Midlands 62 E3
Darley N Yorks 94 D5
Darley Bridge Derby 76 C2
Darley Head N Yorks 94 D4
Darlingscott Warwick 51 E7
Darlington D'lington 101 C7
Darliston Shrops 74 F2
Darlton Notts 77 B7
Darnall S Yorks 88 F4
Darnick Scot Borders 123 F8
Darowen Powys 58 D5
Darra Aberds 160 D4
Darracott Devon 20 F3
Darras Hall Northum 110 B4
Darrington W Yorks 89 B5
Darsham Suffolk 57 C8
Dartford Kent 29 B6
Dartford Crossing Kent 29 B6
Dartington Devon 7 C5
Dartington Cider Press Centre Devon 7 C5
Dartington Crystal Devon 9 C6
Dartmeet Devon 6 B4
Dartmouth Devon 7 D6
Darton S Yorks 88 D4
Darvel E Ayrs 121 F5
Darwell Hole E Sussex 18 D3
Darwen Blackb'n 86 B4
Datchet Windsor 27 B7
Datchworth Herts 41 C5
Datchworth Green Herts 41 C5
Daubhill Gtr Man 86 D5
Daugh of Kinermony Moray 159 E6
Dauntsey Wilts 37 F6
Dava Moray 158 F4
Davenham Ches 74 B3
Davenport Green Ches 74 B5
Daventry Northants 52 C3
David's Well Powys 48 B2
Davidson's Mains C/Edinb 122 B5
Davidstow Cornw'l 8 F3
Davington Dumf/Gal 115 D5
Daviot Aberds 151 B6
Daviot H'land 157 F8
Davoch of Grange Moray 159 D8
Davyhulme Gtr Man 87 E5
Dawley Telford 61 D6
Dawlish Devon 7 B7
Dawlish Warren Devon 7 B7
Dawn Conwy 83 D8
Daws Heath Essex 42 F4
Daw's House Cornw'l 8 F5
Dawsmere Lincs 79 F7
Dayhills Staffs 75 F6
Daylesford Glos 38 B2
Ddôl-Cownwy Powys 59 C7
Ddrydwy Angl 82 D3
Deadwater Northum 116 E2
Deaf Hill Durham 111 F6
Deal Kent 31 D7
Deal Hall Essex 43 E6
Dean Cumb 98 B2
Dean Devon 6 C5
Dean Devon 20 E4
Dean Dorset 13 C7
Dean Hants 15 C6
Dean Som'set 23 E8
Dean Prior Devon 6 C5
Dean Row Ches 87 F6
Deanburnhaugh Scot Borders 115 C6
Deane Gtr Man 86 D4
Deane Hants 26 D3
Deanich Lodge H'land 163 F7
Deanland Dorset 13 C7
Deans W Loth 122 C3
Deanscales Cumb 98 B2
Deanshanger Northants 53 F5
Deanston Stirl 133 D6
Dearham Cumb 107 F7
Debach Suffolk 57 D6
Debden Essex 55 F6
Debden Essex 41 E7
Debden Cross Essex 55 F6
Debenham Suffolk 57 C5
Dechmont W Loth 122 B3
Deddington Oxon 52 F2
Dedham Essex 56 F4
Dedham Heath Essex 56 F4
Deebank Aberds 151 E5
Deene Northants 65 E6
Deenethorpe Northants 65 E6
Deep Sea World, North Queensferry Fife 134 F3
Deepcar S Yorks 88 E3
Deepcut Surrey 27 D7
Deepdale Cumb 100 F2
Deeping Gate Lincs 65 D8
Deeping St James Lincs 65 D8
Deeping St Nicholas Lincs 66 C2
Deerhill Moray 159 D8
Deerhurst Glos 37 B5
Deerness Orkney 176 F4
Defford Worcs 50 E4
Defynnog Powys 34 B3
Deganwy Conwy 83 D7
Deighton N Yorks 102 D1
Deighton W Yorks 88 C2
Deighton C/York 96 E2
Deiniolen Gwyn 83 E5
Delabole Cornw'l 8 F2
Delamere Ches 74 C2
Delfrigs Aberds 151 B8
Dell Lodge H'land 149 C6
Delliefure H'land 158 F4
Delnabo Moray 149 C7
Delnadamph Aberds 149 D8
Delph Gtr Man 87 D7
Delves Durham 110 E4
Delvine Perth/Kinr 141 E8
Dembleby Lincs 78 F3
Denaby Main S Yorks 89 E5
Denbigh = Dinbych Denbs 72 C4
Denbury Devon 7 C6
Denby Derby 76 E3
Denby Dale W Yorks 88 D3
Denchworth Oxon 38 E3
Dendron Cumb 92 B2
Denel End Beds 53 F8
Denend Aberds 160 E3
Denford Northants 53 B7
Dengie Essex 43 D5
Denham Bucks 40 F3
Denham Suffolk 55 C8
Denham Suffolk 57 B5
Denham Green Bucks 40 F3
Denham Street Suffolk 57 B5
Denhead Aberds 161 C6
Denhead Fife 135 C6
Denhead of Arbilot Angus 143 E5
Denhead of Gray Dundee C 142 F3
Denholm Scot Borders 115 C8
Denholme W Yorks 94 F3
Denholme Clough W Yorks 94 F3
Denio Gwyn 70 D4
Denmead Hants 15 C7
Denmore Aberd C 151 C8
Denmoss Aberds 160 D3
Dennington Suffolk 57 C6
Denny Falk 133 F7
Denny Lodge Hants 14 D4
Dennyloanhead Falk 133 F7
Denshaw Gtr Man 87 C7
Denside Aberds 151 E7
Densole Kent 31 E6
Denston Suffolk 55 D8
Denstone Staffs 75 E8
Dent Cumb 100 F2
Denton Cambs 65 F8
Denton D'lington 101 C7
Denton E Sussex 17 D8
Denton Gtr Man 87 E7
Denton Kent 31 E6
Denton Lincs 77 F8
Denton Norfolk 69 F5
Denton Northants 53 D6
Denton N Yorks 94 E4
Denton Oxon 39 D5
Denton's Green Mersey 86 E2
Denver Norfolk 67 D6
Denwick Northum 117 C8
Deopham Norfolk 68 D3
Deopham Green Norfolk 68 E3
Depden Suffolk 55 D8
Depden Green Suffolk 55 D8
Deptford London 28 B4
Deptford Wilts 24 F5
Derby Derby C 76 F3
Derbyhaven I/Man 84 F2
Dereham Norfolk 68 C2
Deri Caerph 35 D5
Derril Devon 8 D5
Derringstone Kent 31 E6
Derrington Staffs 62 B2
Derriton Devon 8 D5
Derry Hill Wilts 24 B4
Derryguaig Arg/Bute 137 E5
Derrythorpe N Lincs 90 D2
Dersingham Norfolk 80 D2
Dervaig Arg/Bute 137 C5
Derwen Denbs 72 D4
Derwenlas Powys 58 E4
Desborough Northants 64 F5
Desford Leics 63 D8
Detchant Northum 125 F6
Detling Kent 29 D8
Deuddwr Powys 60 C2
Devauden Monmouths 36 E1
Devil's Bridge Ceredig'n 47 B6
Devizes Wilts 24 C5
Devol Invercl 120 B3
Devon & Exeter Racecourse Devon 10 F4
Devonport Plym'th 6 D2
Devonside Clack 133 E8
Devoran Cornw'l 3 C6
Dewar Scot Borders 123 E6
Dewlish Dorset 13 E5
Dewsbury W Yorks 88 B3
Dewsbury Moor W Yorks 88 B3
Dewshall Court Heref'd 49 F6
Dhoon I/Man 84 D4
Dhoor I/Man 84 C4
Dhowin I/Man 84 B4
Dial Post W Sussex 17 C5
Dibden Hants 14 D5
Dibden Purlieu Hants 14 D5
Dickleburgh Norfolk 68 F4
Didbrook Glos 51 F5
Didcot Oxon 39 F5
Diddington Cambs 54 C2
Diddlebury Shrops 60 F5
Didley Heref'd 49 F6
Didling W Sussex 16 C2
Didmarton Glos 37 F5
Didsbury Gtr Man 87 E6
Didworthy Devon 6 C4
Digby Lincs 78 D3
Digg H'land 152 C5
Diggerland, Cullompton Devon 10 D5
Diggerland, Langley Park Durham 110 E5
Diggle Gtr Man 87 D8
Digmoor Lancs 86 D2
Digswell Park Herts 41 C5
Dihewid Ceredig'n 46 D3
Dilham Norfolk 69 B6
Dilhorne Staffs 75 E6
Dillarburn S Lanarks 121 E8
Dillington Cambs 54 C2
Dilston Northum 110 C2
Dilton Marsh Wilts 24 E3
Dilwyn Heref'd 49 D6
Dinas Carms 45 F4
Dinas Gwyn 70 D3
Dinas Cross Pembs 45 F2
Dinas Dinlle Gwyn 82 F4
Dinas-Mawddwy Gwyn 59 C5
Dinas Powys V/Glam 22 B3
Dinbych = Denbigh Denbs 72 C4
Dinbych-y-Pysgod = Tenby Pembs 32 D2
Dinder Som'set 23 E7
Dinedor Heref'd 49 F7
Dingestow Monmouths 36 C1
Dingle Mersey 85 F4
Dingleden Kent 18 B5
Dingley Northants 64 F4
Dingwall H'land 157 D6
Dinlabyre Scot Borders 115 E8
Dinmael Conwy 72 E4
Dinnet Aberds 150 E3
Dinnington Som'set 12 C2
Dinnington S Yorks 89 F6
Dinnington Tyne/Wear 110 B5
Dinorwic Gwyn 83 E5
Dinton Bucks 39 C7
Dinton Wilts 24 F5
Dinwoodie Mains Dumf/Gal 114 E4
Dinworthy Devon 8 C5
Dippen N Ayrs 119 D7
Dippenhall Surrey 27 E6
Dipple Moray 159 D7
Dipple S Ayrs 112 D2
Diptford Devon 6 D5
Dipton Durham 110 D4
Dirdhu H'land 149 B6
Dirleton E Loth 135 F7
Dirt Pot Northum 109 E8
Discoed Powys 48 C4
Discovery Point Dundee C 135 B6
Diseworth Leics 63 B8
Dishes Orkney 176 D5
Dishforth N Yorks 95 B6
Disley Ches 87 F7
Diss Norfolk 56 B5
Disserth Powys 48 D2
Distington Cumb 98 B2
Ditchampton Wilts 25 F5
Ditcheat Som'set 23 F8
Ditchingham Norfolk 69 E6
Ditchling E Sussex 17 C7
Ditherington Shrops 60 C5
Dittisham Devon 7 D6
Ditton Halton 86 F2
Ditton Kent 29 D8
Ditton Green Cambs 55 D7
Ditton Priors Shrops 61 F6
Divach H'land 147 B7
Divlyn Carms 47 F6
Dixton Glos 50 F4
Dixton Monmouths 36 C2
Dobcross Gtr Man 87 D7
Dobwalls Cornw'l 5 C7
Doc Penfro = Pembroke Dock Pembs 44 E4
Doccombe Devon 10 F2
Dochfour Ho. H'land 157 F7
Dochgarroch H'land 157 E7
Docking Norfolk 80 D3
Docklow Heref'd 49 D7
Dockray Cumb 99 B5
Dockroyd W Yorks 94 F3
Dodburn Scot Borders 115 D7
Doddinghurst Essex 42 E1
Doddington Cambs 66 E3
Doddington Kent 30 D3
Doddington Lincs 78 B2
Doddington Northum 125 F5
Doddington Shrops 49 B8
Doddiscombsleigh Devon 10 F3
Dodford Northants 52 C4
Dodford Worcs 50 B4
Dodington S Gloucs 24 A2
Dodleston Ches 73 C7
Dods Leigh Staffs 75 F7
Dodworth S Yorks 88 D4
Doe Green Warrington 86 F3
Doe Lea Derby 76 C4
Dog Village Devon 10 E4
Dogdyke Lincs 78 D5
Dogmersfield Hants 27 D5
Dogridge Wilts 37 F7
Dogsthorpe Peterbro 65 D8
Dol-for Powys 58 D5
Dol-y-Bont Ceredig'n 58 F3
Dol-y-cannau Powys 48 E4
Dolanog Powys 59 C7
Dolau Powys 48 C3
Dolau Rh Cyn Taff 34 F3
Dolbenmaen Gwyn 71 C6
Dolfach Powys 59 D6
Dolfor Powys 59 F8
Dolgarrog Conwy 83 E7
Dolgellau Gwyn 58 C4
Dolgran Carms 46 F3
Dolhendre Gwyn 72 F2
Doll H'land 165 D5
Dollar Clack 133 E8
Dolley Green Powys 48 C4
Dollwen Ceredig'n 58 F3
Dolphin Flints 73 B5
Dolphinholme Lancs 92 D5
Dolphinton S Lanarks 122 E4
Dolton Devon 9 C7
Dolwen Conwy 83 D8
Dolwen Powys 59 D6
Dolwyd Conwy 83 D8
Dolwyddelan Conwy 83 F7
Dolyhir Powys 48 D4
Doncaster S Yorks 89 D6
Doncaster Racecourse S Yorks 89 D7
Dones Green Ches 74 B3
Donhead St Andrew Wilts 13 B7
Donhead St Mary Wilts 13 B7
Donibristle Fife 134 F3
Donington Lincs 78 F5
Donington on Bain Lincs 91 F6
Donington South Ing Lincs 78 F5
Donisthorpe Leics 63 C7
Donkey Town Surrey 27 C7
Donnington Glos 38 B1
Donnington Heref'd 50 F2
Donnington Shrops 61 D5
Donnington Telford 61 C7
Donnington W Berks 26 C2
Donnington W Sussex 16 D2
Donnington Wood Telford 61 C7
Donyatt Som'set 11 C8
Doonfoot S Ayrs 112 C3
Dorback Lodge H'land 149 C6
Dorchester Dorset 12 E4
Dorchester Oxon 39 E5
Dorchester Abbey, Wallingford Oxon 39 E5
Dordon Warwick 63 D6
Dore S Yorks 88 F4
Dores H'land 157 F6
Dorking Surrey 28 E2
Dormansland Surrey 28 E5
Dormanstown Redcar/Clevel'd 102 B3
Dormington Heref'd 49 E7
Dormston Worcs 50 D4
Dornal S Ayrs 105 B6
Dorney Bucks 27 B7
Dornie H'land 155 H4
Dornoch H'land 164 F4
Dornock Dumf/Gal 108 C2
Dorrery H'land 169 D5
Dorridge W Midlands 51 B6
Dorrington Lincs 78 D3
Dorrington Shrops 60 D4
Dorsington Warwick 51 E6
Dorstone Heref'd 48 E5
Dorton Bucks 39 C6
Dorusduain H'land 146 B2
Dosthill Staffs 63 E6
Dottery Dorset 12 E2
Doublebois Cornw'l 5 C6
Dougarie N Ayrs 119 C5
Doughton Glos 37 E5
Douglas I/Man 84 E3
Douglas S Lanarks 121 F8
Douglas & Angus Dundee C 142 F4
Douglas Water S Lanarks 121 F8
Douglas West S Lanarks 121 F8
Douglastown Angus 142 E4
Doulting Som'set 23 E8
Dounby Orkney 176 D1
Doune H'land 163 D8
Doune Stirl 133 D6
Doune Park Aberds 160 B4
Douneside Aberds 150 D3
Dounie H'land 164 E2
Dounreay H'land 168 C4
Dousland Devon 6 C3
Dovaston Shrops 60 B3
Dove Cottage and Wordsworth Museum Cumb 99 D5
Dove Holes Derby 75 B7
Dovenby Cumb 107 F7
Dover Kent 31 E7
Dover Castle Kent 31 E7
Dovercourt Essex 57 F6
Doverdale Worcs 50 C3
Doveridge Derby 75 F8
Doversgreen Surrey 28 E3
Dowally Perth/Kinr 141 E7
Dowbridge Lancs 92 F4
Dowdeswell Glos 37 C6
Dowlais Merth Tyd 34 D4
Dowland Devon 9 C7
Dowlish Wake Som'set 11 C8
Down Ampney Glos 37 E8
Down Hatherley Glos 37 B5
Down St Mary Devon 10 D2
Down Thomas Devon 6 D3
Downcraig Ferry N Ayrs 129 E6
Downderry Cornw'l 5 D8
Downe London 28 C5
Downend I/Wight 15 F6
Downend S Gloucs 23 B8
Downend W Berks 26 B2
Downfield Dundee C 142 F3
Downgate Cornw'l 5 B8
Downham Essex 42 E3
Downham Lancs 93 E7
Downham Northum 124 F4
Downham Market Norfolk 67 D6
Downhead Som'set 23 E8
Downhill Perth/Kinr 141 F7
Downhill Tyne/Wear 111 D6
Downholland Cross Lancs 85 D4
Downholme N Yorks 101 E6
Downies Aberds 151 E8
Downley Bucks 39 E8
Downside Som'set 23 E8
Downside Surrey 28 D2
Downton Hants 14 E3
Downton Wilts 14 B2
Downton on the Rock Heref'd 49 B6
Dowsby Lincs 65 B8
Dowsdale Lincs 66 C2
Dowthwaitehead Cumb 99 B5
Doxey Staffs 62 B3
Doxford Northum 117 B7
Doxford Park Tyne/Wear 111 D6
Doynton S Gloucs 24 B2
Draffan S Lanarks 121 E7
Dragonby N Lincs 90 C3
Drakeland Corner Devon 6 D3
Drakemyre N Ayrs 120 D2
Drake's Broughton Worcs 50 E4
Drakes Cross Worcs 51 B5
Drakewalls Cornw'l 6 B2
Draughton Northants 53 B5
Draughton N Yorks 94 D3
Drax N Yorks 89 B7
Draycote Warwick 52 B2
Draycott Derby 76 F4
Draycott Glos 51 F6
Draycott Som'set 23 D6
Draycott in the Clay Staffs 63 B5
Draycott in the Moors Staffs 75 E6
Drayford Devon 10 C2
Drayton Leics 64 E5
Drayton Lincs 78 F5
Drayton Norfolk 68 C4
Drayton Oxon 52 E2
Drayton Oxon 38 E4
Drayton Portsm'th 15 D7
Drayton Som'set 12 B2
Drayton Worcs 50 B4
Drayton Bassett Staffs 63 D5
Drayton Beauchamp Bucks 40 C2
Drayton Manor Park, Tamworth Staffs 63 D5
Drayton Parslow Bucks 39 B8
Drayton St Leonard Oxon 39 E5
Dre-fach Ceredig'n 46 E4
Dre-fach Carms 33 C7
Dreamland Theme Park, Margate Kent 31 B7
Drebley N Yorks 94 D3
Dreemskerry I/Man 84 C4
Dreenhill Pembs 44 D4
Drefach Carms 46 F2
Drefach Carms 33 C6
Drefelin Carms 46 F2
Dreghorn N Ayrs 120 F3
Drellingore Kent 31 E6
Drem E Loth 123 B8
Dresden Stoke 75 E6
Dreumasdal W Isles 170 G3
Drewsteignton Devon 10 E2
Driby Lincs 79 B6
Driffield ER Yorks 97 D6
Driffield Glos 37 E7
Drigg Cumb 98 E2
Drighlington W Yorks 88 B3
Drimnin H'land 137 C6
Drimpton Dorset 12 D2
Drimsynie Arg/Bute 131 E7
Drinisiadar W Isles 173 J4
Drinkstone Suffolk 56 C3
Drinkstone Green Suffolk 56 C3
Drishaig Arg/Bute 131 D7
Drissaig Arg/Bute 130 D5
Drochil Scot Borders 122 E4
Drointon Staffs 62 B4
Droitwich Spa Worcs 50 C3
Droman H'land 166 D3
Dron Perth/Kinr 134 C3
Dronfield Derby 76 B3
Dronfield Woodhouse Derby 76 B3
Drongan E Ayrs 112 C4
Dronley Angus 142 F3
Droxford Hants 15 C7
Droylsden Gtr Man 87 E7
Druid Denbs 72 E4
Druidston Pembs 44 D3
Druimarbin H'land 138 B4
Druimavuic Arg/Bute 138 E4
Druimdrishaig Arg/Bute 128 C2
Druimindarroch H'land 145 E6
Druimyeon More Arg/Bute 118 A3
Drum Arg/Bute 128 C4
Drum Perth/Kinr 134 D2
Drumbeg H'land 166 F3
Drumblade Aberds 160 D2
Drumblair Aberds 160 D3
Drumbuie Dumf/Gal 113 F5
Drumbuie H'land 155 G3
Drumburgh Cumb 108 D2
Drumburn Dumf/Gal 107 C6
Drumchapel Glasg C 120 B5
Drumchardine H'land 157 E6
Drumchork H'land 162 F2
Drumclog S Lanarks 121 F6
Drumderfit H'land 157 D7
Drumeldrie Fife 135 D6
Drumelzier Scot Borders 122 F4
Drumfearn H'land 145 B6
Drumgask H'land 148 E2
Drumgley Angus 142 D4
Drumguish H'land 148 E3
Drumin Moray 159 F5
Drumlasie Aberds 150 D5
Drumlemble Arg/Bute 118 E3
Drumligair Aberds 151 C8
Drumlithie Aberds 151 F6
Drummoddie Dumf/Gal 105 E7
Drummond H'land 157 C7
Drummore Dumf/Gal 104 F5
Drummuir Moray 159 E7
Drummuir Castle Moray 159 E7
Drumnadrochit H'land 147 B8
Drumnagorrach Moray 160 C2
Drumoak Aberds 151 E6
Drumpark Dumf/Gal 107 A5
Drumphail Dumf/Gal 105 C6
Drumrash Dumf/Gal 106 B3
Drumrunie H'land 163 D5
Drums Aberds 151 B8
Drumsallie H'land 138 B3
Drumstinchall Dumf/Gal 107 D5
Drumsturdy Angus 142 F4
Drumtochty Castle Aberds 143 B6
Drumtroddan Dumf/Gal 105 E7
Drumuie H'land 152 E5
Drumuillie H'land 148 B5
Drumvaich Stirl 133 D5
Drumwhindle Aberds 161 E6
Drunkendub Angus 143 E6
Drury Flints 73 C6
Drury Square Norfolk 68 C2
Drusillas Park, Polegate E Sussex 18 E2
Dry Doddington Lincs 77 E8
Dry Drayton Cambs 54 C4
Drybeck Cumb 100 C1
Drybridge Moray 159 C8
Drybridge N Ayrs 120 F3
Drybrook Glos 36 C3
Dryburgh Scot Borders 123 F8
Dryhope Scot Borders 115 B5
Drylaw C/Edinb 122 B5
Drym Cornw'l 2 C5
Drymen Stirl 132 F3
Drymuir Aberds 161 D6
Drynoch H'land 153 F5
Dryslwyn Carms 33 B6
Dryton Shrops 61 D5
Dubford Aberds 160 B5
Dubton Angus 143 D5
Duchally H'land 163 C7
Duchlage Arg/Bute 129 B8
Duck Corner Suffolk 57 E7
Duckington Ches 73 D8
Ducklington Oxon 38 D3
Duckmanton Derby 76 B4
Duck's Cross Beds 54 D2
Duddenhoe End Essex 55 F5
Duddingston C/Edinb 123 B5
Duddington Northants 65 D6
Duddleswell E Sussex 17 B8
Duddo Northum 124 E5
Duddon Ches 74 C2
Duddon Bridge Cumb 98 F4
Dudleston Shrops 73 F7
Dudleston Heath Shrops 73 F7
Dudley Tyne/Wear 111 B5
Dudley W Midlands 62 E3
Dudley Port W Midlands 62 E3
Dudley Zoological Gardens W Midlands 62 E3
Duffield Derby 76 E3
Duffryn Newp 35 F6
Duffryn Neath P Talb 34 E2
Dufftown Moray 159 F7
Duffus Moray 159 C5
Dufton Cumb 100 B1
Duggleby N Yorks 96 C4
Duirinish H'land 155 G3
Duisdalemore H'land 145 B7
Duisky H'land 138 B4
Dukestown Bl Gwent 35 C5
Dukinfield Gtr Man 87 E7
Dulas Angl 82 C4
Dulcote Som'set 23 E7
Dulford Devon 11 D5
Dull Perth/Kinr 141 E5
Dullatur N Lanarks 121 B7
Dullingham Cambs 55 D7
Dulnain Bridge H'land 149 B5
Duloe Beds 54 C2
Duloe Cornw'l 5 D7
Dulsie H'land 158 E3
Dulverton Som'set 10 B4
Dulwich London 28 B4
Dumbarton W Dunb 120 B3
Dumbleton Glos 50 F5
Dumcrieff Dumf/Gal 114 D4
Dumfries Dumf/Gal 107 B6
Dumgoyne Stirl 132 F4
Dummer Hants 26 E3
Dumpford W Sussex 16 B2
Dumpton Kent 31 C7
Dun Angus 143 D6
Dun Charlabhaigh W Isles 172 D4
Dunain Ho. H'land 157 E7
Dunalastair Perth/Kinr 140 D4
Dunan H'land 153 G6
Dunans Arg/Bute 129 A5
Dunball Som'set 22 E5
Dunbar E Loth 124 B2
Dunbeath H'land 165 B8
Dunbeg Arg/Bute 130 B4
Dunblane Stirl 133 D7
Dunbog Fife 134 C4
Duncanston Aberds 150 B4
Duncanston H'land 157 D6
Dunchurch Warwick 52 B2
Duncote Northants 52 D4
Duncow Dumf/Gal 114 F2
Duncraggan Stirl 132 D4
Duncrievie Perth/Kinr 134 D3
Duncton W Sussex 16 C3
Dundas Ho. Orkney 176 H3
Dundee Dundee C 142 F4
Dundeugh Dumf/Gal 113 F5
Dundon Som'set 23 F6
Dundonald S Ayrs 120 F3
Dundonnell H'land 162 F4
Dundonnell Hotel H'land 162 F4
Dundonnell House H'land 163 F5
Dundraw Cumb 108 E2
Dundreggan H'land 147 C6
Dundreggan Lodge H'land 147 C6
Dundrennan Dumf/Gal 106 E4
Dundry N Som'set 23 C7
Dunecht Aberds 151 D6
Dunfermline Fife 134 F2
Dunfield Glos 37 E8
Dunford Bridge S Yorks 88 D2
Dungworth S Yorks 88 F3
Dunham Notts 77 B8
Dunham Massey Gtr Man 86 F5
Dunham-on-the-Hill Ches 73 B8
Dunham Town Gtr Man 86 F5
Dunhampton Worcs 50 C3
Dunholme Lincs 78 B3
Dunino Fife 135 C7
Dunipace Falk 133 F7
Dunira Perth/Kinr 133 B6
Dunkeld Perth/Kinr 141 E7
Dunkerton Bath/NE Som'set 24 D2
Dunkeswell Devon 11 D6
Dunkeswick N Yorks 95 E6
Dunkirk Kent 30 D4
Dunkirk Norfolk 81 E8
Dunk's Green Kent 29 D7
Dunlappie Angus 143 C5
Dunley Hants 26 D2
Dunley Worcs 50 C2
Dunlichity Lodge H'land 157 F7
Dunlop E Ayrs 120 E4
Dunmaglass Lodge H'land 147 B8
Dunmore Arg/Bute 128 D2
Dunmore Falk 133 F8
Dunnet H'land 169 B7
Dunnichen Angus 143 E5
Dunninald Angus 143 D7
Dunning Perth/Kinr 134 C2
Dunnington ER Yorks 97 D7
Dunnington Warwick 51 D5
Dunnington C/York 96 D2
Dunnockshaw Lancs 87 B6
Dunollie Arg/Bute 130 B4
Dunoon Arg/Bute 129 C6
Dunragit Dumf/Gal 105 D5
Dunrobin Castle Museum & Gardens H'land 165 D5
Dunrostan Arg/Bute 128 B2
Duns Scot Borders 124 D3
Duns Tew Oxon 38 B4
Dunsby Lincs 65 B8
Dunscore Dumf/Gal 113 F8
Dunscroft S Yorks 89 D7
Dunsdale Redcar/Clevel'd 102 C4
Dunsden Green Oxon 26 B5
Dunsfold Surrey 27 F8
Dunsford Devon 10 F3
Dunshalt Fife 134 C4
Dunshillock Aberds 161 D6
Dunskey Ho. Dumf/Gal 104 D4
Dunsley N Yorks 103 C6
Dunsmore Bucks 40 D1
Dunsop Bridge Lancs 93 D6
Dunstable Beds 40 B3
Dunstall Staffs 63 B5
Dunstall Common Worcs 50 E3
Dunstall Green Suffolk 55 C8
Dunstan Northum 117 C8
Dunstan Steads Northum 117 B8
Dunster Som'set 21 E8
Dunster Castle, Minehead Som'set 21 E8
Dunston Lincs 78 C3
Dunston Norfolk 68 D5
Dunston Staffs 62 C3
Dunston Tyne/Wear 110 C5
Dunsville S Yorks 89 D7
Dunswell ER Yorks 97 F6
Dunsyre S Lanarks 122 E3
Dunterton Devon 5 B8
Duntisbourne Abbots Glos 37 D6
Duntisbourne Leer Glos 37 D6
Duntisbourne Rouse Glos 37 D6
Duntish Dorset 12 D4
Duntocher W Dunb 120 B4
Dunton Beds 54 E3
Dunton Bucks 39 B8
Dunton Norfolk 80 D4
Dunton Bassett Leics 64 E2
Dunton Green Kent 29 D6
Dunton Wayletts Essex 42 E2
Duntulm H'land 152 B5
Dunure S Ayrs 112 C2
Dunvant Swan 33 E6
Dunvegan H'land 152 E3
Dunvegan Castle H'land 152 E3
Dunwich Suffolk 57 B8
Dunwood Staffs 75 D6
Dupplin Castle Perth/Kinr 134 C2
Durdar Cumb 108 D4
Durgates E Sussex 18 B3
Durham Durham 111 E5

Durham Cathedral Durham 111 E5
Durisdeer Dumf/Gal 113 D8
Durisdeermill Dumf/Gal 113 D8
Durkar W Yorks 88 C4
Durleigh Som'set 22 F4
Durley Hants 15 C6
Durley Wilts 25 C7
Durnamuck H'land 162 E4
Durness H'land 167 C6
Durno Aberds 151 B6
Duror H'land 138 D3
Durran Arg/Bute 131 E5
Durran H'land 169 C6
Durrington Wilts 25 E6
Durrington W Sussex 16 D5
Dursley Glos 36 E4
Durston Som'set 11 B7
Durweston Dorset 13 D6
Dury Shetl'd 175 G6
Duston Northants 52 C5
Duthil H'land 148 B5
Dutlas Powys 48 B4
Duton Hill Essex 42 B2
Dutson Cornw'l 8 F5
Dutton Ches 74 B2
Duxford Cambs 55 E5
Duxford Oxon 38 E3
Duxford Airfield (Imperial War Museum), Sawston Cambs 55 E5
Dwygyfylchi Conwy 83 D7
Dwyran Angl 82 E4
Dyce Aberd C 151 C7
Dye House Northum 110 D2
Dyffryn Bridg 34 E2
Dyffryn Carms 32 B4
Dyffryn Pembs 44 B4
Dyffryn Ardudwy Gwyn 71 E6
Dyffryn Castell Ceredig'n 58 F4
Dyffryn Ceidrych Carms 33 B8
Dyffryn Cellwen Neath P Talb 34 D2
Dyke Lincs 65 B8
Dyke Moray 158 D3
Dykehead Angus 142 C3
Dykehead N Lanarks 121 D8
Dykehead Stirl 132 E4
Dykelands Aberds 143 C7
Dykends Angus 142 D2
Dykeside Aberds 160 D4
Dykesmains N Ayrs 120 E2
Dylife Powys 59 E5
Dymchurch Kent 19 C7
Dymock Glos 50 F2
Dyrham S Gloucs 24 B2
Dyrham Park S Gloucs 24 B2
Dysart Fife 134 E5
Dyserth Denbs 72 B4

E

Eachwick Northum 110 B4
Eadar Dha Fhadhail W Isles 172 E3
Eagland Hill Lancs 92 E4
Eagle Lincs 77 C8
Eagle Barnsdale Lincs 77 C8
Eagle Moor Lincs 77 C8
Eaglescliffe Stockton 102 C2
Eaglesfield Cumb 98 B2
Eaglesfield Dumf/Gal 108 B2
Eaglesham E Renf 121 D5
Eaglethorpe Northants 65 E7
Eairy I/Man 84 E2
Eakley Lanes M/Keynes 53 D6
Eakring Notts 77 C6
Ealand N Lincs 89 C8
Ealing London 40 F4
Eals Northum 109 D6
Eamont Bridge Cumb 99 B7
Earby Lancs 94 E2
Earcroft Blackb'n 86 B4
Eardington Shrops 61 E7
Eardisland Heref'd 49 D6
Eardisley Heref'd 48 E5
Eardiston Shrops 60 B3
Eardiston Worcs 49 C8
Earith Cambs 54 B4
Earl Shilton Leics 63 E8
Earl Soham Suffolk 57 C6
Earl Sterndale Derby 75 C7
Earl Stonham Suffolk 56 D5
Earle Northum 117 B5
Earley Wokingham 27 B5
Earlham Norfolk 68 D5
Earlish H'land 152 C4
Earls Barton Northants 53 C6
Earls Colne Essex 42 B4
Earl's Croome Worcs 50 E3
Earl's Green Suffolk 56 C4
Earlsdon W Midlands 51 B8
Earlsferry Fife 135 E6
Earlsfield Lincs 78 F2
Earlsford Aberds 160 E5
Earlsheaton W Yorks 88 B3
Earlsmill Moray 158 D3
Earlston Scot Borders 123 F8
Earlston E Ayrs 120 F4
Earlswood Monmouths 36 E1
Earlswood Surrey 28 E3
Earlswood Warwick 51 B6
Earnley W Sussex 16 E2
Earsairidh W Isles 171 L3
Earsdon Tyne/Wear 111 B6
Earsham Norfolk 69 F6
Earswick C/York 96 D2
Eartham W Sussex 16 D3
Easby N Yorks 102 D3
Easby N Yorks 101 D6
Easdale Arg/Bute 130 D3
Easebourne W Sussex 16 B2
Easenhall Warwick 52 B2
Eashing Surrey 27 E7
Easington Bucks 39 C6
Easington Durham 111 E7
Easington ER Yorks 91 C7
Easington Northum 125 F7
Easington Oxon 52 F2
Easington Oxon 39 E6
Easington Redcar/Clevel'd 103 C5
Easington Colliery Durham 111 E7
Easington Lane Tyne/Wear 111 E6
Easingwold N Yorks 95 C8
Easole Street Kent 31 D6
Eassie Angus 142 E3
East Aberthaw V/Glam 22 C2
East Adderbury Oxon 52 F2
East Allington Devon 7 E5
East Anstey Devon 10 B3
East Appleton N Yorks 101 E7
East Ardsley W Yorks 88 B4
East Ashling W Sussex 16 D2
East Auchronie Aberds 151 D7
East Ayton N Yorks 103 F7
East Bank Bl Gwent 35 D6
East Barkwith Lincs 91 F5
East Barming Kent 29 D8
East Barnby N Yorks 103 C6
East Barnet London 41 E5
East Barns E Loth 124 B3
East Barsham Norfolk 80 D5
East Beckham Norfolk 81 D7
East Bedfont London 27 B8
East Bergholt Suffolk 56 F4
East Bilney Norfolk 68 C2
East Blatchington E Sussex 17 D8
East Boldre Hants 14 D4
East Brent Som'set 22 D5
East Bridgford Notts 77 E6
East Buckland Devon 21 F5
East Budleigh Devon 11 F5
East Burrafirth Shetl'd 175 H5
East Burton Dorset 13 F6
East Butsfield Durham 110 E4
East Butterwick N Lincs 90 D2
East Cairnbeg Aberds 143 B7
East Calder W Loth 122 C3
East Carleton Norfolk 68 D4
East Carlton Northants 64 F5
East Carlton W Yorks 94 E5
East Chaldon Dorset 13 F5
East Challow Oxon 38 F3
East Chiltington E Sussex 17 C7
East Chinnock Som'set 12 C2
East Chisenbury Wilts 25 D6
East Clandon Surrey 27 D8
East Claydon Bucks 39 B7
East Clyne H'land 165 D6
East Coker Som'set 12 C3
East Combe Som'set 22 F3
East Common N Yorks 96 F2
East Compton Som'set 23 E8
East Cottingwith ER Yorks 96 E3
East Cowes I/Wight 15 E6
East Cowick ER Yorks 89 B7
East Cowton N Yorks 101 D8
East Cramlington Northum 111 B5
East Cranmore Som'set 23 E8
East Creech Dorset 13 F7
East Croachy H'land 148 B2
East Croftmore H'land 149 C5
East Curthwaite Cumb 108 E3
East Dean E Sussex 18 F2
East Dean Hants 14 B3
East Dean W Sussex 16 C3
East Down Devon 20 E5
East Drayton Notts 77 B7
East Ella Kingston/Hull 90 B4
East End Dorset 13 E7
East End ER Yorks 91 B6
East End Hants 14 E4
East End Hants 15 B7
East End Hants 26 C2
East End Herts 41 B7
East End Kent 18 B5
East End N Som'set 23 B6
East End Oxon 38 C3
East Farleigh Kent 29 D8
East Farndon Northants 64 F4
East Ferry Lincs 90 E2
East Fortune E Loth 123 B8
East Garston W Berks 25 B8
East Ginge Oxon 38 F4
East Goscote Leics 64 C3
East Grafton Wilts 25 C7
East Grimstead Wilts 14 B3
East Grinstead W Sussex 28 F4
East Guldeford E Sussex 19 C6
East Haddon Northants 52 C4
East Hagbourne Oxon 39 F5
East Halton N Lincs 90 C5
East Ham London 41 F7
East Hanney Oxon 38 E4
East Hanningfield Essex 42 D3
East Hardwick W Yorks 89 C5
East Harling Norfolk 68 F2
East Harlsey N Yorks 102 E2
East Harnham Wilts 14 B2
East Harptree Bath/NE Som'set 23 D7
East Hartford Northum 111 B5
East Harting W Sussex 15 C8
East Hatley Cambs 54 D3
East Hauxwell N Yorks 101 E6
East Haven Angus 143 F5
East Heckington Lincs 78 E4
East Hedleyhope Durham 110 E4
East Hendred Oxon 38 F4
East Herrington Tyne/Wear 111 D6
East Heslerton N Yorks 96 B5
East Hoathly E Sussex 18 D2
East Horrington Som'set 23 E7
East Horsley Surrey 27 D8
East Horton Northum 125 F6
East Huntspill Som'set 22 E5
East Hyde Beds 40 C4
East Ilkerton Devon 21 E6
East Ilsley W Berks 38 F4
East Keal Lincs 79 C6
East Kennett Wilts 25 C6
East Keswick W Yorks 95 E6
East Kilbride S Lanarks 121 D6
East Kirkby Lincs 79 C6
East Knapton N Yorks 96 B4
East Knighton Dorset 13 F6
East Knoyle Wilts 24 F3
East Kyloe Northum 125 F6
East Lambrook Som'set 12 C2
East Lamington H'land 157 B8
East Langdon Kent 31 E7
East Langton Leics 64 E4
East Langwell H'land 164 D4
East Lavant W Sussex 16 D2
East Lavington W Sussex 16 C3
East Layton N Yorks 101 D6
East Leake Notts 64 B2
East Learmouth Northum 124 F4
East Leigh Devon 9 D8
East Lexham Norfolk 67 C8
East Lilburn Northum 117 B6
East Linton E Loth 123 B8
East Liss Hants 15 B8
East Looe Cornw'l 5 D7
East Lound N Lincs 89 E8
East Lulworth Dorset 13 F6
East Lutton N Yorks 96 C5
East Lydford Som'set 23 F7
East Mains Aberds 151 E5
East Malling Kent 29 D8
East March Angus 142 F4
East Marden W Sussex 16 C2
East Markham Notts 77 B7
East Marton N Yorks 94 D2
East Meon Hants 15 B7
East Mere Devon 10 C4
East Mersea Essex 43 C6
East Mey H'land 169 B8
East Molesey Surrey 28 C2
East Morden Dorset 13 E7
East Morton W Yorks 94 E3
East Ness N Yorks 96 B2
East Newton ER Yorks 97 F8
East Norton Leics 64 D4
East Nynehead Som'set 11 B6
East Oakley Hants 26 D3
East Ogwell Devon 7 B6
East Orchard Dorset 13 C6
East Ord Northum 125 D5
East Panson Devon 9 E5
East Peckham Kent 29 E7
East Pennard Som'set 23 F7
East Perry Cambs 54 C2
East Portlemouth Devon 6 F5
East Prawle Devon 7 F5
East Preston W Sussex 16 D4
East Putford Devon 9 C5
East Quantoxhead Som'set 22 E3
East Rainton Tyne/Wear 111 E6
East Ravendale NE Lincs 91 E6
East Raynham Norfolk 80 E4
East Rhidorroch Lodge H'land 163 E6
East Rigton W Yorks 95 E6
East Rounton N Yorks 102 D2
East Row N Yorks 103 C6
East Rudham Norfolk 80 E4
East Runton Norfolk 81 C7
East Ruston Norfolk 69 B6
East Saltoun E Loth 123 C7
East Sleekburn Northum 117 F8
East Somerton Norfolk 69 C7
East Stockwith Lincs 89 E8
East Stoke Dorset 13 F6
East Stoke Notts 77 E7
East Stour Dorset 13 B6
East Stourmouth Kent 31 C6
East Stowford Devon 9 B8
East Stratton Hants 26 F3
East Studdal Kent 31 E7
East Suisnish H'land 153 F6
East Taphouse Cornw'l 5 C6
East-the-Water Devon 9 B6
East Thirston Northum 117 E7
East Tilbury Thurr'k 29 B7
East Tisted Hants 26 F5
East Torrington Lincs 90 F5
East Tuddenham Norfolk 68 C3
East Tytherley Hants 14 B3
East Tytherton Wilts 24 B4
East Village Devon 10 D3
East Wall Shrops 60 E5
East Walton Norfolk 67 C7
East Wellow Hants 14 B4
East Wemyss Fife 134 E5
East Whitburn W Loth 122 C2
East Williamston Pembs 32 D1
East Winch Norfolk 67 C6
East Winterslow Wilts 25 F7
East Wittering W Sussex 15 E8
East Witton N Yorks 101 F6
East Woodburn Northum 116 F5
East Woodhay Hants 26 C2
East Worldham Hants 26 F5
East Worlington Devon 10 C2
East Worthing W Sussex 17 D5
Eastbourne E Sussex 18 F3
Eastbridge Suffolk 57 C8
Eastburn W Yorks 94 E3
Eastbury Herts 40 E3
Eastbury W Berks 25 B8
Eastby N Yorks 94 D3
Eastchurch Kent 30 B3
Eastcombe Glos 37 D5
Eastcote London 40 F4
Eastcote Northants 52 D4
Eastcote W Midlands 51 B6
Eastcott Cornw'l 8 C4
Eastcott Wilts 24 D5
Eastcourt Wilts 37 E6
Eastcourt Wilts 25 C7
Easter Ardross H'land 157 B7
Easter Balmoral Aberds 149 E8
Easter Boleskine H'land 147 B8
Easter Compton S Gloucs 36 F2
Easter Cringate Stirl 133 F6
Easter Davoch Aberds 150 D3
Easter Earshaig Dumf/Gal 114 D3
Easter Fearn H'land 164 F3
Easter Galcantray H'land 158 E2
Easter Howgate Midloth 122 C5
Easter Howlaws Scot Borders 124 E3
Easter Kinkell H'land 157 D6
Easter Lednathie Angus 142 C3
Easter Milton H'land 158 D3
Easter Moniack H'land 157 E6
Easter Ord Aberds 151 D7
Easter Quarff Shetl'd 175 K6
Easter Rhynd Perth/Kinr 134 C3
Easter Row Stirl 133 E6
Easter Silverford Aberds 160 B4
Easter Skeld Shetl'd 175 J5
Easter Whyntie Aberds 160 B3
Eastergate W Sussex 16 D3
Easterhouse Glasg C 121 C6
Eastern Green W Midlands 63 F6
Easterton Wilts 24 D5
Eastertown Som'set 22 D5
Eastertown of Auchleuchries Aberds 161 E7
Eastfield N Lanarks 121 C8
Eastfield N Yorks 103 F8
Eastfield Hall Northum 117 D8
Eastgate Durham 110 F2
Eastgate Norfolk 81 E7
Eastham Mersey 85 F4
Eastham Ferry Mersey 85 F4
Easthampstead Brackn'l 27 C6
Eastheath Wokingham 27 C6
Easthope Shrops 61 E5
Easthorpe Essex 43 B5
Easthorpe Leics 77 F8
Easthorpe Notts 77 D7
Easthouses Midloth 123 C6
Eastington Devon 10 D2
Eastington Glos 36 D4
Eastington Glos 37 C8
Eastleach Martin Glos 38 D2
Eastleach Turville Glos 38 D1
Eastleigh Devon 9 B6
Eastleigh Hants 14 C5
Eastling Kent 30 D3
Eastmoor Derby 76 B3
Eastmoor Norfolk 67 D7
Eastney Portsm'th 15 E7
Eastnor Heref'd 50 F2
Eastoft N Lincs 90 C2
Eastoke Hants 15 E8
Easton Cambs 54 B2
Easton Cumb 108 D2
Easton Cumb 108 B4
Easton Devon 10 F2
Easton Dorset 12 G4
Easton Hants 26 F3
Easton Lincs 65 B6
Easton Norfolk 68 C4
Easton Som'set 23 E7
Easton Suffolk 57 D6
Easton Wilts 24 B3
Easton Grey Wilts 37 F5
Easton-in-Gordano N Som'set 23 B7
Easton Maudit Northants 53 D6
Easton on the Hill Northants 65 D7
Easton Royal Wilts 25 C7
Eastpark Dumf/Gal 107 C7
Eastrea Cambs 66 E2
Eastriggs Dumf/Gal 108 C2
Eastrington ER Yorks 89 B8
Eastry Kent 31 D7
Eastville Bristol 23 B8
Eastville Lincs 79 D7
Eastwell Leics 64 B4
Eastwick Herts 41 C7
Eastwick Shetl'd 174 F5
Eastwood Notts 76 E4
Eastwood Southend 42 F4
Eastwood W Yorks 87 B7
Eathorpe Warwick 51 C8
Eaton Ches 74 C2
Eaton Ches 75 C5
Eaton Leics 64 B4
Eaton Norfolk 68 D5
Eaton Notts 77 B7
Eaton Oxon 38 D4
Eaton Shrops 60 F3
Eaton Shrops 60 F5
Eaton Bishop Heref'd 49 F6
Eaton Bray Beds 40 B2
Eaton Constantine Shrops 61 D5
Eaton Green Beds 40 B2
Eaton Hastings Oxon 38 E2
Eaton on Tern Shrops 61 B6
Eaton Socon Cambs 54 D2
Eavestone N Yorks 94 C5
Ebberston N Yorks 103 F6
Ebbesbourne Wake Wilts 13 B7
Ebbw Vale = Glyn Ebwy Bl Gwent 35 D5
Ebchester Durham 110 D4
Ebford Devon 10 F4
Ebley Glos 37 D5
Ebnal Ches 73 E8
Ebrington Glos 51 E6
Ecchinswell Hants 26 D2
Ecclaw Scot Borders 124 C3
Ecclefechan Dumf/Gal 107 B8
Eccles Scot Borders 124 E3
Eccles Gtr Man 87 E5
Eccles Kent 29 C8
Eccles on Sea Norfolk 69 B7
Eccles Road Norfolk 68 E3
Ecclesall S Yorks 88 F4
Ecclesfield S Yorks 88 E4
Ecclesgreig Aberds 143 C7
Eccleshall Staffs 62 B2
Eccleshill W Yorks 94 F4
Ecclesmachan W Loth 122 B3
Eccleston Ches 73 C8
Eccleston Lancs 86 C3
Eccleston Mersey 86 E2
Eccleston Park Mersey 86 E2
Eccup W Yorks 95 E5
Echt Aberds 151 D6
Eckford Scot Borders 116 B3
Eckington Derby 76 B4
Eckington Worcs 50 E4
Ecton Northants 53 C6
Edale Derby 88 F2
Edburton W Sussex 17 C6
Edderside Cumb 107 E7
Edderton H'land 164 F4
Eddistone Devon 8 B4
Eddleston Scot Borders 122 E5
Eden Camp Museum, Malton N Yorks 96 B3
Eden Park London 28 C4
Edenbridge Kent 28 E5
Edenfield Lancs 87 C5
Edenhall Cumb 109 F5
Edenham Lincs 65 B7
Edensor Derby 76 C2
Edentaggart Arg/Bute 129 A8
Edenthorpe S Yorks 89 D7
Edentown Cumb 108 D3
Ederline Arg/Bute 130 E4
Edern Gwyn 70 D3
Edgarley Som'set 23 F7
Edgbaston W Midlands 62 F4
Edgcott Bucks 39 B6
Edgcott Som'set 21 F7
Edge Shrops 60 D3
Edge End Glos 36 C2
Edge Green Ches 73 D8
Edge Hill Mersey 85 F4
Edgebolton Shrops 61 B5
Edgefield Norfolk 81 D6
Edgefield Street Norfolk 81 D6
Edgeside Lancs 87 B6
Edgeworth Glos 37 D6
Edgmond Telford 61 C7
Edgmond Marsh Telford 61 B7
Edgton Shrops 60 F3
Edgware London 40 E4
Edgworth Blackb'n 86 C5
Edinample Stirl 132 B4
Edinbane H'land 152 D4
Edinburgh C/Edinb 123 B5
Edinburgh Castle C/Edinb 123 B5
Edinburgh Crystal Visitor Centre, Penicuik Midloth 122 C5
Edinburgh Zoo C/Edinb 122 B5
Edingale Staffs 63 C6
Edingight Ho. Moray 160 C2
Edingley Notts 77 D6
Edingthorpe Norfolk 69 A6
Edingthorpe Green Norfolk 69 A6
Edington Som'set 23 F5
Edington Wilts 24 D4
Edintore Moray 159 E8
Edith Weston Rutl'd 65 D6
Edithmead Som'set 22 E5
Edlesborough Bucks 40 C2
Edlingham Northum 117 D7
Edlington Lincs 78 B5
Edmondsham Dorset 13 C8
Edmondsley Durham 110 E5
Edmondthorpe Leics 65 C5
Edmonstone Orkney 176 D4
Edmonton London 41 E6
Edmundbyers Durham 110 D3
Ednam Scot Borders 124 F3
Ednaston Derby 76 E2
Edradynate Perth/Kinr 141 D5
Edrom Scot Borders 124 D4
Edstaston Shrops 74 F2
Edstone Warwick 51 C6
Edvin Loach Heref'd 49 D8
Edwalton Notts 77 F5
Edwardstone Suffolk 56 E3
Edwinsford Carms 46 F5
Edwinstowe Notts 77 C6
Edworth Beds 54 E3
Edwyn Ralph Heref'd 49 D8
Edzell Angus 143 C5
Efail Isaf Rh Cyn Taff 34 F4
Efailnewydd Gwyn 70 D4
Efailwen Carms 32 B2
Efenechtyd Denbs 72 D5
Effingham Surrey 28 D2
Effirth Shetl'd 175 H5
Efford Devon 10 D3
Egdon Worcs 50 D4
Egerton Gtr Man 86 C5
Egerton Kent 30 E3
Egerton Forstal Kent 30 E2
Eggborough N Yorks 89 B6
Eggbuckland Plym'th 6 D3
Eggington Beds 40 B2
Egginton Derby 63 B6
Egglescliffe Stockton 102 C2
Eggleston Durham 100 B4
Egham Surrey 27 B8
Egleton Rutl'd 65 D5
Eglingham Northum 117 C7
Egloshayle Cornw'l 4 B5
Egloskerry Cornw'l 8 F4
Eglwys-Brewis V/Glam 22 C2
Eglwys Cross Wrex 73 E8
Eglwys Fach Ceredig'n 58 E3
Eglwysbach Conwy 83 D8
Eglwyswen Pembs 45 F3
Eglwyswrw Pembs 45 F3
Egmanton Notts 77 C7
Egremont Cumb 98 C2
Egremont Mersey 85 E4
Egton N Yorks 103 D6
Egton Bridge N Yorks 103 D6
Eight Ash Green Essex 43 B5
Eignaig H'land 138 E1
Eil H'land 148 C4
Eilanreach H'land 145 B8
Eilean Darach H'land 163 F5
Eileanach Lodge H'land 157 C6
Einacleite W Isles 172 F4
Eisgean W Isles 173 G6
Eisingrug Gwyn 71 D7
Elan Village Powys 47 C8
Elberton S Gloucs 36 F3
Elburton Plym'th 6 D3
Elcho Perth/Kinr 134 B3
Elcombe Swindon 37 F8
Eldernell Cambs 66 E3
Eldersfield Worcs 50 F3
Elderslie Renf 120 C4
Eldon Durham 101 B7
Eldrick S Ayrs 112 F2
Eldroth N Yorks 93 C7
Eldwick W Yorks 94 E4
Elfhowe Cumb 99 E6
Elford Northum 125 F7
Elford Staffs 63 C5
Elgin Moray 159 C6
Elgol H'land 153 H6
Elham Kent 31 E5
Elie Fife 135 D6
Elim Angl 82 C3
Eling Hants 14 C4
Elishader H'land 152 C6
Elishaw Northum 116 E4
Elkesley Notts 77 B6
Elkstone Glos 37 C6
Ellan H'land 148 B4
Elland W Yorks 88 B2
Ellary Arg/Bute 128 C2
Ellastone Staffs 75 E8
Ellemford Scot Borders 124 C3
Ellenbrook I/Man 84 E3
Ellenhall Staffs 62 B2
Ellen's Green Surrey 27 F8
Ellerbeck N Yorks 102 E2
Ellerburn N Yorks 103 F6
Ellerby N Yorks 103 C5
Ellerdine Heath Telford 61 B6
Ellerhayes Devon 10 D4
Elleric Arg/Bute 138 E4
Ellerker ER Yorks 90 B3
Ellerton ER Yorks 96 F3
Ellerton Shrops 61 B7
Ellesborough Bucks 39 D8
Ellesmere Shrops 73 F8
Ellesmere Port Ches 73 B8
Ellingham Norfolk 69 E6
Ellingham Northum 117 B7
Ellingstring N Yorks 101 F6
Ellington Cambs 54 B2
Ellington Northum 117 E8
Elliot Angus 143 F6
Ellisfield Hants 26 E4
Ellistown Leics 63 C8
Ellon Aberds 161 E6
Ellonby Cumb 108 F4
Ellough Suffolk 69 F7
Elloughton ER Yorks 90 B3
Ellwood Glos 36 D2
Elm Cambs 66 D4
Elm Hill Dorset 13 B6
Elm Park London 41 F8
Elmbridge Worcs 50 C4
Elmdon Essex 55 F5
Elmdon W Midlands 63 F5
Elmdon Heath W Midlands 63 F5
Elmers End London 28 C4
Elmesthorpe Leics 63 E8
Elmfield I/Wight 15 E7
Elmhurst Staffs 62 C5
Elmley Castle Worcs 50 E4
Elmley Lovett Worcs 50 C3
Elmore Glos 36 C4
Elmore Back Glos 36 C4
Elmscott Devon 8 B4
Elmsett Suffolk 56 E4
Elmstead Market Essex 43 B6
Elmsted Kent 30 E5
Elmstone Kent 31 C6
Elmstone Hardwicke Glos 37 B6
Elmswell ER Yorks 97 D5
Elmswell Suffolk 56 C3
Elmton Derby 76 B5
Elphin H'land 163 C6
Elphinstone E Loth 123 B6
Elrick Aberds 151 D7
Elrig Dumf/Gal 105 E7
Elsdon Northum 117 E5
Elsecar S Yorks 88 E4
Elsenham Essex 41 B8
Elsfield Oxon 39 C5
Elsham N Lincs 90 C4
Elsing Norfolk 68 C3
Elslack N Yorks 94 E2
Elson Shrops 73 F7
Elsrickle S Lanarks 122 E3
Elstead Surrey 27 E7
Elsted W Sussex 16 C2
Elsthorpe Lincs 65 B7
Elstob Durham 101 B8
Elston Notts 77 E7
Elston Wilts 25 E5
Elstone Devon 9 C8
Elstow Beds 53 E8
Elstree Herts 40 E4
Elstronwick ER Yorks 97 F8
Elswick Lancs 92 F4
Elsworth Cambs 54 C4
Elterwater Cumb 99 D5
Eltham London 28 B5
Eltisley Cambs 54 D3
Elton Cambs 65 E7
Elton Ches 73 B8
Elton Derby 76 C2
Elton Glos 36 C4
Elton Heref'd 49 B6
Elton Notts 77 F7
Elton Stockton 102 C2
Elton Green Ches 73 B8
Elvanfoot S Lanarks 114 C2
Elvaston Derby 76 F4
Elveden Suffolk 56 B2
Elvingston E Loth 123 B7
Elvington Kent 31 D6
Elvington C/York 96 E2
Elwick Hartlep'l 111 F7
Elwick Northum 125 F7
Elworth Ches 74 C4
Elworthy Som'set 22 F2
Ely Cambs 66 F5
Ely Card 22 B3
Ely Cathedral and Museum Cambs 66 F5
Emberton M/Keynes 53 E6
Embleton Cumb 107 F8
Embleton Northum 117 B8
Embo H'land 165 E5
Embo Street H'land 165 E5
Emborough Som'set 23 D8
Embsay N Yorks 94 D3
Emery Down Hants 14 D3
Emley W Yorks 88 C3
Emmbrook Wokingham 27 C5
Emmer Green Reading 26 B5
Emmington Oxon 39 D7
Emneth Norfolk 66 D4
Emneth Hungate Norfolk 66 D5
Empingham Rutl'd 65 D6
Empshott Hants 27 F5
Emstrey Shrops 60 C5
Emsworth Hants 15 D8
Enborne W Berks 26 C2
Enchmarsh Shrops 60 E5
Enderby Leics 64 E2
Endmoor Cumb 99 F7
Endon Staffs 75 D6
Endon Bank Staffs 75 D6
Enfield London 41 E6
Enfield Wash London 41 E6
Enford Wilts 25 D6
Engamoor Shetl'd 175 H4
Engine Common S Gloucs 36 F3
Englefield W Berks 26 B4
Englefield Green Surrey 27 B7
Englesea-brook Ches 74 D4
English Bicknor Glos 36 C2
English Frankton Shrops 60 B4
Englishcombe Bath/NE Som'set 24 C2
Enham-Alamein Hants 25 E8
Enmore Som'set 22 F4
Ennerdale Bridge Cumb 98 C2
Enoch Dumf/Gal 113 D8
Enochdhu Perth/Kinr 141 C7
Ensay Arg/Bute 136 D4
Ensbury Bournem'th 13 E8
Ensdon Shrops 60 C4
Ensis Devon 9 B7
Enstone Oxon 38 B3
Enterkinfoot Dumf/Gal 113 D8
Enterpen N Yorks 102 D2
Enville Staffs 62 F2
Eolaigearraidh W Isles 171 K3
Eorabus Arg/Bute 136 F4
Eòropaidh W Isles 172 B8
Epperstone Notts 77 E6
Epping Essex 41 D7
Epping Green Essex 41 D7
Epping Green Herts 41 D5
Epping Upland Essex 41 D7
Eppleby N Yorks 101 C6
Eppleworth ER Yorks 97 F6
Epsom Surrey 28 C3
Epsom Racecourse Surrey 28 D3
Epwell Oxon 51 E8
Epworth N Lincs 89 D8
Epworth Turbary N Lincs 89 D8
Erbistock Wrex 73 E7
Erbusaig H'land 155 H3
Erchless Castle H'land 156 E5
Erddig Wrex 73 E7
Erdington W Midlands 62 E5
Eredine Arg/Bute 131 E5
Eriboll H'land 167 D6
Ericstane Dumf/Gal 114 C3
Eridge Green E Sussex 18 B2
Erines Arg/Bute 128 C3
Eriswell Suffolk 55 B8
Erith London 29 B6
Erlestoke Wilts 24 D4
Ermine Lincs 78 B2
Ermington Devon 6 D4
Erpingham Norfolk 81 D7
Errogie H'land 147 B8
Errol Perth/Kinr 134 B4
Erskine Renf 120 B4
Erskine Bridge Renf 120 B4
Ervie Dumf/Gal 104 C4
Erwarton Suffolk 57 F6
Erwood Powys 48 E2
Eryholme N Yorks 101 D8
Eryrys Denbs 73 D6
Escomb Durham 101 B6
Escrick N Yorks 96 E2
Esgairdawe Carms 46 E5
Esgairgeiliog Powys 58 D4
Esh Durham 110 E4
Esh Winning Durham 110 E4
Esher Surrey 28 C2
Esholt W Yorks 94 E4
Eshott Northum 117 E8
Eshton N Yorks 94 D2
Esk Valley N Yorks 103 D6
Eskadale H'land 157 F5
Eskbank Midloth 123 C6
Eskdale Green Cumb 98 D3
Eskdalemuir Dumf/Gal 115 E5
Eske ER Yorks 97 E6
Eskham Lincs 91 E7
Esprick Lancs 92 F4
Essendine Rutl'd 65 C7
Essendon Herts 41 D5
Essich H'land 157 F7
Essington Staffs 62 D3
Esslemont Aberds 151 B8
Eston Redcar/Clevel'd 102 C3
Eswick Shetl'd 175 H6
Etal Northum 124 F5
Etchilhampton Wilts 24 C5
Etchingham E Sussex 18 C4
Etchinghill Kent 19 B8
Etchinghill Staffs 62 C4
Ethie Castle Angus 143 E6
Ethie Mains Angus 143 E6
Etling Green Norfolk 68 C3
Eton Windsor 27 B7
Eton Wick Windsor 27 B7
Etteridge H'land 148 E2
Ettersgill Durham 100 B3
Ettingshall W Midlands 62 E3
Ettington Warwick 51 E7
Etton ER Yorks 97 E5
Etton Peterbro 65 D8
Ettrick Scot Borders 115 C5
Ettrickbridge Scot Borders 115 B6
Ettrickhill Scot Borders 115 C5
Etwall Derby 76 F2
Eureka!, Halifax W Yorks 87 B8
Euston Suffolk 56 B2
Euximoor Drove Cambs 66 E4
Euxton Lancs 86 C3
Evanstown Bridg 34 F3
Evanton H'land 157 C7
Evedon Lincs 78 E3
Evelix H'land 164 E4
Evenjobb Powys 48 C4
Evenley Northants 52 F3
Evenlode Glos 38 B2
Evenwood Durham 101 B6
Evenwood Gate Durham 101 B6
Everbay Orkney 176 D5
Evercreech Som'set 23 F8
Everdon Northants 52 D3
Everingham ER Yorks 96 E4
Everleigh Wilts 25 D7
Everley N Yorks 103 F7
Eversholt Beds 53 F7
Evershot Dorset 12 D3
Eversley Hants 27 C5
Eversley Cross Hants 27 C5
Everthorpe ER Yorks 96 F5
Everton Beds 54 D3
Everton Hants 14 E3
Everton Mersey 85 E4
Everton Notts 89 E7
Evertown Dumf/Gal 108 B3
Evesbatch Heref'd 49 E8
Evesham Worcs 50 E5
Evington Leics C 64 D3
Ewden Village S Yorks 88 E3
Ewell Surrey 28 C3
Ewell Minnis Kent 31 E6
Ewelme Oxon 39 E6
Ewen Glos 37 E7
Ewenny V/Glam 21 B8
Ewerby Lincs 78 E4
Ewerby Thorpe Lincs 78 E4
Ewes Dumf/Gal 115 E6
Ewesley Northum 117 E6
Ewhurst Surrey 27 E8
Ewhurst Green E Sussex 18 C4
Ewhurst Green Surrey 27 F8
Ewloe Flints 73 C7
Ewloe Grn Flints 73 C6
Ewood Blackb'n 86 B4
Eworthy Devon 9 E6
Ewshot Hants 27 E6
Ewyas Harold Heref'd 35 B7
Exbourne Devon 9 D8
Exbury Hants 14 E5
Exbury Gardens, Fawley Hants 14 D5
Exebridge Som'set 10 B4
Exelby N Yorks 101 F7
Exeter Devon 10 E4
Exeter Cathedral Devon 10 E4
Exford Som'set 21 F7
Exhall Warwick 51 D6
Exley Head W Yorks 94 F3
Exminster Devon 10 F4
Exmouth Devon 10 F5
Exnaboe Shetl'd 175 M5
Exning Suffolk 55 C7
Explosion, Gosport Hants 15 D7
Exton Devon 10 F4
Exton Hants 15 B7
Exton Rutl'd 65 C6
Exton Som'set 21 F8
Exwick Devon 10 E4
Eyam Derby 76 B2
Eydon Northants 52 D3
Eye Heref'd 49 C6
Eye Peterbro 66 D2
Eye Suffolk 56 B5
Eye Green Peterbro 66 D2
Eyemouth Scot Borders 124 C5
Eyeworth Beds 54 E3
Eyhorne Street Kent 30 D2
Eyke Suffolk 57 D7
Eynesbury Cambs 54 D2
Eynort H'land 153 G4
Eynsford Kent 29 C6
Eynsham Oxon 38 D4
Eype Dorset 12 E2
Eyre H'land 152 D5
Eyre H'land 153 F6
Eythorne Kent 31 E6
Eyton Heref'd 49 C6
Eyton Shrops 60 F3
Eyton Wrex 73 E7
Eyton upon the Weald Moors Telford 61 C6

F

Faccombe Hants 25 D8
Faceby N Yorks 102 D2
Facit Lancs 87 C6
Faddiley Ches 74 D2
Fadmoor N Yorks 102 F4
Faerdre Swan 33 D7
Failford S Ayrs 112 B4
Failsworth Gtr Man 87 D6
Fain H'land 156 B2
Fair Green Norfolk 67 C6
Fair Hill Cumb 108 F5
Fair Oak Hants 15 C5
Fair Oak Green Hants 26 C4
Fairbourne Gwyn 58 C3
Fairburn N Yorks 89 B5
Fairfield Derby 75 B7
Fairfield Stockton 102 C2
Fairfield Worcs 50 E5
Fairfield Worcs 50 B4
Fairford Glos 38 D1
Fairhaven Lancs 85 B4
Fairlie N Ayrs 129 E7
Fairlight E Sussex 19 D5
Fairlight Cove E Sussex 19 D5
Fairmile Devon 11 E5
Fairmilehead C/Edinb 122 C5
Fairoak Staffs 74 F4
Fairseat Kent 29 C7
Fairstead Essex 42 C3
Fairstead Norfolk 67 C6
Fairwarp E Sussex 17 B8
Fairy Cottage I/Man 84 D4
Fairy Cross Devon 9 B6
Fakenham Norfolk 80 E5
Fakenham Racecourse Norfolk 80 E5
Fala Midloth 123 C7
Fala Dam Midloth 123 C7
Falahill Scot Borders 123 D6
Falcon Heref'd 49 F8
Faldingworth Lincs 90 F4
Falfield S Gloucs 36 E3
Falkenham Suffolk 57 F6
Falkirk Falk 121 B8
Falkland Fife 134 D4
Falkland Palace Fife 134 D4
Falla Scot Borders 116 C3
Fallgate Derby 76 C3
Fallin Stirl 133 E7
Fallowfield Gtr Man 87 E6
Fallsidehill Scot Borders 124 E2
Falmer E Sussex 17 D7
Falmouth Cornw'l 3 C7
Falsgrave N Yorks 103 F8
Falstone Northum 116 F3
Fanagmore H'land 166 E3
Fangdale Beck N Yorks 102 E3
Fangfoss ER Yorks 96 D3
Fankerton Falk 133 F6
Fanmore Arg/Bute 137 D5
Fannich Lodge H'land 156 C3
Fans Scot Borders 124 E2
Far Bank S Yorks 89 C7
Far Bletchley M/Keynes 53 F6
Far Cotton Northants 52 D5
Far Forest Worcs 50 B2
Far Laund Derby 76 E3
Far Sawrey Cumb 99 E5
Farcet Cambs 66 E2
Farden Shrops 49 B7
Fareham Hants 15 D6
Farewell Staffs 62 C4
Farforth Lincs 79 B6
Faringdon Oxon 38 E2
Farington Lancs 86 B3
Farlam Cumb 109 D5
Farlary H'land 164 D4
Farleigh N Som'set 23 C6
Farleigh Surrey 28 C4
Farleigh Hungerford Som'set 24 D3
Farleigh Wallop Hants 26 E4
Farlesthorpe Lincs 79 B7
Farleton Cumb 99 F7
Farleton Lancs 93 C5
Farley Shrops 60 D3
Farley Staffs 75 E7
Farley Wilts 14 B3
Farley Green Surrey 27 E8
Farley Hill Luton 40 B3
Farley Hill Wokingham 26 C5
Farleys End Glos 36 C4
Farlington N Yorks 96 C2
Farlow Shrops 61 F6
Farmborough Bath/NE Som'set 23 C8
Farmcote Glos 37 B7
Farmcote Shrops 61 E7
Farmington Glos 37 C8
Farmoor Oxon 38 D4
Farmtown Moray 160 C2
Farnborough London 28 C5
Farnborough Hants 27 D6
Farnborough Warwick 52 E2
Farnborough W Berks 38 F4
Farnborough Green Hants 27 D6
Farncombe Surrey 27 E7
Farndish Beds 53 C7
Farndon Ches 73 D8
Farndon Notts 77 D7
Farnell Angus 143 D6
Farnham Dorset 13 C7
Farnham Essex 41 B7
Farnham N Yorks 95 C6
Farnham Suffolk 57 C7
Farnham Surrey 27 E6
Farnham Common Bucks 40 F2
Farnham Green Essex 41 B7
Farnham Royal Bucks 40 F2
Farnhill N Yorks 94 E3
Farningham Kent 29 C6
Farnley N Yorks 94 E5
Farnley W Yorks 95 F5
Farnley Tyas W Yorks 88 C2
Farnsfield Notts 77 D6
Farnworth Gtr Man 86 D5
Farnworth Halton 86 F3
Farr H'land 157 F7
Farr H'land 148 D4
Farr H'land 168 C2
Farr House H'land 157 F7
Farringdon Devon 10 E5
Farrington Gurney Bath/NE Som'set 23 D8
Farsley W Yorks 94 F5
Farthinghoe Northants 52 F3
Farthingloe Kent 31 E6
Farthingstone Northants 52 D4
Fartown W Yorks 88 C2
Farway Devon 11 E6
Fasag H'land 154 E4
Fascadale H'land 137 A6
Faslane Port Arg/Bute 129 B7
Fasnacloich Arg/Bute 138 E4
Fasnakyle Ho. H'land 147 B6
Fassfern H'land 138 B4
Fatfield Tyne/Wear 111 D6
Fattahead Aberds 160 C3
Faugh Cumb 108 D5
Fauldhouse W Loth 122 C2
Faulkbourne Essex 42 C3
Faulkland Som'set 24 D2
Fauls Shrops 74 F2
Faversham Kent 30 C4
Favillar Moray 159 F6
Fawdington N Yorks 95 B7
Fawfieldhead Staffs 75 C7
Fawkham Green Kent 29 C6
Fawler Oxon 38 C3
Fawley Bucks 39 F7
Fawley Hants 15 D5
Fawley W Berks 38 F3
Fawley Chapel Heref'd 36 B2
Faxfleet ER Yorks 90 B2
Faygate W Sussex 28 F3
Fazakerley Mersey 85 E4
Fazeley Staffs 63 D6
Fearby N Yorks 101 F6
Fearn H'land 158 B2
Fearn Lodge H'land 164 F3
Fearn Station H'land 158 B2
Fearnan Perth/Kinr 140 E4
Fearnbeg H'land 154 E3
Fearnhead Warrington 86 E4
Fearnmore H'land 154 D3
Featherstone Staffs 62 D3
Featherstone W Yorks 88 B5
Featherwood Northum 116 D4
Feckenham Worcs 50 C5
Feering Essex 42 B4
Feetham N Yorks 100 E4
Feizor N Yorks 93 C7
Felbridge Surrey 28 F4
Felbrigg Norfolk 81 D8
Felcourt Surrey 28 E4
Felden Herts 40 D3
Felin-Crai Powys 34 B2
Felindre Ceredig'n 46 D4
Felindre Carms 33 B6
Felindre Carms 47 F5
Felindre Carms 33 B8
Felindre Carms 46 F2
Felindre Powys 59 F8
Felindre Swan 33 D7
Felindre Farchog Pembs 45 F3
Felinfach Ceredig'n 46 D4
Felinfach Powys 48 F2
Felinfoel Carms 33 D6
Felingwm isaf Carms 33 B6
Felingwm uchaf Carms 33 B6
Felinwynt Ceredig'n 45 D4
Felixkirk N Yorks 102 F2
Felixstowe Suffolk 57 F6
Felixstowe Ferry Suffolk 57 F7
Felkington Northum 124 E5
Felkirk W Yorks 88 C4
Fell Side Cumb 108 F3
Felling Tyne/Wear 111 C5
Felmersham Beds 53 D7
Felmingham Norfolk 81 E8
Felpham W Sussex 16 E3
Felsham Suffolk 56 D3
Felsted Essex 42 B2
Feltham London 28 B2
Felthorpe Norfolk 68 C4
Felton Heref'd 49 E7
Felton Northum 117 D7
Felton N Som'set 23 C7
Felton Butler Shrops 60 C3
Feltwell Norfolk 67 E7
Fen Ditton Cambs 55 C5
Fen Drayton Cambs 54 C4
Fen End W Midlands 51 B7
Fen Side Lincs 79 D6
Fenay Bridge W Yorks 88 C2
Fence Lancs 93 F8
Fence Houses Tyne/Wear 111 D6
Fengate Norfolk 81 E7
Fengate Peterbro 66 E2
Fenham Northum 125 E6
Fenhouses Lincs 79 E5
Feniscliffe Blackb'n 86 B4
Feniscowles Blackb'n 86 B4
Feniton Devon 11 E6
Fenlake Beds 53 E8
Fenny Bentley Derby 75 D8
Fenny Bridges Devon 11 E6
Fenny Compton Warwick 52 D2
Fenny Drayton Leics 63 E7
Fenny Stratford M/Keynes 53 F6
Fenrother Northum 117 E7
Fenstanton Cambs 54 C4
Fenton Cambs 54 B4
Fenton Lincs 77 D8
Fenton Lincs 77 B8
Fenton Stoke 75 E5
Fenton Barns E Loth 135 F7
Fenton Town Northum 125 F5
Fenwick E Ayrs 120 E4
Fenwick Northum 110 B3
Fenwick Northum 125 E6
Fenwick S Yorks 89 C6
Feochaig Arg/Bute 118 E4
Feock Cornw'l 3 C7
Feolin Ferry Arg/Bute 127 F2
Ferens Art Gallery, Hull Kingston/Hull 90 B4
Ferindonald H'land 145 C6
Feriniquarrie H'land 152 D2
Ferlochan Arg/Bute 138 E3
Fern Angus 142 C4
Ferndale Rh Cyn Taff 34 E4
Ferndown Dorset 13 D8
Ferness H'land 158 E3
Ferney Green Cumb 99 E6
Fernham Oxon 38 E2
Fernhill Heath Worcs 50 D3
Fernhurst W Sussex 16 B2
Fernie Fife 134 C5
Ferniegair S Lanarks 121 D7
Fernilea H'land 153 F4
Fernilee Derby 75 B7
Ferrensby N Yorks 95 C6
Ferring W Sussex 16 D4
Ferry Hill Cambs 66 F3
Ferry Point H'land 164 F4
Ferrybridge W Yorks 89 B5
Ferryden Angus 143 D7

Haunn W Isles 171 J3
Haunton Staffs 63 C6
Hauxley Northum 117 D8
Hauxton Cambs 54 D5
Havant Hants 15 D8
Haven Heref'd 49 D6
Haven Bank Lincs 78 D5
Haven Side ER Yorks 91 B5
Havenstreet I/Wight 15 E6
Havercroft W Yorks 88 C4
Haverfordwest = Hwlffordd Pembs 44 D4
Haverhill Suffolk 55 E7
Haverigg Cumb 92 B1
Havering-atte-Bower London 41 E8
Haveringland Norfolk 81 E7
Haversham M/Keynes 53 E6
Haverthwaite Cumb 99 F5
Haverton Hill Stockton 102 B2
Hawarden = Penarlâg Flints 73 C7
Hawcoat Cumb 92 B2
Hawen Ceredig'n 46 E2
Hawes N Yorks 100 F3
Hawes Side Blackp'l 92 F3
Hawes'Green Norfolk 68 E5
Hawford Worcs 50 C3
Hawick Scot Borders 115 C8
Hawk Green Gtr Man 87 F7
Hawkchurch Devon 11 D8
Hawkedon Suffolk 55 D8
Hawkenbury Kent 30 E2
Hawkenbury Kent 18 B2
Hawkeridge Wilts 24 D3
Hawkerland Devon 11 F5
Hawkes End W Midlands 63 F7
Hawkesbury S Gloucs 36 F4
Hawkesbury Warwick 63 F7
Hawkesbury Upton S Gloucs 36 F4
Hawkhill Northum 117 C8
Hawkhurst Kent 18 B4
Hawkinge Kent 31 F6
Hawkley Hants 15 B8
Hawkridge Som'set 21 F7
Hawkshead Cumb 99 E5
Hawkshead Hill Cumb 99 E5
Hawksland S Lanarks 121 F8
Hawkswick N Yorks 94 B2
Hawksworth Notts 77 E7
Hawksworth W Yorks 94 E4
Hawksworth W Yorks 95 F5
Hawkwell Essex 42 E4
Hawley Hants 27 D6
Hawley Kent 29 B6
Hawling Glos 37 B7
Hawnby N Yorks 102 F3
Haworth W Yorks 94 F3
Hawstead Suffolk 56 D2
Hawthorn Durham 111 E7
Hawthorn Rh Cyn Taff 35 F5
Hawthorn Wilts 24 C3
Hawthorn Hill Brackn'l 27 B6
Hawthorn Hill Lincs 78 D5
Hawthorpe Lincs 65 B7
Hawton Notts 77 D7
Haxby C/York 96 D2
Haxey N Lincs 89 D8
Hay Green Norfolk 66 C5
Hay-on-Wye = Y Gelli Gandryll Powys 48 E4
Hay Street Herts 41 B6
Haydock Mersey 86 E3
Haydock Park Racecourse Mersey 86 E3
Haydon Dorset 12 C4
Haydon Bridge Northum 109 C8
Haydon Wick Swindon 37 F8
Haye Cornw'l 5 C8
Hayes London 28 C5
Hayes London 40 F4
Hayfield Derby 87 F8
Hayfield Fife 134 E4
Hayhill E Ayrs 112 C4
Hayhillock Angus 143 E5
Hayle Cornw'l 2 C4
Haynes Beds 53 E8
Haynes Church End Beds 53 E8
Hayscastle Pembs 44 C3
Hayscastle Cross Pembs 44 C4
Hayshead Angus 143 E6
Hayton Aberd C 151 D8
Hayton Cumb 107 E8
Hayton Cumb 108 D5
Hayton ER Yorks 96 E4
Hayton Notts 89 F8
Hayton's Bent Shrops 60 F5
Haytor Vale Devon 7 B5
Haywards Heath W Sussex 17 B7
Haywood S Yorks 89 C6
Haywood Oaks Notts 77 D6
Hazel Grove Gtr Man 87 F7
Hazel Street Kent 18 B3
Hazelbank S Lanarks 121 E8
Hazelbury Bryan Dorset 12 D5
Hazeley Hants 26 D5
Hazelhurst Gtr Man 87 D7
Hazelslade Staffs 62 C4
Hazelton Glos 37 C7
Hazelton Walls Fife 134 B5
Hazelwood Derby 76 E3
Hazlemere Bucks 40 E1
Hazlerigg Tyne/Wear 110 B5
Hazlewood N Yorks 94 D3
Hazon Northum 117 D7
Heacham Norfolk 80 D2
Head of Muir Falk 133 F7
Headbourne Worthy Hants 26 F3
Headbrook Heref'd 48 D5
Headcorn Kent 30 E2
Headingley W Yorks 95 F5
Headington Oxon 39 D5
Headlam Durham 101 C6
Headless Cross Worcs 50 C5
Headley Hants 26 C3
Headley Hants 27 F6
Headley Surrey 28 D3
Headon Notts 77 B7
Heads S Lanarks 121 E7
Heads Nook Cumb 108 D4
Heage Derby 76 D3
Healaugh N Yorks 95 E7
Healaugh N Yorks 101 E5
Heald Green Gtr Man 87 F6
Heale Devon 20 E5
Heale Som'set 23 E8
Healey Gtr Man 87 C6
Healey Northum 110 D3
Healey N Yorks 101 F6
Healing NE Lincs 91 C6
Heamoor Cornw'l 2 C3
Heanish Arg/Bute 136 F2
Heanor Derby 76 E4
Heanton Punchardon Devon 20 F4
Heapham Lincs 90 F2
Heart of the National Forest Leics 63 C7
Hearthstane Scot Borders 114 B4
Heasley Mill Devon 21 F6
Heast H'land 145 B6
Heath Card 22 B3
Heath Derby 76 C4
Heath and Reach Beds 40 B2
Heath End Hants 26 C3
Heath End Surrey 27 E6
Heath End Warwick 51 C7
Heath Hayes Staffs 62 C4
Heath Hill Shrops 61 C7
Heath House Som'set 23 E6
Heath Town W Midlands 62 E3
Heathcote Derby 75 C8
Heather Leics 63 C7
Heatherfield H'land 153 F5
Heathfield Devon 7 B6
Heathfield E Sussex 18 C2
Heathfield Som'set 11 B6
Heathhall Dumf/Gal 107 B6
Heathrow Airport London 27 B8
Heathstock Devon 11 D7
Heathton Shrops 62 E2
Heatley Warrington 86 F5
Heaton Lancs 92 C4
Heaton Staffs 75 C6
Heaton Tyne/Wear 111 C5
Heaton W Yorks 94 F4
Heaton Moor Gtr Man 87 E6
Heaverham Kent 29 D6
Heaviley Gtr Man 87 F7
Heavitree Devon 10 E4
Hebburn Tyne/Wear 111 C6
Hebden N Yorks 94 C3
Hebden Bridge W Yorks 87 B7
Hebron Angl 82 C4
Hebron Carms 32 B2
Hebron Northum 117 F7
Heck Dumf/Gal 114 F3
Heckfield Hants 26 C5
Heckfield Green Suffolk 57 B5
Heckfordbridge Essex 43 B5
Heckington Lincs 78 E4
Heckmondwike W Yorks 88 B3
Heddington Wilts 24 C4
Heddle Orkney 176 E2
Heddon-on-the-Wall Northum 110 C4
Hedenham Norfolk 69 E6
Hedge End Hants 15 C5
Hedgerley Bucks 40 F2
Hedging Som'set 11 B8
Hedley on the Hill Northum 110 D3
Hednesford Staffs 62 C4
Hedon ER Yorks 91 B5
Hedsor Bucks 40 F2
Hedworth Tyne/Wear 111 C6
Heeley City Farm, Sheffield S Yorks 88 F4
Hegdon Hill Heref'd 49 D7
Heggerscales Cumb 100 C3
Heglibister Shetl'd 175 H5
Heighington D'lington 101 B7
Heighington Lincs 78 C3
Heights of Brae H'land 157 C6
Heights of Kinlochewe H'land 154 D6
Heilam H'land 167 C6
Heiton Scot Borders 124 F3
Hele Devon 20 E4
Hele Devon 10 D4
Helensburgh Arg/Bute 129 B7
Helford Cornw'l 3 D6
Helford Passage Cornw'l 3 D6
Helhoughton Norfolk 80 E4
Helions Bumpstead Essex 55 E7
Hellaby S Yorks 89 E6
Helland Cornw'l 5 B5
Hellesdon Norfolk 68 C5
Hellidon Northants 52 D3
Hellifield N Yorks 93 D8
Hellingly E Sussex 18 D2
Hellington Norfolk 69 D6
Hellister Shetl'd 175 J5
Helm Northum 117 E7
Helmdon Northants 52 E3
Helmingham Suffolk 57 D5
Helmington Row Durham 110 F4
Helmsdale H'land 165 C7
Helmshore Lancs 87 B5
Helmsley N Yorks 102 F4
Helperby N Yorks 95 C7
Helperthorpe N Yorks 97 B5
Helpringham Lincs 78 E4
Helpston Peterbro 65 D8
Helsby Ches 73 B8
Helsey Lincs 79 B8
Helston Cornw'l 3 D5
Helstone Cornw'l 8 F2
Helton Cumb 99 B7
Helwith Bridge N Yorks 93 C8
Hemblington Norfolk 69 C6
Hemel Hempstead Herts 40 D3
Hemingbrough N Yorks 96 F2
Hemingby Lincs 78 B5
Hemingford Abbots Cambs 54 B3
Hemingford Grey Cambs 54 B3
Hemingstone Suffolk 57 D5
Hemington Leics 63 B8
Hemington Northants 65 F7
Hemington Som'set 24 D2
Hemley Suffolk 57 E6
Hemlington M'brough 102 C3
Hemp Green Suffolk 57 C7
Hempholme ER Yorks 97 D6
Hempnall Norfolk 68 E5
Hempnall Green Norfolk 68 E5
Hempriggs House H'land 169 E8
Hempstead Essex 55 F7
Hempstead Medway 29 C8
Hempstead Norfolk 81 D7
Hempstead Norfolk 69 B7
Hempsted Glos 37 C5
Hempton Norfolk 80 E5
Hempton Oxon 52 F2
Hemsby Norfolk 69 C7
Hemswell Lincs 90 E3
Hemswell Cliff Lincs 90 F3
Hemsworth W Yorks 88 C5
Hemyock Devon 11 C6
Hen-feddau fawr Pembs 45 F4
Henbury Bristol 23 B7
Henbury Ches 75 B5
Hendon London 41 F5
Hendon Tyne/Wear 111 D7
Hendre Flints 73 C5
Hendre-ddu Conwy 83 E8
Hendreforgan Rh Cyn Taff 34 F3
Hendy Carms 33 D6
Heneglwys Angl 82 D4
Henfield W Sussex 17 C6
Henford Devon 9 E5
Henghurst Kent 19 B6
Hengoed Caerph 35 E5
Hengoed Powys 48 D4
Hengoed Shrops 73 F6
Hengrave Suffolk 56 C2
Henham Essex 55 F6
Heniarth Powys 59 D8
Henlade Som'set 11 B7
Henley Shrops 49 B7
Henley Som'set 23 F6
Henley Suffolk 57 D5
Henley W Sussex 16 B2
Henley-in-Arden Warwick 51 C6
Henley-on-Thames Oxon 39 F7
Henley's Down E Sussex 18 D4
Henllan Ceredig'n 46 E2
Henllan Denbs 72 C4
Henllan Amgoed Carms 32 B2
Henllys Torf 35 E6
Henlow Beds 54 F2
Hennock Devon 10 F3
Henny Street Essex 56 F2
Henryd Conwy 83 D7
Henry's Moat Pembs 32 B1
Hensall N Yorks 89 B6
Henshaw Northum 109 C7
Hensingham Cumb 98 C1
Henstead Suffolk 69 F7
Henstridge Som'set 12 C5
Henstridge Ash Som'set 12 B5
Henstridge Marsh Som'set 12 B5
Henton Oxon 39 D7
Henton Som'set 23 E6
Henwood Cornw'l 5 B7
Heogan Shetl'd 175 J6
Heol-las Swan 33 E7
Heol Senni Powys 34 B3
Heol-y-Cyw Bridg 34 F3
Hepburn Northum 117 B6
Hepple Northum 117 D5
Hepscott Northum 117 F8
Heptonstall W Yorks 87 B7
Hepworth Suffolk 56 B3
Hepworth W Yorks 88 D2
Herbrandston Pembs 44 E3
Hereford Heref'd 49 E7
Hereford Cathedral Heref'd 49 F7
Hereford Racecourse Heref'd 49 E7
Heriot Scot Borders 123 D6
Heritage Motor Centre, Gaydon Warwick 51 D8
Hermiston C/Edinb 122 B4
Hermitage Scot Borders 115 E8
Hermitage Dorset 12 D4
Hermitage W Berks 26 B3
Hermitage W Sussex 15 D8
Hermon Angl 82 E3
Hermon Carms 46 F2
Hermon Carms 33 B7
Hermon Pembs 45 F4
Herne Kent 31 C5
Herne Bay Kent 31 C5
Herner Devon 9 B7
Hernhill Kent 30 C4
Herodsfoot Cornw'l 5 C7
Herongate Essex 42 E2
Heronsford S Ayrs 104 A5
Herriard Hants 26 E4
Herringfleet Suffolk 69 E7
Herringswell Suffolk 55 B8
Hersden Kent 31 C6
Hersham Cornw'l 8 D4
Hersham Surrey 28 C2
Herstmonceux E Sussex 18 D3
Herston Orkney 176 G3
Hertford Herts 41 C6
Hertford Heath Herts 41 C6
Hertingfordbury Herts 41 C6
Hesket Newmarket Cumb 108 F3
Hesketh Bank Lancs 86 B2
Hesketh Lane Lancs 93 E6
Heskin Green Lancs 86 C3
Hesleden Durham 111 F7
Hesleyside Northum 116 F4
Heslington C/York 96 D2
Hessay C/York 95 D8
Hessenford Cornw'l 5 D8
Hessett Suffolk 56 C3
Hessle ER Yorks 90 B4
Hest Bank Lancs 92 C4
Heston London 28 B2
Hestwall Orkney 176 E1
Heswall Mersey 85 F3
Hethe Oxon 39 B5
Hethersett Norfolk 68 D4
Hethersgill Cumb 108 C4
Hethpool Northum 116 B4
Hett Durham 111 F5
Hetton N Yorks 94 D2
Hetton-le-Hole Tyne/Wear 111 E6
Hetton Steads Northum 125 F6
Heugh Northum 110 B3
Heugh-head Aberds 150 C2
Heveningham Suffolk 57 B7
Hever Kent 29 E5
Hever Castle and Gardens Kent 29 E5
Heversham Cumb 99 F6
Hevingham Norfolk 81 E7
Hewas Water Cornw'l 3 B8
Hewelsfield Glos 36 D2
Hewish N Som'set 23 C6
Hewish Som'set 12 D2
Heworth C/York 96 D2
Hexham Northum 110 C2
Hexham Abbey Northum 110 C2
Hexham Racecourse Northum 110 C2
Hextable Kent 29 B6
Hexton Herts 54 F2
Hexworthy Devon 6 B4
Hey Lancs 93 E8
Heybridge Essex 42 E2
Heybridge Essex 42 D4
Heybridge Basin Essex 42 D4
Heybrook Bay Devon 6 E3
Heydon Cambs 54 E5
Heydon Norfolk 81 E7
Heydour Lincs 78 F3
Heylipol Arg/Bute 136 F1
Heylor Shetl'd 174 E4
Heysham Lancs 92 C4
Heyshott W Sussex 16 C2
Heyside Gtr Man 87 D7
Heytesbury Wilts 24 E4
Heythrop Oxon 38 B3
Heywood Gtr Man 87 C6
Heywood Wilts 24 D3
Hibaldstow N Lincs 90 D3
Hickleton S Yorks 89 D5
Hickling Norfolk 69 B7
Hickling Notts 64 B3
Hickling Green Norfolk 69 B7
Hickling Heath Norfolk 69 B7
Hickstead W Sussex 17 B6
Hidcote Boyce Glos 51 E6
Hidcote Manor Garden, Moreton-in-Marsh Glos 51 E6
High Ackworth W Yorks 88 C5
High Angerton Northum 117 F6
High Bankhill Cumb 109 E5
High Barnes Tyne/Wear 111 D6
High Beach Essex 41 E7
High Bentham N Yorks 93 C6
High Bickington Devon 9 B8
High Birkwith N Yorks 93 B7
High Blantyre S Lanarks 121 D6
High Bonnybridge Falk 121 B8
High Bradfield S Yorks 88 E3
High Bray Devon 21 F5
High Brooms Kent 29 E6
High Bullen Devon 9 B7
High Buston Northum 117 D8
High Callerton Northum 110 B4
High Catton ER Yorks 96 D3
High Cogges Oxon 38 D3
High Coniscliffe D'lington 101 C7
High Cross Hants 15 B8
High Cross Herts 41 C6
High Easter Essex 42 C2
High Eggborough N Yorks 89 B6
High Ellington N Yorks 101 F6
High Ercall Telford 61 C5
High Etherley Durham 101 B6
High Garrett Essex 42 B3
High Grange Durham 110 F4
High Green Norfolk 68 D4
High Green S Yorks 88 E4
High Green Worcs 50 E3
High Halden Kent 19 B5
High Halstow Medway 29 B8
High Ham Som'set 23 F6
High Harrington Cumb 98 B2
High Hatton Shrops 61 B6
High Hawsker N Yorks 103 D7
High Hesket Cumb 108 E4
High Hesleden Durham 111 F7
High Hoyland S Yorks 88 C3
High Hunsley ER Yorks 97 F5
High Hurstwood E Sussex 17 B8
High Hutton N Yorks 96 C3
High Ireby Cumb 108 F2
High Kelling Norfolk 81 C7
High Kilburn N Yorks 95 B8
High Lands Durham 101 B6
High Lane Gtr Man 87 F7
High Lane Heref'd 49 C8
High Laver Essex 41 D8
High Legh Ches 86 F5
High Leven Stockton 102 C2
High Littleton Bath/NE Som'set 23 D8
High Lorton Cumb 98 B3
High Marishes N Yorks 96 B4
High Marnham Notts 77 B8
High Melton S Yorks 89 D6
High Mickley Northum 110 C3
High Mindork Dumf/Gal 105 D7
High Moorland Visitor Centre, Princetown Devon 6 B3
High Newton Cumb 99 F6
High Newton-by-the-Sea Northum 117 B8
High Nibthwaite Cumb 98 F4
High Offley Staffs 61 B7
High Ongar Essex 42 D1
High Onn Staffs 62 C2
High Roding Essex 42 C2
High Row Cumb 108 F3
High Salvington W Sussex 16 D5
High Shaw N Yorks 100 E3
High Spen Tyne/Wear 110 D4
High Stoop Durham 110 E4
High Street Cornw'l 4 D4
High Street Kent 18 B4
High Street Suffolk 57 D8
High Street Suffolk 57 B8
High Street Suffolk 56 E2
High Street Green Suffolk 56 D4
High Throston Hartlep'l 111 F7
High Toynton Lincs 79 C5
High Trewhitt Northum 117 D6
High Valleyfield Fife 134 F2
High Westwood Durham 110 D4
High Wray Cumb 99 E5
High Wych Herts 41 C7
High Wycombe Bucks 40 E1
Higham Derby 76 D3
Higham Kent 29 B8
Higham Lancs 93 F8
Higham Suffolk 55 C8
Higham Suffolk 56 F4
Higham Dykes Northum 110 B4
Higham Ferrers Northants 53 C7
Higham Gobion Beds 54 F2
Higham on the Hill Leics 63 E7
Higham Wood Kent 29 E6
Highampton Devon 9 D6
Highbridge H'land 146 F4
Highbridge Som'set 22 E5
Highbrook W Sussex 28 F4
Highburton W Yorks 88 C2
Highbury Som'set 23 E8
Highclere Hants 26 C2
Highcliffe Dorset 14 E3
Higher Ansty Dorset 13 D5
Higher Ashton Devon 10 F3
Higher Ballam Lancs 92 F3
Higher Bartle Lancs 92 F5
Higher Boscaswell Cornw'l 2 C2
Higher Burwardsley Ches 74 D2
Higher Clovelly Devon 8 B5
Higher End Gtr Man 86 D3
Higher Kinnerton Flints 73 C7
Higher Penwortham Lancs 86 B3
Higher Town I/Scilly 2 E4
Higher Walreddon Devon 6 B2
Higher Walton Lancs 86 B3
Higher Walton Warrington 86 F3
Higher Wheelton Lancs 86 B4
Higher Whitley Ches 86 F4
Higher Wincham Ches 74 B3
Higher Wych Ches 73 E8
Highfield ER Yorks 96 F3
Highfield Gtr Man 86 D5
Highfield N Ayrs 120 D3
Highfield Oxon 39 B5
Highfield S Yorks 88 F4
Highfield Tyne/Wear 110 D4
Highfields Cambs 54 D4
Highfields Northum 125 D5
Highgate London 41 F5
Highland Folk Museum, Aultlairie H'land 148 E3
Highland Folk Museum, Kingussie H'land 148 D3
Highlane Ches 75 C5
Highlane Derby 88 F5
Highlaws Cumb 107 E8
Highleadon Glos 36 B4
Highleigh W Sussex 16 E2
Highley Shrops 61 F7
Highmoor Cross Oxon 39 F7
Highmoor Hill Monmouths 36 F1
Highnam Glos 36 C4
Highnam Green Glos 36 B4
Highsted Kent 30 C3
Highstreet Green Essex 55 F8
Hightae Dumf/Gal 107 B7
Hightown Ches 75 C5
Hightown Mersey 85 D4
Hightown Green Suffolk 56 D3
Highway Wilts 24 B5
Highweek Devon 7 B6
Highworth Swindon 38 E2
Hilborough Norfolk 67 D8
Hilcote Derby 76 D4
Hilcott Wilts 25 D6
Hilden Park Kent 29 E6
Hildenborough Kent 29 E6
Hildersham Cambs 55 E6
Hilderstone Staffs 75 F6
Hilderthorpe ER Yorks 97 C7
Hilfield Dorset 12 D4
Hilgay Norfolk 67 E6
Hill Pembs 32 D2
Hill S Gloucs 36 E3
Hill W Midlands 62 E5
Hill Brow W Sussex 15 B8
Hill Dale Lancs 86 C2
Hill Dyke Lincs 79 E6
Hill End Durham 110 F3
Hill End Fife 134 E2
Hill End N Yorks 94 D3
Hill Head Hants 15 D6
Hill Head Northum 110 C2
Hill Mountain Pembs 44 E4
Hill of Beath Fife 134 E3
Hill of Fearn H'land 158 B2
Hill of Mountblairy Aberds 160 C3
Hill Ridware Staffs 62 C4
Hill Top Durham 100 B4
Hill Top Hants 14 D5
Hill Top W Midlands 62 E3
Hill Top W Yorks 88 C4
Hill Top, Sawrey Cumb 99 E5
Hill View Dorset 13 E7
Hillam N Yorks 89 B6
Hillbeck Cumb 100 C2
Hillborough Kent 31 C6
Hillbrae Aberds 151 B6
Hillbrae Aberds 160 D3
Hillbutts Dorset 13 D7
Hillcliffane Derby 76 E2
Hillcommon Som'set 11 B6
Hillend Fife 134 F3
Hillerton Devon 10 E2
Hillesden Bucks 39 B6
Hillesley Glos 36 F4
Hillfarance Som'set 11 B6
Hillhead Aberds 160 E2
Hillhead Devon 7 D7
Hillhead S Ayrs 112 C4
Hillhead of Auchentumb Aberds 161 C6
Hillhead of Cocklaw Aberds 161 D7
Hillhouse Scot Borders 123 D8
Hilliclay H'land 169 C6
Hillier Gardens and Arboretum Hants 14 B4
Hillingdon London 40 F3
Hillington Glasg C 120 C5
Hillington Norfolk 80 E3
Hillmorton Warwick 52 B3
Hillockhead Aberds 150 C3
Hillockhead Aberds 150 D2
Hillside Aberds 151 E8
Hillside Angus 143 C7
Hillside Mersey 85 C4
Hillside Orkney 176 G3
Hillside Shetl'd 175 G6
Hillswick Shetl'd 174 F4
Hillway I/Wight 15 F7
Hillwell Shetl'd 175 M5
Hilmarton Wilts 24 B5
Hilperton Wilts 24 D3
Hilsea Portsm'th 15 D7
Hilston ER Yorks 97 F8
Hilton Aberds 161 E6
Hilton Cambs 54 C3
Hilton Cumb 100 B2
Hilton Derby 76 F2
Hilton Dorset 13 D5
Hilton Durham 101 B6
Hilton H'land 164 F4
Hilton Shrops 61 E7
Hilton Stockton 102 C2
Hilton of Cadboll H'land 158 B2
Hilton Worcs 50 D4
Himbleton Worcs 50 D4
Himley Staffs 62 E2
Hincaster Cumb 99 F7
Hinckley Leics 63 E8
Hinderclay Suffolk 56 B4
Hinderton Ches 73 B7
Hinderwell N Yorks 103 C5
Hindford Shrops 73 F7
Hindhead Surrey 27 F6
Hindley Gtr Man 86 D4
Hindley Green Gtr Man 86 D4
Hindlip Worcs 50 D3
Hindolveston Norfolk 81 E6
Hindon Wilts 24 F4
Hindringham Norfolk 81 D5
Hingham Norfolk 68 D3
Hinstock Shrops 61 B6
Hintlesham Suffolk 56 E4
Hinton Hants 14 E3
Hinton Heref'd 48 F5
Hinton Northants 52 D3
Hinton Shrops 60 D4
Hinton S Gloucs 24 B2
Hinton Ampner Hants 15 B6
Hinton Blewett Bath/NE Som'set 23 D7
Hinton Charterhouse Bath/NE Som'set 24 D2
Hinton-in-the-Hedges Northants 52 F3
Hinton Martell Dorset 13 D8
Hinton on the Green Worcs 50 E5
Hinton Parva Swindon 38 F2
Hinton St George Som'set 12 C2
Hinton St Mary Dorset 13 C5
Hinton Waldrist Oxon 38 E3
Hints Shrops 49 B8
Hints Staffs 63 D5
Hinwick Beds 53 C7
Hinxhill Kent 30 E4
Hinxton Cambs 55 E5
Hinxworth Herts 54 E3
Hipperholme W Yorks 88 B2
Hipswell N Yorks 101 E6
Hirael Gwyn 83 D5
Hiraeth Carms 32 B2
Hirn Aberds 151 D6
Hirnant Powys 59 B7
Hirst N Lanarks 121 C8
Hirst Northum 117 F8
Hirst Courtney N Yorks 89 B7
Hirwaen Denbs 72 C5
Hirwaun Rh Cyn Taff 34 D3
Hiscott Devon 9 B7
Histon Cambs 54 C5
Hitcham Suffolk 56 D3
Hitchin Herts 40 B4
Hither Green London 28 B4
Hittisleigh Devon 10 E2
Hive ER Yorks 96 F4
Hixon Staffs 62 B4
HMS Victory Portsm'th 15 D7
HMY Britannia C/Edinb 123 B5
Hoaden Kent 31 D6
Hoaldalbert Monmouths 35 B7
Hoar Cross Staffs 62 B5
Hoarwithy Heref'd 36 B2
Hoath Kent 31 C6
Hobarris Shrops 48 B5
Hobbister Orkney 176 F2
Hobkirk Scot Borders 115 C8
Hobson Durham 110 D4
Hoby Leics 64 C3
Hockering Norfolk 68 C3
Hockerton Notts 77 D7
Hockley Essex 42 E4
Hockley Heath W Midlands 51 B6
Hockliffe Beds 40 B2
Hockwold cum Wilton Norfolk 67 F7
Hockworthy Devon 10 C5
Hoddesdon Herts 41 D6
Hoddlesden Blackb'n 86 B5
Hoddom Mains Dumf/Gal 107 B8
Hoddomcross Dumf/Gal 107 B8
Hodgeston Pembs 32 E1
Hodley Powys 59 E8
Hodnet Shrops 61 B6
Hodthorpe Derby 76 B5
Hoe Hants 15 C6
Hoe Norfolk 68 C2
Hoe Gate Hants 15 C7
Hoff Cumb 100 C1
Hog Patch Surrey 27 E6
Hoggard's Green Suffolk 56 D2
Hoggeston Bucks 39 B8
Hogha Gearraidh W Isles 170 C3
Hoghton Lancs 86 B4
Hognaston Derby 76 D2
Hogsthorpe Lincs 79 B8
Holbeach Lincs 66 B3
Holbeach Bank Lincs 66 B3
Holbeach Clough Lincs 66 B3
Holbeach Drove Lincs 66 C3
Holbeach Hurn Lincs 66 B3
Holbeach St Johns Lincs 66 C3
Holbeach St Marks Lincs 79 F6
Holbeach St Matthew Lincs 79 F7
Holbeck Notts 76 B5
Holbeck W Yorks 95 F5
Holbeck Woodhouse Notts 76 B5
Holberrow Green Worcs 50 D5
Holbeton Devon 6 D4
Holborn London 41 F6
Holbrook Derby 76 E3
Holbrook Suffolk 57 F5
Holbrook S Yorks 88 F5
Holburn Northum 125 F6
Holbury Hants 14 D5
Holcombe Devon 7 B7
Holcombe Som'set 23 E8
Holcombe Rogus Devon 11 C5
Holcot Northants 53 C5
Holden Lancs 93 E7
Holdenby Northants 52 C4
Holdenhurst Bournem'th 14 E2
Holdgate Shrops 61 F5
Holdingham Lincs 78 E3
Holditch Dorset 11 D8
Hole-in-the-Wall Heref'd 36 B3
Holefield Scot Borders 124 F4
Holehouses Ches 74 B4
Holemoor Devon 9 D6
Holestane Dumf/Gal 113 E8
Holford Som'set 22 E3
Holgate C/York 95 D8
Holker Cumb 92 B3
Holkham Norfolk 80 C4
Hollacombe Devon 9 D5
Holland Orkney 176 A3
Holland Orkney 176 D5
Holland Fen Lincs 78 E5
Holland-on-Sea Essex 43 C8
Hollandstoun Orkney 176 A6
Hollee Dumf/Gal 108 C2
Hollesley Suffolk 57 E7
Hollicombe Torbay 7 C6
Hollingbourne Kent 30 D2
Hollington Derby 76 F2
Hollington E Sussex 18 D4
Hollington Staffs 75 F7
Hollington Grove Derby 76 F2
Hollingworth Gtr Man 87 E8
Hollins Gtr Man 87 D6
Hollins Green Warrington 86 E4
Hollins Lane Lancs 92 D4
Hollinsclough Staffs 75 C7
Hollinwood Gtr Man 87 D7
Hollinwood Shrops 74 F2
Hollocombe Devon 9 C8
Hollow Meadows S Yorks 88 F3
Holloway Derby 76 D3
Hollowell Northants 52 B4
Holly End Norfolk 66 D4
Holly Grn Worcs 50 E3
Hollybush Caerph 35 D5
Hollybush E Ayrs 112 C3
Hollybush Worcs 50 F2
Hollym ER Yorks 91 B7
Hollywood Worcs 51 B5
Holmbridge W Yorks 88 D2
Holmbury St Mary Surrey 28 E2
Holmbush Cornw'l 4 D5
Holmcroft Staffs 62 B3
Holme Cambs 65 F8
Holme Cumb 92 B5
Holme Notts 77 D8
Holme N Yorks 102 F1
Holme W Yorks 88 D2
Holme Chapel Lancs 87 B6
Holme Green N Yorks 95 E8
Holme Hale Norfolk 67 D8
Holme Lacy Heref'd 49 F7
Holme Marsh Heref'd 48 D5
Holme next the Sea Norfolk 80 C3
Holme-on-Spalding-Moor ER Yorks 96 F4
Holme on the Wolds ER Yorks 97 E5
Holme Pierrepont Notts 77 F6
Holme St Cuthbert Cumb 107 E8
Holme Wood W Yorks 94 F4
Holmer Heref'd 49 E7
Holmer Green Bucks 40 E2
Holmes Chapel Ches 74 C4
Holmesfield Derby 76 B3
Holmeswood Lancs 86 C2
Holmewood Derby 76 C4
Holmfirth W Yorks 88 D2
Holmhead Dumf/Gal 113 F7
Holmhead E Ayrs 113 B5
Holmisdale H'land 152 E2
Holmpton ER Yorks 91 B7
Holmrook Cumb 98 E2
Holmsgarth Shetl'd 175 J6
Holmwrangle Cumb 108 E5
Holne Devon 6 C5
Holnest Dorset 12 D4
Holsworthy Devon 8 D5
Holsworthy Beacon Devon 9 D5
Holt Dorset 13 D8
Holt Norfolk 81 D6
Holt Wilts 24 C3
Holt Worcs 50 C3
Holt Wrex 73 D8
Holt End Hants 26 F4
Holt End Worcs 51 C5
Holt Fleet Worcs 50 C3
Holt Heath Worcs 50 C3
Holt Park W Yorks 95 E5
Holtby C/York 96 D2
Holton Oxon 39 D6
Holton Som'set 12 B4
Holton Suffolk 57 B7
Holton cum Beckering Lincs 90 F5
Holton Heath Dorset 13 E7
Holton le Clay Lincs 91 D6
Holton le Moor Lincs 90 E4
Holton St Mary Suffolk 56 F4
Holwell Dorset 12 C5
Holwell Herts 54 F2
Holwell Leics 64 B4
Holwell Oxon 38 D2
Holwick Durham 100 B4
Holworth Dorset 13 F5
Holy Cross Worcs 50 B4
Holy Island Northum 125 E7
Holybourne Hants 26 E5
Holyhead = Caergybi Angl 82 C2
Holymoorside Derby 76 C3
Holyport Windsor 27 B6
Holystone Northum 117 D5
Holytown N Lanarks 121 C7
Holywell Cambs 54 B4
Holywell Cornw'l 4 D2
Holywell Dorset 12 D3
Holywell E Sussex 18 F2
Holywell Northum 111 B6
Holywell = Treffynnon Flints 73 B5
Holywell Bay Fun Park, Newquay Cornw'l 4 D2
Holywell Green W Yorks 87 C8
Holywell Lake Som'set 11 B6
Holywell Row Suffolk 55 B8
Holywood Dumf/Gal 114 F2
Hom Green Heref'd 36 B2
Homer Shrops 61 D6
Homersfield Suffolk 69 F5
Homington Wilts 14 B2
Honey Hill Kent 30 C5
Honey Street Wilts 25 C6
Honey Tye Suffolk 56 F3
Honeyborough Pembs 44 E4
Honeybourne Worcs 51 E6
Honeychurch Devon 9 D8
Honiley Warwick 51 B7
Honing Norfolk 69 B6
Honingham Norfolk 68 C4
Honington Lincs 78 E2
Honington Suffolk 56 B3
Honington Warwick 51 E7
Honiton Devon 11 D6
Honley W Yorks 88 C2
Hoo Medway 29 B8
Hoo Green Ches 86 F5
Hood Green S Yorks 88 D4
Hooe E Sussex 18 E3
Hooe Plym'th 6 D3
Hooe Common E Sussex 18 D3
Hook ER Yorks 89 B8
Hook London 28 C2
Hook Hants 26 D5
Hook Pembs 44 D4
Hook Wilts 37 F7
Hook Green Kent 18 B3
Hook Green Kent 29 C7
Hook Norton Oxon 51 F8
Hooke Dorset 12 E3
Hookgate Staffs 74 F4
Hookway Devon 10 E3
Hookwood Surrey 28 E3
Hoole Ches 73 C8
Hooley Surrey 28 D3
Hooton Ches 73 B7
Hooton Levitt S Yorks 89 E6
Hooton Pagnell S Yorks 89 D5
Hooton Roberts S Yorks 89 E5
Hop Pole Lincs 65 C8
Hope Derby 88 F2
Hope Devon 6 F4
Hope H'land 167 D6
Hope Powys 60 D2
Hope Shrops 60 D3
Hope Staffs 75 D8
Hope = Yr Hôb Flints 73 D7
Hope Bagot Shrops 49 B7
Hope Bowdler Shrops 60 E4
Hope End Green Essex 42 B1
Hope Green Ches 87 F7
Hope Mansell Heref'd 36 C3
Hope under Dinmore Heref'd 49 D7
Hopeman Moray 158 C5
Hope's Grn Essex 42 F3
Hopesay Shrops 60 F3
Hopley's Green Heref'd 48 D5
Hopperton N Yorks 95 D7
Hopstone Shrops 61 E7
Hopton Shrops 60 B3
Hopton Shrops 61 B5
Hopton Staffs 62 B3
Hopton Suffolk 56 B3
Hopton Cangeford Shrops 60 F5
Hopton Castle Shrops 49 B5
Hopton on Sea Norfolk 69 D8
Hopton Wafers Shrops 49 B8
Hoptonheath Shrops 49 B5
Hopwas Staffs 63 D5
Hopwood Gtr Man 87 D6
Hopwood Worcs 50 B5
Horam E Sussex 18 D2
Horbling Lincs 78 F4
Horbury W Yorks 88 C3
Horcott Glos 38 D1
Horden Durham 111 E7
Horderley Shrops 60 F4
Hordle Hants 14 E3
Hordley Shrops 73 F7
Horeb Ceredig'n 46 E2
Horeb Carms 33 D5
Horeb Carms 33 B6
Horfield Bristol 23 B8
Horham Suffolk 57 B6
Horkesley Heath Essex 43 B5
Horkstow N Lincs 90 C3
Horley Oxon 52 E2
Horley Surrey 28 E3
Hornblotton Green Som'set 23 F7
Hornby Lancs 93 C5
Hornby N Yorks 101 E7
Hornby N Yorks 102 D1
Horncastle Lincs 79 C5
Hornchurch London 41 F8
Horncliffe Northum 124 E5
Horndean Scot Borders 124 E4
Horndean Hants 15 C8
Horndon Devon 6 B3
Horndon on the Hill Thurr'k 42 F2
Horne Surrey 28 E4
Horniehaugh Angus 142 C4
Horning Norfolk 69 C6
Horninghold Leics 64 E5
Horninglow Staffs 63 B6
Horningsea Cambs 55 C5
Horningsham Wilts 24 E3
Horningtoft Norfolk 80 E5
Horns Corner Kent 18 C4
Horns Cross Devon 9 B5
Horns Cross E Sussex 18 C5
Hornsby Cumb 108 D5
Hornsea ER Yorks 97 E8
Hornsea Bridge ER Yorks 97 E8
Hornsey London 41 F6
Hornton Oxon 51 E8
Horrabridge Devon 6 C3
Horringer Suffolk 56 C2
Horringford I/Wight 15 F6
Horse Bridge Staffs 75 D6
Horsebridge Devon 5 B8
Horsebridge Hants 25 F8
Horsebrook Staffs 62 C2
Horsehay Telford 61 D6
Horseheath Cambs 55 E7
Horsehouse N Yorks 101 F5
Horsell Surrey 27 D7
Horseman's Green Wrex 73 E8
Horseway Cambs 66 F4
Horsey Norfolk 69 B7
Horsford Norfolk 68 C4
Horsforth W Yorks 94 F5
Horsham W Sussex 28 F2
Horsham Worcs 50 D2
Horsham St Faith Norfolk 68 C5
Horsington Lincs 78 C4
Horsington Som'set 12 B5
Horsley Derby 76 E3
Horsley Glos 37 E5
Horsley Northum 110 C3
Horsley Northum 116 E4
Horsley Cross Essex 43 B7
Horsley Woodhouse Derby 76 E3
Horsleycross Street Essex 43 B7
Horsleyhill Scot Borders 115 C8
Horsleyhope Durham 110 E3
Horsmonden Kent 29 E7
Horspath Oxon 39 D5
Horstead Norfolk 69 C5
Horsted Keynes W Sussex 17 B7
Horton Bucks 40 C2
Horton Dorset 13 D8
Horton Lancs 93 D8
Horton Northants 53 D6
Horton Shrops 60 B4
Horton S Gloucs 36 F4
Horton Som'set 11 C8
Horton Staffs 75 D6
Horton Swan 33 F5
Horton Wilts 25 C5
Horton Windsor 27 B8
Horton cum Studley Oxon 39 C5
Horton Green Ches 73 E8
Horton Heath Hants 15 C5
Horton-in-Ribblesdale N Yorks 93 B8
Horton Kirby Kent 29 C6
Hortonlane Shrops 60 C4
Horwich Gtr Man 86 C4
Horwich End Derby 87 F8
Horwood Devon 9 B7
Hose Leics 64 B4
Hoselaw Scot Borders 124 F4
Hoses Cumb 98 E4
Hosh Perth/Kinr 133 B7
Hosta W Isles 170 C3
Hoswick Shetl'd 175 L6
Hotham ER Yorks 96 F4
Hothfield Kent 30 E3
Hoton Leics 64 B2
Houbie Shetl'd 174 D8
Houdston S Ayrs 112 E1
Hough Ches 74 D4
Hough Ches 75 B5
Hough Green Halton 86 F2
Hough-on-the-Hill Lincs 78 E2
Hougham Lincs 77 E8
Houghton Cambs 54 B3
Houghton Cumb 108 D4
Houghton Hants 25 F8
Houghton Pembs 44 E4
Houghton W Sussex 16 C4
Houghton Conquest Beds 53 E8
Houghton Green E Sussex 19 C6
Houghton Green Warrington 86 E4
Houghton-le-Side D'lington 101 B7
Houghton-Le-Spring Tyne/Wear 111 E6
Houghton on the Hill Leics 64 D3
Houghton Regis Beds 40 B3
Houghton St Giles Norfolk 80 D5
Houlland Shetl'd 175 H5
Houlland Shetl'd 174 F7
Houlsyke N Yorks 103 D5
Hound Hants 15 D5
Hound Green Hants 26 D5
Houndslow Scot Borders 124 E2
Houndwood Scot Borders 124 C4
Hounslow London 28 B2
Hounslow Green Essex 42 C2
Housay Shetl'd 174 F8
House of Daviot H'land 157 E8
House of Glenmuick Aberds 150 E2
Housesteads Roman Fort Northum 109 C7
Housetter Shetl'd 174 E5
Houss Shetl'd 175 K5
Houston Renf 120 C4
Houstry H'land 169 F6
Houton Orkney 176 F2
Hove Brighton/Hove 17 D6
Hoveringham Notts 77 E6
Hoveton Norfolk 69 C6
Hovingham N Yorks 96 B2
How Cumb 108 D5
How Caple Heref'd 49 F8
How End Beds 53 E8
How Green Kent 29 E5
Howbrook S Yorks 88 E4
Howden Scot Borders 116 B2
Howden ER Yorks 89 B8
Howden-le-Wear Durham 110 F4
Howe H'land 169 C8
Howe Norfolk 69 D5
Howe N Yorks 101 F8
Howe Bridge Gtr Man 86 D4
Howe Green Essex 42 D3
Howe of Teuchar Aberds 160 D4
Howe Street Essex 42 C2
Howe Street Essex 55 F7
Howell Lincs 78 E4
Howey Powys 48 D2
Howgate Midloth 122 D5
Howick Northum 117 C8
Howle Durham 101 B5
Howle Telford 61 B6
Howlett End Essex 55 F6
Howley Som'set 11 D7
Hownam Scot Borders 116 C3
Hownam Mains Scot Borders 116 B3
Howpasley Scot Borders 115 D6
Howsham N Lincs 90 D4
Howsham N Yorks 96 C3
Howslack Dumf/Gal 114 D3
Howtel Northum 124 F4
Howton Heref'd 35 B8
Howtown Cumb 99 C6
Howwood Renf 120 C3
Hoxne Suffolk 57 B5
Hoy Orkney 176 F1
Hoylake Mersey 85 F3
Hoyland S Yorks 88 D4
Hoylandswaine S Yorks 88 D3
Hubberholme N Yorks 94 B2
Hubbert's Bridge Lincs 79 E5
Huby N Yorks 95 E5
Huby N Yorks 95 C8
Hucclecote Glos 37 C5
Hucking Kent 30 D2
Hucknall Notts 77 E5
Huddersfield W Yorks 88 C2
Huddington Worcs 50 D4
Hudswell N Yorks 101 D6
Huggate ER Yorks 96 D5
Hugglescote Leics 63 C8
Hugh Town I/Scilly 2 E4
Hughenden Valley Bucks 40 E1
Hughley Shrops 61 E5
Huish Devon 9 C7
Huish Wilts 25 C6
Huish Champflower Som'set 11 B5
Huish Episcopi Som'set 12 B2
Huisinis W Isles 173 G2
Hulcott Bucks 40 C1
Hulland Derby 76 E2
Hulland Ward Derby 76 E2
Hullavington Wilts 37 F5
Hullbridge Essex 42 E4
Hulme Gtr Man 87 E6
Hulme End Staffs 75 D8
Hulme Walfield Ches 74 C5
Hulver Street Suffolk 69 F7
Hulverstone I/Wight 14 F4
Humber Heref'd 49 D7
Humber Bridge N Lincs 90 B4
Humberston NE Lincs 91 D7
Humbie E Loth 123 C7
Humbleton ER Yorks 97 F8
Humbleton Northum 117 B5
Humby Lincs 78 F3
Hume Scot Borders 124 E3
Humshaugh Northum 110 B2
Huna H'land 169 B8
Huncoat Lancs 93 F7
Huncote Leics 64 E2

Pitmedden Aberds 151 B7
Pitminster Som'set 11 C7
Pitmuies Angus 143 E5
Pitmunie Aberds 151 C5
Pitney Som'set 12 B2
Pitscottie Fife 135 C6
Pitsea Essex 42 F3
Pitsford Northants 53 C5
Pitsmoor S Yorks 88 F4
Pitstone Bucks 40 C2
Pitstone Green Bucks 40 C2
Pitt Rivers Museum (See University Museum) Oxon 39 D5
Pittendreich Moray 159 C5
Pittentrail H'land 164 D4
Pittenweem Fife 135 D7
Pittington Durham 111 E6
Pittodrie Aberds 151 B5
Pitton Wilts 25 F7
Pittswood Kent 29 E7
Pittulie Aberds 161 B6
Pity Me Durham 111 E5
Pityme Cornw'l 4 B4
Pityoulish H'land 148 C5
Pixey Green Suffolk 57 B6
Pixham Surrey 28 D2
Pixley Heref'd 49 F8
Place Newton N Yorks 96 B4
Plaidy Aberds 160 C4
Plains N Lanarks 121 C7
Plaish Shrops 60 E5
Plaistow W Sussex 27 F8
Plaitford Hants 14 C3
Plank Lane Gtr Man 86 E4
Plâs Carms 33 B5
Plas-canol Gwyn 58 C2
Plas Gogerddan Ceredig'n 58 F3
Plas Llwyngwern Powys 58 D4
Plas Mawr, Conwy Conwy 83 D7
Plas Nantyr Wrex 73 F5
Plas-yn-Cefn Denbs 72 B4
Plastow Green Hants 26 C3
Platt Kent 29 D7
Platt Bridge Gtr Man 86 D4
Platts Common S Yorks 88 D4
Plawsworth Durham 111 E5
Plaxtol Kent 29 D7
Play Hatch Oxon 26 B5
Playden E Sussex 19 C6
Playford Suffolk 57 E6
Playing Place Cornw'l 3 B7
Playley Green Glos 50 F2
Plealey Shrops 60 D4
Plean Stirl 133 F7
Pleasington Blackb'n 86 B4
Pleasley Derby 76 C5
Pleasure Island Theme Park NE Lincs 91 D7
Pleasureland Mersey 85 C8
Pleasurewood Hills Family Theme Park, Lowestoft Suffolk 69 E8
Pleckgate Blackb'n 93 F6
Plenmeller Northum 109 C7
Pleshey Essex 42 C2
Plockton H'land 155 G4
Plocrapol W Isles 173 J4
Ploughfield Heref'd 49 E5
Plowden Shrops 60 F3
Ploxgreen Shrops 60 D3
Pluckley Kent 30 E3
Pluckley Thorne Kent 30 E3
Plumbland Cumb 107 F8
Plumley Ches 74 B4
Plumpton Cumb 108 F4
Plumpton E Sussex 17 C7
Plumpton Green E Sussex 17 C7
Plumpton Head Cumb 108 F5
Plumpton Racecourse E Sussex 17 C7
Plumstead London 29 B5
Plumstead Norfolk 81 D7
Plumtree Notts 77 F6
Plungar Leics 77 F7
Plush Dorset 12 D5
Plwmp Ceredig'n 46 D2
Plymouth Plym'th 6 D2
Plympton Plym'th 6 D3
Plymstock Plym'th 6 D3
Plymtree Devon 11 D5
Pockley N Yorks 102 F4
Pocklington ER Yorks 96 E4
Pode Hole Lincs 66 B2
Podimore Som'set 12 B3
Podington Beds 53 C7
Podmore Staffs 74 F4
Point Clear Essex 43 C6
Pointon Lincs 78 F4
Pokesdown Bournem'th 14 E2
Pol a Charra W Isles 171 J3
Polbae Dumf/Gal 105 B6
Polbain H'land 162 C3
Polbathic Cornw'l 5 D8
Polbeth W Loth 122 C3
Polchar H'land 148 D4
Pole Elm Worcs 50 E3
Polebrook Northants 65 F7
Polegate E Sussex 18 E2
Poles H'land 164 E4
Polesden Lacey, Dorking Surrey 28 D2
Polesworth Warwick 63 D6
Polgigga Cornw'l 2 D2
Polglass H'land 162 D4
Polgooth Cornw'l 4 D4
Poling W Sussex 16 D4
Polkerris Cornw'l 5 D5
Polla H'land 167 D5
Pollington ER Yorks 89 C7
Polloch H'land 138 C1
Pollok Glasg C 121 C5
Pollok House Glasg C 121 C5
Pollokshields Glasg C 121 C5
Polmassick Cornw'l 3 B8
Polmont Falk 122 B2
Polnessan E Ayrs 112 C4
Polnish H'land 145 E7
Polperro Cornw'l 5 D7
Polruan Cornw'l 5 D6
Polsham Som'set 23 E7
Polstead Suffolk 56 F3
Poltalloch Arg/Bute 130 F4
Poltimore Devon 10 E4
Polton Midloth 123 C5
Polwarth Scot Borders 124 D3
Polyphant Cornw'l 8 F4
Polzeath Cornw'l 4 B4
Ponders End London 41 E6
Pondersbridge Cambs 66 E2
Pondtail Hants 27 D6
Ponsanooth Cornw'l 3 C6
Ponsworthy Devon 6 B5
Pont Aber Carms 33 B8
Pont Aber-Geirw Gwyn 71 E8
Pont-ar-gothi Carms 33 B6
Pont ar Hydfer Powys 34 B2
Pont-ar-llechau Carms 33 B8
Pont Cwm Pydew Denbs 72 F4
Pont Cyfyng Conwy 83 F7
Pont Cysyllte Wrex 73 E6
Pont Dolydd Prysor Gwyn 71 D8
Pont-faen Powys 47 F8
Pont Fronwydd Gwyn 58 B5
Pont-gareg Pembs 45 E3
Pont-Henri Carms 33 D5
Pont-Llogel Powys 59 C7
Pont Pen-y-benglog Gwyn 83 E6
Pont Rhyd-goch Conwy 83 E6
Pont-Rhyd-sarn Gwyn 59 B5
Pont Rhyd-y-cyff Bridg 34 F2
Pont-rhyd-y-groes Ceredig'n 47 B6
Pont-rug Gwyn 82 E5
Pont Senni = Sennybridge Powys 34 B3
Pont-siân Ceredig'n 46 E3
Pont-y-gwaith Rh Cyn Taff 34 E4
Pont-y-pant Conwy 83 F7
Pont y Pennant Gwyn 59 B6
Pont-y-Pŵl = Pontypool Torf 35 D6
Pont yclun Rh Cyn Taff 34 F4
Pont yr Afon-Gam Gwyn 71 C8
Pont-yr-hafod Pembs 44 C4
Pontamman Carms 33 C7
Pontantwn Carms 33 C5
Pontardawe Neath P Talb 33 D8
Pontarddulais Swan 33 D6
Pontarsais Carms 33 B5
Pontblyddyn Flints 73 C6
Pontbren Araeth Carms 33 B7
Pontbren Llwyd Rh Cyn Taff 34 D3
Pontefract W Yorks 89 B5
Pontefract Racecourse W Yorks 88 B5
Ponteland Northum 110 B4
Ponterwyd Ceredig'n 58 F4
Pontesbury Shrops 60 D3
Pontfadog Wrex 73 F6
Pontfaen Pembs 45 F2
Pontgarreg Ceredig'n 46 D2
Ponthir Torf 35 E7
Ponthirwaun Ceredig'n 45 E4
Pontllanfraith Caerph 35 E5
Pontlliw Swan 33 D7
Pontllyfni Gwyn 82 F4
Pontlottyn Caerph 35 D5
Pontneddfechan Powys 34 D3
Pontnewydd Torf 35 E6
Pontrhydfendigaid Ceredig'n 47 C6
Pontrhydyfen Neath P Talb 34 E1
Pontrilas Heref'd 35 B7
Pontrobert Powys 59 C8
Ponts Green E Sussex 18 D3
Pontshill Heref'd 36 B3
Pontsticill Merth Tyd 34 C4
Pontwgan Conwy 83 D7
Pontyates Carms 33 D5
Pontyberem Carms 33 C6
Pontycymer Bridg 34 E3
Pontyglasier Pembs 45 F3
Pontypool = Pont-y-Pŵl Torf 35 D6
Pontypridd Rh Cyn Taff 34 F4
Pontywaun Caerph 35 E6
Pooksgreen Hants 14 C4
Pool Cornw'l 3 B5
Pool W Yorks 94 E5
Pool o'Muckhart Clack 134 D2
Pool Quay Powys 60 C2
Poole Poole 13 E8
Poole Keynes Glos 37 E6
Poolend Staffs 75 D6
Poolewe H'land 154 B4
Pooley Bridge Cumb 99 B6
Poolfold Staffs 75 D5
Poolhill Glos 36 B4
Poolsbrook Derby 76 B4
Pootings Kent 29 E5
Pope Hill Pembs 44 D4
Popeswood Brackn'l 27 C6
Popham Hants 26 E3
Poplar London 41 F6
Popley Hants 26 D4
Porchester Notts 77 E5
Porchfield I/Wight 15 E5
Porin H'land 156 D4
Poringland Norfolk 69 D5
Porkellis Cornw'l 3 C5
Porlock Som'set 21 E7
Porlock Weir Som'set 21 E7
Port Ann Arg/Bute 128 B4
Port Appin Arg/Bute 138 E3
Port Askaig Arg/Bute 126 C4
Port Bannatyne Arg/Bute 129 D5
Port Carlisle Cumb 108 C2
Port Charlotte Arg/Bute 126 D2
Port Clarence Stockton 102 B2
Port Driseach Arg/Bute 128 C4
Port e Vullen I/Man 84 C4
Port Ellen Arg/Bute 126 E3
Port Elphinstone Aberds 151 C6
Port Erin I/Man 84 F1
Port Erroll Aberds 161 E7
Port Eynon Swan 33 F5
Port Gaverne Cornw'l 8 F2
Port Glasgow Inverci 120 B3
Port Henderson H'land 154 C3
Port Isaac Cornw'l 4 A4
Port Lamont Arg/Bute 129 C5
Port Lion Pembs 44 E4
Port Logan Dumf/Gal 104 E4
Port Mholair W Isles 172 E8
Port Mor H'land 144 F4
Port Mulgrave N Yorks 103 C5
Port Nan Giùran W Isles 172 E8
Port nan Long W Isles 170 C4
Port Nis W Isles 172 B8
Port of Menteith Stirl 132 D4
Port Quin Cornw'l 4 A4
Port Ramsay Arg/Bute 138 E2
Port St Mary I/Man 84 F2
Port Sunlight Mersey 85 F4
Port Talbot Neath P Talb 34 E1
Port Tennant Swan 33 E7
Port Wemyss Arg/Bute 126 D1
Port William Dumf/Gal 105 E7
Portachoillan Arg/Bute 128 E2
Portavadie Arg/Bute 128 D4
Portbury N Som'set 23 B7
Portchester Hants 15 D7
Portclair H'land 147 C7
Portencalzie Dumf/Gal 104 B4
Portencross N Ayrs 119 B8
Portesham Dorset 12 F4
Portessie Moray 159 C8
Portfield Gate Pembs 44 D4
Portgate Devon 9 F6
Portgordon Moray 159 C7
Portgower H'land 165 C7
Porth Cornw'l 4 C3
Porth Rh Cyn Taff 34 E4
Porth Navas Cornw'l 3 D6
Porth Tywyn = Burry Port Carms 33 D5
Porth-y-waen Shrops 60 B2
Porthaethwy = Menai Bridge Angl 83 D5
Porthallow Cornw'l 3 D6
Porthallow Cornw'l 5 D7
Porthcawl Bridg 21 B7
Porthcothan Cornw'l 4 B3
Porthcurno Cornw'l 2 D2
Porthgain Pembs 44 B3
Porthill Shrops 60 C4
Porthkerry V/Glam 22 C2
Porthleven Cornw'l 2 D5
Porthlechog Angl 82 B4
Porthmadog Gwyn 71 D6
Porthmeor Cornw'l 2 C3
Portholland Cornw'l 3 B8
Porthoustock Cornw'l 3 D7
Porthpean Cornw'l 4 D5
Porthtowan Cornw'l 3 B5
Porthyrhyd Carms 33 C6
Porthyrhyd Carms 47 F6
Portincaple Arg/Bute 129 A7
Portington ER Yorks 96 F3
Portinnisherrich Arg/Bute 131 D5
Portinscale Cumb 98 B4
Portishead N Som'set 23 B6
Portkil Arg/Bute 129 B7
Portknockie Moray 159 C8
Portlethen Aberds 151 E8
Portling Dumf/Gal 107 D5
Portloe Cornw'l 3 C8
Portmahomack H'land 165 F6
Portmeirion Gwyn 71 D6
Portmeirion Village Gwyn 71 D6
Portmellon Cornw'l 3 B9
Portmore Hants 14 E4
Portnacroish Arg/Bute 138 E3
Portnahaven Arg/Bute 126 D1
Portnalong H'land 153 F4
Portnaluchaig H'land 145 E6
Portnancon H'land 167 C6
Portnellan Stirl 132 B3
Portobello C/Edinb 123 B6
Porton Wilts 25 F6
Portpatrick Dumf/Gal 104 D4
Portreath Cornw'l 3 B5
Portree H'land 153 E5
Portscatho Cornw'l 3 C7
Portsea Portsm'th 15 D7
Portskerra H'land 168 C3
Portskewett Monmouths 36 F2
Portslade Brighton/Hove 17 D6
Portslade-by-Sea Brighton/Hove 17 D6
Portsmouth Portsm'th 15 E7
Portsmouth W Yorks 87 B7
Portsmouth Sea Life Centre Portsm'th 15 E7
Portsonachan Arg/Bute 131 C6
Portsoy Aberds 160 B2
Portswood S'hampton 14 C5
Porttanachy Moray 159 C7
Portuairk H'land 137 B5
Portway Heref'd 49 F6
Portway Worcs 51 B5
Portwrinkle Cornw'l 5 E8
Poslingford Suffolk 55 E8
Postbridge Devon 6 B4
Postcombe Oxon 39 E7
Postling Kent 19 B8
Postwick Norfolk 69 D5
Potholm Dumf/Gal 115 F6
Potsgrove Beds 40 B2
Pott Row Norfolk 80 E3
Pott Shrigley Ches 75 B6
Potten End Herts 40 D3
Potter Brompton N Yorks 97 B5
Potter Heigham Norfolk 69 C7
Potter Street Essex 41 D7
Potterhanworth Lincs 78 C3
Potterhanworth Booths Lincs 78 C3
Potteries Museum & Art Gallery, Stoke-on-Trent Stoke 75 E5
Potterne Wilts 24 D4
Potterne Wick Wilts 24 D5
Potternewton W Yorks 95 F6
Potters Bar Herts 41 D5
Potter's Cross Staffs 62 F2
Potterspury Northants 53 E5
Potterton Aberds 151 C8
Potterton W Yorks 95 F7
Potto N Yorks 102 D2
Potton Beds 54 E3
Poughill Cornw'l 8 D4
Poughill Devon 10 D3
Poulshot Wilts 24 D4
Poulton Glos 37 D8
Poulton Mersey 85 E4
Poulton-le-Fylde Lancs 92 F3
Pound Bank Worcs 50 B2
Pound Green E Sussex 18 C2
Pound Green I/Wight 14 F4
Pound Green Worcs 50 B2
Pound Hill W Sussex 28 F3
Poundfield E Sussex 18 B2
Poundland S Ayrs 112 F1
Poundon Bucks 39 B6
Poundsgate Devon 6 B5
Poundstock Cornw'l 8 E4
Powburn Northum 117 C6
Powderham Devon 10 F4
Powderham Castle Devon 10 F4
Powerstock Dorset 12 E3
Powfoot Dumf/Gal 107 C8
Powick Worcs 50 D3
Powis Castle, Welshpool Powys 60 D2
Powmill Perth/Kinr 134 E2
Poxwell Dorset 12 F5
Poyle Slough 27 B8
Poynings W Sussex 17 C6
Poyntington Dorset 12 C4
Poynton Ches 87 F7
Poynton Green Telford 61 C5
Poystreet Green Suffolk 56 D3
Praa Sands Cornw'l 2 D4
Pratt's Bottom London 29 C5
Praze Cornw'l 2 C4
Praze-an-Beeble Cornw'l 2 C5
Predannack Wollas Cornw'l 3 E5
Prees Shrops 74 F2
Prees Green Shrops 74 F2
Prees Heath Shrops 74 F2
Prees Higher Heath Shrops 74 F2
Prees Lower Heath Shrops 74 F2
Preesall Lancs 92 E3
Preesgweene Shrops 73 F6
Prenderguest Scot Borders 124 D5
Prendwick Northum 117 C6
Prengwyn Ceredig'n 46 E3
Prenteg Gwyn 71 C6
Prenton Mersey 85 F4
Prescot Mersey 86 E2
Prescott Shrops 60 B4
Pressen Northum 124 F4
Prestatyn Denbs 72 A4
Prestbury Ches 75 B6
Prestbury Glos 37 B6
Presteigne = Llanandras Powys 48 C5
Presthope Shrops 61 E5
Prestleigh Som'set 23 E8
Preston Scot Borders 124 D3
Preston Brighton/Hove 17 D7
Preston Devon 7 B6
Preston Dorset 12 F5
Preston E Loth 123 B8
Preston ER Yorks 97 F7
Preston Glos 37 D7
Preston Glos 50 F2
Preston Herts 40 B4
Preston Kent 30 C4
Preston Kent 31 C6
Preston Lancs 86 B3
Preston Northum 117 B7
Preston Rutl'd 65 D5
Preston Shrops 60 C5
Preston Suffolk 56 D3
Preston Wilts 24 B5
Preston Wilts 25 B7
Preston Bagot Warwick 51 C6
Preston Bissett Bucks 39 B6
Preston Bowyer Som'set 11 B6
Preston Brockhurst Shrops 60 B5
Preston Brook Halton 86 F3
Preston Candover Hants 26 E4
Preston Capes Northants 52 D3
Preston Crowmarsh Oxon 39 E6
Preston Gubbals Shrops 60 C4
Preston Hall Museum, Stockton-on-Tees Stockton 102 C2
Preston on Stour Warwick 51 E7
Preston on the Hill Halton 86 F3
Preston on Wye Heref'd 49 E5
Preston Plucknett Som'set 12 C3
Preston-under-Scar N Yorks 101 E5
Preston upon the Weald Moors Telford 61 C6
Preston Wynne Heref'd 49 E7
Prestonmill Dumf/Gal 107 D6
Prestonpans E Loth 123 B6
Prestwich Gtr Man 87 D6
Prestwick Northum 110 B4
Prestwick S Ayrs 112 B3
Prestwood Bucks 40 D1
Price Town Bridg 34 E3
Prickwillow Cambs 67 F5
Priddy Som'set 23 D7
Priest Hutton Lancs 92 B5
Priest Weston Shrops 60 E2
Priesthaugh Scot Borders 115 D7
Primethorpe Leics 64 E2
Primrose Green Norfolk 68 C3
Primrose Valley N Yorks 97 B7
Primrosehill Herts 40 D3
Princes Gate Pembs 32 C2
Princes Risborough Bucks 39 D8
Princethorpe Warwick 52 B2
Princetown Caerph 35 C5
Princetown Devon 6 B3
Prinknash Abbey, Gloucester Glos 37 C5
Prion Denbs 72 C4
Prior Muir Fife 135 C7
Prior Park Northum 125 D5
Priors Frome Heref'd 49 F7
Priors Hardwick Warwick 52 D2
Priors Marston Warwick 52 D2
Priorslee Telford 61 C7
Priory Church, Lancaster Lancs 92 C4
Priory Wood Heref'd 48 E4
Priston Bath/NE Som'set 23 C8
Pristow Green Norfolk 68 F4
Prittlewell Southend 42 F4
Privett Hants 15 B7
Prixford Devon 20 F4
Probus Cornw'l 3 B7
Proncy H'land 164 E4
Prospect Cumb 107 E8
Prudhoe Northum 110 C3
Ptarmigan Lodge Stirl 132 D2
Pubil Perth/Kinr 140 E1
Puckeridge Herts 41 B6
Puckington Som'set 11 C8
Pucklechurch S Gloucs 23 B8
Pucknall Hants 14 B4
Puckrup Glos 50 F3
Puddinglake Ches 74 C4
Puddington Ches 73 B7
Puddington Devon 10 C3
Puddledock Norfolk 68 E3
Puddletown Dorset 13 E5
Pudleston Heref'd 49 D7
Pudsey W Yorks 94 F5
Pulborough W Sussex 16 C4
Puleston Telford 61 B7
Pulford Ches 73 D7
Pulham Dorset 12 D5
Pulham Market Norfolk 68 F4
Pulham St Mary Norfolk 68 F5
Pulloxhill Beds 53 F8
Pumpherston W Loth 122 C3
Pumsaint Carms 47 E5
Puncheston Pembs 32 B1
Puncknowle Dorset 12 F3
Punnett's Town E Sussex 18 C3
Purbrook Hants 15 D7
Purewell Dorset 14 E2
Purfleet Thurr'k 29 B6
Puriton Som'set 22 E5
Purleigh Essex 42 D4
Purley London 28 C4
Purley W Berks 26 B4
Purlogue Shrops 48 B4
Purls Bridge Cambs 66 F4
Purse Caundle Dorset 12 C4
Purslow Shrops 60 F3
Purston Jaglin W Yorks 88 C5
Purton Glos 36 D3
Purton Glos 36 D3
Purton Wilts 37 F7
Purton Stoke Wilts 37 E7
Pury End Northants 52 E5
Pusey Oxon 38 E3
Putley Heref'd 49 F8
Putney London 28 B3
Putsborough Devon 20 E3
Puttenham Herts 40 C1
Puttenham Surrey 27 E7
Puxton N Som'set 23 C6
Pwll Carms 33 D5
Pwll-glas Denbs 72 D5
Pwll-Meyric Monmouths 36 E2
Pwll-trap Carms 32 C3
Pwll-y-glaw Neath P Talb 34 E1
Pwllcrochan Pembs 44 E4
Pwllgloyw Powys 48 F2
Pwllheli Gwyn 70 D4
Pycombe W Sussex 17 C6
Pye Corner Newp 35 F7
Pye Green Staffs 62 C3
Pyewipe NE Lincs 91 C6
Pyle I/Wight 15 G5
Pyle = Y Pîl Bridg 34 F2
Pylle Som'set 23 F8
Pymoor Cambs 66 F4
Pyrford Surrey 27 D8
Pyrton Oxon 39 E6
Pytchley Northants 53 B6
Pyworthy Devon 8 D5

Q

Quabbs Shrops 60 F2
Quadring Lincs 78 F5
Quainton Bucks 39 C7
Quarley Hants 25 E7
Quarndon Derby 76 E3
Quarrier's Homes Inverci 120 C3
Quarrington Lincs 78 E3
Quarrington Hill Durham 111 F6
Quarry Bank W Midlands 62 F3
Quarry Bank Mill, Wilmslow Ches 87 F6
Quarryford E Loth 123 C8
Quarryhill H'land 164 F4
Quarrywood Moray 159 C5
Quarter S Lanarks 121 D7
Quatford Shrops 61 E7
Quatt Shrops 61 F7
Quebec Durham 110 E4
Quedgeley Glos 37 C5
Queen Adelaide Cambs 67 F5
Queen Camel Som'set 12 B3
Queen Charlton Bath/NE Som'set 23 C8
Queen Dart Devon 10 C3
Queen Oak Dorset 24 F2
Queen Street Kent 29 E7
Queen Street Wilts 37 F7
Queenborough Kent 30 B3
Queenhill Worcs 50 F3
Queen's Head Shrops 60 B3
Queen's Park Beds 53 E8
Queen's Park Northants 53 C5
Queen's View Centre, Loch Tummel Perth/Kinr 141 D5
Queensbury W Yorks 94 F4
Queensferry C/Edinb 122 B4
Queensferry Flints 73 C7
Queenstown Blackp'l 92 F3
Queenzieburn N Lanarks 121 B6
Quemerford Wilts 24 C5
Quendale Shetl'd 175 M5
Quendon Essex 55 F6
Queniborough Leics 64 C3
Quenington Glos 37 D8
Quernmore Lancs 92 D5
Quethiock Cornw'l 5 C8
Quholm Orkney 176 E1
Quicks Green W Berks 26 B3
Quidenham Norfolk 68 F3
Quidhampton Hants 26 D3
Quidhampton Wilts 25 F6
Quilquox Aberds 161 E6
Quina Brook Shrops 74 F2
Quindry Orkney 176 G3
Quinton Northants 53 D5
Quinton W Midlands 62 F3
Quintrell Downs Cornw'l 4 C3
Quixhill Staffs 75 E8
Quoditch Devon 9 E6
Quoig Perth/Kinr 133 B7
Quorndon Leics 64 C2
Quothquan S Lanarks 122 F2
Quoyloo Orkney 176 D1
Quoyness Orkney 176 F1
Quoys Shetl'd 174 B8
Quoys Shetl'd 175 G6

R

Raasay Ho. H'land 153 F6
Rabbit's Cross Kent 29 E8
Raby Mersey 73 B7
Rachan Mill Scot Borders 122 F4
Rachub Gwyn 83 E6
Rackenford Devon 10 C3
Rackham W Sussex 16 C4
Rackheath Norfolk 69 C5
Racks Dumf/Gal 107 B7
Rackwick Orkney 176 G1
Rackwick Orkney 176 B3
Radbourne Derby 76 F2
Radcliffe Gtr Man 87 D5
Radcliffe Northum 117 D8
Radcliffe on Trent Notts 77 F6
Radclive Bucks 52 F4
Radcot Oxon 38 E2
Raddery H'land 157 D8
Radernie Fife 135 D6
Radford Semele Warwick 51 C8
Radipole Dorset 12 F4
Radlett Herts 40 E4
Radley Oxon 39 E5
Radmanthwaite Notts 76 C5
Radmoor Shrops 61 B6
Radmore Green Ches 74 D2
Radnage Bucks 39 E7
Radstock Bath/NE Som'set 23 D8
Radstone Northants 52 E3
Radway Warwick 52 E2
Radway Green Ches 74 D4
Radwell Beds 53 D8
Radwell Herts 54 F3
Radwinter Essex 55 F7
Radyr Card 35 F5
RAF Museum, Hendon London 41 F5
Rafford Moray 158 D4
Ragdale Leics 64 C3
Raglan Monmouths 35 D8
Ragley Hall Warwick 51 D5
Ragnall Notts 77 B8
Rahane Arg/Bute 129 B7
Rainford Mersey 86 D2
Rainford Junction Mersey 86 D2
Rainham London 41 F8
Rainham Medway 30 C2
Rainhill Mersey 86 E2
Rainhill Stoops Mersey 86 E3
Rainow Ches 75 B6
Rainton N Yorks 95 B6
Rainworth Notts 77 D5
Raisbeck Cumb 100 D1
Raise Cumb 109 E7
Rait Perth/Kinr 134 B4
Raithby Lincs 91 F7
Raithby Lincs 79 C6
Rake W Sussex 16 B2
Rakewood Gtr Man 87 C7
Ram Carms 46 E4
Ram Lane Kent 30 E3
Ramasaig H'land 153 E2
Rame Cornw'l 3 C6
Rame Cornw'l 6 E2
Rameldry Mill Bank Fife 134 D5
Ramnageo Shetl'd 174 C8
Rampisham Dorset 12 D3
Rampside Cumb 92 C2
Rampton Cambs 54 C5
Rampton Notts 77 B7
Ramsbottom Gtr Man 87 C5
Ramsbury Wilts 25 B7
Ramscraigs H'land 165 B8
Ramsdean Hants 15 B8
Ramsdell Hants 26 D3
Ramsden Oxon 38 C3
Ramsden Bellhouse Essex 42 E3
Ramsden Heath Essex 42 E3
Ramsey Cambs 66 F2
Ramsey Essex 57 F6
Ramsey I/Man 84 C4
Ramsey Forty Foot Cambs 66 F3
Ramsey Heights Cambs 66 F2
Ramsey Island Essex 43 D5
Ramsey Mereside Cambs 66 F2
Ramsey St Mary's Cambs 66 F2
Ramseycleuch Scot Borders 115 C5
Ramsgate Kent 31 C7
Ramsgill N Yorks 94 B4
Ramshorn Staffs 75 E7
Ramsnest Common Surrey 27 F7
Ranais W Isles 172 F7
Ranby Lincs 78 B5
Ranby Notts 89 F7
Rand Lincs 78 B4
Randwick Glos 37 D5
Ranfurly Renf 120 C3
Rangag H'land 169 E6
Rangemore Staffs 63 B5
Rangeworthy S Gloucs 36 F3
Rankinston E Ayrs 112 C4
Ranmoor S Yorks 88 F4
Ranmore Common Surrey 28 D2
Rannerdale Cumb 98 C3
Rannoch School Perth/Kinr 140 D2
Rannoch Station Perth/Kinr 139 D8
Ranochan H'land 145 E8
Ranskill Notts 89 F7
Ranton Staffs 62 B2
Ranworth Norfolk 69 C6
Raploch Stirl 133 E6
Rapness Orkney 176 B4
Rascal Moor ER Yorks 96 F4
Rascarrel Dumf/Gal 106 E4
Rashiereive Aberds 151 B8
Raskelf N Yorks 95 B7
Rassau Bl Gwent 35 C5
Rastrick W Yorks 88 B2
Ratagan H'land 146 C2
Ratby Leics 64 D2
Ratcliffe Culey Leics 63 E7
Ratcliffe on Soar Leics 63 B8
Ratcliffe on the Wreake Leics 64 C3
Rathen Aberds 161 B7
Rathillet Fife 135 B5
Rathmell N Yorks 93 D8
Ratho C/Edinb 122 B4
Ratho Station C/Edinb 122 B4
Rathven Moray 159 C8
Ratley Warwick 51 E8
Ratlinghope Shrops 60 E4
Rattar H'land 169 B7
Ratten Row Lancs 92 E4
Rattery Devon 6 C5
Rattlesden Suffolk 56 D3
Rattray Perth/Kinr 142 E1
Raughton Head Cumb 108 E3
Raunds Northants 53 B7
Ravenfield S Yorks 89 E5
Ravenglass Cumb 98 E2
Ravenglass and Eskdale Railway & Museum Cumb 98 E2
Raveningham Norfolk 69 E6
Ravenscar N Yorks 103 D7
Ravenscraig Inverci 129 C7
Ravensdale I/Man 84 C3
Ravensden Beds 53 D8
Ravenseat N Yorks 100 D3
Ravenshead Notts 77 D5
Ravensmoor Ches 74 D3
Ravensthorpe Northants 52 B4
Ravensthorpe W Yorks 88 B3
Ravenstone Leics 63 C8
Ravenstone M/Keynes 53 D6
Ravenstonedale Cumb 100 D2
Ravenstown Cumb 92 B3
Ravenstruther S Lanarks 122 E2
Ravensworth N Yorks 101 D6
Raw N Yorks 103 D7
Rawcliffe ER Yorks 89 B7
Rawcliffe C/York 95 D8
Rawcliffe Bridge ER Yorks 89 B7
Rawdon W Yorks 94 F5
Rawmarsh S Yorks 88 E5
Rawreth Essex 42 E3
Rawridge Devon 11 D7
Rawtenstall Lancs 87 B6
Raxton Aberds 161 E5
Raydon Suffolk 56 F4
Raylees Northum 117 E5
Rayleigh Essex 42 E4
Rayne Essex 42 B3
Rayners Lane London 40 F4
Raynes Park London 28 C3
Reach Cambs 55 C6
Read Lancs 93 F7
Reading Reading 26 B5
Reading Street Kent 19 B6
Reagill Cumb 99 C8
Rearquhar H'land 164 E4
Rearsby Leics 64 C3
Reaster H'land 169 C7
Reawick Shetl'd 175 J5
Reay H'land 168 C4
Rechullin H'land 154 E4
Reculver Kent 31 C6
Red Dial Cumb 108 E2
Red Hill Worcs 50 D3
Red House Glass Cone, Wordsley W Midlands 62 F2
Red Houses Jersey 17
Red Lodge Suffolk 55 B7
Red Rail Heref'd 36 B2
Red Rock Gtr Man 86 D3
Red Roses Carms 32 C3
Red Row Northum 117 E8
Red Street Staffs 74 D5
Red Wharf Bay Angl 82 C5
Redberth Pembs 32 D1
Redbourn Herts 40 C4
Redbourne N Lincs 90 E3
Redbrook Glos 36 C2
Redbrook Wrex 74 E2
Redburn H'land 157 C6
Redburn H'land 158 E3
Redburn Northum 109 C7
Redcar Redcar/Clevel'd 102 B4
Redcar Racecourse Redcar/Clevel'd 102 B4
Redcastle Angus 143 D6
Redcastle H'land 157 E6
Redcliff Bay N Som'set 23 B6
Redding Falk 122 B2
Reddingmuirhead Falk 122 B2
Reddish Gtr Man 87 E6
Redditch Worcs 50 C5
Rede Suffolk 56 D2
Redenhall Norfolk 69 F5
Redesdale Camp Northum 116 E4
Redesmouth Northum 116 F4
Redford Aberds 143 B7
Redford Angus 143 E5
Redford Durham 110 F3
Redfordgreen Scot Borders 115 C6
Redgorton Perth/Kinr 134 B2
Redgrave Suffolk 56 B4
Redhill Aberds 160 E3
Redhill Aberds 151 D6
Redhill N Som'set 23 C7
Redhill Surrey 28 D3
Redhouse Arg/Bute 128 D3
Redhouses Arg/Bute 126 C3
Redisham Suffolk 69 F7
Redland Bristol 23 B7
Redland Orkney 176 D2
Redlingfield Suffolk 57 B5
Redlynch Som'set 23 F9
Redlynch Wilts 14 B3
Redmarley D'Abitot Glos 50 F2
Redmarshall Stockton 102 B1
Redmile Leics 77 F7
Redmire N Yorks 101 E5
Redmoor Cornw'l 5 C5
Rednal Shrops 60 B3
Redpath Scot Borders 123 F8
Redpoint H'land 154 D3
Redruth Cornw'l 3 B5
Redvales Gtr Man 87 D6
Redwick Newp 35 F8
Redwick S Gloucs 36 F2
Redworth D'lington 101 B7
Reed Herts 54 F4
Reedham Norfolk 69 D7
Reedness ER Yorks 89 B8
Reeds Beck Lincs 78 C5
Reepham Lincs 78 B3
Reepham Norfolk 81 E6
Reeth N Yorks 101 E5
Regaby I/Man 84 C4
Regoul H'land 158 D2
Reiff H'land 162 C3
Reigate Surrey 28 D3
Reighton N Yorks 97 B7
Reighton Gap N Yorks 97 B7
Reinigeadal W Isles 173 H5
Reiss H'land 169 D8
Rejerrah Cornw'l 4 D2
Releath Cornw'l 3 C5
Relubbus Cornw'l 2 C4
Relugas Moray 158 E3
Remenham Wokingham 39 F8
Remenham Hill Wokingham 39 F7
Remony Perth/Kinr 140 E4
Rempstone Notts 64 B2
Rendcomb Glos 37 D7
Rendham Suffolk 57 C7
Rendlesham Suffolk 57 D7
Renfrew Renf 120 C5
Renhold Beds 53 D8
Renishaw Derby 76 B4
Rennington Northum 117 C8
Renton W Dunb 120 B3
Renwick Cumb 109 E5
Repps Norfolk 69 C7
Repton Derby 63 B7
Reraig H'land 155 H4
Rescobie Angus 143 D5
Resipole H'land 137 B8
Resolis H'land 157 C7
Resolven Neath P Talb 34 D2
Reston Scot Borders 124 C4
Reswallie Angus 143 D5
Retew Cornw'l 4 D4
Retford Notts 89 F8
Rettendon Essex 42 E3
Rettendon Place Essex 42 E3
Revesby Lincs 79 C5
Revesby Bridge Lincs 79 C6
Rew Street I/Wight 15 E5
Rewe Devon 10 E4
Reydon Suffolk 57 B8
Reydon Smear Suffolk 57 B8
Reymerston Norfolk 68 D3
Reynalton Pembs 32 D1
Reynoldston Swan 33 E5
Rezare Cornw'l 5 B8
Rhaeadr Gwy = Rhayader Powys 47 C8
Rhandirmwyn Carms 47 E6
Rhayader = Rhaeadr Gwy Powys 47 C8
Rhedyn Gwyn 70 D3
Rhemore H'land 137 C6
Rhencullen I/Man 84 C3
Rhes-y-cae Flints 73 B5
Rhewl Denbs 72 C5
Rhewl Denbs 73 E5
Rhian H'land 164 C2
Rhicarn H'land 162 B4
Rhiconich H'land 166 D4
Rhicullen H'land 157 B7
Rhidorroch Ho. H'land 163 E5
Rhifail H'land 168 E2
Rhigos Rh Cyn Taff 34 D3
Rhilochan H'land 164 D4
Rhiroy H'land 163 F5
Rhisga = Risca Caerph 35 E6
Rhiw Gwyn 70 E3
Rhiwabon = Ruabon Wrex 73 E7
Rhiwbina Card 35 F5
Rhiwbryfdir Gwyn 71 C7
Rhiwderin Newp 35 F6
Rhiwlas Gwyn 83 E5
Rhiwlas Gwyn 72 F3
Rhiwlas Powys 73 F5
Rhodes Gtr Man 87 D6
Rhodes Minnis Kent 31 E5
Rhodesia Notts 77 B5
Rhodiad Pembs 44 C2
Rhondda Rh Cyn Taff 34 E3
Rhonehouse or Kelton Hill Dumf/Gal 106 D4
Rhoose = Y Rhws V/Glam 22 C2
Rhôs Carms 46 F2
Rhôs Neath P Talb 33 D8
Rhos-fawr Gwyn 70 D4
Rhos-hill Pembs 45 E3
Rhos-on-Sea Conwy 83 C8
Rhos-y-brithdir Powys 59 B8
Rhos-y-garth Ceredig'n 46 B5
Rhos-y-gwaliau Gwyn 72 F3
Rhos-y-llan Gwyn 70 D3
Rhos-y-Madoc Wrex 73 E7
Rhos-y-meirch Powys 48 C4
Rhosamman Carms 33 C8
Rhosbeirio Angl 82 B3
Rhoscefnhir Angl 82 D5
Rhoscolyn Angl 82 D2
Rhoscrowther Pembs 44 E4
Rhosesmor Flints 73 C6
Rhosgadfan Gwyn 82 F5
Rhosgoch Angl 82 C4
Rhosgoch Powys 48 E3
Rhoshirwaun Gwyn 70 E2
Rhoslan Gwyn 71 C5
Rhoslefain Gwyn 58 D2
Rhosllanerchrugog Wrex 73 E6
Rhosmaen Carms 33 B7
Rhosmeirch Angl 82 D4
Rhosneigr Angl 82 D3
Rhosnesni Wrex 73 D7
Rhosrobin Wrex 73 D7
Rhossili Swan 33 F5
Rhosson Pembs 44 C2
Rhostryfan Gwyn 82 F4
Rhostyllen Wrex 73 E7
Rhosybol Angl 82 C4
RHS Garden, Wisley Surrey 27 D8
Rhu Arg/Bute 128 D3
Rhu Arg/Bute 129 B7
Rhuallt Denbs 72 B4
Rhuddall Heath Ches 74 C2
Rhuddlan Ceredig'n 46 E3
Rhuddlan Denbs 72 B4
Rhue H'land 162 E4
Rhulen Powys 48 E3
Rhunahaorine Arg/Bute 118 B4
Rhuthun = Ruthin Denbs 72 D5
Rhyd Gwyn 71 C7
Rhyd Powys 59 D6
Rhyd-Ddu Gwyn 83 F5
Rhyd-moel-ddu Powys 48 B2
Rhyd-Rosser Ceredig'n 46 C4
Rhyd-uchaf Gwyn 72 F3
Rhyd-wen Gwyn 58 C4
Rhyd-y-clafdy Gwyn 70 D4
Rhyd-y-foel Conwy 72 B3
Rhyd-y-fro Neath P Talb 33 D8
Rhyd-y-gwin Swan 33 D7
Rhyd-y-meirch Monmouths 35 D7
Rhyd-y-meudwy Denbs 72 D5
Rhyd-y-pandy Swan 33 D7
Rhyd-y-sarn Gwyn 71 C7
Rhyd-yr-onen Gwyn 58 D3
Rhydaman = Ammanford Carms 33 C7
Rhydargaeau Carms 33 B5
Rhydcymerau Carms 46 F4
Rhydd Worcs 50 E3
Rhydding Neath P Talb 33 E8
Rhydfudr Ceredig'n 46 C4
Rhydlewis Ceredig'n 46 E2
Rhydlios Gwyn 70 D2
Rhydlydan Conwy 83 F8
Rhydness Powys 48 E3
Rhydowen Ceredig'n 46 E3
Rhydspence Heref'd 48 E4
Rhydtalog Flints 73 D6
Rhydwyn Angl 82 C3
Rhydycroesau Shrops 73 F6
Rhydyfelin Ceredig'n 46 B4
Rhydyfelin Rh Cyn Taff 34 F4
Rhydymain Gwyn 58 B5
Rhydymwyn Flints 73 C6
Rhyl = Y Rhyl Denbs 72 A4
Rhymney = Rhymni Caerph 35 D5
Rhymni = Rhymney Caerph 35 D5
Rhynd Fife 135 B6
Rhynd Perth/Kinr 134 B3
Rhynie Aberds 150 B3
Rhynie H'land 158 B2
Ribbesford Worcs 50 B2
Ribblehead N Yorks 93 B7
Ribbleton Lancs 93 F5
Ribchester Lancs 93 F6
Ribigill H'land 167 D7
Riby Lincs 91 D5
Riby Cross Roads Lincs 91 D5
Riccall N Yorks 96 F2
Riccarton E Ayrs 120 F4
Richards Castle Heref'd 49 C6
Richings Park Bucks 27 B8
Richmond London 28 B2
Richmond N Yorks 101 D6
Rickarton Aberds 151 F7
Rickinghall Suffolk 56 B4
Rickleton Tyne/Wear 111 D5
Rickling Essex 55 F5
Rickmansworth Herts 40 E3
Riddings Cumb 108 B4
Riddings Derby 76 D4
Riddlecombe Devon 9 C8
Riddlesden W Yorks 94 E3
Riddrie Glasg C 121 C6
Ridge Dorset 13 F7
Ridge Hants 14 C4
Ridge Wilts 24 F4
Ridge Green Surrey 28 E4
Ridge Lane Warwick 63 E6
Ridgebourne Powys 48 C2
Ridgehill N Som'set 23 C7
Ridgeway Cross Heref'd 50 E2
Ridgewell Essex 55 E8
Ridgewood E Sussex 17 C8
Ridgmont Beds 53 F7
Riding Mill Northum 110 C3
Ridleywood Wrex 73 D8
Ridlington Norfolk 69 A6
Ridlington Rutl'd 64 D5
Ridsdale Northum 116 F5
Riechip Perth/Kinr 141 E7
Riemore Perth/Kinr 141 E7
Rienachait H'land 166 F2
Rievaulx N Yorks 102 F3
Rievaulx Abbey N Yorks 102 F3
Rift House Hartlep'l 111 F7
Rigg Dumf/Gal 108 C2
Riggend N Lanarks 121 B7
Rigsby Lincs 79 B7
Rigside S Lanarks 121 F8
Riley Green Lancs 86 B4
Rileyhill Staffs 62 C5
Rilla Mill Cornw'l 5 B7
Rillington N Yorks 96 B4
Rimington Lancs 93 E8
Rimpton Som'set 12 B4
Rimswell ER Yorks 91 B7
Rinaston Pembs 44 C4
Ringasta Shetl'd 175 M5
Ringford Dumf/Gal 106 D3
Ringinglow S Yorks 88 F3
Ringland Norfolk 68 C4
Ringles Cross E Sussex 17 B8
Ringmer E Sussex 17 C8
Ringmore Devon 6 E4
Ringorm Moray 159 E6
Ring's End Cambs 66 D3
Ringsfield Suffolk 69 F7
Ringsfield Corner Suffolk 69 F7
Ringshall Herts 40 C2
Ringshall Suffolk 56 D4
Ringshall Stocks Suffolk 56 D4
Ringstead Norfolk 80 C3
Ringstead Northants 53 B7
Ringwood Hants 14 D2
Ringwould Kent 31 E7
Rinmore Aberds 150 C3
Rinnigill Orkney 176 G2
Rinsey Cornw'l 2 D4
Riof W Isles 172 E4
Ripe E Sussex 18 D2
Ripley Derby 76 D3
Ripley Hants 14 E2
Ripley N Yorks 95 C5
Ripley Surrey 27 D8
Riplingham ER Yorks 97 F5
Ripon N Yorks 95 B6
Ripon Cathedral N Yorks 95 B6
Ripon Racecourse N Yorks 95 C6
Rippingale Lincs 65 B7
Ripple Kent 31 E7
Ripple Worcs 50 F3
Ripponden W Yorks 87 C8
Rireavach H'land 162 E4
Risabus Arg/Bute 126 E3
Risbury Heref'd 49 D7
Risby Suffolk 55 C8
Risca = Rhisga Caerph 35 E6
Rise ER Yorks 97 E7
Riseden E Sussex 18 B3
Risegate Lincs 66 B2
Riseholme Lincs 78 B2
Riseley Beds 53 C8
Riseley Wokingham 26 C5
Rishangles Suffolk 57 C5
Rishton Lancs 93 F7
Rishworth W Yorks 87 C8
Rising Bridge Lancs 87 B5
Risley Derby 76 F4
Risley Warrington 86 E4
Risplith N Yorks 94 C5
Rispond H'land 167 C6
Rivar Wilts 25 C8
Rivenhall End Essex 42 C4
River Bank Cambs 55 C6
Riverhead Kent 29 D6
Rivington Lancs 86 C4
Roa Island Cumb 92 C2
Roachill Devon 10 B3
Road Green Norfolk 69 E5
Roade Northants 53 D5
Roadhead Cumb 108 B5
Roadmeetings S Lanarks 122 E2
Roadside H'land 169 C6
Roadside of Catterline Aberds 143 B8
Roadside of Kinneff Aberds 143 B8
Roadwater Som'set 22 F2
Roag H'land 153 E3
Roath Card 22 B3
Rob Roy and Trossachs Visitor Centre, Callander Stirl 132 D5
Robert Burns Centre, Dumfries Dumf/Gal 107 B6
Roberton Scot Borders 115 C7
Roberton S Lanarks 114 B2
Robertsbridge E Sussex 18 C4
Roberttown W Yorks 88 B2
Robeston Cross Pembs 44 E3
Robeston Wathen Pembs 32 C1
Robin Hood W Yorks 88 B4
Robin Hood's Bay N Yorks 103 D7
Roborough Devon 9 C7
Roborough Devon 6 C3
Roby Mersey 86 E2
Roby Mill Lancs 86 D3
Rocester Staffs 75 F8
Roch Pembs 44 C3
Roch Gate Pembs 44 C3

Thornholme ER Yorks 97 C7
Thornley Durham 110 F4
Thornley Durham 111 F6
Thornliebank E Renf 120 D5
Thorns Suffolk 55 D8
Thorns Green Ches 87 F5
Thornsett Derby 87 F8
Thornthwaite Cumb 98 B4
Thornthwaite N Yorks 94 D4
Thornton Angus 142 E3
Thornton Bucks 53 F5
Thornton ER Yorks 96 E3
Thornton Fife 134 E4
Thornton Lancs 92 E3
Thornton Leics 63 D8
Thornton Lincs 78 C5
Thornton Mersey 85 D4
Thornton Middlesbro 102 C2
Thornton Northum 125 E5
Thornton Pembs 44 E4
Thornton W Yorks 94 F4
Thornton Curtis N Lincs 90 C4
Thornton Heath London 28 C4
Thornton Hough Mersey 85 F4
Thornton in Craven N Yorks 94 E2
Thornton-le-Beans N Yorks 102 E1
Thornton-le-Clay N Yorks 96 C2
Thornton-le-Dale N Yorks 103 F6
Thornton le Moor Lincs 90 E4
Thornton-le-Moor N Yorks 102 F1
Thornton-le-Moors Ches 73 B8
Thornton-le-Street N Yorks 102 F2
Thornton Rust N Yorks 100 F4
Thornton Steward N Yorks 101 F6
Thornton Watlass N Yorks 101 F7
Thorntonhall S Lanarks 121 D5
Thorntonloch E Loth 124 B3
Thorntonpark Northum 124 E5
Thornwood Common Essex 41 D7
Thornydykes Scot Borders 124 E2
Thoroton Notts 77 E7
Thorp Arch W Yorks 95 E7
Thorpe Derby 75 D8
Thorpe ER Yorks 97 E5
Thorpe Lincs 91 F8
Thorpe Norfolk 69 E7
Thorpe Notts 77 E7
Thorpe N Yorks 94 C3
Thorpe Surrey 27 C8
Thorpe Abbotts Norfolk 57 B5
Thorpe Acre Leics 64 B2
Thorpe Arnold Leics 64 B4
Thorpe Audlin W Yorks 89 C5
Thorpe Bassett N Yorks 96 B4
Thorpe Bay Southend 43 F5
Thorpe by Water Rutl'd 65 E5
Thorpe Common Suffolk 57 F6
Thorpe Constantine Staffs 63 D6
Thorpe Culvert Lincs 79 C7
Thorpe End Norfolk 69 C5
Thorpe Fendykes Lincs 79 C7
Thorpe Green Essex 43 B7
Thorpe Green Suffolk 56 D3
Thorpe Hesley S Yorks 88 E4
Thorpe in Balne S Yorks 89 C6
Thorpe in the Fallows Lincs 90 F3
Thorpe Langton Leics 64 E4
Thorpe Larches Durham 102 B1
Thorpe-le-Soken Essex 43 B7
Thorpe le Street ER Yorks 96 E4
Thorpe Malsor Northants 53 B6
Thorpe Mandeville Northants 52 E3
Thorpe Market Norfolk 81 D8
Thorpe Marriot Norfolk 68 C4
Thorpe Morieux Suffolk 56 D3
Thorpe on the Hill Lincs 78 C2
Thorpe Park, Chertsey Surrey 27 C8
Thorpe St Andrew Norfolk 69 D5
Thorpe St Peter Lincs 79 C7
Thorpe Salvin S Yorks 89 F6
Thorpe Satchville Leics 64 C4
Thorpe Thewles Stockton 102 B2
Thorpe Tilney Lincs 78 D4
Thorpe Underwood N Yorks 95 D7
Thorpe Waterville Northants 65 F7
Thorpe Willoughby N Yorks 95 F8
Thorpeness Suffolk 57 D8
Thorrington Essex 43 C6
Thorverton Devon 10 D4
Thrandeston Suffolk 56 B5
Thrapston Northants 53 B7
Thrashbush N Lanarks 121 C7
Threapland Cumb 107 F8
Threapland N Yorks 94 C2
Threapwood Ches 73 E8
Threapwood Staffs 75 E7
Threave Gardens Dumf/Gal 106 C4
Three Ashes Heref'd 36 B2
Three Bridges W Sussex 28 F3
Three Burrows Cornw'l 3 B6
Three Chimneys Kent 18 B5
Three Cocks Powys 48 F3
Three Counties Showground, Malvern Worcs 50 E2
Three Crosses Swan 33 E6
Three Cups Corner E Sussex 18 C3
Three Holes Norfolk 66 D5
Three Leg Cross E Sussex 18 B3
Three Legged Cross Dorset 13 D8
Three Oaks E Sussex 18 D5
Threehammer Common Norfolk 69 C6
Threekingham Lincs 78 F3
Threemile Cross Wokingham 26 C5
Threemilestone Cornw'l 3 B6
Threemiletown W Loth 122 B3
Threlkeld Cumb 99 B5
Threshfield N Yorks 94 C2
Thrigby Norfolk 69 C7
Thringarth Durham 100 B4
Thringstone Leics 63 C8
Thrintoft N Yorks 101 E8
Thriplow Cambs 54 E5
Throckenholt Lincs 66 D3
Throcking Herts 54 F4
Throckley Tyne/Wear 110 C4
Throckmorton Worcs 50 E4
Throphill Northum 117 F7
Thropton Northum 117 D6
Throsk Stirl 133 E7
Throwleigh Devon 9 E8
Throwley Kent 30 D3
Thrumpton Notts 76 F5
Thrumster H'land 169 E8
Thrunton Northum 117 C6
Thrupp Glos 37 D5
Thrupp Oxon 38 C4
Thrushelton Devon 9 F6
Thrussington Leics 64 C3
Thruxton Hants 25 E7
Thruxton Heref'd 49 F6
Thrybergh S Yorks 89 E5
Thulston Derby 76 F4
Thundergay N Ayrs 119 B5
Thundersley Essex 42 F3
Thundridge Herts 41 C6
Thurcaston Leics 64 C2
Thurcroft S Yorks 89 F5
Thurgarton Norfolk 81 D7
Thurgarton Notts 77 E6
Thurgoland S Yorks 88 D3
Thurlaston Leics 64 E2
Thurlaston Warwick 52 B2
Thurlbear Som'set 11 B7
Thurlby Lincs 65 C8
Thurlby Lincs 78 C2
Thurleigh Beds 53 D8
Thurlestone Devon 6 E4
Thurloxton Som'set 22 F4
Thurlstone S Yorks 88 D3
Thurlton Norfolk 69 E7
Thurlwood Ches 74 D5
Thurmaston Leics 64 D3
Thurnby Leics 64 D3
Thurne Norfolk 69 C7
Thurnham Kent 30 D2
Thurnham Lancs 92 D4
Thurning Norfolk 81 E6
Thurning Northants 65 F7
Thurnscoe S Yorks 89 D5
Thurnscoe East S Yorks 89 D5
Thursby Cumb 108 D3
Thursford Norfolk 81 D5
Thursford Collection, Fakenham Norfolk 81 D5
Thursley Surrey 27 F7
Thurso H'land 169 C6
Thurso East H'land 169 C6
Thurstaston Mersey 85 F3
Thurston Suffolk 56 C3
Thurstonfield Cumb 108 D3
Thurstonland W Yorks 88 C2
Thurton Norfolk 69 D6
Thurvaston Derby 76 F2
Thuxton Norfolk 68 D3
Thwaite N Yorks 100 E3
Thwaite Suffolk 56 C5
Thwaite St Mary Norfolk 69 E6
Thwaites W Yorks 94 E3
Thwaites Brow W Yorks 94 E3
Thwing ER Yorks 97 B6
Tibbermore Perth/Kinr 134 B2
Tibberton Glos 36 B4
Tibberton Telford 61 B6
Tibberton Worcs 50 D4
Tibenham Norfolk 68 F4
Tibshelf Derby 76 C4
Tibthorpe ER Yorks 97 D5
Ticehurst E Sussex 18 B3
Tichborne Hants 26 F3
Tickencote Rutl'd 65 D6
Tickenham N Som'set 23 B6
Tickhill S Yorks 89 E6
Ticklerton Shrops 60 E4
Ticknall Derby 63 B7
Tickton ER Yorks 97 E6
Tidcombe Wilts 25 D7
Tiddington Oxon 39 D6
Tiddington Warwick 51 D7
Tidebrook E Sussex 18 C3
Tideford Cornw'l 5 D8
Tideford Cross Cornw'l 5 C8
Tidenham Glos 36 E2
Tideswell Derby 75 B8
Tidmarsh W Berks 26 B4
Tidmington Warwick 51 F7
Tidpit Hants 13 C8
Tidworth Wilts 25 E7
Tiers Cross Pembs 44 D4
Tiffield Northants 52 D5
Tifty Aberds 160 D4
Tigerton Angus 143 C5
Tigh-na-Blair Perth/Kinr 133 C6
Tighnabruaich Arg/Bute 128 C4
Tighnafiline H'land 162 F2
Tigley Devon 7 C5
Tilbrook Cambs 53 C8
Tilbury Thurr'k 29 B7
Tilbury Juxta Clare Essex 55 E8
Tile Cross W Midlands 63 F5
Tile Hill W Midlands 51 B7
Tilehurst Reading 26 B4
Tilford Surrey 27 E6
Tilgate W Sussex 28 F3
Tilgate Forest Row W Sussex 28 F3
Tillathrowie Aberds 159 F8
Tilley Shrops 60 B5
Tillicoultry Clack 133 E8
Tillingham Essex 43 D5
Tillington Heref'd 49 E6
Tillington W Sussex 16 B3
Tillington Common Heref'd 49 E6
Tillyarblet Angus 143 C5
Tillybirloch Aberds 151 D5
Tillycorthie Aberds 151 B8
Tillydrine Aberds 151 E5
Tillyfour Aberds 150 C4
Tillyfourie Aberds 150 C5
Tillygarmond Aberds 151 E5
Tillygreig Aberds 151 B7
Tillykerrie Aberds 151 B7
Tilmanstone Kent 31 D7
Tilney All Saints Norfolk 67 C5
Tilney High End Norfolk 67 C5
Tilney St Lawrence Norfolk 66 C5
Tilshead Wilts 24 E5
Tilstock Shrops 74 F2
Tilston Ches 73 D8
Tilstone Fearnall Ches 74 C2
Tilsworth Beds 40 B2
Tilton on the Hill Leics 64 D4
Timberland Lincs 78 D4
Timbersbrook Ches 75 C5
Timberscombe Som'set 21 E8
Timble N Yorks 94 D4
Timperley Gtr Man 87 F5
Timsbury Bath/NE Som'set 23 D8
Timsbury Hants 14 B4
Timsgearraidh W Isles 172 E3
Timworth Green Suffolk 56 C2
Tincleton Dorset 13 E5
Tindale Cumb 109 D6
Tingewick Bucks 52 F4
Tingley W Yorks 88 B3
Tingrith Beds 53 F8
Tingwall Orkney 176 D2
Tinhay Devon 9 F5
Tinshill W Yorks 95 F5
Tinsley S Yorks 88 E5
Tintagel Cornw'l 8 F2
Tintagel Castle Cornw'l 8 F2
Tintern Abbey Monmouths 36 D2
Tintern Parva Monmouths 36 D2
Tintinhull Som'set 12 C3
Tintwistle Derby 87 E8
Tinwald Dumf/Gal 114 F3
Tinwell Rutl'd 65 D7
Tipperty Aberds 151 B8
Tipsend Norfolk 66 E5
Tipton W Midlands 62 E3
Tipton St John Devon 11 E5
Tiptree Essex 42 C4
Tir-y-dail Carms 33 C7
Tirabad Powys 47 E7
Tiraghoil Arg/Bute 136 F4
Tirley Glos 37 B5
Tirphil Caerph 35 D5
Tirril Cumb 99 B7
Tisbury Wilts 13 B7
Tisman's Common W Sussex 27 F8
Tissington Derby 75 D8
Titchberry Devon 8 B4
Titchfield Hants 15 D6
Titchmarsh Northants 53 B8
Titchwell Norfolk 80 C3
Tithby Notts 77 F6
Titley Heref'd 48 C5
Titlington Northum 117 C7
Titsey Surrey 28 D5
Tittensor Staffs 75 F5
Tittleshall Norfolk 80 E4
Tiverton Ches 74 C2
Tiverton Devon 10 C4
Tivetshall St Margaret Norfolk 68 F4
Tivetshall St Mary Norfolk 68 F4
Tividale W Midlands 62 E3
Tivy Dale S Yorks 88 D3
Tixall Staffs 62 B3
Tixover Rutl'd 65 D6
Toab Orkney 176 F4
Toab Shetl'd 175 M5
Toadmoor Derby 76 D3
Tobermory Arg/Bute 137 C6
Toberonochy Arg/Bute 130 E3
Tobha Mor W Isles 170 G3
Tobhtarol W Isles 172 E4
Tobson W Isles 172 E4
Tocher Aberds 160 E3
Tockenham Wilts 24 B5
Tockenham Wick Wilts 37 F7
Tockholes Blackb'n 86 B4
Tockington S Glouc 36 F3
Tockwith N Yorks 95 D7
Todber Dorset 13 B6
Todding Heref'd 49 B6
Toddington Beds 40 B3
Toddington Glos 50 F5
Todenham Glos 51 F7
Todhills Cumb 108 C3
Todlachie Aberds 151 C5
Todmorden W Yorks 87 B7
Todrig Scot Borders 115 C7
Todwick S Yorks 89 F5
Toft Cambs 54 D4
Toft Lincs 65 C7
Toft Hill Durham 101 B6
Toft Hill Lincs 78 C5
Toft Monks Norfolk 69 E7
Toft next Newton Lincs 90 F4
Toftrees Norfolk 80 E4
Tofts H'land 169 C8
Toftwood Norfolk 68 C2
Togston Northum 117 D8
Tokavaig H'land 145 B6
Tokers Green Oxon 26 B5
Tolastadh a Chaolais W Isles 172 E4
Tolastadh bho Thuath W Isles 172 D8
Toll Bar S Yorks 89 D6
Toll End W Midlands 62 E3
Toll of Birness Aberds 161 E7
Tolland Som'set 22 F3
Tollard Royal Wilts 13 C7
Tollbar End W Midlands 51 B8
Toller Fratrum Dorset 12 E3
Toller Porcorum Dorset 12 E3
Tollerton Notts 77 F6
Tollerton N Yorks 95 C8
Tollesbury Essex 43 C5
Tolleshunt D'Arcy Essex 43 C5
Tolleshunt Major Essex 43 C5
Tolm W Isles 172 E7
Tolpuddle Dorset 13 E5
Tolvah H'land 148 E4
Tolworth London 28 C2
Tomatin H'land 148 B4
Tombreck H'land 157 F7
Tomchrasky H'land 147 C5
Tomdoun H'land 146 D4
Tomich H'land 147 B6
Tomich H'land 157 B7
Tomich House H'land 157 E6
Tomintoul Aberds 149 E7
Tomintoul Moray 149 C7
Tomnaven Moray 159 F8
Tomnavoulin Moray 149 B8
Ton-Pentre Rh Cyn Taff 34 E3
Tonbridge Kent 29 E6
Tondu Bridg 34 F2
Tonfanau Gwyn 58 D2
Tong Shrops 61 D7
Tong W Yorks 94 F5
Tong Norton Shrops 61 D7
Tonge Leics 63 B8
Tongham Surrey 27 E6
Tongland Dumf/Gal 106 D3
Tongue H'land 167 D7
Tongue End Lincs 65 C8
Tongwynlais Card 35 F5
Tonna Neath P Talb 34 E1
Tonwell Herts 41 C6
Tonypandy Rh Cyn Taff 34 E3
Tonyrefail Rh Cyn Taff 34 F4
Toot Baldon Oxon 39 D5
Toot Hill Essex 41 D8
Toothill Hants 14 C4
Top of Hebers Gtr Man 87 D6
Topcliffe N Yorks 95 B7
Topcroft Norfolk 69 E5
Topcroft Street Norfolk 69 E5
Toppesfield Essex 55 F8
Toppings Gtr Man 86 C5
Topsham Devon 10 F4
Torbay Torbay 7 D7
Torbeg N Ayrs 119 D6
Torboll Farm H'land 164 E4
Torbrex Stirl 133 E6
Torbryan Devon 7 C6
Torcross Devon 7 E6
Tore H'land 157 D7
Torinturk Arg/Bute 128 D3
Torksey Lincs 77 B8
Torlum W Isles 170 E3
Torlundy H'land 139 B5
Tormarton S Glouc 24 B2
Tormisdale Arg/Bute 126 D1
Tormitchell S Ayrs 112 E2
Tormore N Ayrs 119 C5
Tornagrain H'land 157 E8
Tornahaish Aberds 149 D8
Tornaveen Aberds 150 D5
Torness H'land 147 B8
Toronto Durham 101 B6
Torpenhow Cumb 108 F2
Torphichen W Loth 122 B2
Torphins Aberds 150 D5
Torpoint Cornw'l 6 D2
Torquay Torbay 7 C7
Torquhan Scot Borders 123 E7
Torran Arg/Bute 130 E4
Torran H'land 155 F6
Torran H'land 157 B8
Torrance E Dunb 121 B6
Torrans Arg/Bute 137 F5
Torranyard N Ayrs 120 E3
Torre Torbay 7 C7
Torridon H'land 154 E5
Torridon Ho. H'land 154 E4
Torrin H'land 153 G6
Torrisdale H'land 167 C8
Torrisdale-Square Arg/Bute 118 C4
Torrish H'land 165 C6
Torrisholme Lancs 92 C4
Torroble H'land 164 D2
Torry Aberd C 151 D8
Torry Aberds 159 F8
Torryburn Fife 134 F2
Torterston Aberds 161 D7
Torthorwald Dumf/Gal 107 B7
Tortington W Sussex 16 D4
Tortworth S Glouc 36 E4
Torvaig H'land 153 E5
Torver Cumb 98 E4
Torwood Falk 133 F7
Torworth Notts 89 F7
Tosberry Devon 8 B4
Toscaig H'land 155 G3
Toseland Cambs 54 C3
Tosside N Yorks 93 D7
Tostock Suffolk 56 C3
Totaig H'land 152 D3
Totaig H'land 155 H4
Tote H'land 152 E5
Totegan H'land 168 C3
Tothill Lincs 91 F8
Totland I/Wight 14 F4
Totnes Devon 7 C6
Toton Notts 76 F5
Totronald Arg/Bute 136 C2
Totscore H'land 152 C4
Tottenham London 41 E6
Tottenhill Norfolk 67 C6
Tottenhill Row Norfolk 67 C6
Totteridge London 41 E5
Totternhoe Beds 40 B2
Tottington Gtr Man 87 C5
Totton Hants 14 C4
Touchen End Windsor 27 B6
Tournaig H'land 154 B4
Toux Aberds 161 C6
Tovil Kent 29 D8
Tow Law Durham 110 F4
Toward Arg/Bute 129 D6
Towcester Northants 52 E4
Towcester Racecourse Northants 52 E5
Towednack Cornw'l 2 C3
Tower End Norfolk 67 C6
Tower Knowe Visitor Centre, Kielder Water Northum 116 F2
Tower of London London 41 F6
Towersey Oxon 39 D7
Towie Aberds 150 C3
Towie Aberds 161 B5
Towiemore Moray 159 E7
Town End Cambs 66 E4
Town End Cumb 99 F6
Town Row E Sussex 18 B2
Town Yetholm Scot Borders 116 B4
Townend W Dunb 120 B4
Towngate Lincs 65 D8
Townhead Cumb 108 F5
Townhead Dumf/Gal 106 E3
Townhead S Ayrs 112 D2
Townhead S Yorks 88 D2
Townhead of Greenlaw Dumf/Gal 106 C4
Townhill Fife 134 F3
Townsend Bucks 39 D7
Townsend Herts 40 D4
Townshend Cornw'l 2 C4
Towthorpe C/York 96 D2
Towton N Yorks 95 F7
Towyn Conwy 72 B3
Toxteth Mersey 85 F4
Toynton All Saints Lincs 79 C6
Toynton Fen Side Lincs 79 C6
Toynton St Peter Lincs 79 C7
Toy's Hill Kent 29 D5
Trabboch E Ayrs 112 B4
Traboe Cornw'l 3 D6
Tradespark H'land 158 D2
Tradespark Orkney 176 F3
Trafford Park Gtr Man 87 E5
Trago Mills, Newton Abbot Devon 7 B6
Trallong Powys 34 B3
Tranent E Loth 123 B7
Tranmere Mersey 85 F4
Trantlebeg H'land 168 D3
Trantlemore H'land 168 D3
Tranwell Northum 117 F7
Trapp Carms 33 C7
Traprain E Loth 123 B8
Traquair Scot Borders 123 F6
Trawden Lancs 94 F2
Trawsfynydd Gwyn 71 D8
Tre-Gibbon Rh Cyn Taff 34 D3
Tre-Taliesin Ceredig'n 58 E3
Tre-vaughan Carms 32 B4
Tre-wyn Monmouths 35 B7
Trealaw Rh Cyn Taff 34 E4
Treales Lancs 92 F4
Trearddur Angl 82 D2
Treaslane H'land 152 D4
Trebah Garden, Mawnan Smith Cornw'l 3 D6
Trebanog Rh Cyn Taff 34 E4
Trebanos Neath P Talb 33 D8
Trebartha Cornw'l 5 B7
Trebarwith Cornw'l 8 F2
Trebetherick Cornw'l 4 B4
Treborough Som'set 22 F2
Trebudannon Cornw'l 4 C3
Trebullett Cornw'l 5 B8
Treburley Cornw'l 5 B8
Trebyan Cornw'l 5 C5
Trecastle Powys 34 B2
Trecenydd Caerph 35 F5
Trecwn Pembs 44 B4
Trecynon Rh Cyn Taff 34 D3
Tredavoe Cornw'l 2 D3
Treddiog Pembs 44 C3
Tredegar Bl Gwent 35 D5
Tredegar Newydd = New Tredegar Caerph 35 D5
Tredington Glos 37 B6
Tredington Warwick 51 E7
Tredinnick Cornw'l 4 B4
Tredomen Powys 48 F3
Tredunnock Monmouths 35 E7
Tredustan Powys 48 F3
Treen Cornw'l 2 D2
Treeton S Yorks 88 F5
Tref-y-Clawdd = Knighton Powys 48 B4
Trefaldwyn = Montgomery Powys 60 E2
Trefasser Pembs 44 B3
Trefdraeth Angl 82 D4
Trefdraeth = Newport Pembs 45 F2
Trefecca Powys 48 F3
Trefechan Ceredig'n 58 F2
Trefeglwys Powys 59 E6
Trefenter Ceredig'n 46 C5
Treffgarne Pembs 44 C4
Treffynnon Pembs 44 C3
Treffynnon = Holywell Flints 73 B5
Trefgarn Owen Pembs 44 C3
Trefil Bl Gwent 35 C5
Trefilan Ceredig'n 46 D4
Trefin Pembs 44 B3
Treflach Shrops 60 B2
Trefnanney Powys 60 C2
Trefnant Denbs 72 B4
Trefonen Shrops 60 B2
Trefor Angl 82 C3
Trefor Gwyn 70 C4
Treforest Rh Cyn Taff 34 F4
Trefriw Conwy 83 E7
Trefynwy = Monmouth Monmouths 36 C2
Tregadillett Cornw'l 8 F4
Tregaian Angl 82 D4
Tregare Monmouths 35 C8
Tregaron Ceredig'n 47 D5
Tregarth Gwyn 83 E6
Tregeare Cornw'l 8 F4
Tregeiriog Wrex 73 F5
Tregele Angl 82 B3
Tregidden Cornw'l 3 D6
Treglemais Pembs 44 C3
Tregole Cornw'l 8 E3
Tregonetha Cornw'l 4 C4
Tregony Cornw'l 3 B8
Tregoss Cornw'l 4 C4
Tregoyd Powys 48 F4
Tregroes Ceredig'n 46 E3
Tregurrian Cornw'l 4 C3
Tregynon Powys 59 E7
Trehafod Rh Cyn Taff 34 E4
Treharris Merth Tyd 34 E4
Treherbert Rh Cyn Taff 34 E3
Trekenner Cornw'l 5 B8
Treknow Cornw'l 8 F2
Trelan Cornw'l 3 E6
Trelash Cornw'l 8 E3
Trelassick Cornw'l 4 D3
Trelawnyd Flints 72 B4
Trelech Carms 45 F4
Treleddyd-fawr Pembs 44 C2
Trelewis Merth Tyd 35 E5
Treligga Cornw'l 8 F2
Trelights Cornw'l 4 B4
Trelill Cornw'l 4 B5
Trelissick Cornw'l 3 C7
Trelissick Garden, Feock Cornw'l 4 F3
Trellech Monmouths 36 D2
Trelleck Grange Monmouths 36 D1
Trelogan Flints 85 F2
Trelystan Powys 60 D2
Tremadog Gwyn 71 C6
Tremail Cornw'l 8 F3
Tremain Ceredig'n 45 E4
Tremaine Cornw'l 8 F4
Tremar Cornw'l 5 C7
Trematon Cornw'l 5 D8
Tremeirchion Denbs 72 B4
Trenance Cornw'l 4 C3
Trenarren Cornw'l 3 B9
Trench Telford 61 C6
Treneglos Cornw'l 8 F4
Trenewan Cornw'l 5 D6
Trent Dorset 12 C3
Trent Vale Stoke 75 E5
Trentham Stoke 75 E5
Trentham Gardens, Newcastle-under-Lyme Staffs 75 F5
Trentishoe Devon 20 E5
Treoes V/Glam 21 B8
Treorchy = Treorci Rh Cyn Taff 34 E3
Treorci = Treorchy Rh Cyn Taff 34 E3
Tre'r-ddôl Ceredig'n 58 E3
Trerule Foot Cornw'l 5 D8
Tresaith Ceredig'n 45 D4
Tresawle Cornw'l 3 B7
Trescott Staffs 62 E2
Trescowe Cornw'l 2 C4
Tresham Glos 36 E4
Tresillian Cornw'l 3 B7
Tresinwen Pembs 44 A4
Treskinnick Cross Cornw'l 8 E4
Tresmeer Cornw'l 8 F4
Tresparrett Cornw'l 8 E3
Tresparrett Posts Cornw'l 8 E3
Tressait Perth/Kinr 141 C5
Tresta Shetl'd 175 H5
Tresta Shetl'd 174 D8
Treswell Notts 77 B7
Trethosa Cornw'l 4 D4
Trethurgy Cornw'l 4 D5
Tretio Pembs 44 C2
Tretire Heref'd 36 B2
Tretower Powys 35 B5
Treuddyn Flints 73 D6
Trevalga Cornw'l 8 F2
Trevalyn Wrex 73 D7
Trevanson Cornw'l 4 B4
Trevarren Cornw'l 4 C4
Trevarrian Cornw'l 4 C3
Trevarrick Cornw'l 3 B8
Trevaughan Carms 32 C2
Treveighan Cornw'l 5 B5
Trevellas Cornw'l 4 D2
Treverva Cornw'l 3 C6
Trevethin Torf 35 D6
Trevigro Cornw'l 5 C8
Treviscoe Cornw'l 4 D4
Trevone Cornw'l 4 B3
Trewarmett Cornw'l 8 F2
Trewassa Cornw'l 8 F3
Trewellard Cornw'l 2 C2
Trewen Cornw'l 8 F4
Trewennack Cornw'l 3 D5
Trewern Powys 60 C2
Trewethern Cornw'l 4 B5
Trewidland Cornw'l 5 D7
Trewint Cornw'l 8 E3
Trewint Cornw'l 8 F4
Trewithian Cornw'l 3 C7
Trewoofe Cornw'l 2 D3
Trewoon Cornw'l 4 D4
Treworga Cornw'l 3 B7
Treworlas Cornw'l 3 C7
Treyarnon Cornw'l 4 B3
Treyford W Sussex 16 C2
Trezaise Cornw'l 4 D4
Triangle W Yorks 87 B8
Trickett's Cross Dorset 13 D8
Triffleton Pembs 44 C4
Trimdon Durham 111 F6
Trimdon Colliery Durham 111 F6
Trimdon Grange Durham 111 F6
Trimingham Norfolk 81 D8
Trimley Lower Street Suffolk 57 F6
Trimley St Martin Suffolk 57 F6
Trimley St Mary Suffolk 57 F6
Trimpley Worcs 50 B2
Trimsaran Carms 33 D5
Trimstone Devon 20 E3
Trinafour Perth/Kinr 140 C4
Trinant Caerph 35 D6
Tring Herts 40 C2
Tring Wharf Herts 40 C2
Trinity Angus 143 C6
Trinity Jersey 17
Trisant Ceredig'n 47 B6
Trislaig H'land 138 B4
Trispen Cornw'l 4 D3
Tritlington Northum 117 E8
Trochry Perth/Kinr 141 E6
Trodigal Arg/Bute 118 D3
Troed rhiwdalar Powys 47 D8
Troedyraur Ceredig'n 46 E2
Troedyrhiw Merth Tyd 34 D4
Tromode I/Man 84 E3
Trondavoe Shetl'd 174 F5
Troon Cornw'l 3 C5
Troon S Ayrs 120 F3
Trosaraidh W Isles 171 J3
Trossachs Hotel Stirl 132 D4
Troston Suffolk 56 B2
Trottiscliffe Kent 29 C7
Trotton W Sussex 16 B2
Troutbeck Cumb 99 B5
Troutbeck Cumb 99 D6
Troutbeck Bridge Cumb 99 D6
Trow Green Glos 36 D2
Trowbridge Wilts 24 D3
Trowell Notts 76 F4
Trowle Common Wilts 24 D3
Trowley Bottom Herts 40 C3
Trows Scot Borders 124 F2
Trowse Newton Norfolk 68 D5
Trudoxhill Som'set 24 E2
Trull Som'set 11 B7
Trumaisgearraidh W Isles 170 C4
Trumpan H'land 152 C3
Trumpet Heref'd 49 F8
Trumpington Cambs 54 D5
Trunch Norfolk 81 D8
Trunnah Lancs 92 E3
Truro Cornw'l 3 B7
Truro Cathedral Cornw'l 4 E3
Trusham Devon 10 F3
Trusley Derby 76 F2
Trusthorpe Lincs 91 F9
Trysull Staffs 62 E2
Tubney Oxon 38 E4
Tuckenhay Devon 7 D6
Tuckhill Shrops 61 F7
Tuckingmill Cornw'l 3 B5
Tuddenham Suffolk 55 B8
Tuddenham St Martin Suffolk 57 E5
Tudeley Kent 29 E7
Tudhoe Durham 111 F5
Tudorville Heref'd 36 B2
Tudweiliog Gwyn 70 D3
Tuesley Surrey 27 E7
Tuffley Glos 37 C5
Tufton Hants 26 E2
Tufton Pembs 32 B1
Tugby Leics 64 D4
Tugford Shrops 61 F5
Tullibardine Perth/Kinr 133 C8
Tullibody Clack 133 E7
Tullich Arg/Bute 131 D6
Tullich H'land 148 B2
Tullich Muir H'land 157 B8
Tullie House, Carlisle Cumb 108 D3
Tulliemet Perth/Kinr 141 D6
Tulloch Aberds 143 B7
Tulloch Aberds 160 E5
Tulloch Perth/Kinr 134 B2
Tulloch Castle H'land 157 C6
Tullochgorm Arg/Bute 131 F5
Tulloes Angus 143 E5
Tullybannocher Perth/Kinr 133 B6
Tullybelton Perth/Kinr 141 F7
Tullyfergus Perth/Kinr 142 E2
Tullymurdoch Perth/Kinr 142 D1
Tullynessle Aberds 150 C4
Tumble Carms 33 C6
Tumby Woodside Lincs 79 D5
Tummel Bridge Perth/Kinr 140 D4
Tunga W Isles 172 E7
Tunstall ER Yorks 97 F9
Tunstall Kent 30 C2
Tunstall Lancs 93 B6
Tunstall Norfolk 69 D7
Tunstall N Yorks 101 E7
Tunstall Stoke 75 D5
Tunstall Suffolk 57 D7
Tunstall Tyne/Wear 111 D6
Tunstead Derby 75 B8
Tunstead Gtr Man 87 D8
Tunstead Norfolk 81 E8
Tunworth Hants 26 E4
Tupsley Heref'd 49 E7
Tupton Derby 76 C3
Tur Langton Leics 64 E4
Turgis Green Hants 26 D4
Turin Angus 143 D5
Turkdean Glos 37 C8
Turleigh Wilts 24 C3
Turn Lancs 87 C6
Turnastone Heref'd 49 F5
Turnberry S Ayrs 112 D2
Turnditch Derby 76 E2
Turners Hill W Sussex 28 F4
Turners Puddle Dorset 13 E6
Turnford Herts 41 D6
Turnhouse C/Edinb 122 B4
Turnworth Dorset 13 D6
Turriff Aberds 160 C4
Turton Bottoms Blackb'n 86 C5
Turves Cambs 66 E3
Turvey Beds 53 D7
Turville Bucks 39 E7
Turville Heath Bucks 39 E7
Turweston Bucks 52 F4
Tushielaw Scot Borders 115 C6
Tutbury Staffs 63 B6
Tutnall Worcs 50 B4
Tutshill Glos 36 E2
Tuttington Norfolk 81 E8
Tutts Clump W Berks 26 B3
Tuxford Notts 77 B7
Twatt Orkney 176 D1
Twatt Shetl'd 175 H5
Twechar E Dunb 121 B7
Tweedmouth Northum 125 D5
Tweedsmuir Scot Borders 114 B3
Twelve Heads Cornw'l 3 B6
Twemlow Green Ches 74 C4
Twenty Lincs 65 B8
Twerton Bath/NE Som'set 24 C2
Twickenham London 28 B2
Twickenham Stadium London 28 B2
Twigworth Glos 37 B5
Twineham W Sussex 17 C6
Twinhoe Bath/NE Som'set 24 D2
Twinstead Essex 56 F2
Twinstead Green Essex 56 F2
Twiss Green Warrington 86 E4
Twiston Lancs 93 E8
Twitchen Devon 21 F6
Twitchen Shrops 49 B5
Two Bridges Devon 6 B4
Two Dales Derby 76 C2
Two Mills Ches 73 B7
Twycross Leics 63 D7
Twycross Zoo, Ashby-de-la-Zouch Leics 63 D7
Twyford Bucks 39 B6
Twyford Derby 63 B7
Twyford Hants 15 B5
Twyford Leics 64 C4
Twyford Lincs 65 B6
Twyford Norfolk 81 E6
Twyford Wokingham 27 B5
Twyford Common Heref'd 49 F7
Twyn-y-Sheriff Monmouths 35 D8
Twynholm Dumf/Gal 106 D3
Twyning Glos 50 F3
Twyning Green Glos 50 F4
Twynllanan Carms 34 B1
Twynmynydd Carms 33 C7
Twywell Northants 53 B7
Ty-draw Conwy 83 F8
Ty-hen Carms 32 B4
Ty-hen Gwyn 70 D2
Ty-mawr Angl 82 C4
Ty Mawr Carms 46 E4
Ty Mawr Cwm Conwy 72 E3
Ty-nant Conwy 72 E3
Ty-nant Gwyn 59 B6
Ty-uchaf Powys 59 B7
Tyberton Heref'd 49 F5
Tyburn W Midlands 62 E5
Tycroes Carms 33 C7
Tycrwyn Powys 59 C8
Tydd Gote Lincs 66 C4
Tydd St Giles Cambs 66 C4
Tydd St Mary Lincs 66 C4
Tyddewi = St David's Pembs 44 C2
Tyddyn-mawr Gwyn 71 C6
Tye Green Essex 55 F6
Tye Green Essex 42 B3
Tye Green Essex 41 D7
Tyldesley Gtr Man 86 D4
Tyler Hill Kent 30 C5
Tylers Green Bucks 40 E2
Tylorstown Rh Cyn Taff 34 E4
Tylwch Powys 59 F6
Tyn-y-celyn Wrex 73 F5
Tyn-y-coed Shrops 60 B2
Tyn-y-fedwen Powys 72 F5
Tyn-y-ffridd Powys 72 F5
Tyn-y-graig Powys 48 D2
Ty'n-y-groes Conwy 83 D7
Ty'n-y-maes Gwyn 83 E6
Tyn-y-pwll Angl 82 C4
Ty'n-yr-eithin Ceredig'n 47 C5
Tyncelyn Ceredig'n 46 C5
Tyndrum Stirl 139 F7
Tyne Tunnel Tyne/Wear 111 C6
Tyneham Dorset 13 F6
Tynehead Midloth 123 D6
Tynemouth Tyne/Wear 111 C6
Tynemouth Sea Life Centre Tyne/Wear 111 B6
Tynewydd Rh Cyn Taff 34 E3
Tyninghame E Loth 124 B2
Tynron Dumf/Gal 113 E8
Tynygongl Angl 82 C5
Tynygraig Ceredig'n 47 C5
Tŷ'r-felin-isaf Conwy 83 E8
Tyrie Aberds 161 B6
Tyringham M/Keynes 53 E6
Tythecott Devon 9 C6
Tythegston Bridg 21 B7
Tytherington Ches 75 B6
Tytherington S Glouc 36 F3
Tytherington Som'set 24 E2
Tytherington Wilts 24 E4
Tytherleigh Devon 11 D8
Tywardreath Cornw'l 5 D5
Tywyn Conwy 83 D7
Tywyn Gwyn 58 D2

U

Uachdar W Isles 170 E3
Uags H'land 155 G3
Ubbeston Green Suffolk 57 B7
Ubley Bath/NE Som'set 23 D7
Uckerby N Yorks 101 D7
Uckfield E Sussex 17 B8
Uckington Glos 37 B6
Uddingston S Lanarks 121 C6
Uddington S Lanarks 121 F8
Udimore E Sussex 19 D5
Udny Green Aberds 151 B7
Udny Station Aberds 151 B8
Udston S Lanarks 121 D6
Udstonhead S Lanarks 121 E7
Uffcott Wilts 25 B6
Uffculme Devon 11 C5
Uffington Lincs 65 D7
Uffington Oxon 38 F3
Uffington Shrops 60 C5
Ufford Peterbro 65 D7
Ufford Suffolk 57 D6
Ufton Warwick 51 C8
Ufton Nervet W Berks 26 C4
Ugadale Arg/Bute 118 D4
Ugborough Devon 6 D4
Uggeshall Suffolk 69 F7
Ugglebarnby N Yorks 103 D6
Ughill S Yorks 88 E3
Ugley Essex 41 B8
Ugley Green Essex 41 B8
Ugthorpe N Yorks 103 C5
Uidh W Isles 171 L2
Uig Arg/Bute 129 B6
Uig H'land 152 C4
Uig H'land 152 D2
Uigen W Isles 172 E3
Uigshader H'land 152 E5
Uisken Arg/Bute 136 G4
Ulbster H'land 169 E8
Ulceby Lincs 79 B7
Ulceby N Lincs 90 C5
Ulceby Skitter N Lincs 90 C5
Ulcombe Kent 30 E2
Uldale Cumb 108 F2
Uley Glos 36 E4
Ulgham Northum 117 E8
Ullapool H'land 163 E5
Ullenhall Warwick 51 C6
Ullenwood Glos 37 C6
Ulleskelf N Yorks 95 E8
Ullesthorpe Leics 64 F2
Ulley S Yorks 89 F5
Ullingswick Heref'd 49 E7
Ullinish H'land 153 F4
Ullock Cumb 98 B2
Ulnes Walton Lancs 86 C3
Ulpha Cumb 98 E3
Ulrome ER Yorks 97 D7
Ulsta Shetl'd 174 E6
Ulva House Arg/Bute 137 E5
Ulverston Cumb 92 B2
Ulwell Dorset 13 F8
Umberleigh Devon 9 B8
Unapool H'land 166 F4
Unasary W Isles 171 H3
Underbarrow Cumb 99 E6
Undercliffe W Yorks 94 F4
Underhoull Shetl'd 174 C7
Underriver Kent 29 D6
Underwood Notts 76 D4
Undy Monmouths 35 F8
Unifirth Shetl'd 175 H4
Union Cottage Aberds 151 E7
Union Mills I/Man 84 E3
Union Street E Sussex 18 B4
University Museum, Oxford Oxon 39 D5
Unstone Derby 76 B3
Unstone Green Derby 76 B3
Unthank Cumb 108 F4
Unthank Cumb 109 E6
Unthank End Cumb 108 F4
Up Cerne Dorset 12 D4
Up Exe Devon 10 D4
Up Hatherley Glos 37 B6
Up Holland Lancs 86 D3
Up Marden W Sussex 15 C8
Up Nately Hants 26 D4
Up Somborne Hants 25 F8
Up Sydling Dorset 12 D4
Upavon Wilts 25 D6
Upchurch Kent 30 C2
Upcott Heref'd 48 D5
Upend Cambs 55 D7
Upgate Norfolk 68 C4
Uphall W Loth 122 B3
Uphall Station W Loth 122 B3
Upham Devon 10 D3
Upham Hants 15 B6
Uphampton Worcs 50 C3
Uphill N Som'set 22 D5
Uplawmoor E Renf 120 D4
Upleadon Glos 36 B4
Upleatham Redcar/Clevel'd 102 C4
Uplees Kent 30 C3
Uploders Dorset 12 E3
Uplowman Devon 10 C5
Uplyme Devon 11 E8
Upminster London 42 F1
Upnor Medway 29 B8
Upottery Devon 11 D7
Uppark, Petersfield Hants 15 C8
Upper Affcot Shrops 60 F4
Upper Ardchronie H'land 164 F3
Upper Arley Worcs 61 F7
Upper Arncott Oxon 39 C6
Upper Astrop Northants 52 F3
Upper Badcall H'land 166 E3
Upper Basildon W Berks 26 B3
Upper Beeding W Sussex 17 C5
Upper Benefield Northants 65 F6
Upper Bighouse H'land 168 D3
Upper Boddington Northants 52 D2
Upper Borth Ceredig'n 58 F3
Upper Boyndlie Aberds 161 B6
Upper Brailes Warwick 51 F8
Upper Breakish H'land 155 H2
Upper Breinton Heref'd 49 E6
Upper Broadheath Worcs 50 D3
Upper Broughton Notts 64 B3
Upper Bucklebury W Berks 26 C3
Upper Burnhaugh Aberds 151 E7
Upper Caldecote Beds 54 E2
Upper Catesby Northants 52 D3
Upper Chapel Powys 48 E2
Upper Church Village Rh Cyn Taff 34 F4
Upper Chute Wilts 25 D7
Upper Clatford Hants 25 E8
Upper Clynnog Gwyn 71 C5
Upper Cumberworth W Yorks 88 D3
Upper Cwm-twrch Powys 34 C1
Upper Cwmbran Torf 35 E6
Upper Dallachy Moray 159 C7
Upper Dean Beds 53 C8
Upper Denby W Yorks 88 D3
Upper Denton Cumb 109 C6
Upper Derraid H'land 158 F4
Upper Dicker E Sussex 18 E2
Upper Dovercourt Essex 57 F6
Upper Druimfin Arg/Bute 137 C6
Upper Dunsforth N Yorks 95 C7
Upper Eathie H'land 157 C8
Upper Elkstone Staffs 75 D7
Upper End Derby 75 B7
Upper Farringdon Hants 26 F5
Upper Framilode Glos 36 C4
Upper Glenfintaig H'land 147 F5
Upper Gornal W Midlands 62 E3
Upper Gravenhurst Beds 54 F2
Upper Green Monmouths 35 C7
Upper Green W Berks 25 C8
Upper Grove Common Heref'd 36 B2
Upper Hackney Derby 76 C2
Upper Hale Surrey 27 E6
Upper Halistra H'land 152 D3
Upper Halling Medway 29 C7
Upper Hambleton Rutl'd 65 D6
Upper Hardres Court Kent 31 D5
Upper Hartfield E Sussex 29 F5
Upper Haugh S Yorks 88 E5
Upper Heath Shrops 61 F5
Upper Hellesdon Norfolk 68 C5
Upper Helmsley N Yorks 96 D2
Upper Hergest Heref'd 48 D4
Upper Heyford Northants 52 D4
Upper Heyford Oxon 38 B4
Upper Hill Heref'd 49 D6
Upper Hopton W Yorks 88 C2
Upper Horsebridge E Sussex 18 D2
Upper Hulme Staffs 75 C7
Upper Inglesham Swindon 38 E2
Upper Inverbrough H'land 158 F2
Upper Killay Swan 33 E6
Upper Knockando Moray 159 E5
Upper Lambourn W Berks 38 F3
Upper Leigh Staffs 75 F7
Upper Lenie H'land 147 B8
Upper Lochton Aberds 151 E5
Upper Longdon Staffs 62 C4
Upper Lybster H'land 169 F7
Upper Lydbrook Glos 36 C3
Upper Maes-coed Heref'd 48 F5
Upper Midway Derby 63 B6
Upper Milovaig H'land 152 E2
Upper Minety Wilts 37 E7
Upper Mitton Worcs 50 B3
Upper North Dean Bucks 39 E8
Upper Obney Perth/Kinr 141 F7
Upper Ollach H'land 153 F6
Upper Padley Derby 76 B2
Upper Pollicott Bucks 39 C7
Upper Poppleton C/York 95 D8
Upper Quinton Warwick 51 E6
Upper Ratley Hants 14 B4
Upper Rissington Glos 38 C2
Upper Rochford Worcs 49 C8
Upper Sandaig H'land 145 B7
Upper Sanday Orkney 176 F4
Upper Sapey Heref'd 49 C8
Upper Seagry Wilts 37 F6
Upper Shelton Beds 53 E7
Upper Sheringham Norfolk 81 C7
Upper Skelmorlie N Ayrs 129 D7
Upper Slaughter Glos 38 B1
Upper Soudley Glos 36 C3
Upper Stondon Beds 54 F2
Upper Stowe Northants 52 D4
Upper Stratton Swindon 38 F1
Upper Street Hants 14 C2
Upper Street Norfolk 69 C6
Upper Street Norfolk 69 C6
Upper Street Suffolk 56 F5
Upper Strensham Worcs 50 F4
Upper Sundon Beds 40 B3
Upper Swell Glos 38 B1
Upper Tean Staffs 75 F7
Upper Tillyrie Perth/Kinr 134 D3
Upper Tooting London 28 B3
Upper Tote H'land 152 D6
Upper Town N Som'set 23 C7
Upper Treverward Shrops 48 B4
Upper Tysoe Warwick 51 E8
Upper Upham Wilts 25 B7
Upper Wardington Oxon 52 E2
Upper Weald M/Keynes 53 F5
Upper Weedon Northants 52 D4
Upper Wield Hants 26 F4
Upper Winchendon Bucks 39 C7
Upper Witton W Midlands 62 E4
Upper Woodend Aberds 151 C5
Upper Woodford Wilts 25 F6
Upper Wootton Hants 26 D3
Upper Wyche Worcs 50 E2
Upperby Cumb 108 D4
Uppermill Gtr Man 87 D7
Uppersound Shetl'd 175 J6
Upperthong W Yorks 88 D2
Upperthorpe N Lincs 89 D8
Upperton W Sussex 16 B3

Uppertown Derby 76 C3
Uppertown H'land 169 B8
Uppertown Orkney 176 G3
Uppingham Rutl'd 65 E5
Uppington Shrops 61 D6
Upsall N Yorks 102 F2
Upshire Essex 41 D7
Upstreet Kent 31 C6
Upthorpe Suffolk 56 B3
Upton Cambs 54 B2
Upton Ches 73 C8
Upton Cornw'l 8 D4
Upton Dorset 12 F5
Upton Dorset 13 E7
Upton Hants 14 C4
Upton Hants 25 D8
Upton Leics 63 E7
Upton Lincs 90 F2
Upton Mersey 85 F3
Upton Norfolk 69 C6
Upton Notts 77 D7
Upton Notts 77 B7
Upton Northants 52 C5
Upton Oxon 39 F5
Upton Peterbro 65 D8
Upton Slough 27 B7
Upton Som'set 10 B4
Upton W Yorks 89 C5
Upton Bishop Heref'd 36 B3
Upton Cheyney S Gloucs 23 C8
Upton Cressett Shrops 61 E6
Upton Cross Cornw'l 5 B7
Upton Grey Hants 26 E4
Upton Hellions Devon 10 D3
Upton House Warwick 51 E8
Upton Lovell Wilts 24 E4
Upton Magna Shrops 61 C5
Upton Noble Som'set 24 F2
Upton Pyne Devon 10 E4
Upton St Leonard's Glos 37 C5
Upton Scudamore Wilts 24 E3
Upton Snodsbury Worcs 50 D4
Upton upon Severn Worcs 50 E3
Upton Warren Worcs 50 C4
Upwaltham W Sussex 16 C3
Upware Cambs 55 B6
Upwell Norfolk 66 D4
Upwey Dorset 12 F4
Upwood Cambs 66 F2
Uradale Shetl'd 175 K6
Urafirth Shetl'd 174 F5
Urchfont Wilts 24 D5
Urdimarsh Heref'd 49 E7
Ure Shetl'd 174 F4
Ure Bank N Yorks 95 B6
Urgha W Isles 173 J4
Urishay Common Heref'd 48 F5
Urlay Nook Stockton 102 C1
Urmston Gtr Man 87 E5
Urpeth Durham 110 D5
Urquhart H'land 157 D6
Urquhart Moray 159 C6
Urquhart Castle, Drumnadrochit H'land 147 B8
Urra N Yorks 102 D3
Urray H'land 157 D6
Ushaw Moor Durham 110 E5
Usk = Brynbuga Monmouths 35 D7
Usselby Lincs 90 E4
Usworth Tyne/Wear 111 D6
Utkinton Ches 74 C2
Utley W Yorks 94 E3
Uton Devon 10 E3
Utterby Lincs 91 E7
Uttoxeter Staffs 75 F7
Uttoxeter Racecourse Staffs 75 F8
Uwchmynydd Gwyn 70 E2
Uxbridge London 40 F3
Uyeasound Shetl'd 174 C7
Uzmaston Pembs 44 D4

V

Valley Angl 82 D2
Valley Truckle Cornw'l 8 F2
Valleyfield Dumf/Gal 106 D3
Valsgarth Shetl'd 174 B8
Valtos H'land 152 C6
Van Powys 59 F6
Vange Essex 42 F3
Varteg Torf 35 D6
Vatten H'land 153 E3
Vaul Arg/Bute 136 F2
Vaynor Merth Tyd 34 C4
Veensgarth Shetl'd 175 J6
Velindre Powys 48 F3
Vellow Som'set 22 F2
Veness Orkney 176 D4
Venn Green Devon 9 C5
Venn Ottery Devon 11 E5
Vennington Shrops 60 D3
Venny Tedburn Devon 10 E3
Ventnor I/Wight 15 G6
Ventnor Botanic Garden I/Wight 15 G6
Vernham Dean Hants 25 D8
Vernham Street Hants 25 D8
Vernolds Common Shrops 60 F4
Verwood Dorset 13 D8
Veryan Cornw'l 3 C8
Vicarage Devon 11 F7
Vickerstown Cumb 92 C1
Victoria Cornw'l 4 C4
Victoria S Yorks 88 D2
Victoria and Albert Museum London 28 B3
Vidlin Shetl'd 174 G6
Viewpark N Lanarks 121 C7
Vigo Village Kent 29 C7
Vinehall Street E Sussex 18 C4
Vine's Cross E Sussex 18 D2
Viney Hill Glos 36 D3
Virginia Water Surrey 27 C8
Virginstow Devon 9 E5
Vobster Som'set 24 E2
Voe Shetl'd 175 G6
Voe Shetl'd 174 E5
Vowchurch Heref'd 49 F5
Voxter Shetl'd 174 F5
Voy Orkney 176 E1

W

Wackerfield Durham 101 B6
Wacton Norfolk 68 E4
Wadbister Shetl'd 175 J6
Wadborough Worcs 50 E4
Waddesdon Bucks 39 C7
Waddesdon Manor, Aylesbury Bucks 39 C7
Waddingham Lincs 90 E3
Waddington Lancs 93 E7
Waddington Lincs 78 C2
Wadebridge Cornw'l 4 B4
Wadeford Som'set 11 C8
Wadenhoe Northants 65 F7
Wadesmill Herts 41 C6
Wadhurst E Sussex 18 B3
Wadshelf Derby 76 B3
Wadsley S Yorks 88 E4
Wadsley Bridge S Yorks 88 E4
Wadworth S Yorks 89 E6
Waen Denbs 72 C5
Waen Denbs 72 C3
Waen Fach Powys 60 C2
Waen Goleugoed Denbs 72 B4
Wag H'land 165 B7
Wainfleet All Saints Lincs 79 D7
Wainfleet Bank Lincs 79 D7
Wainfleet St Mary Lincs 79 D8
Wainfleet Tofts Lincs 79 D7
Wainhouse Corner Cornw'l 8 E3
Wainscott Medway 29 B8
Wainstalls W Yorks 87 B8
Waitby Cumb 100 D2
Waithe Lincs 91 D6
Wake Lady Green N Yorks 102 E4
Wakefield W Yorks 88 B4
Wakehurst Place Garden, Crawley W Sussex 28 F4
Wakerley Northants 65 E6
Wakes Colne Essex 42 B4
Walberswick Suffolk 57 B8
Walberton W Sussex 16 D3
Walbottle Tyne/Wear 110 C4
Walcot Lincs 78 F3
Walcot N Lincs 90 B2
Walcot Shrops 60 F3
Walcot Telford 61 C5
Walcot Swindon 38 F1
Walcot Green Norfolk 68 F4
Walcote Leics 64 F2
Walcote Warwick 51 D6
Walcott Lincs 78 D4
Walcott Norfolk 69 A6
Walden N Yorks 101 F5
Walden Head N Yorks 100 F4
Walden Stubbs N Yorks 89 C6
Waldersey Cambs 66 D4
Walderslade Medway 29 C8
Walderton W Sussex 15 C8
Walditch Dorset 12 E2
Waldley Derby 75 F8
Waldridge Durham 111 D5
Waldringfield Suffolk 57 E6
Waldringfield Heath Suffolk 57 E6
Waldron E Sussex 18 D2
Wales S Yorks 89 F5
Walesby Lincs 90 E5
Walesby Notts 77 B6
Walford Heref'd 49 B5
Walford Heref'd 36 B2
Walford Shrops 60 B4
Walford Heath Shrops 60 C4
Walgherton Ches 74 E3
Walgrave Northants 53 B6
Walhampton Hants 14 E4
Walk Mill Lancs 93 F8
Walkden Gtr Man 86 D5
Walker Tyne/Wear 111 C5
Walker Art Gallery Mersey 85 E8
Walker Barn Ches 75 B6
Walker Fold Lancs 93 E6
Walkerburn Scot Borders 123 F6
Walkeringham Notts 89 E8
Walkerith Lincs 89 E8
Walkern Herts 41 B5
Walker's Green Heref'd 49 E7
Walkerville N Yorks 101 E7
Walkford Dorset 14 E3
Walkhampton Devon 6 C3
Walkington ER Yorks 97 F5
Walkley S Yorks 88 F4
Walkley Clogs, Hebden Bridge W Yorks 87 B3
Wall Northum 110 C2
Wall Staffs 62 D5
Wall Bank Shrops 60 E5
Wall Heath W Midlands 62 F2
Wall under Heywood Shrops 60 E5
Wallaceton Dumf/Gal 113 F8
Wallacetown S Ayrs 112 D2
Wallacetown S Ayrs 112 B3
Wallands Park E Sussex 17 C8
Wallasey Mersey 85 E4
Wallcrouch E Sussex 18 B3
Wallingford Oxon 39 F6
Wallington London 28 C3
Wallington Hants 15 D6
Wallington Herts 54 F3
Wallington House, Ponteland Northum 117 F6
Wallis Pembs 32 B1
Walliswood Surrey 28 F2
Walls Shetl'd 175 J4
Wallsend Tyne/Wear 111 C5
Wallston V/Glam 22 B3
Wallyford E Loth 123 B6
Walmer Kent 31 D7
Walmer Bridge Lancs 86 B2
Walmersley Gtr Man 87 C6
Walmley W Midlands 62 E5
Walpole Suffolk 57 B7
Walpole Cross Keys Norfolk 66 C5
Walpole Highway Norfolk 66 C5
Walpole Marsh Norfolk 66 C4
Walpole St Andrew Norfolk 66 C5
Walpole St Peter Norfolk 66 C5
Walsall W Midlands 62 E4
Walsall Arboretum W Midlands 62 E4
Walsall Wood W Midlands 62 D4
Walsden W Yorks 87 B7
Walsgrave on Sowe W Midlands 63 F7
Walsham le Willows Suffolk 56 B3
Walshaw Gtr Man 87 C5
Walshford N Yorks 95 D7
Walsoken Cambs 66 C4
Walston S Lanarks 122 E3
Walsworth Herts 54 F3
Walters Ash Bucks 39 E8
Walterston V/Glam 22 B2
Walterstone Heref'd 35 B7
Waltham Kent 30 E5
Waltham NE Lincs 91 D6
Waltham Abbey Essex 41 D6
Waltham Chase Hants 15 C6
Waltham Cross Herts 41 D6
Waltham on the Wolds Leics 64 B5
Waltham St Lawrence Windsor 27 B6
Walthamstow London 41 F6
Walton Cumb 108 C5
Walton Derby 76 C3
Walton Leics 64 F2
Walton Mersey 85 E4
Walton M/Keynes 53 F6
Walton Peterbro 65 D8
Walton Powys 48 D4
Walton Som'set 23 F6
Walton Staffs 75 F5
Walton Suffolk 57 F6
Walton Telford 61 C5
Walton Warwick 51 D7
Walton W Yorks 88 C4
Walton W Yorks 95 E7
Walton Cardiff Glos 50 F4
Walton East Pembs 32 B1
Walton Hall Warrington 86 F4
Walton-in-Gordano N Som'set 23 B6
Walton-le-Dale Lancs 86 B3
Walton on Thames Surrey 28 C2
Walton on the Hill Staffs 62 B3
Walton on the Hill Surrey 28 D3
Walton-on-the-Naze Essex 43 B8
Walton on the Wolds Leics 64 C2
Walton-on-Trent Derby 63 C6
Walton West Pembs 44 D3
Walwen Flints 73 B6
Walwick Northum 110 B2
Walworth D'lington 101 C7
Walworth Gate D'lington 101 B7
Walwyn's Castle Pembs 44 D3
Wambrook Som'set 11 D7
Wanborough Surrey 27 E7
Wanborough Swindon 38 F2
Wandsworth London 28 B3
Wangford Suffolk 57 B8
Wanlockhead Dumf/Gal 113 C8
Wansford ER Yorks 97 D6
Wansford Peterbro 65 E7
Wanstead London 41 F7
Wanstrow Som'set 24 E2
Wanswell Glos 36 D3
Wantage Oxon 38 F3
Wapley S Gloucs 24 B2
Wappenbury Warwick 51 C8
Wappenham Northants 52 E4
Warbleton E Sussex 18 D3
Warblington Hants 15 D8
Warborough Oxon 39 E5
Warboys Cambs 66 F3
Warbreck Blackp'l 92 F3
Warbstow Cornw'l 8 E4
Warburton Gtr Man 86 F5
Warcop Cumb 100 C2
Ward End W Midlands 62 F5
Ward Green Suffolk 56 C4
Warden Kent 30 B4
Warden Northum 110 C2
Wardhill Orkney 176 D5
Wardington Oxon 52 E2
Wardlaw Scot Borders 115 C5
Wardle Ches 74 D3
Wardle Gtr Man 87 C7
Wardley Rutl'd 64 D5
Wardlow Derby 75 B8
Wardy Hill Cambs 66 F4
Ware Herts 41 C6
Ware Kent 31 C6
Wareham Dorset 13 F7
Warehorne Kent 19 B6
Waren Mill Northum 125 F7
Warenford Northum 117 B7
Warenton Northum 125 F7
Wareside Herts 41 C6
Waresley Cambs 54 D3
Waresley Worcs 50 B3
Warfield Brackn'l 27 B6
Warfleet Devon 7 D6
Wargrave Wokingham 27 B5
Warham Norfolk 80 C5
Warhill Gtr Man 87 E7
Wark Northum 109 B8
Wark Northum 124 F4
Warkleigh Devon 9 B8
Warkton Northants 53 B6
Warkworth Northants 52 E2
Warkworth Northum 117 D8
Warlaby N Yorks 101 E8
Warland W Yorks 87 B7
Warleggan Cornw'l 5 C6
Warlingham Surrey 28 D4
Warmfield W Yorks 88 B4
Warmingham Ches 74 C4
Warmington Northants 65 E7
Warmington Warwick 52 E2
Warminster Wilts 24 E3
Warmlake Kent 30 D2
Warmley S Gloucs 23 B8
Warmley Tower S Gloucs 23 B8
Warmonds Hill Northants 53 C7
Warmsworth S Yorks 89 D6
Warmwell Dorset 13 F5
Warndon Worcs 50 D3
Warnford Hants 15 B7
Warnham W Sussex 28 F2
Warninglid W Sussex 17 B6
Warren Ches 75 B5
Warren Pembs 44 F4
Warren Heath Suffolk 57 E6
Warren Row Windsor 39 F8
Warren Street Kent 30 D3
Warrington M/Keynes 53 D6
Warrington Warrington 86 F4
Warsash Hants 15 D5
Warslow Staffs 75 D7
Warter ER Yorks 96 D4
Warthermarske N Yorks 94 B5
Warthill N Yorks 96 D2
Wartling E Sussex 18 E3
Wartnaby Leics 64 B4
Warton Lancs 86 B2
Warton Lancs 92 B4
Warton Northum 117 D6
Warton Warwick 63 D6
Warwick Warwick 51 C7
Warwick Bridge Cumb 108 D4
Warwick Castle Warwick 51 C7
Warwick on Eden Cumb 108 D4
Warwick Racecourse Warwick 51 C7
Wasbister Orkney 176 C2
Wasdale Head Cumb 98 D3
Wash Common W Berks 26 C2
Washaway Cornw'l 4 C5
Washbourne Devon 7 D5
Washfield Devon 10 C4
Washfold N Yorks 101 D5
Washford Som'set 22 E2
Washford Pyne Devon 10 C3
Washingborough Lincs 78 B3
Washington Tyne/Wear 111 D6
Washington W Sussex 16 C5
Wasing W Berks 26 C3
Waskerley Durham 110 E3
Wasperton Warwick 51 D7
Wasps Nest Lincs 78 C3
Wass N Yorks 95 B8
Watchet Som'set 22 E2
Watchfield Oxon 38 E2
Watchfield Som'set 22 E5
Watchgate Cumb 99 E7
Watchhill Cumb 107 E8
Watcombe Torbay 7 C7
Watendlath Cumb 98 C4
Water Devon 10 F2
Water Lancs 87 B6
Water End ER Yorks 96 F3
Water End Herts 40 C3
Water End Herts 41 D5
Water Newton Cambs 65 E8
Water Orton Warwick 63 E5
Water Stratford Bucks 52 F4
Water Yeat Cumb 98 F4
Waterbeach Cambs 55 C5
Waterbeck Dumf/Gal 108 B2
Watercress Line (Mid Hants Railway), Alton Hants 26 F4
Waterden Norfolk 80 D4
Waterfall Staffs 75 D7
Waterfoot E Renf 121 D5
Waterfoot Lancs 87 B6
Waterford Hants 14 E4
Waterford Herts 41 C6
Waterhead Cumb 99 D5
Waterhead Dumf/Gal 114 E4
Waterheads Scot Borders 122 D5
Waterhouses Durham 110 E4
Waterhouses Staffs 75 D7
Wateringbury Kent 29 D7
Waterloo Gtr Man 87 D7
Waterloo H'land 155 H2
Waterloo Mersey 85 E4
Waterloo N Lanarks 121 D8
Waterloo Norfolk 68 C5
Waterloo Perth/Kinr 141 F7
Waterloo Poole 13 E8
Waterloo Shrops 74 F2
Waterloo Port Gwyn 82 E4
Waterlooville Hants 15 D7
Watermeetings S Lanarks 114 C2
Watermillock Cumb 99 B6
Watermouth Castle, Ilfracombe Devon 20 E4
Waterperry Oxon 39 D6
Waterrow Som'set 11 B5
Water's Nook Gtr Man 86 D4
Waters Upton Telford 61 C6
Watersfield W Sussex 16 C4
Watershed Mill Visitor Centre, Settle N Yorks 93 C8
Waterside Aberds 161 F7
Waterside Blackb'n 86 B5
Waterside Cumb 108 E2
Waterside E Ayrs 112 D4
Waterside E Ayrs 120 E4
Waterside E Dunb 121 B6
Waterside E Renf 120 D5
Waterstock Oxon 39 D6
Waterston Pembs 44 E4
Watford Herts 40 E4
Watford Northants 52 C4
Watford Gap W Midlands 62 D5
Wath N Yorks 94 C4
Wath N Yorks 95 B6
Wath N Yorks 96 B2
Wath Brow Cumb 98 C2
Wath upon Dearne S Yorks 88 D5
Watley's End S Gloucs 36 F3
Watlington Norfolk 67 C6
Watlington Oxon 39 E6
Watnall Notts 76 E5
Watten H'land 169 D7
Wattisfield Suffolk 56 B4
Wattisham Suffolk 56 D4
Wattlesborough Heath Shrops 60 C3
Watton ER Yorks 97 D6
Watton Norfolk 68 D2
Watton at Stone Herts 41 C6
Wattston N Lanarks 121 B7
Wattstown Rh Cyn Taff 34 E4
Wauchan H'land 146 F2
Waulkmill Lodge Orkney 176 F2
Waun Powys 59 D5
Waun-y-clyn Carms 33 D5
Waunarlwydd Swan 33 E7
Waunclunda Carms 47 F5
Waunfawr Gwyn 82 F5
Waungron Swan 33 D6
Waunlwyd Bl Gwent 35 D5
Wavendon M/Keynes 53 F7
Waverbridge Cumb 108 E2
Waverton Ches 73 C8
Waverton Cumb 108 E2
Wavertree Mersey 85 F4
Wawne ER Yorks 97 F6
Waxham Norfolk 69 B7
Waxholme ER Yorks 91 B7
Way Kent 31 C7
Way Village Devon 10 C3
Wayfield Medway 29 C8
Wayford Som'set 12 D2
Waymills Shrops 74 E2
Wayne Green Monmouths 35 C8
Wdig = Goodwick Pembs 44 B4
Weachyburn Aberds 160 C3
Weald Oxon 38 D3
Weald and Downland Open Air Museum, Chichester W Sussex 16 C2
Wealdstone London 40 F4
Weardley W Yorks 95 E5
Weare Som'set 23 D6
Weare Giffard Devon 9 B6
Wearhead Durham 109 F8
Weasdale Cumb 100 D1
Weasenham All Saints Norfolk 80 E4
Weasenham St Peter Norfolk 80 E4
Weatherhill Surrey 28 E4
Weaverham Ches 74 B3
Weaverthorpe N Yorks 97 B5
Webheath Worcs 50 C5
Wedderlairs Aberds 161 E5
Wedderlie Scot Borders 124 D2
Weddington Warwick 63 E7
Wedgwood Visitor Centre, Barlaston Staffs 75 F6
Wedhampton Wilts 25 D5
Wedmore Som'set 23 E6
Wednesbury W Midlands 62 E3
Wednesfield W Midlands 62 D3
Weedon Bucks 39 C8
Weedon Bec Northants 52 D4
Weedon Lois Northants 52 E4
Weeford Staffs 62 D5
Week Devon 10 C2
Week St Mary Cornw'l 8 E4
Weeke Hants 26 F2
Weekley Northants 65 F5
Weel ER Yorks 97 F6
Weeley Essex 43 B7
Weeley Heath Essex 43 B7
Weem Perth/Kinr 141 E5
Weeping Cross Staffs 62 B3
Weethley Gate Warwick 51 D5
Weeting Norfolk 67 F7
Weeting Heath NNR Norfolk 67 F7
Weeton ER Yorks 91 B7
Weeton Lancs 92 F3
Weeton N Yorks 95 E5
Weetwood Hall Northum 117 B6
Weir Lancs 87 B6
Weir Quay Devon 6 C2
Welborne Norfolk 68 D3
Welbourn Lincs 78 D2
Welburn N Yorks 96 C3
Welburn N Yorks 102 F4
Welbury N Yorks 102 D1
Welby Lincs 78 F2
Welches Dam Cambs 66 F4
Welcombe Devon 8 C4
Weld Bank Lancs 86 C3
Weldon Northum 117 E7
Welford Northants 64 F3
Welford W Berks 26 B2
Welford-on-Avon Warwick 51 D6
Welham Leics 64 E4
Welham Notts 89 F8
Welham Green Herts 41 D5
Well Hants 27 E5
Well Lincs 79 B7
Well N Yorks 101 F7
Well End Bucks 40 F1
Well Heads W Yorks 94 F3
Well Hill Kent 29 C5
Well Town Devon 10 D4
Welland Worcs 50 E2
Wellbank Angus 142 F4
Welldale Dumf/Gal 107 C8
Wellesbourne Warwick 51 D7
Welling London 29 B5
Wellingborough Northants 53 C6
Wellingham Norfolk 80 E4
Wellingore Lincs 78 D2
Wellington Cumb 98 D2
Wellington Heref'd 49 E6
Wellington Som'set 11 B6
Wellington Telford 61 C6
Wellington Heath Heref'd 50 E2
Wellington Hill W Yorks 95 F6
Wellow Bath/NE Som'set 24 D2
Wellow I/Wight 14 F4
Wellow Notts 77 C6
Wellpond Green Herts 41 B7
Wells Som'set 23 E7
Wells Cathedral Som'set 23 E7
Wells Green Ches 74 D3
Wells-next-the-Sea Norfolk 80 C5
Wellsborough Leics 63 D7
Wellswood Torbay 7 C7
Wellwood Fife 134 F2
Welney Norfolk 66 E5
Welsh Bicknor Heref'd 36 C2
Welsh End Shrops 74 F2
Welsh Frankton Shrops 73 F7
Welsh Highland Railway, Caernarfon Gwyn 82 E4
Welsh Highland Railway, Porthmadog Gwyn 71 D6
Welsh Hook Pembs 44 C4
Welsh National Velodrome Newp 35 F7
Welsh Newton Heref'd 36 C1
Welsh St Donats V/Glam 22 B2
Welshampton Shrops 73 F8
Welshpool = Y Trallwng Powys 60 D2
Welton Cumb 108 E3
Welton ER Yorks 90 B3
Welton Lincs 78 B3
Welton Northants 52 C3
Welton Hill Lincs 90 F4
Welton le Marsh Lincs 79 C7
Welton le Wold Lincs 91 F6
Welwick ER Yorks 91 B7
Welwyn Herts 41 C5
Welwyn Garden City Herts 41 C5
Wem Shrops 60 B5
Wembdon Som'set 22 F4
Wembley London 40 F4
Wembley Stadium London 40 F4
Wembury Devon 6 E3
Wembworthy Devon 9 D8
Wemyss Bay Invercl 129 D6
Wenallt Ceredig'n 47 B5
Wenallt Gwyn 72 E3
Wendens Ambo Essex 55 F6
Wendlebury Oxon 39 C5
Wendling Norfolk 68 C2
Wendover Bucks 40 D1
Wendron Cornw'l 3 C5
Wendy Cambs 54 E4
Wenfordbridge Cornw'l 5 B5
Wenhaston Suffolk 57 B8
Wennington Cambs 54 B3
Wennington London 41 F8
Wennington Lancs 93 B6
Wensley Derby 76 C2
Wensley N Yorks 101 F5
Wentbridge W Yorks 89 C5
Wentnor Shrops 60 E3
Wentworth Cambs 55 B5
Wentworth S Yorks 88 E4
Wenvoe V/Glam 22 B3
Weobley Heref'd 49 D6
Weobley Marsh Heref'd 49 D6
Wereham Norfolk 67 D6
Wergs W Midlands 62 D2
Wern Powys 59 C6
Wern Powys 60 C2
Wernffrwd Swan 33 E6
Wernyrheolydd Monmouths 35 C7
Werrington Cornw'l 8 F5
Werrington Peterbro 65 D8
Werrington Staffs 75 E6
Wervin Ches 73 B8
Wesham Lancs 92 F4
Wessington Derby 76 D3
West Acre Norfolk 67 C7
West Adderbury Oxon 52 F2
West Allerdean Northum 125 E5
West Alvington Devon 6 E5
West Amesbury Wilts 25 E6
West Anstey Devon 10 B3
West Ashby Lincs 79 B5
West Ashling W Sussex 16 D2
West Ashton Wilts 24 D3
West Auckland Durham 101 B6
West Ayton N Yorks 103 F7
West Bagborough Som'set 22 F3
West Barkwith Lincs 91 F5
West Barnby N Yorks 103 C6
West Barns E Loth 124 B2
West Barsham Norfolk 80 D5
West Bay Dorset 12 E2
West Beckham Norfolk 81 D7
West Bedfont Surrey 27 B8
West Benhar N Lanarks 121 C8
West Bergholt Essex 43 B5
West Bexington Dorset 12 F3
West Bilney Norfolk 67 C7
West Blatchington Brighton/Hove 17 D6
West Bowling W Yorks 94 F4
West Bradford Lancs 93 E7
West Bradley Som'set 23 F7
West Bretton W Yorks 88 C3
West Bridgford Notts 77 F5
West Bromwich W Midlands 62 E4
West Buckland Devon 21 F5
West Buckland Som'set 11 B6
West Burrafirth Shetl'd 175 H4
West Burton N Yorks 101 F5
West Burton W Sussex 16 C3
West Butterwick N Lincs 90 D2
West Byfleet Surrey 27 C8
West Caister Norfolk 69 C8
West Calder W Loth 122 C3
West Camel Som'set 12 B3
West Challow Oxon 38 F3
West Chelborough Dorset 12 D3
West Chevington Northum 117 E8
West Chiltington W Sussex 16 C4
West Chinnock Som'set 12 C2
West Chisenbury Wilts 25 D6
West Clandon Surrey 27 D8
West Cliffe Kent 31 E7
West Clyne H'land 165 D5
West Clyth H'land 169 F7
West Coker Som'set 12 C3
West Compton Dorset 12 E3
West Compton Som'set 23 E7
West Cowick ER Yorks 89 B7
West Cranmore Som'set 23 E8
West Cross Swan 33 F7
West Cullery Aberds 151 D6
West Curry Cornw'l 8 E4
West Curthwaite Cumb 108 E3
West Darlochan Arg/Bute 118 D3
West Dean Wilts 14 B3
West Dean W Sussex 16 C2
West Deeping Lincs 65 D8
West Derby Mersey 85 E4
West Dereham Norfolk 67 D6
West Didsbury Gtr Man 87 E6
West Ditchburn Northum 117 B7
West Down Devon 20 E4
West Drayton London 27 B8
West Drayton Notts 77 B7
West Ella ER Yorks 90 B4
West End Beds 53 D7
West End ER Yorks 96 F5
West End ER Yorks 97 F7
West End Hants 15 C5
West End Lancs 86 B5
West End Norfolk 68 D2
West End Norfolk 69 C8
West End N Som'set 23 C6
West End N Yorks 94 D4
West End Oxon 38 D4
West End S Lanarks 122 E2
West End Suffolk 69 F7
West End Surrey 27 C7
West End S Yorks 89 D7
West End Wilts 13 B7
West End Wilts 24 B4
West End W Sussex 17 C6
West End Green Hants 26 C4
West Farleigh Kent 29 D8
West Felton Shrops 60 B3
West Fenton E Loth 135 F6
West Ferry Dundee C 142 F4
West Firle E Sussex 17 D8
West Ginge Oxon 38 F4
West Grafton Wilts 25 C7
West Green Hants 26 D5
West Greenskares Aberds 160 B4
West Grimstead Wilts 14 B3
West Grinstead W Sussex 17 B5
West Haddlesey N Yorks 89 B6
West Haddon Northants 52 B4
West Hagbourne Oxon 39 F5
West Hagley Worcs 62 F3
West Hall Cumb 109 C5
West Hallam Derby 76 E4
West Halton N Lincs 90 B3
West Ham London 41 F7
West Handley Derby 76 B3
West Hanney Oxon 38 E4
West Hanningfield Essex 42 E3
West Hardwick W Yorks 88 C5
West Harnham Wilts 14 B2
West Harptree Bath/NE Som'set 23 D7
West Hatch Som'set 11 B7
West Head Norfolk 67 D5
West Heath Ches 74 C5
West Heath Hants 27 D6
West Heath Hants 26 D3
West Helmsdale H'land 165 C7
West Hendred Oxon 38 F4
West Heslerton N Yorks 96 B5
West Hill Devon 11 E5
West Hill ER Yorks 97 C7
West Hill N Som'set 23 B6
West Hoathly W Sussex 28 F4
West Holme Dorset 13 F6
West Horndon Essex 42 F2
West Horrington Som'set 23 E7
West Horsley Surrey 27 D8
West Horton Northum 125 F6
West Hougham Kent 31 E6
West Houlland Shetl'd 175 H4
West-houses Derby 76 D4
West Huntington C/York 96 D2
West Hythe Kent 19 B8
West Ilsley W Berks 38 F4
West Itchenor W Sussex 15 D8
West Keal Lincs 79 C6
West Kennett Wilts 25 C6
West Kilbride N Ayrs 120 E2
West Kingsdown Kent 29 C6
West Kington Wilts 24 B3
West Kinharrachie Aberds 161 E6
West Kirby Mersey 85 F3
West Knapton N Yorks 96 B4
West Knighton Dorset 12 F5
West Knoyle Wilts 24 F3
West Kyloe Northum 125 E6
West Lambrook Som'set 12 C2
West Langdon Kent 31 E7
West Langwell H'land 164 D3
West Lavington Wilts 24 D5
West Lavington W Sussex 16 B2
West Layton N Yorks 101 D6
West Lea Durham 111 E7
West Leake Notts 64 B2
West Learmouth Northum 124 F4
West Leigh Devon 9 D8
West Lexham Norfolk 67 C8
West Lilling N Yorks 96 C2
West Linton Scot Borders 122 D4
West Liss Hants 15 B8
West Littleton S Gloucs 24 B2
West Looe Cornw'l 5 D7
West Luccombe Som'set 21 E7
West Lulworth Dorset 13 F6
West Lutton N Yorks 96 C5
West Lydford Som'set 23 F7
West Lyng Som'set 11 B8
West Lynn Norfolk 67 B6
West Malling Kent 29 D7
West Malvern Worcs 50 E2
West Marden W Sussex 15 C8
West Marina E Sussex 18 E4
West Markham Notts 77 B7
West Marsh NE Lincs 91 C6
West Marton N Yorks 93 D8
West Meon Hants 15 B7
West Mersea Essex 43 C6
West Midlands Safari Park, Kidderminster Worcs 50 B3
West Milton Dorset 12 E3
West Minster Kent 30 B3
West Molesey Surrey 28 C2
West Monkton Som'set 11 B7
West Moors Dorset 13 D8
West Morriston Scot Borders 124 E2
West Muir Angus 143 C5
West Ness N Yorks 96 B2
West Newham Northum 110 B3
West Newton ER Yorks 97 F7
West Newton Norfolk 67 B6
West Norwood London 28 B4
West Ogwell Devon 7 B6
West Orchard Dorset 13 C6
West Overton Wilts 25 C6
West Park Hartlep'l 111 F7
West Parley Dorset 13 E8
West Peckham Kent 29 D7
West Pelton Durham 110 D5
West Pennard Som'set 23 F7
West Pentire Cornw'l 4 C2
West Perry Cambs 54 C2
West Putford Devon 9 C5
West Quantoxhead Som'set 22 E3
West Rainton Durham 111 E6
West Rasen Lincs 90 F4
West Raynham Norfolk 80 E4
West Retford Notts 89 F7
West Rounton N Yorks 102 D2
West Row Suffolk 55 B7
West Rudham Norfolk 80 E4
West Runton Norfolk 81 C7
West Saltoun E Loth 123 C7
West Sandwick Shetl'd 174 E6
West Scrafton N Yorks 101 F5
West Sleekburn Northum 117 F8
West Somerset Railway, Minehead Som'set 21 E8
West Somerton Norfolk 69 C7
West Stafford Dorset 12 F5
West Stockwith Notts 89 E8
West Stoke W Sussex 16 D2
West Stonesdale N Yorks 100 D3
West Stoughton Som'set 23 E6
West Stour Dorset 13 B5
West Stourmouth Kent 31 C6
West Stow Suffolk 56 B2
West Stowell Wilts 25 C6
West Strathan H'land 167 C7
West Stratton Hants 26 E3
West Street Kent 30 D3
West Tanfield N Yorks 95 B5
West Taphouse Cornw'l 5 C6
West Tarbert Arg/Bute 128 D3
West Thirston Northum 117 E7
West Thorney W Sussex 15 D8
West Thurrock Thurr'k 29 B6
West Tilbury Thurr'k 29 B7
West Tisted Hants 15 B7
West Tofts Norfolk 67 E8
West Tofts Perth/Kinr 141 F8
West Torrington Lincs 90 F5
West Town Hants 15 E8
West Town N Som'set 23 C6
West Tytherley Hants 14 B3
West Tytherton Wilts 24 B4
West Walton Norfolk 66 C4
West Walton Highway Norfolk 66 C4
West Wellow Hants 14 C3
West Wemyss Fife 134 E5
West Wick N Som'set 23 C5
West Wickham Cambs 55 E7
West Wickham London 28 C4
West Williamston Pembs 32 D1
West Willoughby Lincs 78 E2
West Winch Norfolk 67 C6
West Winterslow Wilts 25 F7
West Wittering W Sussex 15 E8
West Witton N Yorks 101 F5
West Woodburn Northum 116 F4
West Woodhay W Berks 25 C8
West Woodlands Som'set 24 E2
West Worldham Hants 26 F5
West Worlington Devon 10 C2
West Worthing W Sussex 16 D5
West Wratting Cambs 55 D7
West Wycombe Bucks 39 E8
West Wylam Northum 110 C4
West Yell Shetl'd 174 E6
Westacott Devon 20 F4
Westbere Kent 31 C5
Westborough Lincs 77 E8
Westbourne Bournem'th 13 E8
Westbourne Suffolk 56 E5
Westbourne W Sussex 15 D8
Westbrook W Berks 26 B2
Westbury Bucks 52 F4
Westbury Shrops 60 D3
Westbury Wilts 24 D3
Westbury Leigh Wilts 24 D3
Westbury-on-Severn Glos 36 C4
Westbury on Trym Bristol 23 B7
Westbury-sub-Mendip Som'set 23 E7
Westby Lancs 92 F3
Westcliff-on-Sea Southend 42 F4
Westcombe Som'set 23 F8
Westcote Glos 38 B2
Westcott Bucks 39 C7
Westcott Devon 10 D5
Westcott Surrey 28 E2
Westcott Barton Oxon 38 B4
Westdean E Sussex 18 F2
Westdene Brighton/Hove 17 D6
Wester Aberchalder H'land 147 B8
Wester Balgedie Perth/Kinr 134 D3
Wester Culbeuchly Aberds 160 B3
Wester Dechmont W Loth 122 C3
Wester Denoon Angus 142 E3
Wester Fintray Aberds 151 C7
Wester Gruinards H'land 164 E2
Wester Lealty H'land 157 B7
Wester Milton H'land 158 D3
Wester Newburn Fife 135 D6
Wester Quarff Shetl'd 175 K6
Wester Skeld Shetl'd 175 J4
Westerdale H'land 169 D6
Westerdale N Yorks 102 D4
Westerfield Shetl'd 175 H5
Westerfield Suffolk 57 E5
Westergate W Sussex 16 D3
Westerham Kent 28 D5
Westerhope Tyne/Wear 110 C4
Westerleigh S Gloucs 23 B9
Westerton Angus 143 D6
Westerton Durham 110 F5
Westerton W Sussex 16 D2
Westerwick Shetl'd 175 J4
Westfield Cumb 98 B1
Westfield E Sussex 18 D5
Westfield Heref'd 50 E2
Westfield H'land 169 C5
Westfield N Lanarks 121 B7
Westfield Norfolk 68 D2
Westfield W Loth 122 B2
Westfields Dorset 12 D5
Westfields of Rattray Perth/Kinr 142 E1
Westgate Durham 110 F2
Westgate N Lincs 89 D8
Westgate Norfolk 81 C5
Westgate on Sea Kent 31 B7
Westhall Aberds 151 B5
Westhall Suffolk 69 F7
Westham Dorset 12 G4
Westham E Sussex 18 E3
Westham Som'set 23 E6
Westhampnett W Sussex 16 D2
Westhay Som'set 23 E6
Westhead Lancs 86 D2
Westhide Heref'd 49 E7
Westhill Aberds 151 D7
Westhill H'land 157 E8
Westhope Heref'd 49 D6
Westhope Shrops 60 F4
Westhorpe Lincs 78 F5
Westhorpe Suffolk 56 C4
Westhoughton Gtr Man 86 D4
Westhouse N Yorks 93 B6
Westhumble Surrey 28 D2
Westing Shetl'd 174 C7
Westlake Devon 6 D4
Westleigh Devon 9 B6
Westleigh Devon 11 C5
Westleigh Gtr Man 86 D4
Westleton Suffolk 57 C8
Westley Shrops 60 D3
Westley Suffolk 56 C2
Westley Waterless Cambs 55 D7
Westlington Bucks 39 C7
Westlinton Cumb 108 C3
Westmarsh Kent 31 C6
Westmeston E Sussex 17 C7
Westmill Herts 41 B6
Westminster London 28 B4
Westminster Cathedral London 28 B3
Westmuir Angus 142 D3
Westness Orkney 176 D2
Westnewton Cumb 107 E8
Westnewton Northum 124 F5
Westoe Tyne/Wear 111 C6
Weston Bath/NE Som'set 24 C2
Weston Ches 74 D4
Weston Devon 11 F6
Weston Dorset 12 G4
Weston Halton 86 F3
Weston Hants 15 B8
Weston Herts 54 F3
Weston Lincs 66 B2
Weston Notts 77 C7
Weston Northants 52 E3
Weston N Yorks 94 E4
Weston Shrops 61 E5
Weston Shrops 61 B5
Weston Staffs 62 B3
Weston W Berks 25 B8
Weston Beggard Heref'd 49 E7
Weston by Welland Northants 64 E4
Weston Colville Cambs 55 D7
Weston Coyney Stoke 75 E6
Weston Favell Northants 53 C5
Weston Green Cambs 55 D7
Weston Green Norfolk 68 C4
Weston Heath Shrops 61 C7
Weston Hills Lincs 66 B2
Weston-in-Gordano N Som'set 23 B6
Weston Jones Staffs 61 B7
Weston Longville Norfolk 68 C4
Weston Lullingfields Shrops 60 B4
Weston-on-the-Green Oxon 39 C5
Weston-on-Trent Derby 63 B8
Weston Park Staffs 62 C2
Weston Patrick Hants 26 E4
Weston Rhyn Shrops 73 F6
Weston-Sub-Edge Glos 51 E6
Weston-super-Mare N Som'set 22 C5
Weston Turville Bucks 40 C1
Weston under Lizard Staffs 62 C2
Weston under Penyard Heref'd 36 B3
Weston under Wetherley Warwick 51 C8
Weston Underwood Derby 76 E2
Weston Underwood M/Keynes 53 D6
Westonbirt Glos 37 F5
Westonbirt Arboretum, Tetbury Glos 37 F5
Westoncommon Shrops 60 B4
Westoning Beds 53 F8
Westonzoyland Som'set 23 F5
Westow N Yorks 96 C3
Westport Arg/Bute 118 D3
Westport Som'set 11 C8
Westrigg W Loth 122 C2
Westruther Scot Borders 124 E2
Westry Cambs 66 E3
Westville Notts 76 E5
Westward Cumb 108 E2
Westward Ho! Devon 9 B6
Westwell Kent 30 E3
Westwell Oxon 38 D2
Westwell Leacon Kent 30 E3
Westwick Cambs 54 C5
Westwick Durham 101 C5
Westwick Norfolk 81 E8
Westwood Devon 10 E5
Westwood Wilts 24 D3
Westwoodside N Lincs 89 E8
Wetheral Cumb 108 D4
Wetherby W Yorks 95 E7
Wetherby Racecourse W Yorks 95 E7
Wetherden Suffolk 56 C4
Wetheringsett Suffolk 56 C5
Wethersfield Essex 55 F8
Wethersta Shetl'd 174 G5
Wetherup Street Suffolk 56 C5
Wetley Rocks Staffs 75 E6
Wettenhall Ches 74 C3
Wetton Staffs 75 D8
Wetwang ER Yorks 96 D5
Wetwood Staffs 74 F4
Wexcombe Wilts 25 D7
Wexham Street Bucks 40 F2
Weybourne Norfolk 81 C7
Weybread Suffolk 68 F5
Weybridge Surrey 27 C8
Weycroft Devon 11 E8
Weydale H'land 169 C6
Weyhill Hants 25 E8
Weymouth Dorset 12 G4
Weymouth Sea Life Park Dorset 12 F4
Whaddon Bucks 53 F6
Whaddon Cambs 54 E4
Whaddon Glos 37 C5
Whaddon Wilts 14 B2
Whale Cumb 99 B7
Whaley Derby 76 B5
Whaley Bridge Derby 87 F8
Whaley Thorns Derby 76 B5
Whaligoe H'land 169 E8
Whalley Lancs 93 F7
Whalton Northum 117 F7
Wham N Yorks 93 C7
Whaplode Lincs 66 B3
Whaplode Drove Lincs 66 C3
Whaplode St Catherine Lincs 66 B3
Wharfe N Yorks 93 C7
Wharles Lancs 92 F4
Wharncliffe Side S Yorks 88 E3
Wharram-le-Street N Yorks 96 C4
Wharton Ches 74 C3
Wharton Green Ches 74 C3
Whashton N Yorks 101 D6
Whatcombe Dorset 13 D6
Whatcote Warwick 51 E8
Whatfield Suffolk 56 E4
Whatley Som'set 11 D8
Whatley Som'set 24 E2
Whatlington E Sussex 18 D4
Whatstandwell Derby 76 D3
Whatton Notts 77 F7
Whauphill Dumf/Gal 105 E8
Whaw N Yorks 100 D4
Wheatacre Norfolk 69 E7
Wheatcroft Derby 76 D3
Wheathampstead Herts 40 C4
Wheathill Shrops 61 F6
Wheatley Devon 10 E4
Wheatley Hants 27 E5
Wheatley Oxon 39 D5
Wheatley S Yorks 89 D6
Wheatley W Yorks 87 B8
Wheatley Hill Durham 111 F6
Wheaton Aston Staffs 62 C2
Wheddon Cross Som'set 21 F8
Wheedlemont Aberds 150 B3
Wheelerstreet Surrey 27 E7
Wheelock Ches 74 D4
Wheelock Heath Ches 74 D4
Wheelton Lancs 86 B4
Wheen Angus 142 B3
Wheldrake C/York 96 E2
Whelford Glos 38 E1
Whelpley Hill Bucks 40 D2
Whempstead Herts 41 B6
Whenby N Yorks 96 C2
Whepstead Suffolk 56 D2
Wherstead Suffolk 57 E5
Wherwell Hants 25 E8
Wheston Derby 75 B8
Whetsted Kent 29 E7
Whetstone Leics 64 E2

Distance table

How to use this table

Distances are shown in miles and kilometres with estimated journey times in hours and minutes.

For example: the distance between Dover and Fishguard is 331 miles or 533 kilometres with an estimated journey time of 6 hours, 20 minutes.

Estimated driving times are based on an average speed of 60mph on Motorways and 40mph on other roads. Drivers should allow extra time when driving at peak periods or through areas likely to be congested.

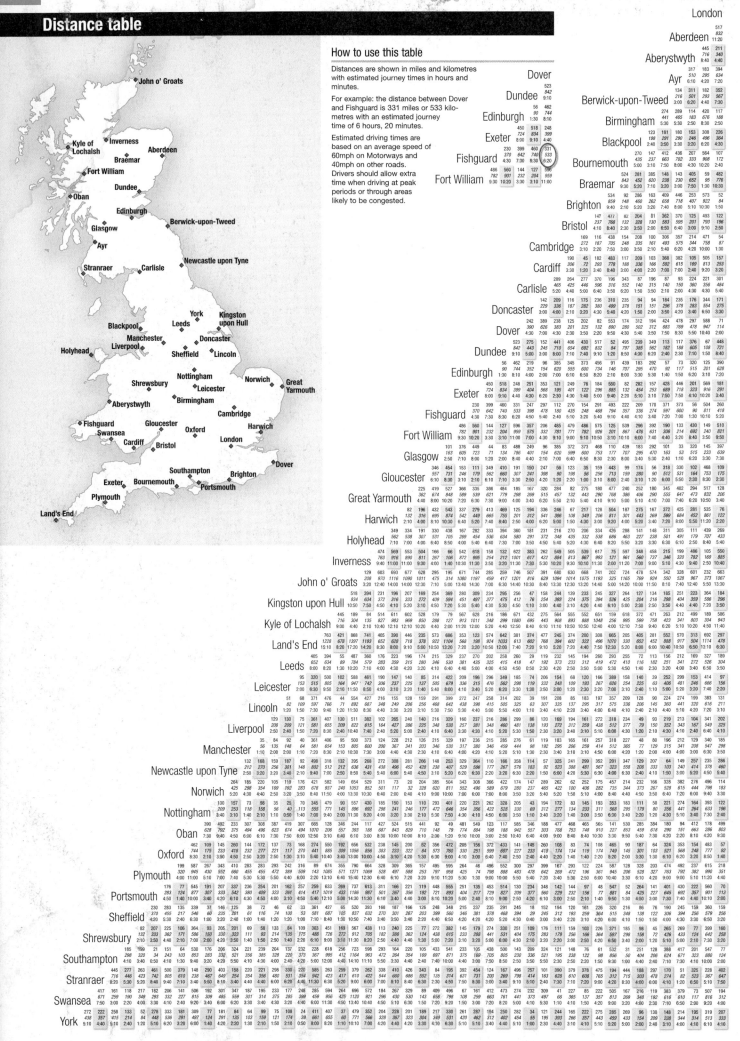